POPULAR TALES

OF

THE WEST HIGHLANDS

Volume 1

POPULAR TALES

OF

THE WEST HIGHLANDS

ORALLY COLLECTED

With a Translation
BY THE LATE J. F. CAMPBELL

———

NEW EDITION

———

VOLUME I

Birlinn

© New Preface, Hugh Andrew 1994

This edition by Birlinn Ltd 1994
Birlinn Ltd
13 Roseneath Street
Edinburgh EH9 1JH

Typeset in Monotype Plantin
by ROM-Data Ltd, Falmouth and
printed in Finland by
Werner Soderstrom OY

A CIP record for this book is available
from the British Library

ISBN 1 874744 15 7

Popular Tales of the West Highlands Volumes 1, 2 and 3
by J.F. Campbell were originally published in 1860 and
1861 by Edmonston and Douglas, Edinburgh

Chuidich Comhairle nan Leabhraichean am foillsichear
le cosgaisean an leabhair seo

Do

IAIN MAC SHEORAIS

MAC CALLEN MOR

MARQUESS OF LORNE.

———

MY DEAR LORNE,
 I dedicate this collection of West Country Stories to
you as the son of my Chief, in the hope that it may add to the interest
which you already feel in a people, of whom a large number look
with respect on "Mac Callen Mor" as the head of their tribe. I know
that the poorest Highlanders still feel an honest pride whenever
their chiefs, or men of their name, earn distinction; and many of
"Clan Dhiarmaid" take a warm interest in you.
 Amidst curious rubbish you will find sound sense if you look for
it. You will find the creed of the people, as shewn in their stories,
to be, that wisdom and courage, though weak, may overcome
strength, and ignorance, and pride; that the most despised is often
the most worthy; that small beginnings lead to great results.
 You will find perseverance, frugality, and filial piety rewarded;
pride, greed, and laziness punished. You will find much which tells
of barbarous times; I hope you will meet nothing that can hurt, or
should offend.
 If you follow any study, even that of a popular tale, far enough,
it will lead you to a closed door, beyond which you cannot pass till
you have searched and found the key, and every study will lead the
wisest to a fast locked door at last; but knowledge lies beyond these
doors, and one key may open the way to many a store which can
be reached, and may be turned to evil or to good.
 That you may go on acquiring knowledge, selecting the good,
and rejecting the evil; that you, like Conal in the story, may gather
gold, and escape unharmed from the giant's land, is the earnest
wish of your affectionate kinsman,

J. F. CAMPBELL.

SEPTEMBER, 1860.

Preface

John Francis Campbell of Islay is among the greatest of many great Scots of Victorian times. Born in 1821 and heir to Islay until 1847 when his father, in hopeless debt, was forced to sell the estate, John Francis ended up in the service of his cousin, the eighth Duke. It was patronage that was to prove invaluable. His drive, energy, and scientific enthusiasm saw him placed on Royal Commissions on Heating and Ventilating, Lighthouses, and Coal. In this capacity he made friends with some of the greatest men of his day. In between times he wrote popular books on geology, was an expert in optics and produced a method of recording hours of sunshine which, refined later, still remains in use today.

A keen traveller, he had a lifelong fascination with Scandinavia, visiting at least eleven times in his life, and was an extraordinary linguist. In 1873 he claimed modestly to know 'pretty well' English, Gaelic, French, Italian, Spanish, German, Norwegian, Danish, Swedish, Latin, and Greek, and to have some acquaintance with another fifteen languages.

In 1859 his friend, Sir George Dasent, published 'Popular Tales from the Norse'. It was an immense influence on Campbell. With an unusually broadminded approach, his parents had allowed him to mingle with the Highland community in general, and he was thus exposed to the vast wealth of storytelling at an early age. His linguistic abilities, voracious curiosity, scientific training, and love of the Highlands and their people, left him perfectly placed to collect the riches around him. The collection of folktales was a relatively recent and relatively haphazard procedure. Campbell, with his network of paid informants, concern for accuracy, and cross checking procedures established standards which were to be benchmarks until the advent of recording techniques.

What we have in print is merely the tip of the iceberg, produced in four volumes between 1860 and 1862 and an instant success. Following this the Duke of Argyll released him from all other duties and allowed him to become a full time collector. The result of this legacy was over a million and a quarter words. Much of the collection, gathered from a number of sources, is uneven in quality, much is still unstudied, but this vast legacy remains a staggering achievement by any standard. It had one further effect. The actual act of collecting the tales led to their preservation – the story telling necessary to collect, led to the tales being passed on, but also heightened the prestige of the teller.

Campbell died in 1885. His obituary in the 'Scotsman' stated that he was

> ' . . . a man of great ability who might have gone further than he did if his efforts had been more concentrated.'

Perhaps a slightly churlish epitaph for one of the greatest men of his age.

Hugh Andrew

Publishers Note: The volume reproduced here simply reprints the actual tales. The notes on the Ossianic controversy have been superseded and are of largely historical interest. They have therefore been omitted.

It is hoped that it will be possible to reproduce the two further collections from Campbell's work, published respectively in 1940 and 1960, 'More West Highland Tales.'

It is also worth reminding readers that although Campbell strove for accuracy in his translations, he was translating into the style of his time, hence the very Victorian feel to much of the English.

CONTENTS

NAME.	TOLD BY

Contents

xiii

Contents

NAME.	TOLD BY

INTRODUCTION.

THE FAIRY EGG, AND WHAT CAME OUT OF IT.

ON the stormy coasts of the Hebrides, amongst seaweed and shells, fishermen and kelp-burners often find certain hard, light, floating objects, somewhat like flat chestnuts, of various colours—grey, black, and brown, which they call sea-nuts, strand-nuts, and fairy-eggs. Where they are most common, they are used as snuff-boxes, but they are also worn and preserved as amulets, with a firm or sceptical belief in their mysterious virtues. Old Martin, who wrote of the Western Isles in 1703, calls them "Molluka beans," and tells how they were then found, and worn, and used as medicine; how they preserved men from the evil eye, and cured sick cattle by a process as incomprehensible as mesmerism. Practical Highland-men of the present day call the nuts trash, and brand those who wear them, like their ancestors a hundred and fifty years ago, as ignorant and superstitious; but learned botanists, too wise to over-look trifles, set themselves to study even fairy-eggs; and believing them to be West Indian seeds,* stranded in Europe, they planted them, and some (from the Azores) grew. Philosophers, having discovered what they were, used them to demonstrate the existence of the Gulf Stream, and it is even said that they formed a part of one link in that chain of reasoning which led Columbus to the New World.

So within this century, men have gathered nursery tales. They set themselves earnestly to learn all that they could concerning them; they found similar tales common to many languages; they traced them back for centuries; they planted them in books, and at last the Brothers Grimm, their predecessors and their followers, have raised up a pastime for children to be "a study fit for the energies of grown men and to all the dignity of a science."

* *Mimosa scandens*, great pod-creeper. *Mucuna ureus.*

So at least says the learned author of the translation of "Norse Tales," and there are many who agree with him.

Men have now collected stories from most parts of the world. They have taken them from the dictation of American Indians, South Sea Islanders, Lapps and Samoydes, Germans and Russians. Missionaries have published the fables of African savages; learned men have translated Arabic, Sanscrit, and Chinese manuscripts; even Egyptian papyri have been dug up, and forced to yield their meaning, and all alike have furnished tales, very similar to stories now told by word of mouth. But as some of these are common to races whose languages have been traced to a common origin, it is now held that nursery stories and popular tales have been handed down together with the languages in which they are told; and they are used in striving to trace out the origin of races, as philologists use words to trace language, as geologists class rocks by the shells and bones which they contain, and as natural philosophers used fairy-eggs in tracing the Gulf Stream.

The following collection is intended to be a contribution to this new science of "Storyology." It is a museum of curious rubbish about to perish, given as it was gathered in the rough, for it seemed to me as barbarous to "polish" a genuine popular tale, as it would be to adorn the bones of a Megatherium with tinsel, or gild a rare old copper coin. On this, however, opinions vary, but I hold my own, that stories orally collected can only be valuable if given unaltered; besides, where is the model story to be found?

Practical men may despise the tales, earnest men condemn them as lies, some even consider them wicked; one refused to write any more for a whole estate; my best friend says they are all "blethers." But one man's rubbish may be another's treasure; and what is the standard of value in such a pursuit as this?

"And what are you going to do with them stories, Mr. Camal?" said a friend of mine, as he stood amongst the brown sea-weed, at the end of a pier, on a fine summer's evening, and watched my departure in a tiny boat.

"Print them, man, to be sure."

My friend is famous for his good stories, though they are of another kind, and he uses tobacco; he eyed me steadily for a moment, and then he disposed of the whole matter monosyllabically, but forcibly,

"Huch!!"

It seemed to come from his heart.

Said a Highland coachman to me one day, "The luggage is very heavy. I will not believe but there is stones in the portmanteaus! They will be pickin' them up off the road, and takin' them away with them; I have seen them myself;" and then, having disposed of geology, he took a sapient pinch of snuff.

So a benighted Englishman, years ago in Australia, took up his quarters in a settler's hut, as he told me. Other travellers came in, and one had found a stone in a dry river-course which he maintained to be partly gold. The rest jeered at him till he threw away his prize in a pet; and then they all devoured mutton chops and damper, and slept like sensible men.

So these tales may be gold or dross according to taste. Many will despise them, but some may take an interest in the pastime of their humble countrymen; some may be amused; those who would learn Gaelic will find the language of the people who told the stories; and those who would compare popular tales of different races, may rest assured that I have altered nothing; that these really are what they purport to be—stories orally collected in the West Highlands since the beginning of 1859. I have but carried drift rubbish from the place where I found it to a place where it may be seen and studied by those who care to take the trouble.

The resemblance which the collection bears to others already made, is a strong argument for the common origin of the stories, and of the people who tell them. But, as a foundation for argument, I am bound to give the evidence on which I have formed my belief in their antiquity, for the stories would be rubbish indeed if they were not genuine traditions.

This is the account given by Mr. Hector MacLean, parish schoolmaster at Ballygrant in Islay, whom I have known from his boyhood, and who, at my request, collected stories last summer in the Long Island:—

> "In the Islands of Barra, the recitation of tales during the long winter nights is still very common. The people gather in crowds to the houses of those whom they consider good reciters to listen to their stories. They appear to be fondest of those tales which describe exceedingly rapid changes of place in very short portions of time, and have evidently no respect for the unities. During the recitation of those tales, the emotions of the reciters are occasionally very strongly excited, and so also are those of the listeners, almost shedding tears at one time, and giving way to loud laughter at another. A good many

of them firmly believe in all the extravagance of these
stories.

"They speak of the Ossianic heroes with as much feeling,
sympathy, and belief in their existence and reality as the
readers of the newspapers do of the exploits of the British
army in the Crimea or in India; and whatever be the extravagance of the legends they recite respecting them, it is exceedingly remarkable that the same character is always ascribed to
the same hero in almost every story and by almost every
reciter. Fingal, or rather Fionn, is never called the king of any
country or territory, but the king of the Finn, a body of men
who were raised, according to the traditions current in the
Long Island and other parts of the Highlands, in Ireland and
in the Highlands, to defend both countries against foreign
invaders, more especially against the Scandinavians. The
origin these illiterate people assign to them, according to the
traditions handed down to them, is, that the largest and
strongest bodied young men and women were selected and
married together in order to produce a brave and powerful
race capable of withstanding and repelling the incursions of
foreign foes. Any hero that came west, east, north or south,
and 'Cothrom na Fînne' (the chance of the Finne), is the term
still used for fair-play in the Highlands.

"In no tale or tradition related to me regarding these heroes
have I heard the name, 'Righ Mhòr-bheinn' (King of
Morven), ascribed to Fionn; nor have I heard him described
as the king of any territory or country—always 'Righ na Fînne
or Fèinne.' Fèinn or Fînn is the plural of Fiann, which is
probably derived from Fiadh dhuine; either a wild man, from
his strength and bravery, or else the man of deer, from their
maintaining themselves by hunting deer, extensive tracts of
land being allotted to them for that purpose. The last etymol-
ogy I believe myself to be the correct one.

"The most of the people in Barra and South Uist are Roman
Catholics, can neither read nor write, and hardly know any
English. From these circumstances it is extremely improbable
that they have borrowed much from the literature of other
nations. In North Uist and Harris these tales are nearly gone,
and this, I believe, to be owing partly to reading, which in a
manner supplies a substitute for them, partly to bigoted
religious ideas, and partly to narrow utilitarian views."

This clear statement is accompanied by a description of each of the men who contributed, from which it appears in detail that the greater number speak Gaelic only, that many of them can neither read nor write, and that they are clever though uneducated; and this account I know to be correct in some cases, from my own personal knowledge of the men. Hector Urquhart, now gamekeeper at Ardkinglas, whom I have known for many years, agrees with MacLean in his account of the telling of these stories in other districts in former times.

This is his account:—

"In my native place, Pool-Ewe, Ross-shire, when I was a boy, it was the custom for the young to assemble together on the long winter nights to hear the old people recite the tales or sgeulachd, which they had learned from their fathers before them. In these days tailors and shoemakers went from house to house, making our clothes and shoes. When one of them came to the village we were greatly delighted, whilst getting new kilts at the same time. I knew an old tailor who used to tell a new tale every night during his stay in the village; and another, an old shoemaker, who, with his large stock of stories about ghosts and fairies, used to frighten us so much that we scarcely dared pass the neighbouring churchyard on our way home. It was also the custom when an *aoidh*, or stranger, celebrated for his store of tales, came on a visit to the village, for us, young and old, to make a rush to the house where he passed the night, and choose our seats, some on beds, some on forms, and others on three-legged stools, etc., and listen in silence to the new tales; just as I have myself seen since, when a far-famed actor came to perform in the Glasgow theatre. The goodman of the house usually opened with the tale of *Famhair Mor* (great giant) or some other favourite tale, and then the stranger carried on after that. It was a common saying, 'The first tale by the goodman, and tales to daylight by the *aoidh*,' or guest. It was also the custom to put riddles, in the solving of which all in the house had to tax their ingenuity. If one of the party put a riddle which was not solved that night, he went home with the title of King of Riddles. Besides this, there was usually in such gatherings a discussion about the *Fein*, which comes from FIANTAIDH, giant; the Fiantaidh were a body of men who volunteered to defend their country from the invasions and inroads of the Danes and

Norwegians, or *Lochlinnich*. FIUNN, who was always called King of the Fein, was the strongest man amongst them, and no person was admitted into the company who was less in height than he, however much taller. I remember the old black shoemaker telling us one night that FIUNN had a tooth which he consulted as an oracle upon all important occasions. He had but to touch this tooth, and whatever he wanted to know was at once revealed to him.

"The above is all I can at present readily call to mind of the way in which the evenings were spent in the Highlands thirty or forty years ago. The minister came to the village in 1830, and the schoolmaster soon followed, who put a stop in our village to such gatherings; and in their place we were supplied with heavier tasks than listening to the old shoemaker's fairy tales. From that period till I collected the few in this collection, I have not heard a tale recited. On going to visit my friends last summer, I expected that I would get some old tales among them, but I found that the most of the old men who used to relate them in my young days had died, and the few who were then alive of them were so old that they had lost their memories, so that I only got but a trifle to what I expected.

March 1860. "HECTOR URQUHART."

John Dewar, a labourer, whom I never saw, but who has written and sent me many stories, agrees with the others. These men have never met, and have acted independently; and yet, in many cases, I have received versions of the same story from each and from other sources, and I have myself heard the same incidents repeated by their authorities, and by others whom they had never seen; sometimes even the very words.

The name of every narrator is given with his story, and I am satisfied on direct evidence that most of these were known in the Highlands at least forty years ago. Now, for the benefit of those who know as little of the subject as I did, let me give the theory of the distribution of popular tales, as I have gathered it from the able introduction to the Norse Tales and other sources, and then let me point out the bearing of this collection on that theory.

It is supposed that the races known as Indo-European came from Central Asia at some very early period, and passed over Europe, separating and settling down as nations; retaining words of their original language, and leaving the traces of their religion and history everywhere as popular tales; and that they found the land occupied. Each wave, it is said, "pushed onwards those who went before," but, as it seems to me, each in turn must have stopped as it arrived at the great sea, and there the waves of this stream of men must have mingled and stagnated.

As the flotsam and jetsam of American rivers and of the Gulf Stream is constantly drifting northwards and eastwards, and finds a resting-place on some western shore, so the traces of the great human stream, which is supposed to have flowed westwards, should be found in greatest abundance stranded at the western sea. If this be correct, and if the plains of Asia sent migratory hordes eastwards as well as westwards, the tales and languages of the far East and West should most resemble each other, and should also resemble more than others the oldest forms of the myths and languages of those from whom they sprang. Brittany, Scandinavia, Ireland, and the west of Scotland, from their geographical position, should contain more of this light mental *debris* than Central Europe; for the same reason that more of the floating rubbish of American rivers is found on the shores of Europe than anywhere on the great ocean; and if mankind had a common origin, and started from the plains of Asia, and if popular tales really are old traditions, then the tales of Ceylon should resemble those of Barra, and those of Japan should resemble the others, because men travelling eastwards and arrived at Japan, could not easily advance further. Mr. Oliphant tells us that both in China and in Japan groups are commonly seen listening to professional story-tellers in the streets, and it is to be hoped that some one will enable us to judge of their talents.

Be that as it may, fairy-eggs are not the only foreign products found on the shores of the Hebrides, and the people who dwell there know stories of larger growth than mere nursery tales. Great logs of drift-wood find their way to shore, and are turned to use. Such a log I once found, and used myself, long ago. It was half buried in the sand; it had been long tossed by the sea, and battered against rocks, for it was heavy with water, splintered and ground. No tree like it grew like it grew anywhere near. There was no mark of a tool on it. The stumps of its roots and branches remained, and it seemed as if it had been torn up and wafted to its resting-place by winds and waves alone. I have no doubt that it came from America. Had it been insignificant and useless, like a fairy-egg, we might have left it, or preserved it as a curiosity; but it was a useful log, and we were a party of chilled otter hunters, so, after a few speculations, we hoisted the prize on our shoulders, carried it to our dwelling, a neighbouring cave, and there we burned it. I see it often, hissing and spluttering, and lighting up the bivouac with its red glare. Its ashes may be there still, but that tree is a tree no longer; its origin and wanderings cannot now be traced; it has shared the fate of many a popular tale. It was found and used up.

Such a log I lately saw in South Uist. No tool mark was on it; it had lost its own foliage, but it was covered with a brown and white marine foliage of seaweed and dead barnacles, and it was drilled in all directions by these curious sea-shells, which are supposed by the people to be embryo geese. It was sound, though battered, and a worthy Celtic smith was about to add it to the roof of a cottage, which he was making of boulders and turf. It was about to share the fate of many popular tales, and become a part of something else. It may be recognised as an American production hereafter, and its history is deeply marked on it, though if forms part of a house by this time. So a genuine popular tale may be recognised in a play or a romance.

Another such tree I saw in Benbecula, with bark still on the roots, and close to it lay a squared log, and near that a mast with white paint and iron bindings, blocks and crosstrees, still attached to it. A few miles off was a stranded ship, with her cargo and fittings, a wreck about to be sold, and turned to any use that the new owners might think fit. All these were about to be changed, and as it was with drift-wood in the Highlands, so, as I imagine, it has been with popular tales everywhere. They are as old as the races who tell them, but the original ideas, like the trees from which logs, masts, and ships are made, have been broken up, cut, carved, and ornamented—lost and found—wrecked, destroyed, broken, and put together again; and though the original shape is hard to find, the fragments may be recognized in books, and wherever else they may now be found.

But as there are quiet spots in the world where drift-wood accumulates undisturbed, so there are quiet spots where popular tales flourish in peace, because no man has interfered with them. In Spitzbergen, according to the accounts given me by Norwegian bear hunters and adventurous English nobles, trees, such as those occasionally found in Scotland, are piled in heaps. Trees, logs, broken spars, and wreck, gather and bleach and decay together, because there are no men on that wild shore to use them. So in the islands where the western "wanderers," "Albanich," settled down, and where they have remained for centuries, old men and women are still found who have hardly stirred from their native islands, who speak only Gaelic, and cannot read or write, and yet their minds are filled with a mass of popular lore, as various as the wreck piled on the shores of Spitzbergen. If such as these get hold of the contents of a story book, they seem unconsciously to extract the incidents, and reject all the rest,—to select the true wood, and throw away foreign ornament, just as they chip off the paint of a stranded mast, or scrape the sea-weed off a log when they build it into a roof. I have given one specimen of a story, which I believe to be derived from the "Arabian Nights," though it is quite impossible that the man who told it to Hector MacLean, and who told it to me also, in nearly the same words, can have got it directly from any book; for he cannot read at all, and he does not understand English.

I have found very little notice of these West Highland prose tales in books, but they are referred to. In 1703, Martin says that his countrymen then told long tales about Fin MacCoul, but he adds that he will not trouble the reader with them.

In 1780, Dr. Smith, in his book on Gaelic poetry, says, that prosaic tales should be preserved in the same manner may seem strange, but so it is. He condemns the "urskels" as "later tales," unworthy of notice, probably because they were different from the poetry of which he collected so much.

Gaelic dictionaries mention "legends" as sources from which words have been taken. Amongst the Gaelic MSS. now in the Advocates' Library, there are several which contain tales similar to those now told in the Highlands. One passage about the sailing of boat, which I have got, with variations, from a great many people living in various parts of the Highlands, I find in a MS. which was lent to me by the secretary of the Celtic Society of London. It is dated 23d December 1808, signed Alexander Stewart, A.M., and marked, Poems of Ossian. It contains 7721 lines of Gaelic, mostly poetry, which by the references seem to have been copied from something else. The passage to which I refer, occurs in a "Fragment of a Tale," p. 17, which occupies thirty-seven folio pages, and treats of carrying off a lady from an island, and her recovery by her husband.

Dr. MacLeod, the best of living Gaelic scholars, printed one old tale, somewhat altered, with a moral added, in his "Leabhar nan Cnoc," in 1834, but even his efforts to persevere and use this old lore were unsuccessful.

Those, then, who understood Gaelic, thought popular tales unworthy of notice; those who did not understand Gaelic, could know nothing about them; and there are many now living in the

Highlands, who speak Gaelic and yet believed, till they searched at my request, that stories had become extinct in their districts. One good Highlander, who has helped me much, Mr. James Robertson, living at Inveraray, so believed, till he heard his own nursemaid repeat No. 17, and a neighbouring fisherman tell No. 6. In the Highlands, as elsewhere, society is arranged in layers, like the climates of the world. The dweller on an Indian plain little dreams that there is a region of perpetual frost in the air above him; the Esquimaux does not suspect the slumbering volcano under his feet; and the dwellers in the upper and lower strata of society, everywhere, know as little of each other's ways of life as the men of the plain know of the mountaineers in the snow.

Highland stories then, have been despised by educated men, and they are as yet unchanged popular tales. It so happened that a piper was the instructor of my babyhood. He was a stalwart, kindly, gentle man, whose face is often before me, though he has long since gone to his rest. From him I first heard a few of the tales in this collection. They had almost faded from my memory, but I remembered their existence, and I knew where to search, so I began at the beginning of 1859 by writing to my Highland friends, of all degrees, for stories of all kinds, true stories excepted; and here let me thank them cordially for the trouble which they have taken, for they are too numerous to thank in detail.

I begged for the very words used by the people who told the stories, with nothing added, or omitted, or altered. Those who could wrote Gaelic, those who could not did their best in English,— translated, at first or second-hand, from Gaelic; and when I had so gathered many versions of a story, I thought I might safely conclude that it had been known in the country for many years, and was essentially a popular tale.

My next step was to go at Easter to a Highland district, near the lowlands, where a gamekeeper had marked down a lot of tale-tellers, and I was soon convinced that there was plenty of game, though hard to get.

This difficulty may be worth some explanation, for it exists elsewhere, and bears on the collection of tales everywhere. Highland peasants and fishermen, especially those dwelling near the lowlands, are shy and proud, and even more peculiarly sensitive to ridicule than peasants elsewhere. Many have a lurking belief in the truth of the stories which they tell, and a rooted conviction that any one with a better education will laugh at the belief, and the story, and the narrator and his language, if he should be weak enough to venture on English, and betray his knowledge of Sgeultachd and his creed. He cannot imagine that any one out of his own class can possibly be amused by his frivolous pastimes. No one ever has hitherto. He sees every year a summer flood of tourists of all nations pouring through his lochs and glens, but he knows as little of them as they know of him. The shoals of herrings that enter Loch Fyne know as much of the dun deer on the hill-side, as Londoners and Highland peasants know of each other. Each gets an occasional peep at the other as the deer may see the herrings capering in the loch—each affects the other slowly but surely, as the herrings do drive away the wild deer by attracting men to catch them; but the want of a common language here as elsewhere, keeps Highlands and Lowlands, Celt and Saxon, as clearly separate as oil and water in the same glass.

The first step, then, towards the acquisition of a story is to establish confidence. It may be that the would-be collector sees before him a strapping lad dressed in the garb of a west country fisherman—a rough blue bonnet, jacket, and trousers. He steps out and ranges up alongside. The Highlander glances from under his bushy eyebrows, and sees with his sharp grey eyes that the new comer is a stranger. He looks rather like a Saxon; Highland curiosity is strong, and he longs to ask whence he comes; but politeness is stronger, and it would be uncivil to begin questioning at once. So with a nervous kick of one foot, and a quick shy glance, the fisherman jerks out, "It's a fine day." "Tha n' latha briagh" (the day is fine), replies the stranger; and as he speaks, the whole face and manner of his companion change as if by magic; doubt and hesitation, suspicion and curiosity, become simple wonder; his eyes and his heart open wide at the sound of his native tongue, and he exclaims, "You have Gaelic! You will take my excuse by your leave, but what part of the Gaeldom are you from?" And then having found out all that is to be discovered, the ice being broken, and confidence established, it oozes out gradually that the fisherman knows a story, and after much persuasion he tells it, while he rows the gentleman who can talk Gaelic across a Highland loch. At parting, he adds that he has only told it to please a "Gael," and that he would not have said one word to a Gall (stranger). But the man who is fluent in his boat, is shy and backward when set down to repeat his story for transcribing, and it is only when set with one of his neighbours whom he knows, that his story is got on paper.

Or it may be an old dame in a tall white mutch with a broad black silk band, a red cloak, and clean white apron. She is 70, and can walk ten miles; she has known all the neighbouring families for generations. If you can claim cousinship with any, she is your friend; but she *will* praise the ancestors and tell of the adventures of Rob Roy the Gregorach, the last of the freebooters. "But, Mary, can you say Murachag and Mionachag?" "Huch! my dear, that is an ursgeul that is nonsense. The Good Being bless you, I knew your grandmother," etc., etc. So one must rest contented with the fact, that old Mary knows one tale, and probably many more, which a week's persuasion might perhaps extract.

Or it may be a pretty lass, whose eye twinkles with intelligence at every catch-word, thrown out as a bait, but whom nothing will induce to confess that she knows the foolish tales which the minister has condemned.

Or it is an old wandering vagabond of a tinker, who has no roof but the tattered covering of his tent. He has pitched it in a quarry under a giant fir, the knarled roots, half bare, hardly support the tree on the edge of a red clay bank, and form a kind of hollow, a "cos," in which the tinker and his tribe have nestled at odd times for years. A thin blue smoke is curling amongst the blackened roots, and winding itself about the noble tree. A stately mansion and a wide domain, and a blue highland loch, with a shoal of brown herring boats, can be seen through the wood from the door of the tinker's tent; and there he lies, an old man past eighty, who has been a soldier, and "has never seen a school"; too proud to beg, too old to work; surrounded by boxes and horn spoons, with shaggy hair and naked feet, as perfect a nomad as the wildest Lapp or Arab in the whole world. It is easy to make friends with such men. A kind word in their native language is all that is required, but to get their stories is another affair. "Donald, did you ever see the like of *this*?" Up starts the old man on his elbow,—"Och! och! that's a fairy arrow, I have seen that; och! och! no fairy arrow will ever hit the man who has that—no fire will ever burn the house where that is. That's lucky, well! well!" and the old man sinks down on his bed of fern. But the elf shot has hit the mark, and started a train of thought, which leads at last to a wild weird story; but before that story can be written, the whole tribe decamp, and are lost for a time.

The first difficulty, then, was the nature of the people who knew the stories; and the second, the want of men able and willing to write Gaelic. It was easy to write English versions of tales heard in Gaelic, but I wanted the Gaelic as it was told, and I had neither time nor ability to write it down myself. I therefore sought out two men on whom I could rely, to collect and write for me, and the largest share of this book has been collected and written by them. One is Mr. Hector Urquhart, gamekeeper at Ardkinglas on Loch Fyne; the other, Mr. Hector MacLean, schoolmaster at Ballygrant in Islay, who has superintended the printing of the Gaelic. They entered into the spirit of the work at once, and they have executed their share of it with the greatest fidelity. But while these are my chief aids, I am largely indebted to many others for written Gaelic; for example, to one of my earliest friends, Mrs. MacTavish; to the Rev. Mr. MacLauchlan of Edinburgh; to Alexander Fraser, Esq., of Mauld, near Beauly; to many of the schoolmasters on the estate of Sir Kenneth MacKenzie; to Mr. Donald Torrie, Benbecula; and to many others, including John Dewar, a self-educated man of advanced age, whose contribution does him the greatest credit.

The next step was to spend a summer holiday in studying the actual condition of this popular lore, where I had found that it existed in the greatest profusion. I landed at Lochmaddy in North Uist, and walked with a knapsack to the sound of Barra, and back to Stornoway; crossing the sound of Harris in a fishing boat. I found a population differing from that of the mainland, perhaps the least changed from their old ways of any people in the kingdom. Gaelic is their usual, often their only language. Every English word which has crept in has a Gaelic head and tail. Many, I know not how many, "have no English" at all, and have never been taught to read. In many islands the people are living undisturbed, where their ancestors have lived time out of mind. They are a small, active, intelligent race, with dark hair and eyelashes, and grey eyes; quick, clever, and pugnacious. I had expected to find traces of Norwegian occupation in the people and their language. I watched carefully for Norwegian words and features; and I found the people a complete contrast to Norwegian peasants, whom I know well, who are large, bony, light-haired fair men, sagacious rather than quick; and generally slow to anger.

I could find nothing Scandinavian, except certain names of places, and certain ruins, which it is the fashion to attribute to the Lochliners. Even the houses and the old agricultural implements, where they are still used, are peculiar. For example, the old crooked spade still used in islands in the sound of Barra, and elsewhere, has no resemblance to any agricultural implement that I have ever seen anywhere out of the West Highlands. It is in fact a foot plough used without horses. It is remarkable that a steam plough should be at work at the same time, on the east coast of Cromarty at Tarbert. Every horse I met on the road stopped of his own accord. Every man asked my news, "whence I took the walking," where I lived, and why I came? Saddles were often sacks, stirrups a loop of twisted bent, bridles the same, and bits occasionally wood. Dresses were coarse, but good; but there was an air of kindly politeness over all, that is not to be found in homespun dresses in any other country that I know. When I was questioned, I answered, and told my errand, and prospered. "I was not a drover come to buy cattle at the fair;" "Neither was I a merchant though I carried a pack." "I was the gentleman who was after Sgialachdan." My collector had made my name known. I spoke Gaelic, and answered questions. I am one of themselves, so I got on famously.

Men and women of all ages could and did tell me stories, children of all sizes listened to them; and it was self-evident that people generally knew and enjoyed them. Elsewhere I had been told, that thirty or forty years ago, men used to congregate and tell stories; here, I was told, that they now spend whole winter nights about the fire listening to these old world tales. The clergy, in some places, had condemned the practice, and there it had fallen into disuse; stories seemed to be almost exterminated in some islands, though I believe they were only buried alive; but in other places this harmless amusement is not forbidden; and there, in every cluster of houses, is some one man famed as "good at sgialachdan," whose house is a winter evening's resort. I visited these, and listened, often with wonder, at the extraordinary power of memory shown by untaught old men.

It is perhaps beyond the province of a mere collector of old tales to be serious; but surely Gaelic books containing sound information would be a vast boon to such a people. The young would read them, and the old would understand them. All would take a warmer interest in Canada and Australia, where strong arms and bold spirits are wanted, if they knew what these countries really are. If they heard more of European battles, and knew what a ship of war is now, there would be more soldiers and sailors from the Isles in the service of their country, At all events, the old spirit of popular romance is surely not an evil spirit to be exercised, but rather a good genius to be controlled and directed. Surely stories in which a mother's blessing, well earned, leads to success; in which the poor rise to be princes, and the weak and courageous overcome giants; in which wisdom excels brute force,—surely even such frivolities are better pastime than a solitary whisky bottle, or sleep, or grim silence; for that seems the choice of amusements if tales are forbidden and Gaelic books are not provided for men who know no other language; and who, as men, must be amused now and then.

I have never heard a story, whose point was obscenity, publicly told in a Highland cottage; and I believe that such are rare. I *have* heard them where the rough polish of more modern ways has replaced the polished roughness of "wild" Highlanders; and that where even the bagpipes have been almost abolished as profane.

I have heard the music of the "Cider Cellars" in a parlour, even in polished England, when I had failed to extract anything else from a group of comfortably-dressed villages. A half-polished human gem is but a spoiled crystal anywhere; and I prefer the rough diamond or the finished jewel.

But this is foreign to my work; my visits were to the tellers of old stories, and had nothing to do with political economy and public morals. I paid my visits, and heard the stories; and a goodly audience often gathered to share the treat, and all seemed marvellously to enjoy it. If there was an occasional coarse word spoken, it was not coarsely meant.

Let me describe one of these old story men as a type of his kind. I trust he will not be offended, for he was very polite to me. His name is MacPhie; he lives at the north end of South Uist, where the road ends at a sound, which has to be forded at the ebb to get to Benbecula. The house is built of a double wall of loose boulders, with a layer of peat three feet thick between the walls. The ends are round, and the roof rests on the inner wall, leaving room for a crop of yellow gowans. A man might walk round the roof on the top of the wall. There is but one room, with two low doors, one on each side of the house. The fire is on the floor; the chimney is a hole above it; and the rafters are hung with pendants and festoons of shining black peat reek. They are of birch from the mainland, American drift wood, or broken wreck. They support a covering of turf and straw, and stones, and heather ropes, which keep out the rain well enough.

The house stands on a green bank, with grey rocks protruding through the turf; and the whole neighbourhood is pervaded by cockle shells, which indicate the food of the people and their fishing pursuits. In a neighbouring kiln there were many cart-loads about to be burned, to make that lime which is so durable in the old castles. The owner of the house, whom I visited twice, is seventy-nine. He told me nine stories, and like all the others, declared that there was no man in the islands who knew them so well. "He could not say how many he knew;" he seemed to know versions of nearly everything I had got; and he told me plainly that my versions were good for nothing. "Huch! Thou hast not got them right at all." "They came into his mind," he said, "sometimes at night when he could not sleep,—old tales that he had not heard for threescore years."

He had the manner of a practised narrator, and it is quite evident he is one; he chuckled at the interesting parts, and laid his withered finger on my knee as he gave out the terrible bits with due solemnity. A small boy in a kilt, with large round glittering eyes, was standing mute at his knee, gazing at his wrinkled face, and devouring every word. The boy's mother first boiled, and then mashed, potatoes; and his father, a well grown man in tartan breeks, ate them. Ducks and ducklings, a cat and a kitten, some hens and a baby, all tumbled about on the clay floor together, and expressed their delight at the savoury prospect, each in his own fashion; and three wayfarers dropped in and listened for a spell, and passed their remarks till the ford was shallow. The light came streaming down the chimney, and through a single pane of glass, lighting up a tract in the blue mist of the peat smoke, and fell on the white hair and brown withered face of the old man, as he sat on a low stool with his feet to the fire; and the rest of the dwelling, with all its plenishing of boxes and box-beds, dishes and dresser, and gear of all sorts, faded away through shades of deepening brown, to the black darkness of the smoked roof and the "peat corner." There we sat, and smoked and talked for hours, till the tide ebbed; and then I crossed the ford by wading up to the waist, and dried my clothes in the wind in Benbecula.

Another man of the same stamp, Patrick Smith, lives near the sound of Barra; and a third, "Donald MacDonald MacCharles MacIntyre," in Benbecula; and I heard of plenty more, whom I had not time to visit. I found them to be men with clear heads and wonderful memories, generally very poor and old, living in remote corners of remote islands, and speaking only Gaelic; in short, those who have lived most at home, furthest from the world, and who have no source of mental relaxation beyond themselves and their neighbours.

At Gearrloch on the mainland, some old namesakes of mine are of the same stamp, but in these regions the schoolmaster has made himself at home. Tales have been forbidden, but other lore has been provided. There are many well attended English schools, so old men have access to books and newspapers through their children. Tradition is out of fashion and books are in.

Farther east stories are still rarer, and seem to be told rather by women than by men. The long romances of the west give place to stories about ghosts and fairies, apparitions, and dreams—stories which would be told in a few words, if at all, in the islands. Fairy belief is becoming a fairy tale. In another generation it will grow into a romance, as it has in the hands of poets elsewhere, and then the whole will either be forgotten or carried from people who must work to "gentles" who can afford to be idle and read books. Railways, roads, newspapers, and tourists, are slowly but surely doing their accustomed work. They are driving out romance; but they are not driving out the popular creed as to supernaturals. That creed will survive when the last remnant of romance has been banished, for superstition seems to belong to no one period in the history of civilization, but to all. It is as rife in towns as it is amongst the hills, and is not confined to the ignorant.

I have wandered amongst the peasantry of many countries, and this trip but confirmed my old impression. There are few peasants that I think so highly of, none that I like so well. Scotch Highlanders have faults in plenty, but they have the bearing of Nature's own gentlemen—the delicate, natural tact which discovers, and the good taste which avoids, all that would hurt or offend a guest. The poorest is ever the readiest to share the best he has with the stranger. A kind word kindly meant is never thrown away, and whatever may be the faults of this people, I have never found a boor or a churl in a Highland bothy.

Celts have played their part in history, and they have a part to play still in Canada and Australia, where their language and character will leave a trace, if they do not influence the destiny of these new worlds. There are hundreds in those distant lands whose language is still Gaelic, and to whom these stories are familiar, and if this book should ever remind any of them of the old country, I shall not have worked in vain in the land which they call "Tir nam Beann, 's nan Gleann, 's nan Gaisgeach."*

So much, then, for the manner of collecting the tales, and the people who told them. The popular lore which I found current in the west, and known all over the Highlands in a greater or less degree amongst the poorer classes, consists of:—

1st. That which is called Seanachas na Finne, or Feinnie, or Fiann, that is, the tradition or old history of the Feene.

This is now the rarest of any, and is commonest, so far as I know,

* The land of Hills, and Glens, and Heroes.

in Barra and South Uist. There are first fragments of poems which may have been taken from the printed book, which goes by the name of the History of the Finne in the Highlands, and the Poems of Ossian elsewhere. I never asked for these, but I was told that the words were "sharper and deeper" than those in the printed book.

There are, secondly, poetical fragments about the same persons, which, to the best of my knowledge, are not in any printed book. I heard some of these repeated by three different men.

Patrick Smith, in South Uist, *intoned* a long fragment; I should guess, about 200 lines. He recited it rapidly to a kind of chant. The subject was a fight with a Norway witch, and Fionn, Diarmaid, Oscar and Conan, were named as Irish heroes. There were "ships fastened with silver chains, and kings holding them;" swords, spears, helmets, shields, and battles, were mentioned; in short, the fragment was the same in style and machinery as the famous Poems; and it was attributed to Ossian. The repetition began with a short prose account of what was to follow. Smith is sixty, and says that he cannot read. He does not understand English. He says that such poems used to be so chanted commonly when he was young. The same account of the manner of reciting similar poems was given me by a clergyman in Argyllshire, who said that, within his recollection, the "death of Cuchullin" used to be so recited by an old man at the head of Loch Awe.

Donald Macintyre, in Benbecula, recited a similar fragment, which has since been written and sent to me. The subject is a dialogue between a lady and a messenger returning from battle, with a number of heads on a withy; the lady asks their story, and the messenger tells whose heads they were, and how the heroes fell. It sounded better than it reads, but the transcriber had never written Gaelic before.

John Campbell, generally known as "Yellow John," living in Strath Gearrloch, about twelve miles west of Flowerdale, repeated a similar fragment, which lasted for a quarter of an hour. He said he had known it for half a century. He is a very old man, and it is difficult to follow him, and the poetry was mingled with prose, and with "said he," "said she." It was the last remnant of something which the old man could only remember imperfectly, and which he gave in broken sentences; but here again the combat was with a Norway witch, and the scene, Ireland. Fionn, Diarmaid and other such names appeared. Diarmaid had "his golden helm on his head;" his "two spears on his shoulder;" his "Narrow-pointed shield on his left arm;" his "small shield on his right;" his sword was "leafy," (?) leaf-shaped. And the old man believed that Diarmaid, the Irish hero, was his ancestor, and his own real name O'Duine. He spoke of "his chief MacCalain," and treated me with extra kindness, as a kinsman. "Will you not take some more" (milk and potatoes). "Perhaps we may never see each other again. Are we not both Campbells?"

I heard of other men who could repeat such poems, and I have heard of such men all my life; but as I did not see out to gather poems, I took no trouble to get them.

Two chiefs, I think one was MacLeod, sent their two fools to gather bait on the shore; and to settle a bet which fool was the best, they strewed gold on the path. One fool stopped to gather it, but the other said, "When we are at 'golding,' let us be 'golding,' and when we are at bait-making, let us be bait-making," and he stuck to his business. My business was prose, but it may not be out of place to state my own opinion about the Ossian controversy, for I have been asked more than once if I had found any trace of such poems.

I believe that there were poems of very old date, of which a few fragments still exist in Scotland as pure traditions. That these related to Celtic worthies who were popular heroes before the Celts came from Ireland, and answer to Arthur and his knights elsewhere. That the same personages have figured in poems composed, or altered, or improved, or spoilt by bards who lived in Scotland, and by Irish bards of all periods; and that these personages have been mythical heroes amongst Celts from the earliest of times. That "the poems" were orally collected by Macpherson, and by men before him, by Dr. Smith, by the committee of the Highland Society, and by others, and that the printed Gaelic is old poetry, mended and patched, and pieced together, and altered, but on the whole a genuine work. Manuscript evidence of the antiquity of similar Gaelic poems exists. Some were printed in 1807, under the authority of the Highland Society of London, with a Latin translation, notes, etc., and were reprinted in 1818. MacPherson's "translation" appeared between 1760 and 1762, and the controversy raged from the beginning, and is growling still; but the dispute now is, whether the poems were originally *Scotch* or *Irish*, and how much MacPherson altered them. It is like the quarrel about the chameleon, for the languages spoken in Islay and Rathlin are identical, and the language of the poems is difficult for me, though I have *spoken* Gaelic from my childhood. There is no doubt at all that Gaelic poems on such subjects existed long before MacPherson was born; and it is equally certain that there is no composition in the Gaelic language which bears the smallest resemblance in style to the peculiar kind of prose in which it pleased MacPherson to translate. The poems have a peculiar rhythm, and a style of their own which is altogether lost in his English translation. But what concerns me is the popular belief, and it seems to be this—"Mac-Pherson must have been a very dishonest person when he allowed himself to pass as the author of Ossian's poems." So said a lady, one of my earliest friends, whose age has not impaired her memory, and so say those who are best informed, and understand the language.

The illiterate seem to have no opinion on the subject. So far as I could ascertain, few had heard of the controversy, but they had all heard scraps of poems and stories about the Finne, all their lives; and they are content to believe that "Ossian, the last of the Finne," composed the poems, wrote them, and burned his book in a pet, when he was old and blind, because St. Patrick, or St. Paul, or some other saint, would not believe his wonderful stories.

Those who would study "the controversy," will find plenty of discussion; but the report of the Highland Society appears to settle the question on evidence. I cannot do better than quote from Johnson's Poets the opinion of a great author, who was a great translator, who, in speaking of his own work, says:—

> "What must the world think ... After such a judgment passed by so great a critick, the world who decides so often, and who examines so seldom; the world who, even in matters of literature, is almost always the slave of authority? Who will suspect that so much learning should mistake, that so much accuracy should be misled, or that so much candour should be biassed? ... I think that no translation ought to be the ground of criticism, because no man ought to be condemned upon another man's explanation of his meaning... ." (Postscript to the Odyssey, Pope's Homer, Johnson's Poets, pp. 279, 280.

And to that quotation let me add this manuscript note, which I found in a copy of the Report of the Highland Society on the poems of Ossian; which I purchased in December 1859; and which came from the library of Colonel Hamilton Smith, at Plymouth.

> "The Reverend Dr. Campbell, of Halfway Tree, Lisuana, in Jamaica, often repeated to me in the year 1709, 1801, and

1802, parts of Ossian in Gaelic; and assured me that he had possessed a manuscript, long the property of his family, in which Gaelic poems, and in particular, whole pieces of Ossian's compositions were contained. This he took out with him on his first voyage to the West Indies in 1780, when his ship was captured by a boat from the Santissima Trinidata, flagship of the whole Spanish fleet; and he, together with all the other passengers, lost nearly the whole of their baggage, among which was the volume in question. In 1814, when I was on the staff of General Sir Thomas Graham, now Lord Lyndoch, I understood that Mr. MacPherson had been at one time his tutor; and, therefore, I asked his opinion respecting the authenticity of the Poems. His lordship replied that he never had any doubts on the subject, he having seen in Mr. MacPherson's possession several manuscripts in the Gaelic language, and heard him speak of them repeatedly; he told me some stronger particulars, which I cannot now note down, for the conversation took place during the action of our winter campaign.

(Signed) "CHARLES HAMN. SMITH, Lt.-Col."

The Colonel had the reputation of being a great antiquary, and had a valuable library. James MacPherson, a "modest young man, who was master of Greek and Latin," was "procured" to be a preceptor to "the boy Tommy," who was afterwards Lord Lyndoch (according to a letter in a book printed for private circulation). As it appears to me, those who are ignorant of Gaelic, and now-a-days maintain that "MacPherson composed Ossian's Poems," are like critics who, being ignorant of Greek, should maintain that Pope wrote the Odyssey, and was the father of Homer; or, being ignorant of English, should declare that Tennyson was the father of King Arthur and all his knights, because he has published one of many poems which treat of them. It was different when Highlanders were "rebels;" and it was petty treason to deny that they were savages.

A glance at "Johnson's Tour in the Hebrides," will show the feeling of the day. He heard Gaelic songs in plenty, but would not believe in Gaelic poems. He appreciated the kindness and hospitality with which he was treated; he praised the politeness of all ranks, and yet maintained that their language was "the rude speech of a barbarous people, who had few thoughts to express, and were content, as they conceived grossly, to be grossly understood."

He could see no beauty in the mountains which men now flock

to see. He saw no fish in fording northern rivers, and explains how the winter torrents sweep them away; the stags were "perhaps not bigger than our fallow-deer;" the waves were not larger than those on the coast of Sussex; and yet, though the Doctor would not believe in Gaelic poems, he did believe that peat grew as it was cut, and that the vegetable part of it probably caused a glowing redness in the earth of which it is mainly composed; and he came away willing to believe in the second sight, though not quite convinced.

That sturdy old Briton, the great lexicographer, who is an honour to his country, was not wholly free from national prejudice; he erred in some things; he may have erred in a matter of which he could not well judge; he did not understand Gaelic; he did not believe in traditions; he would not believe in the translations; and MacPherson seems to have ended by encouraging the public belief that he was the author of poems which had gained so wide a celebrity.

Matters have changed for the better since those days; Celt and Saxon are no longer deadly foes. There still exists, as I am informed, an anti-Celtic society, whose president, on state occasions, wears three pairs of trousers; but it is no longer penal to dispense with these garments; and there are Southerns who discard them altogether, when they go north to pursue the little stags on the ugly hills, and catch fish in the torrents.

There are Celtic names in high places, in India, and at home; and an English Duke is turning the Gaelic of Ossian's poems into English verse.

This, however, is foreign to my subject, though it bears somewhat on the rest of the traditions of the Finne. I have stated my own opinion because I hold it, not because I wish to influence those who differ from me. I have no wish to stir up the embers of an expiring controversy, which was besprinkled with peculiarly acrid ink, and obscured by acid fumes. I neither believe that MacPherson composed Ossian, nor that Ossian composed all the poems which bear his name. I am quite content to believe Ossian to have been an Irishman, or a Scotsman, or a myth, on sufficient evidence.

Besides these few remnants of poetry which still survive, I find a great many prose tales relating to the heroes of the poems; and as these personages certainly were popular heroes in Ireland and in Scotland centuries ago, I give what I have gathered concerning them, with the conviction that it is purely Celtic tradition.*

* See page 256 of "Scotland in the Middle Ages," by Cosmo Innes, Edmunston and Douglas, 1860, for evidence taken from "The fathers of our Scotch literature," and the Report of the Highland Society.

The Seannachas of the Fine consists, then, of poetry already printed; fragments which are not in print, so far as I know, and which are now very rare; and prose tales which are tolerably common, but rapidly disappearing.

In all these, according to tradition, Fionn, Diarmaid, and the rest, are generally represented as Irish worthies. The scene is often laid in Ireland; but there are hundreds of places in Scotland in which some of the exploits are said to have been performed. I know not how many cairns are supposed to contain the bones of the wild boar, whose bristles wounded the feet of Diarmaid when he paced his length against the hair; Kyle Reay, in Skye, is named after a giant warrior who leaped the strait. There are endless mountains bearing Ossianic names in all parts of Scotland, and even in the Isle of Man the same names are to be found mixed up with legends. In April 1860, I met a peasant near Ramsey who knew the name of Fin MacCoul, though he would not say a word about him to me. In Train's history of the Island, published by Mary Quiggin, 1845, at page 359, is this note:—

"In a letter, dated 20th September, 1844, from a highly respected correspondent in the Isle of Man, he says—'Are you aware that the septennial appearance of the island, said to be submerged in the sea by enchantment near Port Soderick, is expected about the end of this month?' Though the spell by which this fancified island has been bound to the bottom of the ocean since the days of the great Fin MacCoul, and its inhabitants transformed in blocks of granite, might, according to popular belief, be broke by placing a bible on any part of the enchanted land when at its original altitude above the waters of the deep, where it is permitted to remain only for the short space of thirty minutes. No person has yet had the hardihood to make the attempt, lest, in case of failure, the enchanter, in revenge, might cast his club over Mona also."

And in Cregeen's Manks dictionary, by the same publisher, 1835, is this Manks proverb—

"Ny three geayghn s' feayrey dennee Fion M'Cooil,
Geay henneu, as geay huill,
As geay fo ny shiauill."

Which I understand to mean—

> The three coldest winds that came to Fion M'Cooil,
> Wind from a thaw, wind from a hole,
> And wind from under the sails.

In short, I believe that the heroes of Ossian belong to the race, not to any one set of poems, or to any single branch of the Celtic language.

2d. There are tales, not necessarily about the Fin, consisting partly of plain narrative and dialogue, which vary with every narrator, and probably more or less every time the story is told; and partly of a kind of measured prose, which is unlike anything I know in any other language. I suspect that these have been compositions at some time, but at what time I cannot even guess.

These almost always relate to Ireland and Scandinavia; to boats, knights, swords, and shields. There are adventures under ground, much battle, generally an island with fire about it (perhaps Iceland), and a lady to be carried off. There is often an old woman who has some mysterious vessel of balsam which brings the dead to life, and a despised character who turns out to be the real hero, sometimes a boaster who is held up to ridicule. I believe these to be bardic recitations fast disappearing and changing into prose; for the older the narrator is, the less educated, and the farther removed from the rest of the world, the more his stories are garnished with these passages. "Fin MacCumhal goes go Graffee," published in 1857, from Mayo, is evidently a translation of a tale of this kind. In all these, the scene is laid in Eirinn and Lochlan, now Ireland and Scandinavia; and these would seem to have been border countries. Perhaps the stories relate to the time when the Scandinavians occupied part of the Western Isles.

3d. There is popular history of events which really happened within the last few centuries: of this, I have gathered none, but I heard a great deal in a very short time, and I have heard it all my life. It is a history devoid of dates, but with clear starting points. The event happened at the time of Shamas (James) at the battle of Shirra Muir; at Inverlochy; after Culloden. The battle was between MacNeill and MacLeod. MacLeod came from *that* castle. They met on *that* strand. The dead are buried *there*. Their descendants now live in such a place. He was the last man hanged in Harris. *That* is called the slab of lamentation, from which the MacLeans embarked for Ireland when the MacDonalds had conquered them, and taken the land. MacLean exposed his wife on the Lady Rock because she had made his servant blow up one of the ships of the

Spanish Armada, for jealousy of the Spanish lady who was on board. The history is minute and circumstantial, and might be very interesting if faithfully collected, but it is rather local than national, and is not within the scope of my work. It is by far the most abundant popular lore, and has still a great hold on the people. The decision of a magistrate in a late case of "Sapaid" (broken heads) was very effective, because he appealed to this feeling. It was thus described to me: "Ah! he gave it to them. He leant back in his chair, and spoke grandly for half an hour. He said you are as wild men fighting together in the days of King Shamas."

4th. There are tales which relate to men and women only, and to events that might have happened anywhere at any time. They might possibly be true, and equally true, whether the incidents happened to an Eastern sage or a wise old Highlander. Such tales as Nos. 19 and 20. These are plentiful, and their characteristic is sagacity and hidden meaning.

5th. There are children's tales, of which some are given. They are in poetry and prose as elsewhere, and bear a general resemblance to such tales all over the world. The cat and the mouse play parts in the nursery drama of the Western Isles, as well as in "Contes et Apologues Indiens inconnus jusqu' a ce jour," etc.; a translation into French, by Mr. Stanislaus Julien, in 1860, of Chinese books, which were translated into that language from Sanscrit in 1565, by a Chinese doctor, and President of the Ministry of Justice, who composed "The Forest of Comparisons," in twenty-four volumes, divided into 20 classes, and subdivided into 508 sections, after twenty years of hard labour, during which he abstracted about 400 works. This is the name of one; Fo-choue-kiun-nieou-pi-king.

Let those who call Gaelic hard, try that; or this: Tchong-king-siouen-tsi-pi-yu-king.

Let those who contemn nursery rhymes, think of the French savant, and the Chinese cabinet minister, and the learning which they have bestowed on the conversations of cats and mice.

6th. Riddles and puzzles, of which there are a very great number. They are generally descriptive, such as, "No bigger than a barley corn, it covers the king's board"—(the eye). I have given a few. If any despise riddles, let them bear in mind that the Queen of Sheba is believed to have propounded riddles to Solomon, and that Samson certainly proposed a riddle to the Philistines. I am told that riddles are common in India now.

7th. Proverbs, in prose and in verse, of which 1515 were printed in 1819, and many more are still to be got. Many are evidently very old from their construction, and some are explained by the stories, for example, "Blackberries in February" has no very evident meaning, but a long story explains that difficulties may by vanquished. A king's son was sent by a stepmother to get "that which grew, and is neither crooked nor straight"—(sawdust); "Blackberries in February," which he found growing in a charnel-house; and a third thing, equally easy to find when the way was known.

8th. There are songs, of which there are a vast number, published and unpublished, of all sorts and kinds, sung to wild and peculiar tunes. They are condemned and forbidden in some districts, and are vanishing rapidly from all. These used to be sung continually within my recollection, and many of them are wild, and, to my ear, beautiful. There are songs composed in a particular rhythm for rowing, for washing clothes by dancing on them; songs whose rhythm resembles a piobroch; love songs; war songs; songs which are nearly all chorus, and which are composed as they are sung. The composer gives out a single line applicable to anything then present, and the chorus fills up the time by singing and clapping hands, till the second line is prepared. I have known such lines fired at a sportsman by a bevy of girls who were waulking blankets in a byre, and who made the gun and the dog the theme of several stanzas. Reid's Bibliotheca Scoto-Celtica, 1832, gives a list of eighty-one Gaelic books of poetry printed since 1785. There are hymn books, song books, and poetry composed by known and unknown bards, male and female. Of the former, Mackenzie, in his Beauties of Gaelic poetry, gives a list of thirty-two, with specimens of their works and a short biography. Of the latter class, the unknown poets, there are many at the present day; and who is to guess their number in times when men did nothing but fight and sing about their battles? A very few of these bards have become known to the world by name, and, in all probability their merits never will be known. Let any one translate Sir Patrick Spens or Annie Laurie into French or Greek, or read a French translation of Waverley, and the effect of translation on such compositions will be evident.

9th. The romantic popular tales of which this collection mainly consists.

I presume that I have said enough as to their collection, and that I may now point out what seems to me to be their bearing on the scientific part of the subject; that I may take them as tradition, and argue from them as from established facts. I have endeavoured to show how, when, and where I got the stories; each has its own separate pedigree, and I have given the original Gaelic, with the closest translation which I was able to make.

Now, let me mention the works in which I have found similar tales, and which are within the reach of all who can read English. First—Tales from the Norse, translated by G. W. Dasent, published 1859. Many of the Gaelic tales collected in 1859 resemble these very closely. The likeness is pointed out in the notes.

It is impossible that the book could have become known to the people who told the stories within the time, but if it were, a manuscript which has been lent to me by the translator, proves that the stories were known in Scotland before the translation from the Norse was made public.

It is a verbatim copy made by a clergyman from a collection of fourteen tales, gathered by "Peter Buchan, editor of the Ancient Ballads and Songs of the North of Scotland." It is dated 1848, Glasgow; and signed, Alexander B. Grosart. The tales are written in English, and versions of all except three, had previously come to me in Gaelic. For example, (No. 2), The Battle of the Birds closely resembles "The Master Maid" from Norway, but it still more resembles Mr. Peter Buchan's "Greensleeves," found in Scotland thirteen years before the Norse tales were translated. The manuscript was sent by Mr. Grosart, after he had read the Norse tales, and it seems to be clearly proved that these stories are common to Norway and Scotland.

I have found very few stories of the kind amongst the peasantry of the low country, though I have sought them. I find such names as Fingal in Mr. Buchan's stories, and I know them to be common in the islands where the scene is often laid. The language is not that of any peasantry, and I have come to the conclusion that this collection is mostly derived from Gaelic, directly or indirectly, perhaps from the shoals of West Highlanders and Irishmen who used to come down as shearers every harvest, and who are now scattered all over Scotland as farm-servants and drovers, and settled in Edinburgh and Glasgow as porters. I know from one of these, a drover, who goes every year to the south with cattle, that he has often entertained lowland farm-servants by telling in English the stories which he learned as child in South Uist. I know of men in Paisley, Greenock, and Edinburgh, who are noted for their knowledge of sgeulachd. But while I hold that this particular collection was not told in this form by lowland Scotch peasants, I know that they still do tell such stories occasionally, and I also know that Englishmen of the lower ranks do the same. I met two tinkers in

St. James's Street in February with black faces and a pan of burning
coals each. They were followed by a wife, and preceded by a mangy
terrier with a stiff tail. I joined the party, and one told me a version
of "the man who travelled to learn what shivering meant," while
we walked together through the park to Westminster. It was clearly
the popular tale which exist in Norse, and German, and Gaelic, and
it bore the stamp of the mind of the class, and of the man, who told
it in his own peculiar dialect, and who dressed the actors in his own
ideas. A cutler and a tinker travel together, and sleep in an empty
haunted house for a reward. They are beset by ghosts and spirits of
murdered ladies and gentlemen, and the inferior, the tinker, shows
most courage, and is the hero. "He went into the cellar to draw
beer, and there he found a little chap a-sittin' on a barrel with a red
cap on 'is 'ed; and sez he, sez he, 'Buzz.' 'Wot's buzz?' sez the tinker.
'Never you mind wot's buzz,' sez he. 'That's mine; don't you go
for to touch it,' " etc., etc., etc.

In a less degree many are like the German stories of the brothers
Grimm. That collection has been translated, and a book so well
known may possibly have found its way into the Highlands. It is
impossible to speak with certainty; but when all the narrators agree
in saying that they have known their stories all their lives, and when
the variation is so marked, the resemblance is rather to be attributed
to common origin than to books. I only once heard of such a book
in the Highlands. It was given to a gamekeeper in Sutherland for
his children, and was condemned, and put out of the way as trash.

The Gaelic stories resemble in some few cases the well-known
tales of Hans Andersen, founded on popular tales told in Denmark.

And they resemble sundry other books which are avowedly
founded on popular tales collected in various countries.

Some are like the French tales of the Countess D'Aulnoy which
have been translated. One is like part of Shakespeare, but it is still
more like the Italian story in Boccaccio, from which part of Cymbeline is supposed to be taken. Perhaps Shakespeare may have
founded Cymbeline on a popular tale then current in England as
well as in Italy.

A few resemble the Arabian Nights, and in some cases I believe
that the stories have been derived from early English translations
of that well-known book. I used myself to read an edition of 1815
to my piper guardian, in return for his ursgeuls, but he seemed more
inclined to blame the tyranny of the kings than to admire the
Eastern stories.

MacLean has himself told the story of Aladdin in Gaelic as his share of a winter night's entertainment, and I have heard of several people of the poorer class who know the Arabian Nights well. But such stories are easily known after a little experience has been gained. The whole of a volume is run together, the incidents follow in their order, or in something like it. The difference in style is as marked as the contrast between a drift tree and a wrecked vessel, but as it is curious to trace the change from Eastern ways as seen through an English translation of a French view of the original Arabic, I give specimens. These contain the incidents embodied in stories in the Arabian Nights, but the whole machinery and decoration, manners and customs, are now as completely West Highland as if the tales had grown there. But for a camel which appears, I would almost give up my opinion, and adopt that of MacLean, who holds that even these are pure traditions.

In support of his view it may be said that there are hundreds of other books as well known in England as those mentioned above, of which neither I nor my collectors have ever found a trace. Jack and the Bean-stalk, and Jack the Giant-killer, Beauty and the Beast, and the Sleeping Beauty in the Woods, as known in England, are unknown in the Highlands. None of the adventures of Mr. Pickwick, or Sam Weller, or Jack Shepherd, or Gulliver, or Robinson Crusoe, are mixed up with the prose tales. No part of the story of Wallace, as told in the "Scottish Chiefs," or of "Waverley," is to be found in popular history. There is nothing like "The Mysteries of London." There are none of the modern horrors of which ballads have been made, such as "Sad was the day when James Greenacre first got acquainted with Sarah Gale." There are no gorgeous palaces, and elegant fairies; there are no enchanters flying in chariots drawn by winged griffins; there are no gentle knights and noble dames; no spruce cavaliers and well-dressed ladies; no heroes and heroines of fashionable novels; but, on the contrary, everything is popular. Heroes are as wild, and unkempt, and savage as they probably were in fact, and kings are men as they appear in Lane's translations of the Arabian Nights.

Eastern tale tellers knew what Haroun al Raschid must have suffered when he put on the fisherman's clothes, and Mr. Lane has not scrupled to follow the original Arabic.

If the people of the West Highlands have added book stories to their traditions, they have selected those only which were taken from peasants like themselves in other countries, and they have stripped off all that was foreign to their own manners. The people have but taken back their own.

Besides books accessible to all English readers, I find similar stories in books beyond the reach of the people. I have pointed out in the notes all that were within my reach, and came under my notice, but this part of the subject is a study, and requires time to acquire knowledge which I do not possess.

Such, then, is the evidence which bears on the immediate origin of the stories. I believe them to be pure traditions, very little affected by modern books, and, if at all, only by those which are avowedly taken from popular tales. A trip of five days in the Isle of Man in April 1860 has but confirmed this opinion.

That island, in spite of its numerous rulers, is still peculiarly Celtic. It has belonged to Norwegians. English, Scotch, Welsh, and Irish have fought for it. It has a Law Court with a Norwegian name held on a mound; half the names in the island are Norse, such as Laxey (Salmon isthmus), Langness, Snafell; but these names are not understood by the people who live at the places. Peel has a descriptive Gaelic name, which means island port; a Salmon is Braddan, not Lax; and of the poorer classes living in the mountain farms, and on the points and distant corners of the island, there are still many who can hardly speak anything but Manks. Their hair is dark; the sound of their voices, even their houses, are Celtic. I know one turf dwelling which might be a house in North Uist. There was the fire on the floor, the children seated around it, the black haired Celtic mother on a low stool in front,—the hens quarrelling about a nest under the table, in which several wanted to lay eggs at once.

"Get out, Polly! Drive her out, John!" And then John, the son, drove out Polly, the hen, with a stick; and the hen said "Gurr-r-m;" and ran in under the table again and said, "Cluck, cluck," and laid the egg then and there. There was the same kindly hospitable manner in the poorest cottage; and I soon found that a Scotch Highlander could speak Manks as soon as he could acquire the art of mispronouncing his own language to the right amount, and learn where to introduce the proper English word. "La fine"—fine day—was the salutation everywhere; and the reply, "Fine, fine." But though nouns are almost the same, and the language is but a dialect of Gaelic, the foreigner was incomprehensible, because he could not pronounce as they did; and I was reduced to English. Now this island is visited every summer by shoals of visitors from the mainland; steam-boats bring them from Liverpool, a thousand at a time, and they sweep over the whole country. If visitors import stories, here there are plenty of strangers, and I was a stranger myself. If stories are imported in books, here are the books also. The first picture I saw on landing was a magnificent Bluebeard in a shop window. He was dressed as an Eastern potentate, and about to slice off his wife's head with a crooked scimitar, while the two brothers rode up to the gate on prancing steeds, with horror on their faces and swords in their hands. But there was not a trace of any of that kind of story to be found amongst the peasants with whom I spoke in the Isle of Man.

I found them willing to talk, eager to question, kindly, homely folk, with whom it was easy to begin an acquaintance. I heard everywhere that it *used* to be common to hear old men telling stories about the fire in Manks; but any attempt to extract a story, or search out a queer old custom, or a half-forgotten belief, seemed to act as a pinch of snuff does on a snail.

The Manksman would not trust the foreigner with his secrets; his eye twinkled suspiciously, and his hand seemed unconsciously to grasp his mouth, as if to keep all fast. After getting quite at ease with one old fellow over a pipe, and having learned that a neighbour's cow had born a calf to the "Taroo ustey," water bull, I thought I might fish for a story, and told one as a bait.

"That man, if he had two pints, would tell you stories by the hour," said a boy. "Oh, yes, they used to tell plenty of stories," said the old man, "Skyll, as we call them."

Here was the very word mispronounced, "sgeul," so my hopes rose. "Will you tell me a story now?" "Have you any churches in your country?" "Yes, and chapels; but will you tell me a story?" "What you got to sell in your bag?" "What a shame now, for you, an old Mananach, not to tell me a story when I have told you one, and filled your pipe and all." "What do you pay for the tobacco?" "Oh, will you not tell the man a story?" said the boy. "I must go and saw now," said the old man; and so we parted.

But though this was the usual thing, it was not always so; and it soon became evident that the stories given in Train's history of the Isle of Man, are nearly all known to the people now; and these are of the same nature as some known in the Highlands of Scotland; some are almost identical; and nearly all the Manks customs are common to the Western Isles.

Thus I heard of Fairies, "Ferish," who live in green mounds, and are heard at times dressing mill-stones in haunted mills; of Taroo Ustey, the water bull; of Dinny Mara, the sea man, and of the Mermaid; of Caval Ustey, the water horse; of Fion MacCooil; of a city under the waves; of a magic island seen in the far west. I heard of giants. No one would tell about them; but in a book I found how

Goddard Crovan threw a vast boulder at his scolding wife, and how a Norman baron, named "Kitter" and his cook; "Eaoch," and his magic sword, "Macabuin," made by "Loan Maclibhuin, the dark smith of Drontheim;" and "Hiallusnan-urd, the one-legged hammerman,"—are all woven into a story, and mixed up with such Norwegian names as Olave and Emergaid, exactly as a story is jumbled together in the Western Isles of Scotland.

I got some stories which I have not found in the Manks books, so I give them here, in the hope that some Manksman may be induced to gather the popular lore of his own country. This from a woman who lives near the Calf of Man.

"Did you ever hear tell of the Glashan?"

"No; tell me about the Glashan."

"Well, you see, in the old times they used to be keeping the sheep in the folds; and one night an old man forgot to put them in, and he sent out his son, and he came back and said the sheep were all folded, but there was a year-old lamb, oasht, playing the mischief with them; and that was the Glashan.

"You see they were very strong, and when they wanted a stack threshed, though it was a whole stack, the glashan would have it threshed for them in one night.

"And they were running after the women. There was one of them once caught a girl, and had a hould of her by the dress, and he sat down and he fell asleep; and then she cut away all the dress, you see, round about this way, and left it in his fist and ran away; and when he awoke, he threw what he had over his shoulder, this way; and he said (something in Manks which I could not catch).

"Well, you see, one night the ould fellow sent all the women to bed, and he put on a cap and a woman's dress, and he sat down by the fire and he began to spin; and the young glashans, they came in, and they began saying something in Manks that means 'Are you turning the wheel? are you trying the reel?' Well, the ould glashan, he was outside, and he knew better than the young ones; he knew it was the ould fellow himself, and he was telling them, but they did not mind him; and so the ould man threw a lot of hot turf, you see, it was turf they burned then, over them and burned them; and the ould one said (something in Manks). 'You'll not understand that, now?' 'Yes, I do, pretty nearly.' 'Ah, well.' And so the glashans went away and never came back any more."

"Have you many stories like that, guidwife?" "Ay," said she, "there were plenty of people that could tell these stories once. When I was a little girl, I used to hear them telling them in Manks over the fire at night; but people is so changed with pride now that they care for nothing."

Now here is a story which is all over the Highlands in various shapes. Sometimes it is a Brollichan son of the Fuath, or a young water horse transformed into the likeness of a man, which attacks a lonely woman, and gets burned or scalded, and goes away to his friends outside. In the islands, the woman generally says her name is Myself; and the goblin answers, when asked who burned him, "Myself." This Manks story is manifestly the same, though this incident is left out. I have heard it in Lewis, and in many places besides, and part of it is best omitted.

The Glashan, as I found out afterwards, frequented neighbouring farms till within a very late period. He wore no clothes, and was hairy; and, according to Train's history, Phynodderee, which means something hairy, was frightened away by a gift of clothes— exactly as the Skipness long-haired Gruagach was frightened away by the offer of a coat and a cap. The Manks brownie and the Argyllshire one each repeated a rhyme over the clothes; but the rhymes are not the same, though they amount to the same thing.

Here, then, is a Gaelic popular tale and belief in Man; and close to it I found a story which has a counterpart in Grimm. I heard it from my landlady at Port Erin, and I met two Manksmen afterwards who knew it—

"The fish all gathered once to choose a king; and the fluke, him that has the red spots on him, stayed at home to make himself pretty, putting on his red spots, to see if he would be king, and he was too late, for when he came the herring was king of the sea. So the fluke curled his mouth on one side, and said, 'A simple fish like the herring, king of the sea!' and his mouth has been to one side ever since."

It seems, too, that the Manks version of "Jack the Giant Killer" varies from the English; for

"Jack the Giant Killer,
Varv a Vuchd in the river,"

killed a pig in the river; and the English hero did nothing of the sort. In short, the Isle of Man has its own legends, which have their own peculiarities; they resemble others, and do not seem to be taken from books. The same class of people tell them there as elsewhere; the difficulty of getting at them is the same; and the key to the secret is the native language. From what I gleaned in a five days' walk, I am sure that a good Manksman might yet gather a large harvest within a very narrow space. And now to return to my own subject.

I find that men of all ranks resemble each other; that each branch of popular lore has its own special votaries, as branches of literature have amongst the learned; that one man is the peasant historian and tells of the battles of the clans; another, a walking peerage, who knows the descent of most of the families in Scotland, and all about his neighbours and their origin; others are romancers, and tell about the giants; others are moralists, and prefer the sagacious prose tales, which have a meaning, and might have a moral; a few know the history of the Feni, and are antiquarians. Many despise the whole as frivolities; they are practical moderns, and answer to practical men in other ranks of society.

But though each prefers his own subject, the best Highland story-tellers know specimens of all kinds. Start them, and it seems as if they would never stop. I timed one, and he spoke for an hour without pause or hesitation, or verbal repetition. His story was Connall Gulban, and he said he could repeat fourscore. He recited a poem, but despised "Bardism"; and he followed me six miles in the dark to my inn, to tell me numbers 19 and 20, which I have condensed; for the very same thing can be shortly told when it is not a composition. For example.

In telling a story, narrative and dialogue are mixed; what the characters have told each other to do is repeated as narrative. The people in the story tell it to each other, and branch off into discussions about their horses and houses and crops, or anything that happens to turn up. One story grows out of another, and the tree is almost hidden by a foliage of the speaker's invention. Here and there comes a passage repeated by rote, and common to many stories, and to every good narrator. It seems to act as a rest for the memory. Now and then, an observation from the audience starts an argument. In short, one good story in the mouth of a good narrator, with a good audience, might easily go rambling on for a whole winter's night, as it is said to do.

The "Slim Swarthy Champion used to last for four hours." Connall Gulban "used to last for three evenings. Those that wanted to hear the end had to come back." One of my collectors said it would take him a month to write it down, but I am bound to add

that he has since done it in a very much shorter time. I have heard
of a man who fell asleep by the fire, and found a story going on
when he awoke next morning. I have one fragment on which (as I
am told) an old man in Ross-shire used to found twenty-four
stories, all of which died with him.

There are varieties in public speakers amongst the people as
amongst their representatives, for some are eloquent, some terse,
some prosy.

But though a tale may be spun out to any extent, the very same
incidents can be, and often are, told in a few words, and those tales
which have been written for me are fair representations of them as
they are usually told. They are like a good condensed report of a
rambling speech, with extraneous matter left out. One narrator said
of the longest story which I had then got—"It is but the contents;"
but I have more than once asked a narrator to tell me the story
which he had previously told to one of my collectors, and a collector
to write down a story which I had previously heard, and I have
always found the pith, often the very words. In no instance have I
found anything added by those whom I employed, when their work
was subjected to this severe test.

This is the account which one of my collectors gives of the old
customs of his class—he is a workman employed by the Duke of
Argyll; he tells me that he is self-educated; and as he repeats some
of the stories which he has written, from memory, his account of
the way in which he acquired them is valuable.

> I remember, upwards of fifty years ago, when I was a boy, my
> father lived in the farest north house, in the valley called
> Glen-na Callanach. I also used to be with my grandfather; he
> lived near Terbert, Lochlomond side. I remember, in the
> winter nights, when a few old people would be together, they
> would pass the time with telling each other stories, which they
> had by tradition. I used to listen attentively, and hear them
> telling about the ceatharnaich, or freebooters, which used to
> come to plunder the country, and take away cattle; and how
> their ancestors would gather themselves togather to fight for
> their property, the battles they fought, and the kind of weap-
> ons they used to fight with; the manners of their ancestors,
> the dress they used to wear, and different hardships they had
> to endure.
>
> I was also sometimes amused, listening to some people
> telling Gaelic romances, which we called sgeulachds. It was

customary for a few youngsters to gather into one house, and whither idle or at some work, such as knitting stockings or spinning, they would amuse each other with some innocent diversion, or telling sgeulachds. Us that was children was very fond of listening to them, and the servant maid that was in my father's house would often tell us a sgeulachd to keep us queit.

In those days, when people killed their Marte cow they keept the hide, and tanned it for leather to themselves. In those days every house was furnished with a wheel and a reel; the women spun, and got their webs woven by a neighbouring weaver; also, the women was dyers for themselves, so that the working class had their leather, their linen, and their cloth of their own manufacturing; and when they required the help of a shoemaker, or of a tailor, they would send for them. The tailors and shoemakers went from house to house, to work wherever they were required, and by travelling the country so much, got acquaint with a great maney of the traditionary tales, and divulged them through the country; and as the country people made the telling of these tales, and listening to hear them, their winter night's amusement, scarcely aney part of them would be lost. Some of these romances is supposed to be of great antiquity, on account of some of the Gaelic words being out of use now. I remember, about forty years ago, of being in company with a man that was watching at night; he wished me to stop with him, and he told me a (sgeulachd) romance; and last year I heard a man telling the same story, about therty miles distante from where I had heard it told forty years before that; and the man which told me the tale could not tell me the meaning of some of the old Gaelic words that was in it. At first I thought they were foreign words, but at last I recollected to have heard some of them repeated in Ossian's poems, and it was by the words that was before, and after them, that I understood the meaning of them. The same man told me another story, which he said he learned from his granfather, and Denmark, Swedden, and Noraway was named in it in Gaelic, but he forgot the name of the two last-named places.

It appears likely to me, that some of these tales was invented by the Druids, and told to the people as sermons; and by these tales the people was caused to believe that there was fairies which lived in little conical hills, and that the fairies had the power of being either visible or invisible, as they thought proper, and that they had the power of enchanting people, and of taking them away and make fairies of them; and that the Druids had charms which would prevent that; and they would give these charms to the people for payment; and maney stories would be told about people being taken away by the fairies, and the charms which had to be used to break the spell, and get them back again; and others, on account of some neglidgeance, never got back aney more.

Also that there was witches; people which had communication with an evil spirit, from which they got the power of changing themselves into aney shape they pleased; that these witches often put themselves in the shape of beasts, and when they were in the shape of beasts, that they had some evil design in view, and that it was dangerous to meet them. Also that they could, and did, sometimes take away the produce of people's dairy, and sometimes of the whole farm. The Druidical priests pretended that they had charms that would prevent the witches from doing aney harm, and they would give a charm for payment. When the first day of summer came, the people was taught to put the fire out of their houses, and to place it on some emince near the house for to keep away the witches, and that it was not safe for them to kindle a fire in their house aney more, until they bought it from beil's druide. That fire was called beil-teine (beils-fire), and the first day of summer was called beil-fires day; and also when the first night of winter came, the people would gather fuel and make blazing fire for to keep away the witches, or at least to deprive them of the power of taking away the produce of the farm, and then they would go to the Druid and buy a kindling of what was called the holy fire. The Druids also caused the people to believe that some families had been enchanted and changed into beasts, and as the proper means had not been used, the spell was never broken; and that swans, seals, and marmaids had been different beings, familys that had been enchanted.

Beil or Beul was the name which the Druids gave their god, and the Druids of Beil pretended to be the friends of the people; they pretended to have charms to cure different kinds of diseases, and also charms to prevent fairies, ghosts, and witches, from annoying or harming people. It is a well-known fact, that the superstitions of the Druids has been handed down from generation to generation for a great maney ages, and is not wholy extinct yet; and we have reason to believe that some of the tales, which was invented in those days for to fright the people, has been told and kept in remembrance in the self and same manner. The priests of Beil was the men that was called Druids, the miracles which they pretended to perform was called meurbheileachd (beil-fingering), and their magic which they pretended to perform was called druichd (druidisem), and we have plenty of reason to believe superstitious tales as well as superstition, originated among the Druids.

JOHN DEWAR.

"J. Campbell, Esq.
"SIR—I hope you will correct aney errors that you may find on this piece which I wrote."

I have corrected only two or three errors in spelling, and the writing is remarkably clear, but I have left some words which express the Gaelic pronunciation of English.

The derivation of MIORBHULL, *a marvel*, from the finger of Bel, was suggested by Dr. Smith (see Armstrong's Dic.)

J.F.C.

Now let me return to the cottage of old Macphie, where I heard a version of the Sea-Maiden, and let me suppose that one of the rafters is the drift log which I saw about to be added to a roof in the same island.

The whole roof is covered with peat soot, but that may be scraped away, and the rough wood appears. There are the holes of boring sea shells, filled with sand and marine products. It is evident that the log came by sea, that it did not come in a ship, and that it was long enough in warm salt water for the barnacles to live and die, and for their dwellings to be filled with sea rubbish; that it floated through latitudes where barnacles live. The fairy eggs, which are picked up on the same shore, point to the West Indies as a stage on the way. Maps of ocean currents shew the gulf-stream flowing from the Gulf of Mexico past the Hebrides, but the tree is a fir, for there is a bit of bark which proves the fact, and it appears that pines grow between 40° and 60° in America. It is therefore possible that the rafter was once an American fir tree, growing in the Rocky Mountains; that it was swept into the Mississippi, and carried to the Gulf of Mexico; drifted by the gulf-stream past the West India Islands to the Hebrides, and stranded by a western gale on its voyage to

Spitzbergen. But all this must have happened long ago, for it is now a rafter covered with the soot of generations. That rafter is a strange fact, it is one of a series, and has to be accounted for. There it is, and a probable account of its journey is, that it came from East to West without the help of man, in obedience to laws which govern the world.

That smoked rafter certainly was once a seed in a fir-cone, somewhere abroad. It grew to be a pine tree; it must have been white with snow in winter, and green in summer, and glittering with rain drops and hoar-frost in bright sunshine at various times and seasons. The number of years it stood in the forest can be counted by the rings in the wood. It is certain that it was torn up by the roots, for the roots are there still. It may have formed a part of one of these wonderful natural rafts of the Mississippi, of which one in 1816 was "No less than ten miles in length, two hundred and twenty yards wide, and eight feet deep."* It has been to warm seas, and has worn a marine dress of green and brown since it lost its own natural dress of green branches. Birds must have sat on it in the forest,—crabs and shells have lived on it at sea, and fish must have swam about it; and yet it is now a rafter, hung with black pendants of peat smoke. A tree that grew beside it may now be in Spitzbergen amongst walrusses. Another may be a snag in the Mississippi amongst alligators, destined to become a fossil tree in a coal field. Part of another may be a Yankee rocking chair, or it may be part of a ship in any part of the World, or the tram of a cart, or bit of a carriage, or a wheel-barrow, or a gate post, or anything that can be made of fir wood anywhere; and the fate of stories may be as various as that of fir trees, but their course may be guessed at by running a back scent overland, as I have endeavoured to follow the voyage of a drift log over sea.

Macphie's story began thus:—"There was a poor old fisher in Skye, and his name was Duncan;" and every version of the story which I have found in the highlands, and I have found many, is as highland as the peat-reek on the rafters. The same story is known in many districts in Scotland, and it is evident, that it has been known there for many years. It is a curious fact. It is worth the trouble of looking under what is purely highland, to see if its origin can be discovered.

First, then, the incidents are generally strung together in a particular order in the Highlands, but, either separately or together,

* Lyell's Principles of Geology, p. 267.

every incident in the story is to be found in some shape in other languages. Norse has it as "Shortshanks." Irish has it. German has it. It is in the Italian of Straparola as "Fortunio." In the French of le Cabinet des Feés, 1785. It is in every language in Europe as "St. George and the Dragon." It is in Mr. Peter Buchan's English of 1847 as part of "Greensleeves." It is in "Perseus and Andromeda." The scene of that story is placed in Syria, and it is connected with Persia. There is something in Sanscrit about Indra, a god who recovered the stolen cattle of the gods, but here the scent is very cold, and the hound at fault, though it seems that the Sanscrit hero was the sun personified, and that he had horses of many colours, including red and white, which were always feminine, as the horses in Gaelic stories are, and which had wings and flew through the air. These were "Svankas," with beautiful steps. "Rohitas," red or brown; Gaelic horses are often described as "Seang," "Ruadh"; and here seems to be a clue which is worth the attention of Eastern scholars.

There is a mermaid in the story, and mermaids are mentioned in Irish, and in Arabic, and in Manks, and Italian: men even assert that they have seen mermaids in the sea within the last few years, amongst the Hebrides and off Plymouth.

There are creatures, Falcon, Wolf and Lion. Two of them were natives within historic times, one is still; but the third is a foreigner. There is an Otter, and a Sea Monster, and in other tales, there are Bears and Doves, and other animals; but every one of them, except the monster, is to be found on the road to the land where Sanscrit was spoken, and all these, and many more, played their part in popular tales elsewhere, while no real animal is ever mentioned which is peculiar to lands out of the road which leads overland to India.

Nearly all these have Gaelic names, and most of them are still living within a few days' journey of the Hebrides under other names. I saw a live wolf from a diligence one fine morning in Brittany, and I have seen bears in Scandinavia and in Germany. The only far-fetched animal is the Lion, and in another story a similar creature appears as "Cu Seang." Here is a fresh scent—for Sing is Lion in India—and *may* once have meant Lion in Gaelic; for though Leomhan is the word now used, Seang is applied to anything slender and active. Shune is a dog in Sanscrit, Siunnach a fox in Gaelic, and there are many other Gaelic words which point to the "eastern origin of Celtic nations." The story cannot have crossed the sea from the West. It is therefore probable that it came from the East, for it is not of home growth, and the question is, how did it get to Barra?

It seems to have been known along a certain track for many ages. It is possible that it came from the far East with the people, and that it has survived ever since. It is hard to account for it otherwise. Those who have most studied the subject so account for popular tales elsewhere, and therefore, Donald Macphie's story of the Sea-Maiden acquires an interest not all its own.

Much has been written, and said, and discovered about the popular migrations which have poured from East to West, and which are moving on still. Philology has mapped out the course of the human stream, and here, in the mind of an old fisherman, unable to read, or to speak any language but his own, is the end of a clue which seems to join Iran and Eirinn; as a rafter in his hut may link him with the Rocky Mountains.

Admit that this so-called fiction, and others like it, *may* be traditions, which have existed from the earliest of times, and every word and incident acquires an interest, for it may lead to something else.

The story certainly grew in the mind of man, as a tree grows from a seed, but when or where? It has certainly been told in many languages. It is worth inquiring how many races have told it.

The incidents, like drift trees, have been associated with people and events, as various as birds, fish, alligators, walrusses, and men; mountain ranges, and ocean currents. They have passed through the minds of Ovid and Donald Macphie. They have been adorned by poets, painted by artists, consecrated by priests,—for St. George is the patron saint of England; and now we find that which may have sprung from some quarrel about a cow, and which has passed through so many changes, dropping into forgetfulness in the mind of an old fisherman, and surrounded with the ideas which belong to his every-day life. Ideas differing from those of the people who first invented the story, as the snow of the Rocky Mountains differs from peat-reek.

Now, to look forwards, and follow in imagination the shoals of emigrants from Germany, Scandinavia, France, Ireland, and Scotland, who are settled in clumps, or scattered over America and Australia; to think of the stories which have been gathered in Europe from these people alone, and which they have most certainly carried with them, and will tell their children; and then the route of popular tales hereafter, and their spread in former ages, can be traced and may be guessed.

I have inquired, and find that several Islanders, who used to tell
the stories in Gaelic, are now settled in Australia and Canada. One
of my relatives was nearly overwhelmed with hospitality in an
Australian village, by a colony of Argyllshire Celts, who had found
out that he was a countryman.

I was lately told of a party of men who landed in South America,
and addressed a woman whom they found in a hut, in seven
different languages; but in vain. At last, one of them spoke Gaelic,
which he had not done for many years, and she answered, "Well,
it is to thyself I would give the speech," for she was a native of
Strathglas.

There is a Gaelic population in Upper Canada: there are Highland regiments in India: many of the Arctic explorers were Highlanders, and most of the servants of the Hudson's Bay Company
still are: Dr. Livingstone is in South Africa; and what is true of
Highlanders is equally true of Germans and Scandinavians, they
are spread over the world. In short, the "migration of races," and
"the diffusion of popular tales," is still going on, the whole human
race is mingling together, and it is fair to argue from such facts, and
to try to discover that which is unknown from that which is proved.

What is true of one Gaelic story is true of nearly all; they contain
within themselves evidence that they have been domesticated in the
country for a long time, and that they came from the East, but they
belong to the people now, wherever they came from; and they seem
also to belong to the language.

Poems and compositions clearly do. In the prose tales, when
animals speak, they talk in their natural key, so long as they speak
Gaelic, and for that reason, among others, I believe them to be old
traditions. The little birds speak in the key of all little birds (ee);
they say, "beeg, beeg." The crow croaks his own music when he
says, "gawrag, gawrag." When driven to say, "silly, silly," he no
longer speaks the language of nature. Grimm's German frog says,
"warte, warte," he sings, "mach mir auf," and talks his own
language. So does his Gaelic relative, in No. 33, when he says,—

> "A chaomhag, a chaomhag,
> An cuimhneach leat
> An gealladh beag
> A thug thu aig
> An tobar dhomh,
> A ghaoil, a ghaoil?"

He then imitates the quarking and gurgling of real frogs in a pond

in spring, in sounds which no Saxon letters can express; but when
he sings,—

> "Open the door, my hinney, my heart,
> Open the door, my ain wee thing,
> And mind the words that you and I spak',
> Down in the meadow, at the well spring,"

he is speaking in a foreign tongue, though the story has been
domesticated in the Lowlands of Scotland for many a long day, and
is commonly told there still. The Scotch story has probably been
found and polished by some one long ago, but when the frog comes
"loup, louping," he is at home in Low Country Scotch, and these
words are probably as old as the story and the language.

If Motherwell's beautiful nursery songs were to be collected from
oral recitation anywhere, they would prove themselues Scotch by
this test: The watch-dog says, "wouff, wouff;" the hen is "chuckie;"
the chickens, "wheetle, wheeties;" the cock is "cockie-leerie-law;"
the pigeon, "croodle-doo;" the cow says, "moo." And so also the
wood-pigeon who said, "Take two sheep, Taffy take two," spoke
English; but the blackcock, and cuckoo, and cock, in the Norse
tales, who quarrelled about a cow, are easily known to be foreigners
when they speak English, for the original Norse alone gives their
true note. The Gaelic stories, tried by this test, certainly belong to
the language as they do to the people; and now let us see if they can
teach us anything about the people, their origin, and their habits,
past and present.

First, the manners are generally those of the day. The tales are
like the feasts of the pauper maniac, Emperor of the world, who
confided to his doctor that all his rich food tasted of oatmeal brose.
Kings live in cottages, and sit on low stools. When they have
coaches, they open the door themselves. The queen saddles the
king's horse. The king goes to his own stable when he hears a noise
those. Sportsmen use guns. The fire is on the floor. Supernatural
old women are found spinning "beyond" it, in the warm place of
honour, in all primitive dwellings, even in a Lapland tent. The
king's mother puts on the fire and sleeps in the common room, as
a peasant does. The cock sleeps on the rafters, the sheep on the
floor, the bull behind the door. A ladder is a pole, with pegs stuck
through it. Horses put their noses "into" bridles. When all Ireland
passes in review before the princess, they go in at the front door
and out at the back, as they would through a bothy; and even the
unexplained personage, the daughter of the king of the skies, has

maids who chatter to her as freely as maids do to Highland mistresses. When the prince is at death's door for love of the beautiful lady in the swan's down robe, and the queen mother is in despair, she goes to the kitchen to talk over the matter.

The tales represent the actual, every-day life of those who tell them, with general fidelity. They have done the same, in all likelihood, time out of mind, and that which is not true of the present is, in all probability, true of the past; and therefore something may be learned of forgotten ways of life.

If much is of home growth, if the fight with the dragon takes place at the end of a dark, quiet Highland loch, where real whales actually blow and splash, there are landscapes which are not painted from nature, as she is seen in the Isles, and these may be real pictures seen long ago by our ancestors. Men ride for days through forests, though the men who tell of them live in small islands, where there are only drift trees and bog pine. There are traces of foreign or forgotten laws or customs. A man buys a wife as he would a cow, and acquires a right to shoot her, which is acknowledged as good law.

Cæsar tells of the Gauls, that "men have the power of life and death over their wives, as well as their children." It appears that an Iceland betrothal was little more than the purchase of a wife; and in this the story may be a true picture of the past.

Men are bound with the binding of the three smalls—waist, ankles, and wrists—tightened and tortured. The conqueror almost invariably asks the conquered what is his "eirig," an old law term for the price of men's blood, which varied with the rank of the injured man; and when the vanquished has revealed his riches, the victor takes his life, and the spoil; his arms, combs, basins, dresses, horses, gold and silver; and such deeds may have been done. The tales which treat of the wars of Eirinn and Lochlann, and are full of metrical prose, describe arms and boats, helmet, spears, shields, and other gear; ships that are drawn on shore, as Icelandic ships really were; boats and arms similar to those which are figured on old stones in Iona and elsewhere, and are sometimes dug out of old graves and peat mosses. I believe them to be descriptions of real arms, and dresses, manners, and events.

For example, the warriors always abuse each other before they fight. So do the heroes of Ossian; so do the heroes of Homer; so do soldiers now. In the *Times* of the 29th of December 1859, in a letter from the camp at Ceuta in this passage:—

"While fighting, even when only exchanging long shots, the Moors keep up a most hideous howling and shrieking, vituperating their enemies in bad Spanish, and making the mountains resound with the often-repeated epithet of '*perros*' (dogs). To this the Spaniards condescend not to reply, except with bullets, although in the civil war it was no unusual thing to hear Carlist and Christina skirmishers abusing each other, and especially indulging in unhandsome reflections upon each others' Sovereign."

Again, the fights are single combats, in which individuals attack masses and conquer. So were the Homeric combats. What will be the story told in Africa by the grandson of the Moor here described, when he sits on his flat roof or in his central court in Tetuan, as I have done with one of the Jews now ruined; he will surely tell of his ancestor's deeds, repeat the words in which Achmed abused the unbeliever, and tell how he shot some mystical number of them with a single ball.

"Upon the whole they stood their ground very stoutly, and some of them gave proof of great courage, advancing singly along the ridge until they caught sight of the first Spaniards posted below it, when they discharged their *espingardas* and retreated."

"Stories" had begun in Morocco, by the 9th of January 1860, when the next letter appeared:—

"The Moors have been giving out fantastical histories of their victories over the Spaniards, of their having taken redoubts, which they might have held had they thought it worth while, and in which they would have captured guns if the Christians had not been so prudent as to remove them beforehand. These are mere fables."

It may be so, but Moors seem to have fought as wild, brave, undisciplined troops have always fought—as Homer's Greeks fought, as Highlanders fought, and as Fionn and his heroes fought, according to tradition. Omit the magic of Maghach Colgar, forget that Moors are dark men, and this might be an account of Diarmid and Conan in the story, or of their descendants as they were described in 1745 by those who were opposed to them:—

"The Moors are generally tall powerful men, of ferocious aspect and great agility, and their mode of coming on, like so many howling savages, is not calculated to encourage and give confidence to lads who for the first time find themselves in action. It seems nearly impossible to make them prisoners. In one encounter (most of these little actions are made up of a number of small fights between a few companies of Spaniards and detached bodies of the Moors, who seem to have no idea of attacking in battalion or otherwise than irregularly), in which a number of Moors were killed, one of them was surrounded by four Cazadores, who came down upon him with fixed bayonets, shouting and signing to him not to fire, and that they would give him quarter. The Moor took no heed of their overtures, levelled his long gun, and shot one of them, whereupon he was, of course, put to death by the others."

So, looking to facts now occurring, and to history, "traditional fictions" look very true, for battles are still a succession of single combats, in which both sides abuse each other, and after which they boast. War is rapine and cruel bloodshed, as described by old fishermen in Barra, and by the *Times'* correspondent at Tetuan; and it is not altogether the chivalrous pastime which poets have sung.

In another class of tales, told generally as plain narrative, and which seem to belong to savage times, a period appears to be shadowed out when iron weapons were scarce, and therefore magical; perhaps before the wars of Eirinn and Lochlann began; when combs were inventions sufficiently new and wonderful to be magical also; when horses were sacred, birds sooth-sayers; apples, oak trees, wells, and swine, sacred or magical. In these the touch of the cold steel breaks all spells; to relieve an enchanted prince it was but necessary to cut off his head; the touch of the cold sword froze the marrow when the giant's heads leaped on again. So Hercules finished the Hydra with iron, though it was hot. The white sword of light which shone so that the giant's red-haired servant used it as a torch when he went to draw water by night, was surely once a rare bright steel sword, when most swords were of bronze, as they were in early times, unless it is still older, and a mythological flash of lightning.

This CLAIDHEAMH GEAL SOLUIS is almost always mentioned as the property of giants, or of other super-natural beings, and is one of the magic gifts for which men contend with them, and fight with each other; and in this the Gaelic tradition agrees with other popular lore.

Fionn had a magic sword forged by a fairy smith, according to a story sent me from Islay, by Mr. Carmichael. King Arthur had a magic sword. The Manks hero, "Olave" of Norway, had a sword with a Celtic name, "Macabuin," made by a smith who was surely a Celt,—"Loan Maclibhuin," though he was "The dark Smith of Drontheim" in the story.* King Arthur and his sword belong to the Bretons and to many other languages, besides Welsh; and the Bretons have a wild war song, "The wine of the Gauls, and the dance of the sword," which is given in Barzaz Breiz (1846).†

There is a magic sword in the Volsung tale, called "Gram," which was the gift of Odin;‡ and a famous sword in the Niebelungen lied; and there are famous swords in many popular tales; but an iron sword was a god long ago amongst the Scythians.§ "An antique iron sword" was placed on a vast pile of brushwood as a temple in every district, at the seat of government, and served as the image of Mars. Sacrifices of cattle and of horses were made to it, and "more victims were offered thus than to all the rest of their gods." Even men were sacrificed; and it is said that the weapons found in Scythian tombs are usually of bronze, "but the sword at the great tomb at ketch was of iron." It seems, then, that an iron sword really was once worshipped by a people with whom iron was rare. Iron is rare, while stone and bronze weapons are common in British tombs, and the sword of these stories is a personage. It shines, it cries out—the lives of men are bound up in it. In one story a fox changes himself into the sword of light, and the edge of the real sword being turned towards a wicked "muime," turned all her spells back upon herself, and she fell a withered fagot.

And so this mystic sword may, perhaps, have been a god amongst the Celts, or the god of the people with whom Celts contended somewhere on their long journey to the west. It is a fiction now, but it may be founded on fact, and that fact probably was the first use of iron.

* Train's History of the Isle of Man, vol. 2, p. 177.
† The Gaelic word for a sword proves that English, French, Breton, and Gaelic have much in common—(Eng.) glave, (Fr.) glaive, (Breton) korol ar c' hleze—dance of the sword, (Gaelic) claidheamh—pronounced, glaive, the first letter being a soft "c," or hard "g," the word usually spelt, *clay* more. Languages said to be derived from Latin do not follow their model so closely as these words do one another—(Lat.) gladius, (Spanish) espada, (Italian) spada; and the northern tongues seem to have preferred some original which resembles the English word, sword. If "spada" belongs to the language from which all these are supposed to have started, these seem to have used it for a more peaceful iron weapon, a spade.
‡ Norse Tales, Introduction, 62.
§ At page 54 of Rawlinson's Herodotus, vol. 3, is the translation of the passage in which this worship is described.

Amongst the stories described in the index to the Gaelic MSS. in Edinburgh is one in which the hero goes to Scythia and to Greece, and ends his adventures in Ireland. And in the "Chronicles of the Eri," 1822, by O'Connor, chief of the prostrated people of his nation, Irish is usually called "the Phœnician dialect of the Scythian language." On such questions I will not venture. Celts may or may not be Scythians, but as a collector of curiosities, I may fairly compare my museum with other curious things; and the worship of the Scimitar, 2200 years ago, by a people who are classed with the Indo-European races, appears to have some bearing on all magic swords from the time of Herodotus down to the White Sword of Light of the West Highlands.

If iron weapons, to which supernatural virtues are ascribed, acquired their virtue when iron was rare, and when its qualities were sufficiently new to excite wonder—then other things made of iron should have like virtues ascribed to them, and the magic should be transferred from the sword to other new inventions; and such is the case.

In all popular tales of which I know anything, some mysterious virtue is attributed to iron; and in many of them a gun is the weapon which breaks the spells. In the West it is the same.

A keeper told me that he was once called into a house by an old woman to cure her cow, which was "bewitched," and which was really sick. The ceremony was performed, according to the directions of the old woman, with becoming gravity. The cow was led out, and the gun loaded, and then it was solemnly fired off over the cow's back, and the cure was supposed to be complete.

In the story of the hunter, when the widow's son aims at the enchanted deer, he sees through the spell, only when he looks over the sight, and while the gun is cocked, but when he has aimed three times, the spell is broken and the lady is free.

So in a story (I think Irish) which I have read somewhere, a man shoots from his hip at a deer, which seems to be an old man whenever he looks over the sight. He aims well, and when he comes up finds only the body of a very old man, which crumbles into dust, and is carried away by the wind, bit by bit, as he looks at it. An iron weapon is one of the guards which the man takes into the fairy hill in the story of the Smith, No. 28. A sharpshooter fires off his gun to frighten the troll in "the Old Dame and her Hen;" the boy throws the steel from his tinder box over the magic horse, and tames him at once in the Princess on the Glass Hill.* And so on throughout,

* Norse Tales, Nos. 3 and 13.

iron is invested with magic power in popular tales and mythology; the last iron weapon invented, and the first, the gun and the sword, are alike magical; a "bit of a rusty reaping hook" does equally good service, and an old horse shoe is as potent a spell against the powers of evil as any known; for one will be found on most stable doors in England.

Now comes the question, Who were these powers of evil who cannot resist iron? These fairies who shoot *stone* arrows, and are of the foes to the human race? Is all this but a dim, hazy recollection of war between a people who had iron weapons and a race who had not? the race whose remains are found all over Europe?

If these were wandering tribes they had leaders, if they were warlike they had weapons. There is a smith in the pantheon of many nations. Vulcan was a smith; Thor wielded a hammer; even Fionn had a hammer, which was heard in Lochlann when struck in Eirinn, according to the story found midway in Barra. Fionn may have borrowed his hammer from Thor long ago, or both may have got theirs from Vulcan, or all three may have brought hammers with them from the land where some primeval smith wielded the first sledge hammer, but may not all these smith gods be the smiths who made iron weapons for those who fought with the skin-clad warriors who shot flint arrows, and who are now bogles, fairies, and demons?

In any case, tales about smiths seem to belong to mythology, and to be common property. Thus the Norse smith, who cheated the evil one,* has an Irish equivalent in the Three Wishes,† and a Gaelic story, "The Soldier," is of the same class, and has a Norse equivalent in the Lad and the Deil. There are many of the same class in Grimm; and the same ideas pervade them all. There is war between the smiths and soldiers, and the devil; iron, and horses' hoofs, hammers, swords, and guns come into play; the fiend is a fool, and he has got the worst of the fight; according to the people, at all events, ever since St. Dunstan took him by the nose with a pair of tongs. In all probability the fiend of popular tales is own brother to the Gruagach and Glashan, and was once a skin-clad savage, or the god of a savage race.

If this theory be correct, if these are dim recollection of savage times and savage people, then other magic gear, the property of giants, fairies, and bogles, should resemble things which are precious now amongst savage or half civilized tribes, or which really

* Norse Tales, 16, 53.
† Carletou. Dublin, 1846. P. 330.

have been prized amongst the old inhabitants of these islands, or of other parts of the world; and such is often the case.

The work of art which is most sought after in Gaelic tales, next to the white glave of light, is a pair of combs.

CIR MHIN OIR AGUS CIR GHARBH AIRGIOD, a fine golden comb and a coarse comb of silver, are worth a deadly fight with the giants in many a story.

The enchanted prince, when he ceases to be a raven, is found as a yellow ringletted beautiful man, with a golden comb in the one hand and a silver comb in the other. Maol a' Chliobain invades the giant's house to steal the same things for the king. When the coarse comb is forgotten the king's coach falls as a withered faggot. In another story which I have, it is said of a herd who had killed a giant and taken his castle, "He went in and he opened the first room and there was not a thing in it. He opened another, and it was full of gold and silver and the treasures of the world. Then he opened a drawer, and he took a comb out of it, and when he would give a sweep with it on the one side of his head, a shower of gold would fall out of that side; and when he would give a sweep on the other side, a shower of silver would fall from that side. Then he opened another room, and it was full of every sort of food that a man might think there had ever been."

And so in many other instances the comb is a treasure for which men contend with giants. It is associated with gold, silver, dresses, arms, meat, and drink; and it is magical.

It is not so precious in other collections of popular tales, but the same idea is to be traced in them all. There is a water-spirit in Grimm which catches two children, and when they escape they throw behind them a brush, a comb, and a mirror, which replace the stone, the twig, and the bladder of water, which the Gaelic prince finds in the ear of the filly, and throws behind him to arrest the giant who is in pursuit. In the nix of the mill pond an old woman gives a golden comb to a lady, and she combs her black hair by the light of the moon at the edge of a pond, and the water-spirit shews the husband's head. So also in Snow White the wicked queen combs the hair of the beautiful princess with a poisoned comb, and throws her into a deadly magic sleep. That princess is black, white, and red, like the giant in No. 2, and like the lady in Conal; and like a lady in a Breton story; and generally foreign stories in which combs are mentioned as magical, have equivalents in Gaelic. For example, the incidents in the French story of Prince Cherie, in which gifted children comb jewels from their hair, bear a general resemblance to many Gaelic and German stories. Now there is a reason for everything, though it is not always easy to find it out; and the importance of the comb in these stories may have a reason also.

In the first place, though every civilized man and woman now owns a comb, it is a work of art which necessarily implies the use of tools, and considerable mechanical skill. A man who had nothing but a knife could hardly make a comb; and a savage with flint weapons would have to do without. A man with a comb, then, implies a man who has made some progress in civilization; and a man without a comb, a savage, who, if he had learned its use, might well covet such a possession. If a black-haired savage, living in the cold north, were to comb his hair on a frosty night, it is to be presumed that the same thing would happen which now takes place when fair ladies or civilized men comb their hair. Crackling sparks of electricity were surely produced when men first combed their hair with a bone comb; and it seems to need but a little fancy and a long time to change the bright sparks into brilliant jewels, or glittering gold and silver and bright stars, and to invest the rare and costly thing which produced such marvels with magic power.

There is evidence throughout all popular tales that combs were needed. Translations are vague, because translators are bashful; but those who have travelled amongst half civilized people, understand what is meant when the knight lays his head on the lady's knee, and she"dresses his hair." In German, Norse, Breton, and Gaelic, it is the same.

From the mention of the magic comb, then, it appears that these legends date from an early, rude period, for the time when combs were so highly prized, and so little used, is remote.

In Wilson's "Prehistoric Annals of Scotland," page 424, is a drawing of an old bone comb of very rude workmanship, found in a burgh in Orkney, together with part of a deer's horn and a human skeleton; another was found in a burgh in Caithness; a third is mentioned; and I believe that such combs are commonly found in old British graves.

At page 554, another drawing is given of one of a pair of combs found in a grave in Orkney. The teeth of the comb were fastened between plates of bone, rivetted together with copper nails, and the comb was decorated with ornamental carvings. With these, brooches of a peculiar form were discovered. Similar brooches are commonly found in Denmark. I have seen many of them in museums at Bergen and Copenhagen; and I own a pair which were found in an old grave in Islay, together with an amber bead and some fragments of rusted iron.

A bronze comb is also mentioned at page 300, as having been found in Queen Mary's Mount, a great cairn near the battlefield of Langside, which was pulled to pieces to build stone dykes, and which was found to contain rude arms, bones, rings of bituminous shale, and other things which are referred to very early prehistoric ages.

At page 500 Mr. Wilson mentions a great number of monuments in Scotland on which combs are represented, together with two-handed mirrors and symbols, for which deep explanations and hidden meanings have been sought and found. Combs, mirrors, and shears are also represented on early Roman tombs, and hidden meanings have been assigned to them; but Mr. Wilson holds that these are but indications of the sex of the buried person. Joining all this together, and placing it besides the *magic* attributed to combs in these Highland stories, this view appears to be the most reasonable. The sword of the warrior is very commonly sculptured on the old gravestones in the Western Isles. It is often twisted into a cross, and woven with those endless knots which resemble certain eastern designs. Strange nondescript animals are often figured about the sword, with tails which curl, and twist, and sprout into leaves, and weave themselves into patterns. Those again resemble illuminations in old Irish and Gaelic manuscripts, and when the most prized of the warrior's possessions is thus figured on his tomb, and is buried with him, it is but reasonable to suppose that the comb, which was so valued as to be buried with its owner, was figured on the monument for the same reason; and that sword and comb were, in fact, very highly prized at some period by those who are buried in the tombs, as the stories now represent that they were by men and giants.

So here again the popular fictions seem to have a foundation of fact.

Another magical possession is the apple. It is mentioned more frequently in Gaelic tales than in any collection which I know, but the apple plays its part in Italian, German, and Norse also. When the hero wishes to pass from Islay to Ireland he pulls sixteen apples and throws them into the sea, one by one, and he steps from one to the other. When the giant's daughter runs away with the king's son, she cuts an apple into a mystical number of small bits, and each bit talks. When she kills the giant she puts an apple under the hoof of the magic filly and he dies, for his life is in the apple, and it is crushed. When the byre is cleansed, it is so clean that a golden apple would run from end to end and never raise a stain. There is a gruagach who has a golden apple, which is thrown at all comers, and unless they are able to catch it they die; when it is caught and thrown back by the hero, Gruagach an Ubhail dies. There is a game called cluich an ubhail, the apple play, which seems to have been a deadly game whatever it was. When the king's daughter transports the soldier to the green island on the magic tablecloth, he finds magic apples which transform him, and others which cure him, and by which he transforms the cruel princess and recovers his magic treasures. In German a cabbage does the same thing.

When the two eldest idle king's sons go out to herd the giant's cattle, they find an apple tree whose fruit moves up and down as they vainly strive to pluck it.

And so on throughout, whenever an apple is mentioned in Gaelic stories it has something marvellous about it.

So in German, in the Man of Iron, a princess throws a golden apple as a prize, which the hero catches three times and carries off and wins.

In Snow White, where the poisoned comb occurs, there is a poisoned magic apple also.

In the Old Griffin, the sick princess is cured by rosy-cheeked apples.

In the Giant with the Three Golden Hairs, one of the questions to be solved is, why a tree which used to bear golden apples does not now bear leaves? and the next question is about a well.

So in the White Snake, a servant who acquires the knowledge of the speech of birds by tasting a white snake, helps creatures in distress, gets their aid, and procures a golden apple from three ravens, which "flew over the sea even to the end of the world, where stands the tree of life." When he had got the apple he and his princess ate it, and married and lived happily ever after.

So in Wolf's collection, in the story of the Wonderful Hares, a golden apple is the gift for which the finder is to gain a princess; and that apple grew on a sort of tree of which there was but one in the whole world.

In Norse it is the same; the princess on the Glass Hill held three golden apples in her lap, and he who could ride up the hill and carry off the apples was to win the prize; and the princess rolled them down to the hero, and they rolled into his shoe.

The good girl plucked the apples from the tree which spoke to her when she went down the well to the underground world; but the ill-tempered step-sister thrashed down the fruit; and when the time of trial came, the apple tree played its part and protected the good girl.

So in French, a singing apple is one of the marvels which the Princess Belle Etoile, and her brothers and her cousin, bring from the end of the world, after all manner of adventures; and in that story the comb, the stars, and jewels in the hair, the talking soothsaying bird, the magic water, the horse, the wicked step-mother, and the dragon, all appear; and there is a Gaelic version of that story. In short, that French story agrees with Gaelic stories, and with a certain class of German tales; and contains within itself much of the machinery and incident which is scattered elsewhere, in collections of tales gathered in modern times amongst the people of various countries.

So again in books of tales of older date, and in other languages, apples and marvels are associated.

In Straparola is an Italian story remarkably like the Gaelic Sea Maiden, and clearly the same in groundwork as Princess Belle Etoile. A lady, when she has lost her husband, goes off to the Atlantic Ocean with three golden apples; and the mermaid who had swallowed the husband, shews first his head, then his body to the waist, and then to the knees; each time for a golden apple; and the incidents of that story are all to be found elsewhere, and most of them are in Gaelic.

So again, in the Arabian Nights, there is a long story, The Three Apples, which turns upon the stealing of one, which was a thing of great price, though it was not magical in the story.

So in classical times, an apple of discord was the prize of the fairest; and the small beginning from which so much of all that is most famous in ancient lore takes its rise; three golden apples were the prize of one of the labours of Hercules, and these grew in a garden which fable has placed far to the westwards, and learned commentators have placed in the Cape Verde Islands.

So then it appears that apples have been mysterious and magical from the earliest of times; that they were sought for in the west, and valued in the east; and now when the popular tales of far west are examined, apples are the most important of natural productions, and invested with the magic which belongs to that which is old and rare, and which may once have been sacred.

It is curious that the forbidden fruit is almost always mentioned in English as an apple; and this notion prevails in France to such a degree, that when that mad play, La Proprieté c'est le Vol, was acted in Paris in 1846, the first scene represented the Garden of Eden with a tree, and a board on which was written "il est défendu de manger de ces pommes."

And it is stated in grave histories that the Celtic priests held apples sacred; so here again popular tales hold their own.

Again, supposing tales to be old traditions, something may be gleaned from them of the past. Horses, for example, must once have been strange and rare, or sacred, amongst the Celts, as among other races.

The horses of the Vedas, which drew the chariot of the sun, appear to have been confused with the sungod of Indian mythology. Horses decided the fate of kingdoms in Persia, according to Herodotus. They were sacred when Phæton drove the chariot of the sun. The Scandinavian gods had horses, according to the Edda. They are generally supernatural in Grimm's German stories, in Norse tales, in French, and in many other collections. They are wonderful in Breton tales.

When the followers of Columbus first took horses to America, they struck terror into the Indians, and they and their riders were demigods; because strange and terrible.

Horses were surely feared, or worshipped, or prized, by Celts, for places are named after them. Penmarch in Brittany, means horse-head or hill. Ardincaple in Scotland means the mare's height, and there are many other places with similar names.

In Gaelic tales, horses are frequently mentioned, and more magic properties are attributed to them than elsewhere in popular lore.

In No. 1, horses play a very prominent part; and in some versions of that tale, the heroine is a lady transformed into a grey mare. It is to be hoped, for the hero's sake, that she did not prove herself the better horse when she resumed her human form.

In No. 3, there is a horse race. In No. 4, there are mythical horses; and in an Irish version of that story, told me in August 1860, by an Irish blind fiddler on board the Lochgoihead boat, horses again play their part, with hounds and hawks. In No. 14, there are horses; in one version there is a magic "powney." In 22, a horse again appears, and gives the foundation for the riddle on which the story turns. In 40, a horse is one of the prizes to be gained. In 41, the horse plays the part of bluebeard. In 48, a horse is to be hanged as a thief. In 51, the hero assumes the form of a horse. In many other tales which I have in manuscript, men appear as horses, and reappear as men; and horses are marvellous. In one tale, a man's son is sent to a warlock and becomes a horse, and all sorts of creatures besides. In another, a man gets a wishing grey filly from the wind, in return for some meal which the wind had blown away; and there is a whole series of tales which relate to water-horses, and which seem, more than all the rest, to shew the horse as a degraded god, and as it would seem, a water-god, and a destroyer.

I had intended to group all these stories together, as an illustration of this part of the subject, but time and space are wanting. These shew that in the Isle of Man, and in the Highlands of Scotland, people still firmly believe in the existence of a water-horse. In Sutherland and elsewhere, many believe that they have seen these fancied animals. I have been told of English sportsmen who went in pursuit of them, so circumstantial were the accounts of those who believed that they had seen them. The witnesses are so numerous, and their testimony agrees so well, that there must be some old deeply-rooted Celtic belief which clothes every dark object with the dreaded form of the EACH UISGE. The legends of the doings of the water kelpie all point to some river god reduced to be a fuath or bogle. The bay or grey horse grazes at the lake-side, and when he is mounted, rushes into the loch and devours his rider. His back lengthens to suit any number; men's hands stick to his skin; he is harnessed to a plough, and drags the team and the plough into the loch, and tears the horses to bits; he is killed, and nothing remains but a pool of water; he falls in love with a lady, and when he appears as a man and lays his head on her knee to be dressed, the frightened lady finds him out by the sand amongst his hair. "Tha gainmheach ann." There is sand in it, she says, and when he sleeps she makes her escape. He appears as an old woman, and is put to bed with a bevy of damsels in a mountain shealing, and he sucks the blood of all, save one, who escapes over a burn, which, waterhorse as he is, he dare not cross. In short, these tales and beliefs have led me to think that the old Celts must have had a destroying water-god, to whom the horse was sacred, or who had the form of a horse.

Unless there is some such foundation for the stories, it is strange to find the romances of boatmen and fishermen inhabiting small islands, filled with incidents which seem rather to belong to a wandering, horse-riding tribe. But the tales of Norwegian sailors are similar in this respect; and the Celtic character has in fact much which savours of a tribe who are boatmen by compulsion, and would be horsemen if they could. Though the Western islanders are fearless boatmen, and brave a terrible sea in very frail boats, very few of them are in the royal navy, and there are not many who are professed sailors. On the other hand, they are bold huntsmen in the far north of America. I do not think that they are successful farmers anywhere, though they cling fondly to a spot of land, but they are famous herdsmen at home and abroad. On the misty hills of old Scotland or the dry plains of Australia, they still retain the qualities which made a race of hunters, and warriors, and herdsmen, such as are represented in the poems of Ossian, and described in history; and even within the small bounds which now contain the Celtic race in Europe, their national tastes appear in strong relief. Every deer-stalker will bear witness to the eagerness of Highlanders in pursuit of their old favourite game, the dun deer; the mountaineer shews what he is when his eye kindles and his nostril dilates at the sight of a noble stag; when the gillie forgets his master in his keenness, and the southern lags behind; when it is "bellows to mend," and London dinners are remembered with regret. Tyree is famous for its breed of ponies: it is a common bit of Highland "chaff" to neigh at a Tyree man, and other islands have famous breeds also. It is said that men almost starving rode to ask for a meal in a certain place, and would not sell their ponies; and though this is surely a fiction, it rests on the fact that the islanders are fond of horses. At fairs and markets all over the Highlands ponies abound. Nothing seems to amaze a Highlander more than to see any one walk who can afford to ride; and he will chase a pony over a hill, and sit in misery on a packsaddle when he catches the beast, and endure discomfort, that he may ride in state along a level road for a short distance.

Irish Celts, who have more room for locomotion, cultivate their national taste for horse flesh in a higher degree. An Irish hunter is valued by many an English Nimrod; all novels which purport to represent Irish character paint Irishmen as bold riders, and Irish peasants as men who take a keen interest in all that belongs to hunting and racing. There is not, so far as I know, a single novel founded on the adventures of an Irish or Highland sailor or farmer, though there are plenty of fictitious warriors and sportsmen in prose and in verse. There are endless novels about English sailors, and sportsmen, and farmers, and though novels are fictions, they too rest on facts. The Celts, and Saxons, and Normans, and Danes, and Romans, who help to form the English race, are at home on shore and afloat, whether their steeds are of flesh and blood, or, as the Gaelic poet says, of brine. The Celtic race are most at home amongst their cattle and on the hills, and I believe it to be strictly in accordance with the Celtic character to find horses and chariots playing a part in their national traditions and poems of all ages.

I do not know enough of our Welsh cousins to be able to speak of their tastes in this respect; but I know that horse racing excites a keen interest in Britany, though the French navy is chiefly manned by Breton and Norman sailors, and Breton ballads and old Welsh romances are full of equestrian adventures. And all this supports the theory that Celts came from the east, and came overland; for horses would be prized by a wandering race.

So hounds would be prized by the race of hunters who chased the Caledonian boars as well as the stags; and here again tradition is in accordance with probability, and supported by other testimony. In No. 4 there are mystical dogs; a hound, GADHAR is one of the links in No. 8; a dog appears in No. 11; a dog, who is an enchanted man, in No. 12; there is a phantom dog in No. 23; there was a "spectre hound in Man;" and there are similar ghostly dogs in England, and in many European countries besides.

In 19, 20, 31, 38, and a great many other tales which I have in manuscript, the hound plays an important part. Sometimes he befriends his master, at other times he appears to have something diabolical about him; it seems as if his real honest nature had overcome a deeply-rooted prejudice, for there is much which savours of detestation as well as of strong affection. Dog, or son of the dog, is a term of abuse in Gaelic as elsewhere, though cuilein is a form of endearment, and the hound is figured beside his master, or at his feet, on many a tombstone in the Western Isles. Hounds are mentioned in Gaelic poetry and in Gaelic tales, and in the earliest accounts of the Western Isles; and one breed still survives in these long-legged, rough, wiry-haired stag-hounds, which Landseer so loves to paint.

In one story, for which I have no room, but which is well worthy of preservation, a step-mother sends two step-children, a brother and sister, out into the world to seek their fortune. They live in a cottage with three bare yellow porkers, which belong to the sister. The brother sells one to a man for a dog with a green string, and so gets three dogs, whose names are Knowledge, FIOS; Swift, LUATH; Weighty, TROM. The sister is enraged, and allies herself with a giant who has a hot coal in his mouth. Knowledge tells his master the danger which awaits him: how the giant and his sister had set a venomous dart over the door. Swiftness runs in first, and saves his master at the expense of his own tail, and then the three dogs upset a caldron of boiling water over the giant, who is hid in a hole in the floor, and so at the third time the giant is killed, and the only loss is a bit of the tail of Luath.

Then the king's son goes to dwell with a beautiful lady; and after a time he goes back to visit his sister, armed with three magic apples. The sister sets three venomous porkers at him, and he, by throwing the apples behind him, hinders them with woods, and moors, and lakes, which grow up from the apples; but they follow. The three dogs come out and beat the three pigs, and kill them, and then the king's son get his sister to come with him, and she was as a servant-maid to the prince and the fine woman with whom he lived. Then the sister put GATH NIMH, a poisonous sting or thorn, into the bed, and the prince was as though he were dead for three days, and he was buried. But Knowledge told the other two dogs what to do, and they scraped up the prince, and took out the thorn; and he came alive again and went home, and set on a fire of grey oak, and burned his sister. And John Crawfurd, fisherman at Lochlong-head, told John Dewar "that he left the man, and the woman, and the dogs all happy and well pleased together." This curious story seems to shew the hog and the dog as foes. Perhaps they were but the emblems of rival tribes, perhaps they were sacred amongst rival races; at all events, they were both important personages at some time or other, for there is a great deal about them in Gaelic lore.

The boar was the animal which Diarmid slew, and which caused his death when he paced his length against the bristles,—the venomous bristles pierced a mole in his foot. It was a boar which was sent out to find the body of the thief in that curious story, an gillie currach; and in a great many other stories, boars appear as animals of the chase. The Fiantaichean or Feen, whomsoever they were, are always represented as hunting wild boars, as tearing a boar to bits by main force, or eating a whole boar. Cairns, said to have been raised over boars, are shewn in many parts of Scotland still. I myself once found a boar's tusk in a grave accidentally discovered, close to the bridge at Pool-Ewe. There were many other bones, and a rough flint, and a lot of charcoal, in what seemed to be a shallow human grave, a kind of stone coffin built up with loose slabs.

"Little pigs" play their part in the nursery lore of England. Everybody who has been young and has toes, must know how

"This little pig went to market,
And this little pig staid at home—
This little pig got roast beef,

And this little pig got none;
And this little pig went wee, wee, wee, all the way home."

There is a long and tragic story which has been current amongst
at least three generations of my own family regarding a lot of little
pigs who had a wise mother, who told them where they were to
build their houses, and how, so as to avoid the fox. Some of the
little pigs would not follow their mother's counsel, and built houses
of leaves, and the fox got in and said, "I will gallop, and I'll trample,
and I'll knock down your house," and he ate the foolish, little,
proud pigs; but the youngest was a wise little pig, and, after many
adventures, she put an end to the wicked fox when she was almost
vanquished, bidding him look into the caldron to see if the dinner
was ready, and then tilting him in headforemost. In short, pigs are
very important personages in the popular lore of Great Britain.

We are told by history that they were sacred amongst the Gauls,
and fed on acorns in the sacred oak groves of the Druids, and there
is a strong prejudice now amongst Highlanders against eating pig's
flesh.

So oak trees are mythical. Whenever a man is to be burned for
some evil deed, and men are always going to be roasted, fagots of
"grey," probably green oak, are fetched. There is a curious story
which the Rev. Mr. MacLachlan took down from the recitation of
an old man in Edinburgh, in which a mythical old man is shut up
in an oak tree, which grows in the court of the king's palace; and
when the king's son lets his ball roll into a split in the tree by chance,
the old man tells the boy to fetch an axe and he will give him the
ball, and so he gets out, and endows the Prince with power and
valour. He sets out on his journey with a red-headed cook, who
personates him, and he goes to lodge with a swine-heard; but by
the help of the old man of the great tree, BODACH NA CRAOIBHE
MOIRE, he overcomes a boar, a bull, and a stallion, and marries the
king's daughter, and the red-headed cook is burnt.

So then, in these traditions, swine and oak trees are associated
together with mythical old men and deeds of valour, such as a race
of hunters might perform, and admire, and remember. Is it too
much to suppose that these are dim recollections of pagan times?
DRUIDH is the name for magician, DRAOCHD for magic. It is surely
not too much to suppose that the magicians were the Druids, and
the magic their mysteries; that my peasant collectors are right, when
they maintain that GRUAGACH, the long-haired one, was a "pro-
fessor" or "master of arts," or "one that taught feats of arms;" that

the learned Gruagach, who is so often mentioned, was a Druid in his glory, and the other, who, in the days of Johnson, haunted the island of Troda as "Greogaca," who haunted the small island of Inch, near Easdale, in the girlhood of Mrs. MacTavish, who is remembered still, and is still supposed to haunt many a desolate island in the far west, is the phantom of the same Druid, fallen from his high estate, skulking from his pursuers, and really living on milk left for him by those whose priest he had once been.

> "The small island of Inch, near Easdale, is inhabited by a brownie, which has followed the Macdougalls of Ardincaple for ages, and takes a great interest in them. He takes care of their cattle in that island night and day, unless the dairymaid, when there in summer with the milk cattle, neglects to leave warm milk for him at night in a knocking-stone in the cave, where she and the herd live during their stay in the island. Should this perquisite be for a night forgot, they will be sure in the morning to find one of the cattle fallen over the rocks with which the place abounds. It is a question whether the brownie has not a friend with whom he shares the contents of the stone, which will, I daresay, hold from two to three Scotch pints."

Mrs. MacTavish, 1859, Islay.

If the manners and customs of druids are described as correctly as modern manners really are, then something may be gathered concerning druidical worship; but without knowledge, which I have no time to acquire, the full bearing of traditions on such a subject cannot be estimated.

The horse and the boar, the oak tree and the apple, then, are often referred to. Of mistletoe I have found no trace, unless it be the sour herb which brings men to life, but that might be the "soma," which plays such a part in the mythology of the Vedas, or the shamrock, which was sacred in Ireland.

Wells are indicated as mysterious in a great many tales—poison wells and healing wells—and some are still frequented, with a half belief in their virtue; but such wells now often have the name of some saint affixed to them.

Birds are very often referred to as soothsayers—in No. 39 especially; the man catches a bird and says it is a diviner, and a gentleman buys it as such. It was a bird of prey, for it lit on a hide, and birds of prey are continually appearing as bringing aid to men, such as the raven, the hoodie, and the falcon. The little birds

especially are frequently mentioned. I should therefore gather from
the stories that the ancient Celts drew augury from birds as other
nations did, and as it is asserted by historians that the Gauls really
did. I should be inclined to think that they possessed the domestic
fowl before they became acquainted with the country of the wild
grouse, and that the cock may have been sacred, for he is a foe and
a terror to uncanny beings, and the hero of many a story; while the
grouse and similar birds peculiar to this country are barely mentioned. The cat plays a considerable part, and appears as a transformed princess; and the cat may also have been sacred to some
power, for cats are the companions of Highland witches, and of
hags all the world over, and they were sacred to gods in other lands;
they were made into mummies in Egypt, together with hawks and
other creatures which appear in Highland tales. Ravens were Odin's
messengers; they may have been pages to some Celtic divinity also.
Foxes, and otters, and wolves, and bears all appear in mythical
characters. Serpents were probably held in abhorrence, as they have
been by other races, but the serpent gave wisdom, and is very
mythical.

Old Macdonald, travelling tinker, told me a long story, of which
one scene represented an incantation more vividly to me than
anything I have ever read or heard. "There was a king and a knight,
as there was and will be, and as grows the fir tree, some of it crooked
and some of it straight, and he was a king of Eirinn," said the old
tinker, and then came a wicked stepmother, who was incited to evil
by a wicked henwife. The son of the first queen was at school with
twelve comrades, and they used to play at shinny every day with
silver shinnies and a golden ball. The henwife, for certain curious
rewards, gave the stepdame a magic shirt, and she sent it to her
step-son, "Sheen Billy," and persuaded him to put it on; he refused
at first, but complied at last, and the shirt was a BEITHIR (great
snake) about his neck. Then he was enchanted and under spells,
and all manner of adventures followed; but at last he came to the
house of a wise woman who had a beautiful daughter, who fell in
love with the enchanted prince, and said she must and would have
him.

"It will cost thee much sorrow," said the mother.

"I care not," said the girl, "I must have him."

"It will cost thee thy hair."

"I care not."

"It will cost thee thy right breast."

"I care not if it should cost me my life," said the girl.

And the old woman agreed to help her to her will. A caldron was prepared and filled with plants; and the king's son was put into it stripped to the magic shirt, and the girl was stripped to the waist. And the mother stood by with a great knife, which she gave to her daughter.

Then the king's son was put down in the caldron, and the great serpent, which appeared to be a shirt about his neck, changed into its own form, and sprang on the girl and fastened on her; and she cut away the hold, and the king's son was freed from the spells. Then they were married, and a golden breast was made for the lady. And then they went through more adventures, which I do not well remember, and which the old tinker's son vainly strove to repeat in August, 1860, for he is far behind his father in the telling of old Highland tales.

The serpent, then, would seem to be an emblem of evil and wisdom in Celtic popular mythology.

There is something mysterious about rushes. The fairies are found in a bush of rushes; the great caldron of the Feen is hid under a bush of rushes; and in a great many other instances TOM LUACHARACH appears. I do not know that the plant is mentioned in foreign tales, but it occurs several times in border minstrelsy.

If the Druids worshipped the sun and moon, there is very little direct reference to such worship in highland stories now. There are many highland customs which point to solar worship, but these have been treated of by abler pens, and I have nothing to add on that head.

There is yet another animal which is mythical—the water-bull. He certainly belongs to Celtic mythology, as the water-horse does, for he is known in the Isle of Man and all over the islands.

There are numerous lakes where the water-bulls are supposed to exist, and their progeny are supposed to be easily known by their short ears. When the water-bull appears in a story he is generally represented as friendly to man. I have a great many accounts of him, and his name in Skye is Tarbh Eithre.

There is a gigantic water bird, called the Boobrie, which is supposed to inhabit the fresh water and sea lochs of Argyllshire. I have heard of him nowhere else; but I have heard of him from several people.

He is ravenous and gigantic, gobbles up sheep and cows, has webbed feet, a very loud hoarse voice, and is somewhat like a cormorant. He is reported to have terrified a minister out of his propriety, and it is therefore to be assumed that he is of the powers of evil. And there are a vast number of other fancied inhabitants of earth, air, and water, enough to form a volume of supernatural history, and all or any of these may have figured in Celtic mythology; for it is hard to suppose that men living at opposite ends of Scotland, and peasants in the Isle of Man, should invent the same fancies unless their ideas had some common foundation.

Besides these animals, there is a whole supernatural world with superhuman gigantic inhabitants.

There are continual fights with these giants, which are often carried on without arms at all—mere wrestling matches, which seem to have had certain rules. It is somewhere told of the Germans that they in their forests fought with clubs, and the Celtic giants may once have been real men. Hercules fought with a club. Irishmen use shillelahs still, and my west country friends, when they fight now-a-days, use barrel staves instead of swords, and use them well, if not wisely; but whether giants were men or myths, they are always represented as strange, lubberly beings, whose dealings with men invariably end in their discomfiture. There are giants in Herodotus and, I believe, in every popular mythology known. There are giants in Holy Writ. They spoke an unknown tongue everywhere. They said "Fee fo fum" in Cornwall. They say "Fiaw fiaw foaghrich" in Argyll, and these sounds may possibly be corruptions of the language of real big burly savages, now magnified into giants.

The last word might be the vocative of the Gaelic for stranger, ill pronounced, and the intention may be to mimic the dialect of a foreigner speaking Gaelic.

An Italian organ-grinder once found his way to the west, and sang "Fideli, fidela, fidelin-lin-la." The boys caught the tune, and sang it to the words, "Deese creepe Signaveete ha," words with as much meaning as "Fee fo fum," but which retain a certain resemblance to an Italian sound.

If the giants were once real savages, they had the sense of smell peculiarly sharp, according to the Gaelic tales, as they had in all others which treat of them, and they ate their captives, as it is asserted that the early inhabitants of Scotland did, as Herodotus says that Scyths did in his time, and as the Feejee islanders did very lately, and still do. A relative of mine once offered me a tooth as a relic of such a feast; it had been presented to him in the Feejee islands by a charming dark young lady, who had just left the banquet, but had not shared in it. The Highland giants were not so big but that their conquerors wore their clothes; they were not so strong that men could not beat them, even by wrestling. They were not quite savages; for though some lived in caves, others had houses and cattle, and hoards of spoil. They had slaves, as we are told that Scotch proprietors had within historic times. In "Scotland in the Middle Ages," p. 141, we learn that Earl Waldev of Dunbar made over a whole tribe to the Abbot of Kelso in 1170, and in the next page it is implied that these slaves were mostly Celts. Perhaps those Celts who were not enslaved had their own mountain view of the matter, and looked down on the Gall as intrusive, savage, uncultivated, slave-owning giants.

Perhaps the mountain mists in like manner impeded the view of the dwellers on the mountain and the plain, for Fin MacCoul was a "God in Ireland," as they say, and is a "rawhead and bloody bones" in the Scottish lowlands now.

Whatever the giants were they knew some magic arts, but they were always beaten in the end by men.

The combats with them are a Gaelic proverb in action:—

"Theid seoltachd thar spionnaidh."

Skill goes over might, and probably, as it seems to me, giants are simply the nearest savage race at war with the race who tell the tales. If they performed impossible feats of strength, they did no more than Rob Roy, whose "putting stone" is now shewn to Saxon tourists by a Celtic coachman, near Bunawe, in the shape of a boulder of many tons, though Rob Ruadh lived only a hundred years ago, near Inverary, in a cottage which is now standing, and which was lately inhabited by a shepherd.

The Gaelic giants are very like those of Norse and German tales, but they are much nearer to real men than the giants of Germany and Scandinavia, and Greece and Rome, who are almost, if not quite, equal to the gods. Famhairan are little more than very strong men, but some have only one eye like the Cyclops.

Their world is generally, but not always, under ground; it has castles, and parks, and pasture, and all that is to be found above the earth. Gold, and silver, and copper, abound in the giant's land; jewels are seldom mentioned, but cattle, and horses, and spoil of dresses, and arms, and armour, combs, and basins, apples, shields, bows, spears, and horses, are all to be gained by a fight with the giants. Still, now and then a giant does some feat quite beyond the power of man; such as a giant in Barra, who fished up a hero, boat and all, with his fishing-rod, from a rock, and threw him over his head, as little boys do "cuddies" from a pier-end. So the giants may be degraded gods after all.

But besides "popular tales," there are fairy tales, which are not told as stories, but facts. At all events, the creed is too *recent* to be lightly spoken of.

Men do believe in fairies, though they will not readily confess the fact. And though I do not myself believe that fairies *are*, in spite of the strong evidence offered, I believe there once was a small race of people in these islands, who are remembered as fairies, for the fairy belief is not confined to the Highlanders of Scotland. I have given a few of the tales which have come to me as illustrations in No. 27.

"*They*" are always represented as living in green mounds. They pop up their heads when disturbed by people treading on their houses. They steal children. They seem to live on familiar terms with the people about them when they treat them well, to punish them when they ill treat them. If giants are magnified, these are but men seen through the other end of the telescope, and there are such people now. A Lapp is such a man—he is a little, flesh-eating mortal—having control over the beasts, and living in a green mound—when he is not living in a tent, or sleeping out of doors, wrapped in his deer-skin shirt. I have lived amongst them and know them and their dwellings pretty well. I know one which would answer to the description of a fairy mound exactly. It is on the most northern peninsula in Europe, to the east of the North Cape, close to the sea, in a sandy hollow near a burn. It is round—say, twelve feet in diameter—and it is sunk three feet in the sand; the roof is made of sticks and covered with turf. The whole structure, at a short distance, looks exactly like a conical green mound about four feet high. There was a famous crop of grass on it when I was there, and the children and dogs ran out at the door and up to the top when we approached, as ants run on an ant hill when disturbed. Their fire was in the middle of the floor, and the pot hung over it from the roof. I lately saw a house in South Uist found in the sand hills close to the sea. It was built of loose boulders, it was circular, and had recesses in the sides, it was covered when found, and it was full of sand; when that was removed, stone querns and combs of bone were found, together with ashes, and near the level of the top there was a stratum of bones and teeth of large grass-eating animals. I know not what they were, but the bones were splintered and broken, and mingled with ashes and shells, oysters, cockles, and wilks (periwinkles), shewing clearly the original level of the ground, and proving that this was a dwelling almost the same as a Lapp "Gam" at Hopseidet.

Now, let us see what the people of the Hebrides say of the fairies. There was a woman benighted with a pair of calves, "and she went for shelter to a knoll, and she began driving the peg of the tether into it. The hill opened, and she heard as though there was a pot hook 'gleegashing,' on the side of the pot. A woman put up her head, and as much as was above her waist, and said, 'What business hast thou to disturb this tulman, in which I make my dwelling.' " This might be a description of one of my Lapp friends, and probably is a description of such a dwelling as I saw in South Uist. If the people slept as Lapps sleep, with their feet to the fire, a woman outside might have driven a peg very near one of the sleepers, and she might have stood on a seat and poked her head out of the chimney.

The magic about the beasts is but the mist of antiquity; and the fairy was probably a Pict. Who will say who the Pict may have been? Probably the great Clibric hag was one, and of the same tribe.

"In the early morning she was busy milking the hinds; they were standing all about the door of the hut, till one of them ate a hank of *blue* worsted hanging from a nail in it." So says the "fiction," which it is considered a sin to relate. Let me place some facts from my own journal beside it.

"Wednesday, August 22, 1850. Quickjok, Swedish Lapland.—In the evening the effect of the sunlight through the mist and showers was most beautiful. I was sketching, when a small man made his appearance on the opposite side of the river and began to shout for a boat. The priest exclaimed that the Lapps had come down, and accordingly the diminutive human specimen was fetched, and proved to be a Lapp who had established his camp about seven miles off, near Vallespik. He was about twenty-five years old, and with his high blue cap on could stand upright under my arm."

I had been wandering about Quickjok for a week, out on Vallespik frequently, searching for the Lapps, with the very glass which I had previously used to find deer close to Clibric, which is but a small copy of the Lapland mountain.

"Thursday, 23rd.—Started to see the deer, with the priest and the Clockar, and Marcus, and the Lapp. The Lapp walked like a deer himself, aided by a very long birch pole, which he took from its hiding place in a fir tree. I had hard work to keep up with him. Marcus and the priest were left behind. Once up through the forest, it was cutting cold, and we walked up to the 'cota' in two hours and a quarter. The deer was seen in the distance, like a brown speck on the shoulder of Vallespik; and with the glass I could make out that a small mortal and two dogs were driving them home. The cota is a permanent one, made in the shape of a sugar loaf, with birch sticks, and long flat stones and turf. There are two exactly alike, and each has a door, a mere narrow slit, opening to the west, and a hole in the roof to let out the smoke. I crept in, and found a girl of about fifteen, with very pretty eyes, sitting crouched up in a corner, and looking as scared as one of her own fawns. The priest said, that if we had come without our attendant genius, the small Lapp, she would have fainted, or run away to the hills. I began to sketch her, as she sat looking modest in her dark corner, and was rejoicing in the extreme stillness of my sitter, when, on looking up from some careful touch, I found that she had vanished through the door-way. I had to bribe her with bread and butter before she could be coaxed back. A tremendous row of shouting and barking outside now announced the arrival of the deer, so I let my sitter go, and off she ran as fast as she could. I followed more leisurely to the spot where the deer were gathered, on a stony hillside. There were only about 200; the rest had run off up wind on the way from the mountains, and all the other Lapps were off after them, leaving only my pretty sitter, the boy, and a small woman with bleared eyes, as ugly as sin, his sister.

"How I wished for Landseer's pencil as I looked at that scene! Most of the deer were huddled close together; hinds and calves chewing the cud with the greatest placidity, but here and there some grand old fellows, with wide antlers, stood up against the sky line, looking magnificent. I tried to draw, but it was hopeless; so I sat down, and watched the proceedings of my hosts.

"First, each of the girls took a coil of rope from about her neck, and in a twinkling it was pitched over the horns of a hind. The noose was then slipped round the neck, and a couple of turns of rope round the nose, and then the wild milkmaid set her foot on the halter and proceeded TO MILK THE HIND, into a round birch bowl with a handle. Sometimes she sat, at others she leant her head on the deer's dark side, and knelt beside her. I never saw such a succession of beautiful groups.

"Every now and then some half-dozen deer would break out of the herd and set off to the mountain, and then came a general skurry. The small Lapp man, with his long birch pole, would rush screaming after the stragglers; and his two gaunt, black, rough, half-starved dogs would scour off, yelping, in pursuit. It generally ended in the hasty return of the truants, with well-bitten houghs for their pains; but some fairly made off, at a determined long trot, and vanished over the hill. It was very curious to be thus in the midst of a whole herd of creatures so like our own wild deer, to have them treading on my feet and poking their horns against my sketch-book as I vainly tried to draw them, and to think that they who had the power to bid defiance to the fleetest hound in Sweden should be so perfectly tame as to let the small beings who herded them so thump, and bully, and tease them. The milking, in the meantime, had been progressing rapidly; and after about an hour the pretty girl, who had been dipping her fingers in the milk-pail and licking up the milk all the time, took her piece of bread and butter, and departed with her charge, munching as she went.

"The blear-eyed one, and the boy, and our party, went into the cota, and dined on cold roast reiper and reindeer milk. The boy poured the milk from a small keg, which contained the whole product of the flock; and having given us our share, he carefully licked up all that remained on the outside of the keg, and set it down in a corner. It was sweet and delicious, like thick cream. Dinner over, we desired the Lapp to be ready in the morning (to accompany me), and with the clocker's dog, 'Gueppe,' went reiper-shooting. The clocker himself, with a newly-slaughtered reindeer calf on his shoulders, followed; and so we went home."

A few days afterwards, I was at another camp, on another hill, where the same scene was going on. "In a tent I found a fine-looking Lapp woman sitting on a heap of skins, serving out coffee, and handing reindeer cream to the clocker with a silver spoon. She had silver bracelets, and a couple of silver rings; and altogether, with her black hair, and dark brown eyes glittering in the fire-light, she looked eastern and magnificent." Her husband had many trinkets, and they had, amongst other articles, a comb, which the rest seemed much to need.

Her dress was blue, so were most of the dresses, and one of her possessions was a bone contrivance for weaving the bands which all wore round their ankles. She must have had blue yarn somewhere, for her garters were partly blue.

I spent the whole of the next day in the camp, and watched the whole operations of the day.

"After dinner, the children cracked the bones with stones and a knife, after they had polished the outside, and sucked up the marrow; and then the dogs, which did not dare to steal, were called in their turn, and got the remains of the food in wooden bowls, set apart for their especial use."

The bones in the hut in South Uist might have been the remains of such a feast by their appearance.

"The cota was a pyramid of sods and birch sticks, about seven feet high, and twelve or fourteen in diameter. There were three children, five dogs, an old woman, Marcus, and myself, inside; and all day long the handsome lady from the tent next door, with her husband, and a couple of quaint-looking old fellows in deer-skin shirts, kept popping in to see how I got on. It was impossible to sit upright for the slope of the walls, as I sat cross-legged on the ground."

This might be a description of the Uist hut itself, and its inhabitants, as I can fancy them.

"The three dogs (in the tent), at the smallest symptom of a disturbance, plunged out, barking, to add to the row; they popped in by the same way under the canvas, so they had no need of a door."

So did the dogs in the story of Seantraigh; they ran after the stranger, and stopped to eat the bones. And it is remarkable that all civilized dogs fall upon and worry the half-savage black Lapp dogs, and bark at their masters whenever they descend from their mountains, as the town dogs did at the fairy dogs. In short, these extracts might be a fair description of the people, and the dwellings, and the food, and the dogs described as fairies, and the hag, and the tulman, in stories which I have grouped together; told in Scotland within this year by persons who can have no knowledge of what is called the "Finn theory," and given in the very words in which they came to me, from various sources.

Lord Reay's forester must surely have passed the night in a Lapp cota on Ben Gilbric, in Sutherland, when Lapps were Picts; but when was that? Perhaps in the youth of the fairy of whom the following story was told by a Sutherland gamekeeper of my acquaintance.

THE HERDS OF GLEN ODHAR.—A wild romantic glen in Strath Carron is called Glen Garaig, and it was through this that a woman was passing carrying an infant wrapped in her plaid. Below the path, overhung with weeping birches, and nearly opposite, run a very deep ravine, known as Glen Odhar, the dun glen. The child, not yet a year old, and which had not spoken or attempted speech, suddenly addressed his mother thus:—

S lionmhor bo mhaol odhar,   Many a dun hummel cow,
Le laogh na gobhal   With a calf below he,

Chunnaic mise ga'm bleoghan	Have I seen milking
Anns a' ghleann odhar ud thall,	In that dun glen yonder,
Gun chu, gun duine,	Without dog, without man,
Gun bhean, gun ghille,	Without woman, without gillie,
Ach aon duine,	But one man,
'S e liath.	And he hoary.

The good woman flung down the child and plaid and ran home, where, to her great joy, her baby boy lay smiling in its cradle.

Fairies then milked deer, as Lapps do. They lived under ground, like them. They worked at trades especially smith work and weaving. They had hammers and anvils, and excelled in their use, but though good weavers, they had to steal wool and borrow looms. Lapps do work in metal on their own account; they make their own skin dresses, but buy their summer clothes. A race of wanderers could not be weavers on a large scale, but they can and do weave small bands very neatly on hand-looms; and they alone make these. There are savages now in South Africa, who are smiths and miners, though they neither weave nor wear clothes. Fairies had hoards of treasure—so have Lapps. A man died shortly before one of my Tana trips, and the whole country side had been out searching for his buried wealth in vain. Some years ago the old silver shops of Bergen and Trondhjem overflowed with queer cups and spoons, and rings, silver plates for waist belts, old plate that had been hidden amongst the mountains, black old silver coins that had not seen the light for years. I saw the plate and bought some, and was told that, in consequence of a religious movement, the Lapps had dug up and sold their hoards. Fairies are supposed to shoot flint arrows, and arrows of other kinds, at people now. Men have told me several times that they had been shot at: one man had found the flint arrow in an ash tree; another had heard it whiz past his ear; a third had pulled a slender arrow from a friend's head. If that be so, my argument fails, and fairies are *not* of the past; but Californian Indians now use arrow-heads which closely resemble those dug up in Scotland, in Denmark, and, I believe, all over Europe. Fairies are conquered by Christian symbols. They were probably Pagans, and, if so, they may have existed when Christianity was introduced. They steal men, women, and children, and keep them in their haunts. They are not the only slave owners in the world. They are supernatural, and objects of a sort of respect and wonder. So are gipsies where they are rare, as in Sweden and Norway; so are the Lapps themselves, for they are professed wizards. I have known a

terrified Swedish lassie whip her horse and gallop away in her cart
from a band of gipsies, and I have had the advantage of living in
the same house with a Lapp wizard at Quickjok, who had prophe-
sied the arrival of many strangers, of whom I was one. Spaniards
were gods amongst the Indians till they taught them to know better.
Horses were supernatural when they came, and on the whole, as it
appears, there is much more reason to believe that fairies were a
real people, like the Lapps, who are still remembered, than that
they are "creatures of imagination" or "spirits in prison," or "fallen
angels;" and the evidence of their actual existence is very much
more direct and substantial than that which has driven, and seems
still to be driving, people to the very verge of insanity, if not beyond
it, in the matter of those palpable-impalpable, visible-invisible
spirits who rap double knocks upon dancing deal boards.

I am inclined to believe in the former existence of fairies in this
sense, and if for no other reason, because all the nations of Europe
have had some such belief, and they cannot all have invented the
same fancy. The habitation of Highland fairies are green mounds,
they therefore, like the giants, resemble the "under jordiske" of the
north, and they too may be degraded divinities.

It seems then, that Gaelic tales attribute supernatural qualities
to things which are mentioned in popular tales elsewhere, and that
Gaelic superstitions are common to other races; and it seems worth
inquiry whether there was anything in the known customs of Celtic
tribes to make these things valuable, and whether tradition is
supported by history.

In the first place, then, who are Celts now? Who were their
ancestors? Who are their relations? and where have Gaelic tribes
appeared in history.

I believe that little is really known about the Gael; and in
particular, the origin of the West Highlanders has been very keenly
disputed. One thing is clear, they speak a language which is almost
identical with the Irish of the north of Ireland, and they are the same
people. The dialect of Irish, which varies most from Scotch Gaelic,
is clearly but another form of the same tongue. Manks is another;
and these three are closely related to Welsh and Breton, though the
difference is very much greater. Gaelic, Irish, and Manks vary from
each other about as much as Norse, Swedish, and Danish. Welsh
and Breton vary from the rest about as much as German and Dutch
do from the Scandinavian languages. There are variations in Gaelic,
and I believe there are in all the five surviving Celtic dialects, as
there are in the languages of different countries in England, of every

valley in Norway and Sweden, of every German district, and of every part of France, Spain, and Italy. But one who knows Gaelic well, can make himself understood throughout the Highlands, as freely as an Englishman can in England, though he may speak with a Northumbrian burr, or a west country twang, or like a true Cockney.

These, then, form the Celtic clan, the people of the west of Scotland, the Irish, the Manks, the Welsh, and the Breton. Who their relations are, and who their ancestors, are questions not easily answered, though much has been written on the subject. The following is a brief outline of what is given as Celtic history by modern writers whose works I have consulted lately:—

According to Henri Martin, the French historian,* the whole of Central Europe, France, and Spain, were once overrun by a race calling themselves Gael, and best known as Gauls. This people is generally admitted to have been of the same stock as Germans, Latins, Greeks, and Slavonians, and to have started from Central Asia at some unknown epoch. They are supposed to have been warlike, to have been tatooed like modern New Zealanders, and painted like North American Indians, to have been armed with stone weapons like the South Sea Islanders and California Indians; but shepherd, as well as hunters, and acquainted with the use of wheat and rye, which they are supposed to have brought with them from Asia. One great confederation of tribes of this race was known to ancient historians, as Κελτοι. They were represented as fair and rosy-cheeked, large-chested, active, and brave, and they found the Euskes settled in the south of France, who were dark-complexioned, whose descendants are supposed to be the Euscualdonec or Basques of the Pyrennees, and who are classed with the Lapps of the north of Europe, and with tribes now dwelling in the far north of Asia. I have seen faces in Barra very like faces which I had seen shortly before at St. Sebastian in Spain. A tribe of Gauls made their way into Italy, and have left traces of their language there, in the names of mountains chains and great rivers. There are named "Amhra," or "Ombres," and Amhra is translated Valliant. This invasion is calculated to have taken place about 1500 B.C.

The Gael were followed by Kimri or Cimbri, a kindred people of a darker complexion, speaking a kindred language, and their descendants are supposed to be the Welsh and Bretons. These in

* Histoire de France, par Henri Martin; 1855

turn occupied the interior of eastern Europe, and were followed by the Scyths, and these, says the French historian, were Teutons.

According to the learned author of the essay on the Cimmerians, in the third volume of Rawlinson's Herodotus, p. 184, it is almost beyond doubt that a people known to their neighbours as Cimmerii, Gimiri, or probably Gomerini, attained a considerable power in Western Asia and Eastern Europe within the period indicated by the dates B.C. 800, 600, or even earlier.

These people are traced to the inhabitants of Wales and Gael and Cymri are admitted by all to be Κελτοι; and still keep up their old character for pugnacity by quarrelling over their pedigrees.

Celts were undoubtedly the primitive inhabitants of Gaul, Belgium, and the British Islands, possibly also of Spain and Portugal; but no word of the language spoken by these ancient Cimbri has been preserved by ancient authors, except the name, "and perhaps the name Cimmerii may have included many Celtic tribes not of the Cymric branch." These Gauls appeared everywhere in Europe; and, in particular, they who had probably been driven out by the Scythians invaded Scythia, intermixed with the people, and formed the people known in history as Celto-Scythians; who the Scyths were (according to the author) appears to be uncertain. All that remains of their language is a list of words, picked out of the works of ancient authors; and knowing what modern authors make of words which they pick up by ear, such a list is but a narrow foundation on which to build. Still on that list it has been decided that Scyths spoke a language which has affinity with Sanscrit, and in that list, as it seems to me, there are several words which resemble Gaelic more closely than the Sanscrit words given with them. And so, according to this theory, the Basques were found in Europe by the first Gael, and these were driven westwards by Kimri, and these again by Scythians, and these by Teutons, and all these still occupy their respective positions. The Basques and Lapps pushed aside; The Gael in Scotland and Ireland, driven far to the westwards; the Kimri driven westwards into Wales and Brittany; the Scyths lost or absorbed; and the Teutons occupying their old possessions, as Germans, Saxons, English, Scandinavians, and all their kindred tribes; and of all these the Basques and their relatives alone speak a language which cannot be traced to a common unknown origin, from which Sanscrit also came.

Whatever then throws light on the traditions of the first invaders of Europe is of interest to all the rest, for, according to this theory, they are all of the same clan. They are all branches of the same old stock which grew in Central Asia, and which has spread over great part of the world, and whatever is told of Gauls is of interest to all branches of Celts.

Rome was taken by Gauls about 390 B.C.; Greece was invaded by Gauls about 297 B.C., and they are then described as armed with great swords and lances, and wearing golden collars, and fighting savagely. At the end of the third century B.C., according to the French historian, Gaul might have been a common name for the greatest part of Europe, for Gauls were everywhere.

Now, what manner of men were these Gauls, when men saw them who could describe them?

All the Gauls kept their hair untouched by iron, and raised it like a mane towards the top of the head. As to the beard, some shaved it, others wore it of a moderate length. The chiefs and the nobles shaved the cheeks and the chin, and let their mustache grow to all their length. (Histoire de France, page 33.)

Their eyes were blue or sea-green, and shone under this thick mass of hair, of which the blond hue had been changed by lime-water to a flaming tint.

Their mustaches were "Rousses," which is the only word I know which will translate ruadh.

The warrior was armed with an enormous sabre on his left thigh; he had two darts in his hand, or a long lance; he carried a four-cornered shield, painted of various brilliant colours, with bosses representing birds or wild animals; and on his head was a helmet topped with eagles' wings, floating hair, or horns of wild animals; his clothes were particoloured and he wore "brighis;" he was always fighting at home or abroad; he was a curious inquiring mortal, always asking questions; and truly he must have been a formidable savage that old French Gaul. Men's heads were nailed at the gates of his towns and his houses, beside trophies of the chase, much as modern Gael now hang up the trophies of their destructive skill, in the shape of pole-cats and crows.

The chiefs kept human heads embalmed and preserved, like archives of family prowess, of the Dyaks of Borneo and the New Zealanders still do, or did very lately. The father had the power of life and death over his wife and children, and exercised it too by burning the guilty wife; and, though some chiefs had several wives, and there are some scandalous stories of the manner and customs of the inhabitants of the island; women were consulted together with men by the chiefs on matters of moment, and held a high place amongst the Gauls of France.

Now, this short description of the Gauls, rapidly gleaned from the pages of two modern books of high authority and great research, after my Gaelic stories were collected, agrees with the picture which the Gaelic tales give of their mythical heroes in many particulars. They have long beautiful yellow hair, Leadanach, Buidh, Boidheach. They are Ruadh, Rousses. They have large swords, claidheamh, sometimes duileagach, leaf-shaped. They cast spears and darts, Sleadh. They are always asking questions, and their descendants have not lost the habit yet. Their dwellings are surrounded by heads stuck on staves, stob. They have larders of dead enemies. When a man is described as ragged and out of order, it is almost always added that his beard had grown over his face; and though beards are coming into fashion now, it is not a highland fashion to wear a beard; and many a stinging joke have I heard aimed at a bearded man by modern Highlanders. The shields of the warriors are Bucaideach, bossed; Balla-bhreachd, dotted and variegated; Bara-chaol, with slender point; "with many a picture to be seen on it, a lion, a cremhinach, and a deadly snake;" and such shields are figured on the Iona tombs. The ancient Gauls wore helmets which represented beasts. The enchanted king's sons, when they came home to their dwellings, put off cochal, the husk, and become men; and when they go out, they resume the cochal and become animals of various kinds. May this not mean that they put on their armour. They marry a plurality of wives in many stories. In short, the enchanted warriors are, as I verily believe, nothing but real men, and their manners real manners, seen through a haze of centuries, and seen in the same light as they are seen in other popular tales, but, mayhap, a trifle clearer, because the men who tell of them are the descendants of the men described, and have mixed less with other men.

I do not mean that the tales date from any particular period, but that traces of all periods may be found in them—that various actors have played the same parts time out of mind, and that their manners and customs are all mixed together, and truly, though confusedly, represented—that giants and fairies, and enchanted princes were men; that Rob Roy may yet wear many heads in Australia, and be a god or an ogre, according to taste—that tales are but garbled popular history, of a long journey through forests and wilds, inhabited by savages and wild beasts: of events that occurred on the way from east to west, in the year of grace, once upon a time.

Tales certainly are historical in this sense when they treat of Eirinn and Lochlann, for the islands were the battlefield of the Celts and Scandinavians, and though they lack the precision of more modern popular history, they are very precise as to Irish names and geography. "They went to Cnoc Seannan in Ireland." Conall was called Gulbanach from Beinn Gulbain in Ireland. There is the "king of Newry," and many other places are named according to their Gaelic names, never as they are named in English. The same is true of the manuscript tales in the Advocates' Library. Places about Loch Awe are named, and the characters pass backwards and forwards between Ireland and Argyll, as we are told they really did when the Irish Celts invaded and possessed that part of the west of Scotland, and that invasion is clearly referred to in more than one popular tradition still current. When Lochlann is mentioned, it is further off, and all is uncertain. The king's son, not the king himself, is usually the hero. Breacan *Mac* Righ Lochlainn is named, or the son of the king of Lochlann, without a name at all, but the Irish kings often have a whole pedigree; thus Connall Gulbanach MacIulin MacArt Mac some one else, king of Ireland, and I lately heard a long story about "Magnus."

This again is like distorted, undated popular history of true events. They are clearly seen at home, the very spot where the action took place is pointed to; less clearly in Ireland, though people and places are named; they are dimly seen in Lochlann, and beyond that everything is enlarged, and magical, and mysterious and grotesque. Real events are distorted into fables and magnified into supernatural occurrences, for the Gaelic proverbs truly say, "There are long horns on cattle in mist" or "in Ireland," and "Far away fowls have fine feathers."

But whether the stories are history or mythology, it is quite clear that they are very old, that they belong to a class which is very widely spread, and that they were not made by living men.

All story-tellers agree in saying that they learned them as traditions long ago; and if all those whose names are given had been inclined to tell "stories" in another sense, they could not have made and told the same stories at opposite ends of Scotland, almost simultaneously, to different people. James Wilson could not have told Connall Cra-bhuidhe to Hector MacLean in Islay, about the same time that Neil Gillies was telling Conal Crobhi to me at Inverary, and a very short time before Hector Urquhart got No. 8 from Kenneth MacLean in Gairloch. An old fisherman and an old porter could not have combined to tell a "story" which was in Straparola, in Italian, in 1567, to Hector MacLean in Barra, in 1859, and to the Rev. Mr. MacLauchlan in Edinburgh, in 1860, unless these stories were popular facts, though despised as fictions; and they are curious facts too, for the frame of Conal is common to old German manuscripts, and some of the adventures are versions of those of Ulysses. There are many proverbs which are only explained when the story is known; for example, "blackberries in February" means nothing; but when explained by the story, the meaning is clearly the idea which an acquaintance of mine once embodied in a French toast, as "les impossibilités accomplies." The stories do not change rapidly, for I have gone back to a reciter after the lapse of a year, and I have heard him again repeat in Gaelic, what I had translated from his dictation, with hardly a change (vol. 1).

I have now no doubt that the popular tales are very old; that they are old "Allabanaich," Highlanders and wanderers; that they have wandered, settled, and changed, with those who still tell them; and call themselves "Albannaich," men whose wandering spirit is not yet extinct, though they were settled in their present abodes "before the memory of man."

There was and is, a wandering spirit in the whole race, if Celts are Indo-Europeans. In the people who delighted in the adventures of Ulysses and Æneas, a longing spirit of western adventure, which was shewn in the fabled Atalantis, and the Island of the Seven Cities and St. Brandon—the spirit which drove the hordes of Asia to Europe, and urged Columbus to discover America, and which still survives in "the Green Isle of the great deep," "Eilean uaine an iomal torra domhain," of which so much is told, which Highland fancy still sees on the far western horizon, and which as "FLATHINNIS," the Isle of Heroes, has now been raised from an earthly paradise to mean Heaven.

Much has been said about highland superstitions, and highlanders of the east and west, like their southern neighbours, have many, but they are at least respectable from their age; and because they are so widely spread over the world, I believe them to be nearly all fictions founded on facts.

Thirteen Highlanders would eat their potatoes together without fear, and one of them might spill the salt without a shudder. I never heard of a Celtic peasant consulting his table as an oracle, or going to a clairvoyant; but plenty of them dream dreams and see visions, and believe in them as men in Bible history did of old.

A man had been lost in crossing the dangerous ford, five or six miles of sand or rock, between Benbecula and North Uist, shortly before I was there in 1859. I was told the fact, and it was added incidentally, "And did he not come to his sister in a dream, and tell her where to find him? and she went to the place, and got him there, half buried in sand, after the whole country side had been looking for him in vain." Here is a similar story from Manchester:—

"FULFILMENT OF A DREAM.—An inquest was held last evening at Sheffield, before Mr. Thomas Badger, coroner, on the body of Mr. Charles Holmes, button manufacturer, Clough House Lane, who had been found drowned on Monday morning, in the Lead-mill dam in that town. The deceased left his home on Saturday night in company with his wife; they walked through the town together, and about nine o'clock, at which time they were at the top of Union Street, he said to her, 'I'm going to leave thee here, Fanny.' She said, 'Are you?' and he replied, 'Yes, I want to see an old friend who is going to Birmingham on Monday, and he is to be here.' She said to him, 'Well, Charlie, don't stop long, because I do feel queer about that dream,' and he replied, 'Oh, don't say that; I'll just have a glass, and then come home. Go and get the supper ready, and I'll come directly.' She then left him. When he got into the house he was invited to drink with his friend, but he exhibited some reluctance, saying that on the night before his wife had dreamed that she saw him dead in a public-house, and that she had dreamed a similar dream about a week before. Unfortunately, however, he yielded to the temptation, got drunk, and did not leave the public-house till after twelve. He was accompanied part of the way home by his friend, and was never afterwards seen alive. Near his house are the Lead-mill dams, and, in consequence of his not returning home, his wife felt convinced that he had fallen in and got drowned. A search was made, and on Monday morning his body was found in the water, and was removed to the Royal Standard public-house, where his wife saw the body, and identified it as that of her husband; The jury returned a verdict of 'Found drowned,' and recommended that an opening in the wall, near the dam, through which it is supposed he had fallen, should be built up."—*Manchester Examiner.*

There are plenty of lowlanders as well as "ignorant" Highlanders who think that they are seers, without the aid of a deal board through which to look into futurity, by the help of a medium, and it is by no means uncommon, as I am told, for the Astronomer-Royal to receive English letters asking his advice, *ex officio.*

It may not be out of place to add a word as to the spoken Gaelic of these tales; the mode of writing it; and the English of the translation. First, then, it is admitted by all that the Gaelic of the West Highlands is a branch of the old Celtic stock, that is to say, the language of some of the oldest invaders or inhabitants of Europe of whom anything is known. Why it is I know not, but from works on philology it appears that the Highland dialect has been least studied, and for that reason, if for no other, it is perhaps best worth the trouble. I thought it best to ignore all that had been said or written on the subject, to go direct to those who now speak the language, especially to those who speak no other tongue; to men who use words as they use their feet and hands, utterly unconscious of design; who talk as nature and their parents taught them; and who are as innocent of philology as their own babies when they first learn to say "Abbi."

I requested those who wrote for me to take down the words as they were spoken, and to write as they would speak themselves; and the Gaelic of the tales is the result of such a process. The names of the writers are given, and I am satisfied that they have done their work faithfully and well. The Gaelic then is *not* what is called "classical Gaelic." It is generally the Gaelic of the people—pure from the source.

Next, as to orthography. I chose one man, Mr. Hector MacLean, whom I know to be free from prejudice, and who knows the rules of Gaelic spelling, to correct the press, and I asked him to spell the sounds which he heard, according to the principles of Gaelic orthography, whenever he wrote anything down himself; and in correcting the press for the work of others, to correct nothing but manifest mistakes, and this he has done, as it appears to me, very well.

In Gaelic there are certain vowels, and combinations of them, which represent certain sounds; and they are all sounded, and always in the same manner, *according to theory*, but in practice it is a very different matter. In speaking Gaelic, as is the case in other languages, various modes of pronouncing the same vowels exist in various districts. The consonants meet and contend and extinguish each other, and change the sound of the vowels in Gaelic more than in any other language which I know; but they fight by rule, and the conquered and the slain encumber the words which are their battlefields, as dead or dying consonants standing beside the silent *h* which kills or controls them. One difficulty in writing Gaelic from dictation is to ascertain, in words of doubtful meaning, whether the sound *v* is to be expressed by *bh* or *mh*. The first letter was once at the head of a small regiment of letters, and sounded his own note *m* or *b*, and so he regulated the meaning of the rest, but having fallen in with an *h* in an oblique case, and being changed thereby to *v*, the whole history of the word must be known before it can be settled whether it should begin with *mh* or *bh*, and it is much more difficult in other cases, where the letter is silenced altogether. My mother, if Gaelic, might become *vy vother*—father, *ather*, but the sounds would be spelt *mhother, fhather*. The meaning in a book depends on the spelling, but in speaking, it is a different matter. There are shades of sound which an ear used to a language can detect, but which letters are wholly unfitted to express.

Gaelic scholars, then, who have a standard for Gaelic writing, and who adhere to it strictly, will probably find much which will appear to them erroneous spelling.

An English scholar reading Sir Walter Scott's novels will find plenty of words which are not in Johnson's Dictionary, and a student of Pickwick will find much in Sam Weller's conversation which he will not discover in that form in Shakspeare.

Had I found stories in the Isle of Wight I should have spelt good morning good marnin, because it is so pronounced; falbh is spelt folbh when a story comes from some of the Western Islands, because it is so pronounced there; and for the same reason iad is spelt eud. I have no doubt there are errors. I can only vouch for having chosen men who did their best in a very difficult matter; for I do not believe that there are ten men now living who would write a hundred lines of Gaelic off hand and spell them in the same way. I very much doubt if ten men ever did live at the same time who would have agreed as to Gaelic spelling; and I know that I find forms of words in books which I have very rarely heard in conversation. For example, the plural in IBH (*iv*) is very rare; the common form is AN.

The spelling of the first book printed in the Gaelic language, Bishop Carswell's Prayer-book, 1567, is not the same as the spelling of the Gaelic Bible. The Gaelic names in old charters are not spelt according to modern rule. The old Gaelic manuscripts in the Advocates' Library are spelt in various ways. Every man who has written Gaelic for me, spells words variously. Manks spelling is phonetic. Irish spelling is different; and where there is so little authority, I hope to be forgiven if I have ventured to ask men to follow their own own road. I hope they will be forgiven if they have taken a short cut to obtain a certain object, and if they have left the beaten path.

For the translation I am responsible, and I feel that the English needs excuse. It has been the fashion so far to translate Gaelic freely; that is, to give the sense of the passage without caring much for the sense of words. One result is, that dictionaries give so many meanings that they are almost useless to any one ignorant of Gaelic. There are many words in these tales which were new to me, and I have repeatedly been driven to gather their meaning from the context, or to ask for it at the source, because of the multitude of contradictory explanations given in dictionaries. Let me take one word as an example. In the first tale the hero meets CU SEANG NA COILL' UAINE, and the meaning turned on the word SEANG. To that word the following meanings are attached:—Slender, slender-waisted, hungry, hungry-looking, lank, lean, active, handsome, strong; (applied to a shirt-front), fine; "Sad am I this day arising the breast of my shirt is not *seang*;" (applied to food in a proverb), meat makes men "seang;" (applied to hinds in an ode), neat; (applied to a horse), spirited; also slim, small, small-bellied, gaunt, nimble, agile; (applied to lady), slender-waisted. On looking further it appears that SEANGAN is an ant; that SHUNKA is the Dakotah for all animals of the dog species, and that the word came to be applied to a horse, as spirit dog, when horses came first to that country; and it further appears that there is a word in broad Scotch which nearly fits the Gaelic, SWANK; that SING means a lion in India; and that the horses of the sun were swankas with beautiful steps in Sanscrit. It seemed to me that the phrase might be thus freely translated "The Forest Lion."

But though it seemed to me possible I might be entirely wrong, so I gave the meaning of the words, about which there could be no mistake:—

CU SEANG NA COILL' UAINE.
Dog slim of the wood green.

My belief is, that the word was an adjective, descriptive of the qualities of a lion wherever their likeness is to be found—as strength, activity, high courage, bold bearing, slender form, hunger, satiety; but I did not venture to translate CU SEANG by "*lion*," nor by "*grey hound*," as I was advised to do. I translated it by those words which seem to give the present meaning of the Gaelic. CU, a dog; SEANG, slim; and the phrase stands, "The slim dog of the green wood."

And so throughout I have aimed at giving the present real meaning of every separate word, but so as to give its true meaning in the passage in which it occurs. Where I have not been able to do both, I have tried to keep as close as I could to the original idea involved. For example, "In the mouth of night" is new to English, but it is comprehensible, and it is the exact meaning of the phrase commonly used to express the first coming on of darkness. The expression is poetical. It seems to refer to some old mythical notion that the sun went into a cave or a tent to sleep, for "Take thy sleep in thy cave" is a line in Ossian's "Address to the Sun," and though it was suggested to me to alter this translation, and make it "good English," I thought it best to adhere to my original plan. Generally where the phrase occurs it is translated "in the mouth of night," though I was advised to write, "in the dusk," "in the evening," "at nightfall," "in the mantle of night," "at twilight," "in the grey of the evening."

I admit that all these phrases express ideas which might be attached to the words; but what could an unfortunate student make of a passage in which a word meaning *mouth* according to all dictionaries, should seem to mean *mantle*, or *fall*, or *grey*. It is very much easier to write naturally and translate freely; and as I have tried hard to make my translation a close one, I hope the bad English will be forgiven.

Those only who have tried to turn Gaelic into English can understand the difficulty. There are in fact many Gaelic phrases which will not go into English at all. For example, THA SO AGAM (I have this), *is this at me, or with me, or by me*, is a phrase which cannot be rendered for want of a word equivalent to AG or AIG, which expresses position and possession, and is combined with *am, ad, e, inn, ibh*, and changed to aca to express the persons. Gaelic will not bear literal translation into English, but I have tried to give the real meaning of every word as nearly as I could, and to give it by using the English word which most resembled the Gaelic; and thus I have unexpectedly fallen in with a number of English words which seem to have the same origin as Gaelic, if they are not survivors of the language of the ancient Britons. I have translated CLAIDHEAMH, pronounced Claiv, by glave, TRAILL by thrall, and so throughout wherever I have thought of an English word that resembled a word admitted to be Gaelic.

It is my own opinion, and it is that of Mr. MacLean, that the Gaelic language is the same from Cape Clear in Ireland to Cape Wrath in Scotland, though there are many dialects, and there is much variety. The language was taught to me by a native of Lorn, and he was chosen by the advice of men well able to judge, as a native of the district where the best Gaelic was then supposed to be spoken. Speaking from my own experience, I can converse freely in Lorn Gaelic with Scotch Highlanders in every district of Scotland, and with natives of Rathlin. I can make my way with natives of the North of Ireland, but I cannot converse with the natives of some Irish districts. I could not make the Manksmen understand me, but I can readily understand most of the words in Manks and in Irish, when pronounced separately.

There are a very great many words in Welsh and in Breton which I can understand, or trace when they are separately spoken, but the difference in these is much wider. Peasants come from Connaught to Islay, and in a very short time converse freely, though their accent betrays them; but an Argyllshire Highlander is known in the north by his accent, just as a Yorkshireman would be found out in Somersetshire. An Islay man is detected in Mull, and a native of one parish in Islay is detected when he speaks in another; but though there are such shades of difference, a Highlander used to hear languages variously spoken should have no difficulty in understanding any dialect of Gaelic spoken in Scotland, and most of the Irish dialects. But which of all these is the best, who is to decide? The author of a very good dictionary says, under the word COIG, that "in the islands of Argyllshire every word is pronounced just as Adam spoke it." Dr. Johnson pronounced the whole to be the rude speech of a barbarous people; and the Saxon knew as much of Gaelic as the Celt did of Adam. One Gaelic scholar wished to change the island words; a good Highlander told me that Dalmally was the best place for Gaelic, another was all for Western Ross. Nobody has a good word for Sutherland Gaelic, but it is very pure nevertheless in some districts; north country men are all for Inverness. I have heard excellent Gaelic in the Long Island. On the whole, I am inclined to think that dialect the best which resembles the largest number of others, and that is the dialect spoken by the most illiterate in the islands, and on the promontories furthest to the west. I will not venture to name any district, because I have no wish to contend with the natives of all the others.

The spirit of nationality is one which has a large development amongst my countrymen, and the subject of language brings it out in strong relief. It is but a phase of human nature, a result of the quality which phrenologists describe as combativeness, and it seems to be common to all the races classed as Indo-European.

It is a common opinion in England that one Englishman can thrash three Frenchmen; and I have no doubt that a similar opinion prevails in France, though I do not know the fact. Highlanders believe that lowlanders generally are soft and effeminate; lowlanders think that mountaineers are savages. An Irish Celt detests his brother Celt over the water. A Scotch Celt calls another Eireannach when he abuses him, but let a common foe appear and they will all combine.

England, Ireland, and Scotland are up in arms, with rifles on their shoulders, at a hint of the approach of a Frenchman; but they joined France with heart and hand to fight the Russian and the Chinese; and as soon as the battle was over, they came back and fought at home.

The English lion stirred up the Scotch lion in the English press, and the northern lion growled over his wrongs. Ireland began to tell of the tyrant Saxon, and a stranger might think that the Union was about to fall to pieces. It is not so; it is but a manifestation of superfluous energy which breaks out in the other "union" over the water, and makes as much noise there as steam blowing off elsewhere.

I maintain that there is chronic war in every part of her Majesty's dominions. Not long ago a dispute arose about a manner of catching herrings. One set of men caught them with drift-nets, another with dragnets, and one party declared that the other violated the law; blood got up, and at last a whole fleet of fishing-boats left their ground and sailed twenty miles down to attack the rival fleet in form. A gun-boat joined the party, and peace was preserved; but it was more the result of a calm, which enabled the light row-boats to escape from the heavier sailing fleet. Both parties spoke the same language, and on any subject but herrings, they would have backed each other through the world.

The purchase of an orange, and a box on the ear, grew into a serious riot in a northern town last year. The fight spread as from a centre, and lasted three days; but here it developed itself into a fight between Celt and Saxon. Both sides must have been in the wrong, and I am quite sure they were both ignominiously defeated, although they may hold the contrary.

Every election in the three kingdoms is a shameful riot, according to some public organ, whose party get the worst of it.

There is a regular stand-up fight in Paris periodically, the rest of Europe goes to war in earnest at every opportunity, and when there are no national or class wars, men fight as individuals all over the world. I was once at Christmas at a hurling match in Ireland. The game was played on ice on a lake, and after some hours the owner of the lake sent down a Scotch butler with bread and cheese and whisky for the players. They gathered about the cart in perfect good humour, when suddenly, without cause, an excited banker's clerk shouted, "Hurro for——" (the nearest post town), and performed a kind of war dance on the outside edge of his skates, flourishing a stick wildly, and chanting his war song, "I'll bet ere a man in England, Ireland, or SCOTLAND." A knobby stick rose up in the crowd, and the Scotch butler was down; but an Irish boy who had not opened his mouth was the next. He went head-foremost into a willow bush amongst the snow, and three men in frieze great-coats kicked him with nailed shoes. In ten minutes the storm was over, the butler was up again in his cart dispensing the refreshments, the man in the bush was consoling himself with a dram, and all was peace. But that night the country party took up a position behind a stone wall, and when the others came, they sallied forth and there was a battle-royal.

So I have seen a parish shinty match in the Highlands become so hot and furious, that the leaders were forced to get two pipers and march their troops out of the field in opposite directions, to prevent a civil war of parishes.

And so, a part of her Majesty's guards having gone out to exercise at Clewer, and being stationed as "the enemy" at some point, obstinately refused to "retreat in disorder;" but stood their ground with such determination, that the officers had to sound the retreat on both sides to prevent a serious battle.

So at Eton, shins were broken in my tutor's football match against my dame's; and boys injured themselves in rowing frantically for the honour of upper or lower sixes.

Two twins, who were so like, that one used to skip round a pillar and answer to his brother's name, and who probably would have died for each other, still fought in private so earnestly, that one carried the mark of a shovel on his forehead for many a long day; and so boys fight, and men fight, individually and collectively, as parties, races, and nations, all over Europe, if not all over the world.

I decline to state my opinion as to which Gaelic is the best, for that is a peculiarly delicate subject, my countrymen having ceased to use their dirks, are apt to fight with pens, and I would rather see the children of the Gael, in this as in other matters fighting shoulder to shoulder against foes, and working side by side with their friends.

The Gaelic language is essentially descriptive, rich in words, which by their sound alone express ideas. The thundering sound of the waves beating on the shore is well expressed by TONN, a wave; LUNN, a heavy Atlantic swell.

The harsh rattling and crushing of thunder by TAIRNEANACH.

The plunge of a heavy body thrown into deep water by TUNN, plunge.

The noise of small stones and fine gravel streaming seawards from a beach in the undertow is heard in SCRITHEAN, gravel.

The tinkling of shells as they slip and slide on the sand at the edge of the sea is heard in SLIGEAN, shells.

The hard sharp knocking of stones in CLACH, a stone, and thence all manner of compound ideas follow as CLACHAN, a village; CLACHAIR, a mason; CLACHARAN, a stone-chat.

The names of domestic animals usually resemble their notes. Bo, a cow; gobhar, a goat; caora, a sheep; laogh, a calf. Words such as barking, growling, squealing, coughing, sneezing, suggest the idea by the sound, as they do in English. Many names of beasts and birds, which are not of this class, are descriptive in another sense. The grouse are the reddish brown cock and hen; the fox, the reddish brown dog; the wolf, the fierce dog; the sandpiper, the little driolichan of the strand. The crow is the flayer, the falcon, the darter; the otter the brown or black beast.

It is a language full of metaphorical and descriptive expressions. "He went to the beginning of fortune;" "he put the world under his head;" "he took his own body home;" "he went away"—that is, he went home sick, and he died. "There were great masses of rain, and there was night and there was darkness." "Ye must not be out amidst the night, she is dark."

It is rich in words expressive of war, by no means rich in words belonging to the arts. CRANN, a tree, means a mast, the bar of a door, a plough, and many other things made of wood. BEAIRT means a loom, a block and tackling, and engines of various kinds.

It seems to contain words to express the great features of nature, which can be traced in the names of rivers and mountains in a great part of Europe, such as EAS, a rapid (pr. ace); ATH (pr. A. and Av.), a ford; AMHAINN, OBHAINN, ABHAINN, a river, variously pronounced, *avain, a-wen, ovain, o-in, o-un, o-n.* Calais I take to be CALA, a harbour; the word has no meaning in French. Boulogne might be BEUL OBHAINN, river's mouth; Donau, the Danube, might mean the brown river. Tana might mean the shallow, and both are descriptive.

Rhine might mean the division, and there is a district in Islay whose name is pronounced exactly as the name of the great German river. Balaclava is exceedingly like the name of an Islay farm, and might mean kite's town, BAILE CHLAMHAIN; but though such resemblances can hardly fail to occur to any one who knows the Gaelic language, it requires time and careful study to follow out such a subject, and it is foreign to my purpose. There are plenty of Gaelic words which closely resemble words in other European languages. Amongst the few Sanscrit words which I have been able to glean from books, I find several which resemble Gaelic words of similar meaning—JWALA, light flame, has many Gaelic relations in words which mean shining, fire, lightning, the moon, white, swan.

DYU, day, is like an diugh, to-day; MIRAH, the ocean, like muir, mara, the sea; but this again is foreign to my purpose.

My wish has been simply to gather some specimens of the wreck so plentifully strewn on the coasts of old Scotland, and to carry it where others may examine it; rather to point out where curious objects worth some attention may be found, than to gather a great heap. I have not sought for stranded forests. I have not polished the rough sticks which I found; I have but cut off a very few offending splinters, and I trust that some may be found who will not utterly despise such rubbish, or scorn the magic which peasants attribute to a fairy egg.

POSTSCRIPT

September 1860.

The stories marked XVII.*a*, XVII.*b*, XVII.*c*, XVII.*d*, in the first volume were intended for the second, but it has been found more convenient to place them in Vol. I. Those which were to have been given as specimens of tales probably derived from the "Arabian Nights," have been left out to make room for others.

In August and September 1860 I again visited the Western Highlands, carrying with me nearly the whole of these two volumes in print. I have repeatedly made the men who told the stories to my collectors repeat them to me, while I compared their words with the book. In two instances I have made men repeat stories which I had myself written down in English from their Gaelic, and I have found no important variation in any instance. I find that the story is generally much longer as told, but that it is lengthened by dialogue, which has often little to do with the incidents, though sometimes worth preservation. I have now seen most of the men whose names are mentioned, and I have myself heard versions of nearly every story in the book repeated, either by those from whom they were got, or by people who live far from them,—for instance, John Mackinnon, stableman at Broadford, in Skye, told me in September a version of No. 18, which contains nearly all the incidents which I had before got from Islay, and several which were new to me.

Including those which are printed, I have more than two hundred stories written down in Gaelic. I have about an equal number written in English from Gaelic, and I have heard a great many more, while Mr. Hector MacLean, Mr. Dewar, Mr. Carmichael, Mr. Torrie, Mr. Fraser, and others, are still writing down for me, in the Long Island, in Argyllshire, and elsewhere.

If I have time and opportunity, I hope hereafter to arrange these materials; to place the incidents in *each* story according to the majority of versions, and so strive to get the old form of the legends; for I am convinced that much is to be learned from this despised old rubbish, though it must be sifted before it can be turned to proper use.

In conclusion, I would tender my thanks once more to all those who have given me their assistance. In particular, I wish to express my sense of obligation to the Rev. Thomas Maclauchlan, Free Church Gaelic minister in Edinburgh, who has contributed many stories, written down by himself from the dictation of one of his parishioners, and who has himself published a volume of Celtic gleanings.

I am also much indebted to the Rev. Mr. Beatson, minister of Barra, who aided Mr. MacLean in his search for legends, and who showed much kindness to myself; and I have received assistance from other clergymen of various persuasions, including the Rev. Thomas Pattison in Islay. I am happy to have it in my power to mention such names; for the strange idea possesses the people in many districts, that to repeat the most harmless sgeulachd is a grievous sin, and that fables, and poems, and novels of every sort ought to be put down and exterminated, because they are fictions. That spirit, if strong enough and put in action, would sweep away much of the literature of ancient and modern times; and it seems strange to have to remonstrate against it now-a-days. Still, strange as it may seem, the spirit exists, and I am grateful for the support of enlightened liberal men. Surely the best treatment for "Superstition," if this be superstition, is to drag it into light, the very worst to dignify it by persecution, and strive to hide it.

1

THE YOUNG KING OF EASAIDH RUADH.

From James Wilson, blind fiddler, Islay.

The young king of Easaidh Ruadh, after he got the heirship to himself, was at much merry making, looking out what would suit him, and what would come into his humour. There was a GRUAGACH near his dwelling, who was called Gruagach carsalach donn—(The brown curly long-haired one.)

He thought to himself that he would go to play a game with him. He went to the Seanagal (soothsayer) and he said to him—"I am made up that I will go to game with the Gruagach carsalach donn." "Aha!" said the Seanagal, "art thou such a man? Art thou so insolent that thou art going to play a game against the Gruagach carsalach donn? 'Twere my advice to thee to change thy nature and not to go there." "I wont do that," said he. " 'Twere my advice to thee, if thou shouldst win of the Gruagach carsalach donn, to get the cropped rough-skinned maid that is behind the door for the worth of thy gaming, and many a turn will he put off before thou gettest her." He lay down that night, and if it was early that the day came, 'twas earlier than that that the king arose to hold gaming against the Gruagach. He reached the Gruagach, he blessed the Gruagach, and the Gruagach blessed him. Said the Gruagach to him, "Oh young king of Easaidh Ruadh, what brought thee to me to-day? Wilt thou game with me?" They began and they played the game. The king won. "Lift the stake of thy gaming so that I may get (leave) to be moving." "The stake of my gaming is to give me the cropped rough-skinned girl thou hast behind the door." "Many a fair woman have I within besides her," said the Gruagach. "I will take none but that one." "Blessing to thee and cursing to thy teacher of learning" They went to the house of the Gruagach, and the Gruagach set in order twenty young girls. "Lift now thy choice from amongst these." One was coming out after another, and every one that would come out she would say, "I am she; art thou not silly that art not taking me with thee?" But the Seanagal had asked him to take none but the last one that would come out. When the last one came out, he said, "This is mine." He went with her, and when they were a bit from the house, her form altered, and she is the loveliest woman that was on earth. The king was going home full of joy at getting such a charming woman.

He reached the house, and he went to rest. If it was early that the day arose, it was earlier than that that the king arose to go to game with the Gruagach. "I must absolutely go to game against the Gruagach to-day," said he to his wife. "Oh!" said she, "that's my father, and if thou goest to game with him, take nothing for the stake of thy play but the dun shaggy filly that has the stick saddle on her."

The king went to encounter the Gruagach, and surely the blessing of the two to each other was not beyond what it was before. "Yes!" said the Gruagach, "how did thy young bride please thee yesterday?" "She pleased fully." "Hast thou come to game with me to-day?" "I came." They began at the gaming, and the king won from the Gruagach on that day. "Lift the stake of thy gaming, and be sharp about it." "The stake of my gaming is the dun shaggy filly on which is the stick saddle."

They went away together. They reached the dun shaggy filly. He took her out from the stable, and the king put his leg over her and she was the swift heroine! He went home. His wife had her hands spread before him, and they were cheery together that night. "I would rather myself," said his wife, "that thou shouldest not go to game with the Gruagach any more, for if he wins he will put trouble on thy head." "I won't do that," said he, "I *will* go to play with him to-day."

He went to play with the Gruagach. When he arrived, he thought the Gruagach was seized with joy. "Hast thou come?" he said. "I came." They played the game, and, as a cursed victory for the king, the Gruagach won that day. "Lift the stake of thy game," said the young king of Easaidh Ruadh, "and be not heavy on me, for I cannot stand to it." "The stake of my play is," said he, "that I lay it as crosses and as spells on thee, and as the defect of the year, that the cropped rough-skinned creature, more uncouth and unworthy than thou thyself, should take thy head, and thy neck, and thy life's look off, if thou dost not get for me the GLAIVE OF LIGHT of the king of the oak windows." The king went home, heavily, poorly, gloomily. The young queen came meeting him, and she said to him, "Mohrooai! my pity! there is nothing with thee tonight." Her face and her splendour gave some pleasure to the king when he looked on her brow, but when he sat on a chair to draw her towards him, his heart was so heavy that the chair broke under him.

"What ails thee, or what should ail thee, that thou mightest not tell it to me?" said the queen. The king told how it happened. "Ha!" said she, "what should'st thou mind, and that thou hast the best wife in Erin, and the second best horse in Erin. If thou takest my advice, thou wilt come (well) out of all these things yet."

If it was early that the day came, it was earlier than that that the queen arose, and she set order in everything, for the king was about to go on his journey. She set in order the dun shaggy filly, on which was the stick saddle, and though he saw it as wood, it was full of sparklings with gold and silver. He got on it; the queen kissed him, and she wished him victory of battlefields. "I need not be telling thee anything. Take thou the advice of thine own she comrade, the filly, and she will tell thee what thou shouldest do." He set out on his journey, and it was not dreary to be on the dun steed.

She would catch the swift March wind that would be before, and the swift March wind would not catch her. They came at the mouth of dusk and lateness, to the court and castle of the king of the oak windows.

Said the dun shaggy filly to him, "We are at the end of the journey, and we have not to go any further; take my advice, and I will take thee where the sword of light of the king of the oak windows is, and if it comes with thee without scrape or creak, it is a good mark on our journey. The king is now at his dinner, and the sword of light is in his own chamber. There is a knob on its end, and when thou catchest the sword, draw it softly out of the window 'case.' " He came to the window where the sword was. He caught the sword and it came with him softly till it was at its point, and then it gave a sort of a "sgread." "We will now be going," said the filly. "It is no stopping time for us. I know the king has felt us taking the sword out." He kept his sword in his hand, and they went away, and when they were a bit forward, the filly said, "We will stop now, and look thou whom thou seest behind thee." "I see" said he, "a swarm of brown horses coming madly." "We are swifter ourselves than these yet," said the filly. They went, and when they were a good distance forward, "Look now," said she; "whom seest thou coming?" "I see a swarm of black horses, and one white-faced black horse, and he is coming and coming in madness, and a man on him." "That is the best horse in Erin; it is my brother, and he got three months more nursing than I, and he will come past me with a whirr, and try if thou wilt be so ready, that when he comes past me, thou wilt take the head off the man who is on him; for in the time of passing he will look at thee, and there is no sword in his court will take off his head but the very sword that is in thy hand." When this man was going past, he gave his head a turn to look at him, he drew the sword and he took his head off, and the shaggy dun filly caught it in her mouth.

This was the king of the oak windows. "Leap on the black horse," said she, "and leave the carcass there, and be going home as fast as he will take thee home, and I will be coming as best I may after thee." He leaped on the black horse, and, "Moirë!" he was the swift hero, and they reached the house long before day. The queen was without rest till he arrived. They raised music, and they laid down woe. On the morrow, he said, "I am obliged to go to see the Gruagach to-day, to try if my spells will be loose." Mind that it is not as usual the Gruagach will meet thee. He will meet thee furiously, wildly, and he will say to thee, didst thou get the sword? and say thou that thou hast got it; he will say, how didst thou get it? and thou shalt say, if it were not the knob that was on its end I had not got it. He will ask thee again, how didst thou get the sword? and thou wilt say, if it were not the knob that was on its end, I had not got it. Then he will give himself a lift to look what knob is on the sword, and thou wilt see a mole on the right side of his neck, and stab the point of the sword in the mole; and if thou dost not hit the mole, thou and I are done. His brother was the king of the oak windows, and he knows that till the other had lost his life, he would not part with the sword. The death of the two is in the sword, but there is no other sword that will touch them but it." The queen kissed him, and she called on victory of battlefields (to be) with him, and he went away.

The Gruagach met him in the very same place where he was before. "Didst thou get the sword?" "I got the sword." "How didst thou get the sword?" "If it were not the knob that was on its end I had not got it," said he. "Let me see the sword." "It was not laid on me to let thee see it." "How didst thou get the sword?" "If it were not the knob that was on its end, I got it not." The Gruagach gave his head a lift to look at the sword; he saw the mole; he was sharp and quick, and he thrust the sword into the mole, and the Gruagach fell down dead.

He returned home, and when he returned home, he found his

set of keepers and watchers tied back to back, without wife, or horse, or sweetheart of his, but was taken away.

When he loosed them, they said to him, "A great giant came and he took away thy wife and thy two horses." "Sleep will not come on mine eyes nor rest on mine head till I get my wife and my two horses back." In saying this, he went on his journey. He took the side that the track of the horses was, and he followed them diligently. The dusk and lateness were coming on him, and no stop did he make until he reached the side of the green wood. He saw where there was the forming of the site of a fire, and he thought that he would put fire upon it, and thus he would put the night past there.

He was not long here at the fire, when "CU SEANG of the green wood came on him.

He blessed the dog, and the dog blessed him.

"Oov! oov!" said the dog, "Bad was the plight of thy wife and thy two horses here last night with the big giant." "It is that which has set me so pained and pitiful on their track to-night; but there is no help for it." "Oh! king," said the dog, "thou must not be without meat." The dog went into the wood. He brought out creatures, and they made them meat contentedly. "I rather think myself," said the king, "that I may turn home; that I cannot go near that giant." "Don't do that," said the dog. "There's no fear of thee, king. Thy matter will grow with thee. Thou must not be here without sleeping." "Fear will not let me sleep without a warranty." "Sleep thou," said the dog, "and I will warrant thee." The king let himself down, stretched out at the side of the fire, and he slept. When the watch broke, the dog said to him, "Rise up, king, till thou gettest a morsel of meat that will strengthen thee, till thou wilt be going on thy journey. Now," said the dog, "if hardship or difficulty comes on thee, ask my aid, and I will be with thee in an instant." They left a blessing with each other, and he went away. In the time of dusk and lateness, he came to a great precipice of rock, and there was the forming of the site of a fire.

He thought he would gather dry fuel, and that he would set on fire. He began to warm himself, and he was not long thus when the hoary hawk of the grey rock came on him. "Oov! oov!" said she, "Bad was the plight of thy wife and thy two horses last night with the big giant." "There is no help for it," said he. "I have got much of their trouble and little of their benefit myself." "Catch courage," said she. "Thou wilt get something of their benefit yet. Thou must not be without meat here," said she. "There is no contrivance for getting meat," said he. "We will not be long getting meat," said the falcon. She went, and she was not long when she came with three ducks and eight blackcocks in her mouth. They set their meat in order, and they took it. "Thou must not be without sleep," said the falcon. "How shall I sleep without a warranty over me, to keep me from any one evil that is here." "Sleep thou, king, and I will warrant thee." He let himself down, stretched out, and he slept.

In the morning, the falcon set him on foot. "Hardship or difficulty that comes on thee, mind, at any time, that thou wilt get my help." He went swiftly, sturdily. The night was coming, and the little birds of the forest of branching bushy trees, were talking about the briar roots and the twig tops; and if they were, it was stillness, not peace for him, till he came to the side of a great river that was there, and at the bank of the river there was the forming of the site of a fire. The king blew a heavy, little spark of fire. He was not long here when there came as company for him the brown otter of the river. "Och! och!" said the otter, "Bad was the plight of thy wife and thy two horses last night with the giant." "There is no help for it. I got much of their trouble and little of their benefit." "Catch courage, before mid-day to-morrow thou wilt see thy wife. Oh! King, thou must not be without meat," said the otter. "How is meat to be got here?" said the king. The otter went through the river, and she came and three salmon with her, that were splendid. They made meat, and they took it. Said the otter to the King, "Thou must sleep." "How can I sleep without any warranty over me?" "Sleep thou, and I will warrant thee." The king slept. In the morning, the otter said to him, "Thou wilt be this night in presence of thy wife." He left blessing with the otter. "Now," said the otter, "if difficulty be on thee, ask my aid and thou shalt get it." The king went till he reached a rock, and he looked down into a chasm that was in the rock, and at the bottom he saw his wife and his two horses, and he did not know how he should get where they were. He went round till he came to the foot of the rock, and there was a fine road for going in. He went in, and if he went it was then she began crying. "Ud! ud!" said he, "this is bad! If thou art crying now when I myself have got so much trouble coming about thee." "Oo!" said the horses, "set him in front of us, and there is no fear for him, till we leave this." She made meat for him, and she set him to rights, and when they were a while together, she put him in front of the horses. When the giant came, he said, "The smell of the stranger is within." Says she, "My treasure! My joy and my cattle! there is nothing but the smell of the litter of the horses." At the end of a while he went to give meat to the horses, and the horses began at him, and they all but killed him, and he hardly crawled from them. "Dear thing," said she, "they are like to kill thee. "If I myself had my soul to keep, it's long since they had killed me," said he. "Where, dear, is thy soul? By the books I will take care of it." "It is," said he, "in the Bonnach stone." When he went on the morrow, she set the Bonnach stone in order exceedingly. In the time of dusk and lateness, the giant came home. She set her man in front of the horses. The giant went to give the horses meat and they mangled him more and more. "What made thee set the Bonnach stone in order like that?" said he. "Because thy soul is in it." "I perceive that if thou didst know where my soul is, thou wouldst give it much respect." "I would give (that)," said she. "It is not there," said he, "my soul is; it is in the threshold." She set in order the threshold finely on the morrow. When the giant returned, he went to give meat to the horses, and the horses mangled him more and more. "What brought thee to set the threshold in order like that?" "Because thy soul is in it." "I perceive if thou knewest where my soul is, that thou wouldst take care of it." "I would take that," said she. "It is not there that my soul is," said he. "There is a great flagstone under the threshold. There is a wether under the flag. There is a duck in the wether's belly, and an egg in the belly of the duck, and it is in the egg that my soul is." When the giant went away on the morrow's day, they raised the flagstone and out went the wether. "If I had the slim dog of the greenwood, he would not be long bringing the wether to me." The slim dog of the greenwood came with the wether in his mouth. When they opened the wether, out was the duck on the wing with the other ducks. "If I had the Hoary Hawk of the grey rock, she would not be long bringing the duck to me." The Hoary Hawk of the grey rock came with the duck in her mouth; when they split the duck to take the egg from her belly, out went the egg into the depth of the ocean. "If I had the brown otter of the river, he would not be long bringing the egg to me." The brown otter came and the egg in her mouth, and the queen caught the egg, and she crushed it between her two hands. The giant was coming in the lateness, and when she crushed the egg, he fell down dead, and he has never yet moved out of that. They took with them a great deal of his gold and silver. They passed a cheery night with the brown otter of the river, a night with the hoary falcon of the grey rock, and a night with the slim dog of the greenwood. They came home and they set in order "a CUIRM CURAIDH CRIDHEIL," a hearty hero's feast, and they were lucky and well pleased after that.

Received June 9, 1859.

An old man, of the name of Angus MacQueen, who lived at Ballochroy, near Portaskaig, in Islay, "who could recite Ossian's Poems," taught this more than forty years ago (say 1820) to James Wilson, blind fiddler in Islay who recited it to Hector MacLean, schoolmaster, Islay.

The Gaelic is dictated and written by Islay men.

RIGH OG EASAIDH RUAGH.

Bha rìgh òg Easaidh Ruagh an dèigh dha'n oighreachd fhaotainn da fèin ri mòran àbhachd, ag amharc a mach dè a chordadh ris,'s dè thigeadh r 'a nadur. Bha gruagach fagus d'a chomhnuidh ris an abradh iad a ghruagach charsalach dhonn. Smaointich e ris fèin gun rachadh e a dh' iomairt cluiche ris. Dh'fhalbh e thun an t-seanaghail, 's thubhairt e ris, "Tha mi air a dheanadh suas gun d'thèid mi dh' iomairt cluiche ris a' ghruagach charsalach dhonn." "Aha," arsa 'n seanagheal, "an duine mar so thu? am bheil thu cho uaibhreach 's gu bheil thu a' dol a dh' iomairt cluiche ris a a' ghruagach charsalach dhonn? B'e mo chomhairle dhuit do nadur atharrachadh 's gun dol ann." "Cha dean mi sin." "Be'e mo chomhairle dhuit ma bhùidneas thu air a' ghruagach charsalach dhonn, an nighean mhaol charrach a tha cùl an doruis fhaotainn air son brìgh do chluiche, 's cuiridh e ioma car dheth mu'm faigh thu i." Chaidh e laidhe 'n oidhche sin, 's ma 's moch a thainig an latha 's moiche na sin a dh' èirich an rìgh a chumail cluiche ris a'ghruagaich. Ràinig e a ghruagach. Bheannaich e do'n ghruagaich 's bheannaich a ghruagach dà. Thuirt a ghruagach ris, "A righ òg Easaidh Ruagh, dè thug a' m'ionnsuidh an diugh thu? an iomair thu cluiche rium?" Thòisich iad's dh' iomair iad an cluiche. Bhùidhinn an rìgh. "Tog brìgh do chluiche 's gu'm faighinn a bhi 'g imeachd." " 'S e brigh mo chluiche thu thoirt domh na nighin maoil carraich a th' agad air cùl an doruis." " 'S iomad boireannach maiseach a th'agamsa stigh a bharrachd urra." "Cha ghabh mi gin ach i siod." "Beannachd dhuitse 's mollachd do d' oid-ionnsachaidh." Chàidh iad gu tigh na gruagaich 's chuir a' ghruagach an òrdugh fichead nighean òg. "Tog a nis do roghainn asda sin." Bha té 'tighinn a mach an dèigh té, 's a h-uile té 'thigeadh a mach, theireadh i, "is mis' i, 's amaideach thu nach 'eil 'g am thobh-airtse leat;" ach dh'iarr an seanaghal air gun gin a ghabhail ach an té dheireadh a thigeadh a mach. 'Nuair a thainig an te mu dheireadh a mach, thuirt e "So mo thè-sa." Dh' fholbh e leatha 's 'nuair a bha iad stàtuinn o'n tigh dh'atharraich a cruth, agus 's i boireannach a b'àille 'bha air thalamh. Bha'n rìgh 'dol dachaidh làn toil-inntinn leithid de bhoireannach maiseach fhaotainn. Ràinig e'n tigh. Chaidh e laidhe. Ma 's moch a thainig an latha, is moiche na sin a dh'èirich an rìgh, 'dhol a dh'iomairt cluiche ris a ghruagaich. "Is èigin domh dol a dh'iomairt cluiche ris a ghruagaich an diugh," ars' e r'a bhean. "Oh," ars' ise, "sin m'athair's ma thèid thu dh'iomairt cluiche ris, na gabh ni sam bith airson brigh do chluiche ach an loth pheallagach odhar a tha 'n diollaid mhaid' urra. Dh'fholbh an rìgh, 's choinnich a ghruagach e, 's gu cinnteach cha robh 'm beannachadh na bu tàire na bha e roimhe aig an dithis ri chéile. "Seadh," ars' a ghruagach "demur a chòrd do bhean òg riut an dé?" "Chord gu h-iomlan." "An d' thàinig thu dh'iomairt cluiche rium an diugh?" "Thàinig." Thòisich iad air a' chluiche, 's bhuidhinn an rìgh air a' ghruagaich an latha sin. "Tog brìgh do chluiche 's bi ealamh leis." " 'S e brìgh mo chluiche gum faigh mi an loth pheallagach odhar air a' bheil an dòllaid mhaide." Dh' fholbh iad còmhla. Ràinig iad an loth pheallagach odhar, thug e mach as an stàbull i,'s chuir an rìgh a chas thairte, 's b'e 'n curaidh i. Chaidh e dhachaidh; bha làmhan sgaoilt' aig a' bhean roimhe; 's bha iad gu sùnndach comhla an oidhche sin. "B'fhearr leam fèin," ursa 'bhean, "nach rachadh thu 'dh'iomairt cluiche ris a' ghruagach tuillidh, chionn ma bhuidhneas e cuiridh e dragh ann ad cheann." "Cha dean mi sin; thèid mi dh'iomairt cluiche ris an diugh." Chaidh e dh'iomairt cluiche ris a' ghruagaich. 'N uair a ràinig e, thar leis gun do ghabh a ghruagach boch. "An d'thàinig thu?" "Thàinig." Dh'iomair iad an cluiche, 's mar bhuaidh mhollachd do'n rìgh bhuidhinn a' ghruagach an latha sin. "Tog brìgh do chluiche," arsa rìgh òg Eas Ruagh, " 's na bi trom orm, chionn cha-n urrainn mi seasamh ris." "S'e brìgh mo chluiche-sa," urs' esan, "gu bheil mi 'cur mar chroisean, 'us mar gheasan ort, 'us mar *sheisean* na bliadhna, am beathach maol, carrach is mithreubhaiche 's is mi-threònaiche na thu fèin, a thoirt do chinn 's do mhuineil 's do choimhead-beatha dhiot, mar am faigh thu dhomhsa claidheamh soluis rìgh nan uinneagan daraich." Chaidh an rìgh dachaidh gu trom, bochd, duibhthaimhasach. Thàinig a bhànrighinn òg na chomhdhail's thubhairt i ris, "Mo thruaighe! cha 'n ni 'sam bith leat a nochd." Thug a h-aoidh agus a h-ailleachd rud-eigin de thoilinntinn do n rìgh, nur a dh' amhairc e air a gnùis; ach nur a shuidh e air cathair a tharruinn e d' a ionnsuidh, thug e osann as, is sgoilt a chathair fodha. "Dè th' ort, na bhiodh ort, nach fhaodadh thu innseadh dhomhsa?" ars' a bhanrigh. Dh' innis an

righ demur a thachair. "Ud," ars' ise, "de amhail a chuireas thu air,
's gur ann agad a tha 'bhean is fheàrr 'an Eirinn, 's an darra each is
fheàrr 'an Eirinn. Ma ghabhas thu mo chomhairle-sa thig thu as
gach ni dhiubh sin fhathasd." Ma 's moch a thàinig an latha 's
moiche na sin a dh' èirich a bhànrighinn, 's a chuir i uidheam air
gach ni chum gum bitheadh an rìgh 'dol air a thurus. Chuir i 'n
òrdugh an loth pheallagach, odhar, air an robh 'n dìollaid mhaide;
's ged a chitheadh esan 'na maid' i, bha i làn dhealrach le òr is
airgeid. Chaidh e air a muin. Phòg a' bhanrigh e, 's ghuidh i buaidh
làrach leis. Cha ruig mise leas a bhi 'g innseadh ni sam bith dhuit,
gabh thusa comhairle do bhana-chompanaich féin, an loth, 's
innsidh i duit dè 's còir dhuit a dheanamh. Ghabh e mach air a
thurus; 's cha bu chianalach a bhi air muin na steud odhar.
Bheireadh i air a' ghaoth luath Mhairt a bhiteadh roimhpe, 's cha
bheireadh á ghaoth luath mhàirt urra. Thàinig iad am beul an
athaidh 's an anamoich gu cùirt agus cathair righ nan uinneagan
daraich. Urs' an loth pheallagach odhar ris, "Tha sinn aig ceann
turuis, 's cha-n' eil againn ri dol na 's fhaide, gabh thusa mo
chomhairle-sa 's bheir mi thu far am bheil claidheamh soluis rìgh
nan uinneagan daraich, 's ma thig e leat gun sgread gun sgrioch, 's
comharradh maith air ar turus e. Tha 'n righ nis aig a dhinneir, 's
tha 'n claidheamh soluis 'n a sheòmbar fèin; tha cnap air a cheann,
's nur a bheireas thu air a chlaidheamh tarruinn gu réidh mach a
"CASE" na h-uinneig e." Thàinig e gus an uinneig far an robh an
claidheamh. Rug e air a claidheamh 's thàinig e leis gu réidh gus an
robh e aig a bhàrr, 's thug e seòrsa sgread as an sin. "Bithidh sinn
a nis, arsa 'n loth, aig imeachd, cna-n àm stad duinn e, tha fios agam
gun do mhothaich an righ dhuinn a toirt a chlaidheimh a mach.
Ghléidh esan an claidheamh 'n a laimh 's dh' fholbh iad, 's 'n uair
a bha iad treis air an aghaidh, thuirt an loth, "Stadaidh sinn a nis
's amhaircidh thu co 'chi thu 'd dheigh." "Chi mi," ars' esan,
"sgaoth dh' eachaibh donna 'tighinn air bhàinidh." " 'S luaithe sinn
féin na iad sin fathasd." Dh' fhalbh iad 's 'n uair a bha iad astar
maith air an aghaidh, "amhairc a nis" ars' ise "co 'chi thu teachd."
"Chi mi sgaoth dh' eacha dubha, agus aon each blàr dubh, 's e a
tighinn air a chuthach, 's duin' air a mhuin." " 'S e sin an t-each is
fheàrr an Eirinn, 's e mo bhràthair a th' ann, 's fhuair e ràidhe
banaltrachd a bharrachd ormsa, agus thig e seachad ormsa le
sreann, 's feuch am bi thu cho tapaidh 's 'nur a thig e seachad ormsa
an d' thoir thu 'n ceann de 'n fhear a th' air a mhuin; chionn an àm
dol seachad amhaircidh e ortsa, 's cha-n 'eil claidheamh 'n a chùirt
a bheir an ceann deth, ach a 'cheart chlaidheamh a tha 'd laimh."

'N uair a bha 'm fear so 'dol seachad thug e amhadh air a cheann
a dh' amharc air; tharruinn esan an claidheamh 'us thug e 'n ceann
deth, 's cheap an loth pheallagach 'n a beul e. B' e so rìgh nan
uinneagan daraich. "Leum air muin an eich dhuibh," urs' ise, " 's
fag a chlosach an siod, 's bi 'dol dachaidh cho luath 's a bheir e
dachaidh thu, 's bithidh mise 'tighinn mar is fheàrr a dh' fhaodas
mi 'n 'ur déigh." Leum e air muin an eich dhuibh, 's am Moire b'
e 'n curaidh e, 's ràinig iad an tigh fada roimh latha. Bha 'bhan-rìgh
gun laidhe gus an d' ràinig e. Thog iad ceòl 's leag iad bròn. An la'r
na mhàireach thuirt esan, " 's éigin dòmhsa dol a dh'amharc na
gruagaich an diugh, feuch am bi mo gheasan ma sgaoil."
"Cuimhnich nach ann mar a b-àbhaist a dh' amaiseas a gruagach
ort. Coinnichidh e thu gu feargach fiadhaich 's their e riut, 'an
d'fhuair thu 'n claidheamh?' 's abair thusa gun d'fhuair. Their e
riut ciod e mar a fhuair thu e? 'is their thusa, 'mar b'e an cnap a
bh'air a cheann cha d'fhuair mi e.' Foigh-nichidh e rithisd diot,
'demur a fhuair thu 'n claidheamh,' 's their thusa, 'mar b'e an cnap
a bh'air a cheann cha d' fhuair mi e.' Bheir e 'n so togail air a dh'
amharc ciod e 'n cnap a th' air a chlaidheamh 's chì thu ball-dorain
taobh deas a mhuneil, agus stob bàrr a chlaidheimh anns a bhall-
dorain 's mar amais thu air a bhall-dorain, tha thuso 's mise réidh.
B' e 'bhràthair rìgh nan uinneagan daraich e, 's tha fhios aige gus
an cailleadh am fear eile 'bheatha nach dealaicheadh e ris a
chlaidheamh. Tha bàs an dithis 's a chlaidheamh; ach cha-n 'eil
claidheamh eile dhear-gas orr' ach e." Phòg a bhanrigh e, 's ghuidh
i buaidh làrach leis, 's dh' fholbh e. Thachair a gruagach air anns
cheart àit' an robh e roimhid. "An d' fhuair thu 'n claidheamh?"
"Fhuair mi 'n claidheamh." "Dèmur a fhuair thu 'n claidheamh?"
"Mur b'e an cnap a bh' air a cheann cha n' fhaighinn e." "Leig
fhaicinn domh an claidheamh." "Cha robh e mar fhiachaibh orm
a leigeil fhaicinn duit." "Demur a fhuair thu 'n claidheamh?" "Mur
b'e an cnap a bh' air a cheann cha d' fhuair mi e." Thug a gruagach
togail air a cheann a dh' amharc air a chlaidheamh. Chunnaic esan
am ball-dorain. Bha e urrant' ealamh; shàth e 'n claidheamh anns
a bhall-dorain, 's thuit a ghruagach sìos marbh. Thill e dhachaidh,
's 'n uair a thill e dhachaidh, fhuair e luchd gleidhidh agus coimhead
ceangailt' an sin cùl ri eùl; 's gun bhean, no each, no leannan aige,
gun a bhi air an tiort air folbh. 'N uair a dh' fhuasgail e iad, thubhairt
iad ris, "Thàinig famhair mòr agus thug e air folbh do bhean agus
do dhà each." "Cha d' théid cadal air mo shùil no fois air mo
cheum, gus am faigh mi mo bhean agus mo dhà each air an ais. Le
so a ràdh dh' fholbh e air a thurus; ghabh e 'n taobh a bha lorg nan

each, 's lean e gu dian iad. Bha 'n t-athadh 's an t-anamoch a tighinn air, 's cha d' rinneadh stad leis gus an d' ràinig e taobh na coill' uaine. Chunnaic e far an robh làrach cruthachadh gealbhain, 's smaointich e gun cuireadh e tein' air, 's gun cuireadh e seachad an oidhch' ann. Cha b' fhad 'a bha e 'n so aig a ghealbhan gus an d' thàinig cu seang na coill' uain' air. Bheannaich e do 'n chù, 's bheannaich an cù dà. "Ubh! ùbh!" ars' an cù "b' olc diol do mhnatha 's do dhà each an so an raoir aig an fhamhair mhòr." " ' 'S e sin a chuir mise cho peanasach truagh air an tòir a nochd, ach cha-n' 'eil arach' air." "A righ," ars' an cù, "cha-n fhaod thu bhi gun bhiadh." Chaidh an cù stigh do 'n choille, thug e mach beathaichean, 's rinn iad am biadh gu tlachdmhor. "Tha dùil agam féin," ars' an rìgh, "gum faod mi tilleadh dhachaidh, nach urrainn mi dol a chòir an fhamhair sin." "Na dean sin," ars' an cù; "cha-n eagal duit a righ, cinn'idh do ghnothuch leat. Cha-n 'fhaod thu bhi so gun chadal." "Cha leig an t-eagal domh cadal 's gun bharantas orm." "Caidil thus'," ars' an cù, " 's barantachaidh mis' thu." Leig an righ e féin na shìneadh taobh an teine 's chaidil e. Nur a bhrisd an fhàire thubhairt an cù ris, "Eirich," a rìgh, " 'us gun gabhadh thu greim bìdh a neartaicheas thu, 's gum bitheadh thu dol air do thurus. Nis," ars' an cù, "ma thig cruadhchas no càs ort, iarr mo chuideachadh, 's bithidh mi agad a thiotadh." Dh' fhàg iad beannachd aig a chéile 's dh' fholbh e. An àm an athaidh 's an ammoich, thàinig e gu h-ailbhinn mhòr creige, agus bha cruthachadh làrach gealbhain ann. Smaointich e gun cruinneachadh e connadh, 's gun cuireadh e air teine. Thòisich e air a gharadh, 's cha b' fhada bha e mar so 'n uair a thàinig seobhag liath na creige glais' air. "Ubh! ùbh!" ars' ise, b' olc diol do mhnatha 's do dhà each an rair aig an fhamhair mhòr." "Cha-n' 'eil arach' air," ars' esan, "fhuair mi féin mòran d' an dragh is beagan d' an àbhachd. "Glac misneach," ars' ise, "gheobh thu rudeigin d' an àbhachd fhathasd. Cha n' fhaod thu bhi gun bhiadh an so," ars' ise. "Cha-n' 'eil seòl air biadh fhaotainn ars esan." "Cha-n fhada bhitheas sinn a faotainn bidh." Dh' fholbh i 's cha b'fhada bha i n' uair a thàinig i 's tri lachan 's ochd coilich dhubha 'n a beul. Chuir iad an ordugh am biadh 's ghabh iad e. "Cha-n fhaod thu bhi gun chadal," ars' an t-seobhag. "Demur a chaidleas mi gun bharantas 'sam bith orm gu mo dhìon o aon olc a tha 'n so?" "Caidil thusa, rìgh, 's barantachaidh mis' thu." Leig e e féin 'n a shineadh, 's chaidil e. Anns a mhaidinn chuir an t-seobhag air a chois e. Cruadhchas no càs a thig ort, cuimhnich aig àm sam bith gum faigh thu mo chuideachadhsa. Dh' fholbh e gu dian, foghainteach, luath,

laidir. Bha 'n latha folbh 's an oidhche tighinn, 's eunlaith bheaga
na coille craobhaich, dosraiche, dualaich, a' gabhail ma bhun nam
preas 's ma bhàrr nan dos; 's mu bha, cha bu tàmh 's cha bu chlos
dàsan e, gus an d' thàinig e gu taobh aimhne mhòr a bha sin, agus
aig bruach na h-aimhne bha cruthachadh làrach gealbhain. Shéid
an rìgh srachdanach trom teine. Cha b'fhada bha e 'n so 'n uair a
thàinig ann an companas ris doran donn na h-aimhne. "Och," ars'
an doran, "b'olc dìol do mhnatha 'n so an rair aig an fhamhair."
"Cha-n 'eil arach' air, fhuair mise mòran d'an dragh is beagan d'
an àbhachd." "Glac misneach, fo mheadhon latha màireach chì thu
do bhean. A rìgh, cha 'n fhaod thu bhi gun bhaidh," ars' an doran.
"Demur a gheibhear biadh an so," ars' an rìgh. Dh fholbh an doran
feadh na h-abhann, 's thainig e 's tri bradain leis a bha ciatach. Rinn
iad biadh is ghabh iad e. Thuirt an doran ris an rìgh, "feumaidh tu
cadal." "Demur a chaidleas mi 's gun bharantachadh sam bith
orm?" "Caidil thusa 's barantachaidh mis' thu an nochd." Chaidil
an rìgh. Anns a mhaduinn, thuirt an doran ris, bithidh thu an nochd
an làthair do mhnatha. Dh fhàg e beannachd aig an doran. "Nis,"
ars' an doran, "ma bhitheas càs ort, iarr mo chuideachadh-sa, 's
gheobh thu e." Dh 'fholbh an rìgh gus an d' ràinig e creag, 's dh'
amhairc e sìos ann an glomhas a bha 's a chreig, 's aig a ghrunnd
chunnaic e a bhean agus a dhà each, 's cha robh fios aige demur a
gheobheadh e far an robh iad. Ghabh e mu 'n cuairt gus an d'
thàinig e gu bun na creige, 's bha rathad ciatach a dhol a stigh.
Chaidh e stigh, 's ma chaidh, 's ann a thòisich is' air caoineadh.
"Ud! ud!" ars' esan, " 's olc so, mi féin a dh' fhaotainn na huibhir
de dhragh a tighinn ma d' thuaiream, ma 's ann a caoineadh a tha
thu nis." "U," arsa na h-eich, "cuir thus' air' ur beulthaobh-ne e,
's cha-n eagal da gus am fàg sinne so." Rinn i biadh dà, 's chur i air
dòigh e, 's 'n air a bha iad treis comhla chuir i air beulthaobh nan
each e. 'N uair a thàinig am famhair thubhairt e, "THA BOLADH AN
FHARBHALAICH A STIGH. Ars' ise, "M' ullaidh, is m'aighear, is m'
fheudail, cha-n' eil ann ach boladh a bhalaidh bhreuna de na
h-eachaibh." An ceann treis chaidh e 'thoirt bidh do na h-eich, 's
thòisich na h-eich air, 's cha mhòr nach do mharbh iad e, 's cha d'
rinn e ach snàgan air éigin uatha. "Ghràidh," ars' ise, "tha iad a
brath do mharbhadh." "Na'm b' ann agam féin a bhitheadh 'm
anam g'a ghleidheadh 's fhad' o'n a mharbh iad mi," ars' esan. "C'
ait' a ghràidh am bheil d' anam? An leòbhra, gabhaidh mise cùram
deth." "Tha e," ars' esan, "ann an clach nam bonnach." Nur a dh'
fholbh esan an l'ar na mhàireach, chuir ise òrdugh clach nam
bonnach gu fuathasach. An am an athaidh 's an anmoich thàinig

am famhair a stigh. Chuir ise a fear air beulthaobh nan each. Chaidh am famhair a thoirt bidh do na h-eich, 's leadair iad e na bu mhotha 's na bu mhotha. "Ciod e 'thug ort clach nam bonnach a chur an òrdugh mur sin?" ars' esan. "Chionn gu bheil d' anam innte." "Tha mi 'g aithneachadb nam bitheadh fios agad c' aite 'bheil m' anam, gun d' thugadh thu t'aire mhaith dhà." "Bheireadh." "Cha-n ann an ain a tha m'anam 's ann a tha e 'sa starsaich." Chuir ise an ordugh an starsach gu gasd' an la 'r na mhàireach. Nur a thill am famhair chaidh e thoirt bìdh do na h-eich 's leadair na h-eich e na bu mhotha 's na bu mhotha. "Dé 'thug ort an starsach a chuir an ordugh mar sud?" "Chionn gu bheil d' anam innte." "Tha mi 'g aithneachadh na 'm bitheadh fios agad far am bheil m' anam gun gabhadh tù cùram dheth." "Ghabhadh," ars' ise. "Cha-n' ann an sin a tha m' anam, ars' esan. Tha leac mhòr fo 'n starsaich, tha molt fo 'n leachd, tha lach 'am broinn a mhuilt, agus tha ubh am broinn na lacha, agus 's ann anns an ubh a tha m' anam. 'N uair a dh' fholbh am famhair an la'r na mhàireach thog iad an leac, 's a mach a thug am molt. Na 'm bitheadh agamsa cù seang na coill'uaine, cha b' fhad 'a bhitheadh e 'toirt a' mhuilt a m' ionnsuidh. Thainig cù seang na coill' uaine ugus am molt 'n a bheul. 'N uair a dh'fhosgail iad am molt, a mach a bha 'n lach air iteagach leis na lachan eile. Na'm bitheadh agamsa seobhag liath na creige glaise, cha b'fhada'bhitheadh i 'toirt na lach a m'ionnsuidh. Thàinig seobhag liath na creige glaise 's an lach 'n a beul. 'N uair a sgoilt iad an lach a thoirt an uibhe a 'broinn mach a ghabh an t-ubh ann an doimhneachd a chuain. Na'm bitheadh agamsa doran donn na h-amhann, cha b'fhada bhitheadh i 'toirt a m' ionnsuidh an uibhe. Thàinig an doran donn 's an t-ubh na beul, 's rug a bhanrigh air an ubh 's phronn i eadar a da laimh e. Bha 'm famhair a tighinn anns an athamanachd, 's 'n uair a phronn ise 'n t-ubh thuit e sìos marbh, 's cha do charaich e as a sin fhathasd. Thug iad mòran leo de dh 'òr 's de dh' airgeid. Chuir iad oidhche shunndach seachad aig doran donn na h-abhann, oidhch' aig seobhag liath na creige glaise, agus oidhch' aig cù seang na coill' uaine. Thàinig iad dachaidh 's chuir iad an òrdugh cuirm chridheil, 's bha iad gu sona, toilichte 'n a dhéigh sin.

2.   I have another version of this tale, written by Hector Urquhart, told by John Campbell, living at Strath Gairloch, Ross-shire, received June 27, 1859. It is very well told. It varies a little from the Islay version, but the resemblance is so close, that to print it entire would be repetition. It contains many characteristic phrases which

the other has not got, so I give this abstract. The Gaelic is as it came to me.

THE "SGEULACHD" OF THE WIDOW'S SON.—There was once a widow's son, and he was often stalking (SEALG). On a day of days and he stalking, he "sits" at the back of a knoll, before the sun and behind the wind (RI AGHAIDH GREINE'S RI CUL NA GAOITHE), and there came the way a youth, like a picture (OGANACH DEALBHANACH), riding a blue filly (FAILORE GORM), and he sits beside him. They played at cards, and the widow's son won, and when evening came the youth said, "What is the stake of thy gaming?" (CE DHE BUIDH DO CHLUICHE?) and he said, "the blue filly under thee." He took her home, and she changed into the finest woman that man ever saw. Next day he went stalking, and on coming home in the mouth of night (AM BEUL NA OIDHCHE), he learned that the big giant had taken away his sweetheart—CHA NEIL COMAS AIR AS EISE ACH NA BO MHISE BO TREASA CHA MHEALLADH EISE FAD I. "There is no help for it," said he, "but were I the stronger, he would not allure her far."

DH'ERICH MAC NA BANNTRICH. The widow's son arose, 's CHAIDH E NA CHRIOSIBH IALLA S' NA IALLA GAISGICH, and he went into his belts of thongs and his thongs of warrior, 'S DH'FHALBH E LE CEUMANIBH GU TUISLEAG DOMH MHEANMNACH, and he went with leaping strides, cheerful to me (or? *Doimhainneachd*—of deepness) S' DHEANADH E MILE THORAN NA SLEIBH LEIS NA H UILLE CEUM A DHEANADH E, and he would make a thousand knolls of the hill with every step he made, 'S B' FHEAR DHA NAMHAID A SHEACHANADH NA TACHAIRT AN LATHA SIN RIS, and his foe had better avoid him than meet that day with him. He saw a little hut "in the mouth of night," and though far away, not long to reach it, AIR A THUBHADH LE ITEAGAN GARBHA NAN EUN A MUIGH S LE ITEAGAN MINE NAN EUN A STEACH, thatched with coarse feathers of the birds without, and with fine feathers of the birds within, AGUS RUITHAG AN T UBHAL BHON DARNA CEAN DHON A CHIN EILE LE CHO COMHRAD S'A BHA E, and the apple would run from one end to the other end, so even it was. He went in and found no man, but two great fires on the fire-place (CHAGAILT) on the floor. SUIL DA DUG E, glance that he gave he saw a falcon coming in with a heath hen in her claws, and the next glance it was, GILLE BRIAGH BUIDH, a braw yellow lad, who spoke as in the Islay version, entertained him and told him in the morning to call on SEABHAG SUIL GHORM GHLENNA FEIST—the blue-eyed falcon of Glen Feist. Next day it was the same, and he came, AIR CIARADH DON FHEISGAR, at the turning-dun of the evening, to a second hut, thatched like the other, S' BHA SNATHNEAN BEAG SUARACH SIODA CUMAIL DION A DHROMA RIS, and there was a little sorry silken thread, keeping the thatch of its back on. DOBHRAN DONN, otter

brown, come in with a salmon, and became a man, and spoke as the
other, and told him in the morning to call on DOBHRAN DONN SRUTH
AN T' SHIUL—Brown otter of sail stream. The third day was the same,
the hut was the same, but that there were two great fires on each
fire-place, and there came in MADADH MOR, big dog, with a hare by
the throat, who became the finest man, AIR AN DUG E ROSK RIAMH,
he ever turned face to; who said as the others did—"It was late when
the big giant went past with thy sweetheart on his shoulder." At
parting he told him to call on MADADH GLAS DRIOM AN T-SHLEIBHE—
grey dog of mountain back in time of need. That night he saw, TIGH
MOR GEAL AN AN GLEANN FADA FAISICH, a big white house in a long
desert glen, and saw his sweetheart with a golden comb in her hand,
and she would take a while at combing her hair, and a while at
weeping, and when she saw him she said—"My pity, what brought
thee here? the giant will kill thee." "Two shares of fear on him, and
the smallest share on me," said the widow's son.

She had laid it as crosses and as spells on the giant, not to come
near her for a day and a year, and they were together in the giant's
house till evening.

She hid him, and had a long talk with the giant when he came
home, who was wheedled, as in the other story, into telling first that
his life (BETHA) was in (CARN GLAS UD THALL) yonder grey cairn.
The lady was addressed as NIGHINN RIGH CHOIGE MUGH—O daughter of king of COIGE MUGH, which kingdom is not within my
geographical studies.

The giant came home, and found the grey cairn dressed out and
ornamented, and after a deal of persuasion, gave out that his life was
in SEANN STOC DARRICH—an old oak stump on the bank of yonder
river. So the next day that was dressed out, and when he came home
he said, "Do thou make the stock braw, BRIAGH, every day. On the
third day they split the oak stump with an axe, and a hare leaped out.
"There now is the giant's life away," said the king's daughter, "and
he will come without delay and kill thee, and not spare me." Grey
dog of mountain back was called, and brought the hare, and a salmon
leaped out into the river. Brown otter of sail stream brought the
salmon, and a heath hen sprang out. Blue-eyed falcon of Glen Feist
brought the bird, and the giant came roaring—"King's daughter, let
me have my life and thou shalt have the little chest of gold and the
little chest of silver that is in yonder grey cairn." The widow's son
answered, "I will have that, and I will have this;" and he seized the
axe, and the stock fell, and the giant was dead. And the widow's son
and the daughter of King Coige Mugh, in Erin, staid in the house
and the land of the giant, and their race was there when I was there
last.

The warrior's dress of thongs is remarkable, and something like it is described in another tale. There is a curious picture at Taymouth of a man, supposed to be the Regent Murray, in a Highland dress, which may be the dress described. The upper part is composed of strips of some ornamental material, which might be stamped gilded leather; the rest of the dress is a linen shirt, with ruffles, and a plaid wrapped about the body in the form of a modern kilt, and belted plaid; he wears stockings and shoes of a peculiar pattern: the head-dress is a bonnet with an ostrich plume; the arms, a dirk and a long ornamented gun.

There is another picture at Dytchley, in Oxfordshire, which represents an ancestor of Lord Dillon in an Irish costume. The dress consists solely of a very short garment like a shirt, coloured, and very much ornamented with tags, which might be leather. The gentleman is armed with a spear, and the dress is probably a masquerade representation of a real Irish dress of some period.

I would here remark that the personages and places in all these tales are like the actors in a play and the scenes. The incidents vary but little, but the kings and their countries vary with every version, though there is a preference for Erin, Ireland; Lochlain, Scandinavia, or rather Denmark and Norway; and Greuge, the Greekdom, Greece.

3. I have a third version of this written by MacLean, told by Donald MacPhie, in South Uist. The old man was very proud of it, and said it was "the HARDEST" story that the transcriber had ever heard. He told me the same.

As often happens with aged reciters, when he repeated it a second time slowly for transcribing, nearly all the curious, "impassioned, and sentimental" language was left out. This is MacLean's account, and it entirely agrees with my own experience of this man, who is next thing to a professional reciter (see introduction). This version is the most curious of the three. I hope some day to get it better copied, so I do not abstract it now It is nearer the Ross-shire version than the Islay story, and carries the scene to Greece from Ireland. The reciter is 79, and says he learned it in his youth from an old man of the name of John MacDonald, Aird a Mhachair.

The principle on which gaming is carried on in this and in other tales is peculiar. The stake is rather a ransom, for it is always settled after the game is decided.

The game played is TAILEASG, which Armstrong translates as sport, game, mirth, chess, backgammon, draughts.

This story resembles in some particulars—

1. The Gaelic tale published by Dr. MacLeod, printed page 30, Leobhar Nan Cnoc. 1834
2. The Sea Maiden, in present collection, and the stories referred to in the notes.

3. The Giant who had no Heart in his Body. Norse Tales. 1859.
4. The Seven Foals, where a horse advises his rider. Norse Tales.
5. Dapplegrim, where the same occurs, where there are two horses, and where the rider hides about the horses. Norse Tales.
6. Fortunio, where the horse also advises his rider.
7. This also resembles a part of the "Arabian Nights," where the Calender is changed into a monkey, and the princess fights a genius in various shapes.
8. "The Ball of Crystal," Grimm, where the power of an enchanter is in *a crystal ball*, in *an egg*, in *a fiery bird*, in *a wild ox*.
9. The Three Sisters, page 52, where a little key is found in *an egg*, in *a duck*, in *a bull*. This book is an English translation (1845) of Volks Märchen, by Musaeus, 1872. Said to have been published in English in 1790.
10. Another version of the Sea Maiden recited to me in South Uist. The soul of the Sea Maiden was in *an egg*, in *a goose*, in *a ram*, in *a wild bull*, and was got by the help of *an otter, a falcon, a wolf* and *a lion*.

Lempriere—Ægyptus—Kneph or Knouphis—A God represented as a *ram*. He was the soul of the world; his symbol a circle, in the centre of which is a serpent with the head of a hawk, or a globe with a serpent turned round it. Together with mind, the primitive matter was given, both produced from the same great principle, existing in it from all eternity, imperishable. The primitive matter was rude and shapeless when the spirit imparted to it the power of motion, and gave it the form of a sphere. This became the sphere *or egg* of the world which *Kneph let fall from his mouth*, when he wished to form all things.

It is warmly contended by Irish writers that the religion of the Celts, and the Celts themselves, came from Phœnicia and Carthage.

If this story be mythological, here is something like it.

We have the *hawk, ram*, and *a bird*; and in the Inverary version we have a *fish* and the *egg*, with the life of bird, beast, fish, and man in it.

There is a place called *Lok Maaien-ker*, in Morbihan, Brittany, a long, dark, underground passage, at the end of which are certain rudely sculptured stones. On one of these is something which bears some faint resemblance to the snake, who appears in the next tale.

There is one word in this tale, "SEANG," which is not given in dictionaries as a substantive. Sing, applied to an Indian prince, means lion, and the beast here described might be one. Seang, as an adjective, means thin, slim, slender, gaunt, and is the root of *Seangan*, an ant.

In Prichard's "Celtic Nations," by Latham, 1856, a Dacota word is quoted—"SUNGKA," which originally comprehended the idea of Dog, Fox, and Wolf.

The word GRUAGACH, which here means some male personage, generally means a maiden. It also means "A female spectre of the class of Brownies to which the Highland dairy-maids made frequent libations of milk—*rarely* THE CHIEF OF A PLACE."—*Armstrong dic.* This word, which has not its common meaning, may help to trace the language. The root is GRUAG, the hair of the head.

A Gruagach used to haunt Skipness Castle, and is still remembered there as a supernatural female who did odd jobs about the house for the maids, and lived in the ruin.

"There was also a Gruagach in Kerrisdale, in Gairloch, in Ross-shire, once upon a time."

This may be the same word as *Groac'h* or *Grac'h*, a name given to the Druidesses, who had colleges in an island near the coasts of Brittany (p. 155, vol. i., Foyer Breton). The story given has many incidents common to the Gaelic stories.

The sword of light is common in Gaelic stories; and stripped of supernatural qualities, the whole thing seems very like an account of some race contending with another, whose chief wore long hair, who had horses and bright (? steel) swords, to which extraordinary virtues were attributed, and who were at the same time beset by savages who lived in caves, and were assisted by other savages represented by creatures.

2

THE BATTLE OF THE BIRDS.

From John Mackenzie, fisherman, near Inverary.

There was once a time when every creature and bird was gathering
to battle. The son of the king of Tethertown* said, that he would
go to see the battle, and that he would bring sure word home to his
father the king, who would be king of the creatures this year. The
battle was over before he arrived all but one (fight), between a great
black raven and a snake, and it seemed as if the snake would get
the victory over the raven. When the King's son saw this, he helped
the raven, and with one blow takes the head off the snake. When
the raven had taken breath, and saw that the snake was dead, he
said, "For thy kindness to me this day, I will give thee a sight. Come
up now on the root of my two wings." The king's son mounted
upon the raven, and, before he stopped, he took him over seven
Bens, and seven Glens, and seven Mountain Moors.

"Now," said the raven, "seest thou that house yonder? Go now
to it. It is a sister of mine that makes her dwelling in it; and I will
go bail that thou art welcome. And if she asks thee, Wert thou at
the battle of the birds? say thou that thou wert. And if she asks,
Didst thou see my likeness? say that thou sawest it. But be sure that
thou meetest me to-morrow morning here, in this place." The
king's son got good and right good treatment this night. Meat of
each meat, drink of each drink, warm water to his feet, and a soft
bed for his limbs.

On the next day the raven gave him the same sight over seven
Bens, and seven Glens, and seven Mountain moors. They saw a
bothy far off, but, though far off, they were soon there. He got good

---

* Na Cathair Shiomain. Heather ropes are used for binding thatch on Highland
cottages.

treatment this night, as before—plenty of meat and drink, and warm water to his feet, and a soft bed to his limbs—and on the next day it was the same thing.

On the third morning, instead of seeing the raven as at the other times, who should meet him but the handsomest lad he ever saw, with a bundle in his hand. The king's son asked this lad if he had seen a big black raven. Said the lad to him, "Thou wilt never see the raven again, for I am that raven. I was put under spells; it was meeting thee that loosed me, and for that thou art getting this bundle. Now," said the lad, "thou wilt turn back on the self-same steps, and thou wilt lie a night in each house, as thou wert before; but thy lot is not to lose the bundle which I gave thee, till thou art in the place where thou wouldst most wish to dwell."

The king's son turned his back to the lad, and his face to his father's house; and he got lodging from the raven's sisters, just as he got it when going forward. When he was nearing his father's house he was going through a close wood. It seemed to him that the bundle was growing heavy, and he thought he would look what was in it.

When he loosed the bundle, it was not without astonishing himself. In a twinkling he sees the very grandest place he ever saw. A great castle, and an orchard about the castle, in which was every kind of fruit and herb. He stood full of wonder and regret for having loosed the bundle—it was not in his power to put it back again—and he would have wished this pretty place to be in the pretty little green hollow that was opposite his father's house; but, at one glance, he sees a great giant coming towards him.

"Bad's the place where thou hast built thy house, king's son," says the giant. "Yes, but it is not here I would wish it to be, though it happened to be here by mishap," says the king's son. "What's the reward thou wouldst give me for putting it back in the bundle as it was before?" "What's the reward thou wouldst ask?" says the king's son. "If thou wilt give me the first son thou hast when he is seven years of age," says the giant. "Thou wilt get that if I have a son," said the king's son.

In a twinkling the giant put each garden, and orchard, and castle in the bundle as they were before. "Now," says the giant, "take thou thine own road, and I will take my road; but mind thy promise, and though thou shouldst forget, I will remember."

The king's son took to the road, and at the end of a few days he reached the place he was fondest of. He loosed the bundle, and the same place was just as it was before. And when he opened the castle-door he sees the handsomest maiden he ever cast eye upon. "Advance, king's son," said the pretty maid; "everything is in order for thee, if thou wilt marry me this very night." "It's I am the man that is willing," said the king's son. And on the same night they married.

But at the end of a day and seven years, what great man is seen coming to the castle but the giant. The king's son minded his promise to the giant, and till now he had not told his promise to the queen. "Leave thou (the matter) between me and the giant," says the queen.

"Turn out thy son," says the giant; "mind your promise." "Thou wilt get that," says the king, "when his mother puts him in order for his journey." The queen arrayed the cook's son, and she gave him to the giant by the hand. The giant went away with him; but he had not gone far when he put a rod in the hand of the little laddie. The giant asked him—"If thy father had that rod what would he do with it?" "If my father had that rod he would beat the dogs and the cats, if they would be going near the king's meat," said the little laddie. "Thou'rt the cook's son," said the giant. He catches him by the two small ankles and knocks him—"Sgleog"—against the stone that was beside him. The giant turned back to the castle in rage and madness, and he said that if they did not turn out the king's son to him, the highest stone of the castle would be the lowest. Said the queen to the king, "we'll try it yet; the butler's son is of the same age as our son." She arrayed the butler's son, and she gives him to the giant by the hand. The giant had not gone far when he put the rod in his hand. "If thy father had that rod," says the giant, "what would he do with it?" "He would beat the dogs and the cats when they would be coming near the king's bottles and glasses." "Thou art the son of the butler," says the giant, and dashed his brains out too. The giant returned in very great rage and anger. The earth shook under the sole of his feet, and the castle shook and all that was in it. "OUT HERE THY SON," says the giant, "or in a twinkling the stone that is highest in the dwelling will be the lowest." So needs must they had to give the king's son to the giant.

The giant took him to his own house, and he reared him as his own son. On a day of days when the giant was from home, the lad heard the sweetest music he ever heard in a room at the top of the giant's house. At a glance he saw the finest face he had ever seen. She beckoned to him to come a bit nearer to her, and she told him to go this time, but to be sure to be at the same place about that dead midnight.

And as he promised he did. The giant's daughter was at his side
in a twinkling, and she said, "Tomorrow thou wilt get the choice
of my two sisters to marry; but say thou that thou wilt not take
either, but me. My father wants me to marry the son of the king of
the Green City, but I don't like him." On the morrow the giant took
out his three daughters, and he said, "Now son of the king of
Tethertown, thou hast not lost by living with me so long. Thou wilt
get to wife one of the two eldest of my daughters, and with her leave
to go home with her the day after the wedding." "If thou wilt give
me this pretty little one," says the king's son, "I will take thee at
thy word."

The giant's wrath kindled, and he said, "Before thou gett'st her
thou must do the three things that I ask thee to do." "Say on," says
the king's son. The giant took him to the byre. "Now," says the
giant, "the dung of a hundred cattle is here, and it has not been
cleansed for seven years. I am going from home to-day, and if this
byre is not cleaned before night comes, so clean that a golden apple
will run from end to end of it, not only thou shalt not get my
daughter, but 'tis a drink of thy blood that will quench my thirst
this night." He begins cleaning the byre, but it was just as well to
keep baling the great ocean. After mid-day, when sweat was blinding him, the giant's young daughter came where he was, and she
said to him, "Thou art being punished, king's son." "I am that,"
says the king's son. "Come over," says she, "and lay down thy
weariness." "I will do that," says he, "there is but death awaiting
me, at any rate." He sat down near her. He was so tired that he fell
asleep beside her. When he awoke, the giant's daughter was not to
be seen, but the byre was so well cleaned that a golden apple would
run from end to end of it. In comes the giant, and he said, "Thou
hast cleaned the byre, king's son?" "I have cleaned it," says he.
"Somebody cleaned it," says the giant. "Thou didst not clean it, at
all events," said the king's son. "Yes, yes!" says the giant, "since
thou wert so active to-day, thou wilt get to this time to-morrow to
thatch this byre with birds' down—birds with no two feathers of
one colour." The king's son was on foot before the sun; he caught
up his bow and his quiver of arrows to kill the birds. He took to the
moors, but if he did, the birds were not so easy to take. He was
running after them till the sweat was blinding him. About mid-day
who should come but the giant's daughter. "Thou art exhausting
thyself, king's son," says she. "I am," said he. "There fell but these
two blackbirds, and both of one colour." "Come over and lay down
thy weariness on this pretty hillock," says the giant's daughter. "It's

I am willing," said he. He thought she would aid him this time, too, and he sat down near her, and he was not long there till he fell asleep.

When he awoke, the giant's daughter was gone. He thought he would go back to the house, and he sees the byre thatched with the feathers. When the giant came home, he said, "Thou hast thatched the byre, king's son?" "I thatched it," says he. "Somebody thatched it," says the giant. "Thou didst not thatch it," says the king's son. "Yes, yes!" says the giant. "Now," says the giant, "there is a fir-tree beside that loch down there, and there is a magpie's nest in its top. The eggs thou wilt find in the nest. I must have them for my first meal. Not one must be burst or broken, and there are five in the nest." Early in the morning the king's son went where the tree was, and that tree was not hard to hit upon. Its match was not in the whole wood. From the foot to the first branch was five hundred feet. The king's son was going all round the tree. She came who was always bringing help to him; "Thou art losing the skin of thy hands and feet." "Ach! I am," says he. "I am no sooner up than down." "This is no time for stopping," says the giant's daughter. She thrust finger after finger into the tree, till she made a ladder for the king's son to go up to the magpie's nest. When he was at the nest, she said, "Make haste now with the eggs, for my father's breath is burning my back." In his hurry she left her little finger in the top of the tree. "Now," says she, "thou wilt go home with the eggs quickly, and thou wilt get me to marry to-night if thou canst know me. I and my two sisters will be arrayed in the same garments, and made like each other, but look at me when my father says, Go to thy wife, king's son; and thou wilt see a hand without a little finger." He gave the eggs to the giant. "Yes, yes!" says the giant, "be making ready for thy marriage."

Then indeed there was a wedding, and it *was* a wedding! Giants and gentlemen, and the son of the king of the Green City was in the midst of them. They were married, and the dancing began, and that was a dance? The giant's house was shaking from top to bottom. But bed time came, and the giant said, "It is time for thee to go to rest, son of the king of Tethertown; take thy bride with thee from amidst those."

She put out the hand off which the little finger was, and he caught her by the hand.

"Thou hast aimed well this time too; but there is no knowing but we may meet thee another way," said the giant.

But to rest they went. "Now," says she, "sleep not, or else thou diest. We must fly quick, quick, or for certain my father will kill thee."

Out they went, and on the blue gray filly in the stable they mounted. "Stop a while," says she, "and I will play a trick to the old hero." She jumped in, and cut an apple into nine shares, and she put two shares at the head of the bed, and two shares at the foot of the bed, and two shares at the door of the kitchen, and two shares at the big door, and one outside the house.

The giant awoke and called, "Are you asleep?" "We are not yet," said the apple that was at the head of the bed. At the end of a while he called again. "We are not yet," said the apple that was at the foot of the bed. A while after this he called again. "We are not yet," said the apple at the kitchen door. The giant called again. The apple that was at the big door answered "You are now going far from me," says the giant. "We are not yet," says the apple that was outside the house. "You are flying," says the giant. The giant jumped on his feet, and to the bed he went, but it was cold—empty.

"My own daughter's tricks are trying me," said the giant. "Here's after them," says he.

In the mouth of day, the giant's daughter said that her father's breath was burning her back. "Put thy hand, quick," said she, "in the ear of the gray filly, and whatever thou findest in it, throw it behind thee." "There is a twig of sloe tree," said he. "Throw it behind thee," said she.

No sooner did he that, than there were twenty miles of black thorn wood, so thick that scarce a weasel could go through it. The giant came headlong, and there he is fleecing his head and neck in the thorns.

"My own daughter's tricks are here as before," said the giant; "but if I had my own big axe and wood knife here, I would not be long making a way through this." He went home for the big axe and the wood knife, and sure he was not long on his journey, and he was the boy behind the big axe. He was not long making a way through the black thorn. "I will leave the axe and the wood knife here till I return," says he. "If thou leave them," said a Hoodie* that was in a tree, "we will steal them."

"You will do that same," says the giant, "but I will set them home." He returned and left them at the house. At the heat of day the giant's daughter felt her father's breath burning her back.

"Put thy finger in the filly's ear, and throw behind thee whatever

* The principal Gaelic vowels bear some resemblance to the cawing of a hoodie. They are all broad A.

thou findest in it." He got a splinter of gray stone, and in a twinkling there were twenty miles, by breadth and height, of great gray rock behind them. The giant came full pelt, but past the rock he could not go.

"The tricks of my own daughter are the hardest things that ever met me," says the giant; "but if I had my lever and my mighty mattock, I would not be long making my way through this rock also." There was no help for it, but to turn the chase for them; and he was the boy to split the stones. He was not long making a road through the rock. "I will leave the tools here, and I will return no more." "If thou leave them," says the hoodie, "we will steal them." "Do that if thou wilt; there is no time to go back." At the time of breaking the watch, the giant's daughter said that she was feeling her father's breath burning her back. "Look in the filly's ear, king's son, or else we are lost." He did so, and it was a bladder of water that was in her ear this time. He threw it behind him and there was a fresh-water loch, twenty miles in length and breadth, behind them.

The giant came on, but with the speed he had on him, he was in the middle of the loch, and he went under, and he rose no more.

On the next day the young companions were come in sight of his father's house. "Now," said she, "my father is drowned, and he won't trouble us any more; but before we go further," says she, "go thou to thy father's house, and tell that thou hast the like of me; but this is thy lot, let neither man nor creature kiss thee, for if thou dost thou wilt not remember that thou hast ever seen me." Every one he met was giving him welcome and luck, and he charged his father and mother not to kiss him; but as mishap was to be, an old grey-hound was in and she knew him, and jumped up to his mouth, and after that he did not remember the giant's daughter.

She was sitting at the well's side as he left her, but the king's son was not coming. In the mouth of night she climbed up into a tree of oak that was beside the well, and she lay in the fork of the tree all that night. A shoemaker had a house near the well, and about mid-day on the morrow, the shoemaker asked his wife to go for a drink for him out of the well. When the shoemaker's wife reached the well, and when she saw the shadow of her that was in the tree, thinking of it that it was her own shadow—and she never thought till now that she was so handsome—she gave a cast to the dish that was in her hand, and it was broken on the ground, and she took herself to the house without vessel or water.

"Where is the water, wife?" said the shoemaker. "Thou

shambling, contemptible old carle, without grace, I have stayed too long thy water and wood thrall."* "I am thinking, wife, that thou hast turned crazy. Go thou, daughter, quickly, and fetch a drink for thy father." His daughter went, and in the same way so it happened to her. She never thought till now that she was so loveable, and she took herself home. "Up with the drink," said her father. "Thou hume-spun† shoe carle, dost thou think that I am fit to be thy thrall." The poor shoemaker thought that they had taken a turn in their understandings, and he went himself to the well. He saw the shadow of the maiden in the well, and he looked up to the tree, and he sees the finest woman he ever saw. "Thy seat is wavering, but thy face is fair," said the shoemaker. "Come down, for there is need of thee for a short while at my house." The shoemaker understood that this was the shadow that had driven his people mad. The shoemaker took her to his house, and he said that he had but a poor bothy, but that she should get a share of all that was in it. At the end of a day or two came a leash of gentlemen lads to the shoemaker's house for shoes to be made them, for the king had come home, and he was going to marry. The glance the lads gave they saw the giant's daughter, and if they saw her, they never saw one so pretty as she. " 'Tis thou hast the pretty daughter here," said the lads to the shoemaker. "She is pretty, indeed," says the shoemaker, "but she is no daughter of mine." "St. Nail!" said one of them, "I would give a hundred pounds to marry her." The two others said the very same. The poor shoemaker said that he had nothing to do with her. "But," said they, "ask her to-night, and send us word to-morrow." When the gentles went away, she asked the shoemaker—"What's that they were saying about me?" The shoemaker told her. "Go thou after them," said she; "I will marry one of them, and let him bring his purse with him." The youth returned, and he gave the shoemaker a hundred pounds for tocher. They went to rest, and when she had laid down, she asked the lad for a drink of water from a tumbler that was on the board on the further side of the chamber. He went; but out of that he could not come, as he held the vessel of water the length of the night. "Thou lad," said she, "why wilt thou not lie down?" but out of that he could not drag till the bright morrow's day was. The shoemaker came to the door of the chamber, and she asked him to take away that lubberly boy. This wooer went and betook himself to his home, but he did not tell the other two how it happened to him. Next came

* Tràill, a slave.
† Peillag, felt, coarse cloth.

the second chap, and in the same way, when she had gone to rest—"Look," she said, "if the latch is on the door." The latch laid hold of his hands, and out of that he could not come the length of the night, and out of that he did not come till the morrow's day was bright. He went, under shame and disgrace. No matter, he did not tell the other chap how it had happened, and on the third night he came. As it happened to the two others, so it happened to him. One foot stuck to the floor; he could neither come nor go, but so he was the length of the night. On the morrow, he took his soles out (of that), and he was not seen looking behind him. "Now," said the girl to the shoemaker, "thine is the sporran of gold; I have no need of it. It will better thee, and I am no worse for thy kindness to me." The shoemaker had the shoes ready, and on that very day the king was to be married. The shoemaker was going to the castle with the shoes of the young people, and the girl said to the shoemaker, "I would like to get a sight of the king's son before he marries." "Come with me," says the shoemaker, "I am well acquainted with the servants at the castle, and thou shalt get a sight of the king's son and all the company." And when the gentles saw the pretty woman that was here they took her to the wedding-room, and they filled for her a glass of wine. When she was going ro drink what is in it, a flame went up out of the glass, and a golden pigeon and a silver pigeon sprung out of it, They were flying about when three grains of barley fell on the floor. The silver pigeon sprang, and he eats that. Said the golden pigeon to him, "If thou hadst mind when I cleared the byre, thou wouldst not eat that without giving me a share." Again fell three other grains of barley, and the silver pigeon sprang, and he eats that, as before. "If thou hadst mind when I thatched the byre, thou wouldst not eat that without giving me my share," says the golden pigeon. Three other grains fall, and the silver pigeon sprang, and he eats that. "If thou hadst mind when I harried the magpie's nest, thou wouldst not eat that without giving me my share," says the golden pigeon; "I lost my little finger bringing it down, and I want it still." The king's son minded, and he knew who it was he had got. He sprang where she was, and kissed her from hand to mouth. And when the priest came they married a second time. And there I left them.

This version of the Battle of the Birds was recited by John Mackenzie, April 1859, and written in Gaelic by Hector Urquhart. The reciter is a fisherman, and has resided for the last thirty-four years at Ceanmore, near Inverary, on the estate of the Duke of Argyll.

He is a native of Lorn. He says he has known it from his youth, and
he has been in the habit of repeating it to his friends on winter nights,
as a pastime, "*He can read English and play the bagpipes, and has a
memory like Oliver and Boyd's Almanac.*" He got this and his other
stories from his father and other old people in Lorn and elsewhere.
He is about sixty years of age, and was employed, April 1859, in
building dykes on the estate of Ardkinglas, where Hector Urquhart
is gamekeeper. In reciting his stories he has all the manner of a
practised narrator; people still frequent his house to hear his tales. I
know the man, and I have heard him recite many. The Gaelic has
some few north country words.

CATH NAN EUN.

Bha am ann uair, anns an robh na h' uile beathach 's eun a
cruinneachadh gu cath. Thubhairt mac rìgh Cathair Shìomain,
"Gu'n rachadh e a dh' fhaicinn a chath, agus gun d' thugadh e fios
cinnteach dhachaidh do dh' athair an rìgh, co a bhiodh 'na rìgh air
na beathaichcan air a bhliadhna so." Bha 'n cath seachad mu 'n
dràinig e, ach eadar aon-fhitheach mòr dubh agus nathair, agus bha
aogas gu'm faigheadh an nathair buaidh air an fhitheach. 'Nuair a
chunnaic mac an rìgh so, chuidich e 'm fitheach, agus le aon bhuille
thugar an ceann do 'n nathair. 'Nuair a leig am fitheach anail, 'sa
chunnaic e gu'n robh an nathair marbh, thubhairt e, "Air son do
choimhneis dhòmhsa an diugh, bheir mise sealladh dhuit; thig a
nios a nis air bun mo dhà sgéithe." Chaidh mac an rìgh suas air
muin an fhithich agus mu 'n do stad e, thug e thairis e air seachd
beanntaibh, seachd glìnn, agus seachd monaidhean. "A nis," ars'
am fitheach, "am bheil thu faicinn an tigh' ud thàll; falbh a nis d'a
'ionnsuidh; 's i piuthar dhòmhsa a tha gabhail còmhnuidh ann agus
théid mis 'an urras gu'r è do bheatha, agus ma dh' fhoighneachdas
i dhìot, 'an robh thu aig Cath nan eun? abair thusa, 'gu'n robh'."
"Agus ma dh' fheòraicheas i dhìot, 'am faca tu mo choltas-sa, abair
thusa 'gu 'm faca, ach bi cinnteach gu'n coinnich thu mise moch
am màireach anns an àite so." Fhuair mac an rìgh gabhail aige gu
maithe 's gu ro mhaith air an oidhche so, biadh dheth gach biadh,
's deoch dheth gach deoch, uisge blàth d'a chasan 's leaba bhog d'a
leasan. Air an ath latha, thug am fitheach an sealladh ceudna dhà
thairis air seachd beanntaibh, seachd glinn, agus seachd
monaidhean. Chunnaic iad bothan fad' uatha ach ge b' fhad uatha,
cha b' fhada 'ga 'ruigheachd. Fhuair e gabhail aig' air an oidhche
so gu maith mar an ceudna; paílteas biadh 's deoch, 's uisge blàth

d'a chasan, 's leaba bhog d'a leasan. Air an treas maduinn an àit an fhithich fhaicinn, mar air na h-uairean roimhe, co thug coinneamh dha, ach an t-òganach a bu dhreachmhoire a chunnaic e riamh, agus pasgan aige na làimh. Dh' fhoighneachd mac an rìgh do 'n òganach so, "Am fac e fitheach mòr dubh?" Thubhairt an t-òganach ris, "Cha 'n 'fhaic thu 'm fitheach tuillidh, oir s mise am fitheach a bha 'sin; bha mi air mo chuir fo gheasaibh agus 'se thusa a choinneachadh a dh' fhuasgail mi, air son sin, tha thu a' faotainn a phasgain so." "Nis," ars' an t-òganach, "pillidh tu air t'ais air a chois-cheum cheudna, agus bithidh tu oidhche anns gach tigh mar a bha thu roimhe; ach am bonn a tha agad ri dhèanamh, 'na fuasgail am pasgan sin a thug mi dhuit, gus am bi thu anns an àite bu mhiannaiche leat a bhith chòmhnuidh." Thug mac an rìgh a chùl air an òganach, agus thug e aghaidh air tigh Athar, agus fhuair e aoidheachd aig peathraichean an fhithich ceart mar a fhuair e 'dol air aghaidh. Nuair a bha e dlùthachadh ri tigh athar, bha e 'dol troimhe choille dhùmhail; air leis gu 'n robh am pasgan a' fàs trom, agus smaoinich e gu 'n sealladh e gu dè a bh' ann. 'Nuair a dh' fhuasgail e 'm pasgan, cha b' ann gun iongantas a chur air fhéin. Ann am prioba na sùla, faicear an aon àite bu bhrèagha a chunnaic e riamh caisteal mòr, agus lios, anns an robh na h-uile seòrsa meas is luibhean mun cuairt air a' chaisteal. Sheas e làn iongantais, agus aithreachais air son am pasgan fhuasgladh. Cha robh 'na chomas a chur air ais a rithist, agus bu mhiann leis an t-àite bòidheach so a bhith air an lagan bhòidheach uaine a bha fa chomhair tigh athar. Ach sùil do 'n d' thug e, faicear famhair mòr, 's e gabhail d'a 'ionnsuidh. " 'S olc an t-àite anns an do thog thu do thigh, a mhic an rìgh," ars' am famhair. "Seadh, ach cha b' ann an so bu mhiannaiche leam e 'bhith, ge do thachair e 'bhith ann gu tabaisteach," arsa mac an rìgh. "Ciod an duais a bheireadh tu air son a chur air ais sa phasgan mar a bha e roimhe?" "Ciod an duais a dh' iarradh tu?" arsa mac an rìgh. "Ma bheir thu dhòmhs' a cheud mhac a bhitheas agad, 'nuair a bhitheas e seachd bliadhna dh' aois," ars' am famhair. "Gheibh thu sin ma bhitheas mac agam," thubhairt mac an rìgh. Ann am prioba na sùla chuir am famhair gach lios is gàrradh is caisteal 'sa phasgan mar a bha iad roimhe. "Nis," ars' am famhair, "gabh thusa do rathad féin, 's gabhaidh mise mo rathad féin, ach cuimhnich do ghealladh 's ged nach cuimhnich thusa, cha di-chuimhnich mise." Thug mac an rìgh an rathad air, 's an ceann beagan làithean ràinig e 'n t-àite bu mhiannaiche leis; dh' fhuasgail e 'm pasgan, agus bha 'n t-àite ceudna dìreach mar a bha e roimhe, agus a nuair a dh' fhosgail e

dorus a chaisteail, faicear an òigh bu dhreachmhoire air an d' thug
e sùil riamh. "Thìg air t-aghaidh, a mhic an righ," ars' an nighean
bhòidheach, "tha gach ni an òrdugh air do shon, ma phòsas tu mise,
an nochd féin." " 'S mis' an duine a bhitheas toileach," thubhairt
mac an righ; agus air an oidhche sin féin phòs iad. Ach an ceann
latha 's seachd bliadhna co 'm fear mòr a chithear a tighinn a dh'
ionnsuidh a chaisteail ach am famhair. Chuimhnich mac an rìgh a
ghealladh do 'n famhair, agus gus a so, cha d' innis e do 'n bhan-rìgh
a ghealladh. "Leig thus' eadar mise 's am famhair," ars' a bhan-righ.
"Cuir a mach do mhac," ars' am famhair; "cuimhnich do
ghealladh." "Gheibh thu sin," ars' an righ, " 'nuair a chuireas a
mhathair an òrdugh e air son a thurais." Sgeadaich a bhan-righ mac
a chòcaire agus thug i do 'n fhamhair air làimh e. Dh' fhalbh am
famhair leis, ach cha b' fhada a chaidh e, 'nuair a chuir e slatag ann
an làimh a ghille-bhig. Dh' fheòraich am famhair dheth, "Na 'm
bitheadh an t-slatag sin aig t-athair, de 'dhèanadh e, leatha?" "Na
'm biodh an t-slat so aig m' athair, ghabhadh e air na coin 's air na
cait na 'm biodh iad a dol a chòir biadh an rìgh," ars' an gille beag.
" 'S tusa mac a chòcaire," ars' am famhair. Beirear air dha chaol
cois' air, agus sgleogar e ris a chloich a bha ri' thaobh. Thill am
famhair air ais a dh' ionnsuidh a chaisteail ann am feirg is cuthach,
's thubhairt e, "Mar cuireadh iad a mach dhàsan mac an rìgh, gu
'm b' e 'chlach a b' àirde a chlach a b' ìsle bhiodh do 'n chaisteal."
Thubhairt a bhan-righ ris an rìgh, "Feuchaidh sinn fathast e, tha
mac a bhuidealair an aon aois ri ar mac féin." Sgeadaich i mac a
bhuidealair, agus thugar do 'n fhamhair e air làimh. Cha deach am
famhair ach goirid, nuair a chuir e 'n t-slatag 'na làimh, "Na 'm
bitheadh an t-slat so aig t-athair," ars' am famhair, "dé a dhèanadh
e leatha?" "Ghabhadh e air na coin 's air na cait 'nuair a bhiodh iad
a tighinn dlùth air botail 's air gloinneachan an rìgh." " 'S tusa mac
a bhuidealair," ars' am famhair, is spad e 'n t-eanchainn as air an
dòigh cheudna. Thill am famhair, ann am feirg is corruich ro mhòr.
Chrith an talamh fo 'bhonn, 's chrith an caisteal 's na bh' ann."
"MACH AN SO DO MHAC," ars' am famhair, "oir ann nam prioba
na sùla 's e chlach is àirde, 'chlach is ìsle bhitheas do 'n aitreabh."
'S e bh' ann gu m b' éiginn mac an rìgh thabhairt do 'n fhamhair.
Thug am famhair e d'a thigh féin, agus thog e mar mhac dha féin
e. Latha do na làithibh 's am famhair bho 'n bhaile, chuala am
t-òganach an ceòl bu bhinne a chual e riamh, ann an seòmar a bha
'm mullach tigh an fhamhair. Sùil do 'n d'thug e, chunnaic an
aghaidh bu bhrèagha a chunnaic e riamh. Smèid i air e thighinn ni
bu dlùithe dhi, agus thubhairt i ris, "E' dh' fhalbh air an am so ach

e bhith cinnteach e 'bhith anns an àite cheudna mu mharbh mheadhain-na h-oidhche so;" agus mar a gheall, choimhlion. Bha nighean an fhamhair ri' thaobh ann am prioba na sùla agus thubhairt i ris, "Am màireach gheibh thu do roghainn ri phosadh dheth mo dhà phiuthar; ach abair thusa nach gabh thu a h-aon dhiubh ach mise; tha m' athair air son gu 'm pòs mi mac rìgh na Cathair uaine, ach 's coma leam è." Air an latha màireach, thug am famhair a mach a thriuir nighean 's thubhairt e, 'Nis, a mhic rìgh na Cathair Shìomain, cha do chaill thu air a bhith leamsa cho fada: gheibh thu air son bean aon do 'n dithis is sine do m' nigheanaibh, agus bithidh cead agad dol dhachaidh leatha, an déigh na bainnse." "Ma bheir thu dhomh an té bheag bhòidheach so," arsa mac an rìgh, "gabhaidh mi air t-fhacal thu." Las fearg an fhamhair, agus thubhairt e, "Ma'm faigh thu sin, feumaidh tu na tri nitheanana a dh' iarras mis' ort a dhèanamh." "Abair romhad," arsa mac an rìgh. Thug am famhair do 'n bhàthaich e. "Nis," ars' am famhair, "tha innear nan ceud damh an so, agus cha deach a chartadh o cheann seachd bliadhna. "Tha mise 'dol o 'n bhaile 'n diugh agus mar bi 'm bàthach so air a chartadh mu 'n d'thig an oidhche cho ghlan 's gu'n ruith ubhall òir o cheann gu ceann dith, cha 'n e mhàin nach faigh thu mo nighean, ach 's e deoch dhe d'fhuil a chaisgeas mo phathadh a nochd." Toisichear air cartadh na bathaich, ach bu cheart cho maith teannadh ri taomadh a chuain mhòir. 'N déigh mheadhoin-latha 's am fallus 'ga 'dhalladh thàinig nighean òg an fhamhair far an robh e 's thubhairt i ris, "Tha thu 'ga'd' phianadh, a mhic an rìgh." "Tha mi 'n sin," arsa mac an rìgh. "Thig a nall," ars' ise, "agus leig do sgìos." "Ni mi sin," ars esan, "cha 'n 'eil ach am bàs a feitheamh orm co dhiu." Shuidh e sìos làimh rithe. Bha e cho sgìth, agus gu 'n do thuit e 'na chadal ri 'taobh. 'Nuair a dhùisg e, cha robh nighean an fhamhair ri fhaicinn; ach bha bhathaich cho glan cairte 's gu 'n ruitheadh ubhall òir bho cheann gu ceann dith. 'Steach thigear am famhair, 's thubhairt e, "Chairt thu 'm bathaich, a mhic an rìgh." "Chairt mi," ars' esan. "Chairt neach éiginn i," ars' am famhair. "Cha do chairt thus' i co dhiu," thubhairt mac an rìgh. "Seadh! Seadh!" ars' am famhair, "bhon a' bha thu co tapaidh an diugh, gheibh thu gus an am so am maireach gu tubhadh a bhathaich so le clòimh eòin gun dà ite air an aon dath." Bha mac an rìgh air a chois roi'n ghrein. Ghlac e a bhogha 's a bhalg-saighead a mharbhadh nan èun. Thug e 'm monadh air, ach ma thug, cha robh na h-eòin cho furasda ri 'm faotainn. Bha e a ruith 'nan déigh, gus an robh am fallus 'ga 'dhalladh. Mu mheadhon-la co 'thigeadh ach nighean an fhamhair. "Tha thu ga'd' phianadh, a mhic an rìgh," ars' ise. "Tha mi," thubhairt esan, "cha do thuit ach an dà lon dubh so, agus iad air aon dath." "Thig a nall, 's leig do sgìos air a chnocan bhòidheach so," arsa nighean an fhamhair. " 'S mi tha toileach," thubhairt esan. Smaoinich e gu n cobhaireadh i air air an àm so cuideachd. Shuidh e sìos làimh rithe, 's cha b'fhad' a bha e 'n sin gus an do thuit e 'na chadal; agus a nuair a dhùisg e, bha nighean an fhamhair air falbh. Smaoinich e tilleadh thun an tighe, 's faicear am bathaich tùghte leis na h-itean. 'Nuair a thàinig am famhair dhachaidh thubhairt e, "Thubh thu 'm bathaich, a mhic an rìgh." "Thubh mi," ars' esan. "Thubh cuid-eiginn i," ars' am famhair. "Cha do thubh thusa i," arsa mac an rìgh. "Seadh! Seadh!" ars' am famhair. " 'Nis," ars' am famhair, "tha craobh ghiubhas ri taobh an loch ud shios agus tha nead pioghaid 'na mullach." "Na h-uibhean a gheibh thu anns an nead, feumaidh iad a bhi agamsa gu mo *cheud-lon, gaidh*; cha 'n fhàod a h-aon a bhith sgàinte no briste, agus 's e còig a tha 'san nead." Moch 'sa mhaduinn, dh'fhalbh mac an rìgh far an robh a chraobh, 's cha robh sin duilich amas oirre. Cha robh a leithbhreac 'sa choill' air fad. Bho 'bonn gu ruig a ceud mheanglan, còig ceud troidh. Bha mac an rìgh à dol ceithir thimchioll air a chraoibh. Thàinig ise 'bha daonnan à dèanamh furtachd dha: "Tha thu air call craiceann nan làmh 's nan cas, a mhic an rìgh." "Ach tha," ars' esan, "cha luaithe shuas na shìos mi." "Cha 'n àm fuireachd so," arsa nighean an fhamhair. Shàth i' meur an déigh meur, gus an d' rinn i fàradh do mhac an rìgh gu dol suas do nead na pioghaid. 'Nuair a bha e aig an 'nead, thubhairt ise, "Dèan cabhag a nuas leis na h-uibheam, oir tha anail m' athar a' losgadh mo dhroma." Leis a chabhaig a bh' air-san, dh' fhàg ise 'lùdag am mullach na craoibhe. "Nis," ars' ise, "thèid thu dhachaidh leis na h-uibhean gu luath, agus gheibh thu mise ri phòsadh a nochd ma dh'aithnicheas tu mi; bithidh mis' agus mo dha phiuthar air ar n-èideadh anns an aon trusgan, agus air ar dèanamh coltach ri' chéile. Ach seall thus' ormsa 'nuair a their m' athair 'falbh le d' mhnaoi, a mhic an rìgh; agus chi thu làimh gun lùdag." Thug e na h-uibhean do'n fhamhair. "Seadh! Seadh!" ars' am famhair, "bi' dèanamh deas chum do phòsadh." 'S ann an sin a bha bhanais, 's b'e bhanais i famhairean 's daoiné uaisle, 's mac rìgh na Cathair uaine 'nam meadhon. Chaidh am pòsadh, 's thòisich an dàmhsa, 's b'e sin an damhsa. Bha tigh an fhamhair air chrith bho 'mhullach gu 'bhonn. Ach thàinig àm dol a luidhe, 's thubhairt am famhair, "Tha 'n t-àm dhuit dol a luidhe, a mhic rìgh na Cathair Shìomain; thoir leat do bhean as am meadhon sin." Chuir ise mach a làimh dheth 'n robh an lùdag agus rug e oirre air làimh. "Dh' amais thu gu maith air an am so cuideachd, ach cha 'n 'eil fios nach coinnich sinn thu air dòigh eile," thubhairt am famhair. Ach a luidhe chaidh iad. "A nis," thuirt ise; "cadal cha dèan thu, air neo bàsaichidh tu; feumaidh sinn teicheadh gu luath, oir gun teagamh marbhaidh m' athair thu." A mach ghabh iad, agus air an loth dhuinn a bha anns an stabull, chaidh iad. "Dèan socair beagan," ara' ise, "agus cluichidh mise cleas air an t-seann laoch." Leum i stigh, agus gheàrr i ubhall 'na naoi earannan, 's chuir, i dà earrann dhith aig ceann na leapa, agus dà earrann aig casan na leapa; dà earrann aig dorus-chadha, agus dà earann aig an dorus-chadha, agus dà earann aig an dorus mhòr, agus a h-aon air taobh a mach an tighe. Dhùisg am famhair, agus ghlaodh e, " 'M bheil sibhse 'nur cadal." "Cha 'n 'eil fathast," ars' an ubhall a bha aig ceann na leapa. An ceann ghreis ghlaodh e rithist, "Cha 'n 'eil fathast," ars' an ubhall a bha aig casan na leapa. Greis an déigh sin, ghlaodh e rithist, "Cha 'n 'eil fathast," thubhairt an ubhal aig dorus a chadha. Ghlaodh am famhair a rithist, 's fhreagair an ubhal a bha aig an dorus mhòr. "Tha sibh a' dol ni's faide uam," ars' am famhair. "Cha 'n 'eil fathast," ars' an ubhal a bha air taobh a mach an doruis. "Tha sibh a teichadh," ars' am famhair. Leum am famhair air a chasan, agus gu ruig an leabaidh chaidh e; ach bha i gu fuar, fàs. "Tha cuilbheartan mo nighean féin a feuchainn rium," thubhairt am famhair. Air an tòir ghabh e," Am beul an latha, thuirt nighean an fhamhair, "Gu 'n robh anail a h-athair a losgadh a droma." "Cuir do làmh gu luath," ars' ise, "ann an cluais na loth dhuinn, agus ge be ni gheibh thu innte tilg 'na d' dhéigh e." "Tha bior do sgitheach an so," thubhairt esan. "Tilg as do dheigh e." Cha luaithe rinn e so, na bha fichead mìle do sgitheach cho tiugh ann 's gum bu ghann do neas dol troimhe. Thàinig am famhair 'na dhian 's siud e 'n coinneamh a chinn 's amhach anns an sgitheach!! "Tha cuilbheartan mo nighean féin an so mar an ceudna," thubhairt am famhair; "ach na 'm biodh agamsa mo thuagh mhòr 's mo chorc choille an so, cha b' fhad' a bhithinn a dèanamh rathad troimhe so." Thill e dhachaidh air son na tuaidh mòire 's na corc choille, agus gun teagamh cha robh e fad a' dèanamh rathad troi 'n sgitheach. "Fàgaidh mi n' tuadh s' a chorc choille 'n so, gus am till mi," ars' esan. "MA DH' FHAGAS, thuirt feannag a bha ann an craobh," goididh sinne iad." "Ni sibh sin fhéin," ars' am famhair, "ach cuiridh mise dhachaidh iad." Thill e agus dh' fhàg e iad aig an tigh. Ann an teas an latha mhothaich ise anail a h'athar a losgadh a droma. "Cuir do mheur ann an cluais na lotha, agus tilg na gheibh thu innte as do dhéigh." Fhuair e sgealb do chlach ghlais 's thilg e as a dhéigh i. Ann am prioba na sùla, bha fichead mìle do chreag mhòr ghlas air leud 's air àirde as an déigh. Thàinig am famhar'na dheann, ach seachad air a' chreag cha robh comas dha dol. "Se cuilbheartan mo nighinn fèin rud as cruaidh' a thachair riamh rium," ars' am famhair. "Ach na 'm biodh agamsa mo gheamhlag 's mo mhatag mhòr, cha b' fhada a bhithinn a dèanamh rathad roimh n' chreig so cuideachd." B'fheudar tilleadh air an son, agus b'e féin gille sgoltadh nan clach. Cha robh e fada a dèanamh rathad troimh 'n chreag. "Fagaidh mi an acfhuinn an so, 's cha thill mi tuillidh." "MA DH' FHAGAS," ars' an fheannag, "goididh sinn' iad." "Tha sin 's a roghainn agad; cha 'n'eil tìom tilleadh ann." Ann am bristeadh na fàire thubhairt nighean an fhamhair, "gu'n robh i mothachainn anail a h-athar a losgadh a droma." "Seall ann an cluais na lotha, a mhic an rìgh, air neo tha sinn cailte." Rinn e so, agus, s' e aotroman làn uisge a bha 'na cluais air an am so. "Tilg 'na d' dhéigh e," arsa nighean an fhamhair. Rinn e so, agus bha loch uisge fichead mìle air fad 's air leud 'nan déigh. Thàinig am famhair air aghaidh, ach leis an astar a bh' aige, bha e ann am meadhoin an loch, agus chaidh e foidhe, 's cha d' éirich e ni's mò. Air an ath latha, bha a chuideachd òg air tighinn am fradharc tigh athar-san. "Nis." ars'ise, "tha m'athair bàite, 's cha chuir e dragh tuillidh òirn. "Ach mu'n d' théid sinn ni 's faide," ars'ise, "rach thusa gu tigh t'athar, agus innis ga'bheil mo leithid-sa agad; ach am bonn a tha agad ri 'dheànamh, na leig le duine na crèutair do phògadh; oir ma ni thu sin, cha bhi cuimhn' agad gu'faca tu riamh mi." Chuir gach neach mar a bha tachairt air fàilte is furan air, 's thug e àithne d'a athair 's d'a mhàthair, gun esan a phògadh; ach mar a bha 'n tubaist 'an dàn, bha sean mhial-chù do ghalla 'steach 's dh' aithnich i e, 's leum i suas ri bheul, agus na dhéigh sin dhi-chuimhnich e nighean an fhamhair. Bha ise 'na suidhe aig taobh an tobair mar a dh' fhàg e i, ach cha robh mac an rìgh a' tighinn. Ann am beul na h-oidhche, streap i suas ann an craobh do dharach a bha ri taobh an tobair. Luidh i ann an gobhall na craoibhe fad na h'oidhche sin. Bha tigh aig greusaiche dlùth do 'n tobar, agus mu mheadhon là a' màireach, dh' iarr an greusaich air a mhnaoi, i 'dhol airson deoch dha as an tobar. 'Nuair a rainig bean a ghreusaiche an tobar, 's a chunnaic i faileas na té a bha anns a chraoibh, air saoilsinn dh'ise gu 'm b'e faileas féin a bh' ann (s' cha do shaoil leatha gu so gu 'n robh i co brèagha), thug i tilgeil do'n chuman a bha 'na làimh, 's bhrist i ris an talamh e, 's thug i'n tigh oirre gun chuinneag gun uisge! "Cait' am bheil an t-uisge, a bhean," thubhairt an greusaiche. "A bhodaich leibidich, shuaraich, gun mhaise, dh' fhan mi tuilidh 's fada 'n am thràill uisge 's connaidh agad." "Tha mi féin a smaoineachadh, a bhean, gu'n deach thu air bhoile; falbh thusa a nighean, gu, luath 's faigh deoch do d' athair. Dh' fhalbh a nighean, agus air an dòigh cheudna thachair dhi. Cha do shaoil leatha gu so gu 'n robh i co tlachdmhor, 's thug i 'n tigh oirre. "Nios an deoch," ars' a h-athair. "A pheallaig bhodiach nam brò, an saoil thu gu 'bheil mise gu bhi 'm thràill uisge agad." Smaoinich an greusaiche bochd gu'n d' thug iad car as am beachd, 's dh 'fhalbh e féin do 'n tobar. Chunnaic e faileas na gruagaiche san tobar, 's dh' amhairc e suas do 'n chraoibh 's faicear am boirionnach bu bhrèagha a chunnaic e riamh. " 'S corrach do shuidheachan ach 's maiseach do ghnùis," thubhairt an greusaiche. "Thig a nuas, oir tha feum dhuit car ùine gheàrr 'nam thigh-sa." Thuig an greusaiche gu'm b'e so am faileas a chuir a chuideachdsan air bhoile. Thug an greusaich i gu thigh 's thubhairt e rithe, "Nach robh aige-san ach bothan bochd, ach bothan bochd, ach gu 'm faigheadh i a cuid dhe na bh' ann." An ceann latha na dhà 'na dhéigh so, tháinig triùir fhleasgach uasal gu tigh a ghreusaiche, airson brògan a dhèanmh dhoibh, 's an rìgh air tighinn dhachaidh, agus e 'dol a phòsadh. Ach sùil do 'n d' thug na fleasgaich, chunnaic iad nighean an fhamhair, 's ma chunnaic, cha 'n fhac iad riamh té co bòidheach rithe. " 'S ann agad a tha 'n nighean bhòidheach an so," thubhairt na fleasgaich ris a ghreusaiche. "Ach cha 'n e mo nighean-sa th' ann." "Nàile!" arsa fear dhiubh, "bheirinn féinn ceùd punnd air son a pòsadh." Thubhairt an dithis eile a leithid cheudna. Thubhairt au greusaiche bochd, "Nach robh gnothuch aige-san ri a dhéanmh rithe." "Ach," ars' iadsan, "farraid thusa dhith 'n nochd, agus leig fios thugainne 'màireach." Nuair a dh' fhalbh na h'-uaislean, dh' fharraid i do'n ghreusaiche, "gu dé sud a bha iad ag radh mu 'm dheibhinnse?" Dh' innis an greusaiche dhith. "Falbh 'nan déigh," ars' ise, "pòsaidh mi fear aca a nochd féin, 's thugadh e leis a sporan airgid." Dh' fhalbh an greusaiche 'nan déigh, 's dh' innis e 'n sin fein. Thill e'n t-òganach. Thug e ceud punnd do 'n ghreusaiche, air-son tochar. "Chaidh i a luidhe, agus an uair a bha aodach an òganaich dheth, dh' iarr i air deoch uisge as a chòrn a bha air a bhòrd air taobh thall an t-seòmair; dh' fhalbh e, ach a' sin cha d' thigeadh e fad na h'-oidhche, is greim aig air an t-soitheach uisge." "Oglaich thu," thubhairt ise, "cairson nach dig thu a luidhe?" ach as a' so cha diongadh e, gus an robh an latha geal am màireach ann. Thainig an greusaiche gu dorus an t-seòmair, agus dh'iarr i air, "an slaodaire ballaich sin a thabhairt air falbh." Dh' fhalbh an suiriche so, 's thug 'e 'n tigh air, ach cha do dh' innis e mar dh' éirich dha do 'n dithis eile. Air an ath oidhche, thàinig an darna fleasgach, agus air an doigh cheudna nuair a chaidh i a luidhe, "Seall," thuirt ise, "am bheil an crann air an dorus." Air a chrann ghabh a lamhan gréim, agus as a' sin cha d' thigeadhe e fad na h-oidhche, as a' so cha d' thigeadh e gu latha geal am maireach. Dh' fhalbh e fo sprochd is nàire. Coma co dhiu, cha d'innis e, mar thachair, do 'n fhleasgach eile, agus air an treas oidhche, thàinig am fear eile, agus mar a thachair do'n dithis eile thachair dha; bha cas air an leabaidh 's cas eile air an urlar, cha d'thigeadh 's cha rachadh e, ach, air an dòigh so bha e fad na h'oidhche. Am màireach thug e 'bhuinn as, 's cha 'n fhacas e' sealtainn 'na dhéigh. "Nis," arsa 'n nighean ris a ghreusaiche, " 's leatsa an sporan òir, cha 'n 'eil feum agam-sa air, 's feàird thus' e, agus cha mhiosde mis' e, airson do chaoimhneis dhomh." Bha na brògan ullamh aig a ghreusaiche, agus air an latha sin féin, bha an rìgh gu pòsadh. Bha 'n greusaiche dol do 'n chaisteal le brògan nan òganach, 's thubhairt an nighean ris a ghreusaiche, "bu mhaith leam sealladh fhaicinn dhe mac an righ, mu'm pòsadh e." "Thig leamsa," ars' an greusaiche, "tha mi mion eòlach air seirbheisich a' chaisteail, agus gheibh thu sealladh air mac an rìgh 's na cuideachd uile." Agus a nuair a chunnaic na h-uaislean am boireannach bòidheach a bha 'n so, thug iad i so sheòmar na bainnse, agus lìon iad gloinne fion dhi. 'Nuair a bha i' dol a dh' òl na bha sa ghloinne, chaidh lasair suas aiste, agus leum calman òir 's calman airgid as a' ghloinne. Bha iad ag itealaich mu 'n cuairt, 'nuair a thuit tri ghràinnean eòrna air an urlar. Leum an calman airgiod, agus ithear sud. Thubhairt an calman òir ris, na'm biodh cuimhn' agad 'nuair a chairt mi 'm bàthaich, CHA 'N ITHEADH TU SIUD GUN CHUID A THOIRT DHOMHSA. A rithist thuit tri gràinnean eòrn' eile, 's leum an calman airgiod agus ithear siud mar an ceudna. "Na'm bitheadh cuimhn' agad 'nuair a thubh mi 'm bàthaich CHA 'N ITHEADH TU SIUD, GUN MO CHUID A THOIRT DHOMHSA," ars' an calman òir. Tuitear tri ghràinnean eile, s leum an calman airgiod, agus ithear siud cuideachd. "Na 'm biodh cuimhn' agad 'nuair a chreach mi nead na pioghaid, CHA 'N'ITHEADH TU SIUD GUN MO CHUID A THOIRT DHOMHSA," ars' an calman òir. "Chaill mi 'n lùdag 'gad' thadhairt a nuas, agus tha i dhìth orm fathast." Chuimhnich mac an rìgh, 's dh' aitnich e co a bh' aige. Leum e far an robh i, 's phòge e i bho làimh gu i beul, agus a nuair a thàinig an sagairt phòg iad an darna h-uair!! Agus dh' fhag mis' an sin iad.

HECTOR URQUHART.

2.   There is another version of this tale current in Islay. It was
taken down from the recitation of Ann Darroch by Hector Maclean.
It is called the "Widow's Son." He goes to seek his fortune, and
comes to a giant's house, where he engages himself as servant for a
peck of gold and a peck of silver. He is sent first to cleanse the seven
byres that have never been cleansed for seven years. All he puts out
at one door comes in at the other. The giant's daughter comes; he
promises to marry her, and she says, "Gather, oh shovel, and put
out, oh grape," and the tools work of themselves, and clear the byres.
Next he has to thatch the byres with feathers, no quills to be upwards.
He gets only one feather, and the giant's daughter takes three grains
of barley, and throws them on the roof. The birds of the air gather,
and thatch the byres in a minute. Next day he has to catch the steed
that had never seen a blink of earth or air. The girl gives him a little
rusty bridle, and the steed comes and puts her head into it. She makes
six little cakes, which she places at the fire, the foot water, the door
of the chamber, the side of the bed, and the kitchen door, and they
mount the steed and ride off. The giant lies down and calls to his
daughter. The cakes answer till there are none left to reply. Then he
rises, takes his clothes, his boots, and his sword of light; he makes
seven miles at each step; he sees seven miles by the light of the
sword—he follows; they hear him coming; the girl gives the widow's
son a golden apple, and tells him to throw it at a mole on her father,
where alone he is vulnerable; he fears that he will miss so small a
mark, so she throws it herself, and the giant is dead in an instant.

They reach a big town. He is told to kiss nothing, or he will forget
the girl and his promise. A big dog comes to meet him, and puts his
paws on his shoulder and kisses him. He takes service with the king,
and at last he is to be married to the king's daughter.

She takes service with a smith, disguised as a man, and "comes on
famously." The smith's daughter falls in love with her, and wants to
marry her. She tells, at last, that she is a girl in search of her own
lover. On a day of days the smith and his daughter and his servant
are invited to the wedding of the widow's son with the king's
daughter. They go, and the giant's daughter sets a golden cock and
a silver hen on the board before the bridegroom. She takes a grain
of barley from her pocket and throws it before them. The cock pecks
the hen and eats the barley; and the hen says, "Gog, Gog, if thou
hadst mind when I cleansed the seven byres for thee, thou wouldst
not do that to me." She does this three times, and the birds remind
him of what has been done; then he knows her, leaps over the board,
catches her by the arm, leaves the king's daughter, and marries her.

3.   There is another version current at Inverary, repeated to me
by a stable boy who was then employed at the ferry of St. Katharines,
and who repeated it in Gaelic while rowing the boat to Inverary. It

began thus:—I will tell you a story about the wren. There was once a farmer who was seeking a servant, and the wren met him, and he said, "What art thou seeking for?" "I am seeking a servant," said the farmer. "Wilt thou take me?" said the wren. "Thee, thou poor creature; what good wouldst thou do?" "Try thou me," said the wren. So he engaged him, and the first work he set him to was threshing in the barn. The wren threshed (what did he thresh with?—a flail to be sure), and he knocked off one grain. A mouse came out and she eats that. "I'll praise thee, and don't do that again," said the wren. He struck again, and he knocked off two grains. Out came the mouse and she eats that. So they arranged a contest that they might know which was the strongest, and there was neither mouse nor rat on earth that did not gather, nor was there bird under heaven that did not come to the battle. The son of a gentleman heard of the fight, and he came also, but he slept before it was over, and when he awoke there was neither "mouse nor rat to be seen; there was but one great black raven." The raven and the man agreed to travel together, and they come to an inn. The gentleman goes in, but the raven is sent to the stable, because the porters and waiters object to the like of a raven. Here he picks out all the horses' eyes, and in the morning there is a disturbance. The gentleman pays and scolds, and they go to another inn, where the raven is sent to the byre, and picks out all the cows' eyes. Then they part. The raven takes out a book, and gives it to his companion with a warning not to open it till he gets home to his father's house. He breaks the charge, looks, and finds himself in a giant's house. There he takes service, and is sent to clean the byre. It had seven doors, it had not been cleaned for seven years, and all that he put out at one door came in at the other. Then came the giant's red-haired daughter, and said, "If thou wilt marry me I will help thee." He consents; and she sets all the grapes and forks about the place to work of themselves, and the byre is cleansed. Then the giant sets him to reach the byre with feathers, and every feather he put on the wind blew away. Then came the giant's girl, and the promise was repeated; and she played a whistle that she had, and he laid his head in her lap, and every bird there was came, and they thatched the byre.

Then the giant sent him to the hill to fetch the gray horse that was seven years old; and she told him that he would meet two black dogs, and she gave him a cake of tallow and half a cheese, and a tether; and she said that the dogs and the horse would kill him unless he gave the dogs the food, and put the tether on the horse. When the dogs ran at him, he put the tallow in the mouth of one, and the cheese in the throat of the other; and when the horse came down the hill to kill him with his mouth open, he put the tether in his mouth and he followed him quietly home. "Now," said she, "we will be off." So they mounted and rode away, but first she took four apples, three she placed about the house, which spoke as in the other tales, the fourth she took with her. When the last of the apples had spoken, the giant rose and followed. Then the girl felt her father's breath on her back, and said, "Search in the horse's ear." And he found a twig. "Throw it behind you," said she; and he threw it, and it became the biggest wood that ever was. The giant came, and returned for his "big axe and his little axe," and he hewed his way through; and the red-haired girl said that she felt her father's breath. "Now," said she to the king's son (here the narrator remembered that he was a prince instead of a young farmer), "see in the filly's ear" (here he remembered that it was a filly). So he looked, and found a bit of stone, threw it, and it became a mountain. The giant came, looked for his big hammer and his little hammer, and smashed his way through the hill, and she felt his breath again. Then he sought in the ear, and found a (something) of water, and threw it, and it became a loch of fresh water. The giant came, and returned for his big scoop and his little scoop, and baled the water out, and he was after them again. Then she said, "My father is coming now, and he will kill us. Get off the filly, king's son," and he got off, and she gave him the apple, and she said, "Now put it under the filly's foot." And he did so; and the filly put her foot on it, and it smashed to bits; and the giant fell over dead, for his heart was in the apple. So they went on to his father's house, and she was made house-keeper, for they were not married; then in a short time she became house-maid, then kitchen-maid, and then hen-wife; and then the king was to be married (he had now become a king); and then first the porter, then the head waiter, and then some other servant, came and courted her. They promise to let her in to the wedding, and give her a fine dress each; and each in turn is admitted into the hen-wife's room; but the first goes to put the lid on the kettle, and is fast by the hands all night; the second is, in like manner, fast to a window which he goes to shut; and the feet of the third stick to the floor. Then she comes to the porter in her dirty dress. He drives her away, but he is at last obliged to give her a fine dress, and let her in. Then she comes to the head waiter, who does the same. Then she comes to the servant, who does the same, but is forced to let her in to the wedding. Then she takes out a golden cock and a silver hen, which she had brought. She sets them on the floor, and they talk. "Dost thou remember how I cleansed byre? Dost thou mind how I thatched the barn? Dost thou remember how I saved thy life?" And so on, till they repeat the whole story, reminding the king how she had been the house-keeper, house-maid, and hen-wife, and faithful throughout. And the king said, "Stop, I will marry thee." And when she said that, she showed the fine dresses that she had got from the porter, and the head waiter, etc., and they were married;

and if they have not died since then, they are alive, merry, and rich.

4. The stable boy said that he had learned this from a very old man, now living near Lochgilphead, who could tell it much better than he could. A gentleman at the inn said that an old woman, now dead, used to tell something like this, and that her raven was the son of the king of Lochlin. The old woman lived near Dalmally, and her daughter is said to be there still, but I have been unable to find her out. On asking for her, and giving my reason, I was told by a waiter that "light had dawned in that district, and that ignorance was banished."

5. A very similar story is well known in South Uist, and a fragment of it is still told in Sutherland.

6. The Uist story told to me by Donald MacCraw, as we walked along the road last September, is called "Mother's Blessing." The lad, so called because he is so good, goes to seek his fortune. He plays cards, and wins from some gentles; then stakes seven years' service against so many thousands, and loses to a black dog who comes in with a looking-glass on every paw. He goes to serve the dog, and is shown a cave where there are a hundred stakes and ninety-nine heads on them. He is set to cleanse the byre, to catch the steed, and to rob the nest. The black dog's daughter helps. She throws out one spadeful, and the litter flies out, "seven spadefuls at each of seven doors for every one he throws out." She gives a rusty bridle for the steed. She strikes the sea with a rod, and makes a way to the island where the nest is, and gives her toes to make a ladder to climb up. He leaves one, and offers one of his own instead. She refuses, because "her father always washes her feet himself." They ride off on the horse—the dog and his company follow. A wood grows and a river flows from things found in the horse's ear, and the dog is defeated but not killed. She gives the lad a treasure which is found under a tuft of rushes. He goes home, speaks to his mother, and forgets all. He builds a palace, and is to be married to a lady, but she is so proud that she will have the widow's hut pulled down. Mother's Blessing will not, so the match is off, but after a time it is on again. The door opens, and in walks the black dog smoking a pipe. He goes to the priest and forbids the ceremony. The priest says, "Begone to thine own place down below." "It's many a long day since *thou* art wanted there," says the dog. The priest defies all fiends, and *will* marry the pair. The dog says, "If I tell all I know thou wilt not." Then he whispers, and the priest is silenced. Then he brings in a fine gentleman, and says to the bride—"There is thy first lover; marry him." And they are married then and there. The dog brings in his own daughter; Mother's Blessing marries her, and the dog danced at the wedding with the priest. MacCraw said there was something left out which his informant would not tell.

7. I have received yet another version of this tale, very well written in Gaelic, from JOHN DEWAR, who, according to his own account of himself, is now (October 1859) residing in Glendaruail, and is about to proceed to Roseneath, where he used to get employment in making stobbs for the fences. He heads his story—"Tales of the Gael in the Winter Nights," and promises to send more. UIRSGEALN NAN GAEL S' NA OIDHCHENAN GEAMHRAIDH.—His Gaelic spelling is rather phonetic—

He heard it from his mother, told nearly as the stable-boy gave it; and has heard it lately in Glendaruail. He first heard an abridgement four or five years before 1812 or 1813, when he learned this from Mary MacCalum, a native of Glen Falloch, at the head of Loch Lomond.

It begins with a quarrel between a mouse and a wren in a barn about a grain of oats, which the mouse *will* eat. The wren brings his twelve birds—the mouse her tribe. The wren says, "Thou hast thy tribe with thee"—"As well as myself," says the mouse. The mouse sticks out her leg proudly, and the wren breaks it with his flail. The creatures of the plain and of the air all joined the quarrel, and there was a pitched battle on a set day. They fought the battle in a field above a king's house; and the fight was so fierce, that there were left but a raven and a snake. The king's son looked out of a window, and saw the snake twined round the raven's neck, and the raven holding the snake's throat in his beak—GOB—and neither dared to let go. Both promised friendship for help, and the king's son slew the serpent—NATHAIR.

The raven lived for a year and a day in the palace, then took the king's son hunting for the first time, and when he was tired, carried him. "And he put his hands about the raven before his wings, and he hopped with him over nine Bens, and nine Glens, and nine Moors." They go to the three sisters, and the king's son gets hospitality, because he comes from the land where the birds set the battle, and brings news of the raven, who is yet alive, and lived with him for a year and a day. Each day the number of glens, and hills, and moors passed over, falls from nine to six and three. The same thing is said by each of the three sisters: "That is a year and a day for thee in this place, and a piece in thy purse on the day when thou goest;" but he keeps tryst, and returns to the raven. On the third day came a mist, and the raven was not to be found; but when the king's son was nearly beat, he looked over a rock, and saw FEAR LEADANACH BUIDHE BOIDHEACH AGUS CIR OIR ANSA N' DARNA LAIMH, AGUS CIR AIRGID SAN LAIMH EILE, a beautiful yellow ringletted man, with a golden comb in the one hand, and a silver comb in the other, who asked if he would take him instead of the raven. He would not, "Nor half-a-dozen such." So the yellow ringletted man told him that he was the FITHEACH CROM DUBH—the black humpy raven that was laid under spells by a bad DRUIDH that knew how to put under spells. He had been set free by coming to his father's house with the king's son. Then he gave him a book, and told him to go with the wind the way it might blow, and to look in the book when he wished to see his father's house, but always from a hill top.

The king's son soon got tired, and looked in the book at the bottom of a glen, and saw his father's house at the bottom of a peat hag, with all the doors and windows shut, and no way to get to it.

Then came a giant, who shewed him the way for the promise of his first son. He shewed him his father's house on the top of a hill, with each door and window open, and got the promise. "And it was the giant who had cast DRUIDHEACHD upon him, that he might see his father's house in the bottom of a peat hag."

"Long after that the old king died, and the son got the kingly chair. He married; he had a son; and he was coming on to be a brave lad, and they were dwelling happily in the castle. The giant came to them, and he asked that the king's son should be sent out to him there, and they were not very willing to do that; but the giant said, unless they sent him out, that the highest stone of the castle would be the lowest presently; and they thought of arraying the cook's son bravely, and sending him out; and they did that. The giant went away with him, and he had a rod in his hand, and when they were a little bit from the house, the giant asked the cook's son—'What would thy father do with this little rod if he had it?' 'I don't know myself,' said the cook's son, 'unless he would beat the dogs away from the meat.' With that the giant understood that he had not got the right one, and he turned back with him, and he asked that the king's son should be sent to him. Then they put brave clothes on the son of the STIUARD, and they sent him out to the giant, but the giant was not long till he did to him as he had done to the cook's son, and he returned with him full of heavy wrath. He said to them, unless they sent out to him there the king's son, that the highest stone in the castle would be the lowest presently, and that he would kill all who were within; and then they were obliged to send out the king's son himself, though it was very grievous; and the giant went away with him. When they were gone a little bit from the castle, the giant showed him the rod that was in his hand and he said—'What would thy father do with this rod if he were to have it?' And the king's son said—'My father has a braver rod than that.' And the giant asked him—'Where will thy father be when he has that brave (briagh) rod?' And the king's son said—'He will be sitting in his kingly chair;' and the giant understood that he had the right one. [*This passage is translated entire, because, as I am told, there is a similar passage in the Volsung tale.*] The giant took him home, and set him to clean the byre that had not been cleansed

for seven years; and in case of failure, threatened 'S E'T FHUIL URAR
ALUIN GHRINN A BHITHIS AGUM A CHASGA M' IOTADH AGUS T' FHEOIL
UR GHRINN MAR MHILLISTAIN FHIACAL. It is thy fresh goodly beautiful blood I will have quenching my thirst, and thy fresh, beautiful
flesh as sweetening of teeth;" and he went to bed.

The king's son failed of course; all that went out at one door came
at in at another. Then came MARI RUADH, Auburn Mary, the giant's
daughter, and made him promise to marry her, and he gave his hand
and his promise. She made him set all the CAIBE and shovels in order,
waved her hand, and they worked alone, and cleaned the byre. "She
took an apple from her pocket—a golden apple—and it would run
from end to end, and would raise no stain in any place, it was so
clean."

The daughter "had been in sewing all day," when her father came
home from hunting, and asked his housewife. Next came the thatch-
ing of the barn with "the feathers of all the birds the giant had ever
killed, to be laid as close as ever they lay on the back of a heather hen
or a black cock." The wind blew them a new promise, "CHATHUDH,"
she shook them as chaff (is shaken on hill tops now), with the wind,
and the wind blew them straight to their own place. The giant came
home from his hunting as usual, and asked—"Housewife, was Auburn Mary out at all to-day?" "No, she was within sewing." He went
out, and brought in SRIAN BHRIAGH SHOILEIR DEARRSACH, a brave,
clear, shiny bridle, and ordered the king's son to catch the FALAIRE,
filly, on yonder hill, and tie her in the stable, or else, &c.

The fine bridle would not do. Then the daughter brought from
the stable, SEAN SRIAN DUBH MEIRGACH, an old, black, rusty bridle
that was behind one of the turf seats, and shook it, and the filly came
and put her nose *into it*.

The giant had the usual talk, but gave no more orders, and his
daughter told the king's son that he would kill him that night, but
that she would save him if he would promise to marry her.

"She put a wooden bench in the bed of the king's son; two wooden
benches in her own bed. She spat at the front of her own bed, and
spat at the side of the giant's bed, and spat at the passage door, and
she set two apples above the giant's bed, ready to fall on him when
he should wake and set him asleep again." And they mounted and
rode away, and set the filly "running with might."

The giant awoke, and shouted—"Rise, daughter, and bring me a
drink of the blood of the king's son." "I will arise," said the spittle,
in front of his bed; and of the apples fell and struck him between the
two shoulders, and he slept. The second time it was—"Rise, wife;"
and the same thing happened. The third time he shouted—"Art thou
rising to give me a drink of the blood of the king's son, Oh wife?"
"Coming with it," said the spittle, "behind the door of the cabh."

Then he lay a while, and got up with an axe, and struck it into the bench in the bed of the king's son. [So did a giant to Jack the giant-killer, and so did Skrymir to Thorr in Gylfi's mocking. Edda (translated by G. W. Dasent, page 54)]. And when he saw what he had, he ran to his daughter's bed, and struck his axe into the two things which he found there. Then he ran into the stable, and then he ran after the fugitives. At the mouth of day, the daughter said—"I feel my father's breath burning me between the two shoulders;" and the king's son took a drop of water from the filly's right ear, and threw it over his shoulder, and it became a lake which the giant could not cross. Then he said—This is a part of my own daughter's tricks; and he called out, FIRE FAIRE, A MHARI RUADH, AGUS NA THUG MISE DHUITSA DO DH'FHOLUM AGUS DO IONNSACHADH, N' E SO MAR A RINN THU ORM MA DHEIREADH. "Feere Faire, Auburn Mary, and all the learning and teaching I have given thee, is it thus thou hast done to me at last?" And, said she, CHAN EILE AGUD AIR ACH A BHI NAS GLIC A RITHISD. "Thou hast for it but to be wiser again." Then he said, if I had MO BHATA DUBH DIONACH FHEIN NACH FACA GAOTH NA GRIAN O CHEAN SEACHD BLIADHNA. My own tight black boat that saw neither wind nor rain since seven years' end. And his daughter said—"Thou has for it but to go and fetch her then."

Next time it was a little stone that was found in the left ear which became a great crag, and was broken through with the big hammer and the little hammer, ORD MOR AGUS ORD BEAG, which broke and pounded a breach through the rock in an instant by themselves. The third time it was the seed of a tree which became a wood, and was cut through by the axes TUATHAN of the giant, which he set to work, and his wife brought up the black dogs.

The fourth time it was a very little tiny drop of water that was found in the left ear, which became a narrow loch, but so deep that the giant could not cross it. He had the usual talk with his daughter, and got the same reply; tried to drink the water, but failed, for a curious reason, then he thought he would leap it, but his foot slipped and he was drowned.

Then came the incident of the kiss and the old greyhound.

She went to the house of a seamstress, and engaged herself, and was a good workwoman. When the king's son was to be married to another, the cook sent one of his underlings to the well for water. She stood on a branch of the tree above the FUARAN cold spring, and when the maid saw her shadow in the well she thought she had grown golden herself, for there was "golden weaving" on the dress of Auburn Mary. And she went back to the cook and said: "Thou art the lad to send me to fetch thee water, and I am a lump of gold." He sent another, with the same result, so he went himself and saw Mary go to the house of the seamstress. The cook told, and they asked about the stranger, but no one knew anything about her, till the hen wife went to the seamstress and found out "that she had come from a shore afar off; that she never saw her like for sewing nor for shape, and if they had her at the wedding, she would make FEARTAN miracles that would astonish them."

The hen wife told the queen, and she was engaged to help to make the dresses. They were pleased with her, and asked her to the wedding, and when there they asked her to show some of her wonderful tricks.

"Then she got a pock, and showed that it was empty; and she gave it a shake, and it grew thick, and she put in her hand and took out a silver hen, and she set it on the ground, and it rose and walked about the house. Then came the golden cock, and the grain of corn, and the pecking, and the hen said—

> "Leig ma choir leam,
> Ma chuid do n' eorna."

Leave me my right, my share of the corn; and the cock pecked her; and she stood out from him, and said—

Geog Geog Geōa.   Geog Geog Geōa.

An cuimhne leat an latha chuir mi m' bathach falamh air do shon?	Dost thou remember the day that I emptied the byre for thee?
'S an cuimhne leat an latha a thubh mi n' sabhal air do shon?	Dost thou remember the day that I thatched the barn for thee?
'S an cuimhne leat an latha ghlac mi n'fhailair air do shon?	Dost thou remember the day that I caught the filly for thee?
'S an cuimhne leat an latha bhàth mi m'athair air do shon?	Dost thou remember the day that I drowned my father for thee?

Then the king's son thought a little and he remembered Auburn Mary, and all she had done for him, and he asked a voice with her apart, and they had a little talk, and she told the king and the queen, and he found the "gin" kin good, and he turned his back on the other one, and he married Auburn Mary, and they made a wedding that lasted seven years; and the last day was no worse than the first day—

> S'ma bha na b'fhearr ann, bha,
> S'mar robh leig da

And if there were better there were,
And if not, let them be.

The tale is ended.
Tha crioch air 'n sgeul.

This version is probably the oldest. It is the most picturesque; it contains nearly all that is in the others, and it is full of the quaint expressions which characterize the telling of Gaelic tales. The quarrel is remarkably like a fable aimed at the greédy *castle* mouse and the sturdy *country* wren, a fable from the country side, for the birds beat the beasts of the plain, the raven beat the snake.

8.   I have still another version, told by Roderick Mackenzie, sawyer, Gairloch, and written by Hector Urquhart. It is called, NIGHEAN DUBH GHEAL DEARG, The Daughter of Black-white Red.

Three sons of the king of Erin were on a day playing shinny on a strand, and they saw birds whose like they had never seen, and one especially. Their father told them that this was MAC SAMHLADH NIGHINN DUBH GHEAL DEARG, and the eldest son said that he would never rest till he got the great beautiful bird for himself. Then his father sent him to the king of France (NA FRAINGE), and he struck palm on latch, and it was asked who it was, and he said that he was the son of Erin's king, going to seek the daughter of Black-white Red. He was entertained, and next day set off to the king of Spain (NA SPAINDE), and did the same; and thence he went to the king of Italy (NA H'EADILT). He gave him an old man, BODACH, and a green boat, and they sailed (and here comes in a bit of the passage which is common to so many stories about hoisting the sails, etc., with one or two lines that I have found nowhere else, and here the three kings seem to replace the three old women, who are always appearing, for they know where the lad is going, and help him on). The old man sailed the boat on shore, and up to the door of Black-white Red, a giant, who as usual said FIU FA FOAGRAICH, and threatened to make a shinny ball of his head, and eat him unless he performed the tasks set him. The giant's eldest daughter came, and he knew her at once, and they played at cards all night. She gave him a tether to catch the little dun shaggy filly, which he would lose unless he put it on the first time.

Next he had to kill, TARBH MOR NA TANICH, the great bull of the cattle, (or perhaps of the earth, TAN). The daughter gave him her father's BOGHA SAIGHEAD, arrow bow, with which he pushed at the bull, and he followed him. He put the big black arrow in his forehead when he got to the house.

The third task was to cleanse the great byre of the seven stalls that had not been cleansed for seven years, or his head to be a football. The daughter came at night as usual and gave him BARA agus

CROMAN, a barrow and a crook, and told him to say CAB CAB A CHROMAIN, CUIR AIR A BHARA A SHLUASAID, CUIR A MACH A BHARA, and the tools worked of themselves.

Then he had three more tasks set. The three daughters put three needles through three holes in a partition, he caught the one without "CHRO." (?) They put out three great pins, and he caught the one that had two "PHLOC" heads. Then they pushed out their little fingers, and he took the one with, CAB AS AN IONGA, a notch in the nail.

"Hugh! huh!" said the giant, "thou hast her now, but to Erin thou goest not; thou must stay with me." At last they got out the barge (BIRLINN). The giant awoke and asked, what was that sound? One of the daughters answered, that it was a OIDHCHE UAMHASACH LE TEIN-ADHAIR 'S TAIRNEANACH, a fearful night with heaven-fire and thunder. "It is well to be under the shelter of a rock," said the giant. The next scrape of the boat it was the same thing, and at the third the barge was out and under sail, but the giant was on foot, aud he threw A CHEARTLEADH DHUBH, his black clue, and the boat sailed stern foremost. The giant sat down in the gravel to haul the boat, and the daughter shot an arrow, ANN AM BONN DUBH AN FHAMHAIR, into the giant's black sole, and there he lay.

Then they got to Erin. He went home first; she staid in the barge, till tired of waiting, she went to a smith's house where she staid with the smith and his mother.

One day the smith heard that the RIDIR was going to be married, and told her. She sent him to the palace to tell the cook that the finest woman he ever saw was living with him, and would marry him if he would bring her part of the wedding feast.

The cook came, and when he saw her, brought a back load of viands. Then they played the same trick to the butler, and he brought a back load of wine every day. Then she asked the smith to make her a golden cock, and a silver hen; and when he could not, she made them herself. Then she asked the butler if she could get a sight of the king's son and the bride, "and the butler was very much pleased that she had asked him, and not the cook, for he was much afraid that the cook was looking after her also." When the gentles saw her they asked her to the dancing room, and then came the cock and hen play, in which the hen said—A CHOILICH DHURDANICH DHUIBH, Thou black murmuring cock, dost thou remember, etc. The prince remembers, marries the true girl, "and there I left them."

This version varies considerably from the others. It is very well told, and I much regret that space will not allow me to give it entire, the more so because the reciter has braved the prejudices of some of his neighbours who object to all fiction. I hope I have said enough to show that this story is worth preservation.

If stories be mythological this contains a serpent. NATHAIR, pronounced *Na-ir,* and a raven, FITHEACH, pronounced *Feeach,* who seem like transformed divinities, for they appear only to start the other characters, and then vanish into some undescribed kingdom. There is one passage (referred to) which resembles Norse mythology.

So far as I can make out, it seems to be best known near Cowal in Argyllshire, though it is known throughout the Highlands.

It would have been easy to construct one version from the eight here mentioned, but I have preferred to give the most complete, entire, and full abstracts of the rest. Many more versions can be got, and I shall be grateful to anyone who will throw light on the story and its origin.

One of the tasks resembles one of those imposed on Hercules. It might have been taken from classical mythology if it stood alone, but Norwegian peasants and West Highlanders could not so twist the story of Hercules into the same shape.

All the Gaelic versions are clearly versions of the same story as the Master Maid, in Dasent's Norse Tales; and there are other traits in other Norse stories, which resemble the Gaelic.

Of the forty-three heroes called Hercules, and mentioned in ancient lore, one, at least, is said to have made long voyages in the Atlantic beyond his own pillars. Another, or the same, was prevented from being present at the hunting of the Caledonian boar, having killed a man in "Calydo," which, by the way, is Gaelic for Black Forest. Another was an Indian, and this may be one of the same clan.

If stories be distorted history of real events, seen through a haze of centuries, then the giants in this tale may be the same people as the Gruagach and his brother in the last. They are here described as a wise learned race, given to magic arts, yellow or auburn haired. (RUADH) possessing horses, and knowing how to tame them—able to put the water between them and their pursuers—able to sew better than the others—better looking—musical—possessing treasure and bright weapons—using king's sons of other races as slaves, and threatening to eat them. If the raven was one, they were given to combing their own golden ringlets with gold and silver combs and the giant maidens dressed the hair of their lovers who laid their heads in their laps, as I have often seen black haired Lapland ladies dress the hair of Lapland swains, and as ladies in popular tales of all lands always do. I will not venture to guess who this race may have been, but the race who contended with them would seem to have been dark complexioned. Nearly all the heroines of Gaelic songs are fair or yellow haired. Those are dark who now most admire yellow locks. A dark Southern once asked if a golden haired youth from the north had dyed his hair, for nothing natural could be so beautiful. Dark

Celts and fair northmen certainly met and fought, and settled and intermarried, on the western isles and coasts, where this tale is current, but I am told that it has traits which are to be found in Eastern manuscripts, which were old long before the wars of the Northmen, of which we know, began. The task I have undertaken is to gather stories, not to account for them, but this much is sure, either Norway got this from Scotland or Scotland from Norway, when they were almost one country, or both got it from the same source. The Gaelic stories resemble each other about as much as they all resemble the Norse. The translation was published in 1859, and this story has been current in the islands at least for 40 years. I can remember to have heard part of it myself more than 20 years ago. I believe there is an Irish version, though I have not met with it in any book. I have traced the story amongst Irish labourers in London, who have told me that they used in their young days to sit about the fire whole winter nights, and tell about the fight between the raven and the snake; about the giants, Fin MacCoul and Conan Maol, "who had never a good word for any one," and similar tales. My informants were from Cork, their language, though difficult, could be made out from a knowledge of Gaelic only.

The bridle described seems to be the old Highland bridle which is still common. It has no bit, but two plates of wood or iron are placed at right angles to the horse's mouth, and are joined above and below by a rope, which is often made of horse-hair, leather, or twisted bent. The horse's nose goes INTO IT.

The ladder is also the Highland ladder still common in cottages. It consists of a long stick with pegs stuck *through* it.

There are many stories in Grimm's German collection which resemble the Battle of the Birds. They have incidents in common, arranged somewhat in the same order; but the German stories, taken together, have a character of their own, as the Gaelic versions have: and both differ from the Norwegian tale. Each new Gaelic version which comes to me (and I have received several since this was written), varies from the rest, but resembles them; and no single version is like any one of the German tales, though German, Norse, and Gaelic all hang together.

3

THE TALE OF THE HOODIE.

From Ann MacGilvray, Islay.—April 1859.

There was ere now a farmer, and he had three daughters. They were waulking* clothes at a river. A hoodie† came round and he said to the eldest one, "M-POS-U-MI, Wilt thou wed me, farmer's daughter?" "I won't wed thee, thou ugly brute. An ugly brute is the hoodie," said she. He came to the second one on the morrow, and he said to her, "M-POS-U-MI, wilt thou wed me?" "Not I, indeed," said she; "an ugly brute is the hoodie." The third day he said to the youngest, M-POS-U-MI, "Wilt thou wed me, farmer's daughter?" "I will wed thee," said she; "a pretty creature is the hoodie," and on the morrow they married.

The hoodie said to her, "Whether wouldst thou rather that I should be a hoodie by day, and a man at night; or be a hoodie at night, and a man by day?" "I would rather that thou wert a man by day, and a hoodie at night," says she. After this he was a splendid fellow by day, and a hoodie at night. A few days after they married he took her with him to his own house.

At the end of three quarters they had a son. In the night there came the very finest music that ever was heard about the house. Every man slept, and the child was taken away. Her father came to the door in the morning, and he asked how were all there. He was very sorrowful that the child should be taken away, for fear that he should be blamed for it himself.

At the end of three quarters again they had another son. A watch was set on the house. The finest of music came, as it came before,

* *Postadh.* A method of washing clothes practised in the Highlands—viz., by dancing on them barefoot in a tub of water.
† Hoodie—the Royston crow—a very common bird in the Highlands; a sly, familiar, knowing bird, which plays a great part in these stories. He is common in most parts of Europe.

about the house; every man slept, and the child was taken away. Her father came to the door in the morning. He asked if every thing was safe; but the child was taken away, and he did not know what to do for sorrow.

Again, at the end of three quarters they had another son. A watch was set on the house as usual. Music came about the house as it came before; every one slept, and the child was taken away. When they rose on the morrow they went to another place of rest that they had, himself and his wife, and his sister-in-law. He said to them by the way, "See that you have not forgotten any thing." The wife said, "I FORGOT MY COARSE COMB." The coach in which they were fell a withered faggot, and he went away as a hoodie.

Her two sisters returned home, and she followed after him. When he would be on a hill top, she would follow to try and catch him; and when she would reach the top of a hill, he would be in the hollow on the other side. When night came, and she was tired, she had no place of rest or dwelling; she saw a little house of light far from her, and though far from her she was not long in reaching it.

When she reached the house she stood deserted at the door. She saw a little laddie about the house, and she yearned to him exceedingly. The housewife told her to come up, that she knew her cheer and travel. She laid down, and no sooner did the day come than she rose. She went out, and when she was out, she was going from hill to hill to try if she could see a hoodie. She saw a hoodie on a hill, and when she would get on the hill the hoodie would be in the hollow, when she would go to the hollow, the hoodie would be on another hill. When the night came she had no place of rest or dwelling. She saw a little house of light far from her, and if far from her she was not long reaching it. She went to the door. She saw a laddie on the floor to whom she yearned right much. The housewife laid her to rest. No earlier came the day than she took out as she used. She passed this day as the other days. When the night came she reached a house. The housewife told her to come up, that she knew her cheer and travel, that her man had but left the house a little while, that she should be clever, that this was the last night she would see him, and not to sleep, but to strive to seize him. She slept, he came where she was, and he let fall a ring on her right hand. Now when she awoke she tried to catch hold of him, and she caught a feather of his wing. He left the feather with her, and he went away. When she rose in the morning she did not know what she should do. The housewife said that he had gone over a hill of poison over which she could not go without horseshoes on her hands and feet. She gave her man's clothes, and she told her to go to learn smithying till she should be able to make horse shoes for herself.

She learned smithying so well that she made horseshoes for her hands and feet. She went over the hill of poison. That same day after she had gone over the hill of poison, her man was to be married to the daughter of a great gentleman that was in the town.

There was a race in the town that day, and every one was to be at the race but the stranger that had come over to poison hill. The cook came to her, and he said to her, Would she go in his place to make the wedding meal, and that he might get to the race.

She said she would go. She was always watching where the bridegroom would be sitting.

She let fall the ring and the feather in the broth that was before him. With the first spoon he took up the ring, with the next he took up the feather. When the minister came to the fore to make the marriage, he would not marry till he should find out who had made ready the meal. They brought up the cook of the gentleman, and he said that *this* was not the cook who made ready the meal.

They brought up now the one who had made ready the meal. He said, "That now was his married wife." The spells went off him. They turned back over the hill of poison, she throwing the horse shoes behind her to him, as she went a little bit forward, and he following her. When they came back over the hill, they went to the three houses in which she had been. These were the houses of his sisters, and they took with them the three sons, and they came home to their own house, and they were happy.

Written down by Hector Maclean, schoolmaster at Ballygrant, in Islay, from the recitation of "Ann MacGilvray, a Cowal woman, married to a farmer at Kilmeny, one Angus Macgeachy from Campbelltown." Sent April 14, 1859.

The Gaelic of this tale is the plain everyday Gaelic of Islay and the West Highlands. Several words are variously spelt, but they are variously pronounced—falbh, folbh, tigh, taighe, taighean. There is one word, Tapaidh, which has no English equivalent; it is like *Tapper* in Swedish.

———

URSGEUL NA FEANNAIG.

Bha tuathanach ann roimhe so; agus bha triùir nighean aige. Bha eud a' postadh aig obhainn. Thàinig feannag mu'n cuairt's thuirt e

ris an té bu shine, "Am pòs thu mise a nighean an tuathanaich."
"Cha phòs mis' thu 'bheathaich ghrànnda: is grannda am beathach
an fheannag," ars'ise. Thàinig e thun na dàrna té an la 'r na
mhàireach, 's thuirt e rithe, "Am pòs thu mise." "Cha phòs mi
féin," ars'ise; " 's grànnda am beathach an fheannag." An treas la
thuirt e ris an te b'òige, "Am phòs thu mise, a nighean an
tuathanaich." "Pòsaidh," ars'ise; "s bòidheach am beathach an
fheannag." An la'r na mhàireach phòs èud. Thuirt an fheannag
rithe, "Cò 'ca is fheàrr leat mise a bhith am fheannag 'san latha
'sam dhuine 'san oidhche, na bhith 'san oidhche am fheannag 's
am dhuine 'san latha?" " 'S fhearr leam thu bhith a'd' dhuine 'san
latha 's a'd' fheannag 'san oidhche," ars'ise. As a dhèigh so bha e
na òganach ciatach 'san latha, 's'na fheannag 's an oidhche. Am
beagan làithean an déigh dhaibh pòsadh thug e leis i 'ga 'thigh féin.
Ann an ceann tri ràithean bha mac aca. Anns an oidhche thàinig
an aon cheòl tìmchiol an taighe bu bhòidhche 'chualas riamh.
Chaidil a h-uile duine, 's thugadh air folbh am pàisde. Thainig a
h-athair thun an doruisd sa mhadainn. Dh' fheòraich e dé mur a
bha h-uile h-aon an siod; 's bha duilichinn mhòr air gun tugadh air
folbh am pàisde, eagal agus gum biodh coir' air a dhèanadh air féin
air a shon. Ann an ceann tri ràithean a rithisd bha mac eile aca.
Chuireadh faire air an tigh. Thàinig ceòl ra bhòidheach mar a
thàinig roimhid timchoill an taighe; chaidil a h-uile duine 's
thugadh air folbh am pàisde. Thàinig a h-athair thun an doruisd sa
mhaidainn dh'fheòraich e an robh gach ni ceart; ach bha 'm pàisde
air a thoirt air folbh, 's cha robh fhiòs aige dé a dhèanadh e leis an
duilichinn. Ann an ceann tri ràithean a rithisd bha mac eile aca.
Chaidh faire 'chur air an tigh mar a b' àbhaist. Thàinig ceòl
timchioll an taighe mar a thàinig roimhid; chaidil gach neach, 's
thugadh am pàisde air folbh. Nur a dh' éiridh iad an la 'r na
mhàireach chaidh iad gu hàite tàmh eile a bha aca, e fein 's a' bhean,
's a' phiuthar chéile. Thuirt e riu air an rathad, "Feuch nach do
dhichuimhnich sibh ni 'sam, bith." Urs' a' bhean,
"DHIOCHUIMHNICH MI MO CHIR GHARBH." Thuit an carbad anns
an robh eud 'na chual chrìonaicch, s dh' fhalbh esan 'na fheannag.
Thill a dha phiuthair dhachaidh 's dh' fholbh ise 'na dhéighsan.
Nur a bhiodh esan air mullach cnoic leanadh ise e feuch am
beireadh i air, 's nur a ruigeadh ise mullach a chnoic bhiodh esan
san lag an taobh eile. Nur a thàing an oidhche 's i sgìth, cha robh
àite tàmh na fuireachd aice. Chunnaic i tigh beag soluisd fada uaithe
's ma b' fhada uaithe cha b' fhada a bha ise 'ga ruigheachd. Nur a
ràinig i an tigh sheas i gu dìblidh aig an dorusd. Chunnaic i balachan

beag feadh an taighe, s theòigh i ris gu h-anabarrach. Thuirt bean an taighe rithe tighinn a nìos, gu robh fios a seud 's a suibhail aice-se. Chaidh i laidhe, 's cha bu luaithe thainig an latha na dh' éiridh i. Chaidh i 'mach, 's nur a bha i 'mach bha i o chnoc gu cnoc feuch am faiceadh i feannag. Chunnaic i feannag air cnoc, 's nur a rachadh ise air a' chnoc bhiodh an fheannag 'san lag, nur a rachadh i do'n lag bhiodh an fheannag air cnoc eile. Nur a thàinig an oidhche cha robh àite taimh na fuireachd aice. Chunnaic i tigh beag soluisd fada uaithe 's ma b' fhada uaithe cha b' fhada 'bha ise 'g a ruigheachd. Chaidh i gus an dorusd. Chunnaic i balachan air an urlar ris an do theòigh i gu ra mhòr. Chuir bean an taighe a laidhe i. Cha bu mhoich' a thàinig an latha na ghabh i 'mach mar a b'àbhaist. Chuir i seachad an latha so mar no làithean eile. Nur a thàinig an oidhche ràinig i tigh. Thuirt bean an taighe rithe tighinn a nìos; gu 'robh fios a seud 's a siubhail aice-se; nach d' rinn a fear ach an tigh fhàgail bho cheann tiota beag; i 'bhith tapaidh, gum b' i siod an oidhche ma dheireadh dhi fhaicinn, 's gun i 'chadal, ach strì ri gréim a dhèanadh air. Chaidil ise, 's thàinig esan far an robh i, 's lig e tuiteam do dh' fhàinn, air a làimh dheas. Nur a dhuisg ise an so thug i làmh air breith air, 's rug i air ite d'a sgéith. Leig e leatha an ite, 's dh' fhalbh e. Nur a dh' éiridh i 'sa mhadainn cha robh fios aice dé a dheànadh i. Thuirt bean an taighe gu'n deach e thairis air cnoc neamh air nach b'urrainn ise dol thairis gun chrùidhean d'a làmhan agus d'a casan. Thug i dhi aodach fir 's thuirt i rithe dol a dh' ionnsachadh na goibhneachd gus am biodh i comasach air crùidhean a dhèanadh dhì féin. Dh' ionnsaich i 'ghoibhneachd cho math 's gun d' rinn i crùidhean d'a làmhan agus d'a casan. Dh 'fholbh i thairis air a chnoc neamh. An latha sin féin an déigh dhi dol thairis air a chnoc neamh bha pòsadh ri bhith aig a fear ri nighean duine uasail mhòir a bha 'sa bhaile. Bha rèis anns a bhaile an latha sin, s bha h-uile h-aon ri bhith aig an rèis ach an coigreach a thàinig thairis air a' chnoc neamh. Thainig an còcaire a h-ionnsuidh, 's thuirt e rithe an rachadh i 'na àite a dhèanadh biadh na bainnse, 's gu 'faigheadh e dol thun na réise. Thuirt i gu' rachadh. Bha i furachail daonnan càite am biodh fear na bainnse 'na shuidhe. Lig i tuiteam do 'n fhàinne agus do 'n ite 'sa bhrot a bha air a bheulaobh. Leis a chiad spàin thog e'm fàinne, s leis an ath spàin thog e 'n ite. Nur a thàinig am ministir a làthair a dheanadh a phòsaidh cha phòsaidh esan gus am faigheadh e fios co a rinn am biadh. Thug iad a' làthair còcaire an duine uasail, 's thuirt esan nach b' e siod an còcaire a rinn am biadh. Thug iad an làthair an so an t-aon a rinn am biadh. Thuirt esan gum b'e siod a' bhean phòsda-san a nis. Dh' fholbh na geasan dheth. Thill iad air an ais thairis air a' chnoc neamh; ise a tilgeil nan crùidhean as a deigh da 'ionnsuidhsan nur a thigeadh i treis air a h-aghaidh, 's esan 'ga leantainn. Nur a thàinig eud air an ais thar a' chnoic, chaidh iad thun nan tri taighean anns an robh ise. B'e sin tri taighean a pheathraichean-san, thug iad leo an tri mic. Thàinig iad dhachaidh g'an tigh féin, 's bha iad gu toilichte.

HECTOR MACLEAN.

2.   I have a great many versions of this tale in Gaelic; for example, one from Cowal, written from memory by a labourer, John Dewar. These are generally wilder and longer than the version here given.

This has some resemblance to an infinity of other stories. For example—Orpheus, Cupid and Psyche, Cinderella's Coach, The Lassie and her Godmother (Norse tales), East o' the Sun and West o' the Moon (ditto), The Master Maid (ditto), Katie Wooden Cloak (ditto), The Iron Stove (Grimm), The Woodcutter's Child (ditto), and a tale by the Countess d'Aulnoy, Prince Cherie.

If this be history, it is the story of a wife taken from an inferior but civilized race. The farmer's daughter married to the Flayer "FEANNAG," deserted by her husband for another in some distant, mythical land, beyond far away mountains, and bringing him back by steady, fearless, persevering fidelity and industry.

If it be mythology, the hoodie may be the raven again, and a transformed divinity. If it relates to races, the superior race again had horses—for there was to be a race in the town, and every one was to be at it, but the stranger who came over the hill; and when they travelled it was in a coach, which was sufficiently wonderful to be magical, and here again the comb is mixed up with the spells.

There is a stone at Dunrobin Castle, in Sutherland, on which a comb is carved with other curious devices, which have never been explained. Within a few hundred yards in an old grave composed of great slabs of stone, accidentally discovered on a bank of gravel, a man's skeleton was found with teeth worn down, though perfectly sound, exactly like those of an old horse. It is supposed that the man must have ground his teeth on dried peas and beans—perhaps on meal, prepared in sandstone querns. Here, at least, is the COMB near to the grave of the farmer. The comb which is so often found with querns in the old dwellings of some pre-historic race of Britons; the comb which is a civilized instrument, and which in these stories is always a coveted object worth great exertions, and often magical.

4

THE SEA-MAIDEN.

From John Mackenzie, fisherman, near Inverary.

There was ere now a poor old fisher, but on this year he was not getting much fish. On a day of days, and he fishing, there rose a sea-maiden at the side of his boat, and she asked him if he was getting fish. The old man answered, and he said that he was not. "What reward wouldst thou give me for sending plenty of fish to thee?" "Ach!" said the old man, "I have not much to spare." "Wilt thou give me the first son thou hast?" said she. "It is I that would give thee that, if I were to have a son; there was not, and there will not be a son of mine," said he, "I and my wife are grown so old." "Name all thou hast." "I have but an old mare of a horse, an old dog, myself and my wife. There's for thee all the creatures of the great world that are mine." "Here, then, are three grains for thee that thou shalt give thy wife this very night, and three others to the dog, and these three to the mare, and these three likewise thou shalt plant behind thy house, and in their own time thy wife will have three sons, the mare three foals, and the dog three puppies, and there will grow three trees behind thy house, and the trees will be a sign, when one of the sons dies, one of the trees will wither. Now, take thyself home, and remember me when thy son is three years of age, and thou thyself wilt get plenty of fish after this." Everything happened as the sea-maiden said, and he himself was getting plenty of fish; but when the end of the three years was nearing, the old man was growing sorrowful, heavy hearted, while he failed each day as it came. On the namesake of the day, he went to fish as he used, but he did not take his son with him.

The sea-maiden rose at the side of the boat, and asked, "Didst thou bring thy son with thee hither to me?" "Och! I did not bring him. I forgot that this was the day." "Yes! yes! then," said the

sea-maiden; "thou shalt get four other years of him, to try if it be
easier for thee to part from him. Here thou hast his like age," and
she lifted up a big bouncing baby. "Is thy son as fine as this one?"
He went home full of glee and delight, for that he had got four other
years of his son, and he kept on fishing and getting plenty of fish,
but at the end of the next four years sorrow and woe struck him,
and he took not a meal, and he did not a turn, and his wife could
not think what was ailing him. This time he did not know what to
do, but he set it before him, that he would not take his son with
him this time either. He went to fish as at the former times, and the
sea-maiden rose at the side of the boat, and she asked him, "Didst
thou bring thy son hither to me?" "Och! I forgot him this time too,"
said the old man. "Go home then," said the sea-maiden, "and at
the end of seven years after this, thou art sure to remember me, but
then it will not be the easier for thee to part with him, but thou shalt
get fish as thou used to do."

The old man went home full of joy; he had got seven other years
of his son, and before seven years passed, the old man thought that
he himself would be dead, and that he would see the sea-maiden
no more. But no matter, the end of those seven years was nearing
also, and if it was, the old man was not without care and trouble.
He had rest neither day nor night. The eldest son asked his father
one day if any one were troubling him? The old man said that some
one was, but that belonged neither to him nor to any one else. The
lad said he *must* know what it was. His father told him at last how
the matter was between him and the sea-maiden. "Let not that put
you in any trouble," said the son; "I will not oppose you." "Thou
shalt not; thou shalt not go, my son, though I should not get fish
for ever." "If you will not let me go with you, go to the smithy, and
let the smith make me a great strong sword, and I will go to the end
of fortune." His father went to the smithy, and the smith made a
doughty sword for him. His father came home with the sword. The
lad grasped it and gave it a shake or two, and it went in a hundred
splinters. He asked his father to go to the smithy and get him
another sword in which there should be twice as much weight; and
so did his father, and so likewise it happened to the next sword—it
broke in two halves. Back went the old man to the smithy; and the
smith made a great sword, its like he never made before. "There's
thy sword for thee," said the smith, "and the fist must be good that
plays this blade." The old man gave the sword to his son, he gave
it a shake or two. "This will do," said he; "it's high time now to
travel on my way." On the next morning he put a saddle on the

black horse that the mare had, and he put the world under his head,* and his black dog was by his side. When he went on a bit, he fell in with the carcass of a sheep beside the road. At the carrion were a great dog, a falcon, and an otter. He came down off the horse, and he divided the carcass amongst the three. Three third shares to the dog, two third shares to the otter, and a third share to the falcon. "For this," said the dog, "if swiftness of foot or sharpness of tooth will give thee aid, mind me, and I will be at thy side." Said the otter, "If the swimming of foot on the ground of a pool will loose thee, mind me, and I will be at thy side." Said the falcon, "if hardship comes on thee, where swiftness of wing or crook of a claw will do good, mind me, and I will be at thy side." On this he went onward till he reached a king's house, and he took service to be a herd, and his wages were to be according to the milk of the cattle. He went away with the cattle, and the grazing was but bare. When lateness came (in the evening), and when he took (them) home they had not much milk, the place was so bare, and his meat and drink was but spare this night.

On the next day he went on further with them; and at last he came to a place exceedingly grassy, in a green glen, of which he never saw the like.

But about the time when he should go behind the cattle, for taking homewards, who is seen coming but a great giant with his sword in his hand. "HIU! HAU!! HOGARAICH!!!" says the giant. "It is long since my teeth were rusted seeking thy flesh. The cattle are mine; they are on my march; and a dead man art thou." "I said, not that," says the herd; "there is no knowing, but that may be easier to say than to do."

To grips they go—himself and the giant. He saw that he was far from his friend, and near his foe. He drew the great clean-sweeping sword, and he neared the giant; and in the play of the battle the black dog leaped on the giant's back. The herd drew back his sword, and the head was off the giant in a twinkling. He leaped on the black horse, and he went to look for the giant's house. He reached a door, and in the haste that the giant made he had left each gate and door open. In went the herd, and that's the place where there was magnificence and money in plenty, and dresses of each kind on the wardrobe with gold and silver, and each thing finer than the other. At the mouth of night he took himself to the king's house, but he took not a thing from the giant's house. And when the cattle were

* Took the world for his pillow.

milked this night there *was* milk. He got good feeding this night, meat and drink without stint, and the king was hugely pleased that he had caught such a herd. He went on for a time in this way, but at last the glen grew bare of grass, and the grazing was not so good.

But he thought he would go a little further forward in on the giant's land; and he sees a great park of grass. He returned for the cattle, and he puts them into the park.

They were but a short time grazing in the park when a great wild giant came full of rage and madness. "Hiu! Haw!! Hoagraich!!!" said the giant. "It is a drink of thy blood that quenches my thirst this night." "There is no knowing," said the herd, "but that's easier to say than to do." And at each other went the men. *There* was the shaking of blades! At length and at last it seemed as if the giant would get the victory over the herd. Then he called on his dog, and with one spring the black dog caught the giant by the neck, and swiftly the herd struck off his head.

He went home very tired this night, but it's a wonder if the king's cattle had not milk. The whole family was delighted that they had got such a herd.

He followed herding in this way for a time; but one night after he came home, instead of getting "all hail" and "good luck" from the dairymaid, all were at crying and woe.

He asked what cause of woe there was this night. The dairymaid said that a great beast with three heads was in the loch, and she was to get (some) one every year, and the lots had come this year on the king's daughter, "and in the middle of the day (to morrow) she is to meet the Uile Bheist at the upper end of the loch, but there is a great suitor yonder who is going to rescue her."

"What suitor is that?" said the herd. "Oh, he is a great General of arms," said the dairymaid, "and when he kills the beast, he will marry the king's daughter, for the king has said, that he who could save his daughter should get her to marry."

But on the morrow when the time was nearing, the king's daughter and this hero of arms went to give a meeting to the beast, and they reached the black corrie at the upper end of the loch. They were but a short time there when the beast stirred in the midst of the loch; but on the general's seeing this terror of a beast with three heads, he took fright, and he slunk away, and he hid himself. And the king's daughter was under fear and under trembling with no one at all to save her. At a glance, she sees a doughty handsome youth, riding a black horse, and coming where she was. He was

marvellously arrayed, and full armed, and his black dog moving
after him. "There is gloom on thy face, girl," said the youth. "What
dost thou here?" "Oh! that's no matter," said the king's daughter.
"It's not long I'll be here at all events." "I said not that," said he.
"A worthy fled as likely as thou, and not long since," said she. "He
is a worthy who stands the war," said the youth. He lay down beside
her, and he said to her, if he should fall asleep, she should rouse
him when she should see the beast making for shore. "What is
rousing for thee?" said she. "Rousing for me is to put the gold ring
on thy finger on my little finger." They were not long there when
she saw the beast making for shore. She took a ring off her finger,
and put it on the little finger of the lad. He awoke, and to meet the
beast he went with his sword and his dog. But there was the
spluttering and splashing between himself and the beast! The dog
was doing all he might, and the king's daughter was palsied by fear
of the noise of the beast. They would now be under, and now above.
But at last he cut one of the heads off her. She gave one roar RAIVIC,
and the son of earth, MACTALLA of the rocks (echo), called to her
screech, and she drove the loch in spindrift from end to end, and
in a twinkling she went out of sight. "Good luck and victory that
were following thee, lad!" said the king's daughter. "I am safe for
one night, but the beast will come again, and for ever, until the
other two heads come off her." He caught the beast's head, and he
drew a withy through it, and he told her to bring it with her there
to-morrow. She went home with the head on her shoulder, and the
herd betook himself to the cows, but she had not gone far when this
great General saw her, and he said to her that he would kill her, if
she would not say that 'twas he took the head off the beast. "Oh!"
says she, " 'tis I will say it, Who else took the head off the beast but
thou!" They reached the king's house, and the head was on the
General's shoulder. But here was rejoicing, that she should come
home alive and whole, and this great captain with the beast's head
full of blood in his hand. On the morrow they went away, and there
was no question at all but that this hero would save the king's
daughter.

   They reached the same place, and they were not long there when
the fearful Uile Bheist stirred in the midst of the loch, and the hero
slunk away as he did on yesterday, but it was not long after this
when the man of the black horse came, with another dress on. No
matter, she knew that it was the very same lad. "It is I am pleased
to see thee," said she. "I am in hopes thou wilt handle thy great
sword to-day as thou didst yesterday. Come up and take breath."

But they were not long there when they saw the beast steaming in the midst of the loch.

The lad lay down at the side of the king's daughter, and he said to her, "If I sleep before the beast comes, rouse me." "What is rousing for thee?" "Rousing for me is to put the ear-ring that is in thine ear in mine." He had not well fallen asleep when the king's daughter cried, "rouse! rouse!" but wake he would not; but she took the ear-ring out of her ear, and she put it in the ear of the lad. At once he woke, and to meet the beast he went, but *there* was Tloopersteich and Tlaperstich, rawceil s'tawceil, spluttering, splashing, raving and roaring on the beast! They kept on thus for a long time, and about the mouth of night, he cut another head off the beast. He put it on the withy, and he leaped on the black horse, and he betook himself to the herding. The king's daughter went home with the heads. The General met her, and took the heads from her, and he said to her, that she must tell that it was he who took the head off the beast this time also. "Who else took the head off the beast but thou?" said she. They reached the king's house with the heads. Then there was joy and gladness. If the king was hopeful the first night, he was now sure that this great hero would save his daughter, and there was no question at all but that the other head would be off the beast on the morrow.

About the same time on the morrow, the two went away. The officer hid himself as he usually did. The king's daughter betook herself to the bank of the loch. The hero of the black horse came, and he lay at her side. She woke the lad, and put another ear-ring in his other ear; and at the beast he went. But if rawceil and toiceil, roaring and raving were on the beast on the days that were passed, this day she was horrible. But no matter, he took the third head off the beast; and if he did, it was not without a struggle. He drew it through the withy, and she went home with the heads. When they reached the king's house, all were full of smiles, and the General was to marry the king's daughter the next day. The wedding was going on, and every one about the castle longing till the priest should come. But when the priest came, she would marry but the one who could take the heads off the withy without cutting the withy. "Who should take the heads off the withy but the man that put the heads on?" said the king.

The General tried them, but he could not loose them; and at last there was no one about the house but had tried to take the heads off the withy, but they could not. The king asked if there were any one else about the house that would try to take the heads off the withy? They said that the herd had not tried them yet. Word went for the herd; and he was not long throwing them hither and thither. "But stop a bit, my lad," said the king's daughter, "the man that took the heads off the beast, he has my ring and my two ear-rings." The herd put his hand in his pocket, and he threw them on the board. "Thou art my man," said the king's daughter. The king was not so pleased when he saw that it was a herd who was to marry his daughter, but he ordered that he should be put in a better dress; but his daughter spoke, and she said that he had a dress as fine as any that ever was in his castle; and thus it happened. The herd put on the giant's golden dress, and they married that same night.

They were now married, and everything going on well. They were one day sauntering by the side of the loch, and there came a beast more wonderfully terrible than the other, and takes him away to the loch without fear, or asking. The king's daughter was now mournful, tearful, blind-sorrowful for her married man; she was always with her eye on the loch. An old smith met her, and she told how it had befallen her married mate. The smith advised her to spread everything that was finer than another in the very same place where the beast took away her man; and so she did. The beast put up her nose, and she said, "Fine is thy jewellery, king's daughter." "Finer than that is the jewel that thou tookest from me," said she. "Give me one sight of my man, and thou shalt get any one thing of all these thou seest." The beast brought him up. "Deliver him to me, and thou shalt get all thou seest," said she. The beast did as she said. She threw him alive and whole on the bank of the loch.

A short time after this, when they were walking at the side of the loch, the same beast took away the king's daughter. Sorrowful was each one that was in the town on this night. Her man was mournful, tearful, wandering down and up about the banks of the loch, by day and night. The old smith met him. The smith told him that there was no way of killing the Uille Bheist but the one way, and this is it—"In the island that is in the midst of the loch is Eillid Chaisfhion—the white footed hind, of the slenderest legs, and the swiftest step, and though she should be caught, there would spring a hoodie out of her, and though the hoodie should be caught, there would spring a trout out of her, but there is an egg in the mouth of the trout, and the soul of the beast is in the egg, and if the eggs breaks, the beast is dead."

Now, there was no way of getting to this island, for the beast would sink each boat and raft that would go on the loch. He thought he would try to leap the strait with the black horse, and even so he did. The black horse leaped the strait, and the black dog with one bound after him. He saw the Eillid, and he let the black dog after her, but when the black dog would be on one side of the island, the Eillid would be on the other side. "Oh! good were now the great dog of the carcass of flesh here!" No sooner spoke he the word than the generous dog was at his side; and after the Eillid he took, and the worthies were not long in bringing her to earth. But he no sooner caught her than a hoodie sprang out of her. " 'Tis now, were good the falcon grey, of sharpest eye and swiftest wing!" No sooner said he this than the falcon was after the hoodie, and she was not long putting her to earth; and as the hoodie fell on the bank of the loch, out of her jumps the trout. "Oh, that thou wert by me now, oh otter!" No sooner said than the otter was at his side, and out on the loch she leaped, and brings the trout from the midst of the loch; but no sooner was the otter on shore with the trout than the egg came from his mouth. He sprang and he put his foot on it. 'Twas then the beast let out a roar, and she said, "Break not the egg, and thou gettest all thou askest." "Deliver to me my wife?" In the wink of an eye she was by his side. When he got hold of her hand in both his hands he let his foot (down) on the egg and the beast died.

The beast was dead now, and now was the sight to be seen. She was horrible to look upon. The three heads were off her doubtless, but if they were, there were heads under and heads over head on her, and eyes, and five hundred feet. But no matter, they left her there, and they went home, and there was delight and smiling in the king's house that night. And till now he had not told the king how he killed the giants. The king put great honour on him, and he was a great man with the king.

Himself and his wife were walking one day, when he noticed a little castle beside the loch in a wood; he asked his wife who was dwelling in it? She said that no one would be going near that castle, for that no one had yet come back to tell the tale, who had gone there.

"The matter must not be so," said he; "this very night I will see who is dwelling in it." "Go not, go not," said she; "there never went man to this castle that returned." "Be that as it pleases," says he. He went; he betakes himself to the castle. When he reached the door, a little flattering crone met him standing in the door. "All hail and good luck to thee, fisher's son; 'tis I myself am pleased to see thee; great is the honour for this kingdom, thy like to be come into it—thy coming in is fame for this little bothy; go in first; honour to the gentles; go on, and take breath." In he went, but as he was going up, she drew the Slachdan druidhach on him, on the back of his head, and at once—there he fell.

On this night there was woe in the king's castle, and on the morrow there was a wail in the fisher's house. The tree is seen withering, and the fisher's middle son said that his brother was dead, and he made a vow and oath, that he would go, and that he would know where the corpse of his brother was lying. He put saddle on a black horse, and rode after his black dog; (for the three sons of the fisher had a black horse and a black dog), and without going hither or thither he followed on his brother's step till he reached the king's house.

This one was so like his elder brother, that the king's daughter thought it was her own man. He stayed in the castle. They told him how it befell his brother; and to the little castle of the crone, go he must—happen hard or soft as it might. To the castle he went; and just as befell the eldest brother, so in each way it befell the middle son, and with one blow of the Slachdan druidhach, the crone felled him stretched beside his brother.

On seeing the second tree withering, the fisher's youngest son said that now his two brothers were dead, and that he must know what death had come on them. On the black horse he went, and he followed the dog as his brothers did, and he hit the king's house before he stopped. 'Twas the king who was pleased to see him; but to the black castle (for that was its name) they would not let him go. But to the castle he must go; and so he reached the castle.— "All hail and good luck to thyself, fisher's son: 'tis I am pleased to see thee; go in and take breath," said she (the crone). "In before me thou crone: I don't like flattery out of doors; go in and let's hear thy speech." In went the crone, and when her back was to him he drew his sword and whips her head off; but the sword flew out of his hand. And swift the crone gripped her head with both hands, and puts it on her neck as it was before. The dog sprung on the crone, and she struck the generous dog with the club of magic; and there he lay. But this went not to make the youth more sluggish. To grips with the crone he goes; he got a hold of the Slachan druidhach, and with one blow on the top of the head, she was on earth in the wink of an eye. He went forward, up a little, and he sees his two brothers lying side by side. He gave a blow to each one with the Slachdan druidhach and on foot they were, and there was the spoil! Gold and silver, and each thing more precious than another, in the crone's castle. They came back to the king's house, and then there was rejoicing! The king was growing old.

The eldest son of the fisherman was crowned king, and the pair of brothers stayed a day and a year in the king's house, and then the two went on their journey home, with the gold and silver of the crone, and each other grand thing which the king gave them; and if they have not died since then, they are alive to this very day.

Written, April 1850, by Hector Urquhart, from the dictation of John Mackenzie, fisherman, Kenmore, near Inverary, who says that he learned it from an old man in Lorn many years ago. He has lived for thirty-six years at Kenmore. He told the tale fluently at first, and then dictated it slowly.

The Gaelic is given as nearly as possible in the words used by Mackenzie, but he thinks his story rather shortened.

———

A MHAIGHDEAN MHARA.

Bha ann roimhe so, sean iasgair bochd, ach air a bhliadhna so, cha robh e faotainn a bheag do dh'iasg. Latha do na laithean 's e 'giasgach, dh' eirich maighdean-mhara ri taobh a bhàta, 's dh' fheòraich i dheth, An robh e faotainn a bheag do dh'iasg? Fhreagair an seann duine, 's thubhairt e nach robh. "De 'n duais a bheireadh tu dhòmhsa airson pailteas éisg a chuir thugad?" "Ach!" ars' an seann duine, "Cha 'n 'eil a bheag agamsa ri sheachnadh." "An toir thu dhomh an cèud mhac a bhitheas agad?" ars' ise. " 'S mise a bheireadh sin dhuit na 'm biodh mac agam; cha robh 's cha bhi mac agamsa," ars' esan; "tha mi féin 's mo bhean air cinntinn co sean. 'Ainmich na bheil agud.' Cha 'n 'eil agamsa ach seann làir eich, seana ghalla choin, mi féin 's mo bhean; sin agadsa na tha chreutairean an t-saoghail mhòr agamsa." "So agad, mata, trì spilgeanan a bheir thu do d' mhnaoi air an oidhche nochd, agus trì eile do 'n ghalla, agus an trì so do 'n chapull, agus an trì so mar an ceudna, cuiridh tu air cùl do thighe; agus 'nan am fein bithidh triùir mhac aig do bhean, tri searraich aig an làir, tri cuileanan aig a ghalla, agus cinnidh tri chraobhan air cùl do thighe, agus bithidh na craobhan 'nan samhladh; 'nuair a bhasaicheas a h-aon do na mic seargaidh té do na craobhan. Nis, thoir do thigh ort, agus coinnich mise dur a bhitheas do mhac tri bliadhna 'dh' aois, 's gheibh thu féin pailteas eisg an déigh so." Thachair na h-uile ni mar a thubhairt a mhaighdean-mhara; agus bha e féin a faotainn pailteas éisg, ach a nuair a bha ceann nan tri bliadhna a dlùthachadh bha an seann duine a fàs cianail, trom-chridheach, 's e 'dol uaithe na h-uile latha mar bha teachd. Air comhainm an latha, chaidh e' dh' iasgachd mar a b'àbhaist, ach cha d'-thug e mhac leis.

Dh' éirich a mhaighdean-mhara ri taobh a bhàta, 's dh' fharraid i, "an d'-thug thu leat do mhac thugam?" "Ach! cha d'-thug, dhi-chuimhnich mi gu 'mi b'e so an latha." "Seadh! seadh! mata," ars' a mhaighdean-mhara, "gheibh thu ceithir bliadhn' eile dheth; faodaidh gur ann is usa dhuit dealachadh ris; so agad a chomhaoise," 'si togail suas leanabh brèagha sultmhor, "am bheil do mhac-sa cho brèagha ris?" Dh' fhalbh e dhachaidh làn sodain is sòlais, a chionn gu 'n d' fhuair e ceithir bliadhn' eile d'a mhac; 's bha e'g-iasgach 'sa' faotainn pailteas éisg. 'Ach an ceann na h-ath cheithir bliadhna, bhuail mulad 's bròn e, 's cha ghabhadh e lòn 's cha dèanadh e tùrn, 's cha robh a' bhean a tuigsinn dè a bha cur air. Air an am so, cha robh fios aige de 'dhèanadh e, ach chuir e roimhe, nach d'-thugadh e leis a mhac air an uair so nis mò. Dh'-fhalbh e dh' iasgach mar air na h-uairean roimhe, 's dh'èirich a mhaighdean-mhara ri taobh a bhàta, 's dh' fheòraich i dheth, "An d' thug thu thugam do mhac?" "Ach dhi-chuimhnuich mi e air an uair so cuideachd," ars' an seann duine. "Falbh dhachaidh, mata," ars' a mhaighdean-mhara, "agus an ceann seachd bliadhna na dheigh so, tha thu cinnteach mis' a choinneachadh; ach cha 'n ann an sin is usa dhuit dealachadh ris; ach gheibh thu iasg mar a b-àbhaist dhuit."

Chaidh an seann duine dhachaidh làn aoibhneis: fhuair e seachd bliadhn' eile d'a mhac! agus mu'n rachadh seachd bliadhna seachad, bha 'n seann duine a smuaineachadh gu 'm biodh e féin marbh, agus nach faiceadh e 'mhaighdean-mhara tuillidh. Ach coma co dhiu, bha ceann nan seachd bliadhna so a dlùthachadh cuideachd, agus ma 'bha cha robh an seann duine gun chùram a's trioblaid. Cha robh fois aige a latha na dh' oidhche. Dh' fheòraich am mac bu shine d'a athair, aon latha, an robh ni air bith a' cuir dragh air? Thubhairt an seann duine gu'n robh, ach nach buineadh sin dhàsan, na do neach air bith eile. Thubhairt an t-òganach gu 'm feumadh e fios fhaotainn air, 's dh'innis athair dha mu dheireadh mar a bha chuis eadar e féin 'sa mhaighdean-mhara. "Na cuireadh sin cùram 'sam bith oirbh," ars' am mac: "Cha téid, mise na 'r n-aghaidh." "Cha teid, cha teid, a mhic, ged nach faighinn iasg a chaoidh." "Mur leig sibh dhomh dol maille ribh, rachaibh do'n cheàrdach, agus deanadh an gobha claidheamh mòr làidir dhòmhsa, 's falbhaidh mi air ceann an fhortaín." Chaidh athair do 'n cheardaich, 's rinn an gobha claidheamh. Rug an t-òganach air 's thug e crathadh na dhà air, 's dh' fhalbh e 'na cheud spealg. Dh' iarr e air 'athair dol do'n cheàrdaich, agus claidheamh eile fhaotainn deanta, anns am bitheadh a dhà uiread do chudthrom; agus mar so rinn athair, agus air an dòigh cheudna thachair do 'n chlaidheamh; bhrist e na dha leth. Air ais chaidh an seann duine do'n cheàrdaich, agus rinn an gobha claidheamh mòr; a leithid, cha d' rinn e riamh roimhe. "So agad do chlaidheamh," ars' an gobha, " 's feumaidh an dorn a bhi maith a chluicheas an lann so." Thug an seann duine an claidheamh d'a mhac; thug e crathadh na dithis air; "Ni so feum," ars' am mac, " 's mithich a nis triall air mo thuras," ars' esan. Air maduinn an ath latha, chuir e dìollaid air an each dubh a bha aig an làir, agus thug e 'n saoghal fuidh' cheann 's an cùth dubh ri thaobh. 'N uair a chaidh e greis air aghaidh, thachair carcais caora ris aig taobh an rathaid. Aig a charcais bha madadh mòr, seabhag, agus dòbhran. Theirin e bhàr an eich, agus roinn e a' chlosach eadar an triùir. Tri trianan do'n mhadadh, da thrian do'n dòbhran, agus trian do'n t-seabhag. "Airson so," ars' am madadh, "Ma ni luathas chas na géire fiacail cobhair dhuit, cuimhnich ormsa, agus bithidh mi ri d' thaobh." Thubhairt an dòbhran, "Ma ni snàmh coise air grunnd linne fuasgladh ort, cuimhnich ormsa agus bithidh mi ri 'd' thaobh." Ars' an t-seabhag, "Ma thig cruaidh chàs ort, far an deàn luathas itean na crom ionga feum, cuimhnich ormas, 's bithidh mi ri 'd' thaobh." Ghabh e 'n so air aghaidh, gus an d'ràinig e tigh rìgh, 's ghabh e muinntearas gu bhi 'na bhuachaille, agus 's ann a réir 's na bhitheadh do bhainne aig a chrodh a bhiodh a thuarasdal. Chaidh e air falbh leis a chrodh, ach cha robh an t-ionaltradh ach lom. 'Nuair a thàinig an t-anmoch, 's a thug e dhachaidh iad, cha robh 'bheag do bhainn' aca, bha 'n t-àite co lom, 's cha robh 'bhaidh na 'dheoch ach suarrach air an oidhche so. Air an ath latha, ghabh e air adhart ni b' fhaide leo, agus mu dheireadh thàinig e gu àite anabarrach feurach, ann an gleann uaine nach fac e riamh a leithid. Ach mu am dha dol mu chùl a chruidh gu 'n tabhairt dhachaidh, co a chithear a' tighinn ach famhair mòr, 'sa chlaidheamh 'na làimh. "Hiu! Hau! Hoagraich!" ars' am famhair, " 's fada bho 'n bha meirg air m' fhiaclan ag iarraidh do chuid feola: 's leamsa 'n crodh, tha iad air mo chrìch, agus is duine marbh thusa." "Cha dubhairt mi sin," ars' am buachaille; "cha 'n 'eil fios nach usa sin a ràdh na dhèanamh."

Ann am badaibh a' cheile gabhar e féin 's am famhair. Chunnaic e gu 'n robh e fada bho a charaid 's dlu d'a nàmhaid. Tharruing e 'n claidheamh mòr nach fhagadh fuigheal beum, agus dhlùthaich e ris an fhamhair, agus ann am mireadh a chatha leum an cù dubh air cùl an fhamhair, 's tharruing am buachaill' a chlaidheamh 's bha 'n ceann do 'n fhamhair ann am prioba na sùil. Leum e air muin an eich dhuibh, agus chaidh e shealltainn airson tigh an fhamhair. Ràinig e 'n dorus, agus leis a' chabhaig, a bha air an fhamhair, dh' fhàg e gach geata 's gach dorus fosgailte. 'Steach chaidh am buachaille, agus 'sann an sin a bha 'n greadhnachas, òr 's airgiod ann am pailteas, 's trusgain dheth gach seòrsa air am faitheam le òr 's airgiod, 's gach ni bu rìomhaiche na cheile. Am beul na h-oidche thug e caisteal an rìgh air, ach cha d' thug e dad air bith leis a tigh an fhamhair; agus a nuair a chaidh an crodh a bhleoghan, 's ann an sin a bha 'm bainne. Fhuair e de bheatha mhaith air an oidhche so, biadh 's deoch gun ghainne, agus bha an rìgh anabarrach toilichte, gu 'n d' fhuair e greim air a leithid do bhuachaille. Chaidh e air aghaidh air son ùine air an dòigh so, ach mu dheireadh, dh' fhàs an gleann lom do dh' fheur, agus cha robh an t-ionaltradh cho maith. Ach smaoinich e gun rachadh e air aghaidh beagan ni b'fhaide a' stigh air còir an fhamhair, agus faicear pàirce mhòr do fheur. Thill e airson a chruidh agus cuirear a stigh do 'n phàirce iad. Cha robh iad ach goirid ag ionaltradh 'sa phàirce, 'nuair a thàinig famhair mòr, fiadhaich, lan fearg agus corruich "Héu! hò! hoagraich!" ars' am famhair, " 'se deoch do d' fhuil a chaisgeas mo phathadh a nochd." "Cha 'n' eil fios," ars' am buachaille, "Nach fasa sin a ràdh na dheanamh." Ach na cheile ghabh na fir, 's ann an sin a bha 'n crathadh lann. Mu dheireadh thall bha coltas air gu'm faigheadh am famhair buaidh air a bhuachaille. 'N sin ghlaodh e air a chù, agus le aon leum, rug an cù dubh air amhaich air an fhamhair, 's ghrad bhuail am buachaille an ceann de.

Chaidh e dhachaidh glé sgìth air an oidhche so, ach nu'r thaing, mar a' robh bainne aig crodh an righ! 's bha 'n teaglach air fad co toilichte air son gun d' fhuair iad a' leithid so do bhuachaille. Lean e air a bhuachailleachd air an dòigh so ré uine; ach oidhche 's e air tighinn dhachaidh, an àite do 'n bhanaraich furan's fàilte 'chur air, 's ann a bha iad air fad ri cumha 's ri bròn. Dh' fhoighneachd e de 'n t-aobhar bròin a bha' so an nochd. Thubhairt a bhanarach, gu 'n robh beist mhòr le tri chinn 'san loch, agus gu 'n robh i ri aon fhaotainn a h-uile bliadhna, agus gu 'n d' thàinig an crannchur am bliadhna air nighean an rìgh, " 's mu mheadhon latha 'màireach, tha i ri coinneachainn na huile-bhéist aig ceann shuas an loch; ach tha suiriche mòr an siud a tha 'dol g'a teàrnadh." "De 'n suiriche a tha ann?" thubhairt am buachaille. "O! tha Seanalair mòr airm," thubhairt a' bhanarach, "agus a nuair a mharbhas e 'bhéist, pòsaidh e nighean an rìgh; oir thubhairt an rìgh 'ge b'è theàrnadh a nighean, gu 'faigheadh e i ri phòsadh." Ach air an latha 'maireach, 'nuair a

bha an t-am a dluthachainn, dh' fhalbh nighean an righ 's an
gaisgeach airm so gu coinneamh a thabhairt do 'n bheist, 's rainig
iad an Coire dubh aig ceann shuas an loch. Cha robh iad ach goirid
an sin 'nuair a ghluais a bhéist ann am meadhon an loch; ach air
do'n t-Seanalair an t-uamhas bèiste so fhaicinn le tri chinn, ghabh
e eagal, 's shéap e air falbh 's dh' fhalaich e e fèin, 's bha nighean
an righ fo chrith 's fo eagal, gun neach ann a theàrnadh i. Sùil do
'n d' thug i faicear òganach foghainteach, dreachmhor a marcachd
each dubh 's a' tighinn far an robh i. Bha e air a sgeadachdainn gu
h-anabarrach 's fo làn armachd 's an cù dubh a' siubhal 'na dhéigh.
"Tha gruaim air do ghnùis, a nighean," ars, an t-òganach; "dè tha
thu deanadh an so?" "O! 's coma sin, thubhairt nighean an righ,
cha 'n fhad' a bhitheas mi ann co dhiu." "Cha dubhairt mi sin,"
ars' esan. "Theich laoch cho coltach riutsa, 's cha 'n 'eil fada
uaidhe," thubhairt ise. " 'Se laoch a sheasas cath," ars' an t-
òganach. Shuidh e sìos làimh rithe 's thubhairt e rithe, "Na 'n
tuiteadh esan 'na chadal, i ga 'dhùsgadh 'n uair a chitheadh i 'bhéist
a' deanamh air son tìr." "De 's dùsgadh duit," thubhairt ise? " 'S
dusgadh dhomh am fàinne th' air do mheur a chur air mo lughdag."
Cha b' fhada bha iad an sin, 'n uair a chunnaic i bhéist a dèanamh
gu tìr. Thug i 'm fàinne bhàr a meur, 's chuir i air lughdag an
òganaich e. Dhùisg e, agus an coinneamh na béiste ghabh e, le
'chlaidheamh 's le chù; ach 's ann an sin a bha 'n t-slupartaich 's
an t-slapartaich eadar e féin 's a' bhéist; 's bha 'n cù dèanamh na
b' urrainn e, 's bha nighean an rìgh air bhall-chrith eagail le fuaim
na béiste. Bhiodh iad uair fuidhe 's uair an uachdar, ach ma
dheireadh, gheàrr e fear do na cinn di; thug i aon raibheic aiste, 's
ghoir mac-talla nan creag d'a sgrèuch, 's chuir i 'n loch 'na lasair
bho cheann gu ceann, agus ann am prioba na sùla, chaidh i as an
t-sealladh. "Piseach 's buaidh gu 'n robh ga d' leantainn, òganaich,"
arsa nighean an rìgh, "tha mise sàbhailt air son aon oidhche; ach
thig a bheist a rithist, gu bràth gus an d' thig an dà cheann eile dhi."
Rug e air ceann na béiste, agus tharruing e gad roimhe 's thubhairt
e rithe, i ga' thabhairt leatha 'm màireach an sud. Dh' fhalbh i
dhachaidh 's an ceann air a guallainn, 's thug am buachaille na mairt
air. Ach cha b' fhada bha i air a' rathad 'n uair a choinnich an
Seanalair mòr so i, agus thubhairt e rithe gu marbhadh e i mur
canadh i gur esan a thug an ceann do 'n bhéist. "O! ars' ise, 's mi
their! co eile 'thug an ceann do 'n bheist ach thu." Ràinig iad tigh
an rìgh 's an ceann air guallainn an t-Seanalair; ach 's ann an so a
bha 'n t-aoibhneas, i 'thighinn dhachaidh beò slàn, agus ceann na
béiste làn fola aig a Chaiptean mhòr so 'na làimh. Air an latha

'màireach, dh'fhalbh iad, agus cha robh teagamh sam bith nach teàrnadh an gaisgeach so nighean an rìgh. Ràinig iad an t-àite ceudna, 's cha robh iad fad' an sin, 'n uair a ghluais an uile-bheist oillteil ann am meadhon an loch, 's shèap an gaisgeach air falbh mar a rinn e air an lath' dè. Ach cha b' fhad an déigh so, dur a thàinig fear an eich dhuibh 's deis eile air. Coma co dhiu, dh'aithnich i gur e cheart òganach a bh' ann. " 'S mise tha toilichte d' fhaicinn," ars' ise, "tha mi 'n dòchas gu làimhsich thu do chlaidheamh mòr an diugh mar a rinn thu 'n dè; thig a nìos 's leig t-anail." Ach cha b' fhada bha iad an sin, 'n uair a chunnaic iad a bhéist a *totail* am meadhon an loch. Luidh an t-òganach sìos ri taobh nighean an rìgh, 's thubhairt e rithe, "Ma chaidleas mise mu 'n d'thig a bhéist, dùisg mi." "De as dùsgadh dhuit?" " 'S dùsgadh dhomh a chluais-fhail sin a tha 'na d' chluais, a chuir 'na mo thè féin." Cha mhath a chaidil e 'n uair a ghlaodh nighean an rìgh, "Dùisg! dùisg!" Ach dusgadh cha dèanadh e; ach thug i chluas-fhail as a cluais, agus chuir i 'n cluas an òganaich e, 's air ball dhùisg e, 's an car na béiste chaidh e; ach 's ann an sin a bha 'n t-slupartaich 's an t-slapartaich, raoiceil, 's taoiceil air a bhéist. Lean iad mar so rè ùine fada, 's mu bheul na h-oidhche, gheàrr e 'n ceann eile do 'n bhéist. Chuir e air a' ghad e 's leum e air muin an eich dhuibh, 's thug e 'bhuachailleached air. Dh' fhalbh nighean an rìgh dhachaidh leis na cinn: thachair an Seanalair rithe 's thug e uaipe na cinn, 's thubhairt e rithe, "Gu 'm feumadh i chantainn gu 'm b' esan a thug an ceann do 'n bhéist air an uair so cuideachd." "Co eile a thug an ceann do 'n bhéist ach thu?" thuirt ise. Ràinig iad tigh an rìgh leis na cinn, ach 's ann an sin a bha 'n t-aoibhneas 's an t-aighear. Mha bha an righ subhach an ceud oidhche, bha e nis cinnteach gu 'n teàrnadh an gaisgeach mòr so a nighean, 's cha robh teagamh sam bith nach bitheadh an ceann eile do 'n bhéist air an latha màireach. Mu 'n am cheudna, dh' fhablh an dithis air an latha 'màireach. Dh' fhalaich an t-oifigir e féin mar a b-abhaist: thug nighean an rìgh bruaich an loch oirre, 's thàinig gaisgeach an eich dhuibh, 's luidh e ri' taobh. Dhùisg i 'n t-òlach 's chuir i cluas-fhail 'na chluais eile agus ann am bad na béiste ghabh e. Ach ma bha raoiceil, is 's taoiceil air a bheist air na làithean a chaidh seachad, 's ann an diugh a bha 'n t-uamhas oirre. Ach coma co dhiu, thug e 'n treas ceann do 'n bhéist, 's ma thug cha b' ann gun spàirn. Tharruing e ro 'n ghad e, 's dh' fhalbh i dhachaidh leis na cinn. 'N uair a ràinig iad tigh an righ, bha na h-uile làn gàirdeachas, 's bha 'n Seanalair ri nighean an rìgh a' phòsadh air an ath latha. Bha bhanais a dol air a h-aghaidh 's gach neach mu 'n Chaisteal 's fadal air gus an d' thigeadh an sagairt. Ach a nuair a thainig an sagairt, cha phòsadh i ach an neach a bheireadh na cinn do 'n ghad gun an gad a ghearradh. "Co bheireadh na cinn do 'n ghad ach am fear a chuir na cinn air," thuibhairt an righ. Dh' fheuch an Seanalair iad, ach cha b-urrainn e na cinn fhuasgladh; 's mu dheireadh, cha robh a h'aon mu 'n tigh nach d' fheuch ris' na cinn a thoirt do 'n ghad, ach cha b-urrainn iad. Dh' fhoighneachd an righ, "An robh neach air bith eile mu 'n tigh a dh' fheuchadh ris na cinn a thoirt bhar a ghaid." Thubhairt iad nach d' fheuch am buachaille fathast iad. Chaidh fios air a' bhuachaille, 's cha b' fhada bha esan a tilgeadh fear a null 's a nall diubh. "Ach fan beagan òganoich," arsa nighean an righ: "am fear a thug na cinn do 'n bhéist, tha 'm fàinne agamsa aige, agus mo dhà chluais-fhail." Chuir am buachaille 'làimh 'na phòca, 's thilig e air a bhòrd iad. "S'-tusa mo dhuine-sa," arsa nighean an rìgh. Cha robh an rìgh cho toilichte, 'n uair a chunnaic e gu 'm b'e 'bhuachaille a bha ri' nighean a phòsadh; ach; dh' òrduich e gu feumt' a chur ann an trusgan ni b'fhearr. Ach labhair a nighean, 's thubhairt i, "Gun robh trusgan aige cho rìomhach 'sa bha riamh 'na chaisteal; agus mor so thachair; chuir am buachaille deis' òir an fhamhair, air, agus phòs iad air an oidhche sin fein.

Bha iad a nis pòsda 's na h-uile ni dol air aghaidh gu maith. Bha iad aon lath' a spaisdearachd mu thaobh an locha, 's thàinig béist a b-uamhasaiche na 'n te eile, 's thugar air falbh e gun athadh gun fhoighneachd. Bha nighean an rìgh an so gu dubhach, dèurach, dalla-bhrònach air son a fear-posda. Bha i daonnan 'sa sùil air an loch. Thachair seana ghobha rithe, 's dh' innis i dha mar thachair da céile-pòsda. Chomhairlich an gobha dhi i 'sgaoileadh gach nì bu bhrèagha na chèile anns a cheart àite 'san 'd' thug a bhéist air falbh a duine; agus mar so rinn i. Chuir a bhéist suas a sròn, 's thubhairt i. " 'S brèagh 'd' ailleas a nighean an rìgh." " 'S brèagha na sin an t-àilleagan a thug thu uam," thubhairt ise. "Thoir dhomh aon sealladh do m' dhuine, 's gheibh thu aon ni do na tha thu 'faicinn." Thug a' bhéist suas e. "Aisig dhomh e, 's gheibh thu na tha thu 'faicinn," ars' ise. Rinn a' bhéist mar a thubhairt i; thilig i beo slàn e air bruach an locha. Goirid 'na dheigh sud, 's iad a sràidimeachd ri taobh an loch, thug a bhèist cheudna air falbh nighean an rìgh. Bu bhrònach gach neach a bha 'sa bhaile air an oidhche so. Bha a duine gu dubhach, deurach, a' siubhal sìos agus suas mu bhruachan an locha a latha 's do dh' oidhche. Thachair an seana ghobha ris. Dh' innis an gobha dha, Nach robh dòigh air an uile-bheist a mharbhadh, ach aon dòigh, agus 's e sin—"Anns an eilen 'tha am meadhon an locha tha eilid chaisfhionn as caoile cas 's as luaithe ceum, agus ge do rachadh beirsinn oirre, leumadh feannag aisde, agus ged a rachadh beirsinn air an fheannag, leumadh breac aisde; ach tha ubh am beul a bhric, agus tha anam na béiste 'san ubh 's ma bhristeas an t-ubh, tha a bhéist marbh." Nis cha robh dòigh air faotainn do 'n eilean so, bho 'n chuireadh a bhéist foidh gach bata 's gach ràth, a rachadh air an loch. Smaoinich e gu 'm feuchadh e 'n Caolas a leum leis an each dhubh, agus mar so fhein rinn e. Leum an t-each dubh an Caolas, 's an Cù dubh le aon leum as an déigh. Chunnaic e' n eilid, 's leig e 'n cù dubh 'na déigh, ach an uair a bhiodh an cù air aon taobh do 'n eilean bhiodh an eilid air an taobh eile. "O! bu mhath a nis madadh mòr na closaiche feòla an so." Cha luaithe 'labhair e 'm facal na bha 'm madadh còir ri thaobh, agus an déigh na h-eilid ghabh e 's cha b' fhada 'bha na laoich ga cuir ri talamh; ach cha bu luaithe a rug e oirre, na leum feannag aisde; " 'S ann a nis a bu mhath an t-seobhag ghlas as geire suil 's is làidire sgiath." Cha luaithe thubhairt e so, na bha 'n t-seobhag as déigh 'na feannaig, 's cha b' fhada 'bha i ga cuir ri talamh; agus air tuiteam do 'n fheannaig air bruach an locha, a mach aisde leumtar am breac. "O! nach robh thus' agamsa a nis a dhobhrain." Cha luaith' thubhairt na bha 'n dobhran ri thaobh, agus a mach air an loch leum i, 's thugar am breac a meadhon an loch; Ach cha luaithe bha 'n dòran air tìr leis a bhreac na thainig an t-ubh a mach as a bheul. Ghrad leum esan, 's chuir e 'chas air, 's ann an sin a leig a bhéist raoic aisde, 's thubhairt i, "Na brist an t-ubh, 's gheibh thu na dh' iarras tu." "Aisig dhòmhsa mo bhean." Ann am prioba na sùla bha i ri 'thaobh. Nuair a fhuair e greim air a laimh 'na dha' làimh, leig e chas air an ubh, 's bhàsaich a bhéist. Bha 'bheist marbh a nis, agus 'sann a nis a bha 'n sealladh ri fhaicinn. Bha i uamhasach ri sealltainn oirre, bha na tri chinn di gun teagamh, ach ma bha, bha ceann os-ceann cheann oirre, agus sùilean, 's coig ceud cas. Coma co dhiu, dh' fhàig iad ann a 'sud i, 's chaidh iad dhachaidh. Bha sòlas is gàirdeachas ann an tigh an rìgh air an oidhche so, 's cha d' innis e do 'n rìgh gu so mar a mharbh e na famhairean. Chuir an rìgh urram mòr air, 's bha e 'na dhuine mòr aig an rìgh.

Bha e fein 's a' bhean a' sràidimeachd aon latha, 'n uair a thug e fainear caisteal beag ri taobh an loch, ann an coille. Dh' fharraid e do 'n mhnaoi co bha gabhail còmhnuidh ann? Thubhairt i nach robh neach air bith a' dol a chòir a chaisteal ud, bho nach d'thainig neach air ais fathast a chaidh ann a dh' innseadh sgeùil. "Cha 'n fhaod a chùis a bhi mar sin," ars' esan; "a nochd féin chi mi co' tha gabhail comhnuidh ann." "Cha d' theid, cha d' theid," thubhairt ise, "cha deach duine riamh do 'n chaisteal so a phill air ais." "Biodh sin 's a roghainn aige," ars' esan. Dh' fhalbh e, agus gabhar do 'n chaisteal 's nuair a ràinig e 'n dorus, thachair cailleach bheag, bhrosgulach ris 'na seasamh san dorus. 'Furan 's failte dhuit, a mhic an iasgair 's mi féin a tha toilichte d' fhaicinn; 's mòr an onair do 'n rìoghachd so do leithid a thighinn innte; 's urram do 'n bhothan bheag so thu thighinn a stigh;' gabh a stigh air thoiseach, onair na h-uaisle, 's leig t' anail:" 's a steach ghabh e; ach a nuair a bha e air tì dol suas, tharruing i an slacan-dhruidheachd air an cùl a chinn, 's air ball thuit e 'n sin. "Air an oidhche so bha bròn ann an caisteal an rìgh agus air an latha màireach bha tuireadh ann an tigh an iasgair. Chunnacas a chraobh a seargadh 's thubhairt mac meadhonach an iasgair, "gu 'n robh a bhràthar marbh," 's thug e bòid is briathar gu falbhadh e s gu 'm biodh fios aige cait' an robh corp a bhràthar na luidhe. Chuir e dìollaid air each dubh, 's mharcaich è an déigh a choin duibh (oir bha each dubh 's cù dubh aig triùir mhac an iasgair) agus gun dol a null na nall, lean e air ceum a bhràthair bu sine, gus an dràinig e tigh an rìgh. Bha e so co coltach ri 'bhràthair 's gu 'n d' shaoil le nighean an rìgh gu 'm be duine fein a bh' ann. Dh' fhan e 'n so 'sa chaisteal, 's dh' innis iad dha mar thachair d'a bràthair, agus do chaisteal beag na cailliche dh' fheumadh e' dol bog na cruaidh mar thachradh, 's do 'n chaisteal chaidh e, agus ceart mar a thachair do 'n bhràthair bu sine, anns gach dòigh thachair do 'n mhac mheadhonach, 's le aon bhuille do 'n t-slacan-dhruidheachd, leag a' chailleach e na shìneadh ri' taobh a bhràthar. Air faicinn an darna craobh a' seargadh do mhac òg an iasgair thubhairt e, gu 'n robh a nis a dhithis bhràithrean marbh, agus gu' feumadh fios a bhi aigesan de 'm bàs a thàinig orra. Air muin an eich dhuibh ghabh e, 's lean e 'n cù mar a rinn a bhràthair, agus tigh an rìgh bhuail e mu 'n do stad e. 'Se 'n rìgh bha toilichte fhaicinn, ach do 'n chaisteal dubh (oir 'se so ainm) cha leigadh iad e, ach do 'n chaisteal dh' fheumadh e dol, 's mur sin ràinig e 'n caisteal. "Failte 's furan dhuit féin, a mhic an iasgair, 's mi tha toillichte d'fhaicinn; gabh a steach 's leig t-anail," thuirt ise. " 'Stigh romham thu, a chailleach, 's coma leam sodal a muigh." "Rach a steach 's cluinneam do chòmhradh." A' steach, ghabh a chailleach, agus a nuair a bha a cùl ris, tharruing e a chlaidheamh 's spadar a ceann dhi, ach leum an claidheamh as a laimh, 's ghrad rug a chailleach air a ceann le a da làimh, s cuirear air a h-amhaich e mar' bha e roimhe. Leum an cù air a chaillich, 's bhuail i 'm madadh còir leis an t-slacan-dhruidheachd, 's luidh esan an sin, ach cha deach so air mhithapadh do 'n òlach, 's an sàs sa chaillich gabhar e. Fhuair e gréim air an t-shlacan-dhruidheachd, agus le aon bhuille am mullach a cinn bha i ri talamh ann am prioba na sùl. Chaidh e beagan air aghaidh suas, 's faicear a dha bhràthair na 'n luidhe taobh ri taobh. Thug e buille do gach fear dhiubh, leis an t-slacan dhruidheachd 's air an cois bha iad. Ach 's ann so a bha 'n spuill òir 's airgid, 's gach ni bu luachmhoire na chèile ann an caisteal na cailliche. Thàinig iad air an ais do thigh an rìgh, 's ann an sin a bha 'n gàirdeachas. Bha 'n rìgh a fàs seann, agus chaidh mac bhu shine an iasgair a chrùnadh 'na rìgh, 's dh' fhan an dithis bhràithrean latha 's bliadhna ann an tigh an rìgh, 's dh' fhalbh an dithis a nis dhachadh le òr 's airgiod na cailliche, 's gach nì rìomhach eile 'thug an rìgh dhoibh; 's mar do shiubhail iad uaidh sin tha iad beo gus an latha 'n diugh.

HECTOR URQUHART.

2. Another version of this was told to me in South Uist, by DONALD MACPHIE, aged 79, in September 1859.

There was a poor old fisher in Skye, and his name was Duncan. He was out fishing, and the sea-maiden rose at the side of hisboat, and said, "Duncan, thou art not getting fish." They had a long talk, and made a bargain; plenty of fish for his first son. But he said, "I have none." Then the sea-maiden gave him something, and said, "Give this to thy wife, and this to thy mare, and this to thy dog, and they will have three sons, three foals, and three pups," and so they had, and the eldest son was Iain. When he was eighteen, he found his mother weeping, and learned that he belonged to the mermaid. "Oh," said he, "I will go where there is not a drop of salt water." So he mounted one of the horses and went away. He soon came to the carcase of an old horse, and at it a lion (leon), a wolf (matugally), and a falcon (showag). LEÒMHAN, MADADH-ALLUIDH, SEABHAG or SEOBHAG.

The lion spoke, and *she* asked him to divide the carcass. He did so, and each thanked him, and said, "When thou art in need think of me, and I will be at thy side (*or thou wilt be a lion, a wolf, or a falcon, I am uncertain which he meant*), for we were here under spells till some one should divide this carcass for us."

He went on his way and became a king's herd. He went to a smith and bade him make him an iron staff. He made three. The two first bent, the third did well enough. He went a-herding, and found a fine grass park, and opened it and went in with the cattle. FUATH of the seven heads, and seven humps, and seven necks, came and took six by the tails and went away with them (*so Cacus dragged away cows by the tail*). "Stop," said the herd. The FUATH would not, so they came to grips. Then the fisher's son either thought of the lion, or became one, but at all events a lion seized the giant and put him to earth.

"Thine is my lying down and rising up," said he. "What is thy ransom?" said the herd. The giant said, "I have a white filly that will go through the skies, and a white dress; take them." And the herd took off his heads.

When he went home they had to send for carpenters to make dishes for the milk, there was so much.

The next day was the same. There came a giant with the same number of heads, and took eight cows by their tails, and slung them on his back. The herd and the wolf (or as a wolf) beat him, and got a red filly that could fly through the air, and a red dress, and cut off their heads. And there were still more carpenters wanted, there was so much milk.

The third day came a still bigger giant and took nine cows, and the herd as, or *with* a falcon, beat him, and got a green filly that would go through the sky, and a green dress, and cut his heads off, and there was more milk than ever.

On the fourth day came the Carlin, the wife of the last giant, and mother of the other two, and the fisher's son went up into a tree. "Come down till I eat thee," said she. "Not I," said the herd. "Thou hast killed my husband and my two sons, come down till I eat thee." "Open thy mouth, then, till I jump down," said the herd. So the old Carlin opened her gab, and he thrust the iron staff down her throat, and it came out at a mole on her breast [*this is like the mole of the Gruagach in No. 1*], and she fell. Then he sprang on her, and spoke as before, and got a basin, and when he washed himself in it, he would be the most beautiful man that was ever seen on earth, and a fine silver comb, and it would make him the grandest man in the world; and he killed the Carlin and went home.

[*So far this agrees almost exactly with the next version, but there is a giant added here and a coarse comb left out*].

When the fisher's son came home, there was sorrow in the king's house, for the DRAYGAN was come from the sea. Every time he came there was some one to be eaten, and this time the lot had fallen on the king's daughter.

The herd said that he would go to fight the draygan, and the king said, "No; I cannot spare my herd." So the king's daughter had to go alone. [*The incident of the cowardly knight is here left out*]. Then the herd came through the air on the white filly, with the white dress of the Fuath. He tied the filly to the branch of a tree and went where the king's daughter was, and laid his head in her lap, and she dressed his hair, and he slept. When the draygan came she woke him, and after a severe battle he cut off one head, and the draygan said, "A hard fight tomorrow," and went away. The herd went off in the white filly, and in the evening asked about the battle, and heard his own story. Next day was the same with the red filly and the red dress, and the draygan said, "The last fight to-morrow," and he disappeared. On the third day she scratched a mark on his forehead when his head was in her lap: he killed the draygan, and when he asked about it all, there was great joy, for now the draygan was dead. Then the king's daughter had the whole kingdom gathered, and they took off their head clothes as they passed, but there was no mark. Then they bethought them of the dirty herd, and when he came he would not put off his head gear, but she made him, and saw the mark, and said, "Thou mightest have a better dress." He used his magic comb and basin, and put on a dress, and was the grandest in the company, and they married. It fell out that the king's daughter longed for dulse, and he went with her to the shore to seek it. The sea-maiden rose up and took him. She was sorrowful, and went to the soothsayer and learned what to do.

And she took her harp to the sea shore and sat and played and the sea-maiden came up to listen, for sea-maidens are fonder of music than any other creatures, and when she saw the sea-maiden she stopped. The sea-maiden said, "Play on;" but she said, "No, till I see my man again." So the sea-maiden put up his head. (*Who do you mean? Out of her mouth to be sure. She had swallowed him.*) She played again, and stopped, and then the sea-maiden put him up to the waist. Then she played again and stopped, and the sea-maiden placed him on her palm. Then he thought of the falcon, and became one and flew on shore. But the sea-maiden took the wife.

Then he went to the soothsayer, and he said, "I know not what to do, but in a glen there is TARBH NIMH, a hurtful bull, and in the bull a ram, and in the ram a goose, and in the goose an egg, and there is the soul of the sea-maiden."

Then he called on his three creatures, and by their help got the goose, but the egg fell out in the loch.

Then the lion said *she* knew not what to do, and the wolf said the same. The falcon told of an otter in an island, and flew and seized her two cubs, and the otter dived for the egg to save her cubs. He got his wife, and dashed the egg on the stones, and the mermaid died. And they sent for the fisher and his sons, and the old mother and brothers got part of the kingdom, and they were all happy and lucky after that.

I asked if there was anything about one brother being taken for the other and the naked sword, and was told that the incident was in another story, as well as that of the withering of the three trees. These incidents were in the version of the stable boy; and as they are in Mackenzie's, they probably belong to the story as it was known in Argyllshire.

3. Another version of this was told in April 1859, by John MacGibbon, a lad who was rowing me across Loch Fyne, from St.

Katharine's to Inverary; he said he had heard it from an old man living near Lochgilphead, who could tell many stories, and knew part of the history of the Feine.

The hero was the son of a widow, the youngest of ten; black-skinned and rough "carrach." He went to seek his fortune, and after adventures somewhat like those of the heroes in the other versions, he became like them a king's herd, and was in like manner beset by giants who claimed the pasture. Each fight was preceded by a long and curious parley across a ditch. The giants got larger each day, and last of all came the wife of one, and mother of the other two, who was worst of all.

He got spoil from each, which the conquered giant named as his ransom, and which, as usual, the herd took after killing his foe. From the mother he got a "golden comb, and when he combed his hair with the fine side, he was lovely, and when he combed it with the coarse side, he was hideous again," and a magic basin which made him beautiful when he washed in it. And he got wonderful arms, and dresses, and horses from the giants.

Then the king's daughter was to be given to a giant with three heads who came in a ship. When he leaped on shore, he buried himself to the waist, he was so heavy. The herd was asleep with his head in the lap of the princess, and dressed in the giant's spoil, combed with the fine gold comb, and washed in the magic basin, and beautiful, but nevertheless the princess dressed his hair.

He was awakened each day by biting a joint off his little finger—cutting a patch from the top of his head—and a notch from his ear. Each day he cut off a head, and the giant, when he leaped from the ship on the third day, only sunk to his ankles in the sand, for he had lost two heads.

The third head jumped on again as fast as it was cut off, but at last, by the advice of a hoodie, the cold steel of the sword was held on the neck till the marrow froze, and then the giant was killed, and the herd disappeared as usual.

A red-headed lad, who went to guard the princess, ran away and hid himself, and took the credit each day, but he could not untie the knots with which the heads were bound together on a withy by the herd. Then when all the kingdom had been gathered, the herd was sent for, but he would not come, and he bound three parties of men who were sent to bring him by force.

At last he was entreated to come, and came, and was recognized by the marks, and then he combed his hair, and washed in the magic basin, and dressed in the giant's spoils, and he married the princess, and the Gille Ruadh was hanged.

Here the story ended, but so did the passage of the ferry.

4.   I have another version written by Hector Maclean, from the

dictation of a woman, B. Macaskill, in the small island of Berneray, Aug. 1859.—MAC A GHOBHA, The Smith's Son.

A smith takes the place of the old fisherman. The mermaid rises beside his boat, gets the promise of the son, and sends him fish. (*The three mysterious grains are omitted.*) One son is born to the fisher, and the mermaid lets him remain till he is fourteen years of age.

BHA 'N GILLE 'N SO CHO MOR AN CEAUNN NAN CEITHIR BLIADHNA DIAG! CHA ROBH LEITHID RE BHAIGHIN CHO MOR 'S CHO GARBH 'S CHO FOGHAINTEACH RIS.

The lad was now *so* big at the end of the 14 years! His like was not to be found, so big, so rugged, so formidable as he.

Then he asked his father not to go in the wind of the shore or the sea, for fear the mermaid should catch him, and to make him a staff in which there should be nine stone weight of iron; and he went to seek his fortune. His father made him the staff, and he went, and whom should he meet but MADADH RUADH the fox, MADADH AL-LUIDH the wolf, AGUS AN FHEANNAG, and the hoodie, AGUS OTHAISG ACA GA H'ITHEADH, and eating a year old sheep. He divided the sheep, and the creatures promised to help him, and he went on to a castle, where he got himself employed as a herd, and was sent to a park; "No man ever came alive out of it that ever went into it."

A big giant came and took away one of the cows, and then (SABAID) a fight began, and the herd was undermost, AGUS DE RINN AM BUACHAILL' ACH CUIMHNEACHADH AIR A MHADADH ALLUIDH AGUS GHRAD! BHA 'M BUACHAILL AN AIRD AGUS AM FUAMHAIR FODHA AGUS MHARBH E 'M FUAMHAIR, and what did the herd but remember the wolf, and swift! the herd was above and the giant below, and he killed the giant, and went home with the cattle, and his master said to the BANACHAGAN, "Oh, be good to the herd." (*The spoil, the dresses, and the horses are here all left all out*). The second day it was the same, and he again thought of the wolf, and conquered after he was down.

The third day it was again the same. On the fourth day CAILLEACH MHOR a great carlan came. They fought, and he was undermost again, but thought of the wolf and was up. BAS AS DO CHIONN A CHAILLEACH ARS AM BUACHAILLE DE' T' EIRIG?*

"Death on thy top, Carlin," said the herd, "what's thy value?" "That is not little," said the Carlin, "if thou gettest it. I have three TRUNCANNAN (*an English word with a Gaelic plural*) full of silver. There is a trunk under the foot-board, and two others in the upper end of the castle." "Though that be little, its my own," said he as he killed her.

* EIRIG, a fine for bloodshed, a ransom. Fine anciently paid for the murder of any person. *Scottish Laws—Regiam Majestatem* (Armstrong dic.) *The Laws of the Brets and Scots*, in which every one was valued according to his degree (Innes's "Scotland in the Middle Ages").

On the morrow the king's daughter was to go to the great beast that was on the loch to be killed, and what should the herd do but draw the cattle that way, and he laid his head in her lap and slept, but first told the lady, when she saw the loch trembling, to take off a joint of his little finger. She did so. He awoke, thought of the fox, and took a head, a hump, and a neck off the beast, and he went away, and no one knew that he had been there at all. Next day was the same, but he had a patch cut from his head.

The third day she took off the point of his ear, he awoke, was again beaten by the beast, thought of the fox, and was uppermost, and killed the beast (S' BHA I NA LOCH UISGE N' UAIR A MHARBH E I) and she was a fresh water lake when he had killed her.

(The cowardly general, or knight, or lad, or servant, is here left out.) Then the king's daughter gave out that she would marry the man whose finger fitted the joint which she had cut off and kept in her pocket. Everybody came and cut off the points of their little fingers, but the herd staid away till it was found out by the dairy-maids that he wanted the joint, and then he came and married the lady.

After they were married they went to walk by the shore, and the mermaid rose and took him away. "It is long since thou wert promised to me, and now I have thee perforce," said she. An old woman advised the lady to spread all her dresses on the beach, and she did so in the evening, and the mermaid came, and for the dresses gave back her companion, "and they went at each other's necks with joy and gladness."

In a fortnight the wife was taken away, "and sorrow was not sorrow till now—the lad lamenting his wife." He went to an old man, who said, "There is a pigeon which has laid in the top of a tree; if thou couldst find means to break the egg ANAIL, the breath of the barmaid is in it." SMAOINTICH E AIR AN FHEANNAIG 'S CHAIDH E NA FHEANNAIG 'S LEUM E GO BARR NA CRAOIBHE. He thought on the hoodie, and he became a hoodie (*went into his hoodie*), and he sprang to the top of the tree, and he got the egg, and he broke the egg, and his wife came to shore, and the mermaid was dead.

It is worth remarking the incidents which drop out of the story when told by women and by men. Here the horses and armour are forgotten, but the faithful lover is remembered. The sword is a stick, and the whole thing savours strongly of the every-day experience of the Western Isles, which has to do with fishing, and herding sheep and cattle. It is curious also to remark the variations in the incidents. The hero seems to acquire the qualities of the creatures, or be assisted by them.

5.   I have another version from Barra, but it varies so much, and has so many new incidents, that I must give it entire, if at all. It

most resembles MacGibbon's version. It is called AN 'T IASGAIR the fisher, and was told by Alexander MacNeill, fisherman.

6. I have a sixth version told by John Smith, labourer, living at Polchar in South Uist, who says he learned it about twenty years ago from Angus Macdonald, Balnish. It is called AN GILLE GLAS, the Grey lad. He is a widow's son, goes to seek his fortune, goes to a smith, and gets him to make an iron shinny (*that is a hockey club*), he becomes herd to a gentleman, herds cattle, and is beset by giants whom he kills with his iron club; he gathers the skirt of his grey cassock (*which looks like Odin*), he gets a copper and a silver and a golden castle, servants (or slaves) of various colour and appearance, magic whistles, horses, and dresses, and rescues the daughter of the king of Greece. The part of the cowardly knight is played by a red headed cook. The language of this is curious, and the whole very wild. Unless given entire, it is spoilt.

In another story, also from Berneray, the incident of meeting three creatures again occurs.

There is a lion, a dove, and a rat. And the lion says:—

"What, lad, is thy notion of myself being in such a place as this?"

"Well," said he, "I have no notion, but that it is not there the like of you ought to be; but about the banks of rivers."

It is impossible not to share the astonishment of the lion, and but for the fact that the rat and the dove were as much surprised at their position as the lion, one would be led to suspect that Margaret MacKinnon, who told the story, felt that her lion was out of his element in Berneray. Still he is there, and it seems worth inquiring how he and the story got there and to other strange places.

1st. The story is clearly the same as Shortshanks in Dasent's Norse Tales, 1859. But it is manifest that it is not taken from that book, for it could not have become so widely spread in the islands, and so changed within the time.

2d. It resembles, in some particulars, the Two Brothers, the White Snake, the Nix of the Mill Pond, the Ball of Crystal, in Grimm; and there are similar incidents in other German tales. These have long been published, but I never heard of a copy in the west, and many of my authorities cannot read. It is only necessary to compare any one of the Gaelic versions with any one German tale, or all together, to feel certain that Grimm's collection is not the source from which this story proceeded.

3d. A story in the latest edition of the Arabian Nights (Lane's, 1839), contains the incident of a genius, whose life was not in his body, but in a chest at the bottom of the Circumambient Ocean, but that book is expensive, and quite beyond the reach of peasants and fishermen in the west, and the rest of the story is different.

4th. There is something in Sanscrit about a fight for cattle between a herd and some giants, which has been compared with the classical story of Cacus.—(Mommsen's Roman History).

5th. I am told that there is an Irish "fenian" story which this resembles. I have not yet seen it, but it is said to be taken from a very old Irish MS. (Ossianic Society).

6th. It is clearly the same as the legend of St. George and the Dragon. It is like the classical story of Perseus and Andromeda, but Pegasus is multiplied by three, and like the story of Hercules and Hesione, but Hercules was to have six horses. On the whole, I cannot think that this is taken from any known story of any one people, but that it is the Gaelic version of some old myth. If it contains something which is distorted history, it seems to treat of a seafaring people who stole men and women, and gave them back for a ransom, of a wild race of "giants" who stole cattle and horses, and dresses, and used combs and basins, and had grass parks; and another people who had cattle and wanted pasture, and went from the shore *in* on the giants' land.

If it be mythical, there is the egg which contains the life of the sea-monster, and to get which beast, bird, and fish, earth, air, and water, must be overcome. Fire may be indicated, for the word which I have translated SPINDRIFT, LASAIR, generally means *flame*.

I am inclined to think that it is a very old tale, a mixture of mythology, history, and every-day life, which may once have been intended to convey the moral lesson, that small causes may produce great effects; that men may learn from brutes, Courage from the lion and the wolf, Craft from the fox, Activity from the falcon, and that the most despised object often becomes the greatest. The whole story grows out of a grain of seed. The giant's old mother is more terrible than the giants. The little flattering crone in the black castle more dangerous than the sea monster. The herd thought of the wolf when he fought the giants, but he thought of the fox when he slew the dragon. I can but say with the tale tellers, "dh' fhàg mise n' sin eud." "There I left them," for others to follow if they choose. I cannot say how the story got to the Highlands, and the lion into the mind of a woman in Berneray.

5

CONALL CRA BHUIDHE.

From James Wilson, blind fiddler, Islay.

Conall Cra Bhuidhe was a sturdy tenant in Eirinn: he had four sons. There was at that time a king over every fifth of Eirinn. It fell out for the children of the king that was near Conall, that they themselves and the children of Conall came to blows. The children of Conall got the upper hand, and they killed the king's big son. The king sent a message for Conall, and he said to him—"Oh, Conall! what made thy sons go to spring on my sons till my big son was killed by thy children? but I see that though I follow thee revengefully, I shall not be much the better for it, and I will now set a thing before thee, and if thou wilt do it, I will not follow thee with revenge. If thou thyself, and thy sons, will get for me the brown horse of the king of Lochlann, thou shalt get the souls of thy sons." "Why," said Conall, "should not I do the pleasure of the king, though there should be no souls of my sons in dread at all. Hard is the matter thou requirest of me, but I will lose my own life, and the life of my sons, or else I will do the pleasure of the king."

After these words Conall left the king, and he went home: when he got home he was under much trouble and perplexity. When he went to lie down he told his wife the thing the king had set before him. His wife took much sorrow that he was obliged to part from herself, while she knew not if she should see him more. "Oh, Conall," said she, "why didst not thou let the king do his own pleasure to thy sons, rather than be going now, while I know not if ever I shall see thee more?" When he rose on the morrow, he set himself and his four sons in order, and they took their journey towards Lochlann, and they made no stop but (were) tearing ocean till they reached it. When they reached Lochlann they did not know what they should do. Said the old man to his sons—"stop ye, and we will seek out the house of the king's miller."

When they went into the house of the king's miller, the man asked them to stop there for the night. Conall told the miller that his own children and the children of the king had fallen out, and that his children had killed the king's son, and there was nothing that would please the king but that he should get the brown horse of the king of Lochlann. "If thou wilt do me a kindness, and wilt put me in a way to get him, for certain I will pay thee for it." "The thing is silly that thou art come to seek," said the miller; "for the king has laid his mind on him so greatly that thou wilt not get him in any way unless thou steal him; but if thou thyself canst make out a way, I will hide thy secret." "This, I am thinking," said Conall, "since thou art working every day for the king, that thou and thy gillies should put myself and my sons into five sacks of bran." "The plan that came into thy head is not bad," said the miller. The miller spoke to his gillies, and he said to them to do this, and they put them in five sacks. The king's gillies came to seek the bran, and they took the five sacks with them, and they emptied them before the horses. The servants locked the door, and they went away.

When they rose to lay hand on the brown horse, said Conall, "You shall not do that. It is hard to get out of this; let us make for ourselves five hiding holes, so that if they perceive us we may go in hiding." They made the holes, then they laid hands on the horse. The horse was pretty well unbroken, and he set to making a terrible noise through the stable. The king perceived him. He heard the noise. "It must be that that was my brown horse," said he to his gillies; "try what is wrong with him."

The servants went out, and when Conall and his sons perceived them coming they went into the hiding holes. The servants looked amongst the horses, and they did not find anything wrong; and they returned and they told this to the king, and the king said to them that if nothing was wrong that they should go to their places of rest. When the gillies had time to be gone, Conall and his sons laid the next hand on the horse. If the noise was great that he made before, the noise he made now was seven times greater. The king sent a message for his gillies again, and said for certain there was something troubling the brown horse. "Go and look well about him." The servants went out, and they went to their hiding holes. The servants rummaged well, and did not find a thing. They returned and they told this. "That is marvellous for me," said the king: "go you to lie down again, and if I perceive it again I will go out myself." When Conall and his sons perceived that the gillies were gone, they laid hands again on the horse, and one of them caught him, and if the noise that the horse made on the two former times was great, he made more this time.

"Be this from me," said the king; "it must be that some one is troubling my brown horse." He sounded the bell hastily, and when his waiting man came to him, he said to him to set the stable gillies on foot that something was wrong with the horse. The gillies came, and the king went with them. When Conall and his sons perceived the following coming they went to the hiding holes. The king was a wary man, and he saw where the horses were making a noise. "Be clever," said the king, "there are men within the stable, and let us get them somehow." The king followed the tracks of the men, and he found them. Every man was acquainted with Conall, for he was a valued tenant by the king of Eirinn, and when the king brought them up out of the holes he said, "Oh, Conall art thou here?" "I am, O king, without question, and necessity made me come. I am under thy pardon, and under thine honour, and under thy grace." He told how it happened to him, and that he had to get the brown horse for the king of Eirinn, or that his son was to be put to death. 'I knew that I should not get him by asking, and I was going to steal him.' "Yes, Conall, it is well enough, but come in," said the king. He desired his look-out men to set a watch on the sons of Conall, and to give them meat. And a double watch was set that night on the sons of Conall. "Now, O Conall," said the king, "wert thou ever in a harder place than to be seeing thy lot of sons hanged to-morrow? But thou didst set it to my goodness and to my grace, and that it was necessity brought it on thee, and I must not hang thee. Tell me any case in which thou wert as hard as this, and if thou tellest that, thou shalt get the soul of thy youngest son with thee." "I will tell a case as hard in which I was," said Conall.

"I was a young lad, and my father had much land, and he had parks of year-old cows, and one of them had just calved, and my father told me to bring her home. I took with me a laddie, and we found the cow, and we took her with us. There fell a shower of snow. We went into the herd's bothy, and we took the cow and the calf in with us, and we were letting the shower (pass) from us. What came in but one cat and ten, and one great one-eyed fox-coloured cat as head bard* over them. When they came in, in very deed I myself had no liking for their company. 'Strike up with you,' said the head bard, 'why should we be still? and sing a cronan to Conall Cra-Bhui.' I was amazed that my name was known to the cats themselves. When they had sung the cronan, said the head bard,

'Now, O Conall, pay the reward of the cronan that the cats have sung to thee.' 'Well then,' said I myself, 'I have no reward whatsoever for you, unless you should go down and take that calf.' No sooner said I the word than the two cats and ten went down to attack the calf, and, in very deed, he did not last them long. 'Play up with you, why should you be silent? Make a cronan to Conall Cra-Bhui,' said the head bard. Certainly I had no liking at all for the cronan, but up came the one cat and ten, and if they did not sing me a cronan then and there! 'Pay them now their reward,' said the great fox-coloured cat. 'I am tired myself of yourselves and your rewards,' said I. 'I have no reward for you unless you take that cow down there.' They betook themselves to the cow, and indeed she did not stand them out for long.

" 'Why will you be silent? Go up and sing a cronan to Conall Cra-Bhui,' said the head bard. And surely, oh, king, I had no care for them or for their cronan, for I began to see that they were not good comrades. When they had sung me the cronan they betook themselves down where the head bard was. 'Pay now their reward,' said the head bard; and for sure, oh, king, I had no reward for them; and I said to them, 'I have no reward for you, unless you will take that laddie with you and make use of him.' When the boy heard this he took himself out, and the cats after him. And surely, oh, king, there was "striongan" and catterwauling between them. When they took themselves out, I took out at a turf window that was at the back of the house. I took myself off as hard as I might into the wood. I was swift enough and strong at that time; and when I felt the rustling 'toirm' of the cats after me I climbed into as high a tree as I saw in the place, and (one) that was close in the top; and I hid myself as well as I might. The cats began to search for me through the wood, and they were not finding me; and when they were tired, each one said to the other that they would turn back. 'But,' said the one-eyed fox-coloured cat that was commander-in-chief over them, 'you saw him not with your two eyes, and though I have but one eye, there's the rascal up in the top of the tree.' When he had said that, one of them went up in the tree, and as he was coming where I was, I drew a weapon that I had and I killed him. 'Be this from me!' said the one-eyed one—'I must not be losing my company thus; gather round the root of the tree and dig about it, and let down that extortioner to earth.' On this they gathered about her (the tree), and they dug about her root, and the first branching

* Or commander-in-chief.

root that they cut, she gave a shiver to fall, and I myself gave a shout, and it was not to be wondered at. There was in the neighbourhood of the wood a priest, and he had ten men with him delving, and he said, 'There is a shout of extremity and I must not be without replying to it.' And the wisest of the men said, 'Let it alone till we hear it again.' The cats began, and they began wildly, and they broke the next root; and I myself gave the next shout, and in very deed it was not weak. 'Certainly,' said the priest, 'it is a man in extremity—let us move.' They were setting themselves in order for moving. And the cats arose on the tree, and they broke the third root, and the tree fell on her elbow. I gave the third shout. The stalwart men hasted, and when they saw how the cats served the tree, they began at them with the spades; and they themselves and the cats began at each other, till they were killed altogether—the men and the cats. And surely, oh king, I did not move till I saw the last one of them falling. I came home. And there's for thee the hardest case in which I ever was; and it seems to me that tearing by the cats were harder than hanging to-morrow by the king of Lochlann.

"Od! Conall," said the king, "thou art full of words. Thou hast freed the soul of thy son with thy tale; and if thou tellest me a harder case than thy three sons to be hanged to-morrow, thou wilt get thy second youngest son with thee, and then thou wilt have two sons." "Well then," said Conall, "on condition that thou dost that, I was in a harder case than to be in thy power in prison to-night." "Let's hear," said the king.—"I was there," said Conall, "as a young lad, and I went out hunting, and my father's land was beside the sea, and it was rough with rocks, caves, and geos.* When I was going on the top of the shore, I saw as if there were a smoke coming up between two rocks, and I began to look what might be the meaning of the smoke coming up there. When I was looking, what should I do but fall; and the place was so full of manure, that neither bone nor skin was broken. I knew not how I should get out of this. I was not looking before me, but I was looking over head the way I came—and the day will never come that I could get up there. It was terrible for me to be there till I should die. I heard a great clattering 'tuarneileis' coming, and what was there but a great giant and two dozen of goats with him, and a buck at their head. And when the giant had tied the goats, he came up and he said to me, 'Hao O! Conall, it's long since my knife is rusting in my pouch waiting for thy tender flesh.' 'Och!' said I, 'it's not much thou wilt be bettered by me, though thou should'st tear me asunder; I will make but one meal for thee. But I see that thou art one-eyed. I am a good leech, and I will give thee the sight of the other eye.' The giant went and he drew the great caldron on the site of the fire. I myself was telling him how he should heat the water, so that I should give its sight to the other eye. I got heather and I made a rubber of it, and I set him upright in the caldron. I began at the eye that was well, pretending to him that I would give its sight to the other one, till I left them as bad as each other; and surely it was easier to spoil the one that was well than to give sight to the other.

"When he 'saw' that he could not see a glimpse, and when I myself said to him that I would get out in spite of him, he gave that spring out of the water, and he stood in the mouth of the cave, and he said that he would have revenge for the sight of his eye. I had but to stay there crouched the length of the night, holding in my breath in such a way that he might not feel where I was.

"When he felt the birds calling in the morning, and knew that the day was, he said—'Art thou sleeping? Awake and let out my lot of goats.' I killed the buck. He cried, 'I will not believe that thou art not killing my buck.' 'I am not,' said I, 'but the ropes are so tight that I take long to loose them.' I let out one of the goats, and he was caressing her, and he said to her, 'There thou art thou shaggy, hairy white goat, and thou seest me, but I see thee not.' I was letting them out by the way of one and one, as I flayed the buck, and before the last one was out I had him flayed *bag wise*. Then I went and I put my legs in place of his legs, and my hands in place of his fore legs, and my head in place of his head, and the horns on top of my head, so that the brute might think that it was the buck. I went out. When I was going out the giant laid his hand on me, and he said, 'There thou art thou pretty buck; thou seest me, but I see thee not.' When I myself got out, and I saw the world about me, surely, oh, king! joy was on me. When I was out and had shaken the skin off me, I said to the brute, 'I am out now in spite of thee.' 'Aha!' said he, 'hast thou done this to me. Since thou were so stalwart that thou hast got out, I will give thee a ring that I have here, and keep the ring, and it will do thee good.' 'I will not take the ring from thee,' said I, 'but throw it, and I will take it with me.' He threw the ring on the flat ground, I went myself and I lifted the ring, and I put it on my finger. When he said me then. 'Is the ring fitting thee?' I said to him, 'It is.' He said, 'Where art thou ring?' And the ring said, 'I am here.' The brute went and he betook himself towards where the

* Rifts or chasms, where the sea enters.

ring was speaking, and now I saw that I was in a harder case than ever I was. I drew a dirk. I cut the finger off from me, and I threw it from me as far as I could out on the loch, and there was a great depth in the place. He shouted, 'Where art thou, ring?' And the ring said, 'I am here,' though it was on the ground of ocean. He gave a spring after the ring, and out he went in the sea. And I was as pleased here when I saw him drowning, as though thou shouldst let my own life and the life of my two sons with me, and not lay any more trouble on me.

"When the giant was drowned I went in, and I took with me all he had of gold and silver, and I went home, and surely great joy was on my people when I arrived. And as a sign for thee, look thou, the finger is off me."

"Yes, indeed, Conall, thou art wordy and wise," said the king. "I see thy finger is off. Thou hast freed thy two sons, but tell me a case in which thou ever wert that is harder than to be looking on thy two sons being hanged to-morrow, and thou wilt get the soul of thy second eldest son with thee."

"Then went my father," said Conall, "and he got me a wife, and I was married. I went to hunt. I was going beside the sea, and I saw an island over in the midst of the loch, and I came there where a boat was with a rope before her and a rope behind her, and many precious things within her. I looked myself on the boat to see how I might get part of them. I put in the one foot, and the other foot was on the ground, and when I raised my head what was it but the boat over in the middle of the loch, and she never stopped till she reached the island. When I went out of the boat the boat returned where she was before. I did not know now what I should do. The place was without meat or clothing, without the appearance of a house on it. I raised out on the top of a hill. I came to a glen; I saw in it, at the bottom of a chasm, a woman who had got a child, and the child was naked on her knee, and a knife in her hand. She would attempt to put the knife in the throat of the babe, and the babe would begin to laugh in her face, and she would begin to cry, and she would throw the knife behind her. I thought to myself that I was near my foe and far from my friends, and I called to the woman, 'What art thou doing here?' And she said to me, 'What brought thee here?' I told her myself word upon word how I came. 'Well then,' said she, 'it was so I came also.' She showed me to the place where I should come in where she was. I went in, and I said to her, 'What was in fault that thou wert putting the knife on the neck of the child.' 'It is that he must be cooked for the giant who is here, or else no more of my world will be before me.' I went up steps of stairs, and I saw a chamber full of stripped corpses. I took a lump out of the corpse that was the whitest, and I tied a string to the child's foot, and a string to the lump, and I put the lump in his mouth, and when it went in his throat he would give a stretch to his leg, and he would take it out of his throat, but with the length of the thread he could not take it out of his mouth. I cast the child into a basket of down, and I asked her to cook the corpse for the giant in place of the child. 'How can I do that?' said she, 'when he has count of the corpses.' 'Do thou as I ask thee, and I will strip myself, and I will go amongst the corpses, and then he will have the same count,' said I. She did as I asked her. We put the corpse in the great caldron, but we could not put on the lid. When he was coming home I stripped myself, and I went amongst the corpses. He came home, and she served up the corpse on a great platter, and when he ate it he was complaining that he found it too tough for a child.

" 'I did as thou asked me,' said she. 'Thou hadst count of the corpses thyself, and go up now and count them.' He counted them and he had them. 'I see one of a white body there,' said he. 'I will lie down a while and I will have him when I wake.' When he rose he went up and gripped me, and I never was in such a case as when he was hauling me down the stair with my head after me. He threw me into the caldron, and he lifted the lid and he put the lid into the caldron. And now I was sure I would scald before I could get out of that. As fortune favoured me, the brute slept beside the caldron. There I was scalded by the bottom of the caldron. When she perceived that he was asleep, she set her mouth quietly to the hole that was in the lid, and she said to me 'was I alive.' I said I was. I put up my head, and the brute's forefinger was so large, that my head went through easily. Everything was coming easily with me till I began to bring up my hips. I left the skin of my hips about the mouth of the hole, and I came out. When I got out of the caldron I knew not what to do; and she said to me that there was no weapon that would kill him but his own weapon. I began to draw his spear, and every breath that he would draw I would think I would be down his throat, and when his breath came out I was back again just as far. But with every ill that befell me I got the spear loosed from him. Then I was as one under a bundle of straw in a great wind, for I could not manage the spear. And it was fearful to look on the brute, who had but one eye in the midst of his face; and it was not agreeable for the like of me to attack him. I drew the dart as best I could, and I set it in his eye. When he felt this he gave his head a lift, and he struck the other end of the dart on the top of the cave, and it went through to the back of his head. And he fell cold dead where he was; and thou mayest be sure, oh king, that joy was on me. I myself and the woman went out on clear ground, and we passed the night there. I went and got the boat with which I came, and she was no way lightened, and took the woman and the child over on dry land; and I returned home."

The king's mother was putting on a fire at this time, and listening to Conall telling the tale about the child. "Is it thou," said she, "that were there?" "Well then," said he, " 'twas I." "Och! och!" said she, " 'twas I that was there, and the king is the child whose life thou didst save; and it is to thee that life thanks might be given." Then they took great joy.

The king said, "Oh Conall, thou camest through great hardships. And now the brown horse is thine, and his sack full of the most precious things that are in my treasury."

They lay down that night, and if it was early that Conall rose, it was earlier than that that the queen was on foot making ready. He got the brown horse and his sack full of gold and silver and stones of great price, and then Conall and his four sons went away, and they returned home to the Erin realm of gladness. He left the gold and silver in his house, and he went with the horse to the king. They were good friends evermore. He returned home to his wife, and they set in order a feast; and that was the feast, oh son and brother!

This story, told by a blind man, is a good instance of the way in which a popular tale adapts itself to the mind of everybody. The blinding of the giant and his subsequent address to his pet goat— "There thou art, thou shaggy, hairy, white goat: thou seest me, but I see thee not"—comes from the heart of the narrator. It is the ornament which his mind hangs on the frame of the story.

"James Wilson learnt it from John MacLachlan, an old man at Kilsleven, upwards of forty years ago. The old man would be about eighty years of age at the time."

CRA-BHUIDHE is probably a corruption of some proper name.

CRAG is a paw, a palm. BUIDHE, yellow.

CONALL CRA-BHUIDHE.

Bha Conall crà-bhuidhe na thuathanach foghainnteach ann an

Eirinn. Bha ceathrar mhac aige. Bha anns an am sin rìgh air a h-uile còigeamh do dh' Eirinn. Thuit e mach do chlann an rìgh a bha fagus do Chonall gun deach iad féin agus clann Chonaill thar a' chéile. Fhuair clann Chonaill làmh an uachdar, 's mharbh iad mac mòr an rìgh. Chuir an rìgh fios air Conall 's thuirt e ris, "A Chonaill, dé thug do d' mhicsa dol a leum air mo mhicsa gus an do mharbhadh mo mhac mòr le d' chloinnsa? Ach tha mi faicinn ged a leanuinn le dioghaltas thu nach mòr is fheàirde mi e, agus cuiridh mi nis ma d' choinneamh ni, agus ma ni thu e cha lean mi le dioghaltas thu. Ma gheobh thu féin agus do mhic dòmhsa each donn rìgh Lochlann, gheobh thu anamanna do mhac." "Carson," arsa Conall, "Nach dénainnsa toil an rìgh ged nach biodh anamanna mo mhac air a sgàth idir. Is cruaidh an gnothach a tha thu 'g iarraidh orm, ach caillidh mi mo bheatha féin agus beatha mo mhac air neo ni mi toil an rìgh." An déigh nam briathran so dh 'fhàg Conall an rìgh 's chaidh e dhachaidh. Nur a thàinig e dachaidh bha e fo mhòran trioblaid agus duibh-thiamhas. Nur a chaidh e laidhe dh' innis e d'a bhean an ni chuir an rìgh ma choinneamh. Ghabh a' bhean mòran duilichinn gum b'éigin da dealachadh rìthe féin, 's gun fhios aice 'm faiceadh i tuillidh e. "A Chonaill," ars' ise, "carson nach do leig thu leis an rìgh a thoil féin a dhèanadh ri d' mhic, seach a bhi folbh a nis 's gun fhios'am am faic mi tuillidh thu."

Nur a dh'éiridh iad an la'r na mhàireach chuir e e féin 's a cheithir mic an òrdugh, 's ghabh iad an turas ma thuaiream Lochlann, 's cha d' rinneadh stad leo ach a reubadh cuain gus an d' ràinig iad e. Nur a ràinigh iad Lochlann cha robh fios aca de 'dhèabnadh iad. Arsa'n seann duine ra mhic, "Stadadh sibhse agus iarraidh sinn a mach tigh muillear an rìgh." Nur a chaidh iad a stigh do thigh muillear an rìgh chuir an duine iad a dh' fhantuinn anns an oidhche. Dh'innis Conall do 'n mhuillear gun deach a chlann féin 's clann an rìgh thar a cheile 's gun do mharbh a chlannsan mac an rìgh 's nach robh ni sam bith a thoileachadh an rìgh ach e 'dh 'fhaotainn each donn rìgh Lochlann. "Ma ni thusa rùn orm 's gun cuir thu air dòigh mi gum faigh mi e, gu diongalta paighidh mi air a shon thu," orsa Conall. " 'S amaideach an ni a thàinig thu 'dh 'iarraidh," ars' am muillear, "chionn tha'n rìgh air leagail inntinn air cho mòr 's nach fhaigh thu air dòigh sam bith e mar an goid thu e; ach ma ni thu féin dòigh a mach ceilidh mise rùn ort." " 'S e tha mi smaointeachadh," ars' Conall, "o'n a tha thu 'g obair h-uile latha do 'n rìgh, gun cuireadh thu féin 's do ghillean mi féin 's mo mhic ann an còig saic pruinn." "Cha dona'n seòl a thàinig a'd' cheann," orsa 'm muillear.

Bhruidhinn am muillear r' a ghillean, 's thuirt e riu so a dheanadh, 's chuir iad ann an còig saic iad. Thàinig gillean an rìgh a dh' iarraidh a phruinn, 's thug iad leo na còig saic, 's dhoirt iad air beulthaobh nan each iad. Ghlais na seirbheisich an dorusd, 's dh' fholbh iad. Nur a dh' eirich iad a thoirt làmh air an each dhonn, orsa Conall, "Cha dèan sibh sin, tha e doirbh faotainn as a' so; deanamaid dhuinn féin còig tuill fhalaich, air alt 's ma mhòthachas iad duinn gun d' theid sinn am falach." Rinn iad na tuill. Thug iad an sin làmh air an each. Bha 'n t-each gu math uaibhreach, 's chaidh e gu stararaich fhuathasach feadh an stàbuill. Mhothaich an rìgh dha; chual e 'n stararaich. " 'S éigin gur h-e siod an t-each donn agamsa," urs' e r'a ghillean, "feuchaibh de tha ceàrr air." Chaidh na seirbheisich a mach, 's nur a mhothaich Conall 's a mhic daibh a tighinn chaidh iad 's na tuill fhalaich. Dh' amhairc na seirbheisich feadh nan each, 's cha d' fhuair iad ni sam bith cearr. Thill iad 's dh' innis iad so do 'n rìgh, 's thuirt an rìgh riu, mar an robh stugh cearr iad a dhol d' an aite taimh. Nur a bha ùine aig na gillean a bhith air folbh thug Conall 's a mhic an ath lamh air an each. Ma bu mhòr an stararaich a rinn e roimhe, bu sheachd motha an stararaich a rinn e nis. Chuir an rìgh fios air a ghillean a rìs 's thuirt e gu cinnteach gun robh rudeigin a cur dragh air an each dhonn. "Folbhaibh agus amhaircibh gu math timchioll air," ors' esan. Chaidh na seirbheisich a mach, 's chaidh iadsan do na tuill fhalaich. Rùraich na seirbheisich gu math, 's cha d' fhuair iad ni. Thill iad 's dh' innis iad so. "Tha sin iongantach leamsa," ars' an rìgh. "Theirigeadh sibse 'laidhe rithisd, 's ma mhòthachas mis' a rithisd e, théid mi féin a mach." Nur a mhothaich Conall 's a mhic gun robh na gillean air folbh thug iad lamh a rithisd air an each, 's rug fear ac' air, 's ma bu mhòr an stararaich a rinn an t-each an da shiubhal roimhid, rinn e barrachd air an t-siubhal so. "Bhuam so," urs' an rìgh; " 's éigin gu 'bheil nitheigin a' cur dragh air an each dhonn agamsa." Dh' fhuaim e 'n clag gu deifireach, 's nur a thàinig a theachdaire da 'ionnsuidh thuirt e ris gillean an stàbuill a chur air ghluasad, gun robh rudeigin ceàrr air an each. Thainig na gillean, 's dh' fholbh an rìgh leo. Nur a mhothaich Conall 's a mhic an tòir a' tighinn chaidh iad do na tuill fhalaich. Bha 'n rìgh 'na dhuine furachail, 's chunnaic e far an robh na bha toirt air na h-eich a bhi a' deanadh stararaich. "Bithibh tapaidh," urs' an rìgh, "tha daoine a stigh 's an stàbull, 's faigheamaid iad air alteigin." Lean an rìgh faileachd nan daoine, 's fhuair e iad. Bha h-uile duine eòlach air Conall; chionn bha e 'na thuathanach measail aig rìgh Eireann, 's nur a thug an rìgh nìos as na tuill iad thuirt e "U! Chonaill a' bheil

thu 'n so?" "Tha, rìgh, mi 'n so gun cheist, 's thug an eigin orm
tighinn ann. Tha mi fo d' mhathas agus fo d' onair agus fo d' ghras."
Dh' innis e mar a thachair da, 's gun robh aige 'n t-each donn r'a
fhaotainn do righ Eireann no 'mhac a bhi air a chur gu bàs. "Bha
fhios 'am nach fhaighinn e le iarraidh, 's bha mi 'dol g' a ghoid."
"Seadh, a Chonaill, tha e glé mhath, ach thig a stigh," ars an rìgh.
Dh' iarr e air a luchd coimhead faire chur air mic Chonaill, 's biadh
a thoirt dhaibh; 's chuireadh faire dhùbailt' an oidhche sin air mic
Chonaill. "Nis a Chonaill," ars' an rìgh, "an robh thu 'n àite riabh
na bu chruaidhe na 'bhith 'faicinn do chuid mac 'gan crochadh am
màireach; ach chuir thusa gum' mhathas agus gum' ghras e, 's gur
e 'n éigin a thug ort e, 's cha 'n fhaod mi thusa a chrochadh. Innis
domh càs 'sam bith 'san robh thu cho cruaidh ris a' so, 's ma dh'
innseas thu sin gheobh thu anam do mhic is òige leat." "Innsidh
mi cas cho cruaidh anns' an robh mi," orsa Conall.

"Bha mi ann am ghill'òg, 's bha mòran fearainn aig m' athair, 's
bha paircean bhiorach aige, 's bha te dhiu an deigh breith. Thuirt
mo mhathair rium a toirt dhachaidh. Dh' fholbh mi agus thug mi
leam balachan, agus fhuair sinn a' bhò, 's thug sinn leinn i. Shil fras
shneachda; chaidh sinn a stigh leinn, 's bha sinn a' leigeil dhinn na
froise; dé 'thàinig a stigh ach aona chat deug 's cat mor ruagh cam
na cheannabhard orra. Nur a thàinig iad a stigh, gu dearbh, cha
robh tlachd sam bith agam féin d' an cuideachd. "Suas sibh," ursa
'n ceannabhard, "carson a bhiodh sibh 'nar tàmh, agus seinnibh
crònan do Chonall Crà-bhuidhe." Bha iongantas orm gum' b'
aithne do na cait féin m' ainm. Nur a sheinn iad an crònan, urs' an
ceannabhard, "Nis, a Chonaill, pàigh duais a' chrònain a sheinn na
cait duit." "Mata, ursa mi fein "cha 'n 'eil duais agamsa dhuibh
mar an d' thèid sibh sios agus an laogh sin a ghabhail." Cha bu
luaithe thuirt mi 'm facal na ghabh an da chat deug a sìos an dàil
an laoigh, 's gu dearbh cha do sheas e fada dhaibh. "Suas sibh,
carson a bhiodh sibh, carson a bhiodh sibh 'nar tosd seinnibh
crònan do Chonall Crà-bhuidhe," ars an ceannard. Gu diongalta
cha robh tlachd 'sam bith agam féin d'an crònan, ach a nios a ghabh
an t-aon chat deug, 's mar an do sheinn iad dòmhsa crònan an sin
agus an sin.

"Paigh a nis'nan duais iad," ars an cat mor ruadh. "Tha mi féin
sgith dhibh féin 's de 'r duais," arsa mise, "cha 'n 'eil duais agamsa
dhuibh mar an gabh sibh am mart sin shios." Thug iad thun a
mhairt, 's gu dearbh cha do sheas i fada dhaibh. "Carson a bhios
sibh 'nur tosd theirigibh suas agus seinnibh crònan do Chonall
Crà-bhuidhe," ars an ceannard. Gu cinnteach a rìgh cha robh

amhuil agam dhaibh fèin no d' an crònan, chionn bha mi faicinn nach bu chompanaich mhath iad. Nur a sheinn iad dòmhsa 'n crònan thug iad a sìos orra far an robh an ceannard. "Pàidh a nis an duais," urs' an ceannabhard, " 's gu cinnteach a rìgh cha robh duais agamsa dhaibh, 's thuirt mi riu, "cha 'n 'eil duais agamsa dhuibh mar an d' thoir sibh am balach sin leibh, 's feum a dhèanadh dheth." Nur a chual am balach so thug e 'mach air, 's thug na cait as a dheigh; 's gu cinnteach a rìgh bha striongan eatorra. Nur a chaidh iad a mach ghabh mise mach air uinneag sgroth a bha air taobh cùil an tighe. Thug mi as cho cruaidh 's a dh' fhaodainn a stigh do 'n choille. Bha mi gle luath, làidir 'san am sin. Agus nur a mhothaich mi toirm nan cat a' m' dhéigh streap mi ann an craoibh cho àrd 's a chunnaic mi 'san àite agus a bha dùmhaill anns a bhàrr, 's dh' fhalaich mi mi féin cho math 's a dh' fhaodainn. Thòisich na cait air m'iarraidh feadh na coille, 's cha robh iad 'gam' fhaotainn, agus nur a bha iad sgìth thuirt gach fear r'a chéile gun tilleadh iad, ach thuirt am cat cam, ruadh a bha 'n cheannabhard orra, "Cha 'n fhaca sibhs' e le 'ur da shùil, 's gun agams' ach an aon sùil. Siod an slaightire shuas am bàrr na craoibhe!" Nur a thuirt e sin chaidh fear dhiu suas 'sa chraoibh, 's nur a bha e tigh'n far an robh mi tharruinn mi arm a bh' agam, agus mharbh mi e. "Bhuam so," urs' am fear cam, "cha 'n' fhaod mise 'bhi call mo chuideachd mur so. Cruinnichibh ma bhun na craoibhe, agus cladhachaibh timchioll urra, agus leagaibh an nuas an rògaire gu talamh." Chruinnich iad an so timchioll urra, agus chladhaich iad ma 'bun, agus a chiad fhreumh a gheàrr iad thug i uileann urra gu tuiteam, 's thug mi fèin glaodh asam 's cha bioghnadh e. Bha ann an iomall na coille sagairt agus deich daoin' aig a ruamhar, 's thuirt e. "Tha n' siod glaodh sòraichte cha n 'fhaod mise gun a fhreagairt." Thuirt fear a bu ghlice de na daoine, "Leigeamaid dà gus an cluinn sin a rithisd e." Thòisich na cait 's thòisich iad gu fiadhaich, 's bhrisd iad an ath fhreumh, 's thug mi féin an ath ghlaodh asam, 's gu dearbh cha robh e fann. "Gu cinnteach," ors' an sagairt, " 's duine 'na éigin a th' ann; gluaisemaid." Bha iad a' cuir an òrdugh gu gluasad, 's dh' éiridh na cait air a craoibh gus an do bhrisd iad an treas freumhach, 's thuit a craobh air a h-uileann. Thug mi 'n treas glaodh asam. Dheifirich na daoine foghainteach, 's nur a chunnaic iad an dìol a bh' aig na cait air a chraoibh; thòisich iad urra leis na spàdan, 's thòisich iad féin 's na cait air a cheile, gus an do mharbhadh gu léir iad, na daoin' agus na cait; agus gu cinnteach a rìgh cha do charaich mise gus am faca mi 'n t-aon ma dheireadh a' tuiteam diu. Thainig mi dachaidh, agus sin agad an cas an cruaidhe 'n robh mise riabh, 's air leam gum bu chruaidhe 'bhith gam' leòbadh aig na cait na bhith 'ga m' chrochadh aig rìgh Lochlann a màireach."

"Od a Chonaill," ars an rìgh, " 's briatharach thu; shaor thu anam do mhic le d' naigheachd, agus ma dh' innseas thu dhomh càs is cruaidhe na do thri mic a bhi 'gan crochadh a màireach gheobh thu do dharna mac is òige leat 's bidh an sin da mhac agad." "Mata," orsa Conall, air chùmhnant gun dèan thu sin, bha mi 'n cas a bu chruaidhe na 'bhi agadsa 'nochd am prìosan." "Cluinneam e," urs' an rìgh. "Bha mi 'n siod," orsa Connall, "am ghill' òg 's chaidh mi mach a shealgaireachd, 's bha crìoch m' athar taobh na fairge, 's bha i garbh le creagan, uamhachan, agus geothachan. Nur a bha mi folbh aig bràigh a' cladaich chunnaic mi mar gum biodh toit a' tighinn a nìos eadar da chreag, 's thug mi làmh air amharc de bu chiall do'n toit a bhi tighinn a nìos an siod. Nur a bha mi 'g amharc dè rinn mi ach tuiteam sìos, 's bha 'n t-àite cho làn do leasachadh 's nach do bhrisdeadh cnàimh na craicionn. Cha robh fios'am dé mur a gheobhainn a mach as an so. Cha robh mi 'g amharc romham ach bha mi 'g amharc as mo chionn an rathad a thàinig mi, 's cha d' thig an lath' a gheobhainn suas an sin. Bha e uamhasach leam a bhi 'n sin gus am bàsachainn. Chuala mi tuairneileis mhòr a' tighinn, 's de bha 'n sin ach famhair mòr, 's da dhusan gobhar leis, agus boc air an ceann, 's nur a cheangail am famhair na gobhair thainig e nìos 's thuirt e rium, "Haobh a Chonaill 's fhada mo chorc a' meirgeadh ann a' m' phòca a feitheamh air t-fheòil mhaoth." "Oh," arsa mise, "cha mhor is fheàird thu mise ged a reubas thu mi as a' chéile, cha dean mi ach aon trath dhuit; ach tha mi faicinn gu 'bheil thu air aon sùil, 's léigh math mise 's bheir mi sealladh na shùil eile dhuit." Dh' fholbh am famhair 's tharrainn e 'm brothadair mor air làrach a ghealbhain, 's bha mi féin aig ionnsachadh dha démur a theòigheadh e 'n t-uisge, chum gun d' thugainn a sealladh do 'n t-suil eile. Fhuair mi fraoch, 's rinn mi rubair dheth 's chuir mi 'na sheasamh anns a' brothadair e. Thòisich mi air an t-sùil a bha gu math, a' cur mar fhiachaibh air gun d' thugainn a sealladh do 'n te eile gus an d' fhag mi cho dona r'a chèil' iad; agus gu cinnteach b' fhasa 'n te a bha gu math a mhilleadh na sealladh a thoirt do 'n te eile. Nur a chunnaic e nach bu leur dha leus, 's a thuirt mi féin ris gum faighinn a mach gun taing dha, thug e 'n leum sin as an uisge 's sheas e ann am beul na h-uamha, 's thuirt e gum biodh dìoghladh aig airson sealladh a shuil. Cha robh agam ach fantainn ann am pilleag an sin fad na h-oidhche, 'cumail m' anail a stigh air dhòigh 's nach mòthchadh e càit' an robh mi. Nur a mhothaich e na h-eòin a' gairm anns a mhaidinn, 's a dh' aithnich

e gun robh an lath' ann, thuirt e, "Bheil thu 'd chadal, dùisg agus
leig a mach mo chuid ghobhar." Mharbh mi 'm boc. Ghlaoidh esan,
"Cha chreid mi nach 'eil thu marbhadh mo bhuic." "Cha n'eil,"
orsa mise, "ach tha na ròpaichean cho teann 's gun d' thoir mi fad'
air am fuasgladh. Leig mi mach te de na gobhair, 's bha e ga
criodachadh, 's thuirt e rithe. "Tha thus' an sin a ghobhar, bhàn,
riobagach, roineach, 's chi thusa mise, ach cha 'n fhaic mis' thusa."
Bha mi 'gan cuir a mach a lìon té 's té 's a feannadh a bhuic 's ma'n
robh 'n te ma dheireadh dhiu 'mach bha feannadh-builg agam air.
Dh' fholbh mi 'n so 's chuir mi mo chasan ann an àite 'chasan-
deiridh 's mo làmhan an àite 'chasan-toisich, agus mo cheann an
àite 'chinn, 's na h-adhaircean air mullach mo chinn, air alt 's gun
saoileadh a bhéisd gur e 'm boc a bh' ann. Chaidh mi 'mach. Nur
a bha mi 'dol a mach chuir am famhair a làmh orm, 's thuirt e, "Tha
thus' an sin a bhuic bhòidhich, chi thusa mise ach cha 'n fhaic mis'
thusa." Nur a fhuair mi féin a mach, 's a chunnaic mi 'n saoghal
ma 'n cuairt orm, gu cinnteach a righ bha boch orm. Nur a bha mi
mach, 's a chrath mi dhiom an craicionn, thuirt mi ris a bhéisd,
"Tha mi mach a nis gun taing duit." "Aha," urs' esan, "an d'rinn
thu so orm? O 'n a bha thu cho foghainteach 's gun d' fhuair thu
mach, bheir mi dhuit fàinn' a th' agam an so, 's gléidh am fàinne 's
ni e feum dhuit." "Cha ghabh mi 'm fàinne uait," arsa mise, "ach
tilg e, 's bheir mi leam e." Thilg e 'm fàinn' air a bhlàr, chaidh mi
fein 's thog mi 'm fàinne, 's chuir mi air mo mheur e. Nur a thuirt
e rium an sin, "A' bheil am fàinne freagairt duit?" thuirt mi ris,
"Tha." Urs' esan, "Ca' 'bheil thu fhàinne?" 's thuirt am fàinne.
"Tha mi 'n so." Dh' fholbh a' bhèisd 's thug e ionnsuidh air far an
robh 'm fainne bruidhinn, agus chunnaic mi 'n so gun robh mi 'n
càs na bu chruaidhe na bha mi riabh. Tharruinn mi biodag; ghearr
mi dhìom a' mheur; 's thilg mi uam i cho fhada 's a b' urrainn mi'
mach air an loch, 's bha dòimhneachd mhòr 's an àite. Ghlaoidh
esan, "Càit' a' bheil thu fhainne? 's thuirt am fàinne, "Tha mi 'n
so," ged a bha e 'n grunnd a chuain. Thug e leum as déigh an
fhàinne, 's a mach a ghabh e anns an fhairge 's bha mi cho toilichte
an so nur a chunnaic mi e 'ga bhathadh, 's ged a leigeadh thusa mo
bheatha fein agus beatha mo mhac leam gun mìr dragh a chuir orm.
Nur a bhàthadh am famhair chaidh mi stigh 's thug mi leam na bh'
aige 'dh' òr 's do dh' airgiod, 's chaidh mi dhachaidh, 's gu
cinnteach bha toilinntinn mhòr air mo mhuinntir nur a ràinig mi 's
mar chomharra dhuit fhaic thu 'mheur dhìom.

"Seadh a Chonaill 's briathrach seòlt' thu," ars an righ, "tha mi
faicinn do mheur dhìot. Shaor thu do dha mhac a nis ach innis

domh càs is cruaidhe an robh thu riabh na bhi'g amharc air do dha
mhac 'gan crochadh a màireach 's gheobh thu anam do dharna mic
is sine leat."

"Dh' fholbh an siod m' athair," arsa Conall, "agus fhuair e
dhomh bean, 's bha mi air mo phòsadh. Dh' fholbh mi shealg. Bha
mi folbh taobh na fairge 's chunnaic mi eilean thall am meadhon
an loch, agus thainig mi far an robh bàta an sin, 's ropa roimpe 's
ropa na deigh, 's mòran do neithean nithean luachmhor an taobh
a stigh dhi. Dh' amhaire amhairc mi féin air a bhàta feuch démur
a gheobhainn pairt diu. Chuir mi stigh an darna cas 's bha 'chas
eile air a ghrunnd, 's nur a thog mi mo cheann de ach a bha 'm bàta
nunn am meadhon an loch, 's cha do stad i gus an d' ràinig i 'n
t-eilean. Nur a chaidh mi mach as a bhàta thill am bàta far an robh
i roimhid. Cha robh fiosam an so de' dhèanainn. Bha 'n t-àite gun
bhiadh, gun aodach, gun choltas tighe air. Thog mi mach air
mullach cnoic. Thàinig mi gu gleann. Chunnaic mi ann an grunnd
glomhais bean agus leanabh aice, 's an leanabh ruisgt' air a
glùinean, agus sgian aice 'na làimh. Bheireadh i làmh air an sgian
a chuir air muineal an lèinibh, 's thòiseachadh an leanabh air
gàireachdaich na h-aodann, 's thòiseachadh ise air caoineadh, 's
thilgeadh i 'n sgian air a h-ais. Smaointich mi féin gun robh mi fagus
do m' naimhdean 's fad o m' chairdean, 's ghlaoidh mi ris a
bhoireannach. "De' tha thu 'deanadh an so?" 's thuirt i rium, "De
thug thus' an so?" Dh' innis mi féin di facal air an fhacal mar a
thàinig mi. "Mata," ors' ise, " 's ann mar sin a thainig mise
cuideachd." Sheòl i mi gus an àite 'n d' thiginn a stigh far an robh
i. Chaidh mi stigh, 's thuirt mi rithe, "De bu choireach thu bhi' cur
na sgian air muineal a phàisde?" "Tha gu 'feum mi e 'bhi bruich
airson an fhamhair a tha 'n so, air no cha bhi tuillidh do m' shaoghal
romham." Chaidh mi suas ceumanna staighreach, 's chunnaic mi
seòmar làn do chuirp rùisgte. Thug mi plaibean as a chorp a bu
ghile, agus cheangail mi sreang ri cas a phaisde 's streang ris a
phlaibean, 's chuir mi 'm plaibean 'na bheul, 's nur a bhiodh e' dol'
na mhuineal bheireadh e sìneadh air a chois, 's bheireadh e as a
mhuineal e, ach leis an fhad a bha 's an t-snàthainn cha b-urrainn
e thoirt as a bheul. Thilg mi 'm pàisd' ann am baraille clòimhe, 's
dh' iarr mi urra 'n corp a bhruich do 'n fhamhair an àite phàisde.
"Demur is urrainn mi sin a dheanadh," ars' ise, " 's gu bheil
cunndas aig air na cuirp?" "Dean thusa mar a tha mise 'g iarraidh
ort, 's rùisgidh mise mi féin, 's theid mi 'measg nan corp, 's bidh
an cunndas aig an sin," ursa mise. Rinn i mar a dh' iarr mi urra.
Chuir sin an corp anns a bhrothadair mhòr, ach chu b-urrainn

duinn am brod a chur air. Nur a bha esan a tigh'n dachaidh rùisg mise mi fein 's chaidh mi measg nan corp. Thàinig esan dachaidh, 's chuir ise 'n corp air mias mhòr, 's nur a dh' ith e e bha e a' gearan gun robh e tuillidh is righinn leis do phàisde. "Rinn mise mar a dh' iarr thu," urs' ise, "bha cunndas agad féin air na cuirp, 's theirig suas a nis agus cunnd iad." Chunnd e iad 's bha iad aige. "Tha mi 'faicinn fear corp geal an siod," urs' esan " 's théid mi 'laidhe treis, 's bidh e agam nur a dhùisgeas mi." Nur a dh' éiridh e chaidh e suas 's rug e orm, 's cha robh mi na leithid do chàs riamh, 's nur a bha e 'gam shlaodhadh sios an staighir 's mo cheann as mo dhéigh. Thilg e anns a' choire mi. Thog e 'm brod, 's chuir e 'm brod anns a choire. Bha mi 'n so cinnteach gum bithinn sàglte ma 'm faighinn as an siod. Mar bhuaidh fhortain dòmhsa chaidil a bhéisd taobh a choire. Bha mi 'n sin 'gam sgaltadh le màs a' choire. Nur a mhothaich ise gun robh e 'na chadal chuir i 'beul gu réidh ris an toll a bha 's a' bhrod, 's thuirt i rium an robh mi beò. Thuirt mi gun robh. Chuir mi suas mo cheann, 's bha corrag na beisde cho mòr 's gun deach mo cheann roimhe gu soirbh. Bha h-uile ni tigh'n leam gu soirbh gus an do thòisich mi air toirt a nios mo chruachan. Dh' fhàg mi craicionn nan cruachan ma bheul an tuill, 's thàinig mi as. Nur a fhuair mi 'mach as a choire cha robh fhios'am de' dhèanainn, 's thuirt ise rium nach robh arm sam bith a mharbhadh e ach arm féin. Thòisich mi air tarruinn na sleagh, 's a' h-uile tarruinn a bheireadh e air anail shaoilinn gum bithinn sìos 'na mhuineal, 's nur a chuireadh e 'mach anail bha mi cho fad'a rithisd air m' ais. H-uile h-olc g' an d' fhuaireadh mi fhuair mi n t-sleagh fhuasgladh uaidh. Bha mi 'n sin mar gum bithinn fo ultach cònlaich ann an gaoith mhòr, 's nach b-urrainn mi 'n t-sleagh iomachar, 's b-oillteil a bhi 'g amharc air a bhèisd, 's gun ach aon sùil an clàr aodainn, 's cha b-aobhach do m' leithidsa dol 'na dhàil. Tharruinn mi 'n t-sleagh mar a b'fheàrr a b'urrainn mi, 's chuir mi 'na shùil i. Nur a mhothaich e so thug e togail air a cheann, 's bhuail e ceann eile na sleagh ri driom na h-uamha, 's chaidh i roimhe gu cùl a chinn, 's thuit e fuar, marbh far an robh e, 's gu cinnteach dhuitse a righ bha boch ormsa. Chaidh mi fein 's am boireannach a mach air fearann glan, 's chuir sin seachad an oidhche an sin. Dh' fholbh mi agus fhuair mi m bàta leis an d' thàinig mi, agus cha robh iodramanachd sam bith urra, 's thug mi 'bhean agus am pàisde nunn air talamh tioram, agus thill mi dhachaidh."

Bha mathair an rìgh a' cur air gealbhan 'san am, 's ag éisdeachd ri Conall aig innseadh an naigheachd ma 'n phàisde. "An tus'," urs' ise "bha 'sin." "Mata," urs esan, " 's mi." "Och! och!" ors' ise,

" 's mise 'bha 'n sin, agus 's e 'n rìgh am pàisde d'an do shàbhail thu 'bheatha, agus 's ann ort a dh' fhaodar buidheachas a bheatha thobhairt." Ghabh iad an so toilinntinn mhòr. Urs' an rìgh, "A Chonaill thàinig thu ro chàsan mòr agus 's leat a nis an t-each donn, agus a shachd do na nitheannan is luachmhoire 'th' ann a'm' ionmhas." Chaidh iad a laidhe 'n oidhche, sin 's ma bu mhoch a dh' éiridh Conall bu mhoiche na sin a bha bhanrigh air a cois a 'dheanadh deas. Fhuair e an t-each donn, 's a shachd do dh' òr, 's do dh' airgiod, 's do chlacha luachmhor, 's dh' fholbh an sin Conall 's a cheathrar mac, 's thill iad dachaidh do rìoghachd aighearach Eirinn. Dh' fhàg e 'n tòr 's an t-airgiod aig an tigh, 's chaidh e leis an each thun an rìgh. Chord a féin's an rìgh, 's bha iad 'nan càirdean matha tuillidh. Thill e dhachaidh thun a mhnatha 's chuir iad an òrdugh cuirm, 's b'i chuirm i a mhic 's a bhràthair.

6

THE TALE OF CONAL CROVI.

From Neill Gillies, fisherman, near Inverary.

There was a king over England once, and he had three sons, and they went to France to get learning, and when they came back home they said to their father that they would go to see what order was in the kingdom since they went away; and that was the first place to which they went, to the house of a man of the king's tenants, by name Conal Crobhi.

Conal Crovi had every thing that was better than another waiting for them; meat of each meat, and draughts of each drink. When they were satisfied, and the time came for them to lie down, the king's big son said—

"This is the rule that we have since we came home—The good-wife must wait on me, and the maid must wait on my middle brother, and the guidman's daughter on my young brother." But this did not please Conal Crovi at all, and he said—"I won't say much about the maid and the daughter, but I am not willing to part from my wife, but I will go out and ask themselves about this matter;" and out he went, and he locked the door behind him, and he told his gillie that the three best horses that were in the stable were to be ready without delay; and he and his wife went on one, his gillie and his daughter on another, and his son and the maid on the third horse, and they went where the king was to tell the insult his set of sons had given them.

The king's watchful gillie was looking out whom he should see coming. He called out that he was seeing three double riders coming. Said the king, ha! hah! This is Conal Crovi coming, and he has my three sons under cess,* but if they are, I will not be. When Conal Crovi came the king would not give him a hearing. Then

* Cis, cess, tax, subjection.

Conal Crovi said, when he got no answer, "I will make thy kingdom worse than it is," and he went away, and he began robbing and lifting spoil.

The king said that he would give any reward to any man that would make out the place where Conal Crovi was taking his dwelling.

The king's swift rider said, that if he could get a day and a year he would find out where he was. He took thus a day and a year seeking for him, but if he took it he saw no sight of Conal Crovi. On his way home he sat on a pretty yellow brow, and he saw a thin smoke in the midst of the tribute wood.

Conal Crovi had a watching gillie looking whom he should see coming. He went in and he said that he saw the likeness of the swift rider coming. "Ha, ha!" said Conal Crovi, "the poor man is sent away to exile as I went myself."

Conal Crovi had his hands spread waiting for him, and he got his choice of meat and drink, and warm water for his feet, and a soft bed for his limbs. He was but a short time lying when Conal Crovi cried, "Art thou asleep, swift rider?" "I am not," said he. At the end of a while again he cried, "Art thou asleep?" He said he was not. He cried again the third time, but there was no answer. Then Conal Crovi cried, "On your soles! all within, this is no crouching time. The following will be on us presently." The watchman of Conal Crovi was shouting that he was seeing the king's three sons coming, and a great company along with them. He had of arms but one black rusty sword. Conal Crovi began at them, and he did not leave a man alive there but the three king's sons, and he tied them and took them in, and he laid on them the binding of the three smalls, straitly and painfully and he threw them into the peat corner, and he said to his wife to make meat speedily, that he was going to do a work whose like he never did before. "What is that, my man!" said she. "Going to take the heads off the king's three sons." He brought up the big one and set his head on the block, and he raised the axe. "Don't, don't," said he, "and I will take with thee in right or unright for ever." Then he brought up the younger one, and he did the very same to him. "Don't, don't," said he, "and I will take with thee in right or unright for ever." Then he went, himself and the king's three sons, where the king was.

The watching gillies of the king were looking out when they should see the company coming with the head of Conal Crovi. Then one called out that he was seeing the likeness of the king's three sons coming, and Conal Crovi before them.

"Ha, ha!" said the king, "Conal Crovi is coming, and he has my three sons under cess, but if they are I won't be." He would give no answer to Conal Crovi, but that he should be hanged on a gallows in the early morning of the morrow's day.

Now, the gallows was set up and Conal Crovi was about to be hanged, but the king's big son cried, "I will go in his place." The king's middle son cried, "I will go in his place;" and the king's young son cried, "I will go in his place." Then the king took contempt for his set of sons. Then said Conal Crovi, "We will make a big ship, and we will go steal the three black whitefaced stallions that the king of Eirinn has, and we will make the kingdom of Sasunn as rich as it ever was. When the ship was ready, her prow went to sea and her stern to shore, and they hoisted the chequered flapping sails against the tall tough masts; there was no mast unbent, nor sail untorn, and the brown buckies of the strand were "glagid"ing on her floor. They reached the "Paileas" of the King of Eirinn. They went into the stable, but when Conal Crovi would lay a hand on the black whitefaced stallions, the stallions would let out a screech. The King of Eirinn cried, "Be out lads; some one is troubling the stallions." They went out and they tried down and up, but they saw no man. There was an old hogshead in the lower end of the stable, and Conal Crovi and the king's three sons were hiding themselves in the hogshead. When they went out Conal laid hands on the stallion and the stallion let out a screech, and so they did three times, and at the third turn, one of those who were in the party said, that they did not look in the hogshead. Then they returned and they found the king's three sons and Conal in it. They were taken in to the king, "Ha, ha, thou hoary wretch," said the king, "many a mischief thou didst before thou thoughtest to come and steal my three black stallions."

The binding of the three smalls, straitly and painfully, was put on Conal Crovi, and he was thrown into the peat corner, and the king's three sons were taken up a stair. When the men who were above had filled themselves full of meat and drink, it was then that the king thought of sending word down for Conal Crovi to tell a tale. 'Twas no run for the king's big son, but a leap down to fetch him. Said the king, "Come up here, thou hoary wretch, and tell us a tale." "I will tell that," said he, "if I get the worth of its telling; and it is not my own head nor the head of one of the company." "Thou wilt get that," said the king. "Tost! hush! over there, and let us hear the tale of Conal Crovi":—

"As a young lad I was fishing on a day beside a river, and a great

ship came past me. They said to me would I go as 'pilot' to go to
Rome. I said that I would do it; and of every place as we reached
it, they would ask was that Rome? and I would say that it was not,
and I did not know where in the great world Rome was.

"We came at last to an island that was there, we went on shore,
and I went to take a walk about the island, and when I returned
back the ship was gone. There I was, left by myself, and I did not
know what to do. I was going past a house that was there, and I saw
a woman crying. I asked what woe was on her; she told me that the
heiress of this island had died six weeks ago, and that they were
waiting for a brother of hers who was away from the town, but that
she was to be buried this day.

"They were gathering to the burying, and I was amongst them
when they put her down in the grave; they put a bag of gold under
her head, and a bag of silver under her feet. I said to myself, that
were better mine; that it was of no use at all to her. When the night
came I turned back to the grave.* When I had dug up the grave,
and when I was coming up with the gold and the silver I caught
hold of the stone that was on the mouth of the grave, the stone fell
down and I was there along with the dead carlin. By thy hand, oh,
King of Eirinn! and by my hand, though free, if I was not in a harder
case along with the carlin than I am here under thy compassion,
with a hope to get off."

"Ha! ha! thou hoary wretch, thou camest out of that, but thou
wilt not go out of this."

"Give me now the worth of my ursgeul," said Conal.

"What is that?" said the king.

"It is that the big son of the King of Sasunn, and the big daughter
of the King of Eirinn, should be married to each other, and one of
the black white-faced stallions a tocher for them."

"Thou shalt get that," said the king.

Conal Crovi was seized, the binding of the three smalls laid on
him straitly and painfully, and he was thrown into the peat corner;
and a wedding of twenty days and twenty nights was made for the
young couple. When they were tired then of eating and drinking,
the king said that it were better to send for the hoary wretch, and
that he should tell them how he had got out of the grave.

'Twas no run, but a leap for the king's middle son to go to fetch

* The same word means cave and grave; the grave is dug because western graves
are dug; but the stone falls on the mouth of the grave, probably because the story
came from some country where graves were caves. There is an Italian story in which
this incident occurs—Decameron of Boccacio.

him; he was sure he would get a marriage for himself as he had got for his brother. He went down and he brought him up.

Said the king, "Come up and tell to us how thou gottest out of the grave." "I will tell that," said Conal Crovi, "if I get the worth of telling it; and it is not my own head, nor the head of one that is in the company." "Thou shalt get that," said the king.

"I was there till the day. The brother of the heiress came home, and he must see a sight of his sister; and when they were digging the grave I cried out, oh! catch me by the hand; and the man that would not wait for his bow he would not wait for his sword, as they called that the worst one was there; and I was as swift as one of themselves. Then I was there about the island, not knowing what side I should go. Then I came across three young lads, and they were casting lots. I asked them what they were doing thus. They said 'what was my business what they were doing?' 'Hud! hud!' said I myself, 'you will tell me what you are doing.' Well, then, said they, a great giant took away our sister. We are casting lots which of us shall go down into this hole to seek her. I cast lots with them, and there was but that the next lot fell on myself to go down to seek her. They let me down in a creel. There was the very prettiest woman I ever saw, and she was winding golden thread off a silver windle. Oh! said she to myself, how didst thou come here? I came down here to seek thee; thy three brothers are waiting for thee at the mouth of the hole, and you will send down the creel to-morrow to fetch me. If I be living, 'tis well, and if I be not, there's no help for it. I was but a short time there when I heard thunder and noise coming with the giant. I did not know where I should go to hide myself; but I saw a heap of gold and silver on the other side of the giant's cave. I thought there was no place whatsoever that was better for me to hide in than amidst the gold. The giant came with a dead carlin trailing to each of his shoe-ties. He looked down, and he looked up, and when he did not see her before him, he let out a great howl of crying, and he gave the carlins a little singe through the fire and he ate them. Then the giant did not know what would best keep wearying from him, but he thought that he would go and count his lot of gold and silver; then he was but a short time when he set his hand on my own head. 'Wretch!' said the giant, 'many a bad thing didst thou ever before thou thoughtest to come to take away the pretty woman that I had; I have no need of thee to-night, but 'tis thou shalt polish my teeth early to-morrow.' The brute was tired, and he slept after eating the carlins; I saw a great flesh stake beside the fire. I put the iron spit in the very middle of the fire till it was red. The giant was in his heavy sleep, and his mouth open, and he was snoring and blowing. I took the red spit out of the fire and I put it down in the giant's mouth; he took a sudden spring to the further side of the cave, and he struck the end of the spit against the wall, and it went right out through him. I caught the giant's big sword, and with one stroke I struck the head off him. On the morrow's day the creel came down to fetch myself; but I thought I would fill it with the gold and silver of the giant; and when it was in the midst of the hole, with the weight of the gold and silver, the tie broke. I fell down amidst stones, and bushes, and brambles; and by thy hand, oh, King of Eirinn! and by my hand, though free, I was in a harder case than I am to-night, under thy clemency, with the hope of getting out."

"Ah! thou hoary wretch, thou camest out of that, but thou wilt not go out of this," said the king.

"Give me now the worth of my ursgeul."

"What's that?" said the king.

"It is the middle son of the King of Sasunn, and the middle daughter of the King of Eirinn to be married to each other, and one of the black white-faced stallions as tocher."

"That will happen," said the king.

Conal Crovi was caught and bound with three slender ends, and tossed into the peat corner; and a wedding of twenty nights and twenty days was made for the young couple, there and then.

When they were tired of eating and drinking, the king said they had better bring Conal Crovi up, till he should tell how he got up out of the giant's cave. 'Twas no run, but a spring for the king's young son to go down to fetch him; he was sure he would get a "match" for him, as he got for the rest.

"Come up here, thou hoary wretch," said the king, "and tell us how thou gottest out of the giant's cave." "I will tell that if I get the worth of telling; and it is not my own head, nor the head of one in the company." "Thou wilt get that," said the king. "Tost! silence over there, and let us listen to the sgeulachd of Conal Crovi," said the king.

"Well! I was there below wandering backwards and forwards; I was going past a house that was there, and I saw a woman there, and she had a child in one hand and a knife in the other hand, and she was lamenting and crying. I cried myself to her, 'Hold on thy hand, woman, what art thou going to do?' 'Oh!' said she, 'I am here with three giants, and they ordered my pretty babe to be dead, and cooked for them, when they should come home to dinner.' 'I see,'

said I, 'three hanged men on a gallows yonder, and we will take
down one of them; I will go up in the place of one of them, and
thou wilt make him ready in place of the babe.' And when the giants
came home to dinner, one of them would say, 'This is the flesh of
the babe;' and another would say, 'It is not.' One of them said that
he would go to fetch a steak out of one of those who were on the
gallows, and that he would see whether it was the flesh of the babe
he was eating. I myself was the first that met them; and by thy hand,
oh, King of Eirinn, and by my hand, were it free, if I was not in a
somewhat harder case, when the steak was coming out of me, than
I am to-night under thy mercy, with a hope to get out."

"Thou hoary wretch, thou camest out of that, but thou wilt not
come out of this," said the king.

"Give me now the reward of my ursgeul?"

"Thou wilt get that," said the king.

"My reward is, the young son of the King of Sasunn, and the
young daughter of the king of Eirinn, to be married, and one of the
black stallions as tocher."

There was catching of Conal Crovi, and binding him with the
three slender ends, straitly and painfully, and throwing him down
into the peat corner; and there was a wedding made, twenty nights
and twenty days for the young pair. When they were tired eating
and drinking, the king said that it were best to bring up that hoary
wretch to tell how he came off the gallows. Then they brought
myself up.

"Come up hither, thou hoary wretch, and tell us how thou gottest
off the gallows." "I will tell that," said I myself, "if I get a good
reward." "Thou wilt get that," said the king.

"Well! when the giants took their dinner, they were tired and they
fell asleep. When I saw this, I came down, and the woman gave me
a great flaming sword of light that one of the giants had; and I was
not long throwing the heads off the giants. Then I myself, and the
woman were here, not knowing how we should get up out of the
giant's cave. We went to the farther end of the cave, and then we
followed a narrow road through a rock, till we came to light, and
to the giant's 'biorlinn' of ships.* What should I think, but that I
would turn back and load the biorlinn with the gold and silver of
the giant; and just so I did. I went with the biorlinn under sail till I
reached an island that I did not know. The ship, and the woman,
and the babe were taken from me, and I was left there to come home

* BIOR, a log; LINN a pool; LUINGEANACH, of ships; *naval barge*; or LUNN, handle
of an oar, *oared barge*.

as best I might. I got home once more to Sasunn, though I am here to-night."

Then a woman, who was lying in the chamber, cried out, "Oh, king, catch hold of this man; I was the woman that was there, and thou wert the babe." It was here that value was put on Conal Crovi; and the king gave him the biorlinn full of the giant's gold and silver, and he made the kingdom of Sasunn as rich as it ever was before.

Told by Neill Gillies a fisherman at Inverary, about fifty-five years old, who says that he has known the story, and has repeated it for many years: he learned it from his parents. Written down by
HECTOR URQUHART.

────────

SGEULACHD CHONAIL CHROBHIE.

Bha rìgh air Sasunn aon uair, agus bha triùir mhac aige, 's chaidh iad do 'n Fhraing a dh' fhaotainn ionnsachadh, agus an uair a thill iad dhachaidh, thuirt iad ri 'n athair gun rachadh iad a shealltainn de 'n riaghailt a bha san rìoghachd o n' a dh' fhalbh iad, agus b'e a cheud àite do 'n deach iad do thigh fear do thuathanaich an rìgh do 'm b' ainn Conal Cròbhi. Bha gach ni 'b 'fhearr na chéile aig Conal Cròbhi a feitheamh orra, biadh dheth gach biadh, 's deoch dheth gach deoch. 'Nuair a bha iad subhach 'sa thàinig am dhoibh dol a luidhe, thuirt mac mòr an rìgh, " 'Se so an riaghailt a th' againne bho thàinig sinn dhachaidh, gu 'm bi mise le bean an tighe nochd, agus mo bhràthair meadhonach leis an t-searbhanta, 's mo bhràthair òg le nighean fir an tighe." Ach cha do thaitinn so idir ri Conal Cròbhi, 's thubhairt e, "Mu 'n nighean 's mu'n t-searbhanta cha 'n abair mi mòran, ach cha 'n-'eil mi toilichte dealachadh ri m' bhean, ach théid mise mach agus feòraichidh mi dhiubh fhéin mu thimchioll na cùise so;" agus a mach ghabh e, 's ghlais e 'n dorus na dhéigh 's dh' iarr e air a ghille na tri eich a b' fheàrr a bha anns an stàbull a bhi deas gun dàil. Chaidh e féin 's a' bhean air fear, 's a ghille 's a nighean air fear eile, a mhac 's an searbhanta air an treas each, 's dh' fhalbh iad far an robh an rìgh, a dh' innseadh am masladh a thug a chuid mac dhoibh. Bha gille furachail an rìgh ag amharc a mach co a chitheadh e tighinn. Ghlaodh e gun robh e 'faicinn triùir mharcaiche dùbailte a' tighinn. Thuirt an rìgh, "Ha! hath! so Conal Cròbhi a' tighinn, 's mo thriùir mhacsa fo chìs aige, ach ma tha iadsan, cha bhi mise." 'Nuair a thainig Conal Cròbhi, cha d' thugadh an rìgh éisdeachd dha. Thuirt Conal Cròbhi an sin,

'nuair nach d' fhuair e freagairt, "Ni mise do rìoghachd na 's miosa
na tha i," 's dh' fhalbh e s' dh' fhàg e e, 's thòisich e air robaireachd,
's air togail chreach.

Thuirt an rìgh, gu'n d' thugadh e duais air bith do dhuine a
gheibhadh a mach an t-àite anns an robh Conal Cròbhi a' gabhail
còmhnuidh. Thuirt marcach gemeartach* an righ, na 'm faigheadh
esan latha 's bliadhna, gu 'm faigheadh esan a mach far an robh e.
Thug e mar so latha 's bliadhna, ga 'iarraidh, ach ma thug, cha 'n
fhac e sealladh do Chonal Cròbhi. Air an rathad dhachaidh, shuidh
e air maolan bòidheach buidhe 's chunnaic e caol smuid ann am
meadhom na Coille ùbhlaidh. Bha gille furachail aig Conal Cròbhi
a' sealltainn co 'chitheadh e 'tighinn. Chaidh e stigh, 's thuirt e gun
robh e 'faicinn coslas a mharcaich *ghemeartaich* a' tighinn. "Tha,
tha," thuirt Conal Cròbhi, "Tha 'n duine bochd air a chuir air falbh
air fògradh mar chaidh mi féin." Bha a làmhan sgaoilte aig Conal
Cròbhi a' feitheamh air, 's fhuair e rogha biadh 's deocha, 's burn
blath d'a chasan, 's leaba bhog d'a leasan, Cha robh e ach goirid
'na luidhe 'nuair a ghlaodh Conal Cròbhi, "Am bheil thu 'd chadal,
a mharcaich' ghemeartaich?" "Cha n'eil," thuirt esan. 'N ceann
tacain a rithist, ghlaodh e, "M bheil thu 'n ad' chadal." Thuirt e,
nach robh. Ghlaodh e 'rithist an treas uair, ach cha robh freagradh
ann. Ghlaodh Conal Cròbhi an so, "Air bhur bonn na tha stigh;
cha 'n am crùban a th' ann, bithidh an tòir oirnn an ceartair." Bha
'm fear faire aig Conal Cròbhi a glaodhaich gun robh e 'faicinn triùir
mhac an rìgh a' tighinn le cuideachd mhòr maille riu." Cha robh
do dh' airm aig' ach claidheamh meirgeach dubh. Thòisich Conal
Cròbhi orra, 's cha d' fhag e duine beò, ach triùir mhac an rìgh.
Cheangail e triùir mhac an rìgh an sin 's thug e stigh iad. Chuir e
ceangal nan tri chaoil orra gu daor 's gu docair, 's thilg e ann an
cùil na mòn' iad, 's thuirt e ri 'bhean biadh a dhèanamh gu luath,
gu 'n robh e 'dol a dhèanamh obair nach d' rinn e riamh roimhe a
leithid. "Gu dé sin a dhuine?" thuirt ise. "Dol a thoirt nan ceann
do thriùir mhac an rìgh." Thug e nìos am fear mòr, 's chuir e
'cheann air an ealaig 's thog e 'n tuadh. "Na deàn! na deàn," thuirt
esan, " 's gabhaidh mi leat fhéin an còir 's an eucoir gu bràth." Thug
e nìos an sin am fear meadhonach; chuir e cheann air an ealaig, 's
thog e 'n tuadh. "Na deàn! Na deàn!" thuirt esan, " 's gabhaidh mi
leat fhéin an còir 's an eucoir gu bràth." Thug e nìos an sin am fear
òg, 's rinn e 'leithid eile air. "Na deàn! Na deàn!" thuirt esan, " 's
gabhaidh mi leat an coir 's an eucoir gu bràth." Dh' fhalbh e fhéin

---

* Gemeartach, swift (*not in dictionaries*); probably from CEUM, a pace.

an sin 's triùir mhac an rìgh far an robh an rìgh. Bha gillean furachail an rìgh a' sealltainn a mach, cuin a chitheadh iad a' tighinn a chudeachd le ceann Chonail Chròbhi. Ghlaodh fear amach, gun robh e 'faicinn coslas triùir mhac an rìgh a' tighinn, 's Conal Cròbhi air an toiseach. "Ha! ha!" thuirt an rìgh, "tha Conal Cròbhi a' tighinn 's mo thriùir mhac aige fo chìs, ach ma tha iadsan, cha bhi mise." Cha d'thugadh e freagradh do Chonal Cròbhi, ach gu 'm bitheadh e air a chrochadh air croich air moch maduinn an latha màireach. Nis chaidh a chroich a chuir suas, 's bha Conal Cròbhi gu bhi air a chrochadh; ach ghlaodh mac mòr an rìgh, "Théid mise na àite." Ghlaodh mac meadhonach an rìgh, "Théid mise na àite." Ghlaodh mac og an rìgh, "Théid mise na àite." Ghabh an rìgh mìothlachd an so ri 'chuid mac. Thuirt Conal Cròbhi an sin, "Ni sinn long mhòr agus théid sinn a ghoid nan tri òigeach bhlàra, dhubha a tha aig rìgh Eirinn, 's ni sinn rìoghachd Shasuinn co beartach sa bha i riamh.

'Nuair a bha 'n long deas, chaidh a toiseach ri muir 's a deireadh ri tìr, 's thog iad na siùil bhreaca, bhaidealach ri aghaidh nan crann fada, fulannach, 's cha robh crann gun lùbadh na seòl gun reubadh, 's bha faochagan ruadh a chladaich a glaga-daich air a h-urlar. Ràinig iad pàileas rìgh Eirinn; chaidh iad a stigh do 'n stàbull, ach a nuair a chuireadh Conal Cròbhi a làmh air na h-òigeich bhlàra, dhubha, leigeadh na h-oigeich sgreuch asda. Ghlaodh rìgh Eirinn, "Bithibh a mach, fhearaibh, tha cuideiginn a cur dragh air na h-òigeich." Chaidh iad a mach, 's dh' fheuch iad shìos as shuas ach cha n' fhac iad duine. Bha seann togsaid an ceann shìos an stàbuill, agus bha Conal Cròbhi 's triùir mhac an rìgh 'gam folach fhéin 's an togsaid. 'Nuair a chaidh iadsan a mach, chuir Conal a làmh air an òigeach, ach leig an t-òigeach sgreuch as. Rinn iad so tri uairean, agus air an treas tròmh, thuirt fear do na bha sa chuideachd, nach do sheall iad san togsaid. Sheall iad an sin 's fhuair iad triùir mhac an righ agus Conal anns an togsaid. Chaidh an tabhairt a stigh a dh' ionnsaidh an righ. "Ha! ha! a bhéist liath," thuirt an righ, " 's iomadh cron a rinn thu mu 'n do smaoinich thu tighinn a ghoid nan òigeach dhubh agamsa." Chaidh ceangal nan tri chaoil gu daor 's gu docair a chur air Conal Cròbhi, 's thilgeadh an cùil na moine e, 's chaidh triùir mhac an righ a thoirt an àird staidhir. 'Nuair a lion na fir a bha gu h'àrd iad féin làn do bhiadh, 's do dheoch, 's ann a smaoinich an righ fios a chur a nios air Conal Cròbhi, a dh' innseadh sgeulachd. Cha bu ruith do mhac mòr an righ ach leum sios, g'a iarraidh. Thuirt an righ, "Thig a nios an so, a bhéist liath, 's innis dhuinn sgeulachd." "Innsidh mi sin," thuirt esan, "ma gheibh mi fiach innseadh, 's cha 'n e mo cheann fhéin na ceann aon do 'n chuideachd." "Gheibh thu sin," thuirt an rìgh. "Tosd! thall an sin, 's éisdibh ri sgeulachd Chonail Chrobhi," thuirt an righ!

" 'Nam' ghill' òg, bha mi 'g iasgach latha aig taobh aibhne, 's thàinig long mhòr seachad orm; thuirt iad rium 'an gabhainn a' m' *philot* gu dhol au Ròimh; thuirt mi gu 'n dèanainn e, agus na h-uil' aite, do 'n ruigeamaid, dh' fheòraicheadh iad, am b'e siud an Ròimh? 's theirinn-sa nach b'i, 's cha robh fios agam, c'ait' air an t-saoghal mhòr an robh an Ròimh. Thàinig sinn mu dheireadh gu h-eilean a bha 'n sin. Chaidh sinn air tir agus chaidh mise a ghabhail sràid feadh an eilean, agus dur a thill mi air m' ais, bha 'n long air falbh. Bha mi 'n sin air m' fhàgail leam fhéin, 's cha robh fios agam de a dhèanainn. Bha mi 'dol seachad air tigh a bha 'n sin, 's chunnaic mi bean ri caoineadh. Dh' fheòraich mi dhi de 'm bròn a bha orra? Thuirt i rium 'gu 'n do bhàsaich ban-oighre an eilean so bho cheann sèa seachduinnean agus gu 'n robh i ri 'tìodhlacadh an latha so. Bha iad a' cruinneachadh gus an tiodhlacadh, 's bha mise 'nam measg, 's 'nuair a chuir iad sios anns an uaigh i, chuir iad poc' òir fuidh 'ceann, 's poc' airgid fuidh casan. Thuirt mise rium fhéim, gu 'm b'fheàrr sud agam fhéin, nach robh e gu feum sam bith dh' ise. 'Nuair a thàinig an oidhche thill mi air m' ais gus an uaigh. An uair a chladhaich mi 'n uaigh, 's a bha mi tighinn a nios leis an òr 's leis an airgiod, rug mi air a chlach a bha air beul na huaighe. Thuit a chlach a nuas, 's bha mise còmhladh ris a chailleach mharbh an sin. Air do làimhsa, a righ Eirinn, 's air mo làimh-sa, ge saor e, mur robh mi ni bu chruaidh còmhladh ris a chaillich na tha mi 'n so fo t'iochd-sa, 's dùil ri dol as agam." "Ha! Ha! a bhéist liath, thàinig thu as an sin, ach cha téid thu as an so." "Thoir dhomh a nis fiach m' ursgeul," arsa Conal. "Gu de sin," thuirt an righ. "Tha mac mòr righ Shasuinn, agus nighean mhòr righ Eirinn a bhi air am pòsadh ri 'chéile, agus fear do na h-òigeich bhlàra, dhubha na thocharadh." "Gheibh thu sin, thuirt an righ." Chaidh beireachd air Conal Cròbhi, 's ceangal nan tri chaoil a chuir air gu daor 's gu docair, 's a thilgeil an cùil na moine, 's chaidh banais fichead oidhche 's fichead latha a dhèanamh do 'n chàraid òg. 'Nuair a bha iad sgith an sin ag itheadh 's ag òl, thuirt an righ, gu 'm b' fheàrr fios a chuir air a bhéist liath, 's gu 'n innseadh é gu de mar fhuair é as an uagh. Cha bu ruith ach leum le mac meadhonach an righ gu dol g'a iaraidh. Bha e cinnteach gu 'faigheadh e pòsadh dha fhéin, mar fhuair e d'a bhràthair. Chaidh e sìos 's thug e nios e. Thuirt an righ, "Thig a nios 's innis dhuinn cionnas a fhuair thu as an uaigh." "Innsidh mi sin," thuirt Conal Crobhi, "ma gheibh mi fiach innseadh, 's cha 'n e mo cheann féin, na ceann h-aon a tha sa chuideachd." "Gheibh thu sin," thuirt an righ.

Bha mise an sin gus an latha. Thàinig bràthair na ban-oighre dhachaidh, 's dh' fheumadh e sealladh d'a phiuthar fhaicinn agus dar a bha iad a cladhach na h-uaighe, ghlaodh mise, "O, beir air làimh orm!" 'S am fear nach fanadh ri 'bhogha cha 'n fhanadh ri 'chlaidheamh, 's iad a glaodhaich gu 'n robh am fear bu mhiosa an siud, 's bha mise cho luath ri h-aon aca fhéin. Bha mi 'n sin air feadh an eilean gu 'n fhios dé 'n taobh a rachainn. Thàinig mi 'n sin tarsuinn air triùir ghillean òga, 's iad a cuir chrann.

Dh' fheòraich mi dhiubh, de a bha iad a dèanamh mar siud. Thuirt iad de mo ghnothuchsa de bha iad a dèanamh. "Hud! Hud!" arsa mi fhéin, "innsidh sibh dhomh dé tha sibh a dèanamh." "Mata," thuirt iadsan, "thug famhair mòr air falbh ar piuthar 's tha sin a cuir chrann feuch co againn a théid sìos do 'n toll so g'a h-iarraidh." Chuir mise crann leo 's cha robh ann ach gu'n d' thàinig an crann orm fhéin gu dol sios g' a h-iarraidh. Leig iad sìos mi ann an cliabh. Bha an sin an aon bhoirionnach bu bhòidhche a chunnaic mi riabh, 's i tochras snàth òir far eachan airgid. "O!" thuirt, ise rium, fhéin, "de mar thàinig thusa an so?" "Thàinig mise a nuas gu d' iarraidh; tha do thriuir bhràithrean a feitheamh ort aig beul an tuill, agus cuiridh sibh a nuas an cliabh am màireach gu m' iarraidh-sa. Ma bhitheas mi beò 's maith, 's mar bi cha 'n 'eil atharrach air." Cha robh mi ach goirid an sin a nuair a chuala mi stairum 's stararaich a tighinn aig an fhamhair. Cha robh fios agam càite an rachainn am falach; ach chunnaic mi dùn òir 's airgid an taobh thall uamh an fhamhair. Smaoinich mi nach robh àite air bith a b' fheàrr dhomh dol am folach na 'measg an òir. Thàinig am famhair a stigh, 's cailleach mharbh slaodadh ris gach barrall bròig' aige. Sheall e shòs 's sheall e shuas, 's dar nach fac e is' air thoiseach air, leig e burrall mòr caoinidh as. Thug e dathadh air na cailleachan roimh 'n ghealbhan's dh' ith e iad. Cha robh fhios aig an fhamhair an so de 'n rud a b' fheàrr a chumadh fhadal deth, ach smaointich e gu 'n rachadh e a chunntas a chuid òir a's airgid. Cha robh e ach goirid an sin 'nuair a chuir e làmh air mo cheann fhéin. "A bhéist!" thuirt am famhair, " 's ioma droch rud a rinn thu riamh mu 'n do smaoinich thu tighinn an so a thoirt air falbh a' bhoirinnaich bhòidheach a bh' agam-sa. Cha 'n 'eil feum agamsa ort an nochd, ach 's tu ghlanas m' fhiaclan moch am màireach." Bha a bhéist sgìth 's chaidil e 'n déigh na caillich itheadh. Chunnaic mi bior mòr feòla ri taobh a ghealbhain. Chuir mi 'n teismeadhoin an teine am bior iaruinnn, gus an robh e dearg. Bha 'm famhair 'na throm chadal,

's a bheul fosgailte, 's e 'rùchdail 's a séideil. Thug mi 'm bior dearg
as an teine, 's chuir mi sìos am beul an fhamhair e. Thug e grad
leum gu taobh thall na h-uaimh, 's bhuail e ceann a bhior ris a'
bhalla 's chaidh e mach roi 'n cheann eile. Rug mi air claidheamh
mòr an fhamhair, agus le aon bheum chuir mi 'n ceann dheth. Air
an latha màireach, thàinig an cliabh a nuas gum m' iarraidh fhéin.
Ach smaoinich mi gu 'n lìonainn an cliabh do dh' òr 's do dh' airgiod
an fhamhair, 's dar a bha e 'm meadhon an tuill, le cudthrom an
òir 's an airgid, bhris an iris, thuit mi nuas a measg chlachan, 's
phris, 's dhris, 's air do làimhsa, a rìgh Eirinn, 's air mo làimhs ge
saor e, bha mi 'n càs bu chruaidhe na tha mi nochd fo t'iochdsa 's
dùil agam ri dol as." "Ah! a bhéist liath, thàinig thu as an sin, ach
cha téid thu as an so," ars' an rìgh. "Thoir dhomh a nis fiach m'
ursgeul," arsa Conal. "De sin?" thuirt an rìgh. "Tha mac
meadhonach righ Shasuinn 's nighean mheadhonach rìgh Eirinn a
bhi air am pòsadh ri 'chéile 's fear do na h-òigeich bhlàra, dhubha
mar thochradh." "Tachraidh sin," thuirt an righ. Chaidh beireachd
air Conal Cròbhi 's a cheangal le tri chinn chaoil, sa thilgeadh an
cuil na mòine, 's chaidh banais fichead oidhche 's fichead latha a
dhèanamh do 'n chàraid òig. An sin, 'nuair a bha iad sgìth 'g itheadh
's ag òl, thuirt an righ, gu 'm b'fheàrr dhoibh Conal Cròbhi a thoirt
a nìos gus an innseadh e cionnas a fhuair e nìos a uamh an fhamhair.
Cha bu ruith ach leum le mac òg an rìgh dol sòs g' a iarraidh. Bha
e cinnteach gu 'faigheadh e pòsadh dha fhéin mar fhuair e do chàch.
"Thig a nìos an so, a bhéist liath," thuirt an rìgh, " 's innis duinn
ciamar a fhuair thu a uaigh an fhamhair." "Innsidh mi sin, ma
gheibh mi fiach innseadh, 's cha 'n e mo cheann fhein no ceann
h-aon do na 'bheil sa chuideachd." "Gheibh thu sin," thuirt an righ.
"Tosd! thall an sin, 's eisdeamaid ri sgeulachd Chonail Chròbhi,"
thuirt an righ! (Well), bha mise gu h-ìosal an sin, 's mi
spaisdeireachd air m' ais 's air m' aghaidh. Bha mi 'dol seachad air
tigh a bha 'n sin 's chunnaic mi bean an sin, 's leanabh aice san
darna laimh, 's sgian aice san làimh eile, 's i 'caoinneadh. Ghlaodh
mi fhéin rithe, "Cum air do làmh a bhean; de tha thu dol a
dhèanamh mar sin?" "O!" thuirt ise, "tha mi aig tri famhairean an
so, agus dh' iarr iad orm, mo leanabh bòidheach a bhi marbh 's air
a bhruich air an cionn 'nuair a thigeadh iad dhachaidh gu 'n dinnear.
Chi mi," arsa mise, "triùir dhaoine crochta air croich thall an siud,
bheir sinn a nuas fear dhiubh, agus théid mise suas na àite, 's
deasaichidh tu esan an àite do leinibh." Agus a nuair a thàinig na
famhairean dhachaidh gu 'n dinnear, theireadh fear dhiubh, " 'S e
so feòil an leinibh," 's theireadh fear eile, "cha 'n e." Thuirt fear

dhiubh, gu 'n rachadh e a thoirt staoig a fear do na bha air a chroich, agus gu 'faiceadh e co dhiu 's e feòil an leinibh a bha iad ag itheadh. 'S me fhéin a cheud fhear a thachair orra, 's air do làimh, a rìgh Eirinn, 's air mo làimhsa, ge saor e, mur robh mi ann an cruaidh-chàs ni bu mhò 'nuair a bha 'n staoig a tighinn asam, na tha mi nochd fo t'iochdsa 's dùil ri dol as agam. "A bhéist liath, thàinig thu as an sin, ach cha d' thig thu as an so," ars' an rìgh. "Thoir dhomh a nis duais m' ursgeul." "Gheibh thu sin," ars' an rìgh. "'S e mo dhuais, mac òg rìgh Shasuinn, 's nighean òg rìgh Eirinn a bhi posda, 's fear do na h-òigeich dhubha mar thochradh." Chaidh beireached air Conal Cròbhi, 'sa cheangal le cinn nan tri chaoile gu daor 's gu docair, 's a thilgeadh sìos an cùil na mòine, 's chaidh banais fichead latha 's fichead oidhche a dhèanamh do 'n chàraid òig. 'Nuair a bha iad sgìth 'g itheadh 's a g òl, thuirt an rìgh, gu b' fheàrr a bhéist liath ad a thoirt a nìos, a dh' innseadh de mar thàinig e bhàrr na croiche. Thug iad an so a nìos mi fhéin. "Thig a nìos, a bhéist liath an so, 's innis dhuinn de mar fhuair thu bharr na croiche." "Innsidh mi sin," arsa mi fhéin, "ma gheibh mi duais mhaith." "Gheibh thu sin," thuirt an righ. (Well) a nuair a ghabh na famhairean an dinneir bha iad sgìth, 's thuit iad 'nan cadal. 'Nuair a chunnaic mise so, thàinig mi nuas 's thug a' bhean dhomh claidheamh mòr, lasrach soluis a bha aig fear do na famhairean, 's cha robh mi fada a tilgeadh nan ceann do na famhairean. Bha mi fhéin 's am boirionnach an so gun fhios againn cionnas a gheibheamaid a nìos a' uamh an fhamhair. Dh' fhalbh sinn gu ceann shìos na h-uaimh 's lean sinn an sin rathad cumhang roi chreag gus an d' thàinig sinn gu solus 's gu bior-linn luingeanach an fhamhair. Smuainich mi fhéin gum pillinn air m' ais agus gu 'n luchdaichinn a bhior-linn le òr 's le airgiod an fhamhair, agus mar so fhéin rinn mi. Dh' fhalbh mi leis a bhior-linn fo shèol gus an d' thàinig mi gu h-eilean nach b' aithne dhomh. Chaidh an long, 's am boirionach, 's an leanabh a thoirt uam, 's fagar mise an sin gu tighinn dhachaidh mar a b'fheàrr a dh' fhaodainn. Fhuair mi dhachaidh aon uair eile do Shasunn, ged tha mi 'n so a nochd.

Ghlaodh boirionnach a bha na luidhe san t-seomar, "O a rìgh, beiribh air an duine so. Bu mhise am boirionach a bha 'n sin, 's bu tusa an leanabh." 'S ann an so a bha 'm meas air Conal Cròbhi, 's thug an rìgh dha a bhior-linn làn òir 's airgid an fhamhair 's rinn e rioghachd Shasuinn cho beartach 's a bha i riamh.

This story was told to me at Inveraray, April 25, 1859, by Gillies. It was told with the air of a man telling a serious story, and anxious to tell it correctly. The narrative was interlarded with explanations of the words used, and the incidents described. Those who sat about the fire argued points in the story. These were John MacKenzie, fisherman; John MacDonald, travelling tinker; John Clerk, our host, formerly miller to the Duke of Argyll; and some others, whose names I have forgotten. The story is very correctly written. I took notes at the time, and they agree with the Gaelic as written by Hector Urquhart, from the dictation of Gillies.

7

THE TALE OF CONNAL.

From Kenneth MacLennan, Pool Ewe.

There was a king over Eirinn once, who was named King Cruachan, and he had a son who was called Connal MacRigh Cruachan. The mother of Connal died, and his father married another woman. She was for finishing Connal, so that the kingdom might belong to her own posterity. He had a foster mother, and it was in the house of his foster mother that he made his home. He and his eldest brother were right fond of each other; and the mother was vexed because Connal was so fond of her big son. There was a bishop in the place, and he died; and he desired that his gold and silver should be placed along with him in the grave. Connal was at the bishop's burying, and he saw a great bag of gold being placed at the bishop's head, and a bag of silver at his feet, in the grave. Connal said to his five foster brothers, that they would go in search of the bishop's gold; and when they reached the grave, Connal asked them which they would rather; go down into the grave, or hold up the flagstone. They said that they would hold up the flag. Connal went down; and whatever the squealing was that they heard, they let go the flag and they took to their soles home. Here he was, in the grave on top of the bishop. When the five of foster brothers reached the house, their mother was somewhat more sorrowful for Connal than she would have been for the five. At the end of seven mornings, there went a company of young lads to take the gold out of the bishop's grave, and when they reached the grave they threw the flag to the side of the further wall; Connal stirred below, and when he stirred they went, and they left each arm and dress they had. Connal arose, and he took with him the gold, and arms and dress, and he reached his foster mother with them. They were all merry and lighthearted as long as the gold and silver lasted.

There was a great giant near the place, who had a great deal of gold and silver in the foot of a rock; and he was promising a bag of gold to any being that would go down in a creel. Many were lost in this way; when the giant would let them down, and they would fill the creel, the giant would not let down the creel more till they died in the hole.

On a day of days, Connal met with the giant, and he promised him a bag of gold, for that he should go down in the hole to fill a creel with the gold. Connal went down, and the giant was letting him down with a rope; Connal filled the giant's creel with the gold, but the giant did not let down the creel to fetch Connal, and Connal was in the cave amongst the dead men and the gold.

When it beat the giant to get another man who would go down in the hole, he sent his own son down into the hole, and the sword of light in his lap, so that he might see before him.

When the young giant reached the ground of the cave, and when Connal saw him he caught the sword of light, and he took off the head of the young giant.

Then Connal put gold in the bottom of the creel, and he put gold over him; and then he hid in the midst of the creel, and he gave a pull at the rope. The giant drew the creel, and when he did not see his son, he threw the creel over the top of his head. Connal leaped out of the creel, and the black back of the giant's head (being) towards him, he laid a swift hand on the sword of light, and he took the head off the giant. Then he betook himself to his foster mother's house with the creel of gold and the giant's sword of light.

After this, he went one day to hunt on Sliamh na leirge. He was going forwards till he went into a great cave. He saw, at the upper part of the cave, a fine fair woman, who was thrusting the flesh stake at a big lump of a baby; and every thrust she would give the spit, the babe would give a laugh, and she would begin to weep. Connal spoke, and he said,—"Woman, what ails thee at the child without reason?" "Oh," said she, "since thou art an able man thyself, kill the baby and set it on this stake, till I roast it for the giant." He caught hold of the baby, and he put a plaid that he had on about the babe, and he hid the baby at the side of the cave.

There were a great many dead bodies at the side of the cave, and he set one of them on the stake, and the woman was roasting it.

Then was heard under ground trembling and thunder coming, and he would rather that he was out. Here he sprang in the place of the corpse that was at the fire, in the very midst of the bodies, The giant came, and he asked, "Was the roast ready?" He began to eat, and he said, "Fiu fau hoagrich; it's no wonder that thy own flesh is tough; it is tough on thy brat."

When the giant had eaten that one, he went to count the bodies; and the way he had of counting them was, to catch hold of them by the two smalls of the leg, and to toss them past the top of his head; and he counted them back and forwards thus three or four times; and as he found Connal somewhat heavier, and that he was soft and fat, he took that slice out of him from the back of his head to his groin. He roasted this at the fire, and he ate it, and then he fell asleep. Connal winked to the woman to set the flesh stake in the fire. She did this, and when the spit grew white after it was red, he thrust the spit through the giant's heart, and the giant was dead.

Then Connal went and he set the woman on her path homewards, and then he went home himself. His stepmother sent him and her own son to steal the whitefaced horse from the King of Italy, "Eadailt;" and they went together to steal the whitefaced horse, and every time they would lay hand on him, the whitefaced horse would let out an *ialt* (neigh?). A "company" came out, and they were caught. The binding of the three smalls was laid on them straitly and painfully. "Thou big red man," said the king, "wert thou ever in so hard a case as that?" "A little tightening for me, and a loosening for my comrade, and I will tell thee that," said Connal.

The Queen of the Eadailt was beholding Connal.

Then Connal said:—

> "Seven morns so sadly mine,
> As I dwelt on the bishop's top,
> That visit was longest for me,
> Though I was the strongest myself.
> At the end of the seventh morn
> An opening grave was seen,
> And I would be up before
> The one that was soonest down.
> They thought I was a dead man,
> As I rose from the mould of earth;
> At the first of the harsh bursting
> They left their arms and their dresses.
> I gave the leap of the nimble one,
> As I was naked and bare.
> 'Twas sad for me, a vagabond,
> To enjoy the bishop's gold."

"Tighten well, and right well," said the king; "it was not in one good place that he ever was; great is the ill he has done." Then he was tightened somewhat tighter, and somewhat tighter; and the king said, "Thou great red man, wert thou ever in a harder case than that?" "Tighten myself, and let a little slack with this one beside me, and I will tell thee that."

They did that. "I was," said he,

> "Nine morns in the cave of gold;
> My meat was the body of bones,
> Sinews of feet and hands.
> At the end of the ninth morn
> A descending creel was seen;
> Then I caught hold on the creel,
> And laid gold above and below;
> I made my hiding within the creel;
> I took with me the glaive of light,
> The luckiest turn that I did."

They gave him the next tightening, and the king asked him, "Wert thou ever in case, or extremity, as hard as that?" "A little tightening for myself, and a slack for my comrade, and I will tell thee that."

They did this.

> "On a day on Sliabh na leirge,
> As I went into a cave,
> I saw a smooth, fair, mother-eyed wife,
> Thrusting the stake for the flesh
> At a young unreasoning child. 'Then,' said I,
> 'What causes thy grief, oh wife,
> At that unreasoning child?'
> 'Though he's tender and comely,' said she,
> 'Set this baby at the fire.'
> Then I caught hold on the boy,
> And wrapped my 'maundal' around;
> Then I brought up the great big corpse
> That was up in the front of the heap;
> Then I heard, Turstar, Tarstar, and Turaraich,
> The very earth mingling together;
> But when it was his to be fallen
> Into the soundest of sleep,
> There fell, by myself, the forest fiend;

I drew back the stake of the roast,
And I thrust it into his maw."

There was the Queen, and she was listening to each thing that Connal suffered and said; and when she heard this, she sprang and cut each binding that was on Connal and on his comrade: and she said, "I am the woman that was there;" and to the king, "thou art the son that was yonder."

Connal married the king's daughter, and together they rode the whitefaced horse home; and there I left them.

From HECTOR URQUHART, June 27, 1859. Recited by KENNETH MACLENNAN of Turnaig, Pool Ewe, Ross-shire, aged 70, who learned it from an old man when he was a boy.

SGEULACHD CHONAILL.

Bha righ air Eirinn aon uair da 'm b-ainm righ Cruachan, 's bha mac aige, ris an abradh iad Conall, mac righ Cruachan. Chaochail màthair Chonaill, agus phòs athair bean eile. Bha i air son cuir as do Chonall, chum 's gu'm biodh an rìoghachd aig a sliochd féin. Bha muime chìche aige-san, agus 's ann an tigh a mhuime bha e 'dèanamh a dhachaidh. Bha e fhèin 's a bhràthair bu shine ro mheasail aig a' chéile, agus bha mhàthair gamhlasach air son gu robh Conall cho measail aig a mac mòr. Bha Easbuig anns an àite, agus chaochail e, agus dh' iarr e 'n t-òr 's an t-airgiod aige, a chuir cuide ris anns an uaigh. Bha Conall aig tìodhlacadh an Easbuig, agus chunnaic e pòc mòr òir a dol aig ceann an Easbuig, agus pòc airgid aig a chasan 's an uaigh. Thubhairt Conall ri chuignear chomh-dhaltan, "gu 'rachadh iad air thòir òr an Easbuig," agus nur a ràinig iad an uaigh, dh' fheòraich Conall dhiubh-san. "Co b' fhearr leo dol sìos do 'n uaigh na 'n leac a chumail suas?" Thuirt iadsan gu cumadh iad an leac suas. Chaidh Conall sìos, agus ge b' e sgiamhail a chual' iadsan, leig iad as an leac, agus thug iad na buinn asda dhachaidh. Bha e 'n so 's an uaigh air muin an Easbuig. 'Nuair a ràinig na cuignear bhràithrean altrum an tigh, bha 'm màthair ni bu bhrònaiche airson Chonaill na bhitheadh i airson a Chùigear. An ceann seachd tràithean, dh' fhalbh Cuideachd do ghillean òga a thoirt an òir a uaigh an easbuig' agus nur a ràinig iad an uaigh, thilg iad an leac ri taobh a bhalla thall. Ghluais Conall shìos, agus nur a ghluais, dh' fhalbh iadsan: dh' fhàg iad gach arm 's aodach 'bha aca; dh' eirich Conall, 's thug e leis gach òr, 's gach arm, 's ràinig e mhiume chiche leis. Bha iad uile gu subhach, sòlasach, cho fad, 's a mhair an t-òr 's an t-airgiod. Bha famhair mòr dhlùth do'n àite, aig an robh mòran òir 's airgid ann an Cois Creige, agus bha e 'gealltainn poc òir do neach sam bith a rachadh sìos ann an cliabh. Bha mòran air an call mar so. Nur a leigeadh am famhair sìos iad, 's a lionadh iad an Cliabh, cha chuireadh am famhair sios an cliabh tuillidh, gus am bàsaicheadh iadsan 'san toll. Latha do na làithean, thachair Conall ris an fhamhair, agus gheall e poc òir dha airson a dhol sìos do 'n toll a lionadh cliabh do 'n òr. Chaidh Conall sìos, agus bha 'm famhair 'ga leigeil sìos le ròp. Lìon Conall cliabh an fhamhair do 'n òr, ach cha do leig am famhair sìos an cliabh air thoir Chonaill, 's bha Conall 'san uaigh measg nan daoine marbha, 's an òir. 'Nuair a dh' fhairslich air an fhamhair duine tuillidh fhaotainn a rachadh sìos do 'n toll, chuir e 'mhac fhéin sìos do 'n toll 's an claidheamh soluis air uchd, chum 's gu 'faiceadh e roimhe. Nur a ràinig am famhair òg grund na h-uaimh, 'sa chunnaic Conall e, rug e air a chlaidheamh sholuis, agus thug e 'n ceann do 'n fhamhair òg. Chuir Conall an so òr ann am màs a' chleibh, agus chuir e òr os a cheann: rinn e 'n so fhalach am meadhon a' chléibh: thug e tarruing air an ròp; tharruing am famhair an cliabh, agus dur nach fac e 'mhac 'sa chliabh, thilg e 'n cliabh thar mullach a a chinn. Leum Conall as a' chliabh, 's dubh chùl cinn an fhamhair ris: thug e grad làmh air a' chlaidheamh sholuis, agus thug e 'n ceann do 'n fhamhair. Thug e 'n so tigh a mhuime chìch' air, leis a chliabh òir, 's claidheamh soluis an fhamhair. 'Na dhéigh so, chaidh e latha a shealg so Shliabh na leirge. Bha e gabhail air adhart, gus an deach e stigh, do dh' uaimh mhòr. Chunnaic e 'n uachdar na h-uaimh bean bhàn, bhrèagha 's i putadh bior na feola ri ultach mòr do leanabh, 's na h-uile putadh a bha ise 'toirt do 'n bhior, dhèanadh an leanabh gàire, 's thòisicheadh ise air caoineadh. Labhair Conall, 's thubhairt e, "De fath do bhròin, a bhean, ris an òganach gun chiall." "O!" os ise, "bho 'n is duine tapaidh thu fhéin, marbh an leanabh, 's cuir air a bhior so e, gus an ròist mi e do 'n fhamhair." Rug e air an leanabh, 's chuir e 'n cleòc a bha air mu 'n leanabh, 's dh' fholuich e 'n leanabh am taobh na h-uaimh. Bha mòran do chuirp mharbh' an taobh na h-uaimh, 's chuir e fear dhiubh air a' bhior, 's bha 'm boirionnach 'ga ròstadh. Chualas fo 'n talamh, crith 's toirm a' tighinn, 's b' fhèarr leis gun robh e 'muigh: leum e 'n so an àite 'chuirp a bha ris an teine, an teis-meadhon nan Corp. Thàinig am famhair 's dh' fheòraich e, " 'n robh ròsta bruich." Thòisich e air itheadh, 's thubhairt e, "fiu fou! hoagrich! cha 'n ioghnadh feòil righinn a bhi ort fhéin, 's righinn air d'isean i." Dur a dh' ith am famhair am fear ud, dh fhalbh e chunntadh nan corp, agus se 'n dòigh chunntais a bh' aig orra, beireachd air dhà chaol cois' orra, agus 'gan tillgeadh seachad thar mullach a chinn, agus chunnt e oir ais 's air adhart iad mar so tri no ceithir do dh' uairean; agus bho m a fhuair e Conall ni bu truime, 'se bog reamhar, thug e 'n stiall ud as bho chùl a chinn gu mhanachan. Ròisd e so ris an teine, 's dh'ith e i. Thuit e 'n sin 'na chadal. Smèid Conall air a bhoirionnach, bior na feòla chuir 'san teine. Rinn i so, agus dur a dh' fhàs am bior geal an déigh bhi dearg, shàth e 'm bior troi' chridhe an fhamhair, 's bha 'm famhair marbh. Dh' fhalbh Conall an so, 's chuir e 'bhean air a slighe dhachaidh. Chaidh e 'n so dhachaidh e fhéin. Chuir a mhuime air falbh e sa' mac fhéin a ghoid a Bhlàr-aghan bho rìgh na h-Eadailt, agus dh' fhalbh iad a ghoid a bhlàr-aghan le chéile, agus na h-uile uair a chuireadh iad an làimh air a bhlar-aghan, leigeadh am blàr-aghan (ialt) as. Thàinig cuideachd a mach 's chaidh an glacadh. Chaidh ceangal nan tri chaoil a chuir orra gu daor 's gu daingean. "Fhir mhòr ruaidh," ars' an rìgh, 'n robh thu 'n càs riamh cho cruaidh an sin?" "Teannachadh beag dhomh fhéin, agus lasachadh do m' chompanach 's innsidh mi sin," arsa Conall. Bha banrigh na h-Eadailte 'ga fhaicinn. Thubhairt Conall an sin.

> "Seachd tràth gu bronach dhomh,
> 'S mi chomhnuidh air muin an easbuig.
> 'Sann leamsa 'b' fhad' a' chéilidh sin,
> Ged 'sann leam fhéin bu treise.
> An ceann na seachdamh tràth,
> Chunnacas uaigh 'ga fosgladh,
> 'S ge b'e bo luaithe bhiodh a nuas aca,
> 'S mise a bhiodh suas air thoiseach.
> Shaoil leosan gu 'm bu mharbhan mi,
> Bho 'n uir thalmhaidh 's mi 'g éiridh,
> Ann an toiseach a gharbh-bhristidh,
> Dh' fhag iad an airm 's an eudach,
> Thug mise leum an Uisleagan,
> 'S mi ruisgte, nochdta,
> Bu bhochd dhomhsa 's mi 'm fhògarrach,
> Bhi maitheadh òr do 'n Easbuig."

"Teannaichibh e gu maith 's gu ro mhaith," ars' an rìgh, "cha b' ann an aon àite maith a bha e riamh, 's mòr an t-olc a rinn e." Chaidh an sin a theannachadh ni bu teinne, 's ni bu teinne, 's thubhairt an rìgh, "Fhir mhòir ruaidh, 'n robh thu 'n càs riamh bu chruaidh na sin." "Teannaich mi fhéin, 's leig lasachadh do 'n 'fhear so laimh rium, 's innsidh mi 'n sin." Rinn iad so. Bha mise os esan.

"Naoi tràtha ann an uaimh an òir,
'Se bu bhiadh domh a' cholainn chnàmh,
Feithean chas agus làmh.
An ceann an naoidheadh tràth,
Chunnacas cliabh a' tighinn a mhàn;
Rug mi 'n sin air a' chliabh'
'S chuir mi òr fotham 's òr tharam,
'S rinn mi 'm fholach ann sa 'chliabh,
'S thug mi leam an claidheamh soluis
Tùrn is sona rinn mi riamh."

Thug iad an ath theannachadh dha, s' dh' fhoighneachd an righ dheth, "An robh thu 'n càs na h-eiginn riamh cho chruaidh 'sin?" "Teannachadh beag dhomh fhéin, 's lasachadh do m' chompanach, 's innsidh mi 'n sin." Rinn iad so.

"Latha air sliabh na leirge dhomh
'S mi dol a steach do dh' uamh,
Chunnaic mi bean mhin, bhan, mhathair-shuileach
'Si putadh bior na feòla
Ri òganach, 'se gun chiall.
Thubhairt mìse an sin,
De fàth do bhròin, a bhean,
Ris an òganach 's nach eil ceillidh,
'Oir a mhin oir a mhaise,' ars' ise
'Cuir an leanabh so ri teallach'
Rug mi 'n sin air a mhacan
'S shuain mi mo mhanndal uime
'S thug mi nios an rod mòr colainn
A bha shuas an tùs na tuime
Chuala mi 'n sin, turtar, tartar, agus turaraich
Fior thalamh dol am measg a cheile
Ach air bhith dhàsan tuiteam
Anns an t-suain chadail
'S an do thuit fuathan na coille
Thug mi tarruing air bior an ròstaidh
'S sheòl mi sud ri còrr a ghoile."

Bha a' bhanrigh faicinn 's ag èisdeachd gach ni bha Conall a' fulang 's ag radh, agus dur a chual i so, leum i 's gheàrr i gach ceangal a bha air Conall 's air a chompanach, agus thubhairt i, " 'S mise 'm boirionnach a bha 'n sin, agus ris an righ 's tusa a mac a bha 'n siud." Phòs Conall nighean an righ, 's mharcaich iad le chéile am blàradhan dachaidh. 'S dh fhag mise ann a sin iad.

Recited by Kenneth MacLennan, Turnaig, Pool Ewe, Ross-shire. Written by Hector Urquhart, June 27, 1859.

4. Another story, which seems to be a fragment of this tale made reasonable, forms part of a collection very well written in the Gaelic of Gearrloch, Ross-shire, from the telling of old men, by Mr. Thomas Cameron, schoolmaster, at the request of Osgood H. MacKenzie, Esq., July 1859.

ALEXANDER MACDONALD, INVERASDALE, tells how Uisdean Mor MacIlle Phadraig, a local hero, famous for slaying "Fuathan" (bogles), in a winter that was very cold, on a day of hailing and snowing (sowing and winnowing) was taking the way of "A BHRAIGHE MHOIR" (the great top), and was determined to reach as far as Lochbhraoin. Coming through a place called Lead leachacachan mu Thuath (na Fuath?), he fell in with a woman, and he soon fell in with a new-born child. No house was near, so he killed his horse, put the mother and child inside, and left them in the snow. He went for help, and when he came back he found them warm and well. He took care of them till the woman could do for herself, and the child grew to be an able lad. He was named "MacMhuirich a curach an Eich," which name has stuck to his race to this day.

After this Uisdean came to poverty. On a cold winter's night of hailing and snowing, he was going on a street in Dun Edin (Edinburgh), a woman put her head out of a window and cried, "It is cold this night on Leathad leachachan mu Thuath." "It is," said he. When she heard his Gaelic, she thought she was not far wrong, and asked him in. "What is the hardest 'Cath' that ever befel thee?" said the woman. He repeated the story, and ended with,—"And though I am this night in Dun Edin, many is the hard fight that I have wrestled with." "I am the woman that was there, and this is the child," said she; and she offered him shelter for the rest of his days.

Surely these are Connal, the robber; and the king and his mother; and the king's horse put to a new use, transferred to the Cowgate from Eirinn and Lochlann, and the forests of Germany; brought down from the days of Sindbad, or of Ulysses, or from the fifteenth century, from the age of romance to the nineteenth century and to prose.

5. I have another version of this story, called AN GADAICHE DUBH, The Black Robber, told by Alexander MacNeill, fisherman in Barra, and written by Hector MacLean in August 1859. It varies much from the others. The outline is nearly the same, but the pictures are different. I hope to find room for it.

The story resembles—

1st. The Robber and his Sons, referred to in Grimm's third volume, as taken from a MS. of the fifteenth century. An old robber desires to become an honest man, but his three sons follow their profession, and try to steal the queen's horse. They are caught, and the old robber tells three stories of his own adventures to rescue them.

In the first he is caught by a giant and about to be eaten, but escapes by putting out the giant's eyes with "destructive ingredients." He gets out of a cave by putting on the skin of a sheep. He puts on a gold ring which the giant gave him, which forces him to call out "here I am." He bites off his own finger, and so escapes.

Next—In a wilderness, haunted by strange creatures, he finds a woman about to kill her child as a dinner for some wild men. He makes her cook a hanged thief instead; hangs himself on a tree in place of the cooked thief, and has a slice cut from his side.

Lastly, the giants, frightened by a clap of thunder, run away; he returns to a civilized country, and the queen, as a reward for his stories, liberates the three sons.

2d. Part of this is manifestly the same as the Adventures of Ulysses in the Cave of the Cyclop.—(Odyssey, book ix.)

3d. And the adventure of Sindbad with the giants and dwarfs, on his third voyage (Arabian Nights). The Cat adventure, in the Islay version, may be compared with Sindbad's meeting with the serpents and with the elephants. And

4th. With a Highland story, of some laird of Rasa, whose boat was upset by a company of cats, headed by one large black cat; supposed to be a troop of witches headed by their master.

6.   The incident of being buried in a treasure cave with the dead, is common to the Arabian Nights. *See* Sindbad's Fourth Voyage, and Aladdin; and also,

7.   To the Decameron, second day, novel 5; where a man, after a number of adventures, is lowered into a well by two thieves. He is hauled up with a wheel and a rope by the watch, who are frightened and run away, leaving their arms.

The three meet once more; go to the cathedral, and rise up a marble slab laid over the grave of an archbishop. When "Andreuccio" has gone in and robbed the grave, they send him back for a ring, and drop the slab. The priests come on the same errand as the thieves; he frightens them, gets out with the ring, and returns to Perugia from Naples—"having laid out his money on a ring, whereas the intent of his journey was to have bought horses."

In all these, Greek, Italian, Arabic, German, and Gaelic, there is a general resemblance, but nothing more.

I have given three versions of the same story together, as an illustration of the manner in which popular tales actually exist; and as specimens of language. The men who told the story live as far apart as is possible in the Highlands. I heard one of them tell it; each had his own way of telling the incidents; and each gives something peculiar to himself, or to his locality, which the others leave out. Ewan MacLachlan, in discussing the MSS. in the Advocates' Library in 1812, referring to Dean MacGreggor's MS., written about 1526, says:—"MacDougall is compared to MacRuslainn, the Polyphemus of our winter tales." It would seem, then, that this story has been long known, and it is now widely spread in the Highlands.

The manners and customs of the king and his tenant are very highland, so far as they can be referred to the present day. Probably they are equally true pictures of bygone days. The king's sons probably visited their vassals, and got into all manner of scrapes. The vassals in all probability resented insults, and rebelled, and took to the wild woods and became outlaws. So the mill was probably the resort of idlers and the place for news, as it still is. The king, in all likelihood, lived very near his own stable, for there are no ruins of palaces; and it seems to have been the part of a brave man to submit, without flinching, to have his wrists and ankles tied to the small of his back, and be "tightened" and tortured; and then to recite his deeds as an Indian brave might do.

It seems, too, that "Lochlann," now Scandinavia, was once within easy sail of England and Ireland; and that the King of Lochlann knew the tenants of the neighbouring king. From the history of the Isle of Man, it appears that there really was a king called "Crovan," who is also mentioned by Worsaae (page 287) as the Norwegian Godred Crovan who conquered Man, A.D. 1077. And in this, the stories are probably true recollections of manners and events, so far as they go. When it comes to giants, the story is just as likely to be true in the same sense. There probably was a race of big man-eating savages somewhere on the road from east to west, if not all along the route; for all popular tales agree in representing giants and wild men as living in caves, hoarding wealth, eating men, and enslaving women.

In these stories the caves are described from nature. When Conal walks along the top of the high shore, "rough with caves and goes," and falls into a cave which has an opening below, he does that which is not only possible but probable. I know many caves on the west coast, where a giant might have walked in with his goats from a level sandy beach, near a deep sea, and some where a man might fall into the further end through a hole in a level green sward, and land safely; many are full of all that belongs to a sheep-fold, or a shelter used by goats and cattle, and by the men who take care of them.

I know one where a whole whisky distillery existed not very long ago; I first landed in it from a boat to pick up a wild pigeon; I afterwards scrambled into it from the shore; and I have looked down into it from smooth green turf, through a hole in the roof, into which there flowed a little stream of water. An active man might drop into the far end on a heap of fallen earth.

And here again comes the notion, that the so-called giants had swords so bright, that they shone in the dark like torches, and that they owned riches hid underground in holes.

Perhaps we may believe the whole as very nearly true. It may be that there were really such people, and that they were miners and shepherds; when those who now tell stories about them, were wandering huntsmen armed with stone weapons.

The third version is remarkable as an instance of the way in which poems of greater merit used to be commonly, and still are occasionally recited. "Cuchullin" was partly told, partly recited, by an old man near Lochawe, within the memory of a clergyman who told me the fact. I heard Patrick Smith, in South Uist, and other men, so recite stories in alternate prose and verse, in 1859; and it appears that the Edda was so composed. Poems of the same nature as "the poems of Ossian," if not the poems themselves, were so recited by an old man in Bowmore more than sixty years ago, when my friend Mr. John Crawford, late Governor of Singapore, and a well-known linguist, was a school boy, who spoke little but Gaelic; and when it was as rare to find a man amongst the peasantry in Islay who could speak English, as it is now remarkable to find one who cannot.

8

MURCHAG A'S MIONACHAG.

From Ann Darroch, James Wilson, Hector MacLean, Islay, and many others in other parts of the Highlands.

Moorachug and Meenachug went to gather fruit, and as Moorachug would gather Meenachug would eat. Moorachug went to seek a rod to lay on Meenachug, and she eating his share of fruit.

"What's thy news to-day, oh Voorachai?" said the rod. " 'Tis my own news, that I am seeking a rod to lay on Meenachug, and she eating my share of fruit."

"Thou wilt not get me until thou gettest an axe that will reap me." He reached the axe. "What's thy news to-day, oh Voorachai?" " 'Tis my own news that I am seeking an axe to reap rod—rod to lay on Meenachug—and she eating my share of fruit."

"Thou wilt not get me until thou gettest a stone to smooth me." He reached a stone; "What's thy news to-day, oh Voorachai?" said the stone. " 'Tis my own news that I am seeking stone to smooth axe—axe to reap rod—rod to lay on Meenachaig—and she eating my share of fruit."

"Thou wilt not get me," said the stone, "till thou gettest water will wet me." He reached the water. "What's thy news to-day, oh Voorachai?" said the water. " 'Tis my own news that I am seeking—water to stone—stone to smooth axe—axe to reap rod—rod to lay on Meenachaig—and she eating my share of fruit."

"Thou wilt not get me," said the water, "till thou gettest a deer to swim me." He reached the deer. "What's thy news to-day, oh Voorachai?" said the deer. "Tis my own news, that I am seeking—deer to swim water—water to stone—stone to smooth axe—axe to reap rod—rod to lay on Meenachaig—and she eating my share of fruit."

"Thou wilt not get me," said the deer, "until thou gettest a dog to run me." He reached the dog. "What's thy news to-day, oh Voorachai?" said the dog. " 'Tis my own news that I am seeking—

dog to run deer—deer to swim water—water to stone—stone to smooth axe—axe to reap rod—rod to lay on Meenachaig—and she eating my share of fruit."

"Thou wilt not get me," said the dog, "till thou gettest butter to be rubbed to my feet." He reached the butter. "What's thy news to-day, oh Voorachai?" said the butter. " 'Tis my own news, that I am seeking—butter to feet of dog—dog to run deer—deer to swim water—water to stone—stone to smooth axe—axe to reap rod—rod to lay on Meenachaig—and she eating my share of fruit."

"Thou wilt not get me," said the butter, "till thou gettest a mouse will scrape me." He reached the mouse. "What's thy news to-day, oh Voorachai?" said the mouse. " 'Tis my own news, that I am seeking—mouse to scrape butter—butter to feet of dog—dog to run deer—deer to swim water—water to stone—stone to smooth axe—axe to reap rod—rod to lay on Meenachaig—and she eating my share of fruit."

"Thou wilt not get me," said the mouse, "till thou gettest a cat to hunt me." He reached the cat. "What's thy news to-day, oh Voorachai?" said the cat. " 'Tis my own news, that I am seeking—cat to hunt mouse—mouse to scrape butter—butter to feet of dog—dog to run deer—deer to swim water—water to stone—stone to smooth axe—axe to reap rod—rod to lay on Meenachaig—and she eating my share of fruit."

"Thou wilt not get me," said the cat, "until thou gettest milk for me." He reached the cow. "What's thy news to-day, oh! Voorachai?" said the cow. " 'Tis my own news, that I am seeking—milk for the cat—cat to hunt mouse—mouse to scrape butter—butter to feet of dog—dog to run deer—deer to swim water—water to stone—stone to smooth axe—axe to reap rod—rod to lay on Meenachaig—and she eating my share of fruit."

"Thou wilt not get milk from me till thou gettest a whisp from the barn gillie." He reached the barn gillie. "What's that news to-day, oh, Voorachai?" said the barn gillie. " 'Tis my own news that I am seeking—a whisp for the cow—a cow will shed milk for the cat—cat to hunt mouse—mouse to scrape butter—butter to feet of dog—dog to run deer—deer to swim water—water to stone—stone to smooth axe—axe to reap rod—rod to lay on Meenachaig—and she eating my share of fruit."

"Thou wilt not get a whisp from me," said the barn gillie, "till thou gettest a bonnach for me from the kneading wife." He reached the kneading wife. "What's thy news to-day, oh, Voorachai!" said the kneading wife. "Tis my own news, that I am seeking—bonnach to the barn gillie—whisp to the cow from the barn gillie—milk from the cow to the cat—cat will hunt mouse—mouse will scrape butter—butter to feet of dog—dog to run deer—deer to swim water— water to stone—stone to smooth axe—axe to reap rod—rod to lay on Meenachaig—and she eating my share of fruit."

"Thou wilt not get bonnach from me till thou bringest in water will knead it."

"How will I bring in the water? There is no vessel but that sowen's sieve."

Moorachug took with him the sowen's sieve. He reached the water, and every drop he would put in the sowen's sieve it would go through. A hoodie came over his head, and she cried, "Gawr-rag, gawr-rag, little silly, little silly." "Thou art right, oh hoodie," said Moorachug. "Crèah rooah s' còinneach, crèah rooah s' còinneach," said the hoodie.

Moorachug set crèah rooah s' còinneach, brown clay and moss to it, and he brought in the water to the kneading wife—and he got bonnach from the kneading wife to barn gillie—whisp from the barn gillie to the cow—milk from the cow to the cat—cat to hunt mouse—mouse to scrape butter—butter to feet of dog—dog to run deer—deer to swim water—water to stone—stone to smooth axe— axe to reap rod—rod to lay on Meenachaig—and she eating his share of fruit. And when Moorachug returned Meenachag had just BURST.

This is the best known of all Gaelic tales. It is the infant ladder to learning a chain of cause and effect, and fully as sensible as any of its kind. It used to be commonly taught to children of five or six years of age, and repeated by school boys, and it is still remembered by grown-up people in all parts of the Highlands. There are few variations. In one version the crow was a light bird; in another a gull was introduced, which advised the use of the sand to stuff the riddle.

The tale has sixteen steps, four of which contain double ideas. The English house that Jack built has eleven. The Scotch old woman with the silver penny has twelve. The Norsk cock and hen a-nutting twelve, ten of which are double. The German story in Grimm has five or six, all single ideas. All these are different. In Uist the actors are Biorachan mor agus Biorchan Beag; in Sutherland, Morachan agus Mionachan.

The speech of the Hoodie is always a very close imitation of his note. In another version she says, "CUIR CRIADH RIGHIN RUADH RIS—Put tough red clay to it;" and the gull said, "CUIR POLL BOG RIS—Put soft mud to it;" which is rather the speech of some other bird. There are several rare words in this; for example, "Gadhar," a dog.

———

MURCHADH A'S MIONACHAG.

Dh'fholbh Murchadh a's Mionachag a bhuain sugh, 's mar a bhuaineadh Murchadh dh' itheadh Mionachag. Dh 'fholbh Murchadh a dh' iarraidh slat a ghabhail air Mionachaig 's i 'g itheadh a chuid sugh—"De do naigheachd an diugh a Mhurchaidh?" urs' an t-slat. " 'Se mo naigheachd féin gu 'bheil mi 'g iarraidh Slat a ghabhail air Mionachag 's i 'g itheadh mo chuid sugh." "Cha 'n fhaigh thu mise gus am faigh, thu tuagh a bhuaineas mi." Ràinig e 'n tuagh. "De do naigheachd an diugh a Mhurchaidh?" "Se mo naigheadchd féin gu 'bheil mi 'g iarraidh Tuagh a bhuaineas slat—Slat a ghabhail air Mionachaig 's i 'g itheadh mo chuid sugh"—"Cha 'n fhaigh thu mise gus am faigh thu clach a lìobhas mi." Ràinig e 'chlach. "Dé do naigheachd an diugh a Mhurchaidh?" urs' a' chlach. " 'Se mo naigheachd féin gu 'bheil mi 'g iarraidh Clach a lìobhadh tuagh—Tuagh a bhuain slat—Slat a ghabhail air Mionachaig 's i' g itheadh mo chuid sugh." "Cha n fhaigh thu mis'," urs' a' chlach, "gus am faigh thu uisge a fhliuchas mi." Ràinig e 'n t-uisge—"De do naigheachd an diugh a Mhurchaidh?" urs' an t-uisge. " 'S e mo naigheachd féin gu bheil mi 'g iarraidh Uisge ma chloich—Clach a lìobhadh tuagh—Tuagh a bhuain slat—Slat a ghabhail air Mionachaig 's i 'g itheadh mo chuid sugh." "Cha 'n fhaigh thu mis'," urs' an t-uisge, "gus am faigh thu fiadh a shnámhas mi." Ràinig e 'm fiadh. "Dé do naigheachd an diugh a Mhurchaidh?" urs' am fiadh. " 'Se mo naigheachd féin gu 'bheil mi 'g iarraidh Fiadh a shnàmh uisg'. Uisge ma chloich. Clach a lìobhadh tuagh. Tuagh a bhuain slat. Slat a ghabhail air Mionachaig's i 'g itheadh mo chuid sugh." "Cha 'n fhaigh thu mis'," urs' am fiadh, "gus am faigh thu gadhar a ruitheas mi." Ràinig e 'n gadhar. "De do naigheachd an diugh a Mhurchaidh?" urs' an gadhar. "S e mo naigheachd féin gu 'bheil mi 'g iarraidh Gadhar a ruith fiadh. Fiadh a shnàmh uisg'. Uisge ma chloich. Clach a lìobhadh tuagh. Tuagh a bhuain slat. Slat a ghabhail air Mionachaig 's i 'g itheadh mo chuid sugh." "Cha 'n fhaigh thu mis'," urs' an t-im, "gus am faigh thu luch a sgrìobas mi." "Ràinig e 'n luch. "De do naigheachd an diugh a Murchaidh?" urs' an luch. " 'Se mo naigheachd féin gu 'bheil mi 'g iarraidh Luch a sgrìobadh im. Im chasa gadhair. Gadhar a ruith fiadh. Fiadh a shnàmh uisg'. Uisge ma cloich. Clach a lìobhadh tuagh. Tuagh a bhuain slat. Slat a ghabhail air Mionachaig 's i 'g itheadh mo chuid sugh." "Cha 'n fhaigh thu mis'," urs' an luch, "gus am faigh thu cat a 'shealgas mi." Ràinig e 'n cat. "De do naigheachd an diugh a Mhurchaidh?" urs' an cat. " 'Se mo naigheachd féin gu 'bheil mi 'g iarraidh Cat a shealg luch. Luch a sgrìobadh im. Im chasa gadhair. Gadhar a ruith fiadh. Fiadh a shnàmh uisg'. Uisge ma chloich. Clach a lìobhadh tuagh. Tuagh a bhuain slat. Slat a ghabhail air Mionachaig 's ì 'g itheadh mo chuid sugh." "Cha 'n fhaigh thu mis'," urs' an cat, "gus am faigh thu bainne dhomh." Ràinig e 'bhò." "De do naigheachd an diugh a Mhurchaidh?" urs' a' bhò. " 'Se mo naigheachd féin gu' bheil mi 'g iarraidh Bainne do 'n chat. Cat a shealg luch. Luch a sgrìobadh im. Im chasa gadhar. Gadhar a ruith fiadh. Fiadh a shnàmh uisg'. Uisge ma chloich. Clach a lìobhadh tuagh. Tuagh a bhuain slat. Slat a ghabhail air Mionachaig 's i 'g itheadh mo chuid sugh." "Cha 'n fhaigh thu bainne uamsa, gus am faigh thu sop o 'n ghilleshabhaill." Ràinig e 'n gille-sabhaill. "Dé do naigheachd an diugh a Mhurchaidh?" urs' an gille-sabhaill. " 'Se mo naigheachd féin gu 'bheil mi 'g iarraidh. Sop a gheobh bò. Bo bhligheadh bainne do 'n chat. Cat a shealg luch. Luch a sgrìobadh im. Im chasa gadhar. Gadhar a ruith fiadh. Fiadh a shnàmh uisg'. Uisge ma chloich. Clach a lìobhadh tuagh. Tuagh a bhuain slat. Slat a ghabhail air Mionachaig 's i 'g itheadh mo chuid sugh." "Cha 'n fhaigh thu sop uamsa," urs' an gillesabhaill, "gus am faigh thu Bonnach dhomh o 'n Bhean-fhuinne." Ràinig e 'bhean-fhuinne. "De do naigheachd an diugh a Mhurchaidh?" urs' a' bhean-fhuinne. " 'Se mo naigheachd féin gu 'bheil mi' g iarraidh Bonnach do 'n ghille-shabhaill. Sop do 'n Bho o 'n Ghille-shabhaill. Bainn' o 'n Bho do 'n chat. Cat a shealgas luch. Luch a sgrìobas im. Im chasa gadhair. Gadhar a ruith fiadh. Fiadh a shnàmh uisg'. Uisge ma chloich. Clach a lìobhadh tuagh. Tuagh a bhuain slat. Slat a ghabhail air Mionachaig 's i 'g itheadh mo chuid sugh." "Cha 'n fhaigh thu bonnach uamsa mar an d' thoir thu stigh uisg' a dh' fhuinneas e." "Dé mar a' bheir mi stigh an t-Uisge? Cha 'n 'eil soitheach ann ach an Criathar Cabhrach sin." Thug Murchadh leis an Criathar Cabhrach, 's ràinig e n t-uisge, 's a h-uile deur a chuireadh e 's a' Chriathar Chabhrach rachadh e roimhe. Thàinig Feannag as a chionn 's ghlaoidh i "Gòrrag, gòrrag." "Tha thu ceart, fheannag," ursa Murchadh. "Crèadh ruagh 's còinneach, crèadh ruagh 's còinneach." Chuir Murchadh crèadh ruagh 's còinneach ris, 's thug e 'stigh an t-Uisge, 's fhuair e Bonnach o 'n Bhean-fhuinne do 'n Ghille-shabhaill. Sop o 'n

Ghille-shabhaill do 'n Bhò. Bainn' o 'n Bhò do 'n chat. Cat a shealg luch. Luch a sgrìobadh im. Im chasa gadhair. Gadhar a ruith fiadh. Fiadh a shnàmh uisg'. Uisge ma chloich. Clach a lìobhadh tuagh. Tuagh a bhuain slat. Slat a ghabhaill air Mionachaig 's i 'g itheadh a chuid sugh. 'S nur a thill Murchadh bha Mionachag an déigh SGAINEADH!!

9

THE BROWN BEAR OF THE GREEN GLEN.
From John MacDonald, Travelling Tinker.

There was a king in Erin once, who had a leash of sons. John was the name of the youngest one, and it was said that he was not wise enough; and this good worldly king lost the sight of his eyes, and the strength of his feet. The two eldest brothers said that they would go seek three bottles of the water of the green Isle that was about the heaps of the deep.* And so it was that these two brothers went away. Now the fool said that he would not believe but that he himself would go also. And the first big town he reached in his father's kingdom, there he sees his two brothers there, the blackguards! "Oh! my boys," says the young one, "it is thus you are?" "With swiftness of foot," said they, "take thyself home, or we will have thy life." "Don't be afraid, lads. It is nothing to me to stay with you." Now John went away on his journey till he came to a great desert of a wood. "Hoo, hoo!" says John to himself, "It is not canny for me to walk this wood alone." The night was coming now, and growing pretty dark. John ties the cripple white horse that was under him to the root of a tree, and he went up in the top himself. He was but a very short time in the top, when he saw a bear coming with a fiery cinder in his mouth. "Come down, son of the king of Erin," says he. "Indeed, I won't come. I am thinking I am safer where I am." "But if thou wilt not come down, I will go up," said the bear. "Art thou, too, taking me for a fool?" says John. "A shaggy, shambling creature like thee, climbing a tree!" "But if thou wilt not come down I will go up," says the bear, as he fell out of hand to climb the tree. "Lord! thou canst do that same?" said John; keep back from the root of the tree, then, and I will go down to talk to

*"Eilean uaine a bha 'n iomal torra domhain."

thee." And when the son of Erin's king drew down, they came to chatting. The bear asked him if he was hungry. "Weel! by your leave," said John, "I am a little at this very same time." The bear took that wonderful watchful turn and he catches a roebuck. "Now, son of Erin's king," says the bear, "whether wouldst thou like thy share of the buck boiled or raw?" "The sort of meat I used to get would be kind of plotted boiled," says John; and thus it fell out. John got his share roasted. "Now," said the bear, "lie down between my paws, and thou hast no cause to fear cold or hunger till morning." Early in the morning the Mathon (bear) asked, "Art thou asleep, son of Erin's king?" "I am not very heavily," said he. "It is time for thee to be on thy soles then. Thy journey is long—two hundred miles; but art thou a good horseman, John?" "There are worse than me at times," said he. "Thou hadst best get on top of me, then." He did this, and at the first leap John was to earth.

"Foil! foil!" says John. "What! thou art not bad at the trade thyself. Thou hadst best come back till we try thee again." And with nails and teeth he fastened on the Mathon, till they reached the end of the two hundred miles and a giant's house. "Now, John," said the Mathon, "thou shalt go to pass the night in this giant's house; thou wilt find him pretty grumpy, but say thou that it was the brown bear of the green glen that set thee here for a night's share, and don't thou be afraid that thou wilt not get share and comfort." And he left the bear to go to the giant's house. "Son of Ireland's King," says the giant, "thy coming was in the prophecy; but if I did not get thy father, I have got his son. I don't know whether I will put thee in the earth with my feet, or in the sky with my breath." "Thou wilt do neither of either," said John, "for it is the brown bear of the green glen that set me here." "Come in, son of Erin's king," said he, "and thou shalt be well taken to this night." And as he said, it was true. John got meat and drink without stint. But to make a long tale short, the bear took John day after day to the third giant. "Now," says the bear, "I have not much acquaintance with this giant, but thou wilt not be long in his house when thou must wrestle with him. And if he is too hard on thy back, say thou, 'If I had the brown bear of the green glen here, that was thy master.'" As soon as John went in—"Ai! ai!! or ee! ee!!" says the giant, "If I did not get thy father, I have got his son;" and to grips they go. They would make the boggy bog of the rocky rock. In the hardest place they would sink to the knee; in the softest, up to the thighs; and they would bring wells of spring water from the face of every rock. The giant gave John a sore wrench or two. "Foil! foil!" says he, "if I had here the brown bear of the green glen, thy leap would not be so hearty." And no sooner spoke he the word than the worthy bear was at his side. "Yes! yes!" says the giant, "son of Erin's king, now I know thy matter better than thou dost thyself." So it was that the giant ordered his shepherd to bring home the best wether he had in the hill, and to throw his carcass before the great door. "Now, John," says the giant, "an eagle will come and she will settle on the carcass of this wether, and there is a wart on the ear of this eagle which thou must cut off her with this sword, but a drop of blood thou must not draw." The eagle came, but she was not long eating when John drew close to her, and with one stroke he cut the wart off her without drawing one drop of blood. ("*Och! is not that a fearful lie?*") "Now," said the eagle, "come on the root of my two wings, for I know thy matter better than thou dost thyself." He did this; and they were now on sea, and now on land, and now on the wing, till they reached the Green Isle. "Now, John," says she, "be quick, and fill thy three bottles; remember that the black dogs are away just now." ("*What dogs?*" "*Black dogs; dost thou not know that they always had black dogs chasing the Gregorach!*") When he filled the bottles with the water out of the well, he sees a little house beside him. John said to himself that he would go in, and that he would see what was in it. And the first chamber he opened, he saw a full bottle. ("*And what was in it?*" "*What should be in it but whisky.*") He filled a glass out of it, and he drank it; and when he was going, he gave a glance, and the bottle was as full as it was before. "I will have this bottle along with the bottles of water," says he.

Then he went into another chamber, and he saw a loaf; he took a slice out of it, but the loaf was as whole as it was before. "Ye gods! I won't leave thee," says John. He went on thus till he came to another chamber. He saw a great cheese; he took a slice off the cheese, but it was as whole as ever. "I will have this along with the rest," says he. Then he went to another chamber, and he saw laid there the very prettiest little jewel of a woman he ever saw. "It were a great pity not to kiss thy lips, my love," says John.

Soon after, John jumped on top of the eagle, and she took him on the self same steps till they reached the house of the big giant, and they were paying rent to the giant, and there was the sight of tenants and giants and meat and drink. "Well! John," says the giant, "didst thou see such drink as this in thy father's house in Erin?" "Pooh," says John, "Hoo! my hero; thou other man, I have a drink that *is* unlike it." He gave the giant a glass out of the bottle, but the bottle was as full as it was before. "Well!" said the giant, "I will give

thee myself two hundred notes, a bridle and a saddle for the bottle."
"It is a bargain, then," says John, "but that the first sweetheart I
ever had must get it if she comes the way." "She will get that," says
the giant; but, to make the long story short, he left each loaf and
cheese with the two other giants with the same covenant that the
first sweetheart he ever had should get them if she came the way.

Now John reached his father's big town in Erin, and he sees his
two brothers as he left them—the "blackguardan!" "You had best
come with me, lads," says he, "and you will get a dress of cloth,
and a horse and a saddle and bridle each." And so they did; but
when they were near to their father's house, the brothers thought
that they had better kill him, and so it was that they set on him.
And when they thought he was dead, they threw him behind a dike;
and they took from him the three bottles of water, and they went
home. John was not too long here, when his father's smith came
the way with a cart load of rusty iron. John called out, "Whoever
the Christian is that is there, oh! that he should help him." The
smith caught him, and he threw John amongst the iron; and because
the iron was so rusty, it went into each wound and sore that John
had; and so it was, that John became rough skinned and bald. Here
we will leave John, and we will go back to the pretty little jewel that
John left in the Green Isle. She became pale and heavy; and at the
end of three quarters, she had a fine lad son. "Oh! in all the great
world," says she, "how did I find this?" "Foil! foil!" says the
hen-wife, "don't let that set thee thinking. Here's for thee a bird,
and as soon as he sees the father of thy son, he will hop on the top
of his head." The Green Isle was gathered from end to end, and
the people were put in at the back door and out at the front door;
but the bird did not stir, and the babe's father was not found. Now
here, she said she would go through the world altogether till she
should find the father of the babe. Then she came to the house of
the big giant and sees the bottle. "Ai! ai!!" said she, "who gave thee
this bottle?" Said the giant, "It was young John, son of Erin's king,
that left it." "Well, then, the bottle is mine," said she. But to make
the long story short, she came to the house of each giant, and she
took with her each bottle, and each loaf, and each cheese, till at
length and at last she came to the house of the king of Erin. Then
the five-fifths of Erin were gathered, and the bridge of nobles of the
people; they were put in at the back door and out at the front door,
but the bird did not stir. Then she asked if there was one other or
any one else at all in Erin, that had not been here. "I have a bald
rough-skinned gillie in the smithy," said the smith, "but,"—

"Rough on or off, send him here," says she. No sooner did the bird see the head of the bald rough-skinned gillie, than he took a flight and settles on the bald top of the rough-skinned lad. She caught him and kissed him. Thou art the father of my babe."

"But, John," says the great king of Erin, "It is thou that gottest the bottles of water for me." "Indeed, 'twas I," says John. "Weel, then, what art thou willing to do to thy two brothers?" "The very thing they wished to do to me, do for them;" and that same was done. John married the daughter of the king of the Green Isle, and they made a great rich wedding that lasted seven days and seven years, and thou couldst but hear leeg, leeg, and beeg, beeg, solid sound the peg drawing. Gold a-crushing from the soles of their feet to the tips of their fingers, the length of seven years and seven days.

———

SGEULACHD AIR MATH-GHAMHAINN DONN A GHLINN UAINNE.

Bha rìgh air Eirinn aon uair, aig an robh triùir mhac, 's b' ainm don fhear a b' òige Iain, 's bha e air a radh nach robh e glic na leòir, agus chaill an rìgh saoghalta so sealladh a shùilean, 's lùgh nan cas. Thubhairt an da bhràthair bu shine gun rachadh iadsan air tòir tri botuil uisge do'n eilean uaine a bha 'n iomall torra domhain, agus 'se bh' ann gun d' fhalbh an da bhràthair so. Thubhairt an t-amadan nach creideadh e féin nach falbhadh e cuideachd, agus a cheud bhailemòr do 'n d' thàinig e ann an rìoghachd athar, faicear a dha bhràthair an sin 'nam blaigeartan! "O a bhalacha!" ars' am fear òg, "an ann mar so a tha sibhse." "Air luathas do chas," ars' iadsan, "thoir an tigh ort air neo bithidh do bheatha againn." "Na bitheadh eagal oirbh romham cha 'n fhiach leamsa fanachd maille ribh." Dh'fhalbh Iain an so air a thurus, gus an d' thàinig e gu fàsach mòr do choille. Hu! Huth! ars' Iain ris féin, "Cha 'neil e cneasda dhòmhsa a' choille so a choiseachd leam fhéin." Bha 'n oidhche a' tighinn a nis, 's i fàs gu math dorcha. Ceangailear Iain an t-each bacach, bàn a bha foidhe ri bun craoidhe 's chaidh e féin suas 'na bàrr. Cha robh e ach goirid 'na bàrr gus am fac e math-ghamhainn a' tighinn 's eibhleag theine na bheul. "Thig a nuas, a mhic rìgh Eirinn," ars' esan. "Gu dearbh, cha d' thig, tha mi smaointeachadh gu' bheil mi nis tèaruinte far am bheil mi." "Ach mur d' thig thusa nuas théid mise suas," arsa 'm math-ghamhainn. " 'M bheil thusa 'gam ghabhail 'nam amadan cuideachd," thuirt Iain. Creutair robagach, liobarta coltach riutsa a streapadh chraobh. "Ach mur d' thig thusa nuas, théid mise suas," ars' am math-ghamhainn 's e 'toirt a ghrad làimh air streapadh na craoibhe. " 'S dia ni thu sin fhéin," thuirt Iain. "Fan air t' ais fo bhun na craoibhe, mata, 's théid mi sìos a bhruidhinn riut." Agus dur a theirinn mac rìgh Eirinn a nuas, thàinig iad gu cracaireachd. Dh' fheòrich a' mhath-ghamhainn dheth, 'an robh an t-acras air? "Uill le 'r cead," ars' Iain, "tha beagan orm dheth 'sa cheart am so fein." Thug am math-ghamhainn an sgrìob uallach, aighearach 'ud, 's beirear air boc earba. "A nis, a mhic rìgh Eirinnn," arsa am math-ghamhainn, "Co 's feàrr leat do chuid do 'n bhoc bruich na amh." "An seòrsa bìdh a b' àbhairt dhòmhsa fhaotainn, bhitheadh seòrsa plotadh bruich air," ars' Iain. Agus 'sann a so mar thachair. Fhuair Iain a chuid fhéin ròiste. "A nis," arsa 'm math-ghamhainn, "luidh sìos eadar mo spògan-sa, 's cha 'n eagal fuachd no acrais dhuit gu madainn." Moch 'sa mhadainn, dh' fhoighneachd am math-ghamhainn, "Am bheil thu 'd chadal, a mhic rìgh Eirinn?" "Cha 'n 'eil anabarrach trom," thuirt esan. "Tha 'n t-àm dhuit a bhi air do bhuinn mata, tha 'n t-astar fada, da cheud mìle; ach am bheil thu 'nad 'mharcaiche math, Iain?" "Tha na' s miosa na mi air amannan," thuirt esan. " 'S feàrr dhuit tighinn air mo mhuinn mata." Rinn e so, agus air a cheud leum, bha Iain ri talamh. "Fòil! Fòil!" ars' Iain, "dè 'cha 'n 'eil thu fhein dona air a cheaird! 'S feàrr dhuit tighinn air t-ais gus am feuch sinn a rithist thu;" 's le iongan 's fiaclan ghreimich e ris a mha'ghan, gus an d' ràinig iad ceann an dà cheud mìle, 's tigh famhair. "Nis Iain," arsa 'm ma'ghan, "théid thu chuir seachad na h-oidhche ann an tigh an fhamhair so." Gheibh thu e gu maith gnò, ach abair thusa gur e mathgamhainn donn a' ghlinn uaine, a chuir thusa an so air son cuid oidhche, agus na biodh eagal ort nach fhaigh thu cuid 'us comhnadh. 'S dh' 'fhàg am mathgamhainn e 'dol gu tigh an fhamhair. "A mhic rìgh Eirinn," ars' am famhair, bha 'san targradh thu bhi tighinn, ach mar d' fhuair mi t' athair, fhuair mi 'mhac; cha 'n 'eil fios agam co dhiu chuireas mi 'san talamh thu le m' chasan, no 'san adhar le m'anail." "Cha deàn thu aon chuid do 'n da chuid," thuirt Iain, oir se mathghamhainn donn a' ghlinn uaine a chuir mise 'n so." "Thig a stigh, a mhic rìgh Eirinn," thuirt esan, " 's gheibh thu gabhail agad gu maith a nochd;" agus mar thubhairt b 'fhìor. Fhuair Iain biadh 's deoch gun ghainne; ach gus an sgeulachd fada a dheanamh goirid, thug am mathgamhainn Iain latha an déigh latha gus an treas famhair. "A nis," ars' am mathgamhainn, "cha 'n 'eil mòran eòlais agamsa air an fhamhair so, ach cha bhi thu fada 'na thigh dar a dh' fheumas tu dol a ghleachd ris, agus ma bhitheas e tullidh 's cruaidh air do shon, abair thusa na 'm biodh agamsa ma'ghan donn a ghlinn uaine, b'e sin do maighstir." Co luath 'sa chaidh Iain a stigh, "Ai! Ai! ars' am famhair mòr, mar d'fhuair mi t' athair, fhuair mi 'mhac, agus 'sa chéile ghabh iad; 's dhèanadh iad a bhogan don chreagan— an t-aite bu chruaidhe rachadh iad foidhe gu 'n glùinean 's an t-aite bu bhuige gu 'n sléisdean, 's bheireadh iad fuaranan fior-uisge a h-aodann gach creagain. Thug am famhair fàsgadh goirt na dithis do dh' Iain. "Fòil! Fòil!" thuirt esan, "Na'm biodh agamsa an so mathgamhainn donn a' ghlinn uaine, cha bhiodh do leum co sunndach;" agus cha luaith a labhair e 'm facal na bha am ma'ghan còir ri 'thaobh. "Seadh! Seadh!" ars' am famhair, "a mhic righ Eirinn, tha fios agam a nis air do ghnothach n' is feàrr na tha agad fhéin." 'Se bh' ann gun d-òrduich am famhair do 'n chìobair aige am molt a b' fheàrr a bha 's a' bheinn a thoirt dhachaidh, agus a' chlosach a thilgeadh ma choinneamh an doruis mhòir. "A nis, Iain, ars' am famhair, thig iolaire, agus luidhidh i air closach a mhuilt so, agus tha foinneamh air cluais na h-iolaire so, a dh' fheumas tusa a ghearradh dhi le aon bheum leis a' claidheamh so, ach deur fola cha 'n 'fheud thu tharruinn." Thàinig an iolaire, 's cha robh i fada 'g itheadh dar a theann Iain rithe, 's le aon bheum gheàrr e 'm foinneamh dhi gun aon deur fola a tharruinn. "A nis arsa 'n iolaire, thig air bhun mo dha sgéithe, bho 'n a tha fios agam air do ghnothuch n' is feàrr na th' agad féin." Rinn e so, agus bha iad uair air muir, 's uair air talamh, 's uair air an sgiathan, gus an d' ràinig iad an t-Eilean uaine. "Nis Iain, ars' ise, bi ealamh, 's lìon do bhotuil; cuimhnich gu bheil na coin dhubha air falbh an ceartair." Nuair a lìon a na botuil do 'n uisge as an tobar, faicear tigh beag làimh ris. Thuirt Iain ris féin gu'n rachadh e stigh, s gu 'm faiceadh e dé bh' ann, agus a cheud sòmar a dh' fhosgail e, chunnaic e botull làn do dh-uisge beatha, lìon e gloinne as, 's dh' òl e 'san uair a dh' òl, thug e sùil, 's bha 'm botull cho làn sa bha e roimhe. "Bithidh 'm botull so agam còmhla ris na botuil uisge," ars' esan. Chaidh e 'n sin a stigh do sheomar eile, 's chunnaic e builionn; thug e sliseag as, ach bha 'm builionn cho slàn sa bha e roimhe. "Dia cha 'n fhàg mi thus'," ars' Iain. Chaidh e air aghaidh mar so gus an d' ràinig e seòmar eile; chunnaic e mulachag mhòr chàise, thug e sliseag do 'n mhulachaig, ach bha i cho slàn sa bha i roimhe. "Bithidh so agam còmhla ri càch," ars' esan. Chaidh e 'n so gu seòmar eile, 's faicear 'na luidhe an sin an t-aon àilleagan boirionnaich bu bhoidhche a chunnaic e riamh. "Bu mhòr am beud gun phòg beòil a thoirt dhuit, a ghaoil," ars' Iain. Beagan 'na dheigh so, leum Iain air muin na h-iolaire 's thug i e air a chas cheum cheudna, gus an d-ràinig iad tigh an fhamhair mhòir, 's bha iad a pàidheadh a mhàil do 'n

famhair, agus 's ann an sin a bha 'n sealladh air tuathanaich, 's
famhairean, 's biadh, 's deoch. "Uil, Iain," ars' am famhair, "am
fac thu 'leithid so do dheoch ann an tigh t' athar an Eirinn." "Puth!"
ars' Iain, "hu; a laochain, a dhuine eile, tha deoch agamsa nach
ionann." Thug e gloinne do 'n fhamhair as a bhotul, ach bha 'm
botul cho làn 'sa bha e roimhe. "Mata, ars' am famhair, "bheir mi
fhéin da chèud nott dhuit air son a' bhotuil, srian, agus dìollaid."
" 'S bargain e mata," ars' Iain, "ach gu 'feum an ceud leannan a
bha agamsa fhaotainn ma thig i 'n rathad." "Gheibh i sin," ars' am
famhair, ach gus an sgeulachd fada a dheanamh goirid, dh' fhàg e
gach builionn 's gach mulachag aig an da fhamhair eile, air a'
chumhnant cheudna gu' faigheadh an ceud leannan bha aige-san
iad na 'n d' thigeadh i 'n rathad. Ràinig Iain an so baile mòr athar
ann an Eirinn, 's faicear a dha bhràthair mar dh' fhàg e iad 'nam
blaigeartan. " 'S feàrr dhuibh tighinn dhachaidh leamsa, 'illean,"
ars' esan, 's gheibh sibh deis' eudaich, 's each, 's dìollaid, 's srian
am fear; agus mur so rinn iad; ach dar a bha iad dlùth do thigh an
athair, smaoinich a bhràithrean gum b'fheàrr dhoibh a mharbhadh,
agus 's e bh'ann gun do thòisich iad air, 's dar a shaoil leo e bhi
marbh, thilg iad e air cùl gàrraidh, 's thug iad uaidh na tri botuil
uisge, 's dh' fhalbh iad dhachaidh. Cha robh Iain ro fhada an so,
nuair a thàinig an gobha aig athair an rathad le làn cairt do dh'
iarunn meirgeach. Ghlaodh Iain a mach co air bith an crìosduidh
bha 'n sin, O! e dheanamh cobhair dhàsan. Rug an gobha air, 's
thilg e Iain am measg an iaruinn, agus leis cho meirgeach 'sa bha
'n t-iarrunn, chaidh e ann's gach lot's creuchd a bh' air Iain, agus
's e bh' ann, gun do chinn Iain maol, carrach. Fàgaidh sinn Iain an
so, agus tillidh sinn ris an ailleagan bhòidheach a dh'fhàg Iain 'san
eilean uaine. Chinn i 'n so trom, torrach, breac, ballach, 'san ceann
tri ràithean, bha mac brèagh gille aice. "O air an t-saoghail mhòr,"
ars' ise, "cia mar a fhuair mise so?" "Foil! Foil!" ars' a' chailleach
chearc, "Na cuireadh sin smaointeach ort; so dhuit eun, agus co
luath sa chi e athair do mhic, leumaidh e air mullach a chinn.
Chaidh an t-eilean uaine a chruinneachadh bho cheann gu ceann,
's an sluagh a chur a stigh air an dorus chùil 's amach air an dorus
bheoil, ach cha do ghluais an t-eun, 's cha d' fhuaireadh athair an
leinibh. Thubhairt i 'n so gu falbhadh i feadh an t-saoghail gu leir,
gus am faigheadh i athair a leinibh. Thainig i 'n so gu tigh an
fhamhair mhòir, agus faicear am botul. "Ai! Ai!" deir ise, "co thug
dhuit am botul so?" Thuirt am famhair. " 'Se Iain òg mac rìgh
Eirinn a dh' fhàg e." "Mata 's leamsa am botul," thuirt ise, ach gu
an sgeulachd fad' a dheànamh goirid, thàinig i gu tigh gach famhair,

's thug i leatha gach botul 's gach builionn 's gach mulachag chàise; gus ma dheireadh thall, thàinig i gu tigh rìgh Eirinn. Chaidh 'n so cuig cuigeamh na h-Eirinn a chruinneachadh 's drochaid cheudan na maith. Chaidh an cur a stigh air an dorus chùil, 's a mach air an dorus bheòil, ach cha do ghluais an t-eun. "Dh' fheòraich i 'n so, an robh a h-aon na h-aon idir eile ann an Eirinn nach robh 'n so?" "Tha gille maol, carrach anns a' cheàrdach agamsa," thuirt an gobha ach;" "Car air na dheth, cuir an so e" deir ise: 's cha bo luaithe a chunnaic an t-eun ceann a ghille mhaoil charraich na 'thug e iteag 's luidhear air maol mhullaich a' ghille charrich. Rug i air 's phòg i e." " 'S tusa athair mo leinibh." "Ach Iain," arsa rìgh mòr Eirinn. " 's tusa a fhuair na botuil uisge dhòmhsa." "Ach gu dearbh 's mi," ars' Iain. "Uil, mata, dè tha thu toileach a dhèanamh ri 'd' dhithis bhraithrean?" "A cheart rud a bha iadsan toileach a dhèanamh ormsa, cur as doibh;" agus 's e sin fein a rinneadh. Phòs Iain's nighean rìgh an Eilean Uaine, 's rinn iad banais mhòr ghreadhnach a mhair seachd lathan 's seachd bliadhna 's cha chluinneadh tu ach lig, lig, 's big, big, fuaim tail 's tarruing pinne, òr 'ga phronnadh bho bhonn an coise gu barr am meòir fad sheachd bliadhna 's sheachd lathan.

Written from the recitation of JOHN MACDONALD, travelling tinker. He wanders all over the Highlands, and lives in a tent with his family. He can neither read nor write. He repeats some of his stories by heart fluently, and almost in the same words. I have followed his recitation as closely as possible, but it was exceedingly difficult to keep him stationary for any length of time.

                                        HECTOR URQUHART.

The tinker's comments I got from the transcriber. John himself is a character; he is about fifty years of age; his father, an old soldier, is alive and about eighty; and there are numerous younger branches; and they were all encamped under the root of a tree in a quarry close to Inveraray, at Easter 1859.

The father tells many stories, but his memory is failing. The son told me several, and I have a good many of them written down. They both recite; they do not simply tell the story, but act it with changing voice and gesture, as if they took an interest in it, and entered into the spirit and fun of the tale. They belong to the race of "Cairds," and are as much nomads as the gipsies are.

The father, to use the son's expression, "Never saw a school." He served in the 42d in his youth. One son makes horn spoons, and does not know a single story; the other is a sporting character, a famous fisherman, who knows all the lochs and rivers in the Highlands, makes flies, and earns money in summer by teaching Southerns to fish. His ambition is to become an under-keeper.

This bear story is like a great many others which I have got elsewhere in the Highlands, but I have none told exactly in the same way. It should be much longer, but the wandering spirit of the man would not let him rest to dictate his story. They had to move to an outhouse and let him roam about amongst the shavings, and swing his arms, before this much was got out of him.

I have found the same restlessness amongst wanderers elsewhere. I could never get Lapps to sit still for ten minutes when I tried to draw them; and the air of a house seemed to oppress them. I have hitherto failed in catching an English tinker, whom I let slip one day in London, and to whom I promised good pay if he would come and dictate a story which he had told me. There is a similar wandering population in Norway and Sweden. They own boats and carts, and pretend to magic arts; and are feared and detested by householders as wizards and thieves. It is said that these Norwegian wanderers hold a meeting on a hill near Christiania, once a year, and barter and sell, and exchange whatever they may have acquired in their travels. I have heard a great deal about them from peasants. I have seen them, but very seldom in Norway. I once met a party in the gloaming on a Swedish road, and a little girl, who was following and driving a gentleman in a posting-cart, when she met them, flogged her horse and galloped for dear life.

There is a similar race in Spain, and though they are not all gipsies, they are classed with them. The history of these wanderers would be curious if it could be learned. Borrow's Bible in Spain gives some insight, but there is still much to be known about them. "London Labour and the Poor," and reports on "Ragged Schools," treat of similar people.

This story may be compared with Grimm's Water of Life.

10

THE THREE SOLDIERS.

From James MacLachlan, servant, Islay

There was before a regiment in Dublin in Erin, and it was going a long journey. There was a sergeant, a corporal, and a single soldier, who had sweethearts in the town. They went to see them on the day that they were to go, and they stayed too long, and the regiment left them; they followed it, and they were going and going till the night came on them. They saw a light a long way from them; and if it was a long way from them, it was not long they were in reaching it. They went in, the floor was ready swept, and a fire on it, and no one in; they sat at the fire toasting themselves; they were not long there when the single soldier rose, to whom was the name of John, to look what was in the chamber, because there was a light in it. There was there a board covered with every sort of meat, and a lighted candle on it; he went up, he began to eat, and the rest began to hinder him, for that he had no business with it. When they saw that he did not stop, they went up and they began themselves. There were three beds in the chamber, and one of them went to lie in each bed; they had not laid long when three great red girls came in, and one of them stretched herself near each one of the beds; and when they saw the time fitting in the morning, they rose and went away. When the girls rose, it could not be known that a bit had ever come off the board. They sat and they took their meat. The sergeant said that they had better follow the regiment; and John said that they should not follow it; as long as he could get meat and rest that he would not go. When dinner time came they sat and they took their dinner. The sergeant said they had better go; and John said that they should not go. When supper time came they sat and they took their supper; after supping they went to lie down, each one to his own bed. The girls came this night too, and went to lie down as before. In the morning when they saw the time fitting, they rose and they went away. When the lads rose the board was covered, and it could not be known that a bit had ever come off it. They sat and they took their meat; and when they took their meat, the sergeant said that they *would* go at all events. John said that they should not go. They took their dinner and their supper as they used; they went to lie down; the girls came and they lay down after them. In the morning the eldest gave the sergeant a purse, and every time he would unloose it, it would be full of gold and silver.

She said to the middle one, "What wilt thou give to thine?" "I will give him a towel, and every time he spreads it it will be full of every sort of meat." She gave the towel to the corporal; and she said to the youngest, "What wilt thou give to thine own?" "I will give him a whistle, and every time he plays it he will be in the very middle of the regiment." She gave him the whistle; they left their blessing with them, and they went away. "I wont let it rest here," said John; "I will know who they are before I go further forward." He followed them, and he saw them going down a glen; and when he was about to be down, they came to meet him, crying. "What is the matter with you!" says he. "Much is the matter with us," said they, "that we are under charms, till we find three lads who will spend three nights with us without putting a question to us; and if thou hadst stayed without following us we were free." Is there any way that you can get free but that!" said he. "There is," said they. "There is a tree at the end of the house, and if you come at the end of a day and year and pluck up the tree, we were free." John turned back where the rest were, and he told them how it happened to him; and they gave this advice to each other that they should return back to Dublin again, because it was not worth their while to follow the regiment. They returned back to Dublin.

That night John said,—"I had better go to see the king's daughter to-night." "Thou had'st better stay in the house," said the rest, "than go there."

"I will go there, at all events," says he. He went and he reached the king's house; he struck at the door, one of the gentlewomen asked him what he wanted; and he said that he wished to be speaking to the king's daughter. The king's daughter came where he was, and she asked what business he had with her. "I will give thee a whistle," said he, "and when thou playest it thou wilt be in the middle of such a regiment." When she got the whistle she drove him down stairs, and she shut the door on him. "How went it with thee?" said they. "She wheedled the whistle from me," said he. He did not stop till he had beguiled a loan of the purse from the sergeant. "I had better," said he, "go to see the king's daughter again." He went away and he reached the house; he saw the king's daughter; she wheedled the purse from him, and drove him down stairs, as she did before; and he turned back. He did not stop till he beguiled a loan of the towel from the corporal. He went again where the king's daughter was. "What wilt thou give me this journey?" said she. "A towel, and when it is opened it will be full of every sort of meat." "Let me see it," said she. "We will spread it out," said he. He spread it out, and there was a corner that would not lie right. He said to her to stand on the corner; she stood on it; he stood himself on another corner, and he wished to be in the uttermost isle of the deep; and himself and the king's daughter, and the towel, were in it in five minutes. There was the very prettiest island that man ever saw, and nothing in it but trees and fruits. There they were, going through the island backwards and forwards, and sleep came on him. They came to a pretty little hollow, and he laid his head in her lap; and he took a death grip of her apron, in order that she should not get away without his perceiving her. When he slept she loosed the apron; she left him there; she took the towel with her; she stood on it; she wished herself to be in her father's house, and she was in it. When he awoke he had nothing to get, he had nothing to see but trees and birds; he was then keeping himself alive with the fruits of the island, and hit upon apples; and when he would eat one sort of them they would put a deer's head on him; and when he would eat another sort of them, they would put it off him.

One day he gathered a great many of the apples, and he put the one sort in the one end of the pock, and the other sort in the other end. He saw a vessel going past, he waved to her; a boat came to shore, and they took him on board. The captain took him down to meat, and he left the pock above. The sailors opened the pock to see what was in it; when they saw that apples were in it, they began to eat them. They ate the sort that would put deers' horns on them, and they began fighting till they were like to break the vessel. When the captain heard the row, he came up; and when he saw them, he said, "Thou bad man, what hast thou done to my men now?" "What," said John, "made thy men so impudent that they would go and look into any man's pock?" "What wilt thou give me," said John, "if I leave them as they were before?" The skipper took fright, and he said that he would give him the vessel and cargo at the first port they reached. Here he opened the pock, and he gave them the other sort, and the horns fell off them. It was a cargo of gold was on the ship, and it was to Dublin she was going. When they arrived the captain said to him to be taking care of the vessel and cargo, that he was done with it. "Be patient," said John, "till we see how it goes with us at the end of a few days." He went away on the morrow to sell the apples about the town with nothing on but torn clothes. He went up through the town, and he came opposite the king's house, and he saw the king's daughter with her head out of the window. She asked that a pound of the apples should be sent up to her. He said she should try how they would agree with her first. He threw up an apple to her of the sort that would put a deer's head on her; when she ate the apple there came a deer's head and horns on her. The king sent forth word, that if any man whatsoever could be found, who would heal his daughter, that he should get a peck of gold, and a peck of silver, and herself to marry. She was thus many days and no man coming that could do any good at all. John came to the door with the torn clothes, asking to get in; and when they saw his like, they would not let him in; but she had a little brother who saw them keeping him out, and he told it to his father; and his father said, "Though it were the beggar of the green!" Word went after him that he should return, and he returned. The king said to him, "Could he heal his daughter?" and he said "that he would try it." They took him up to the chamber where she was. He sat, and he took a book out of his pocket, with nothing in it, pretending that he was reading it. "Didst thou," said he, "wheedle a whistle from a poor soldier; when he would play it, it would take him to the middle of the regiment?" "I wheedled," said she. "If that is not found," said he, "I cannot heal thee." "It is," says she. They brought the whistle to him. When he got the whistle he gave her a piece of apple, and one of the horns fell off her. "I can't," said he, "do more to-day, but I will come here to-morrow. Then he went out, and his old comrades met him. The trade they had was to be slaking lime and drawing water for stone masons. He knew them, but they did not know him; he noticed nothing at all, but he gave them ten shillings, and he said to them, "Drink the health of the man who gave them." He left them there, and he returned to the ship. On the morrow he went where the king's daughter was; he took out the book, and he said to her, "Didst thou wheedle a purse from a poor soldier, that would be full of gold and silver every time it was opened?" "I wheedled," said she. "If that is not found," said he, "I cannot heal thee." "It is," said she; and they gave him the purse. When he got the purse he gave her a piece of the apple, and another horn fell off her. "I can

do no more to-day," said he, "but I will come the next night." He
went where his old comrades were, and he gave them other ten
shillings, and he said to them, "To drink the health of the man who
gave them." Then he returned to the vessel. The captain said to him,
"Was he going to take charge of the vessel now?" Said he, "Catch
patience till the end of a day or two, till we see how it goes with us."
He returned the next night to see the king's daughter. He gave a pull
at the book as he used to do,—"Didst thou wheedle," said he, "a
towel from a poor soldier, that would be full of every kind of meat
every time it was undone?" "I wheedled," said she. "If that towel is
not to be found, I cannot cure thee," says he. "It is," says she. They
gave it to him; as quick as he got it, he gave her a whole apple; and
when she ate it she was as she was before. Here he got a peck of gold
and a peck of silver; and they said to him that he would get herself
to marry. "I will come to-morrow," said he. He went the way of his
old comrades this time too; he gave them ten shillings, and he said
to them, "To drink the health of the man who gave them." Said they,
"It would be pleasing to us to know what kind friend is giving us the
like of this every night." "Have you mind," said he, "when we were
in such a place, and that we promised to the three girls that we would
go there again a year from the time." Then they knew him. "That
time has gone past long ago," said they. "It is not gone," said he;
"Next night is the night." He returned where the captain was; he
said to him that himself and his cargo might be off; that he would
not be troubling him; that he had enough. On the morrow he went
past the king's house, and the king's daughter said to him, "Art thou
going to marry me to-day?" "No, nor to-morrow," said he. He
returned where the rest were, and he began to set them in order for
going where they promised. He gave the purse to the sergeant, the
towel to the corporal, and the whistle he kept himself. He bought
three horses, and they went riding with great haste to the place to
which they had promised to go. When they reached the house they
caught the tree, and it came with them at the first pull. The three
girls came so white and smiling where they were, and they were free
from the spells. Every man of them took his own with him; they came
back to Dublin, and they married.

———

URSGEUL.

Bha roimhe so réiseamaid ann am Bailcliath an Eirinn, 's bha i
'folbh air turas fada. Bha séirdsean, corporal, agus saighdear sìngilte

aig an robh leannain anns a' bhaile. Chaidh iad a'm faicinn an latha bha iad ri folbh, 's dh' fhan iad tuillidh is fada, 's dh'fhag an réiseamaid iad. Lean iad i 's bha iad a' folbh 's a' folbh gus an d' thàinig an oidhche orra. Chunnaic iad solus fada uatha, 's ma b' fhada uatha cha b' fhada bha iadsan 'ga ruigheachd. Chaidh iad a stigh. Bha 'n t-ùrlar reidh, sguabte, 's gealbhan air, 's gun duine stigh. Shuidh iad aig a' ghealbhan 'gan garadh. Cha b' fhada 'bha iad mur sin nur a dh' éirich an saighdear singilte, d' am b' ainm Iain, a dh' amharc de 'bha 'san t-seombar, a thaobh gun robh solus ann. Bha 'n sin bord air a chuirneachadh leis a h-uile seòrsa bidh, 's coinneal laist' air. Chaidh e suas; thòisich e air itheadh; 's thòisich càch air a bhacail, o nach robh gnothach aige ris. Nur a chunnaic iad nach do stad e, chaidh iad suas, 's thòisich iad féin. Bha tri leapaichean anns an t-seombar, 's chaidh fear dhiu 'laidhe anns gach leaba.

Cha b' fhada a bha iad 'nan laidhe nur a thàinig tri nigheanan mòra ruagha stigh, 's shin té aca i féin aig beulthaobh gach té de na leapaichean, 's nur a chunnaic iad an t-am iomchuidh anns a' mhaidinn dh' éirich iad, agus dh' fholbh iad.

Nur a dh' éirich na saighdearan cha 'n aithnichte gun d' thàinig mir bhàr a' bhùird riamh. Shuidh iad, 's ghabh iad am biadh. Thuirt an seirdsean gum b' fheàrra dhaibh an réiseamaid a leantainn, 's thuirt Iain nach leanadh. Fhad 'sa gheibheadh e bhiadh 'na thàmh nach folbhadh e. Nur a thàinig an t-am dinnearach, shuidh iad 's ghabh iad an dinneir. Thuirt an séirdsean gum b' fheàrra dhaibh folbh, 's thuirt Iain nach folbhadh. Nur a thàinig am sioparach, shuidh iad 's ghabh iad an siopair. An déigh an sioparach chaidh iad a laidhe, gach fear d'a leaba féin.

Thàinig na nigheanan an oidhche so cuideachd, 's chaidh té laidhe anns a' h-uile leaba dhiu. Anns a' mhaidinn, nur a chunnaic iad an t-am iomchuidh, dh' éirich iad 's dh' fholbh iad.

Nur a dh' éirich na gillean bha 'm bòrd cùirnichte, 's cha 'n aithnichte gun d' thàinig mir riamh dheth. Shuidh iad 's ghabh iad am biadh, 's nur a ghabh iad am biadh thuirt an seirdsean gum folbhadh iad codhiu. Thuirt Iain nach folbhadh. Ghabh iad an dinneir 's an siopair mur a b' àbhaist. Chaidh iad a laidhe.

Thàinig na nigheanan 's laidh iad as an déigh. Anns a' mhaidinn thug an té 'bu shine sporan do 'n t-seirdsean, 's a' h-uile h-uair a dh' fhosgladh e e bhiodh e làn òir is airgid. Urs' i ris an té mheadhonaich, "De 'bheir thusa do t' fhear fein?" "Bheir mise dha tuthailt, 's a' h-uile h-uair a sgaoileas e i bidh i làn de na h-uile seòrsa bìdh." Thug i 'n tuthailt do 'n chorporal, 's thuirt i ris an té b' òige, " Dé 'bheir thusa do t' fhear fein?" "Bheir mi dha fìdeag, 's a' h-uile h-uair a sheinneas e i bidh e 'n teis meadhoin na réiseamaid." Thug i dha an fhìdeag. Dh'fhàg iad beannachd aca 's dh' fholbh iad.

"Cha leig mi leis an so e," urs' Iain, "bidh fhios'am co iad ma 'n d' théid mi na 's faide air m' aghaidh." Lean e iad, 's chunnaic e iad a' dol sìos le gleann, 's nur a bha e thun a bhi shìos thàinig iad 'na choinneamh, 's iad a' caoineadh. "De th' oirbh?" urs' esan. " 'S mòr a th' oirnn," urs' iadsan; "tha sinn fo gheasan gus am faigh sinn tri gillean a laidheas leinn tri oidchean gun cheisd a chur oirnn, 's nam fanadh thusa gun ar leantainn bha sinn ma sgaoil." "Am bheil dòigh sam bith air am faigh sibh ma sgaoil," urs' esan, "ach sin?" "Tha," urs' iadsan; "tha craobh aig ceann an tighe, 's na'n d' thigeadh sibh, an ceann la is bliadhna, 's a' chraobh sin a spìonadh bha sinne ma sgaoil."

Thill Iain air ais far an robh càch; dh' innis e dhaibh mar a thachair dha; 's chuir iad an comhairle r'a cheile gun tilleadh iad air an ais do Bhailecliath a rithisd, chionn nach b' fhiach dhaibh an réiseamaid a leantainn. Thiall iad do Bhailecliath air an ais. An oidhche sin urs' Iain, " 'S fheàrr dhomh dol a dh' amharc nighean an rìgh a nochd." " 'S fheàrra dhuit fantainn aig an tigh," arsa càch, " na dol ann." "Théid mi am codhiù," urs' esan.

Dh' fholbh e 's rainig e tigh an righ. Bhuail e aig an dorus. Dh' fheòraich h-aon de na mnathan uaisle de 'bha dhìth air, 's thuirt e gun robh toil aige 'bhi 'bruidhinn ri nighean an rìigh. Thàinig nighean an rìgh far an robh e, 's dh' fheòraich i dé 'n gnothuch a bh' aige rithe. "Bheir mi dhuit fìdeag," urs' esan, " 's nur a sheinneas thu i bidh thu ann am meadhon a leithid so do reiseamaid." Nur a fhuair ise an fhìdeag bhreab i leis an staighir e, 's dhùin i 'n dorus air. "Démur chaidh dhuit?" urs' iadsan. "Mheall i 'n fhìdeag uam," urs' esan. Cha do stad e gus an do mheall e coingheall de 'n sporan o 'n t-séirdsean. " 'S fheàrra dhomh," urs' esan, "dol a dh' fhaicinn nighean an righ a rithisd."

Dh' fholbh e 's ràinig e 'n tigh. Chunnaic e nighean an rìgh; mheall i 'n sporan uaidhe; bhreab i leis an staighir e mar a rinn i roimhid; 's thill e air ais. Cha do stad e gus an do mheall e coingheall de 'n tuthailt o 'n chorporal.

Chaidh e 'rithisd far an robh nighean an rìgh. "De 'bheir thu dhomh air an t-siubhal so?" urs' ise. "Tuthailt, 's nur a dh' fhosglar i bidh i làn de na h-uile seòrsa bidh." "Leig fhaicinn domh i," urs' ise. "Sgaoilidh sin a mach i," urs' esan. Sgaoil e mach i, 's bha oisean di nach laidheadh gu ceart. Thuirt e rithe seasamh air an oisean.

Sheas i air. Sheas e féin air oisean eile, 's ghuidh e bhi ann an eilean iomallach na doimhne. 'S bha e féin, is nighean an righ, 's an tuthailt ann ann an còig mionaidean. Bha 'sin an aon eilean a bu bhòidhche a chunnaic duine riamh, 's gun ni ann ach craobhan is measan. Bha iad an sin a' folbh feadh an eilean air an ais 's air an aghaidh, 's thàinig an cadal airsan. Thàinig iad gu lagan bòidheach, 's chuir esan a cheann 'na h-uchdse 's rinn e gréim bàis air a h-apran, air alt 's nach fhaigheadh i air folbh gun e mhòthchuinn di. Nur a chaidil esan dh' fhuasgail ise an t-apran; dh' fhàg i 'n sin e; thug i leatha an tuthailt; sheas i urra; ghuidh i bhi 'n tigh a h-athar; 's bha i ann.

Nur a dhùisg esan cha robh ni ri fhaotainn aige, 's cha robh ni ri fhaicinn aige, ach craobhan is eunlaith. Bha e 'n sin a' tighinn beò air measan an eilean, 's dh' amais ubhlan air, 's nur a dh' itheadh e aon seòrsa dhiu chuireadh iad ceann féidh air, 's nur a dh' itheadh e seòrsa eile dhiu chuireadh iad deth e. Aon latha chruinnich e mòran de na h-ubhlan, 's chuir e 'n darna seòrsa ann an aon cheann do 'n phoca, 's an seòrsa éile anns a' cheann eile. Chunnaic e soitheach a' dol seachad; chrath e rithe; thàinig bàta gu tìr; 's thug iad air bòrd e. Thug an caibhtinn sìos e gu biadh, 's dh' fhàg e 'm poca gu h-ard. Dh' fhosgaill na seòladairean am poca a dh' amharc de 'bh 'ann. Nur a chunnaic iad an seòrsa 'chuireadh adhaircean féidh orra. Chinn adhaircean féidh orra, 's thòisich iad air leum air a chéile gus an robh iad a' brath an soitheach a bhrisdeadh. Nur a chuala an caibhtinn an starum thàinig e nìos, s nur a chunnaic e iad thuirt e, " 'Dhroch dhuine dé tha thu an déigh a dhèanadh air mo dhaoine nis?" "De," urs' Iain, "a chuir do dhaoine-sa cho miomhail 's gun rachadh iad a dh' fhaicinn de bhiodh ann am poca duine sam bith? De bheir thu dhomh," urs' Iain, "ma dh' fhàgas mi iad mur a bha iad roimhid?" Ghabh an sgiobair eagal, 's thuirt e gun d' thugadh e dha an soitheach agus an luchd aig a' chiad phort a ruigeadh iad. Dh' fhosgail e 'n so am poca, 's thug e dhaibh an seòrs' eile, 's thuit na h-adhaircean diu. 'S e luchd òir a' bh' air an t-soitheach, agus 's ann a Bhailecliath a bha i 'dol. Nur a ràinig iad thuirt an caibhtinn ris, e 'bhi 'gabhail cùram de 'n t-soitheach 's de 'n luchd, gun robh esan réidh is i. "Dèan faighidinn," urs' Iain, "gus am faic sinn démur a théid duinn ann an ceann beagan làithean."

Dh' fholbh e 'n la 'r na mhàireach a reic nan ubhlan feadh a' bhaile, 's gun air ach aodach srachdte. Chaidh e suas feadh a' bhaile, 's thàinig e ma choinneamh tigh an rìgh, 's chunnaic e nighean an righ 's a ceann a mach air uinneag. Dh' iarr i punnd de na h-ubhlan a chur suas a 'h-ionnsuidh. Thuirt esan i dh' fheacainn

démur a chòrdadh iad rithe an toiseach. Thilg e 'suas ubhal urra
de 'n t-seòrsa 'chuireadh ceann féidh urra. Nur a dh' ith i 'n ubhal
thàinig ceann féidh urra. Chuir an rìgh fios a mach nam faighte
duine sam bith a léighseadh a nighean gum faigheadh e peic òir is
peic airgid, 's i féin r'a phòsadh. Bha i mur sin mòran làithean, 's
gun duine 'tighinn a bha déanadh math sam bith. Thàinig Iain gus
an dorusd leis an aodach shrachdte 'g iarraidh a stigh, 's nur a
chunnaic iad a choslas cha leigeadh iad a stigh e, ach bha bràthair
beag aicise a chunnaic iad 'ga chumail a mach 's dh' innis e d'a
athair e, 's thuirt a h-athair ged a b' e bleidire an lòin a bhiodh ann
a leigeil a stigh. Chaidh fios as a dhéigh a 'thilleadh, agus thill e.
Thuirt an rìgh ris an léighseadh e 'nighean, 's thuirt e gum feuchadh
e ris. Thug iad suas e do 'n t-seombar far an robh i. Shuidh e, 's
thug e 'mach leobhar a phòca 's gun ni sam bith ann, a' leigeil air
gun robh e 'ga 'leubhadh. "An do mheall thusa," urs' esan, "fideag
o shaighdear bochd, nur a sheinneadh e i 'bheireadh e gu meadhon
a réiseamaid." "Mheall," urs' ise. "Mar a' bheil sin air faotainn,"
urs' esan, "cha 'n urrainn mise do leigheas." "Tha," urs' ise. Thug
iad a' ionnsuidh an fhídeag. Nur a fhuair e 'n fhìdeag thug e dhi
pìosa de dh' ubhal, 's thuit fear de na cabair dhi. "Cha 'n urrainn
mi," urs' esan, "tuillidh a dhèanadh an diugh, ach thig mi 'm
màireach."

Dh' fholbh e 'n sin a mach, 's thachair a sheana chompanaich
air, 's e cheaird a bh' aca 'bhi buacadh aoil, 's a' tarruinn uisge do
chlachairean. Dh' aithnich esan iadsan, ach cha d' aithnich iadsan
esan. Cha do leig e rud sam bith air, ach thug e dhaibh deich
tasdain, 's thuirt e riu, "òlaibh deoch slàinte an fhir a thug dhuibh
e."

Dhealaich e 'n sin riu, 's thill e gus an t-soithich. An la 'r na
mhàireach chaidh e far an robh nighean an rìgh. Thug e mach an
leabhar, 's thuirt e rithe, "An do mheall thusa sporan o shaighdear
bochd, a bhiodh làn òir is airgid h-uile h-uair a dh' fhosgailt' e?"
"Mheall," ars' ise. "Mar a' bheil sin air faotainn," urs' esan, "cha
'n urrainn mise do leigheas." "Tha," urs' ise, 's thug ian dha an
sporan. Nur a fhuair e e thug e dhi pìosa do 'n ubhal, 's thuit cabar
eile dhi. "Cha 'n urrainn mi tuillidh a dhèanadh an diugh," urs'
esan, "ach thig mi 'n ath oidhche."

Chaidh e far an robh 'sheana chompanaich, 's thug e dhaibh
deich tasdain eile, 's thuirt e riu deoch slàinte an fhir a thug dhaibh
e òl. Thill e 'n sin thun an t-soithich. Thuirt an caibhtinn ris an
robh e 'dol a ghabhail cùram do 'n t-soitheach a nis. Thuirt esan,
"Glac faighidinn gu ceann latha na dha gus am faic sinn démur a

thèid duinn." Thill e an ath oidhche a dh' fhaicinn nighean an rìgh.
Thug e tarrainn air a leabhar mar a b' àbhaist dha. "An do mheall
thusa," urs' esan, "tuthailt o shaighdear bochd, a bhiodh làn de na
h-uile seòrsa bìdh a' h-uile h-uair a dh' fhosgailt i?" "Mheall," urs'
ise. "Mar a' bheil an tuthailt sin air faotainn cha 'n urrainn mise do
leigheas," urs' esan. "Tha," urs' ise. Thug iad dha i. Cho luath 's
a fhuair esan i thug e ubhal shlàn dhi, 's nur a dh' ith i i bha i mar
a bha i roimhid. Fhuair e 'n sin peic òir is peic airgid, 's thuirt iad
ris gum faigheadh e i féin ri 'pòsadh, "Thig mi 'm màireach," urs'
esan.

Ghabh e rathad a sheana chompanach air an t-siubhal so
cuideachd; thug e deich tasdain daibh; 's thuirt e riu deoch slàinte
an fhir a thug dhaibh e òl. Urs' iadsan, "Bu mhail leinn fios a bhi
againn co an caraid caoimhneil a tha 'toirt duinn a' leithid' a' h-uile
h-oidhche?" "Am bheil cuimhn' agaibh," urs' esan, "Nur a bha sinn
'na leithid so do dh' àite, 's a gheall sin do na tri nigheanan gun
rachamaid ann bliadhna o 'n am sin a rithisd?" Dh' aithnich iad an
sin e. "Chaidh an ùine sin seachad o chionn fada," urs' iadsan. "Cha
deachaidh," urs' esan; " 's i an ath oidhche an oidhche." Thill e far
an robh an caibhtinn, 's thuirt e ris gum faodadh e féin 's a luchd
a bhi folbh, nach biodh esan a' cur dragh air, gun robh na leòir aige.

An la 'r na mhàireach chaidh e seachad tigh an rìgh, 's thuirt
nighean an righ ris, "Am bheil thu dol am' phòsadh an diugh?"
"Cha 'n 'eil na 'màireach," urs' esan. Thill e far an robh càch, 's
thòisich e air cur an òrdugh air son dol far an do gheall iad. Thug
e 'n sporan do 'n séirdsean, an tuthailt do 'n chorporal, 's ghléidh
e féin an fhìdeag. Cheannaich e tri eich, 's dh' fholbh iad air
mharcachd ann an cabhaig mhòir do 'n aite an do gheall iad dol.
Nur a ràinig iad an tigh rug iad air a' chraoibh, is thainig i leis air
a' chiad spìonadh. Thàinig na tri nigheanan gu geal, gàireachdach
far an robh iad, 's bha iad saor o na geasan. Thug a' h-uile fear dhiu
leis a thè féin, 's thàinig iad air an ais do Bhailecliath, 's phòs iad.

Got this tale from a young lad of the name of James M'Lachlin,
who is at present in my own employment. I have had the preceding
tale from him also. He has had them from an old woman that lives
somewhere up the way of Portaskaig, who, he says, can repeat several
more, and to whom I intend immediately to apply.

May 27, 1860.—After speaking to the old woman MacKerrol, I
find that, from age and loss of memory, she is unable now to tell any
of the tales she was wont to repeat.

HECTOR MACLEAN.

Another version of this has been sent by Mr. Osgood Mackenzie from Gairloch. It was recited by HECTOR MACKENZIE at Dibaig, who learned it some years ago from KENNETH MACKENZIE at Dibaig; and it was written by ANGUS MACRAE at Dibaig. This Dibaig version tells how—

1.   There was a soldier, by name Coinneach Buidhe, Kenneth the Yellow, in the army of old, and he belonged to Alba. He deserted, and his master sent a "corpaileir" after him; but the corporal deserted too; and so did a third. They went on till they reached the "yearly wood," in America. After a time, they saw on a certain night, a light which led them to a large house; they found meat and drink, and all that they could desire. They saw no one for a year and a day, except three maidens, who never spoke, but called in at odd times; and as they did not speak, the soldiers were silent.

At the end of the year the maidens spoke, and praised them for their politeness, explained that they were under spells, and for their kindness, gave to the first a cup that would be ever full, and a lamp of light; to the second, a table-cover on which meat was ever; and to the third, a bed in which there would ever be rest for them at any time they chose; and besides, the "TIADHLAICEAN" would make any one who had them get anything he wished. They reached a certain king, whose only daughter pretended to be fond of Kenneth the Yellow, and wheedled him till he gave her the TIADHLAICEAN, when she ordered him to be put in an island in the ocean. When there alone he grew hungry, and ate "abhlan," and a wood like thatch grew through his head, and there remained till he ate "ABHLAN" of another kind, when the wood vanished. He got off in a ship with "ABHLAN" of each sort, and reached the big town of the king where he had been before, where he set up a booth. On a certain day a fair lad came in to sell ABHLAN, and through him the other kind were sold to the king's daughter, and a wood grew on her head. Kenneth the Yellow got back the TIADHLAICEAN, and found his two companions AGUS BHA IAD UILE TUILLEADH ANN AM MEAS AGUS SOIRBHEACHADH GUS A CHRIOCH. And they were all after in worship and prosperousness till the end.

This is manifestly the same story shortened, and made reasonable. It is very well written and spelt according to rule.

3.   I have another version of this told by Hector Boyd, fisherman, Castle Bay, Barra, who says he learned it from John MacNeill, who has left the island; and from Neill MacKinnon, Ruagh Lias. In this the three soldiers are English, Scotch, and Irish. The two last desert; and the first, a sergeant, is sent after them. They persuade him to desert also, and they come to a castle. The Irishman acts the part of John in the Islay version; and the first night they eat and go to sleep, and find dresses when they wake. In the morning they get up and

put on their dresses; and the board was set over with meat and with drink, and they took their TRATH MADAIN, breakfast. They went to take a walk without. The Englishman had a gun, and he saw three swans swimming on a loch, and he began to put a charge in his gun. The swans perceived him, and they cried to him, and they were sure he was going to shoot at them. They came on shore and became three women. "How are these dresses pleasing you?" said they. "The like will be yours every day in the year, and your meat as good as you got; but that you should neither think or order one of us to be with you in lying down or rising up." And so they remained for a year in the castle. One night the Irishman thought of the swans, and in the morning they had nothing but their old dresses.

They went to the loch; the swans came on shore, became women, and gave a purse that would always be full of gold and jewels, to the Englishman; a knife to the Scotchman, and whenever it was opened he would be wherever he wished; and to the Irishman a horn, and when he blew in the small end there would be a thousand soldiers before him; and when he blew in the big end none of them would be seen.

They go to a big town, and build a house on a green hill with money from the purse; and when the house was built, one about went to the town to buy meat. The Irishman fell in love with the king's daughter, and was cheated out of his magic horn; borrowed the purse, and lost that; and then, by the help of the knife, transported himself and the king's daughter to an island which could hardly be seen in the far ocean. And there they were, and there they stayed for seventeen days, eating fruits. One day he slept with his head on her knee, and she looked at her hands and saw how long the nails had grown; so she put her hand in his pocket and took out the knife to pare them. "Oh," said she, "that I were where the nails grew on me," and she was in her father's house. Then he found red apples and grey apples; and no sooner had he eaten some of the red apples than his head was down, and his heels were up, from the weight of the deer's horns that grew on his head. Then he bethought him that one of the grey apples might heal him; and he stretched himself out with his head downwards, and kicked down one of the apples with his feet, and ate it, and the horns fell off him. Then he made baskets, and filled them with the apples; climbed a tree, saw a ship, tore his shirt and waved it on a stick, and was seen.

The skipper was under an oath that he would never leave a man in extremity. They came on shore for him, and were terrified at his beard, thinking that he was the evil spirit. When he got on board, a razor was got, and (as the narrator said) SHEUBHAIG E he was shaved. The ship sailed straight to the king's house. The lady looked out of a window. He sold her a red apple for a guinea. She ate it, the horns grew, and there were not alive those who could take her from that. They thought of saws, and they sent for doctors; and he came, and then there is a scene in which he pretends to read a divining book, and tries saws on the horns, and frightens the lady and recovers the lost gifts. Then he went to his friends, and they went to the swans; and the spells went off them. and they married them.

The story is very well told, especially the last scene; but it is too like the Islay version to make it worth translating at full length.

4.   I have another story, from a Ross-shire man, now in Glasgow, which begins in the same manner, but the incidents are very different.

This story has a counterpart in German, Der Krautesel; and it has a very long pedigree in Grimm's third volume. It seems to be very widely spread, and very old, and to belong to many languages; many versions are given. In one a soldier, one of three, eats apples in a forest, and his nose grows right through the forest, and sixty miles beyond it; and the king's daughter's nose is made to grow, exactly as horns are made to grow on the princess in the Highlands; and she is forced to give up the things which she had got from the soldiers; and which are a purse, a mantle, and a horn of magic power.

In another version, it is a young huntsman who changes a with and her daughter into donkeys, by giving them magic cabbages, which had previously transformed him.

The swans in the third version seem to belong to Sanscrit, as well as to Norse and other languages. In "Comparative Mythology," by Max Muller, Oxford Essays, 1856, a story is given from the Brâhmana of the Yagurveda, in which this passage occurs—"Then he bewailed his vanished love in bitter grief; and went near Kurukshetra. There is a lake there called Anyatahplaksha, full of lotus flowers; and while the king walked along its border, the fairies were playing there in the water in the shape of birds; and Urvasi discovered him, and said, 'That is the man with whom I dwelt so long.' Then her friends said, 'Let us appear to him,' " etc., etc.

The rest of the Eastern story has many Western counterparts, such as "Peter Wilkins and the Flying Ladies," and a story which I have from Islay. The incident of birds which turn out to be enchanted women, occurs in a great many other Gaelic stories; and is in Mr. Peter Buchan's "Green Sleeves" (see introduction); and, as I am told, in the Edda.

BAILECLIATH is Dublin, and takes its Gaelic name from a legend. The name should be Baile àth Cliath, the town of Wattle Ford; either from wattled boats, or a bridge of hurdles; and as it appears, there was a weaver, or tailor, residing at Ath Cliath, Wattle Ford, who got his living by making creels or hurdles, CLIATHAN, for crossing the river. There was a fluent, gabby old man, who was a friend of his;

and from his having such a tongue, the marker of the creels advised
him to become a beggar, as he was sure to succeed. He began, and
got plenty of money. He wore a cap or currachd, and all the coin he
got he buried under a stone, at the end of the wattle bridge. The
bridge maker died; the beggar got ill and kept his cap on, and never
took it off; and when he was dying he asked his wife to bury him in
it; and he was buried with his cap on. The widow's son found out
about the buried treasure, and dug it up; but the beggar's ghost so
tormented the boy, that he had to go to the minister, who advised
them to build a bridge with the money; so they built DROCHAID ATH
CLIATH, and there it is to this very day.

I do not know which of the Dublin bridges is meant, but the story
was got from a woman at Kilmeny in Islay, and this is a mere outline
of it. It is known as the story of the red-haired beggar, Am Bochd
Ruagh.

Bailecliath is a great place in Gaelic songs.

The story of the Three Soldiers is one of which I remember to
have heard a part in my childhood. I perfectly remember contriving
with a companion how we would have given the cruel princess bits
of different kinds of apples, mixed together, so as to make the horns
grow, and fall off time about; but I cannot remember who told me
the story. The version I have given is the most complete, but the
language of the Barra version is better.

There are two or three inconsistencies. They travel on the towel
which had the commissariat, and do not use the locomotive whistle
at all. But there are touches of nature. The mason's labourers
thought the time had passed, but the adventurer did not find time
so long; and he alone remembered the day.

11

THE STORY OF THE WHITE PET.

*From Mrs. MacTavish, widow of the late minister
of Kildalton, Islay.*

There was a farmer before now who had a White Pet (sheep), and
when Christmas was drawing near, he thought that he would kill
the White Pet. The White Pet heard that, and he thought he would
run away; and that is what he did.

He had not gone far when a bull met him. Said the bull to him,
"All hail! White Pet, where art thou going?" "I," said the White Pet,
"am going to seek my fortune; they were going to kill me for
Christmas, and I thought I had better run away." "It is better for
me," said the bull, "to go with thee, for they were going to do the
very same with me."

"I am willing," said the White Pet; "the larger the party the better
the fun."

They went forward till they fell in with a dog.

"All hail! White Pet," said the dog. "All hail! thou dog." "Where
art thou going?" said the dog.

"I am running away, for I heard that they were threatening to kill
me for Christmas."

"They were going to do the very same to me," said the dog, "and
I will go with you." "Come, then," said the White Pet.

They went then, till a cat joined them. "All hail! White Pet," said
the cat. "All hail! oh cat."

"Where art thou going?" said the cat. "I am going to seek my
fortune," said the White Pet, "because they were going to kill me
at Christmas."

"They were talking about killing me too," said the cat, "and I
had better go with you."

"Come on then," said the White Pet.

Then they went forward till a cock met them. "All hail! White Pet," said the cock." "All hail to thyself! oh cock," said the White Pet. "Where," said the cock, "art thou going?" "I," said the White Pet, "am going (away), for they were threatening my death at Christmas."

"They were going to kill me at the very same time," said the cock, "and I will go with you."

"Come, then," said the White Pet.

They went forward till they fell in with a goose. "All hail! White Pet," said the goose. "All hail to thyself! oh goose," said the White Pet. "Where art thou going?" said the goose.

"I," said the White Pet, "am running away because they were going to kill me at Christmas."

"They were going to do that to me too," said the goose, "and I will go with you."

The party went forward till the night was drawing on them, and they saw a little light far away; and though far off, they were not long getting there. When they reached the house, they said to each other that they would look in at the window to see who was in the house, and they saw thieves counting money; and the White Pet said, "Let every one of us call his own call. I will call my own call; and let the bull call his own call; let the dog call his own call; and the cat her own call; and the cock his own call; and the goose his own call." With that they gave out one shout—GAIRE!

When the thieves heard the shouting that was without, they thought the mischief was there; and they fled out, and they went to a wood that was near them. When the White Pet and his company saw that the house was empty, they went in and they got the money that the thieves had been counting, and they divided it amongst themselves; and then they thought that they would settle to rest. Said the White Pet, "Where wilt thou sleep to-night, oh bull?" "I will sleep," said the bull, "behind the door where I used" (to be). "Where wilt thou sleep thyself, White Pet?" "I will sleep," said the White Pet, "in the middle of the floor where I used" (to be). "Where wilt thou sleep, oh dog?" said the White Pet. "I will sleep beside the fire where I used" (to be), said the dog. "Where wilt thou sleep, oh cat?" "I will sleep," said the cat, "in the candle press, where I like to be." "Where wilt thou sleep, oh cock?" said the White Pet. "I," said the cock, "will sleep on the rafters where I used" (to be). "Where wilt thou sleep, oh goose?" "I will sleep," said the goose, "on the midden, where I was accustomed to be."

They were not long settled to rest, when one of the thieves returned to look in to see if he could perceive if any one at all was

in the house. All things were still, and he went on forward to the
candle press for a candle, that he might kindle to make him a light;
but when he put his hand in the box the cat thrust her claws into
his hand, but he took a candle with him, and he tried to light it.
Then the dog got up, and he stuck his tail into a pot of water that
was beside the fire; he shook his tail and put out the candle. Then
the thief thought that the mischief was in the house, and he fled;
but when he was passing the White Pet, he gave him a blow; before
he got past the bull, he gave him a kick; and the cock began to crow;
and when he went out, the goose began to belabour him with his
wings about the shanks.

He went to the wood where his comrades were, as fast as was in
his legs. They asked him how it had gone with him. "It went," said
he, "but middling; when I went to the candle press, there was a
man in it who thrust ten knives into my hand; and when I went to
the fireside to light the candle, there was a big black man lying there,
who was sprinkling water on it to put it out; and when I tried to go
out, there was a big man in the middle of the floor, who gave me a
shove; and another man behind the door who pushed me out; and
there was a little brat on the loft calling out CUIR-ANEES-AN-SHAW-
AY-S-FONI-MI-HAYN-DA—Send him up here and I'll do for him; and
there was a GREE-AS-ICH-E, shoemaker, out on the midden,
belabouring me about the shanks with his apron."

When the thieves heard that, they did not return to seek their lot
of money; and the White Pet and his comrades got it to themselves;
and it kept them peaceably as long as they lived.

———

SGEULACHD A PHEATA BHAIN.

Bha Tuathanach ann roimhe so aig an robh Peata bàn; agus 'n uair
a bha an Nollaig a' teannadh air smuaintich e gu 'marbhabh e 'm
Peata bàn. Chuala am Peata bàn sin agus smuaintich e gun teichadh
e, agus 'se sin a rinn e. Cha deachaidh e fada 'n uair a thachsir
Tarbh air. Thubhairt an tarbh ris, "Fàilte dhuitse a' Pheata bhàin;
càite am bheil thusa a' dol?" "Tha mi," ars' am peata ban, "a' falbh
a dh' iarridh an fhortain, bha iad a' dol a m' mharbhadh a dh'
ionnsuidh na Nollaig agus smuaintich mi gum b' fheàrr domh
teicheadh." "S' feàrr domhsa ars' an Tarbh falbh leat: oir bha iad
a' dol a dhianadh a leithid eile ormsa." "Tha mi toileach," ars' 'm
Peata bàn; mar is mò a' chuideachd 'sann is fheàrr 'n làn-aidhir."
Ghabh iad air 'n aghaidh gus an do thachuir Cù orra. "Fàilte dhuit

a Pheata bhàin," ars' an Cu "Failte dhuit fhé' 'choin." "Càite 'm
bheil thu a' dol?" ars' an Cu. "Tha mi aig teicheadh bho 'n a chuala
mi gun robh iad a' brath mo mharbhabh air son na Nollaig." "Bha
iad a' dol a dhianadh a leithid cheùdna ormsa," ars' an Cu, "agus
falbhaidh mi leibh." "Thig, mata" ars' am Peata bàn. Dh' fhalbh
iad an sin gus an do chomhlaich Cat iad. "Failte dhuit a Pheata
bhàin ars' an cat. Fàilte dhuit fhé' a Chait." "Caite am bheil thu a'
dol?" ars' an Cat. "Tha mi a' dol a dh' iarridh an fhortain," ars' am
Peata ban, "a chionn gu'n robh iad a' dol am' mharbhadh air an
Nollaig." "Bha iad aig iomradh air mise mharbhadh cuideachd,"
ars an Cat, "agus 's féarr dhomh falbh leibh." "Thugainn mata,"
ars' 'm Peata bàn. Ghabh iad an sin air an aghaidh gus an do
choinnich Coileach iad. "Fàilte dhuit a Pheata bhàin," ars' an
Coileach. "Fàilte dhuit fhé'," ars' am Peata bàn. "Caite," ars' an
Coileach, "am bheil thu a dol?" "Tha mi," ars' am Peata bàn, "a'
falbh o 'n a bha iad a mòidhadh mo mharbabh aig an Nollaig."
"Bha iad a' dol am' mharbhabh-sa aig an am cheudna," ars' an
Coileach, "agus theid mi leibh." "Thig mata," ars' am Peata bàn.
Ghabh iad air an aghaidh gus an do thachair giadh orra. "Fàilte
dhuit a Pheata bhàin," ars' an géadh. "Fàilte dhuit fhé' a gheoidh,"
ars' am Peata bàn. "Caite am bheil thu a dol?" ars' an gèadh. "Tha
mise," ars' am Peata ban, "a' teichadh, a chionn gu 'n robh iad a
dol am' mharbhadh aig an Nollaig." "Bha iad a dol a' dhèanadh
sin ormsa cuideachd," ars' an Gèadh, "agus falbhaidh mi leibh."
Ghabh a' chuideachd air an aghaidh gus an robh an oidhche
'teannadh orra, agus chunnaic iad solus beag fada bhuatha 's ge
b'fhada bhuatha cha bh' fhada 'ga ruigheachd. An uair a ràinig iad
an tigh, thubhairt iad ri 'cheile gun amhairceadh iad a stigh air an
uinneag a dh' fhaicinn co a bha anns an tigh; agus chunnaic iad
meairlich a' cunntas airgid; agus thubhairt am Peata bàn,
"Glaoidhidh na uile aon aguinn a ghlaodh féin; glaoidhidh mise mo
ghlaodh; agus glaoidhidh an Tarbh a ghlaodh fein; glaoidhidh an
Cù a ghlaodh fein; agus an Cat a ghlaodh fein; agus an Coileach a
ghlaodh fein; agus an Gèadh a ghlaodh féin." Leis sin thug iad aon
ghàir asda. An uair a chuala na meairlich a' ghàir a bha muidh shaoil
iad gun robh an donas ann, agus theich iad amach, agus dh' falbh
iad do choille a bha dlùth daibh. An uair a chunnaic am Peata bàn
agus a chuideachd gun robh an tigh falamh 'chaidh iad a stigh, agus
fhuair iad an t-airgid a bha aig na meairlich 'ga chunntas, agus roinn
iad eatorra fein e. An sin smuaintich iad gun gabhadh iad mu
thàmh. Thubhairt am Peata bàn, "Caite an caidil thus' an nochd a
Thairbh." "Caidlidh mise," ars' an tarbh, "cùl an doruis far an

àbhaist domh." "Caite an caidil thu fein a Pheata bhàin?" "Caidlidh mise," ars' am Peata bàn am meadhan an ùlair far an àbhaist domh." "Caite an caidil thus' a Choin?" ars' am Peata bàn. "Caidlidh mise taobh an teine far an àbhaist domh," ars' an Cù, "Caite an caidil thus' a Chait?" "Caidlidh mis'," ars' an Cat, "ann am preas nan coinnleann far an toil leam a bhith." "Caite an caidil thus' a Choilich?" ars' am Peata bàn. "Caidlidh mise," ars' an Coileach, "air an spàrr far an àbhaist domh." "Caite an caidil thus a Gheòidh?" "Caidlidh mise," ars' an Géadh air an dùnan far an robh mi cleachte ri bhith."

Cha robh iad fada air gabhail mu thamh an uair a thill fear do na meairlich a dh' amharc a stigh feuch am mòicheadh e an robh aon sa' bith 'san tigh. Bha na uile ni sàmhach agus dh' ealuith e air aghaidh gu preas nan coinnlean airson coinneal a lasadh e dheanadh soluis da, ach an uair a chuir e làmh 'sa bhocsa shàbh an cat ìnean na laimh, ach thug e leis a' choinneal agus dh' fheuch e ri 'lasadh. An sin dh' eirich an cù agus chuir e earball ann am poit uisge bha aig taobh an teine; chrath e earball agus chuir e as a choinneal. Shaoil am meairleach an sin gu robh an donus 'san tigh agus theich e; ach an uair a bha e dol seachad air a' Pheata bhàn thug e buille dha; mun d' fhuar e seachad air an tarbh thug e breab dha; agus thòisich an coileach air glaoidhich; agus an uair a chaidh e mach thòisich an gèadh air a ghreadadh le 'sgiathan mu na luirgnean. Chaidh e don choillidh far an robh a chompanich, co luath 'sa bha 'na chasan. Dh' fheòraich iad dheth cia mar chaidh dha. "Cha deachaidh," ars' esan, "ach meadhonach; an uair a chaidh mi gu preas nan coinnlean bha fear ann a shàth deich sgeanan ann am laimh, agus an uair a chaidh mi gu taobh an teine a lasadh na coinneal bha fear mor, dubh 'na luidhe ann a bha spreadadh uisge urra 'ga cuir as, agus an uair a thug mi làmh air dol amach bha fear mor am meadhan an urlair a thug utag domh, agus fear eil' aig cùl an doruis a phut amach mi, agus bha ablach beag air an fharadh aig glaoidhich amach, " *cuir an nios an so e 's foghnaidh mi fhein dha*," agus bha *Griasaich* amach air an dùnan 'gam ghreadadh mu na casan le apran. A nuair a chual na meairlich sin cha do phill iad a dh' iarridh an cuid airgid, agus fhuair am Peata bàn agus a chompanaich dhaibh fein e, agus chum e socair iad am feadh 'sa bha iad beo.

Mrs. MacTavish got this story from a young girl in her service, November 1859, who learned it in OA, a district of Islay, last year, when she was employed in herding cattle.

It is a version of the same tale as Grimm's "Bremer Stadt Musikanten," which appears to have been long known in Germany in various shapes.

The crowing of the cock is imitated in Gaelic and in German. The Gaelic is closer. "Bringt mir den Schelm her" is not so close to "kikeriki" as the Gaelic words—which I have tried to spell phonetically—are to the note of a cock. There is a bull in the Gaelic tale, instead of an ass; and a sheep and a goose, in addition to the dog, cat, and cock, which are common to both. There are six creatures in the one tale, commonly found about the Highland cottage, which is well described; four in the other, common about German cottages, My own opinion is, that the tale is common to both languages and old, but it might have been borrowed from a book so well known in England as Grimm's Stories are. It is worth remark, that the dog and the cat were to die at Christmas, as well as the sheep and bull, who might reasonably fear to be eaten anywhere, and who have been sacrificed everywhere; the goose, who is always a Christmas dish in the Highlands; and the cock, who should die last of his family, because the toughest. The dog was once sacrificed to Hecate on the 30th of every month; and there was a dog divinity in Egypt. Cats drew the car of Freya, a Norse divinity; they were the companions of Scotch witches, and did wondrous feats in the Highlands. See "Grant Stewart's Highland Superstitions." To roast a cat alive on a spit was a method of raising the fiend and gaining treasure, tried, as it is asserted, not very long ago. I myself remember to have heard, with horror, of a cruel boy, who roasted his mother's cat in an iron pot on a Sunday, while the rest were at church, though it was not said why he did it. A cock has been a sacrifice and sacred amongst many nations; for instance, a cock and a ram's head were emblems of Æsculapius. The crowing of a cock is a terror to all supernatural, unholy beings, according to popular mythology everywhere. When the mother, in these stories, sends her children into the world to seek their fortune, she bakes a cake, and kills a cock. A fowl, as I am informed by a minister in one of the Orkneys, is still, or was lately, buried alive by nurses as a cure for certain childish ailments. In short, the dog, the cat, and the cock may possibly have had good reason to fear death at a religious festival, if this part of their history came from the East with the Celts. The goose also has been sacred time out of mind. Bernacle geese are supposed to be hatched from a seashell. The goose was the great cackler who laid the egg of the world, according to Egyptian inscriptions on coffins. He was the emblem of Seb; he is sacred at the present day in Ceylon. He was sacred in Greece and at Rome; and the Britons would not eat his flesh in the days of Cæsar. Perhaps the custom of eating a goose at Christmas, which, to the best of my knowledge, is peculiar to the Scotch

Highlands, may be a custom begun by the British Christians to mark their conversion, and carried on ever since. Much will be found on this subject in "Rawlinson's Herodotus," p. 122, etc.; in "Mill and Wilson's History of British India;" and in books on Ceylon. At all events, this Gaelic story is well known in Islay, for MacLean writes that he has often heard it, and all the creatures mentioned in it have had to do with mythology at some period somewhere.

I suspect that it is one of the class given in "Contes et Apologues Indiens" (Paris, 1860), a class which includes such well known stories as *"The Goose with the golden Eggs,"* as a man who cut down a tree to get at the fruit (No. 45); *"The Belly and the Members,"* as a quarrel between the head and tail of a serpent (No. 40), a story which somewhat resembles that which is quoted in the introduction, as *"MacLeod's Fool,"* "Le Sage et le Fou" (No. 18); "The two Geese that carried a Tortoise" (No. 14); "Le Jeune Brâmane qui c' est sali le Doight" (No. 64), which is a schoolboy story in Scotland in another shape; "The Ass in the Lion's Skin" (No. 59); "Les Choses impossibles et les Reliques du Bouddha" (No. 110), which has a parallel in Gaelic, in broad Scotch, and in Norse. The Gaelic poet describes impossibilities, such as shell-fish bringing heather from the hill, and the climax is a certain great laird dressed in homespun. The Scotch rhyme came to me from a little boy of five year's old, and is called "The Mantle Joe." It begins " 'Twas on a Monday Mornin' when the Cat crew Day;" There are "Twenty-four Weavers riding on a Paddock;" "A Hare and a Haddie racin' owre the Lea," and such like; and it ends, "Frae Beginning to the End it's a' big Lees." The Norse song was written out for me by an officer on board a steamer, and includes "Two Squirrels taming a Bear," and other such events; and the Sanscrit, which Chinese and French savants have translated, names similar absurd events which might sooner happen than the discovery of the reliques of Buddha. In short, European stories are to be traced in the east, and this White Pet may be one of the kind.

12

THE DAUGHTER OF THE SKIES.

From James MacLauchlan, servant, Islay.

There was there before now a farmer, and he had a leash of daughters, and much cattle and sheep. He went on a day to see them, and none of them were to be found; and he took the length of the day to search for them. He saw, in the lateness, coming home, a little doggy running about a park.

The doggy came where he was—"What wilt thou give me," said he, "if I get thy lot of cattle and sheep for thee?" "I don't know myself, thou ugly thing; what wilt thou be asking, and I will give it to thee of anything I have?" "Wilt thou give me," said the doggy, "thy big daughter to marry?" "I will give her to thee," said he, "if she will take thee herself."

They went home, himself and the doggy. Her father said to the eldest daughter, Would she take him? and she said she would not. He said to the second one, Would she marry him? and she said, she would not marry him, though the cattle should not be got for ever. He said to the youngest one, Would she marry him? and she said, that she would marry him. They married, and her sisters were mocking her because she had married him.

He took her with him home to his own place. When he came to his own dwelling-place, he grew into a splendid man. They were together a great time, and she said she had better go see her father. He said to her to take care that she should not stay till she should have children, for then she expected one. She said she would not stay. He gave her a steed, and he told her as soon as she reached the house, to take the bridle from her head and let her away; and when she wished to come home, that she had but to shake the bridle, and that the steed would come, and that she would put her head into it.

She did as he asked her; she was not long at her father's house when she fell ill, and a child was born. That night men were together at the fire to watch. There came the very prettiest music that ever was heard about the town; and every one within slept but she. He came in and took the child from her. He took himself out, and he went away. The music stopped, and each one awoke; and there was no knowing to what side the child had gone.

She did not tell anything, but so soon as she rose she took with her the bridle, and she shook it, and the steed came, and she put her head into it. She took herself off riding, and the steed took to going home; and the swift March wind that would be before her, she would catch; and the swift March wind that would be after her, could not catch her.

She arrived. "Thou art come," said he. "I came," said she. He noticed nothing to her; and no more did she notice anything to him. Near to the end of three quarters again she said, "I had better go see my father." He said to her on this journey as he had said before. She took with her the steed, and she went away; and when she arrived she took the bridle from the steed's head, and she set her home.

That very night a child was born. He came as he did before, with music; every one slept, and he took with him the child. When the music stopped they all awoke. Her father was before her face, saying to her that she must tell what was the reason of the matter. She would not tell anything. When she grew well, and when she rose, she took with her the bridle, she shook it, and the steed came and put her head into it. She took herself away home. When she arrived he said, "Thou art come." "I came," said she. He noticed nothing to her; no more did she notice anything to him. Again at the end of three quarters, she said, "I had better go to see my father." "Do," said he, "but take care thou dost not as thou didst on the other two journeys." "I will not," said she. He gave her the steed and she went away. She reached her father's house, and that very night a child was born. The music came as was usual, and the child was taken away. Then her father was before her face; and he was going to kill her, if she would not tell what was happening to the children; or what sort of man she had. With the fright he gave her, she told it to him. When she grew well she took the bridle with her to a hill that was opposite to her, and she began shaking the bridle, to try if the steed would come, or if she would put her head into it; and though she were shaking still, the steed would not come. When she saw that she was not coming, she went out on foot. When she arrived, no one was within but the crone that was his mother. "Thou art without a houseman to-day," said the crone; and if thou art quick thou wilt catch him yet. She went away, and she was going till the night came on her. She saw then a light a long way from her; and if it was a long way from her, she was not long in reaching it. When she went in, the floor was ready swept before her, and the housewife spinning up in the end of the house. "Come up," said the housewife, "I know of thy cheer and travel. Thou art going to try if thou canst catch thy man; he is going to marry the daughter of the King of the Skies." "He is!" said she. The housewife rose; she made meat for her; she set on water to wash her feet, and she laid her down. If the day came quickly, it was quicker than that that the housewife rose, and that she made meat for her. She set her on foot then for going; and she gave her shears that would cut alone; and she said to her, "Thou wilt be in the house of my middle sister to-night." She was going, and going, till the night came on her. She saw a light a long way from her; and if it was a long way from her, she was not long in reaching it. When she went in the house was ready swept, a fire on the middle of the floor, and the housewife spinning at the end of the fire. "Come up," said the housewife, "I know thy cheer and travel." She made meat for her, she set on water, she washed her feet, and she laid her down. No sooner came the day than the housewife set her on foot, and made meat for her. She said she had better go; and she gave her a needle would sew by itself. "Thou wilt be in the house of my youngest sister to-night," said she. She was going, and going, till the end of day and the mouth of lateness. She saw a light a long way from her; and if it was a long way from her, she was not long in reaching it. She went in, the house was swept, and the housewife spinning at the end of the fire. "Come up," said she, "I know of thy cheer and travel." She made meat for her, she set on water, she washed her feet, and she laid her down. If the day came quickly, it was quicker than that that the housewife rose; she set her on foot, and she made her meat; she gave her a clue of thread, and the thread would go into the needle by itself; and as the shears would cut, and the needle sew, the thread would keep up with them. "Thou wilt be in the town to-night." She reached the town about evening, and she went into the house of the king's hen wife, to lay down her weariness, and she was warming herself at the fire. She said to the crone to give her work, that she would rather be working than be still. "No man is doing a turn in this town to-day," says the hen wife; "the king's daughter has a wedding." "Ud!" said she to the crone, "give me cloth to sew, or a shirt that will keep my hands going." She gave her shirts to make; she took the shears from her pocket, and she set it to work; she set the needle to work after it; as the shears would cut, the needle would sew, and the thread would go into the needle by itself. One of the king's servant maids came in; she was looking at her, and it caused her great wonder how she made the shears and the needle work by themselves. She went home and she told the king's daughter, that one was in the house of the hen wife, and that she had shears and a needle that could work of themselves. "If there is," said the king's daughter, "go thou over in the morning, and say to her, 'what will she take for the shears.' " In the morning she went over, and she said to her that the king's daughter was asking what would she take for the shears. "Nothing I asked," said she, "but leave to lie where she lay last night." "Go thou over," said the king's daughter, "and say to her that she will get that." She gave the shears to the king's daughter. When they were going to lie down, the king's daughter gave him a sleep drink, so that he might not wake. He did not wake the length of the night; and no sooner came the day, than the king's daughter came where she was, and set her on foot and put her out. On the morrow she was working with the needle, and cutting with other shears. The king's daughter sent the maid servant over, and she asked "what would she take for the needle?" She said she would not take anything, but leave to lie where she lay last night. The maid servant told this to the king's daughter. "She will get that," said the king's daughter. The maid servant told that she would get that, and she got the needle. When they were going to lie down, the king's daughter gave him a sleep drink, and he did not wake that night. The eldest son he had was lying in a bed beside them; and he was hearing her speaking to him through the night, and saying to him that she was the mother of his three children. His father and he himself was taking a walk out, and he told his father what he was hearing. This day the king's daughter sent the servant maid to ask what she would take for the clue; and she said she would ask but leave to lie where she lay last night. "She will get that," said the king's daughter. This night when he got the sleep drink, he emptied it, and he did not drink it at all. Through the night she said to him that he was the father of her three sons; and he said that he was. In the morning, when the king's daughter came down, he said to her to go up, that she was his wife who was with him. When they rose they went away to go home. They came home; the spells went off him, they planted together and I left them, and they left me.

NIGHEAN RIGH NAN SPEUR.

Bha siod ann roimhe so tuathanach, 's triùir nigheanan aige, 's mòran cruidh is chaorach. Dh' fholbh e la' a'm faicinn 's cha robh gin r'a fhaotainn dhiu, 's thug e fad an latha 'gan iarraidh. Chunnaic e, anns an anamoch a' tighinn dachaidh, cuilean beag a' ruith feadh pàirce. Thàinig an cuilean far an robh e, "De bheir thu dhòmhs'," urs' esan, "ma gheobh mi do chuid cruidh is caorach dhuit?" "Cha 'n 'eil fhios'am féin a ruid ghrannda. De bhios thu 'g iarraidh? 's bheir mise dhuit e de ni sam bith a th' agam." "An d' thoir thu dhomh," urs' an cuilean, "do nighean mhòr r'a pòsadh." "Bheir mise dhuit i," urs' esan, "ma ghabhas i féin thu." Chaidh iad dhachaidh, e féin 's an cuilean. Dh' fhoighneachd a h-athair d'a nighean bu shine an gabhadh i e, 's thuirt i nach gabhadh. Thuirt e ris an darna té am pòsadh ise e, 's thuirt i nach gabhadh. Thuirt e ris an darna té am pòsadh ise e, 's thuirt i nach pòsadh, ged nach faighte an crodh gu bràth. Thuirt e ris an té b' òige am pòsadh ise e, 's thuirt i gum pòsadh. Phòs iad, 's bha 'peathraichean a' magadh urra airson gu do phòs i e. Thug e leis dhachaidh i d'a àite féin. Nur a thàinig e g' a àite còmhnuidh féin dh' fhàs e 'na dhuine ciatach. Bha iad còmhla ùine mhòr, 's thuirt ise gum b' fheàrra dhi dol a dh' amharc a h-athar. Thuirt esan rithe i thoirt an aire nach fhanadh i gus am biodh clan aice. Bha i torrach 'san am. Thuirt i nach fanadh. Thug e dhi steud, 's thuirt e rithe, cho luath 's a ruigeadh i 'n tigh an t-srian a thoirt as a ceann, 's a leigeil air folbh, 's nur a bhiodh toil aice tighinn dachaidh nach robh aic' ach an t-srian a chrathadh, 's gun d' thigeadh an steud 's gun cuireadh i 'ceann innte. Rinn i mar a dh' iarr e urra. Cha robh i fad' an tigh a h-athar nur a dh' fhàs i gu bochd 'sa chaidh a h-asaid. An oidhche sin bha daoine cruinn aig a' ghealbhan 'ga 'faire. Thàinig an aona cheòl a bu bhinne chualas riamh feadh a' bhaile, 's chaidil a' h-uile duine stigh ach ise. Thàinig esan a stigh 's thug e uaithe am pàisde. Ghabhe 'mach 's dh' fholbh e. Stad an ceòl, 's dhuisg gach duine, 's cha robh fios de 'n taobh a chaidh am pàisde. Cha d' innis i ni sam bith, ach cho luath 's a dh' 'eiridh i thug i leatha an t-srian, 's chrath i i, 's thàinig an steud, 's chuir i 'ceann innte. Ghabh i air mharcachd urra, 's ghabh an steud air folbh dhachaidh; bheireadh ise air a ghaoith luath Mhàrt a bh' air thoiseach orra, 's cha bheiseadh a ghaoth luath Mhàrt a bha na déigh orra. Ràinig i.

"Thàinig thu," urs' esan. "Thàinig," urs' ise. Cha do leig e rud sam bith air rithe, 's cha mhotha leig ise rud sam bith orra risan.

Dlùth air ceann tri ràithean a rithisd thuirt ise, " 'S fheàrra dhomh
dol a dh' amharc m athar." Thuirt e rithe air an t-siubhal so mar a
thuirt e roimhid. Thug i leatha an steud 's dh' fholbh i. Nur a ràinig
i thug i 'n t-srian a ceann na steud, 's leig i dhachaidh i, 's an oidhche
sin féin chaidh a h-asaid. Thàinig esan mar a rinn e roimhid le ceòl.
Chaidil a' h-uile duine, 's thug e leis am pàisde. Nur a stad an ceòl
dhùisg iad air fad. Bha 'h-athair air a h-aodann ag ràdh rithe gum
feumadh i innseadh de bu chiall de 'n ghnothach. Cha 'n innseadh
ise ni sam bith. Nur a dh' fhàs i gu math, 's a dh' éirich i, thug i
leatha, an t-srian, chrath i i, 's thainig an steud, 's chuir i ceann
innte. Ghabh i air folbh dhachaidh. Nur a ràinig i thuirt esan.
"Thàinig thu." "Thàinig," urs' ise. Cha do leig e rud sam bith aire
rithe, 's cha mhotha 'leig ise urra risan. An ceann tri ràithean a
rithisd thuirt i, " 'S fheàrra dhomh dol a dh' amharc m' athar."
"Dèan," urs' esan, "ach thoir an aire nach dèan thu mar a rinn thu
an da shiubhal roimhid." "Cha dèan," urs' ise. Thug e dhi an steud,
's dh' fholbh i. Ràinig i tigh a h-athar, 's dh' asaideadh i 'n oidhche
sin féin. Thàinig an ceòl mar a b' àbhaist, 's thugadh am pàisd' air
folbh. Bha 'h-athair air a h-aodann an sin, 's e 'dol a 'marbhadh
mar an innseadh i dé 'bha tachairt do na pàisdean, no dé 'n seòrsa
duine a bh' aice. Leis an eagal a chuir e urra dh' innis i dha e. Nur
a dh' fhàs i gu math, thug i leatha an t-srian gu cnoc a bha ma
'coinneamh, 's thòisich i air crathadh na sréine feuch an d'thigeadh
an steud, na'n cuireadh i 'ceann innte, 's ged a bhiodh i 'crathadh
fhathasd cha d' thigeadh an steud. Nur a chunnaic i nach robh i
'tighinn ghabh i mach 'na cois. Nur a ràinig i cha robh duine stigh
ach a' chailleach a bu mhàthair dha. "Tha thusa gun fhear tighe an
diugh," urs' a' chailleach, " 's ma bhios thu tapaidh beiridh thu air
fhathasd."

Ghabh i air folbh, 's bha i 'folbh gus an d' thàinig an oidhche
orra. Chunnaic i 'n sin solus fada uaithe, 's ma b' fhada uaithe cha
b' fhada bha ise 'ga 'ruigheachd. Nur a chaidh i stigh bha urlar réidh
sguabte roimhpe, 's bean an tighe 'sniomh shuas an ceann an tighe.
"Thig a nòis," ursa bean an tighe, "tha fios do sheud 's do shiubhail
agamsa. Tha thu folbh feuch am beir thu air t-fhear. Tha e 'folbh
a phòsadh nighean rìgh nan speur." "Tha!" urs' ise. Dh' éirich bean
an tighe; rinn i biadh dhi; chuir i air uisge 'ghlanadh a cas; 's chuir
i 'laidhe i. Ma bu luatha a thàinig an latha bu luaithe na sin a dh'
éirich bean an tighe 'sa rinn i biadh dhi. Chuir i air a cois i 'n sin
airson folbh, 's thug i dhi siosar a ghearradh leis féin, 's thuirt i rithe.
"Bidh thu ann an tigh mo phiuthar mheadhonachsa nochd." Bha i
'folbh 's a' folbh, gus an d' thàinig an oidhche urra. Chunnaic i

solus fada uaithe,' s ma b' fhada uaithe cha b' fhada bha ise 'ga ruigheachd. Nur a chaidh i stigh bha 'n tigh réidh, sguabte; gealbhan air meadhon an urlair, 's bean an tighe 'sniomh an ceann a' ghealbhain. "Thig a nòis," ursa bean an tighe, "tha fios do sheud 's do shiubhail agamsa." Rinn i biadh dhi; chuir i air uisge; ghlan i 'casan 's chuir i laidhe i. Cha bu luaithe a thàinig an latha na 'chuir bean an tighe air a cois i, 's a rinn i biadh dhi. Thuirt i rithe gum b' fheàrra dhi folbh, 's thug i dhi snàthad a dh' fhuaigheadh leatha féin. Bidh thu ann an tigh mo pheathar is òige a nochd," urs' ise.

Bha i folbh 's a' folbh gu deireadh latha 's beul anamoich. Chunnaic i solus fada uaithe, 's ma b' fhada uaithe cha b' fhada bha ise 'ga ruigheachd. Chaidh i stigh. Bha 'n tigh sguabte, 's bean an tighe 'sniomh os ceann a' ghealbhain. "Thig a nòis," urs' ise, "tha fios do sheud 's do shiubhail agamsa." Rinn i biadh dhi, chuir i air uisge, ghlan i 'casan, 's chuir i laidhe i. Ma bu luath a thàinig an latha, bu luaithe na sin a dh' éirich bean an tighe; chuir i air a cois i, 's rinn i biadh dhi. Thug i dhi ceairsle shnàth 's rachadh an snàthainn anns an t-snàthad leis féin, 's mur a ghearradh an siosar, 's mur a dh' fhuaigheadh an t-snàthad, chumadh a cheairsle snàth ruitha. "Bidh thu anns a' bhaile nochd."

Ràinig i 'm baile ma fheasgar 's chaidh i stigh do thigh chailleach chearc an rìgh. Shuidh i 'leigeil a sgòis; bha i ga garadh aig a' ghealbhan; thuirt i ris a' chaillich obair a' thoirt dhi, gum b' fheàrr leatha 'bhi 'g obair na bhi 'na tàmh. "Cha 'n 'eil duine dèanadh turn 's a' bhaile so 'n diugh," ursa a' chailleach; "tha pòsadh aig nighean an rìgh." "Ud!" urs' ise ris a' chaillich, "thoir dhomh aodach r'a fhuaghal, na léine 'chumas mo làmh air folbh." Thug i dhi léintean r'a dhèanadh. Thug i mach siosar a a pòca; chuir i dh' obair e; chuir i 'n t-snàthad a dh' obair as a dhéigh. Mar a ghearradh an siosar dh' fhuaigheadh an t-snàthad, 's rachadh an snàth anns an t-snàthaid leis féin. Thàinig té do shearbhantan an rìgh stigh; bha i 'g amharc urra; 's bha e cur ioghnadas mòr urra démur a bha i 'toirt air an t-siosar 's air an t-snàthad oibreachadh leotha féin. Chaidh i dhachaidh, 's dh' innis i do nighean an rìgh gun robh té ann an tigh chailleach nan cearc, 's gun robh siosar agus snàthad aice a dh' oibreachadh leotha féin. "Ma tha," ursa nighean an rìgh, "theirig thusa nunn anns a' mhaidinn, 's abair rithe de 'ghabhas i air an t-siosar." Anns a' mhaidinn chaidh i 'nunn, 's thuirt i rithe gun robh nighean an rìgh a' foighneachd dé ghabhadh i air an t-siosar. "Cha 'n iarr mi," urs' ise, "ach cead laidhe far an do laidh i féin an rair." "Theirig thusa nunn," ursa nighean an rìgh, " 's abair rithe gum faigh i sin." Thug i 'n siosar do nighean an rìgh.

Nur a bha iad a' dol a laidhe thug nighean an righ deoch chadail dàsan, air alt 's nach dùisgeadh e. Cha do dhùisg e fad na h-oidhche, 's cha bu luaithe a thàinig an latha na thàinig nighean an rìgh far an robh ise, 'sa chuir i air a cois i. An la 'r na mhàireach bha i 'g obair leis an t-snàthaid, 's a' gearradh le siosar eile. Chuir nighean an rìgh an searbhanta nunn a dh' fhoighneachd dé ghabhadh i air an t-shàthaid. Thuirt i nach gabhadh ni sam bith ach cead laidhe far an do laidh i rair. Dh' innis an searbhanta so do nighean an righ. "Gheobh i sin," ursa nighean an rìgh. Dh' innis an searbhanta gum faigheadh i siod, 's fhuair i 'n t-snàthad. Nur a bha iad a' dol a laidhe thug nighean an rìgh deoch chadail da, 's cha do dhùisg e 'n oidhche sin. Bha 'm mac a bu shine bh' aige ann an leaba làmh riutha, 's bha e 'ga 'cluinntinn a' bruidhinn ris feadh na h-oidhche, 's ag ràdh ris gum b'i màthair a thriùir chloinn'i. Bha athair 's e féin a' gabhail sràid a mach, 's dh' innis e d'a athair dé 'bha e'cluinntinn. An latha so chuir nighean an rìgh an searbhanta a dh' fheòraich de' ghabhadh i air a' cheairsle, 's thuirt i rithe nach iarradh i ach cead laidhe far an do laidh i 'n rair, "Gheobh i sin," ursa nighean an rìgh. An oidhche so nur a fhuair e 'n deoch chadail thaom e i, 's cha d' òl e idir i. Feadh na h-oidhche thuirt ise ris gum b' e athair a triùir mac, 's thuirt esan gum b' e.

Anns a mhaidinn, nur a thàinig nighean an rìgh nuas, thuirt e rithe i 'dhol suas, gum bi 'bhean a bha leis. Nur a dh' eiridh iad dh' fholbh iad airson dol dachaidh. Thàinig iad dachaidh; dh' fholbh na geasan deth. Chuir iad còmhla 's dhealaich mise riutha, 's dhealaich iadsan riumsa.

This is but another version of No. III., "The Hoodie;" but it has certain magic gifts which I have not found in any other Gaelic story; and the *little dog* who goes to the skies, and is about to marry the daughter of the king, and is transformed into a man at home, may turn out to be a Celtic divinity. When so little is known of Celtic mythology, anything may be of use. The raven, the crow, and the serpent, have appeared as transformed beings of superior power. Now, the little dog appears, and there are mystic dogs elsewhere in Gaelic stories, and in other Celtic countries. In the Isle of Man is the well-known "Modey dhu," black dog which used to haunt Peel Castle, and frightened a soldier to death.

In a curious book, written to prove Gaelic to be the original language (History of the Celtic Language, by L. MacLean, 1840), there is a great deal of speculation as to the Farnese Globe; and the dog-star in particular is supposed to have been worshipped by the Druids. Without entering into such a wide field, it is worth notice that "Anubis," the dog-star, was son of Osiris and Nephthys, had the nature of a dog, and was represented with the head of one. He was a celestial double deity, and watched the tropics. The servant lad who told this story; and the old woman, MacKerrol, from whom he learned it, are not likely persons to have heard of Anubis, or the Farnese Globe; so anything got from them may be taken at its value, whatever that may be. The opinion that Celts came from the East by way of Phœnicia, has been held by many, and some one may wish to follow the trial of the little dog; so I give his history as it came to me, rather than fuse it into one story with the Hoodie, as I was at first tempted to do before the plan of this work was decided on.

The beginning of this tale is the Gaelic "Once upon a time."

Bha siod ann roimhe so.

Was yonder in it ere this.

TRIUR is a collective noun of number for three, and answers to *leash*; or to *pair, brace, dozen*, for two; twelve.

STEUD is clearly the same word as steed. It is commonly used in these stories, and I have never heard it used in conversation. It is feminine, like FALAIRE, the other word commonly used for a horse in stories and poetry; and hardly ever in ordinary speech.

Many words are derived from steud, and I do not think that it is imported.

13

THE GIRL AND THE DEAD MAN.

From Ann Darroch, Islay.

There was before now a poor woman, and she had a leash of daughters. Said the eldest one of them to her mother, "I had better go myself and seek for fortune." "I had better," said her mother, "bake a bannock for thee." When the bannock was ready, her mother said to her, "Whether wouldst thou like best the bit and my blessing, or the big bit and my curse?" "I would rather," said she, "the big bit and thy curse." She went away, and when the night was wreathing round her, she sat at the foot of a wall to eat the bannock. There gathered the sreath chuileanach and her twelve puppies, and the little birds of the air about her, for a part of the bannock. "Wilt thou give us a part of the bannock," said they. "I won't give it, you ugly brutes; I have not much for myself." "My curse will be thine, and the curse of my twelve birds; and thy mother's curse is the worst of all." She rose and she went away, and she had not half enough with the bit of the bannock. She saw a little house a long way from her; and if a long way from her, she was not long reaching it. She struck in the door. "Who's there?" "A good maid seeking a master." "We want that," said they, and she got in. She had now a peck of gold and a peck of silver to get; and she was to be awake every night to watch a dead man, brother of the housewife, who was under spells. She had besides, of nuts as she broke, of needles as she lost, of thimbles as she pierced, of thread as she used, of candles as she burned, a bed of green silk over her, a bed of green silk under her, sleeping by day and watching by night. The first night when she was watching she fell asleep; the mistress came in, she struck the magic club on her, she fell down dead, and she threw her out at the back of the midden.

Said the middle one to her mother, "I had better go seek fortune and follow my sister." Her mother baked her a bannock; and she chose the big half and her mother's curse, as her elder sister did, and it happened to her as it happened to her sister.

Said the youngest one to her mother, "I had better myself go to seek fortune too, and follow my sisters." "I had better bake a bannock," said her mother. "Whether wouldst thou rather the little bit and my blessing, or the big bit and my curse?" "I would rather the little bit and your blessing." She went, and the night was wreathing round her, and she sat at the foot of a wall to eat the bannock. There gathered the sreath chuileanach and the twelve puppies, and the little birds of the air about her. "Wilt thou give us some of that?" "I will give, you pretty creatures, if you will keep me company." She gave them some of the bannock; they ate and they had plenty, and she had enough. They clapped their wings about her till she was snug with the warmth. She went, she saw a little house a long way from her; and if it was a long way from her, she was not long reaching it. She struck in the door. "Who's there?" "A good maid seeking a master." "We have need of that." The wages she had were a peck of gold and a peck of silver; of nuts as she broke, of needles as she lost, of thimbles as she pierced, of thread as she used, of candles as she burned, a bed of the green silk over her, and a bed of the green silk under her. She sat to watch the dead man, and she was sewing; on the middle of night he rose up, and screwed up a grin. "If thou dost not lie down properly, I will give thee the one leathering with a stick." He lay down. At the end of a while, he rose on one elbow, and screwed up a grin; and the third time he rose and screwed up a grin. When he rose the third time, she struck him a lounder of the stick; the stick stuck to the dead man, and the hand stuck to the stick; and out they were. They went forward till they were going through a wood; when it was low for her it was high for him; and when it was high for him it was low for her. The nuts were knocking their eyes out, and the sloes taking their ears off, till they got through the wood. After going through the wood they returned home. She got a peck of gold and a peck of silver, and the vessel of cordial. She rubbed the vessel of cordial to her two sisters, and brought them alive. They returned home; they left me sitting here, and if they were well, 'tis well; and if they were not, let them be.

AN NIGHINN AGUS AN DUINE MARBH.

Bha bean bhochd ann roimhe so, 's bha triùir nighean aice. Thuirt an té bu shine dhiu r'a màthair, " 'S fheàrra dhomh fhéin dol a dh' iarraidh an fhortain." " " 'S fheàrra dhòmhs," ursa a màthair, "bonnach a dheasachadh dhuit." Nur a bha 'm bonnach réidh thuirt a mathair rithe, cò'ca 's fheàrr leat a' bhlaidh bheag 's mo bheannachd na 'bhlaidh mhor 's mo mhollachd." " " 'S fheàrr leam," urs' ise, "a' bhlaidh mhòr 's do mhollachd." Dh' fholbh i. Nur a bha 'n oidhche 'casadh urra shuidh i 'chois gàrraidh a dh' itheadh a' bhonnaich. Nur a shuidh i 'dh' itheadh a' bhonnaich chruinnich an t-sreath chuileanach, 's a da chuilean deug, 's eòin bheag an athar timchioll urra airson pàirt de 'n bhonnach. "An d' thoir thu dhuinne pàirt de 'n bhonnach," urs' iadsan. "Cha d' thobhair a bheathaichean grànnda; cha mhòr a th' agam dhomh féin. "Biodh mo mhollachds' agadsa, 's mollachd mo dha eun deug, 's e mollachd do mhàthar is measa dhuit air fad."

Dh' éirich i 's dh' fholbh i, 's cha robh leith a leoir 's a' bhlaidh bhonnaich. Chunnaic i tigh beag fada uaithe, 's ma b' fhada uaithe cha b' fhada bha ise 'ga ruigheachd. Bhuail i'san dorusd. "Co tha siod?" "Searbhantha math aig iarraidh maighstir." "Tha sin a dhith oirnne," urs' iadsan, 's fhuair i 'stigh. Bha peic òir is peic airgid aice r'a fhaotainn, 's i ri aithreachach a' h-uile h-oidhch' a' faire duine marbh, bràthair do bhean an tighe 'bha fo gheasan. Bha aice cuideachd de chnuthan mar a bhrisdeadh i; de shnàthadan mar a chailleadh i; 's do mheurain mar a tholladh i; de shnàth mar a chosdadh i; de choinnlean mar a loisgeadh i; leaba do n t-sìod' uaine thairte; leaba de 'n t-sioda uaine fòiche; codal 'san latha, 's aithreachadh 'san oidhche.

A' chiad oidhche, nur a bha i 'faire, thuit i 'na cadal. Thàinig a banamhaighstir a stigh; bhuail i 'n slachdan draoidheachd urra; thuit i sìos marbh; 's thilg i mach cùl an dùnain i.

Thuirt an té mheadhonach r'a màthair, " 'S fhearra domh dol a dh' iarraidh an fhortain, 's mo phuithar a leantainn." Dheasaich a màthair bonnach, 's roighnich ise an leith mhòr is mollachd a màthar, mar a rinn a piuthar a bu shine. Thachair dhi mar a thachair d'a piuthar.

Thuirt an té b' òige r'a màthair, "S fheàrra dhomh féin dol a dh' iarraidh an fhortain cuideachd, 's mo pheathraichean a leantainn." " 'S fheàrr dhòmhsa bonnach a dheasachadh," urs' a màthair. "Cò'ca 's fheàrr leata a' bhlaidh bheag 's mo bheannachd, na

'bhlaidh mhòr 's mo mhollachd." " 'S fheàrr leam a bhlaidh bheag
's bhur beannachd." Dh' fholbh i. Bha 'n oidhche 'casadh urra, 's
shuidh i 'chois gàrraidh a dh' itheadh a bhonnaich. Chruinnich an
t-sreath chuileanach, 's an da chuilean deug, 's eòin bheag an athar
timchioll urra. "An d' thobhair thu dhuinne rud dheth sin?"
"Bheithir a bheathaichean bòidheach, ma ni sibh comaith rium
féin." Thug i dhaibh rud de 'n bhonnach; dh' ith iad e; 's bha na
leoir acasan 's na leòir aice féin. Chlap iad an sgiathan timchioll
urra, 's bha i 'na falas leis a' bhlàthas.

Dh' fholbh i. Chunnaic i tigh beag fada uaithe, 's ma b' fhada
uaithe cha b' fhada 'bha ise 'ga 'ruigheachd. Bhuail i 'san dorusd.
"Co siod?" "Searbhanta math aig iarraidh maighstir." "Tha sin a
dhìth òirnne." Se 'n tuarasdal a bh' aice peic òir is peic airgid; de
chnuthan mar a bhrisdeadh i; de shnàthadan mar a chailleadh i; de
mheurain mar a tholladh i; de shnàth mar a chosdadh i; de
choinnlean mar a loisgeadh i; leaba de n t-sìod' uaine thairte, 's
leaba de 'n t-sìod uaine fòiche.

Shuidh i 'faire an duine mhairbh, 's bha i fuaghal. Air a'
mheadhon oidhche dh' éirich esan, 's chas e braoisg air. "Mar an
laidh thu sìos mar a th' agad bheir mise aon straoileadh dhuit de
bhata." Laidh e sìos. Ann ceann tacan beag a rithisd dh' éirich e air
a leith-uilinn, 's chas e braoisg air, 's an treas uair dh' éirich e 's
chas e braoisg air!!" Nur a dh' éirich e 'n treas uair bhuail i
straoileadh de 'n bhat' air. Lean am bata ris an duine mharbh; lean
an lamh ris a' bhata! 's a mach a bha iad. Ghabh iad air an aghaidh
gus an robh iad a' dol romh choille. Mar a b' iseal dise b' àrd dhàsan
e, 's mar a b' àrd dhàsan e b' ìseal dise e. Bha na cnuthan a' toirt
nan sùl asda, 's na h-àirnean a' toirt nan cluas dhiutha, gus an d'
fhuair iad romh 'n choille. An déigh dol romh 'n choille thill iad
dachaidh. Fhuair i peic òir is peic airgid, 'sam ballan ìochlaint. Rub
i 'm ballan ìocshlaint r'a da phiuthar, 's thug i beò iad. Thill iad
dhachaidh. Dh' fhàg iad mise a'm 'shuidhe so, 's ma bha iad gu
math 's math, 's mar an robh leigear dhaibh.

This story has some relation to "The man who travelled to learn
what fear was;" but I know nothing quite like it in Gaelic, or in any
other language. Ann Darroch, who told it to Hector MacLean in
May 1859, learned it from an old woman, Margaret Conal, of whom
MacLean writes—

"I have some recollection of her myself; she was wont to repeat
numerous 'ursgeuln' (tales). Her favourite resorts were the kilns,
where the people were kiln-drying their corn; and where she was

frequently rewarded, for amusing them in this manner, by supplies of meal. She was paralytic; her head shook like an aspen leaf, and whenever she repeated anything that was very exciting, her head shook more rapidly; which impressed children with great awe."

Some of the phrases are evidently remembered, and said by heart; the maid's wages, for instance; and the creatures that came to the wandering daughters. The vessel of Balsam occurs often in Gaelic stories, and I cannot make out what it really means. BALLAN IOCSHLAINT, teat, of ichor, of health, seems to be the meaning of the words.

In former days the kilns were not always used for drying corn. It is related that one of the first excisemen who went to the West, found and caught a large party of men kiln-drying malt. He made a seizure of course, and was not a little surprised when he was seized himself, and his arms tied fast behind him. His eyes were bound also; and then he was led to the kiln and set down near the fire; and they gave him the malt to smell and taste; and then they told him it was to be used in making whiskey; and then they gave him a drop, and then a dram, till the gauger was so drunk that they left him there, and departed with their malt kiln-dried and ground.

This I have heard told of the very place which Margaret Conal used to haunt, and of a time when she might have been a little girl; I cannot vouch for the truth of my story, but the kiln and the men about it may be seen now; and such scenes may well account for the preservation of wild stories. A child would not easily forget a story learned amongst a lot of rough farmers, seated at night round a blazing fire, listening to an old crone with palsied head and hands; and accordingly, I have repeatedly heard that the mill, and the kiln, were the places where my informants learned their tales.

There is a word in this tale which the narrator, the translator, the transcriber, the dictionary, and the "old men," have failed to explain. SREATH [?] SOIGH, a bitch (Ross-shire, etc.) CHUILEANACH means some kind of bird, and she has twelve "puppies," DA CHUILEAN DEUG. The narrator maintains that the words are right as she heard them.

14

THE KING WHO WISHED TO MARRY HIS DAUGHTER.
From Ann Darroch, Islay.

There was a king before now, and he married, and he had but one daughter. When his wife departed, he would marry none but one whom her clothes would fit. His daughter one day tried her mother's dress on, and she came and she let her father see how it fitted her. It was fitting her well. When her father saw her he would marry no woman but her. She went, crying where her muime was; and her foster mother said to her, "What was the matter with her?" She said, "That her father was insisting that he would marry her." Her muime told her to say to him, "That she would not marry him till he should get her a gown of the swan's down." He went, and at the end of a day and a year he came, and the gown with him. She went again to take the counsel of her muime. "Say to him," said her muime, "that thou wilt not marry him till he gets thee a gown of the moorland canach." She said this to him. He went, and at the end of a day and year he returned, and a gown of the moorland canach with him. "Say now to him," said her muime, "that thou wilt not marry him till he brings thee a gown of silk that will stand on the ground with gold and silver." At the end of a day and year he returned with the gown. "Say to him now," said her muime, "that thou wilt not marry him till he brings thee a golden shoe, and a silver shoe." He got her a golden shoe and a silver shoe. "Say to him now," said her muime, "that thou wilt not marry him unless he brings thee a kist that will lock without and within, and for which it is all the same to be on sea or on land." When she got the kist, she folded the best of her mother's clothes, and of her own clothes in it. Then she went herself into the kist, and she asked her father to put it out on the sea to try how it would swim. Her father put it out; when it was put out, it was going, and going, till it went out of sight.

It went on shore on the other side; and a herd came where it was, intending to break it, in hopes that there were finding in the chest. When he was going to break it she called out, "Do not so; but say to thy father to come here, and he will get that which will better him for life." His father came, and he took her with him to his own house. It was with a king that he was herd, and the king's house was near him. "If I could get," said she, "leave to go to service to this great house yonder." "They want none," said the herd, "unless they want one under the hand of the cook." The herd went to speak for her, and she went as a servant maid under the hand of the cook. When the rest were going to the sermon; and when they asked her if she was going to it, she said that she was not; that she had a little bread to bake, and that she could not go to it. When they went away, she took herself to the herd's house, and she put on a gown of the down of the swan. She went to the sermon, and she sat opposite the king's son. The king's son took love for her. She went a while before the sermon skailed, she reached the herd's house, she changed her clothes, and she was in before them. When the rest came home, it was talking about the gentlewoman that was at the sermon they were.

The next Sunday they said to her, "Was she going to the sermon;" and she said, "That she was not, that she had a little bread to bake." When they went away, she reached the herd's house, and she put on a gown of the moorland canach; and she went to the sermon. The king's son was seated where he was the Sunday before, and she sat opposite to him. She came out before them, and she changed, and she was at the house before them; and when the rest came home, it was talking about the great gentlewoman that was at the sermon they were. The third Sunday, they said to her, "Was she going to the sermon;" and she said, "That she was not, that she had a little bread to bake." When they went away, she reached the herd's house; she put on the gown that would stand on the ground with gold and silver, and the golden shoe and the silver shoe, and she went to the sermon. The king's son was seated where she was the Sunday before, and she sat where he was. A watch was set on the doors this Sunday. She arose, she saw a cranny, and she jumped out at the cranny; but they kept hold of one of the shoes.

The king's son said, "Whomsoever that shoe would fit, she it was that he would marry."

Many were trying the shoe on, and taking off their toes and heels to try if it would fit them; but there were none whom the shoe would fit. There was a little bird in the top of a tree, always saying as every one was trying on the shoe, "Beeg beeg ha nan doot a heeg ach don tjay veeg a ha fo laiv a hawchkare." "Wee wee, it comes not on thee; but on the wee one under the hand of the cook." When he could get none whom the shoe would fit, the king's son lay down, and his mother went to the kitchen to talk over the matter. "Wont you let me see the shoe?" said she; "I will not do it any harm at all events." "Thou! thou ugly dirty thing, that it should fit thee." She went down, and she told this to her son. "Is it not known," said he, "that it wont fit her at all events? and can't you give it her to please her?" As soon as the shoe went on the floor, the shoe jumped on her foot. "What will you give me," said she, "to let you see the other one?" She reached the herd's house, and she put on the shoes, and the dress that would stand on the floor with gold and silver. When she returned, there was but to send word for a minister, and she herself and the king's son married.

URSGEUL.

Bha 'siod rìgh ann roimhe so, 's phòs e, 's cha robh aige ach an aon nighean. Nur a shiubhail a' bhean cha phòsadh e gin ach te 'fhreagradh a h-aodach dhi. Dh' fheuch a nighean latha aodach a màthar urra, 's thàinig i 's leig i fhaicinn d'a h-athair mar a fhreagradh e dhi. Bha e 'freagairt dhi gu math. Nur a chunnaic a h-athair i, cha phòsadh e bean ach i. Chaidh i 'caoineadh far an robh a muime, 's thuirt a muime rithe dè bh' urra. Thuirt i gun robh a h-athair a' cur roimhe gum pòsadh e i. Thuirt a muime rithe 'ràdh ris nach pòsadh e i gus am faigheadh e dhi guthann de chlòimhe na h-eala.

Dh' fholbh e 's an ceann la is bliadhna thàinig e, 's an guthann leis. Chaidh i 'rithisd a ghabhail comhairl' a muime. "Abair ris," urs' a muime, "Nach pòs thu e gus am faigh e dhuit guthann de chanach an t-sléibhe." Thuirt i so ris. Dh' fholbh e, 's an ceann la is bliadhna thill e 's guthann de chanach an t-sléibhe leis. "Abair ris a nis," urs' a muime, "Nach pòs thu e gus an d'thoir e 't' ionnsuidh guthan sìod a sheasas air an làr le h-òr 's [?]e airgiod." An ceann la is bliadhna thill e leis a ghuthann. "Abair ris a nis," urs' a muime, "Nach pòs thu e gus an d' thoir e 't ionnsuidh bròg òir is bròg airgid." Fhuair e dhi bròg òir is bròg airgid. "Abair ris a nis," ursa a muime, "Nach pòs thu e mar an d' thoir e 't' ionnsuidh cisde a ghlaiseas a mach 's a stigh, 's is coingeis leatha bhi air muir na air tìr."

Nur a fhuair e chisde phaisg i chuid a b' fheàrr de dh' aodach a
màthar 's d'a h-aodach féin innte. Chaidh i féin an sin a stigh 's a'
chisde, 's dh' iarr i air a h-athair a cur a mach air an fhairge feuch
démur a shnàmhadh i. Chuir a h-athair a mach i. Nur a chaidh a
chisd' a mach, bha i folbh 's a' folbh gus an deach i as an t-sealladh.
Chaidh i air tìr air an taobh eile, 's thàinig buachaille far an robh i
airson a brisdeadh, an dúil gun robh feudail anns a' chisde. Nur a
bhu e 'dol a 'brisdeadh ghlaoidh ise, "Na déan; ach abair ri t' athair
tighinn an so, 's gheobh e na 's fheàird e r'a bheò." Thàinig 'athair
's thug e leis g'a thigh féin i. 'S ann aig righ bha'm buachaille, 's
bha tigh an righ dlùth air. "Nam faighinn," urs' ise, "dol air fasdadh
do 'n tigh mhòr so thall." "Cha 'n 'eil gin a dhìth orr', " urs' am
buachaille, "mar am bheil té dhìth orra fo làimh a' chòcaire."
Chaidh am buachaille 's bhruidhin e air a son, 's chaidh i 'na
searbhanta fo làimh a' chòcaire.

Nur a bha càch a' dol do 'n t-searmoin, 's a dh' fheòraidh iad
dhise an robh i dol ann, thuirt i nach robh gun robh beagan arain
aice r'a dheasachadh, 's nach b' urrainn i dol ann. Nur a dh' fholbh
iadsan thug i urra tigh a' bhuachaille, 's chuir i urra guthann de
chlòimhe na h-eala. Chaidh i do 'n t-searmoin, 's shuidh i ma
choinneamh mac an rìgh. Ghabh mac an rìgh gaol urra. Dh' fholbh
ise tacan ma'n do sgaoil an t-searmoin; ràinig i tigh a' bhuachaille;
dh' atharraich i h-aodach; 's bha i stigh rompa. Nur a thàinig càch
dhachaidh 's ann aig iomradh air a' bhean uasal mhòr a bha 's an
t-searmoin, 's thuirt i nach robh, gun robh beagan arain aice r'a
dheasachadh. Nur a dh' fholbh iadsan ràinig i tigh a' bhuachaille,
's chuir i urra guthann de chanach an t-sléibhe, 's chaidh i do 'n
t-searmoin. Bha mac an rìgh 'na shuidhe far an robh ise an
Dòmhnach roimhid, 's shuidh ise ma choinneamh. Thàinig i mach
air thoiseach orra; dh' atharraich i, 's bha i aig an tigh rompa; 's nur
a thàinig càch dhachaidh 's ann aig iomradh air a' bhean uasal mhòr
a bha 'san t-searmoin a bha iad. An treas Dòmhnach thuirte iad
rithe an robh i dol do 'n t-searmoin, 's thuirt i nach robh 'gun robh
beagan arain aice r'a dheasachadh. Nur a dh' fholbh iadsan ràinig
i tigh a bhuachaille; chuir i urra an guthann a sheasadh air an làr le
h-òr 's le h' airgiod; 's a' bhròg airgid; 's chaidh i 'n t-searmoin. Bha
mac an rìgh 'na shuidhe for an robh ise an Dòmhnach roimhid 's
shuidh ise far an robh esan. Chaidh faire 'chur air na dorsan an
Dòmhnach so. Dh' éirich ise. Chunnaic i fruchag, s' leum i mach
air an fhruchaig, ach ghléidh iad gréim air té de na brògan. Thuirt
mac an rìgh té sam bith d'am freagradh a' bhròg gur h' i 'phòsadh
esan. Bha mòran a' feuchainn na bròig orra, 's a' toirt dhiu nan

ladharan agus nan sàiltean feuch am freagradh i dhaibh, ach cha robh gin d'an robh a' bhrog a' freagairt. Bha eun beag am bar craoibhe, 's e daonnan ag ràdh, h-uile té bha feuchainn na bròig urra—"Big, big, cha 'n ann duit a thig, ach do 'n te bhig a tha fo làimh a' chòcaire." Nur nach robh iad a' faotainn gin d'am freagradh a' bhròg laidh mac an rìgh, 's chaidh a' mhàthair do 'n chidsin a dh' iomradh air a' ghnothach. "Nach leig sibh fhaicinn dòmhs' a' bhròg," urs' ise; "cha dèan mi coire urra co dhiu." "Thusa a ruid ghrannda, shalaich! gum freagradh i dhuitse!" Chaidh i sìos 's dh' innis i so d'a mac. "Nach 'eil fhios," urs' esan, "Nach freagair i dhi co dhiu, 's nach fhaod sibh a toirt dhi a 'toileachadh." Cho luath 's a chaidh a' bhròg air an urlar, leum a' bhròg air a cois! "De 'bheir sibh dhòmhs'," urs' ise, " 's an te eile 'leigeil fhaicinn duibh?" Rainig i tigh a bhuachaille, 's chuir urra na brògan, 's an trusgan a sheasadh air an làr le òr 's le airgiod. Nur a thill i cha robh ach fios a chur air ministir, 's phòs i féin is mac an rìgh.

Ann Darroch got this tale from Margaret Connel.

The chest meant by the narrator of this version is clearly the kist, which every well provided highland lass takes to service. Such kists, and such lassies seated on them, may be seen in every highland steam-boat; and still finer kists may be seen in every cottage in Norway, where wood is more plentiful, and kists are on a larger scale. The contents of all are alike; the clothes of generations. The mother's Sunday dresses, and the grandmother's, with some fine shawl, or cap, or bonnet, or something hideous, modern, and fashionable, more prized far than the picturesque old plaid, or bright red cloak of Scotch women, or the endless Norse costumes, which are going out of fashion in the same way. The little bird's note is imitated, and I have tried to spell the speech in English.

2d. I heard a version of this in the island of South Uist, in September 1859, from my companion MacCraw, who got it from a girl then in the inn at the Sound of Benbecula, MORAG A CHOTA BHAIN, Margery White Coats. A king had four daughters, and his wife died, and he said he would marry any one whom his dead wife's clothes would fit. One day the daughters tried, and the youngest only could wear them. The king saw them from a window, and wished to marry her, and she went for advice to her mother's brother. He advised her to promise to marry the king if he would bring her a gown of birds' down, and a gown of the colours of the sky, woven with silver; and when he got that, a gown of the colours of the stars, woven with gold, and glass shoes. When he had got them, she escaped with all her clothes, by the help of her uncle, on a filly, with a magic bridle, she on one side, and her chest of clothes on the other. She rode to a king's palace, hid the chest in a hill under a bush of rushes, turned the filly loose, and went to the palace with nothing on but a white petticoat and a shift. She took service with the cook, and grew dirty and ugly, and slept on a bench by the kitchen fire, and her work was to blow under the great caldron all day long. One day the king's son came home, and was to hold a feast; she went to the queen and asked leave to go, and was refused because she was so dirty. The queen had a basin of water in her hand, and threw it at her, and it broke. She went to the hill, took out the dress of down and silver, and shook her magic bridle; the filly came, and she mounted, and rode to the feast. "The king's son took her by the hand, and took her up as high as any there, and set her on his own lap; and when the feast was over, there was no reel that he danced but he gave it to her." He asked her whence she came, and she said, from the kingdom of Broken Basins; and the prince said that he had never heard of that land, though he had travelled far. She escaped and returned to the cook, and all were talking about the beautiful lady. She asked about her, and was told not to talk about what she did not understand, "a dirty little wretch like her." Then the prince had another feast; and she asked leave again, and the queen refused, and threw a candlestick at her, and it broke, and she did as before. She put on another dress and went; the king's son had eight men on each side of the door to catch her. The same scene went on, and she said she came from the country of Candlesticks—"TIR NAN COILLEARAN," and escaped, leaving a glass shoe. Then the king's son fell sick (of course), and would only marry the woman whom the shoe would fit; and all the ladies came and cut off their toes and heels, but in vain. Then he asked if there was none other. Then a small creature put his head in at the door and said, "If thou didst but know, she whom thou seekest is under the cook." Then he got the history of the basin and candlestick from his mother. The shoe was tried and fitted, and he was to marry Morag. All were in despair, and abused her; but she went out to her chest, shook the magic bridle, and arrayed herself, and came back on the filly, with a "powney" behind with the chest. Then all there that had despised her fell on their knees, and she was married to the prince. "And I did not get a bit there at the wedding," said the girl.

This was told as we walked along the road, and is but a short outline of what was told me, written from notes made in the evening. The man said that the girl told it with a great deal of the queer old language, which he could not remember.

The girl and her chest on the same horse may be seen in the Highlands. The girl, in her white coats and short gown, may be seen blowing the fire in highland inns, the queen's likeness might be found; and the feast is a highland ball; the filly and the magic bridle are common in other stories; the incidents of the basin and candle-stick have an equivalent in Norse; and I got them from a woman at the Sound of Barra afterwards, in another story. This shows what may be lost by dignified travelling. While the man was enjoying himself in the kitchen, the employer was smoking in solitary dignity, up stairs in his bed-room, writing a journal, and utterly unconscious that the game he pursued was so near.

I have other versions of this tale from other sources, and may find room for them hereafter.

The beginning is clearly the same as the French story of "Peau d' Ane," and the end of it is the same as the Norse "Katie Wooden Cloak;" that is the same as Mr. Peter Buchan's "Rashen Coatie" (MSS. collection); and that again has something of "The Sharp Grey Sheep" in Gaelic; and that has to do with half a dozen stories in Grimm; and this is like "Cinderella," and like a Scotch story, quoted in a review of Chambers' Nursery Rhymes in Tait's Edinburgh Magazine.

In fifteen volumes which I explored one fine day, to see if Tait could account for highland stories, I found few popular tales; and of these taken from the German, which I did find, I have found none in the west, so far as I can remember. Tait's stories are polished, but in some of the original poetry legends can be traced.

"Finette Cendron," in the collection of the Contesse d'Aulnoy, belongs to the same class; and the story exists in Straparola, a book which is now very little known, and which deserves to be forgotten, but which contains useful information nevertheless. Those who hold that popular tales are derived from books, will look on Straparola's story as the original. It was printed at Venice in Italian in 1567, that is 293 years ago. Those who hold that popular tales are preserved in all countries, and in all languages alike, will hold that the Italian, German, French, Norse, English, and Gaelic, are all versions of the same story, and that it is as old as the common stock from which all these races sprang.

After working for a year, and weighing all the evidence that has come in my way, I have come to agree with those who hold that popular tales are generally pure traditions; but in order that others may judge, I give the following short outline of the story in Straparola. Favola iv.

Tebaldo, prince of Salerno, promises to his dying wife, that he will only marry another, if he can find one whom a certain ring will fit. After a time the promise becomes known, and it is noised abroad that the prince wishes to marry again. Ladies come; but the ring is too small for one, too large for another, and fits no one. One day, Doralice, the daughter of Tebaldo, tries on her mother's ring, and shows her father that it fits, and then the same strange unnatural wish to marry his daughter seizes the Prince of Salerno that seizes the fathers in the French and Gaelic stories, and caused the Cenci tragedy; but the French and Gaelic stories have something about dresses, which the Italian has not.

Doralice goes to her old nurse for advice, and hides herself in a wardrobe which none could open from without but the nurse, who puts in a supply of a certain liquor, of which a spoonful, however small, would keep a person alive for a long time. The wardrobe is described, and it is such a one as would be found in an Italian palace. The father, having missed the daughter, cannot abide the sight of the wardrobe, orders it to be carried to the piazza by servants, and it is sold to a Genoese merchant. He carries it over sea in a ship to Britannia, and there sells it to the king "Genese."

Here let me remark that the form of the popular tale was exactly the same as it is now, nearly three hundred years ago. The scene is laid somewhere a long way off; the names are those which the narrator happens to know, misapplied; the ornaments are those about him; and the incidents within a certain range, are preserved entire. The story is an old play, with new scenery, and decorations in every country, and with fresh actors in every age.

King Genese of England comes on board the ship, and is taken with the beauty of the wardrobe, buys it, and has it taken to his own chamber. The hidden lady comes out when she is left alone, adorns the chamber, sweeps it and keeps it neat, and at last she is discovered, and the king marries her.

And here the Italian story goes off on quite a different road. It does as popular tales seem to do everywhere else. No sooner has a seeming origin been discovered for one bit, than the whole changes into something else. It is as if some convulsion were to overturn the Vatican, and break the statues once more, and some future antiquary were to try to fit the heads, legs, and arms to the proper bodies. The head of Apollo would not do for the Torso Farnese, but it might seem to fit some strapping Venus, and her arms might go on to some Apollino; and so, when only a few fragments of popular tales are known, it is perfectly hopeless to try to restore them. If all the fragments of all the statues in the Vatican were gathered together, then there might be some hope of mending them; but some are strongly suspected not to wear their own heads even now. If all the fragments of all the popular tales in the world were gathered, something might be reconstructed; but, unless each collector is content to bring his gatherings without alteration, the restorer will have hard work.

But to return to Straparola. The king marries the beautiful lady who keeps his room so tidy in so mysterious a manner, and they have two sons. The wicked Tebaldo, wandering over the world in disguise, arrives in Britain, knows his daughter, obtains access to the palace, murders the two children, and leaves a bloody knife in the Queen's possession. An astrologer is consulted, tells that the knife will be found, and it is found in the Queen's keeping; and she is to die. The astrologer, who knows everything, goes off to the old nurse, who comes at once to England, and tells the king all that has happened. Tebaldo is caught, and torn to pieces by four horses, and his flesh given to rabid dogs.

So end the wicked in many Gaelic tales. "He was torn between horses, burned amongst fires, and his ashes let fly with the wind," is the end of one.

The French story, "Peau d' Ane," is in "les Contes des Fées de Charles Perrault," the wicked father was sent for "Robes," "Couleur du temps," "Couleur du soleil," "Couleur de la Lune," and got them; and then for a donkey's skin, in which the lady disguised herself. But then the French story goes off on another road, for the donkey was precious and magical, and pieces of gold were found in his stall; and he belongs to another class of stories, which have Gaelic relations. (Perrault died 1703).

And so popular tales are woven together in a network which seems to pervade the world, and to be fastened to everything in it. Tradition, books, history, and mythology, hang together; no sooner has the net been freed from one snag, and a mesh gained, than another mesh is discovered; and so, unless many hands combine, the net and the contents will never be brought to shore.

15

THE POOR BROTHER
AND THE RICH.
From Flora MacIntyre, Islay.

There was a poor brother and a rich brother before now. The work that the poor one had, was to be at drains; he hired a gillie, and they had nothing with their mealtime but to take it without sauce. "Had'nt we better," said the gillie, "steal a cow of thy brother's lot?" They went and they did this.

The rich brother was taking a notion that it was they who stole his cow; and he did not know in what way he could contrive to find out if it were they who stole her. He went and he put his mother-in-law in a kist, and he came to seek room for the kist in his brother's house; he put bread and cheese with the crone in the kist; and there was a hole in it, in order that she might find out everything. The gillie found out that the crone was in the kist; he wetted sacks and put them on top of the kist; the water was streaming out of the sacks on the crone, and she was not hearing a word. He went, in the night, where the crone was, and he said to her, "Was she hearing?" "I am not," said she." "Art thou eating a few?" "I am not." "Give me a piece of the cheese, and I will cut it for thee." He cut the cheese, and he stuffed it into her throat till she was choked. The kist was taken home, and the dead crone in it. They buried the crone, and they laid out but little on her.

In the night, said the poor man's gillie to his master, "Is it not lamentable that such and such linen should go with the crone to the cell,* while the children are so much in want of shirts?" He went, and he took a spade with him, and he reached the church-yard. He dug the grave, and he took the crone from the coffin; he took off her the tais dress, he threw her on his back, and he came

* "KILL," cell a small church; hence applied to church-yards.

to the house of the rich brother; he went in with her, and he placed her seated at the fireside, and the tongs between her two feet. When the maid servant rose in the morning, she fell in a faint when she saw the crone before her. The rich brother thrashed his wife because of her mother saying, "that she was about to bring him to bare ruin." He went to the house of his poor brother and told that the crone had come home. "Ah ha!" said the gillie, "because thou didst not spend enough on her living, thou wilt spend it on her dead; I saw the like of this before; thou must lay out a good deal on her."

They bought a good lot of things for the funeral, and they left the one half of it in the house of the poor brother and they buried the crone again. "Is it not lamentable," said the poor brother's gillie to his master, "that such a lot of linen should go on the crone, while thou art so much in want of a shirt thyself?" He went to the cell that night again, he raised the crone, he took off her the tais clothes, and he took her with him on his back; he went into the house of the rich brother, as was usual, and he set the crone standing at the end of the dresser, with her claw full of seeds from the dish of sowens, as if she were eating it. When the man of the house saw her back in the morning, he thrashed his wife soundly, because of her mother. He went then to the house of his poor brother, and he told that the crone had come home again. "Aha!" said the gillie, "because thou didst not spend money on her living, thou wilt spend it on her dead; I saw the like of this before." "Go thou, then, and lay out a good deal on her, for I am tired of her," said the man. He bought a good lot for the crone's funeral, and he took the one half to his master's house. They buried the crone. In the night, said the gillie to his master, "Is it not lamentable that such linen should go with the crone to the cell, while I myself am in such want of a shirt." He took himself to the cell, he raised the crone, he took off her the tais dress, he put her on top of him, and he reached the rich brother's house. He did not get in this journey, so he went with her to the stable, and he tied her on top of a year-old colt. When they rose in the morning, they were well pleased when they did not see the crone before them. He was going from home; he went out to the stable, and he took the mare with him; but he never perceived that the crone was on top of the year-old. When he went away on top of the mare, after him went the year-old with the crone clattering on top of him. He turned back when he saw the crone, and he was like to kill his wife this time. He went to his brother's house and he told that the crone had come back again.

"As thou didst not spend money on her living," said the gillie, "thou must spend it on her dead."

"Go and lay out as thou wilt on her," said he to the gillie, "but keep her away."

He went this time and he bought a good lot for the crone's funeral, and he invited every one in the place. They buried the crone again; and the poor brother was as wealthy as the other, by reason of the funerals.

URSGEUL.

Bha bràthair bochd agus bràthair beairteach ann roimhe so. 'Se 'n obair a bh' aig an fhear bhochd a bhi déanadh dhraintan. Dh' fhasdaidh e gille, 's cha robh mìr aca le am biadh ach 'ga 'ghabhail tur. "Nach fheàrra dhuinn," urs' an gille; "bò de chuid do bhràthar a ghoid." Dh' fholbh iad agus rinn iad so. Bha 'm bràthair beairteach a' gabhail amharuis gur h-iad a ghoid a' bhò, 's cha robh fhios aige dè 'n dòigh a dhèanadh e air faotainn a mach an iad a ghoid i.

Dh' fholbh e 's chuir e 'mhàthair-chéile ann an cisde, 's thàinig e dh' iarraidh rum de 'n chisde ann an tigh a bhràthar. Chuir e aran is càise leis a' chaillich anns a' chisde, 's bha toll urra, air alt gu' mòchadh ise do na h-uile gnothuch. Mhothaich an gille gun robh a' chailleach anns a' chisde. Fhliuch e saic, is thilg e air muinn na cisd' iad. Bha 'n t-uisge 'sruthadh as na saic air a' chaillich, 's cha robh i 'cluinntinn smid. Chaidh e anns an oidhche far an robh a' chailleach, 's thuirt e rithe an robh i cluinntinn. "Cha 'n 'eil," urs' ise. "Am bheil thu 'g itheadh a' bheag?" "Cha 'n 'eil." "Thoir dhòmhsa pìosa de 'n chàise 's gearraidh mi dhuit e." Gheàrr e 'n càise, 's dhinn e 'na muineal e gus an do thachd e i. Chaidh a' chisde 'thoirt dachaidh, 's a' chailleach marbh innte. Thìolaic iad a' chailleach, 's cha d' rinn iad ach cosdas beag urra. Anns an oidhche thuirt gille an fhir bochd r'a mhaighstir, "Nach déisneach a leithid siod de dh' anart a dhol leis a' chaillich do 'n chill, 's cho feumail 's a tha na pàisdean air léintean."

Dh' fholbh e 's thug e leis spàd; ràinig e 'n clagh; chladhaich e 'n uaigh; thug e 'chailleach as a chiste-luidh; thug e dhi an t-ais-aodach; thilg e air a mhuinn i; 's thàinig e gu tigh a' bhràthair bheairteach. Chaidh e stigh leatha, 's chuir e i 'na suidhe aig a' ghealbhan, 's an clotha eadar a da chois. Nur a dh' éiridh an searbhanta anns a' mhaidinn thuit i ann am paiseanadh, nur a

chunnaic i 'chailleach roimpe. Ghabh am bràthair bearteach air a'
bhean airson a màthar ag ràdh gun robh i brath a sgrios. Chaidh e
gu tigh a' bhràthair bhochd, 's dh' innis e gun d' thàinig a' chailleach
dhachaidh. "A ha!" urs' an gille, "O nach do chosd thu r'a beò e
cosdaidh thu r'a marbh e! Chunnaic mise leithid so roimhid.
Feumaidh tu cosdas math a dheanadh urra."

Cheannaich iad cuid mhath de ghnothuichean airson an tòrraidh,
's dh' fhàg iad an darna leith dheth ann an tigh a' bhrathair bhochd.
Thìolaic iad a' chailleach a rithisd. "Nach déisneach," ursa gille
'bhrathair bhochd r'a mhaighstir, "a leithid siod do dh' anart a dhol
air a' chaillich, 's cho feumail 's a tha thu féin air léine."

Chaidh e do 'n chill an oidhche sin a rithisd. Thog e 'chailleach,
's thug e dhith an t-ais-aodach, 's thug e leis air a' mhuinn i. Chaidh
e stigh do thigh a' bhràthair bheairtich mar a b' àbhaist, 's chuir e
'chailleach 'na seasamh aig ceann an dresseir, 's a cròg làn do chàith
as an t-soitheach chabhrach, mar gum biodh i 'ga itheadh. Nur a
chunnaic fear an tighe air a h-ais i anns a mhaidinn, ghabh e air a'
bhean gu h-iomlan airson a màthar. Chaidh e 'n sin do thigh a'
bhrathar bhochd, 's dh' innis e gun d' thàinig a' chailleach
dhachaidh a rithisd. "A ha!" urs' an gille, "O nach do chosd thu r'a
beò e, cosdaidh thu r'a marbh e. Chunnaic mise 'leithid so
roimhid." "Folbh thusa mata 's dean cosdas math urra chionn tha
mise sgìth dhi."

Cheannaich e cuid mhath thun tòrradh na caillich, 's thug e 'n
darna leith thun tigh a' mhaighstir. Thìolaic iad a' chailleach. Anns
an oidhche urs' an gille r'a mhaighstir, "Nach déisneach a' leithid
siod do dh' anart a dol leis a' chaillich do 'n chill, 's mi féin cho
feumail air léine." Thug e 'chill air; thog e chailleach; thug e dhi an
t-ais-aodach; chuir e air a mhuinn i; 's ràinig e tigh a' bhràthar
bheairteach. Cha d' fhuair e stigh air an t-siubhal so. Chaidh e
leatha do 'n stàbull, 's cheangail e i air muinn bliadhnach eich. Nur
a dh' éiridh iad 's a' mhaidinn bha iad gu toilichte, nur nach fhac
iad a' chailleach romhpa. Bha esan a' dol o'n tigh. Chaidh e mach
do 'n stàbull, 's thug e leis an capull, ach cha do mhothaich e gun
robh 'chailleach air muinn a bhliadnaich; nur a dh' fholbh esan air
muinn a chapuill, as a dheigh a bha 'm bliadhnach, 's a' chailleach
a' glaigeileis air a mhuinn. Thill e air ais nur a chunnaic e chailleach,
's theab e bhean a mharbhadh air an uair so. Chaidh e do thigh a'
bhràthar, 's dh' innis e gun d' thainig a' chailleach dhachaidh a
rithisd. "O nach do chosd thu r'a beò e," ars' an gille, "feumaidh
tu 'chosd r'a marbh." "Theirig agus dean do rogha cosdus rithe,"
ars' esan ris a' ghille, "ach cum air folbh i." Chaidh e air an

t-siubhail so agus cheannaich e cuid mhath airson tòrradh na caillich 's chuir e gach duine bha 'san àite. Thìolaic iàd a' chailleach a rithisd, 's bha 'm bràthair bochd cho beairteach ris an fhear eile air tàilleabh nan tòrradh.

One James MacQueen, who lived at Tìrneagan, near Kilmeny, but who is not living now, gave this to one Flora MacIntyre, at Kilmeny, who told it to Hector MacLean.—May 1859.

This story is not like any other that I know. It is one of a kind which is common, in which mortals alone play a part. Some are humorous, and some free. One such has been versified by Allan Ramsay, page 520, vol. 2; and is nearly the same as Tom Totherhouse, the Norse tale.

The expensive funeral was once truly highland; and the invitation to all the world characteristic. It used to be told of one such funeral party, that they dropped the coffin out of a cart on the way over a strand, and never found it out till they got to the churchyard. They returned and finished the funeral, but went home afterwards very drunk; the sons shouting "Horo! it's the carlin's wedding." The funeral dinner was within my memory, and still may be, a solemn feast. Such toasts as "Comfort to the distressed," and "The memory of the deceased," were drank in solemn silence; and the whole matter was conducted with gravity and decorum, but with profuse and necessary hospitality, for the funeral guests had often to travel great distances, and the coffin had to be carried many miles. No Highlander, if his friends can help it, is buried anywhere but at home; coffins may be seen on board the steamers, conveying to the outer islands the bodies of those who have died on the main land. It is a poetic wish to be buried amongst friends, and one that is in full force in the Highlands to this day. The curse of Scotland may occasionally intrude even on such solemn occasions; but a funeral is almost always decorously conducted. In some places, as I am told, a piper may still be seen at the head of the funeral procession, playing a dirge. There is no want of reverence, but death is treated as an ordinary event. I have seen a man's tombstone, with a blank for the date, standing at the end of his house, while he was quite well.

It was lately said of a man who went home to die, "He took his own body home;" and so he did.

There is something mythological about the old woman who will not rest, because enough has not been laid out on her funeral. It may be some remnant of a notion of purgatory; but I suspect it is something heathen.

Romans had to pay their passage, perhaps Celts had to do so likewise.

16

THE KING OF LOCHLIN'S THREE DAUGHTERS.
From Neill Gillies, fisherman, near Inverary.

There was a king over Lochlin, once upon a time, who had a leash of daughters; they went out (on) a day to take a walk; and there came three giants, and they took with them the daughters of the king, and there was no knowing where they had gone. Then the king sent word for the sheanachy, and he asked him if he knew where his lot of daughters had gone. The sheanachy said to the king that three giants had taken them with them, and they were in the earth down below by them, and there was no way to get them but by making a ship that would sail on sea and land; and so it was that the king set out an order, any one who would build a ship that would sail on sea and on land, that he should get the king's big daughter to marry. There was a widow there who had a leash of sons; and the eldest said to his mother on a day that was there, "Cook for me a bannock, and roast a cock; I am going away to cut wood, and to build a ship that will go to seek the daughters of the king." His mother said to him, "Which is better with thee, the big bannock with my cursing, or a little bannock with my blessing?" "Give me a big bannock, it will be small enough before I build a ship." He got a bannock and he went away. He arrived where there was a great wood and a river, and there he sat at the side of the river to take the bannock. A great Uruisg came out of the river, and she asked a part of the bannock. He said that he would not give her a morsel, that it was little enough for himself. He began cutting the wood, and every tree he cut would be on foot again; and so he was till the night came.

When the night came, he went home mournful, tearful, blind sorrowful. His mother asked, "How went it with thee to-day, son?" He said "That it went but black ill; every tree I would cut would be on foot again." A day or two after this the middle brother said that he himself would go; and he asked his mother to cook him a cake and roast him a cock; and in the very way as happened to his eldest brother, so it happened to him. The mother said the very same thing to the young one; and *he* took the little bannock. The Uruisg came, and she asked a part of the cake and the cock. He said to her, "That she should get that." When the Uruisg had eaten her own share of the cake and of the cock, she said to him "That she knew what had brought him there as well as he himself, but he was to go home; but to be sure to meet her there at the end of a day and year; and that the ship would be ready at the end."

It was thus it happened: At the end of a day and a year the widow's young son went, and he found that the Uruisg had the ship floating on the river, fully equipped. He went away then with the ship, and a leash of gentlemen, as great as were in the kingdom, that were to marry the daughters of the king. They were but a short time sailing when they saw a man drinking a river that was there. He asked him, "What art thou doing there?" "I am drinking up this river." "Thou hadst better come with me, and I will give thee meat and wages, and better work than that." "I will do that," said he. They had not gone far forward, when they saw a man eating a stot in a park. "What art thou doing there?" said he.

"I am here going to eat all the stots in this park."

"Thou hadst better go with me, and thou wilt get work, and wages better than raw flesh." "I will do that," said he. They went but a short distance when they saw another man with his ear to the earth. "What art thou doing there?" said he. "I am here hearing the grass coming through earth." "Go with me, and thou wilt get meat, and better wages than to be there with thy ear to the earth." They were thus sailing back and forwards, when the man who was listening said, "That this was the place in which were the king's daughters and the giants." The widow's son, and the three that had fallen in with them, were let down in a creel in a great hole that was there. They reached the house of the big giant. "Ha! ha!" said he, the giant, "I knew well what thou art seeking here. Thou art seeking the king's daughter, but thou wilt not get that, unless thou hast a man that will drink as much water as I." He set the man who was drinking the river to hold drinking against the giant; and before he was half satisfied the giant burst. Then they went where the second giant was. "Ho, hoth! ha, hath!" said the giant, "I know well what sent thee here; thou art seeking the king's daughter; but thou shalt not get her, if thou hast not a man who will eat as much flesh as I." He set the man who was eating the stot to hold the eating of flesh against the giant; but before he was half satisfied the giant burst. Then he went where the third giant was. "Haio!" said the giant, "I know what set thee here; but thou wilt not get the king's daughter, by any means, unless thou stayest a day and a year by me a sgalag" (slave, servant). "I will do that," said he; and he sent up in the basket, first the three men, and then the king's daughters. The three great men were waiting at the mouth of the hole till they should come up, and they went with them where the king was; and they told the king that they themselves had done all the daring deeds that there were.

When the end of a day and year had come, he said to the giant, "that he was going." The giant said, "That he had an eagle that would set him up to the top of the hole." The giant set the eagle away with him, and five stots and ten for a meal for her; but the eagle went not half way up through the hole when she had eaten the stots, and she returned back again.

Then the giant said to him, "Thou must remain by me another day and year, and then I will send thee away." When the end of this year came he sent the eagle away with him, and ten stots and twenty. They went this time well further on than they went before, but she ate the stots and she turned back. "Thou must," said the giant, "stay by me another year, and then I will send thee away." The end of this year came, and the giant sent them away, and three score of stots for the eagle's meat; and when they were at the mouth of the hole the stots were expended, and she was going to turn back; but he took a steak out of his own thigh, and he gave this to the eagle, and with one spring she was on the surface of the earth.

At the time of parting the eagle gave him a whistle, and she said to him, "Any hard lot that comes on thee, whistle and I will be at thy side." He did not allow his foot to stop, or empty a puddle out of his shoe, till he reached the king's big town. He went where there was a smith who was in the town, and he asked the smith if he was in want of a gillie to blow the bellows. The smith said that he was. He was but a short time by the smith, when the king's big daughter sent word for the smith. "I am hearing," said she, "that thou art the best smith in the town; but if thou dost not make for me a golden crown, like the golden crown that I had when I was by the giant, the head shall be taken off thee." The smith came home sorrowfully, lamentably; and his wife asked him his news from the king's house. "There is but poor news," said the smith; "the king's daughter is asking that a golden crown shall be made for her, like the crown that she had when she was under the earth by the giant; but what do I know what likeness was on the crown that the giant had." The bellows-blowing gillie said, "Let not that set thee thinking; get thou for me enough of gold, and I will not be long making the crown." The smith got of gold as he asked, with the king's order. The gillie went into the smithy, and he shut the door; and he began to splinter the gold asunder, and to throw it out of the window. Each one that came the way was gathering the gold, that the bellows lad was hurling out. Here, then, he blew the whistle, and in the twinkling of an eye the eagle came. "Go," said he to the eagle, "and bring here the golden crown that is above the big giant's door." The eagle went, and she was not long on the way, and the crown (was) with her. He gave the crown to the smith. The smith went so merrily, cheerily with the crown where the king's daughter was. "Well then," said she, "if I did not know that it could not be done, I would not believe that this is not the crown I had when I was with the big giant." The king's middle daughter said to the smith, "Thou wilt lose the head if thou dost not make for me, a silver crown, like the one I had when I was by the giant." The smith took himself home in misery: but his wife went to meet him, expecting great news and flattery; but so it was, that the gillie said that he would make a silver crown if he could get enough of silver. The smith got plenty of silver with the king's order. The gillie went, and he did as he did before. He whistled: the eagle came. "Go," said he, "and bring hither here to me, the silver crown that the king's middle daughter had when she was by the giant."

The eagle went, and she was not long on the journey with the silver crown. The smith went merrily, cheerily, with the silver crown to the king's daughter. "Well, then," said she, "it is marvellously like the crown I had when I was by the giant." The king's young daughter said to the smith that he should make a copper crown for her, like the copper crown she had when she was by the giant. The smith now was taking courage, and he went home much more pleasantly this turn. The gillie began to splinter the copper, and to throw it out of each door and window; and now they were from each end of the town gathering the copper, as they were gathering the silver and gold. He blew the whistle, and the eagle was at his side. "Go back," said he, "and bring here hither to me the copper crown that the king's young daughter had when she was by the giant." The eagle went, and she was not long going and coming. He gave the crown to the smith. The smith went merrily, cheerily, and he gave it to the king's young daughter. "Well, then!" said she, "I would not believe that this was not the very crown that I had when I was by the giant underground, if there were a way of getting it." Here the king said to the smith, that he must tell him where he had learned crown making, "for I did not know that the like of thee was in the kingdom." "Well, then," said the smith, "with your leave, oh king, it was not I who made the crowns, but the gillie I have blowing the bellows." "I must see thy gillie," said the king, "till he makes a crown for myself."

The king ordered four horses in a coach, and that they should go to seek the smith's gillie; and when the coach came to the smithy, the smith's gillie was smutty and dirty, blowing the bellows. The horse gillies came, and they asked for the man who was going to look on the king. The smith said, "That was he yonder, blowing the bellows." "Oov! oov!" said they; and they (set) to catch him, and throw him head foremost into the coach, as if they had a dog.

They went not far on their journey when he blew the whistle. The eagle was at his side. "If ever thou didst good for me take me out of this, and fill it full of stones," said he. The eagle did this. The king was out waiting on the coach; and when the king opened the door of the coach, he was like to be dead with the stones bouncing on top of him. There was catching of the horse gillies, and hanging them for giving such an affront to the king.

Here the king sent other gillies with a coach and when they reached the smithy, "Oov! oov!" said they. "Is this the black thing the king sent us to seek?" They caught him, and they cast him into the coach as if they had a turf peat. But they went not far on their way when he blew the whistle, and the eagle was at his side; and he said to her, "Take me out of this, and fill it with every dirt thou canst get." When the coach reached the king's palace, the king went to open the door. Each dirt and rubbish fell about the king's head. Then the king was in a great rage, and he ordered the horse gillies to be hanged immediately. Here the king sent his own confidential servant away; and when he reached the smithy, he caught the black bellows-blowing gillie by the hand. "The king," said he, "sent me to seek thee. Thou hadst better clean a little of the coal off thy face." The gillie did this; he cleaned himself well, and right well; and the king's servant caught him by the hand, and he put him into the coach. They were but a short time going, when he blew the whistle. The eagle came; and he asked her to bring the gold and silver dress that was by the big giant here without delay, and the eagle was not long going and coming with the dress. He arrayed himself with the giant's dress. And when they came to the king's palace, the king came, and he opened the door of the coach, and there was the very finest man the king ever saw. The king took him in, and he told the

king how it happened to him from first to last. The three great men
who were going to marry the king's daughters were hanged, and
the king's big daughter was given him to marry; and they made
them a wedding the length of twenty nights and twenty days; and
I left them dancing, and I know not but that they are cutting capers
on the floor till the day of to-day.

―――――――

SGEULACHD AIR NIGHEANAN RIGH LOCHLAINN

Bha rìgh air Lochlainn aon uair aig an robh triuir nigheanan.
Chaidh iad a mach latha ghabhail sràid, agus thàinig trì famhairean,
's thug iad lèo nigheanan an rìgh, 's cha robh fios c'àite an deach
iad. Chuir an rìgh fios an sin air an t-seanachaidh aige, 's dh'
fheòraich e dheth, "An robh fios aige c'àite an deach a chuid
nigheanan?" Thuirt an seanachaidh ris an rìgh gu 'n d-thug tri
famhairean leo iad, agus gun robh iad anns an talamh gu h-iosal
aca, 's nach robh dòigh air am faotuinn, ach le long a dhèanamh a
sheòladh air muir 's air tìr." Agus 'se bh'ann gun do chuir an rìgh
òrdugh a mach, "Co air bith a thogadh long a sheòladh air muir 's
air tìr, gu' faigheadh e nighean mhòr an rìgh ri phòsadh." Bha
bantrach an sin aig an robh triùir mhac, agus thubhairt am fear 'bu
shine ri 'mhàthair latha bha 'n sin, "Bruich dhòmhsa bonnach 's
ròist coileach; tha mi falbh a ghearradh coille 's a thogail long, a
thèid a dh' iarraidh nigheanan an rìgh." Thuirt a mhàthair
ris, "Cò'ca 's feàrr leat am bonnach mòr le m' mhallachd na 'm
bonnach beag le m' bheannachd." "Thoir dhòmhsa 'm bonnach
mòr; bithidh e beag na leòir mu 'n tog mi long." Fhuair e 'm
bonnach 's dh' fhalbh e. Ràinig e far an robh coille mhòr agus
abhuinn. Shuidh e an sin ri taobh na h-abhunn a ghabhail a'
bhonnaich. Thàinig ùruisg mhòr a mach as an abhuinn, agus dh'iarr
i pàirt do 'n bhonnach. Thubhairt esan nach d' thugadh e mìr dhi,
gun robh e beag na leòir dha féin. Thòisich e air gearradh na coille,
's na h-uile craobh a ghearradh e, bhiodh i air a bonn a rithist; 's
bha e mur sin gus an d' thàinig an oidhche. Nuair a thàinig an
oidhche chaidh e dhachaidh, dubhach, deurach, dalla-bhrònach.
Dh' fhoighnichd a mhàthair dheth, "De mar a chaidh dhuit an
diugh, a mhic." Thubhairt esan, nach deach ach gu dubh dona "Na
h-uile craobh a ghearrainn, bhiodh i air a bonn a rithist." Latha na
dhà an déigh so, thubhairt am bràthair meadhonach, "gu' falbhadh
e fhéin, 's dh' iarr e air a mhàthair, bonnach a bhruich 's coileach
a rostadh; agus air a' cheart dòigh mar thachair d'a bhràthair a bu

shine, thachair dhàsan. Thubhairt a mhàthair a' cheart ni ris an
fhear òg, agus ghabh e 'm bonnach beag, thàinig an ùruisg, 's dh'iarr
i pàirt do 'n bhonnach 's do 'n choileach. Thubhairt e rithe, "Gu
'm faigheadh i sin." Nuair a dh'ith an ùruisg a cuid fhéin do 'n
bhonnach 's do 'n choileach, thubhairt i ris, "Gun robh fios aice-se
dé thug an sud e co maith ris fhéin, ach esan a dhol dachaidh, ach
a bhi cinnteach ise a choinneachainn an sud an ceann latha 's
bliadhna, agus gu 'm bitheadh an long deas air a cheann." 'Sann
mar so a thachair. An ceann latha 's bliadhna dh' fhalbh mac òg na
bantraich, agus fhuair e 'n long air snàmh air an abhuinn fuidh làn
uidheam aig an ùruisg. Dh' fhalbh e an sin leis an luing, agus triùir
dhaoine uaisle cho mòr 'sa bha 'san rìoghachd, a bha gu nigheanan
an rìgh a phòsadh. Cha robh iad ach goirid a seòladh an uair a
chunnaic iad fear ag òl suas abhuinn a bha 'sin. Dh' fheòraich iad
dheth, "De 'tha thu deànamh an sin?" "Tha ag òl suas na h-aibhne
so." " ' 'S feàrr dhuit falbh leam fhéin, 's bheir mi dhuit biadh, 's
tuarasdal, 's obair a's feàrr na sin." "Ni mi sin," ars' esan. Cha
deachaidh iad fad air an aghaidh gus am fac iad fear eile ag itheadh
dhamh ann am pàirc. "De 'tha thu deanamh an sin?" Thubhairt
esan, "Tha mi 'n so a' dol a dh' itheadh na tha dhaimh anns a'
phàirc so." " ' 'S feàrr dhuit falbh leam fhéin, 's gheibh thu obair 's
tuarasdal a's feàrr na feòil amh." "Ni mi sin," thubhairt esan. Cha
deach iad ach goirid dar* a chunnaic iad fear eile 's a' chluas ris an
talamh. "De tha thu deànamh an sin?" Thubhairt esan, "Tha mi
an so a' cluintinn an fheòir a' tighinn troi 'n talamh." "Falbh leam
fhéin 's gheibh thu biadh 's tuarasdal a's feàrr na bhi 'n sin, 's do
chluas ris an talamh." Bha iad mur so a' seòladh air an ais 's air an
aghaidh nuair a thubhairt am fear a bha' g eisteachd, "Gu 'm be
sud an t-àite anns an robh nigheanan an rìgh agus na famhairean."
Chaidh mac na bantraich agus an triùir a thachair orra a leigeil sìos
ann an cliabh, ann an toll mòr a bha 'n sin. Ràinig iad tigh an
fhamhair mhòir. "Ha! ha!" thuirt esan, "tha fios agam gu maith de
'tha thu 'g iarraidh an so; tha thu 'g iarraidh nighean an rìgh, ach
cha 'n 'fhaigh thu sin mar 'eil fear agad a dh' òlas uiread uisge
riumsa." Chuir esan am fear a bha ag òl na h-aibhne a chumail òl
ris an fhamhair, 's mun robh esan leith bhuidheach, sgàin am
famhair. Chaidh iad an sin far an robh an darna famhair. "Ho!
Hoth! Ha! Hath!" thubhairt am famhair, "tha fios agamsa gu maith,
de chuir an so thu; tha thu 'g iarraidh nighean an rìgh, ach cha 'n
fhaigh thu i mar 'eil fear agad a dh' itheas uiread feòla riumsa."

*Dar, from *an tràth*, the time.

Chuir esan am fear a bha 'g' itheadh nan damh a chumail itheadh
feòla ris an fhamhair so: ach mun robh esan leith bhuidheach, sgàin
am famhair. Chaidh iad an sin far an robh an treas famhair. "Haio
"ars' am famhair, "tha fios agamsa de chuir an so thu, ach cha 'n
fhaigh thu nighean an rìgh, idir mur fan thu agamsa latha, 's
bliadhna ann ad sgalaig." "Ni mi sin," thubhairt esan. Chuir e suas
ann an cliabh an toiseach na tri daoine, agus an sin nigheanan an
rìgh. Bha 'n triùir dhaoine mòra aig beul an tuill a' feitheamh gus
an d' thigeadh iad a nios, agus dh' fhalbh iad leo far an robh an
rìgh, 's dh' innis iad do 'n rìgh gu 'm b' iad féin a rinn gach uile
thapachd a bha ann.

    "Nuair a thàinig ceann latha 's bliadhna," thubhairt esan ris an
fhamhair, "gun robh e 'falbh." Thubhairt am famhair, "Gun robh
fiolaire aige-san a chuireadh suas e gu mullach an tuill." Chuir am
famhair an iolaire air falbh leis, agus cùig daimh dheug air son lòn
dhi; ach cha deach an iolaire leith suas troi 'n toll, nuair a dh'ith i
na daimh, agus thill i air a h-ais a rithist. Thubhairt am famhair ris
an sin, "Feumaidh tu fantainn agamsa latha 's bliadhna eile, agus
cuiridh mi 'n sin air falbh thu." Nuair a thàinig ceann na bliadhna
so, chuir e air falbh an iolaire leis, agus deich daimh fhichead.
Chaidh iad air an am so gu maith ni b' fhaide air an aghaidh, na
chaidh iad roimh, ach dh'ith i na daimh, 's thill i air a h-ais. "Feuma
tu," ars' am famhair, "fantainn agamsa bliadhna eile, agus an sin
cuiridh mi air falbh thu." Thàinig ceann na bliadhna so, agus chuir
am famhair air folbh iad, agus tri-fichead damh air son biadh do 'n
iolaire. An uair a bha iad aig beul àrd an tuill, theirig na daimh, 's bha
i 'dol a thilleadh; ach thug esan staoig as a leis fhéin, 's thug e so do
'n iolaire, agus le aon leum bha i air uachdar talamh. An am dealachaidh
thug an iolaire dha feadag agus thubhairt i ris, "cruaidh-chàs sam
bith a thig ort, leig fead agus bithidh mise ri d' thaobh."

    Cha do leig esan stad d'a chois na lodan as a bhròig gus an d'
ràinig e bailie mòr an rìgh. Chaidh e far an robh gobhainn a bha 's
a' bhaile, 's dh' fheòraich e do 'n ghobha, "An robh gille a dhìth
air, airson seideadh a' bhuilg?" Thubhairt an gobha "Gu'n robh."
Cha robh e ach goirid aig a' ghobha, nuair a chuir nighean mhòr
an rìgh fios air a' ghobha. "Tha mi 'cluintinn," ars' ise, "gur tusa
gobhainn a's feàrr 's a' bhaile; ach mur dèan thu dhòmhsa crùn òir
coltach ris a' chrùn òir a bh' agam nuair a bha mi aig an fhamhair,
thèid an ceann a thoirt dhìot." Thàinig an gobha dhachaidh gu
dubhach, brònach, 's dh' fhoighneachd a bhean deth, dé a
naigheachd a tigh an rìgh? "Cha 'n eil ach naigheachd bhochd,"
thuirt an gobha "Tha 'nighean ag iarraidh crùn òir a dheànamh dhi

coltach ris a chrùn a bha aice an uair a bha i fo 'n talamh aig an fhamhair; ach gu de 'fios a tha agamsa de 'n coslas a bha air a' chrùn a bha aig an fhamhair." Thubhairt gille séididh a' bhuilg, "Na cuireadh sin smaointinn ort. Faigh thusa dhòmhsa nis gu leòir do dh' òr, 's cha bhi mise fada a' deànamh a chrùin." Fhuair an gobha na dh' iarr e dh' òr le òrdugh an rìgh. Chaidh an gille stigh do 'n cheàrdaich, 's dhùin e 'n 'dorus, agus thòisich e air spealgadh an òir as a' chéile, 's a thilgeadh a mach air an uinneig. Bha gach neach a thigeadh an rathad a' tional an òir a bha gille a' bhuilg a' smùideadh a mach. Shéid e 'n so an fheadag, agus ann am prioba na sùil, thàinig an iolaire. "Falbh," thubhairt esan ris an iolaire, "agus thoir an so an cruùn òir a tha fos ceann an doruis aig an fhamhair mhòr." Dh' fhalbh an iolaire, 's cha b' fhada bha i air a turus, 'san crùn aice. Thug e 'n crùn do 'n ghobhainn. Dh' fhalbh an gobhainn gu subhach, sunndach leis a' chrùn far an robh nighean an rìgh. "Mata," thubhairt ise, "mur b'e gum bheil fios agam nach gabhadh e deànamh, cha chreidinn nach e so an crùn a bha agam an uair a bha mi leis an fhamhair mhòr." Thubhairt nighean mheadhonach an rìgh ris a' ghobhainn, "Caillidh tu 'n ceann mar dèan thu crùn airgid dhòmhsa coltach ris an fhear a bh' agam an uair a bha mi aig an fhamhair." Thug an gobha an tigh air fo sprochd, ach chaidh a bhean 'na choinneamh an dùl ri naigheachd mòr 's brosguil; ach 'se bh' ann gun d' thubhairt an gille, "gun deànadh esan crùn airgid, na 'm faighadh e na leòir do dh' airgiod." Fhuair an gobha ni's leòir do dh' airgiod le òrdugh an rìgh. Chaidh an gille 's rinn e mar a rinn e roimhe. Leig e fead; thainig an iolaire. "Falbh," thubhairt esan, "agus thoir thugam-sa an so an crùn airgid a bha aig nighean mheadhonach an rìgh an uair a bha i aig an fhamhair." D' fhalbh an iolaire, 's cha b' fhada bha i air a turus leis a' chrùn airgid gu nighean an rìgh. "Mata," thubhairt ise, "tha e anabarrach coltach ris a' chrùn a bh' agam dar a bha mi aig an fhamhair." Thubhairt nighean òg an rìgh ris a ghobha, "E a dheànamh crùn copair dh ise, coltach ris a chrùn chopair a bha aice, nuair a bha i aig an fhamhair. Bha 'n gobha an so a' gabhail misnich, 's chaidh e dhachaidh mòran ni bu toilichte air an trò so. Thòisich an gille air spealgadh a' chopair, 's air a thilgeadh a mach air gach dorus 's uinneag. Bha iad an so as gach ceann do 'n bhaile a' tional a' chopair mar a bha iad a' tional an òir 's an airgid. Shéid e 'n fheadag, 's bha 'n iolaire ri 'thaobh. "Rach air t' ais," thubhairt esan, "agus thoir an so thugamsa an crùn copair a bha aig nighean òg an rìgh an uair a bha i aig an fhamhair." Dh' fhalbh an iolaire, 's cha robh i fada 'dol 'sa' tighinn. Thug e 'n crùn do 'n ghobhainn; dh'

fhalbh an gobhainn gu subhach, sunndach, 's thug e do nighean òg
an righ e. "Mata," thubhairt ise, "cha chreidinn nach b'e so an
dearbh chrùn a bha agam an uair a bha mi aig an fhamhair fo 'n
talamh, na'm biodh dòigh air fhaotainn." Thubhairt an rìgh an so
ris a' ghobhainn, Gu' feumadh e innseadh dhásan, cáite an d'
ionnsaich e deanamh nan crùn, "oir cha robh fios agam gun robh
do leithid 'san ròighachd." "Mata," thubhairt an gobha, "le 'r cead,
a rìgh, cha mhise a rinn na crùin, ach an gille 'tha agam a' séideadh
a' bhuilg." "Feumaidh mi do ghill' fhaicinn," thubhairt an rìgh,
"gus an dèan e crùn dhomh fhéin." Dh' òrdaich an rìgh ceithir eich
ann an chòidse, 's iad a dhol a dh' iarraidh gille a' ghobha. An uair
a thàinig an chòidse a dh' ionnsaidh na ceàrdach, bha gille a' ghobha
gu dubh, salach a' séideadh a' bhuilg. Thàinig na gillean each, 's
dh' fheòraich iad air son an duine a bha 'dol a shealltainn an rìgh.
Thubhairt an gobha gu'm b'e sud e thall a' sèideadh a' bhuilg.
"Ubh! Ubh!" thuirt iadsan, 's iad a beireachd air, 's ga thilgeadh an
comhair a chinn a stigh don chòidse, mar gum bitheadh cù aca.
Cha deach' iad fada air an turus dar a shéid esan an fheadag. Bha
'n iolaire ri 'thaobh. "Ma rinn thu feum riamh dhomh, thoir mise
a mach as so, agus lìon e làn chlach," thubhairt esan. Rinn an iolaire
so. Bha 'n rìgh a mach a feitheadh a chòidse, agus an uair a dh'
fhosgail an rìgh dorus a' chòidse, theab e bhi marbh leis na clachan
a' dòrtadh air a mhuin. Chaidh beireachd air na gillean each, 'san
crochadh airson a leithid do thàmailt a thabhairt do 'n rìgh. Chuir
an rìgh an so air falbh gillean le còidse, agus an uair a ràinig iad a'
cheàrdach, "Ubh! Ubh!" thuirt iadsan, "N'e so an rud dubh a chuir
an rìgh sinn a dh' iarraidh." Rug iad air, 's thilg iad a stigh do 'n
chòids' e, mar gum bitheadh fòid mòine aca. Ach cha deach iad
fada air an slighe, nuair a shéid esan an fheadag, 's bha 'n iolaire ri
'thaobh, 's thubhairt e rithe, "Thoir mise as a' so, agus lìon e do
gach salachar a gheibh thu." Nuair a ràinig an còidse pàileis an righ,
chaidh an righ a dh' fhosgladh an doruis. Thuit gach salachar 's
gach baggaist mu cheann an righ. Bha fearg ro mhòr air an righ, 's
dh' òrdaich e na gillean each a bhi air an crochadh air ball. Chuir
an rìgh a' ghille cinnteach fhéin air falbh, agus an uair a ràinig e a'
cheàrdach, rug e air làimh air gille dubh séididh a' bhuilg. "Chuir
an righ," thuirt esan, "mise gu d' iarraidh 's feàrr dhuit beagan do
'n ghual a ghlanadh dheth t' aodann." Rinn an gille so, ghlan e e
féin gu maith 's gu ro mhaith, 's rug gille an rìgh air làimh air, 's
chuir e stigh do 'n chòids' e. Cha robh iad ach goirid air falbh, dar
a shéid e 'n fheadag. Thàinig an iolaire, 's dh' iarr esan oirre an
deise òir 's airgid a bha aig an fhamhair mhòr a thoirt an sud gun

dàil; 's cha robh an iolaire fada 'dol 's a' tighinn leis an deise. Sgeadaich esan e féin le deise an fhamhair, 's an uair a thàinig iad gu pàileas an rìgh, thàinig an righ, 's dh' fhosgail e dorus a chòidse 's bha 'n sin an aon duine bu bhrèagha a chunnaic an rìgh rìamh. Thug an rìgh stighe, 's dh' innis e do 'n righ mar a dh' éirich dha fo thùs gu deireadh. Chaidh an triùir dhaoine mòra bha 'dol a phòsadh; 's rinn iad banais dhoibh fad fichead oidhche 's fichead latha, 's dh' fhàg mise a' dannsa iad, 's cha 'n'eil fios agamsa nach 'eil iad a' cur nan car air an urlar gus an latha 'n diugh.

This story was written, May 1859, by Hector Urquhart, game-keeper, from the dictation of Neil Gillies, a fisherman and builder of stone dykes, who lives near Inverary. He is now about fifty-five, and says he learned the story from his father, who used to tell it when he was about sixteen or seventeen.

It has something of many other Gaelic tales. In particular, one called "Bolgum Mor," in which there are more gifted men. It has some resemblance to Fortunio; and the part which goes on under ground resembles part of many other popular tales. The Three Giants, with their gold, silver, and copper crowns, are like the Gnomes of the Mine. Similar Giants, ruling over metals, and living in castles made of gold, silver, and copper, are mentioned in a story from South Uist, which resembles the Sea Maiden.

As a whole, No. 16 is unlike anything I know, but nearly every incident has a parallel woven in with something else, and it most resembles Grimm's Golden Goose.

The Enchanted Ship, which could sail on sea or land, belongs to Norse tales and to Norse mythology. The gods had such a ship.

The Eagle is peculiarly eastern: he is but a genius in another shape; the underground treasures are also eastern; and it is worth remark, that two of the daughters are not provided for at all. The three gentlemen were hanged, and the smith's servant married the eldest princess with the golden crown, so the two youngest remain spin-sters. It is suggested by the author of Norse Tales, that similar incidents may show the change from Eastern to Western manners. There would be no hitch, if it were lawful to marry the three ladies in this story; and in the Norse story of Shortshanks, it is suggested that the second brother is added, to make all things proper. In No. 22, a man marries a round dozen.

The clothes of these giants fit the lad, so they were but under-ground men.

There is the usual moral. The least becomes the greatest; but there is a dash of character in the pride of the smith's lad, who will not come till he is taken by the hand by the king's own confidential servant. And this is characteristic of the race. A Celt can be led anywhere, but he will not be driven. The king, who opens his own coach door, is somewhat like a farmer. The coach and four is but the grandest of the vehicles seen in the neighbourhood—one of which was compared by a friend of mine, to "a packing box upon wheels, lined with an old blanket." In the mouth of a city narrator, it would have been a lord mayor's coach, and it probably was a palanquin at one time.

This story may be compared with "The Big Bird Dan," Norse Tales, No. 55. Gifted men are to be found in "The Master Maid," No. 11. Such men are also in German, "How six travelled through the World ;" and, according to the notes in the third volume of Grimm, the story is widely spread, and common to Italian.

17

MAOL A CHLIOBAIN.

From Ann MacGilvray, Islay.

There was a widow ere now, and she had three daughters; and they said to her that they would go to seek their fortune. She baked three bannocks. She said to the big one, "Whether dost thou like best the half and my blessing, or the big half and my curse?" "I like best," said she, "the big half and thy curse." She said to the middle one, "Whether dost thou like best the big half and my curse, or the little half and my blessing?" "I like best," said she, "the big half and thy curse." She said to the little one, "Whether dost thou like best the big half and my curse, or the little half and my blessing?" "I like best the little half and thy blessing." This pleased her mother, and she gave her the two other halves also. They went away, but the two eldest did not want the youngest to be with them, and they tied her to a rock of stone. They went on; but her mother's blessing came and freed her. And when they looked behind them, whom did they see but her with the rock on top of her. They let her alone a turn of a while, till they reached a peat stack, and they tied her to the peat stack. They went on a bit (but her mother's blessing came and freed her), and they looked behind them, and whom did they see but her coming, and the peat stack on the top of her. They let her alone a turn of a while, till they reached a tree, and they tied her to the tree. They went on a bit (but her mother's blessing came and freed her), and when they looked behind them, whom did they see but her, and the tree on top of her.

They saw it was no good to be at her; they loosed her, and let her (come) with them. They were going till night came on them. They saw a light a long way from them; and though a long way from them, it was not long that they were in reaching it. They went in. What was this but a giant's house! They asked to stop the night. They got that, and they were put to bed with the three daughters of the giant. (The giant came home, and he said, "The smell of the foreign girls is within.") There were twists of amber knobs about the necks of the giant's daughters, and strings of horse hair about their necks. They all slept, but Maol a Chliobain did not sleep. Through the night a thirst came on the giant. He called to his bald, rough-skinned gillie to bring him water. The rough-skinned gillie said that there was not a drop within. "Kill," said he, "one of the strange girls, and bring to me her blood." "How will I know them?" said the bald, rough-skinned gillie. "There are twists of knobs of amber about the necks of my daughters, and twists of horse hair about the necks of the rest."

Maol a Chliobain heard the giant, and as quick as she could she put the strings of horse hair that were about her own neck and about the necks of her sisters about the necks of the giant's daughters; and the knobs that were about the necks of the giant's daughters about her own neck and about the necks of her sisters; and she laid down *so* quietly. The bald, rough-skinned gillie came, and he killed one of the daughters of the giant, and he took the blood to him. He asked for MORE to be brought him. He killed the next. He asked for MORE; and he killed the third one.

Maol a Chliobain awoke her sisters, and she took them with her on top of her, and she took to going. (She took with her a golden cloth that was on the bed, and it called out.)

The giant perceived her, and he followed her. The sparks of fire that she was putting out of the stones with her heels, they were striking the giant on the chin; and the sparks of fire that the giant was bringing out of the stones with the points of his feet, they were striking Maol a Chliobain in the back of the head. It is this was their going till they reached a river. (She plucked a hair out of her head and made a bridge of it, and she run over the river, and the giant could not follow her.) Maol a Chliobain leaped the river, but the river the giant could not leap.

"Thou art over there, Maol a Chliobain." "I am, though it is hard for thee." "Thou killedst my three bald brown daughters." "I killed them, though it is hard for thee." "And when wilt thou come again?" "I will come when my business brings me."

They went on forward till they reached the house of a farmer. The farmer had three sons. They told how it happened to them. Said the farmer to Maol a Chliobain, "I will give my eldest son to thy eldest sister, and get for me the fine comb of gold, and the coarse comb of silver that the giant has." "It will cost thee no more," said Maol a Chliobain.

She went away; she reached the house of the giant; she got in unknown; she took with her the combs, and out she went. The giant perceived her, and after her he was till they reached the river. She leaped the river, but the river the giant could not leap. "Thou art over there, Maol a Chliobain." "I am, though it is hard for thee." "Thou killedst my three bald brown daughters." "I killed them, though it is hard for thee." "Thou stolest my fine comb of gold, and my coarse comb of silver." "I stole them, though it is hard for thee." "When wilt thou come again?" "I will come when my business brings me."

She gave the combs to the farmer, and her big sister and the farmer's big son married. "I will give my middle son to thy middle sister, and get me the giant's glave of light." "It will cost thee no more," said Maol a Chliobain. She went away, and she reached the giant's house; she went up to the top of a tree that was above the giant's well. In the night came the bald rough-skinned gillie with the sword of light to fetch water. When he bent to raise the water, Maol a Chliobain came down and she pushed him down in the well and she drowned him, and she took with her the glave of light.

The giant followed her till she reached the river; she leaped the river, and the giant could not follow her. "Thou art over there, Maol a Chliobain." "I am, if it is hard for thee." "Thou killedst my three bald brown daughters." "I killed, though it is hard for thee." "Thou stolest my fine comb of gold, and my coarse comb of silver." "I stole, though it is hard for thee." "Thou killedst my bald rough-skinned gillie." "I killed, though it is hard for thee." "Thou stolest my glave of light." "I stole, though it is hard for thee." "When wilt thou come again?" "I will come when my business brings me." She reached the house of the farmer with the glave of light; and her middle sister and the middle son of the farmer married. "I will give thyself my youngest son," said the farmer, "and bring me a buck that the giant has." "It will cost thee no more," said Maol a Chliobain. She went away, and she reached the house of the giant; but when she had hold of the buck, the giant caught her. "What," said the giant, "wouldst thou do to me: if I had done as much harm to thee as thou hast done to me, I would make thee burst thyself with milk porridge; I would then put thee in a pock! I would hang thee to the roof-tree; I would set fire under thee; and I would set on thee with clubs till thou shouldst fall as a faggot of withered sticks on the floor." The giant made milk porridge, and he made her drink it. She put the milk porridge about her mouth and face, and she laid over as if she were dead. The giant put her in a pock, and he hung her to the roof-tree; and he went away, himself and his men, to get wood to the forest. The giant's mother was within. When the giant was gone, Maol a Chliobain began—" 'Tis I am in the light! 'Tis I am in the city of gold!" "Wilt thou let me in?" said the carlin. "I will not let thee in." At last she let down the pock. She put in the carlin, cat, and calf, and cream-dish. She took with her the buck and she went away. When the giant came with his men, himself and his men began at the bag with the clubs. The carlin was calling, " 'Tis myself that's in it." "I know that thyself is in it," would the giant say, as he laid on to the pock. The pock came down as a faggot of sticks, and what was in it but his mother. When the giant saw how it was, he took after Maol a Chliobain; he followed her till she reached the river. Maol a Chliobain leaped the river, and the giant could not leap it. "Thou art over there, Maol a Chliobain." "I am, though it is hard for thee." "Thou killedst my three bald brown daughters." "I killed, though it is hard for thee." "Thou stolest my golden comb, and my silver comb." I stole, though it is hard for thee." "Thou killedst my bald rough-skinned gillie." "I killed, though it is hard for thee." "Thou stolest my glave of light." "I stole, though it is hard for thee." "Thou killedst my mother." "I killed, though it is hard for thee." "Thou stolest my buck." "I stole, though it is hard for thee." "When wilt thou come again?" "I will come when my business brings me." "If thou wert over here, and I yonder," said the giant, "what wouldst thou do to follow me?" "I would stick myself down, and I would drink till I should dry the river." The giant stuck himself down, and he drank till he burst. Maol a Chliobain and the farmer's youngest son married.

MAOL A CHLIOBAIN.

Bha bainntreach ann roimhe, so 's bha tri nigheanan aice, 's thuirt iad rithe gun rachadh iad a dh' iarraidh an fhortain. Dheasaich i tri bonnaich. Thuirt is ris an té mhòir, "Cò'ca's fheàrr leat, an leith bheag 's mo bheannachd, na'n leith mhòr 's mo mhollachd?" " 'S fheàrr leam," urs' ise, "an leith mhòr 's do mhollachd." Thuirt i ris an te mheadhonaich, "Cò'ca is fheàrr leat an leith mhòr 's mo mhollachd na'n leith bheag 's mo bheannachd?" " 'S fheàrr leam," urs' ise, "an leith mhòr 's do mhollachd." Thuirt i ris an tè bhig,

"Cò'ca is fheàrr leat an leith mhòr 's mo mhollachd n'an leith bheag's mo bheannachd?" 'S fheàrr leam an leith bheag 's do bheannachd. Chòrd so r'a màthair, 's thug i dhi an da leith eile cuideachd.

Dh' fholbh iad, ach cha robh toil aig an dithisd a bu shine an té b' òige 'bhi leò, 's cheangail iad i ri carra cloiche. Ghabh iad air an aghaidh, 's nur a dh' amhairc iad as an déigh, co a chunnaic iad ach ise, 's a' chreag air a muin. Leig'iad leatha car treis gus an d' ràinig iad cruach mhònadh, 's cheangail iad i ris a' chruaich mhònadh. Ghabh iad air an aghaidh treis, 's dh' amhalrc iad 'nan déigh, 's co a chunnaic iad ach ise a' tighinn, 's a' chruach mhònadh air a muin. Leig iad leatha car tacan gus an d' ràinig iad craobh, 's cheangail iad ris a' chraobh i. Ghabh iad air an aghaidh treis, 's nur a dh' amhairc iad 'nan déigh, co a chunnaic iad ach ise a' tighinn, 's a' chraobh air a muin. Chunnaic iad nach robh math a bhith rithe. Dh' fhuasgail iad i, 's leig iad leo i. Bha iad a' folbh gus an d' thàinig an oidhche orra. Chunnaic iad solus fada uatha, 's ma b'fhada uatha cha b'fhada a bha iadsan 'ga 'ruigheachd. Chaidh iad a stigh. Dé a bha 'so ach tigh famhair. Dh' iarr iad fuireachd 'san oidhche. Fhuair iad sin, 's chuireadh a laidhe iad le tri nigheanan an fhamhair.

Bha caran de chneapan òmbair ma mhuinealan nigheanan an fhamhair agus sreanganan gaoisid ma'm muineilsan. Chaidil iad air fad, ach cha do chaidil Maol a chliobain. Feadh na h-oidhche thàinig paghadh air an fhamhair. Ghlaoidh e r'a ghille maol carrach uisge thoirt a 'ionnsuidh. Thuirt an gille maol, carrach, nach robh deur a stigh. "Marbh," urs' esan, "te de na nigheanan coimheach, 's thoir a m' ionnsuidh a fuil." "Demur a dh' aithneachas mi eatorra?" urs' an gille maol, carrach. "Tha caran de chneapan ma mhuinealan mo nigheanansa, 's caran gaoisid ma mhuineil chàich." Chuala Maol a' chliobain am famhair, 's cho clis 's a b'urrainn i, chuir i na sreangannan gaoisid a bha ma 'muineal féin 's ma mhuineail a peathraichean ma mhuineil nigheanan an fhamhair, agus na cneapan a bha ma mhuineil nigheanan an fhamhair ma 'muineal féin, 's ma mhuineil a peathraichean, 's laidh i sìos gu sàmhach. Thàinig an gille maol carrach, 's mharbh e té de nigheanan an fhamhair, 's thug e'n fhuil a 'ionnsuidh. Dh' iarr e tuillidh a thoirt a 'ionnsuidh. Mharbh e an ath té. Dh' iarr e tuillidh, 's mharbh e 'n treas te. Dhùisg Maol a' chliobain a peathraichean, 's thug i leath' air a muin iad, 's ghabh i air folbh. Mhothaich am famhair di, 's lean e i.

Na spreadan teine a bha ise cur as na clachan le a sàiltean, bha iad a' bualadh an fhamhair 'san smigead; 's na spreadan teine a bha

'm famhair a' toirt as na clachan le barraibh a chas, bha iad a'
bualadh Mhaol a' chliobain an cùl a' chinn. " 'Se so a bu dual daibh
gus an d'ràinig iad obhainn. Leum Maol a chliobain an obhainn, s
cha b'urrainn am famhair an obhainn a leum." "Tha thu thall a
Mhaol a chliobain." "Tha ma's oil leat e." "Mharbh thu mo thri
nigheanan maola, ruagha." "Mharbh ma's oil leat e." " 'S cuin a
thig thu 'rithisd?" "Thig nur★ bheir mo ghnothach mi."

Ghabh iad air an aghaidh gus an d' ràinig iad tigh tuathanaich.
Bha aig an tuathanach tri mic. Dh' innis iad mar a thachair dhaibh.
Urs' an tuathanach ri Maol a chliobain, "Bheir mi mo mhac is sine
do 'd phiuthar is sine, 's faigh dhomh cìr mhìn òir 's cìr gharbh
airgid a tha aig an fhamhair." "Cha chosd e tuillidh dhuit," ursa
Maol a chliobain. Dh' fholbh i, 's ràinig i tigh an fhamhair. Fhuair
i stigh gun fhios. Thug i leatha na cìrean, 's ghabh i 'mach.
Mhothaich am famhair di; is as a déigh a bha e gus an d' ràinig e
'n obhainn. Leum ise an obhainn, 's cha b'urrainn am famhair an
obhainn a leum. "Tha thu thall a Mhaol a chliobain." "Tha ma's
oil leat e." "Mharbh thu mo thri nigheanan maola, ruagha."
"Mharbh ma's oil leat e. Ghoid thu mo chìr mhìn òir 's mo chir
gharbh airgid." "Ghoid ma's oil leat e." "Cuin a thig thu 'rithisd?"
"Thig nur bheir mo ghnothach mi."

Thug i na cìrean thun an tuathanaich, 's phòs a piuthar mhòr 's
mac mòr an tuathanaich.

"Bheir mi mo mhac meadhonach do 'd phiuthar mheadhonach,
's faigh dhomh claidheamh soluis an fhamhair." "Cha chosd e
tuillidh dhuit," ursa Maol a chliobain. Ghabh i air folbh, 's ràinig i
tigh an fhamhair. Chaidh i 'suas ann am bàrr craoibh' a bha as
cionn tobar an fhamhair. Anns an oidhche thàinig an gille maol,
carrach, 's an claidheamh soluis leis, a dh' iarraidh uisge. Nur a
chrom e 'thogail an uisge thàinig Maol a chliobain a nuas, 's phut
i sìos 'san tobar e, 's bhàth i e, 's thug i leatha an claidheamh soluis.
Lean am famhair i gus an d' ràinig i an obhainn. Leum i an obhaim,
's cha b'urrainn am famhair a leantainn. "Tha thu thall a Mhaol
a chliobain." "Tha ma's oil leat e." "Mharbh thu mo thri nigheanan
maola, ruagha." "Mharbh ma's oil leat e." "Ghoid tha mo chìr
mhìn òir 's mo chìr gharbh airgid." "Ghoid ma's oil leat e.'
"Mharbh tha mo ghille maol, carrach." "Mharbh ma's oil leat e."
"Ghoid tha tha mo chlaidheamh soluis." "Ghoid ma's oil leat
e." "Cuin a thig thu 'rithisd." "Thig nur bheir mo ghnothach mi."
Ràinig i tigh an tuathanaich leis a' chlaidheamh sholuis, 's phòs

★ Nur, from *an trath*, or *an uair*, the time.

a piuthar mheadhonach, 's mac meadhonach an tuathanaich.

"Bheir mi dhuit féin mo mhac is òige," urs' an tuathanach, 's
thoir am' ionnsuidh, boc a tha aig an fhamhair." "Cha chosd e
tuillidh dhuit," ursa Maol a' chliobain. Dh' fholbh i 's ràinig i tigh
an fhamhair, ach nur a bha gréim aic' air a' bhoc rug am famhair
urra. "De," urs' am famhair, "a dheànadh tus' ormsa na'n deànainn
uibhir coir' ort 's a rinn thus' ormsa." "Bheirinn ort gu 'sgàineadh
thu thu féin le brochan bainne; chuirinn an sin ann am poc' thu;
chrochainn thu ri drìom an tighe; chuirinn teine fodhad; 's
ghabhainn duit le cabair gus an tuiteadh thu 'd chual chrìonaich air
an urlar. Rinn am famhair brochan bainne, 's thuge uire òl. Chuir
ise am brochan bainne m'a beul 's ma h-aodann, 's luidh i seachad
mar gum biodh i marbh. Chuir am famhair am poc' i, 's chroch e
i ri drìom an tighe, 's dh' fholbh e féin 's a dhaoine a dh' iarraidh
fiodh do 'n choille. Bha màthair an fhamhair a stigh. Theireidh
Maol a' chliobain nur a dh' fholbh am famhair, " 'S mise a tha ann
'san t-sòlas 's a mise a tha ann's a' chathair òir." "An leig thu mis'
ann?" urs' a' chailleach. "Cha leig gu dearbh." Ma dheireadh leig
i 'nuas am poca; chuir i stigh a' chailleach, is cat, is laogh, is
soitheach uachdair; thug i leatha am boc; 's dh' fholbh i. Nur a
thàinig am famhair thòisich e féin 's a dhaoine air a' phoca leis na
cabair. Bha 'chailleach a' glaodhach, " 'S mi féin a th' ann." "Tha
fios agam gur tu féin a th' ann," theireadh am famhair, 's e 'g éiridh
air a' phoca. Thàinig am poca 'nuas 'na chual chrìonaich, 's dé 'bha
ann ach a mhàthair. Nur a chunnaic am famhair mur a bha, thug
e as déigh Mhaol a' chliobain. Lean e i gus an d' ràinig i 'n obhainn.
Leum Maol a' chliobain an obhainn, 's cha b'urrainn am famhair
a leum. "Tha thu thall a Mhaol a chliobain." "Tha ma 's oil leat
e." "Mharbh thu mo thri nigheanan maola, ruagha." "Mharbh ma
's oil leat e." "Ghoid thu mo chír mhin òir 's mo chìr gharbh
airgid." "Ghoid ma 's oil leat e." "Mharbh thu mo ghille maol,
carrach." "Mharbh ma's oil leat e." "Ghoid thu mo chlaidheamh
soluis." "Ghoid ma 's oil leat e." "Mharbh thu mo mhàthair."
"Mharbh ma 's oil leat e." "Ghoid thu mo bhoc." "Ghoid ma's oil
leat e." "Cuin a thig thu rithisd?" "Thig nur bheir mo ghnothach
mi." "Na'm biodh thusa bhos 's mise thall," ursa am famhair, "de
'dheànadh thu airson mo leantainn?" "Stopainn mi féin, 's dh'
òlainn gus traoighinn an obhainn." Stop am famhair e féin, 's dh'
òl e gus an do sgàin e. Phòs Maol a chliobain mac òg an
tuathanaich.

This story came to me from four sources. First, the one which I have translated, into which several passages are introduced (in brackets) from the other versions. This was written down by Hector MacLean.

2d. A version got by the same collector from Flora Macintyre, in Islay; received June 16, 1859. In this the whole of the first part is omitted; it begins at the giant's house. The incidents are then nearly the same till she runs away, when she leaps the river with her sisters under her arms. The farmer or king is omitted. She returns, is caught by the giant, tied to a peat-stack, and a rock, which she takes away, and she makes the giant kill; the three cropped red girls: and she kills the cropped rough-skinned gillie: she steals the white glave of light, a fine comb of gold, and a coarse comb of silver. She makes the giant kill his mother, and his dog and cat enticed into a sack; at last she sets the giant to swill the river; he bursts, and she goes home with the spoil. The bit about the sack is worth quoting. She put the crone in the pock, and a cat, and a dog, and a cream-dish with her. When the giant and his men came, they began laying on the pock. The crone cried out, "It's myself thou hast;" and the giant said, "I know, thou she rogue, that it's thou." When they would strike a stroke on the dog, he would give out a SGOL; when they would strike a stroke on the cat, he would give out a MIOG; and when they would strike a stroke on the cream-dish, it would give out a STEALL (a spurt). I have, 3rd. A version very prettily told, at Easter 1859, by a young girl, nursemaid to Mr. Robertson, Chamberlain of Argyll, at Inverary. It was nearly the same as the version translated, but had several phrases well worth preservation, some of which will be found in brackets; such as, "but her mother's blessing came and freed her." The heroine also stole a golden cover off the bed, which called out; and a golden cock and a silver hen, which also called out. The end of the giant was thus: At the end of the last scolding match, the giant said, "If thou wert here, and I yonder, what wouldst thou do?" "I would follow thee over the bridge," said she. So Maol a chliobain stood on the bridge, and she reached out a stick to him, and he went down into the river, and she let go the stick, and he was drowned. "And what become of Maol a chliobain? did she marry the farmer's youngest son?" "Oh, no; she did not marry at all. There was something about a key hid under a stone, and a great deal more which I cannot remember. My father did not like my mother to be telling us such stories, but she knows plenty more,"—and the lassie departed in great perturbation from the parlour.

The 4th version was got by John Dewar from John Crawfort, herring-fisher, Lochlonghead, Arrochar, and was received on the 2d of February 1860. Dewar's version is longer than any, but it came too late. It also contains some curious phrases which the others have not got, some queer old Gaelic words, and some new adventures. The heroine was not only the youngest, but "maol carrach" into the bargain, and the rest called her Maol a Mhoibean; but when they went on their travels she chose the little cake and the blessing. The others tied her to a tree, and a cairn of stones, which she dragged away. Then they let her loose, and she followed them till they came to a burn. "Then the eldest sister stooped to drink a draught from the burn, and there came a small creature, named Bloinigain, and he dabbled and dirtied the burn, and they went on. The next burn they came to the two eldest sisters stooped, one on each side of the burn, to drink a draught; but Bloinigain came and he dabbled and dirtied the burn; and when they had gone on another small distance, they reached another burn; and the youngest sister, whom the rest used to call Maol a Mhoibean, was bent down drinking a draught from the burn, and Bloinigain came and stood at the side of the burn till she had drank her draught, and the other two came; but when they stooped to drink their draught, Bloinigain dabbled the burn, and they went on; and when they came to another burn, the two eldest were almost parched with thirst. Maol a Mhoibean kept Bloinigain back till the others got a drink; and then she tossed Bloinigain heels over head, CAR A MHUILTEAN, into a pool, and he followed them no more."

This Bloinigain plays a great part in another story, sent by Dewar; and his name may perhaps mean "fatty;" BLONAG, fat, suet, lard; BLOINIGEAN-GARAIDH, is spinnage.

The next adventure is almost the very same. The giant's three red-haired polled daughters had PAIDIREANAN of gold about their necks (which word *may* be derived from *pater*, and a name for a rosary), and the others had only strings.

When they fled they came to a great EAS, cataract, and "there was no way of getting over it, unless they could walk on two hairs that were as a bridge across the cataract; and their name was DROCHAID AN DA ROINEAG, the two-hair bridge; and Maol a Mhoibean ran over the eas on the two hairs; but her sisters could not walk on the two hairs, and Maol a Mhoibean had to turn back and carry her sisters, one after one, over the eas on the two-hair bridge." The giant could not cross, and they scolded each other across the river as in the other stories. The giant shouted, "Art thou yonder, Maol a Mhoibean?" and she said "AIR MO NODAIG THA;" and when she had told her deeds, she said, "I will come and go as my business brings me;" and the three sisters went on and took service with the king.

This two-hair bridge over the fall may possibly be a double rainbow; many a time have I sat and watched such a bridge over a fall; and the idea that the rainbow was the bridge of spirits, is old enough.

"Still seem as to my childhood's sight
  A midway station given,
For happy spirits to alight
  Betwixt the earth and heaven."

The Norse gods rode over the bridge, Bif-raust, from earth to heaven; and their bridge was the rainbow which the giants could not cross. There is also a bridge, as fine as a hair, over which the Moslem pass to Paradise; and those who are not helped, fall off and are lost.

The sisters took service; one was engaged to sew, the other to mind the house, and the youngest said she was good at running errands; so at the end of a day and year she was sent for the giant's CABHRAN full of gold, and CABHRAN full of silver; and when she got there the giant was asleep on a chest in which the treasure was.

"Then Maol a Mhoibean thought a while, in what way she should get the giant put off the chest; but she was not long till she thought on a way; and she got a long broad bench that was within, and she set the bench at the side of the chest where the giant was laid; she went out where the burn was, and she took two cold stones from the burn, and she went in where the giant was, and she would put one of the stones in under the clothes, and touch the giant's skin at the end of each little while with the stone; and the giant would lay himself back from her, till bit by bit the giant went back off the chest on to the bench; and then Maol a Mhoibean opened the chest, and took with her the cabhran of gold, and the cabhran of silver." The rest of the adventure is nearly the same as in the other versions; and the eldest sister married the king's eldest son.

The next was the Claidheamh Geal Soluis, white glave of light.

She got in and sat on a rafter on a bag of salt; and as the giant's wife made the porridge, she threw in salt. Then the giant and his son sat and supped, and as they ate they talked of how they would catch Maol, and what they would do to her when they had her; and after supper they went to bed. Then the giant got very thirsty, and he called to his son to get him a drink; and in the time that the giant's son was seeking a CUMAN (cup), Maol a Mhiobean took with her the fill of her SGUIRD (shirt) of salt, and she stood at the outside of the door; and the giant's son said to him "that there was no water within;" and the giant said "That the spring was not far off, and that he should bring in water from the well;" and when the giant's son opened the door, Maol a Mhoibean began to throw salt in his face; and he said to the giant, "That the night was dark, and that it was sowing and winnowing hailstones (GUN ROBH AN OIDHCHE DORCHA AGUS CUR'S CABHADH CLACH-A-MEALLAIN ANN); and thou wilt see a great distance before thee, and a long way behind thee."

When the young giant came out, it was a fine night; and he went to the well with the bright sword, and laid it down beside him; while he stooped to take up the water, Maol followed him, and picked up the sword, and SGUIDS I AN CEANN, she whisked the head off the giant's son. Then came the flight and pursuit, and escape, and scolding match, and the second son of the king married the second sister.

The next adventure was the theft of BOC CLUIGEANACH, the buck with lumps of tangled hair and mud dangling about him. She went over the bridge and into the goats' house, and the goats began at BEUCHDAICH, roaring; and the giant said, "Maol a Mhoibean is amongst the goats;" and he went out and caught her; and he said, "What wouldst thou do to me if thou shouldst find me amongst thy goats, as I found thee?" And she said, "It is (this) that I would kill the best buck that I might have, and I would take out the paunch, and I would put thee in the paunch, and I would hang thee up till I should go to the wood; and I would get clubs of elder, and then I would come home, AGUS SHLACAINN GU BAS THU, and I would belabour thee to death." "And that is what I will do thee," said the giant.

Then comes the bit which is common to several other stories, in various shapes; and which is part of a story in Straparola.

When she was hung up in the goat's paunch, and the giant gone for his elder-wood clubs, Maol a Mhoibean began to say to the giant's wife, "Oh! it's I that am getting the brave sight! Oh! it's I that am getting the brave sight!" as she swayed herself backwards and forwards; and the giant's wife would say to her, "Wilt thou let me in a little while?" and Maol a Mhoibean would say (I will) *not let* (thee in) CHA LEIG, and so on till the wife was enticed into the paunch, and then Maol took the belled buck and went away with him. "AGUS AN UAIR A' B' AIRD ISE B' ISLE EASAN, S' AN NUAIR A B' AIRD ASAN B' ISLE ISE;" and the time she was highest he was lowest, and the time he was highest she was lowest, till they reached the two-hair bridge. The giant came home and belaboured his wife to death, and every blow he struck, the wife would say, "IS MI FHEIN A THA ANN, O 'S MI FHEIN A THA ANN—It is myself that is in it: Oh! it is myself that is in it;" and the giant would say, "I know it is thyself that is in it."

[And in this the giant is like the water-horse in another story, and like the cyclop in the Odyssey, and like all other giants throughout mythology. He was a great, strong, blundering fool, and his family were as stupid as himself.]

Maol married the king's third son, and the king said, "There is one other thing yet of what the giant has that I want, and that is, A SGIATH BHALLABHREAC AGUS A BHOGHA S A DHORLACH—his lumpy bumby shield, and his bow and his quiver, or in poetical language, his variegated bossy shield, and his bow and quiver—and I will give

thee the kingdom if thou wilt get me them." This is a good instance
of what may happen in translating Gaelic into English, one language
into another, which is far removed from it, both in construction and
meaning. BHALLABREAC applies to almost anything that is round or
spotted. The root of the epithet is BALL, which, in oblique cases,
becomes BHALL, vall, and means a spot, a dot, and many other
things. It is the same as the English word ball. A shield was round,
and covered with knobs; a city wall was round, and it was the shield
of the town; an egg was round, and the shell was the shield or the
wall of the egg; a skull is round, and the shield of the brain, and a
head is still called a knob in English slang; a toad-stool is round,—
and so this word ball has given rise to a succession of words, which
at first sight appear to have nothing to do with each other, and the
phrase *might* be translated speckled-wings. The epithet is applied to
clouds and to many things in Gaelic poetry, and has been translated
in many ways, according to the taste of each translator. Those who
felt the beauty of the passages used the words which they found
applicable. Those who do not, may if they choose, search out words
which express their feeling; and so a poem which stands on its own
merit, in its own language, is at the mercy of every translator; and
those who work at Gaelic with dictionaries for guides, may well be
puzzled with the multitude of meanings assigned to words.

So Maol went, and the giant's dog barked at her, and the giant
came out and caught her, and said he would cut her head off; and
she said she would have done worse to him; and "What was that?"
"Put him in sack and roast him;" so he said he would do that, and
put her in, and went for wood. She got her hand out, untied the
string, and put in the dog and cat, and fled with the arms, and the
giant roasted his own dog and cat, AGUS BHA AM MADADH AN 'S AN
SGALAILLE AGUS AN CAT ANNS AN SGIABHUIL—and the dog was in,
and the squalling; and the cat (was) in, and the squealling, and the
giant would say, "FEUCH RUIT A NIS—Try thyself now." When he
found out the trick, he pursued, and when they got to the bridge, his
hand was on her back, and he missed his step and fell into the EAS,
and there he lay. And the king's son and Maol a Mhoibean were
made heirs in the kingdom, and if they wanted any more of the giant's
goods, they got it without the danger of being caught by the giant.

The Gaelic given in Dewar's version is spelt as it came, and is
somewhat Phonetic. The writer knows his own language well, but
has had very little practice in writing it. As he spells in some degree
by ear, his phonetics have their value, as they have in his English
letter given in the introduction.

5.   A gentleman at the inn at Inverary remembered to have heard
a similar story "long ago about a witch that would be running in and
out of a window on a bridge of a single hair."

6. "Kate ill Pratts" is referred to in a review of Chambers' Nursery Rhymes, at page 117, vol. 10; 1853—Tait's Edinburgh Magazine. The story is mentioned as told in Perthshire, and seems to be of the same kind; with a bit of Cinderella, as known in the west, with the advice of the hoodie in Murchadh and Mionachag put in the mouth of a little bird—

> "Stuff wi' fog, and clem wi' clay,
> And then ye'll carry the water away."

These sounds are not imitations of any bird's note, and the Gaelic sounds are; so I am inclined to think the Gaelic older than the low country version.

The story is well known as Little Thumb. It is much the same as Boots and the Troll, Norse Tales, p. 247. It is somewhat like part of Jack and the Bean-stalk. Part of it is like Big Peter and Little Peter, Norse Tales, p. 395; and that is like some German Stories, and like a story in Straparola. The opening is like that of a great many Gaelic Stories, and is common to one or two in Grimm.

There is something in a story from Polynesia, which I have read, in which a hero goes to the sky on a ladder made of a plant, and brings thence precious gifts, much as Jack did by the help of his bean-stalk. In short, this story belongs to that class which is common to all the world, but it has its own distinctive character in the Highlands; for the four versions which I have, resemble each other much more than they do any other of which I know anything.

17*a*.

FABLES.

1. From J. MacLeod, fisherman
on the Laxford, Sutherland.

One day the fox succeeded in catching a fine fat goose asleep by the side of a loch, he held her by the wing, and making a joke of her cackling, hissing and fears, he said,—

"Now, if you had me in your mouth as I have you, tell me what you would do?"

"Why," said the goose, "that is an easy question. I would fold my hands, shut my eyes, say a grace, and then eat you."

"Just what I mean to do," said Rory, and folding his hands, and looking very demure, he said a pious grace with his eyes shut.

But while he did this the goose had spread her wings, and she was now half way over the loch; so the fox was left to lick his lips for supper.

"I will make a rule of this," he said in disgust, "Never in all my life to say a grace again till after I feel the meat warm in my belly."

The wild goose in the Highlands has her true character; she is one of the most wary and sagacious of birds, and a Gaelic proverb says:—

Sealgair thu mar a mharbhas thu Gèadh a's Corr a's Crotach.
Sportsman thou, when killest thou goose, and heron, and curlew?

Rory is a corruption of a Gaelic proper name, which means, one whose hair is of the colour of the fox "Ruadh." The fox is called by various descriptive and other names. BALGAIR, he with the "BALG," bag or quiver, from which the shape of the quiver may be surmised to have resembled the foxes' brush. MADADH RUADH, the red-brown dog. GILLE MARTUINN, the servant of Martin, or perhaps the Martinmas lad, but the true Gaelic, according to my instructor, a

Lorn man, is SIONNACH, pronounced *Shunach*, which is surely the same as the Sanscrit SVAN, dog. SUNUH SHUNI, dog-bitch.

2. From John Campbell, piper; and many other sources lately.

The fox is much troubled by fleas, and this is the way in which he gets rid of them. He hunts about till he finds a lock of wool, and then he takes it to the river, and holds it in his mouth, and so puts the end of his brush into the water, and down he goes slowly. The fleas run away from the water, and at last they all run over the fox's nose into the wool, and then the fox dips his nose under and lets the wool go off with the stream.

This is told as a fact. The place where an "old grey fellow" was seen performing this feat, was mentioned by one of my informants. The fox was seen in the sea near the Caithness hills.

3. "Tha biadh a's ceol an seo," as the fox said when he ate the pipe bag.

This saying I have known from my childhood, and the story attached to it is that the fox being hungry one day, found a bag-pipe, and proceeded to eat the bag, which is generally, or was till lately, made of hide. There was still a remnant of breath in the bag, and when the fox bit it the drone gave a groan, when the fox surprised but not frightened, said:—
"Here is meat and music!"

4. From D. M. and J. Macleod, Laxford, Sutherland.

One day the fox chanced to see a fine cock and fat hen, off which he much wished to dine, but at his approach they both jumped up into a tree. He did not lose heart, but soon began to make talk with them, inviting them at last to go a little way with him. "There was no danger," he said, "Nor fears of his hurting them, for there was peace between men and beasts, and among all animals." At last after much parleying the cock said to the hen, "My dear, do you not see a couple of hounds coming across the field?"
"Yes," said the hen, "and they will soon be here."
"If that is the case, it is time I should be off," said the sly fox, "for I am afraid these stupid hounds may not have heard of the peace."

And with that he took to his heels and never drew breath till he reached his den.

> This fable is very well known, and is probably derived from Æsop, though the narrator did not know the fact. I give it because the authority cannot be impeached, and because equally well-known fables are found in old Chinese books, and are supposed to be common property. This *may* be pure tradition, though I suspect it to be derived indirectly from some book. I myself lately told the fable of the Monkey and the Cats, in Gaelic, to a highlander who was going to law; and it is impossible to be sure of the pedigree of such well-known fables.
>
> The next two are of the same kind, and were new to me when they arrived.

5. THE FOX AND THE FOX-HUNTER.

Once upon a time a Tod-hunter had been very anxious to catch our friend the fox, and had stopped all the earths in cold weather. One evening he fell asleep in his hut; and when he opened his eyes he saw the fox sitting very demurely at the side of the fire. It had entered by the hole under the door provided for the convenience of the dog, the cat, the pig, and the hen.

"Oh! ho!" said the Tod-hunter, "Now I have you." And he went and sat down at the hole to prevent Reynard's escape.

"Oh! ho!" said the fox, "I will soon make that stupid fellow get up." So he found the man's shoes, and putting them into the fire, wondered if that would make the enemy move.

"I shan't get up for that, my fine gentleman," cried the Tod-hunter.

Stockings followed the shoes, coat and trousers shared the same fate, but still the man sat over the hole. At last the fox having set the bed and bedding on fire, put a light to the straw on which his jailor lay, and it blazed up to the ceiling.

"No! That I cannot stand," shouted the man, jumping up; and the fox taking advantage of the smoke and confusion, made good his exit.

> *Note by the Collector.*—This is the beginning of Reineke Fuchs in the Erse. I cannot get any one to write them down in Gaelic, which very few people can *write*. Most of the tales are got from my guide, the gamekeeper; but I have got them from many others.   C. D.
>
> Having told this story to a man whom I met near Oban, as a bait, I was told the following in return.—J. F. C.

6. "The fox is very wise indeed. I don't know whether it is true
or not, but an old fellow told me that he had seen him go to a loch
where there were wild ducks, and take a bunch of heather in his
mouth, then go into the water, and swim down with the wind till
he got into the middle of the ducks, and then he let go the heather
and killed two of them."

7. THE FOX AND THE WRENS.

A fox had noticed for some days, a family of wrens, off which he
wished to dine. He might have been satisfied with one, but he was
determined to have the whole lot,—father and eighteen sons,—and
all so like that he could not tell one from the other, or the father
from the children.

"It is no use to kill one son," he said to himself, "because the old
cock will take warning and fly away with the seventeen. I wish I
knew which is the old gentleman."

He set his wits to work to find out, and one day seeing them all
threshing in a barn, he sat down to watch them; still he could not
be sure.

"Now I have it," he said; "well done the old man's stroke! He
hits true," he cried.

"Oh!" replied the one he suspected of being the head of the
family, "If you had seen my grandfather's strokes, you might have
said that."

The sly fox pounced on the cock, ate him up in a trice, and then
soon caught and disposed of the eighteen sons, all flying in terror
about the barn.

C. D.

This is new to me, but there is something like it in the Battle of
the Birds, where the wren is a farmer threshing in a barn. Why the
wren should wield the flail does not appear, but I suppose there was
some good reason for it "once upon a time."

J. F. C.

8. *From John Dewar, Inveraray, August 27, 1860.*

A fox one day met a cock and they began talking.

"How many tricks canst thou do?" said the fox?"

"Well," said the cock, "I could do three; how many canst thou
do thyself?"

"I could do three score and thirteen," said the fox.

"What tricks canst thou do?" said the cock.

"Well," said the fox, "my grandfather used to shut one eye and give a great shout."

"I could do that myself," said the cock.

"Do it," said the fox. And the cock shut one eye and crowed as loud as ever he could, but he shut the eye that was next the fox, and the fox gripped him by the neck and ran away with him. But the wife to whom the cock belonged saw him and cried out, "Let go the cock; he's mine."

Say thou, " 'SE MO CHOILEACH FHEIN A TH' ANN" (it is my own cock), said the cock to the fox.

Then the fox opened his mouth to say as the cock did, and he dropped the cock, and he sprung up on the top of a house, and shut one eye and gave a loud crow; and that's all there is of that sgeulachd.

I find that this is well-known in the west.

9. HOW THE WOLF LOST HIS TAIL.

One day the wolf and the fox were out together, and they stole a dish of crowdie. Now the wolf was the biggest beast of the two, and he had a long tail like a greyhound, and great teeth.

The fox was afraid of him, and did not dare to say a word when the wolf ate the most of the crowdie, and left only a little at the bottom of the dish for him, but he determined to punish him for it; so the next night when they were out together the fox said:

"I smell a very nice cheese, and (pointing to the moonshine on the ice) there it is too."

"And how will you get it?" said the wolf.

"Well, stop you here till I see if the farmer is asleep, and if you keep your tail on it, nobody will see you or know that it is there. Keep it steady. I may be some time coming back."

So the wolf lay down and laid his tail on the moonshine in the ice, and kept it for an hour till it was fast. Then the fox, who had been watching him, ran in to the farmer and said: "The wolf is there; he will eat up the children,—the wolf!"

Then the farmer and his wife came out with sticks to kill the wolf, but the wolf ran off leaving his tail behind him, and that's why the wolf is stumpy tailed to this day, though the fox has a long brush.

C. D.

This is manifestly the same as the Norse story,—"Why the bear is stumpy tailed?" and it errs in ascribing a stumpy tail to the wolf. There was not time for the "Norse Tales" to become known to the people who told the story, so perhaps this may be a Norse tradition transferred from the bear to the wolf. There is another wolf story in Sutherland, which was told to me by the Duke of Sutherland's head forester in 1848. It was told in Gaelic by a fine old Highlander, who is now dead. His sons have succeeded him, and will probably remember this story which I quote from recollection.

J. F. C.

10. HOW THE LAST WOLF WAS KILLED IN SUTHERLAND.

There was once a time when there were wolves in Sutherland, and a woman that was living in a little town lost one of her children. Well, they went all about the hills looking for the lad, but they could not find him for three days. Well, at the end of that time they gave up, but there was a young lad coming home late through a big cairn of stones, and he heard the crying of a child, and a kind of noise, and he went up to the cairn, and what should he see, in a hole under a big stone, but the boy and two young wolves with him.

Well he was frightened that the old wolf would come, so he went home to the town, and got two others with him, and in the morning they went back to the cairn and they found the hole.

Well, then, one of the lads stopped outside to watch, and the other two went in, and they began to kill the young wolves, and they were squealing, and the old one heard them, and she came running to the place, and slipped between the legs of the lad who was watching, and got her head into the hole, but he held her by the tail.

"What," said the lad who was inside, "is keeping the light from us."

MA BHRISTEAS BUN FIONN BITHIDH FIOS AGAD.

"If the root of Fionn (or if the hairy root) breaks, thou wilt know," said the man outside.

Well, he held on, and the lads that were inside killed the wolf and the young ones, and they took the boy home to his mother, and his family were alive in the time of my grandfather, and they say they were never like other people.

This is manifestly the same as the story of Romulus and Remus, but it appears on very strong evidence that wolves really carry off the suckle children in Oude now, and that these children grow up to be half savages. It is either a fact in natural history, or a tradition,

believed to be a fact in Sutherland and in Oude. I have heard the
same story told in the Highlands of a wild boar, but the boar's tail
would be but a slippery hold.

J. F. C.

According to Innes (Scotland in the Middle Ages, Pp. 125), in
1283, there was an allowance for one hunter of wolves at Stirling;
and there were wild boars fed at the King's expense in 1263, in
Forfarshire. There are plenty of wolves now in Scandinavia, and in
Brittany, and wild boars in Germany, and elsewhere in Europe. The
Gaelic names for wolf are MADADH ALLUIDH, commonly used;
FAOL CHU, ALLA MHADADH, all of which are composed of an
epithet, and a word which now means dog. Dic. etc. MAC TIRE,
Earth's Son; FAOL, Armstrong.

A Boar is TORC, CULLACH, FIADH CHULLACH

The Fox appears as a talking creature in several stories. So does
the Bear in No. IX., and the Wolf and Falcon, No. IV. The Dog
appears in No. XII., the Sheep, Cat, Cock, Goose, Dog, and Bull,
in No. XI.; the Frog in No. XXXIII.; the Cat and the mouse in No.
XLIX. The Rat and the Lion, and the Dove, appear in a story to
which I have referred in No. IV. Other creatures, also, not mentioned
in stories, are gifted with speech, but their speech is generally but a
translation of their notes into Gaelic.

11.   BI GLIC, BI GLIC, *Bee-Gleechk*, be wise, say the Oyster-
catchers, when a stranger comes near their haunts.

12.   GÒRACH, GÒRACH, *Gawrach*, "silly," says the Hoodie, as
he sits on a hillock by the way side and bows at the passengers.

13.   Here is another bit of crow language,—a conversation with
a frog. When it is repeated in Gaelic it can be made absurdly like
the notes of the creatures.

"Ghille Criosda mhic Dhughail cuir a nois do mhàg,

Christ's servant, son of Dugald, put up thy paw.

"Tha eagal orm, tha eagal orm, tha eagal orm."

I fear.

"Gheibh thu còta gorm a's léine. Gheibh thu còta gorm a's
leine."

Thou shalt have a blue coat and a shirt.

Then the frog put up his hand and the hoodie took him to a
hillock and began to eat him, saying,

"Biadh dona lom! 's bu dona riabh thu."

Bad bare meat and bad wert thou ever.

"Caite bheil do ghealladh math a nis?" said the frog.

Where is thy good promise now?

"Sann ag ol a bha sinn an latha sin. Sann ag ol a bha sinn an latha sin."

It is drinking we were on that day.

"Toll ort a ruid ghrannda gur beag feola tha air do chramhan."

"Toll ort!" said the hoodie.

A hole in thee, ugly thing! how little flesh is on thy bones.

Why the frog is called Gilchrist MacDugald, unless the story was made to fit some real event, I do not know. The story used to be told by an old Islay man, Donald Macintyre, to Hector MacLean; and I remember to have heard part of it in my childhood.

The Hoodie has appeared in many places already, and he and his family, the Crows, have been soothsayers time out of mind, and in many lands. A more mischievous, knowing bird does not exist, or one that better deserves his character for wisdom.

The old fable of the bird which dropped a tortoise on a stone, is enacted every day by Hoodies. Any one who will take the trouble to watch, may see hoodies on the shores of the Western Isles, at low tide, flying up into the air and dropping down again.

It will be found that they are trying to drop large stranded mussels and other shells, on the stones on the beach; and if left to their own devices, they will go on till they succeed in cracking the shell, and extracting the inhabitant.

Keepers who trap them most successfully, do it by beating them at their own weapons. They put a bait into a pool of water, and make a show of hiding it, and set the trap on a knoll at some distance. The Hoodie makes a gradual approach, reconnoitering the ground as he advances, and settling on the knolls which command a view, perhaps repeating his song of silly, silly, till he settles on the trap, and next morning his head is on the kennel door with the mortal remains of other offenders.

I suspect that the Hoodie was made a soothsayer because of his natural wisdom.

14.   The Grouse Cock and his wife are always disputing and may be heard on any fine evening or early morning quarrelling and scolding about the stock of food.

This is what the hen says,—

"FAIC THUSA 'N LA UD 'S AN LA UD EILE."

And the cock, with his deeper voice, replies,—

"FAIC THUSA 'N CNOC UD 'S AN CNOC UD EILE."

See thou yonder day, and yon other day.

See thou yonder hill, and yon other hill.

Of all the stories I have gathered and heard, this is all I have about the Grouse. It is remarkable; for if these stories were home-made, and in modern times, they would surely treat of the only bird whose births, deaths, and marriages are chronicled in the newspapers,—and which is peculiar to the British Isles.

15.   The Eagle and the Wren once tried who could fly highest, and the victor was to be king of the birds. So the Wren flew straight up, and the Eagle flew in great circles, and when the Wren was tired he settled on the Eagle's back.
When the Eagle was tired he stopped and
"C' AITE BHEIL THU DHREOLAIN?" URS' AN IOLAIR.
"THA MISE AN SO OS DO CHEANN," URS' AN DREOLAN.
"Where art thou, Wren?" said the Eagle.
"I am here above thee," said the Wren.
And so the Wren won the match.

This was told to me in my childhood, I think, by the Rev. Mr. MacTavish. There is a much better version of the story in Grimm's "King Wren," in which the notes of many creatures are made into German; but this describes the flight of eagle and wren correctly enough. I lately, Sept. 1860, heard it in Skye.

16.   THA FIOS FITHICH AGUD. Thou hast ravens' knowledge, is commonly said to children who are unusually knowing about things of which they have no ostensible means of gaining knowledge.

Odin had two ravens whose names meant Mind and Memory, which told him everything that passed in the world.

17.   NEAD AIR BRIDE; UBH AIR INID; EUN AIR CAISG. MUR AM BI SIN AIG AN FHITHEACH BITHIDH AM BAS.
Nest at Candlemas, egg at Inid, bird at Pash.
If that hath not the Raven, death he hath.

This is rather a bit of popular natural history than anything else, but it shews that the raven is at least as important a personage amongst Celts as the grouse is amongst Saxons.

18.   'S BIGEAD THU SIOD, ARS AN DREOLAN 'N UR THUM E GHOB ANNS AN FHAIRIGE.

Thou'rt lessened by that, said the Wren, when he dipped his beak in the sea.

There are a great number of similar stories current in the islands, but it is very hard to persuade any one that such trifles can be of any value. I have lately heard of a number of stories of the kind. For example—

19.   John Mackinnon, stable-boy at Broadford in Skye, tells that "a man was one day walking along the road with a creel of herrings on his back, and two foxes saw him, and the one, who was the biggest, said to the other, 'Stop thou here, and follow the man, and I will run round and pretend that I am dead.' So he ran round, and stretched himself on the road. The man came on, and when he saw the fox, he was well pleased to find so fine a beast, and he picked him up, and threw him into the creel, and he walked on. But the fox threw the herrings out of the creel, and the other followed and picked them up; and when the creel was empty, the big fox leaped out and ran away, and that is how they got the herrings."

Well, they went on together till they came to a smith's house, and there was a horse tied at the door, and he had a golden shoe, and there was a name on it.

" 'I will go and read what is written on that shoe,' said the big fox, and he went; but the horse lifted his foot, and struck a kick on him, and drove his brains out.

" 'Ghill, ghill, ars an siunnach beag cha sgolair mi 's cha 'n aill leam a bhi.'

" 'Lad, Lad,' said the little fox, 'No scholar me, nor wish I to be;' " and, of course, he got the herrings, though my informant did not say so.

20.   A boy, Alexander Mackenzie, who walked with me from Carbost, in Skye, told that a bee (seillean) met a mouse and said,

> "Teann a nall 'us gun deanamaid tigh."
> "Come over till we make a house."
> "I will not," said Luchag, the mousie.

> Fear dha 'n dug thusa do mhil shamraidh,
> Deanadh e tigh gheamhraidh dhuit.
> Tha tigh agamsa fo thalamh,

>> Nach ruig air gallian na gaoith.
>> Bith tusa an ad isean pheallach
>> A ruidh air barradh nan craobh.

He to whom thou gavest thy summer honey,
Let him make a winter house for thee;
I have a little house under the ground,
That can reach neither cold nor breeze,
Thou wilt be a ragged creature,
Running on the tops of the trees.

21.   The same boy told that there was a mouse in the hill, and
a mouse in a farm.

"It were well," said the hill mouse, "to be in the farm where one
might get things."

Said the farm mouse, " 'S fhearr an t-sith." Better is peace.

22.   The following is not strictly speaking a fable, but it is a sort
of moral tale, and may be classed with fables. It seems to inculcate
a lesson of self-reliance and self-help. I wrote it in English from the
Gaelic repetition of John Mackenzie at Inveraray in 1859, and made
him repeat it in 1860, when I made up several omissions. Other
versions have come to me from other sources, and the tale seems
to be well known in the Highlands. If it is in any book, I have not
been able to find it. Mackenzie says he learned it from a native of
Uist, and I have a very well written version of it, told by Macintyre
in Benbecula, to Mr. Torrie. It is called the "Provost of London,"
and begins with the family history of the hero of the tale. A great
lady fell in love with a poor Highland lad, and he was ashamed of
the love she had taken for him, and went away to an uncle who was
a colonel, and who got him made a major. The lady took to black
melancholy, and he was sent for, and they married. He went to the
wars, bought a small estate, was killed, and his brother-in-law
brought up his son. Then comes the dream, the journey for three
years in Scotland, Ireland, and England; the meeting with "one of
the people of Cambridge," and the rest of the incidents nearly as
they were told to me by Mackenzie, but in different words.

17b.

BAILIE LUNNAIN

Told by John Mackenzie, at Inverary,
to J. F. C. August 1859 and 1860.

There were at some time of the world two brothers in one farm, and they were very great friends, and they had each a son; and one of the brothers died, and he left his brother guardian. When the lad was near to be grown up, he was keeping the farm for his mother almost as well as his father could have done. One night he saw a dream in his sleep, the most beautiful lady that there was in the world, and he dreamed of her three times, and he resolved to marry her and no other woman in the world; and he would not stay in the farm, and he grew pale, and his father's brother could not think what ailed him; and he was always asking him what was wrong with him. "Well, never mind," one day he said, "brother of my father, I have seen a dream, the most beautiful woman that there is in the world, and I will marry no other but she; and I will now go out and search for her over the whole world till I find her."

Said the uncle, "Son of my brother, I have a hundred pounds; I will give them to thee, and go; and when that is spent come back to me, and I will give thee another hundred."

So the lad took the hundred pounds, and he went to France, and then he went to Spain, and all over the world, but he could not find the lady he had seen in his sleep. At last he came to London, and he had spent all his money, and his clothes were worn, and he did not know what he should do for a night's lodging.

Well, as he was wandering about the streets, whom should he see but a quiet-looking respectable old woman; and he spoke to her; and, from less to more, he told her all that had happened to him; and she was well pleased to see a countryman, and she said,

"I, too, am a Highland woman, though I am in this town." And she took him to a small house that she had, and she gave him meat and clothes.

And she said, "Go out now and take a walk; maybe thou mayest see here in one day what thou mightest not see in a year."

On the next day he was out taking a walk about the town, and he saw a woman at a window, and he knew her at once, for she was the lady he had seen in his sleep, and he went back to the old woman.

"How went it with thee this day, Gael?" said she.

"It went well," said he.

"Oh, I have seen the lady I saw in my sleep," said he. And he told her all about it.

Then the old woman asked about the house and the street; and when she knew—"Thou hast seen her," said she. "That is all thou wilt see of her. That is the daughter of the Bailie of London; but I am her foster mother, and I would be right glad if she would marry a countryman of my own. Now, do thou go out on the morrow, and I will give thee fine highland clothes, and thou wilt find the lady walking in such a street: herself and three maidens of company will go out together; and do thou tread on her gown; and when she turns round to see what is the matter, do thou speak to her."

Well, the lad did this. He went out and he found the lady, and he set his foot on her dress, and the gown rent from the band; and when she turned round he said, "I am asking you much grace—it was an accident."

"I was not your fault; it was the fault of the dressmaker that made the dress so long," said she.

And she looked at him; and when she saw how handsome he was, she said, "Will you be so kind as to come home with me to my father's house and take something?"

So the lad went and sat down, and before she asked him anything she set down wine before him and said, "Quicker is a drink than a tale."

When he had taken that, he began and he told her all that happened, and how he had seen her in his sleep, and when, and she was well pleased.

"And I saw thee in my sleep on the same night," said she.

He went away that day, and the old woman that he was lodging with asked him how he had got on, and he told her everything that had happened; and she went to the Bailie's daughter, and told her all the good she could think of about the young lad; and after that he was often at the Bailie's house; and at last the daughter said she would marry him. "But I fear that will not do," said she. "Go home for a year, and when thou comest back I will contrive to marry thee," said she, "for it is the law of this country that no one must be married unless the Bailie himself gives her by the hand to her bridegroom," said she; and she left blessing with him.

Well, the lad went away as the girl said, and he was putting everything in order at home; and he told his father's brother all that had happened to him; but when the year was nearly out he set off for London again, and he had the second hundred with him, and some good oat-meal cakes.

On the road, whom should he meet but a Sassanach gentleman who was going the same road, and they began to talk.

"Where art thou going?" said the Saxon.

"Well, I am going to London," said he

"When I was there last I set a net* in a street, and I am going to see if it is as I left it. If it is well I will take it with me; if not, I will leave it."

"Well," said the other, "that is but a silly thing. How can lintseed be as thou hast left it? It must be grown up and trodden down by ducks and geese, and eaten by hens long ago. I am going to London, too; but I am going to marry the Bailie's daughter."

Well, they walked on together, and at long last the Saxon began to get hungry, and he had no food with him, and there was no house near; and he said to the other, "Wilt thou give me some of thy food?"

"Well," said the Gael, "I have but poor food—oaten bread; I will give you some if you will take it; but if I were a gentleman like you I would never travel without my own mother."

"How can I travel with my mother?" said the Saxon. "She is dead and buried long ago, and rotting in the earth; if not, why should I take her with me?"

And he took the oat cake and ate it, and they went on their way.

They had not gone far when a heavy shower came on, and the Gael had a rough plaid about him, but the Saxon had none; and he said to the other,

"Wilt thou lend me thy plaid?"

"I will lend you a part of it," said the Gael: "but if I were a gentleman like you, I would never travel without my house, and I would not be indebted to any one for favours."

"Thou art a fool," said the Saxon; "my house is four storeys high.

(* To set a net and to sow lint are expressed by the same words.)

How could any man carry a house that is four storeys high about with him?"

But he wrapped the end of the Highlander's plaid about his shoulders, and they went on.

Well, they had not gone far till they came to a small river, and the water was deep after the rain, and there was no bridge, and in those days bridges were not so plentiful as they are now; and the Saxon would not wet his feet, so he said to the Highlander,

"Wilt thou carry me over?"

"Well," said the Gael, "I don't mind if I do; but if I were a gentleman like you, I would never travel without my own bridge, and I would not be in any man's debt for favours."

"Thou art a silly fellow," said the Saxon. "How can any man travel about with a bridge that is made of stone and lime. Thou art but a 'burraidh,' and weighs as much as a house?"

But he got on the back of his fellow-traveller nevertheless, and they travelled on till they got to London. Then the Saxon went to the house of the Bailie, and the other went to the little house of his old countrywoman, who was the foster-mother of the Bailie's daughter.

Well, the Saxon gentleman began to tell the Bailie all that had happened to him by the way; and he said—

"I met with a Gael by the way, and he was a perfect fool—the greatest booby that man ever saw. He told me that he had sown lint here a year ago in a street, and that he was coming to fetch it, if he should find it as he left it, but that if he did not, he would leave it; and how should he find that after a year? He told me I should never travel without my mother, and my house, and my bridge; and how could a man travel with all these things? But though he was nothing but a fool, he was a good-natured fellow, for he gave me some of his food, and lent me a bit of his plaid, and he carried me over a river."

"I know not but he was as wise as the man that was speaking to him," said the Bailie; for he was a wise man. "I'll tell you what he meant," said he.

"Well, I will shew that he was a fool as great as ever was seen," said the Saxon.

"He has left a girl in this town," said the Bailie, "and he is come to see if she is in the same mind as she was when he left her; if so, he will take her with him, if not, he will leave her; and he has set a net," said he. "Your mother nourished you, and a gentleman like you should have his own nourishment with him. He meant that you should not be dependent on him. It was the booby that was with him," said the Bailie. "A gentleman like you should have his own shelter, and your house is your shelter when you are at home. A bridge is made for crossing a river, and a man should always be able to do that without help; and the man was right, and he was no fool, but a smart lad, and I should like to see him," said the Bailie; "and I would go to fetch him if I knew where he was," said he. [According to another version, the house and bridge meant a coach and a saddle-horse.]

Well, the next day the Bailie went to the house where the lad was, and he asked him to come home to his dinner; and the lad came, and he told the Bailie that he had understood all that had been said.

"Now," said he, "as it is the law that no man may be married here unless the Bailie gives him the bride by the hand, will you be so kind as to give me the girl that I have come to marry, if she is in the same mind? I will have everything ready."

And the Bailie said, "I will do that, my smart lad, to-morrow, or whenever thou dost choose. I would go farther than that for such a smart boy," said he.

"Well, I will be ready at such a house to-morrow," said the lad; and he went away to the foster-mother's house.

When the morrow came, the Bailie's daughter disguised herself, and she went to the house of the foster-mother, and the Gael had got a churchman there; and the Bailie came in, and he took his own daughter by the hand; but she would not give her hand to the lad.

"Give thy hand, girl," said the Bailie. "It is an honour for thee to marry such a smart lad." And he gave her to him, and they were married according to law.

Then the Bailie went home, and he was to give his daughter by the hand to the Saxon gentleman that day; but the daughter was not to be found; and he was a widower, and she was keeping the house for him, and they could not find her anywhere.

"Well," said the Bailie, "I will lay a wager that Gael has got her, after all." And the Gael came in with the daughter, and he told them everything just as it had happened, from beginning to the end, and how he had plenty in his own country.

And the Bailie said, "Well, since I myself have given thee my daughter by the hand, it is a marriage, and I am glad that she has got a smart lad like thee for a husband."

And they made a wedding that lasted a year and a day, and they lived happily ever after, and if they have not died since then they are alive yet.

17*c*.

THE SLIM SWARTHY CHAMPION.

From James Wilson, blind fiddler, Islay, 1859.

There was a poor man dwelling in Ard na h-Uamh, and a son was born to him, and he gave him school and learning till he was fourteen years of age. When he was fourteen years of age, he said to his father,

"Father, it is time for me to be doing for myself, if thou wouldst give me a fishing-rod and a basket."

The poor man found every chance till he got a fishing-rod and a basket for him. When he got the fishing-rod and the basket, he went round about Loch Aird na h-Uamh, and took down (by) Loch Thorabais; and after he had fished Loch Thorabais closely, he came to Loch Phort an Eillean;* and after he had fished Loch Phort an Eillean before him, he took out by Loch Allalaidh. He stayed the night in Aird Eileastraidh, and every trout he had he left with a poor woman that was there.

On the morrow he thought that he would rise out, and that he would betake himself to Eirinn. He came to the garden of Aird Inneasdail, and he plucked with him sixteen apples, and then he came to Mull of Otha.† He threw an apple out into the sea, and he gave a step on it: he threw the next one, and he gave a step on it: he threw thus one after one, until he came to the sixteenth, and the sixteenth took him on shore in Eirinn.

When he was on shore he shook his ears, and he thought that it was in no sorry place he would stay.

"He moved as sea heaps from sea heaps,
And as playballs from playballs—

---

* The lake in which is the island where the Lords of the Isles had their dwelling.
† The nearest point to Ireland.

> As a furious winter wind—
> So swiftly, sprucely, cheerily,
> Right proudly,
> Through glens and high-tops,
> And no stop made he
> Until he came
> To city and court of O'Domhnuill.
> He gave a cheery, light leap
> O'er top and turret
> Of court and city
> Of O'Domhuill."*

O'Domhnuill took much anger and rage that such an unseemly ill strippling should come into his court, while he had a doorkeeper for his town.

"I will not believe," said the Champion, but "that thou art taking anger and rage, O'Domhnuill."

"Well, then, I am," said O'Domhnuill, "if I did but know at whom I should let it out."

"My good man," said the Champion, "coming in was no easier for me than going out again would be."

"Thou goest not out," said O'Domhnuill, "until thou tellest me from whence thou camest."

> "I came from hurry-skurry,
> From the end of endless spring.
> From the loved swanny glen—
> A night in Islay and a night in Man,
> A night on cold watching cairns.
> On the face of a mountain
> In the Scotch king's town
> Was I born.
> A soiled, sorry Champion am I,
> Though I happened upon this town."

"What," said O'Domhnuill, "canst thou do, oh Champion? Surely, with all the distance thou hast travelled, thou canst do something."

"I was once," said he, "that I could play a harp."

"Well, then," said O'Domhnuill, "it is I myself that have got the best harpers in the five-fifths of Eirinn, or in the bridge of the first

* The only authority writing this as poetry is the rhythm and alliteration of the original.

of the people, such as—Ruairidh O'Cridheagan, Tormaid
O'Giollagan, and Thaog O'Chuthag."

"Let's hear them playing," said the Champion.

> "They could play tunes and "UIRT" and "ORGAIN,"
> Trampling things, tightened strings,
> Warriors, heroes, and ghosts on their feet.
> Ghosts and spectres, illness and fever,
> They'd set in sound lasting sleep
> The whole great world,
> With the sweetness of the calming tunes
> That the harpers could play."

The music did not please the Champion. He caught the harps,
and he crushed them under his feet, and he set them on the fire,
and made himself a warming, and a sound warming at them.

O'Domhnuill took much lofty rage that a man had come into his
court who should do the like of this to the harps.

"My good man, I will not believe that thou art not taking anger,"
said the Champion.

"Well, then, I am, if I did but know at whom I should let it
out."

"Back, my good man; it was no easier for me to break thy harps
than to make them whole again," said the Champion.

"I will give anything to have them made whole again," said
O'Domhnuill.

"For two times five marks I will make thy harps as good as they
were before," said the Champion.

"Thou shalt get that," said O'Domhnuill.

O'Domhnuill gave him the marks, and he seized on the fill of his
two palms of the ashes, and he made a harp for Ruairidh
O'Cridheagan; and one for Tormaid O'Giollagan; and one for
Thaog O'Chuthag; and a great choral harp for himself.

"Let's hear thy music," said O'Domhnuill.

"Thou shalt hear that, my good man," said the Champion.

The Champion began to play. and och! but he was the boy behind
the harp.

> "He could play tunes, and UIRT and ORGAIN
> Trampling things, tightened strings,
> Warriors, heroes, and ghosts on their feet,
> Ghosts and souls, and sickness and fever,
> That would set in sound lasting sleep

      The whole great world
      With the sweetness of the calming tunes

That the champion could play."

"Thou art melodious, oh Champion!" said O'Domhnuill.

When the harpers heard the Champion playing, they betook themselves to another chamber, and though he had followed on, still they had not come to the fore.

O'Domhnuill went away, and he sent a bidding to meat to the Champion.

"Tell the good man that he will not have that much to gloom on me when I go at mid-day to-morrow," said the Champion.

O'Domhnuill took much proud rage that such a man should come into his court, and that he would not take meat from him. He sent up a fringed shirt, and a storm mantle.

"Where is this going?" said the Champion.

"To thee, oh Champion," said they.

"Say you to the good man that he will not have so much as that to gloom on me when I got at mid-day to-morrow," said the Champion.

O'Domhnuill took much anger and rage that such a man had come into his court and would not either take meat or dress from him. He sent up five hundred Galloglachs to watch the Champion, so that O'Domhnuill might not be affronted by his going out by any way but by the door.

"Where are you going?" said the Champion.

"To watch thee, Champion, so that thou shouldst not go to affront O'Domhnuill, and not to let thee out but as thou shouldst," said they.

"Lie down there," said the Champion, "and I will let you know when I am going."

They took his advice, and they lay down beside him, and when the dawn broke, the Champion went into his garments.

"Where are my watchers, for I am going?" said the Champion.

"If thou shouldst stir," said the great Galloglach, "I would make a sharp sour shrinking for thee with this plough-board in my hand."

The Champion leaped on the point of his pins, and he went over top and turret of court and city of O'Domhnuill.

The Galloglach threw the plough-board that was in his hand, and he slew four and twenty persons of the very people of O'Domhnuill.

Whom should the Champion meet, but the tracking lad of O'Domhnuill, and he said to him—

"Here's for thee a little sour grey weed, and go in and rub it to the mouths of those whom it killed and bring them alive again, and earn for thyself twenty calving cows, and look behind thee when thou partest from me, whom thou shalt see coming."

When the tracking lad did this he saw no being coming, but he saw the Champion thirteen miles on the other side of Luimineach (Limerick).

> "He moved as sea-heaps o' sea-heaps,
> And as playballs o' playballs.
> As a furious winter wind—
> So swiftly, sprucely, cheerily,
> Right proudly,
> Through glens and high tops,
> And he made no stop
> Until he reached
> MacSeathain,* the Southern Earl."

He struck in the door. Said MacSeathain, the southern Earl, "Who's that in the door?"

"I am Duradan o' Duradan, Dust of Dust," said the Champion.

"Let in Dust of Dust," said MacSeathain, the southern Earl; "No being must be in my door without getting in."

They let him in.

"What couldst thou do, Duradan o' Duradan?" said the southern Earl.

"I was on a time, and I could play a juggle," said he.

"Well, then, it is I myself that have the best juggler in the five-fifths of Eirinn, or the bridge of the first of the people, as is Taog Bratach Mac a Cheallaich, rascally Toag, the son of Concealment."

They got up the juggler.

"What," said the southern Earl, "is the trick that thou canst do, Dust of Dust?"

"Well, I was on a time that I could bob my ear off my cheek," said he.

The Champion went and he takes the ear off the cheek.

Said rascally Taog, the son of Concealment: "I could do that myself."

He went and he took down his ear, and up he could not bring it! but the Champion put up his own ear as it was before.

* Seathain is supposed to be John, therefore Johnson.

The Earl took much anger and rage that the ear should be off his juggler.

"For five merks twice over," said the Champion, "I would set the ear as it was before."

He got the five merks twice over, and he put the ear on the juggler as it was before.

"I see," said the Earl, "that the juggling of this night is with thee."

Rascally Taog went away; and though they should have staid there the length of the night, he would not have come near them.

Then the Champion went and he set a great ladder up against the moon, and in one place of it he put a hound and a hare, and in another place of it he put a carl and a girl. A while after that he opened first where he had put the hound and the hare, and the hound was eating the hare; he struck him a stroke of the edge of his palm, and cast his head off. Then he opened again where were the carl and the girl, and the carl was kissing the girl. He struck him a stroke of the edge of his palm, and he cast his head off.

"I would not for much," said the Earl, "that a hound and a carl should be killed at my court.

"Give five merks twice over for each one of them, and I will put the heads on them," said the Champion.

"Thou shalt get that," said the southern Earl.

He got the five merks twice over, and he put the head on the hound and the carl as they were before; and though they should be alive till now, the hound would not have touched a hare, nor the carl a girl, for fear their heads should be taken off.

On the morrow, after their meat in the morning, he went hunting with the Earl. When they were amongst the wood, they heard a loud voice in a knoll (or a bush).

"Be this from me," said Dust of Dust, "I must go to see the foot of the carl MacCeochd." He went out—

> "And moved as sea-heaps o' sea-heaps,
> And as playballs o' playballs;
> As a furious winter wind—
> So swiftly, sprucely, cheerily,
> Right proudly,
> Through glens and high tops,
> And no stop made he
> Until he reached
> The house of the Carl MacCeochd."

He struck at the door. "Who's that?" said the car MacCeochd.

"I," said he, "am the leech's lad."

"Well," said the carl, "many a bad black leech is coming, and they are not doing a bit of good to me."

"Give word to the carl that unless he will not let me in, I will be going," said the Champion.

"Let in the leech's lad; perhaps he is the one in whom is my help," said the carl MacCeochd.

They let him in.

"Rise up, carl MacCeochd, thou art free from thy sores," said the Champion.

Carl MacCeochd arose up, and there was not a man in Eirinn swifter or stronger than he.

"Lie down, carl MacCeochd, thou art full of sores," said the Champion.

The carl MacCeochd lay down, and he was worse than he ever was.

"Thou didst ill," said the carl MacCeochd, "to heal me and spoil me again."

"Thou man here," said the Champion, "I was but shewing thee that I could heal thee."

"I have," said the carl MacCeochd, "but the one daughter in the world, and thou shalt get her and half of all I have, and all my share when I go way, and heal my leg."

"It shall not be so, but send word for every leech that thou hast had, that I might get talking with them," said the leech's lad.

They sent word by running lads through the five-fifths of Eirinn for the leeches that were waiting on the carl, and they came, all thinking that they would get pay, and when they came riding to the house of the carl, the Champion went out and he said to them,

"What made you spoil the leg of the carl MacCeochd, and set himself thus?"

"Well then," said they, "if we were to raise the worth of our drugs, without coming to the worth of our trouble, we would not leave him the worth of his shoe in the world."

Said the leech's lad, "I will lay you a wager, and that is the full of my cap of gold, to be set at the end of yonder dale, and that there are none in Eirinn that will be at it sooner than the carl MacCeochd."

He set the cap full of gold at the end of the dale, and the leeches laid the wager that they could never be.

He went in where the carl MacCeochd was, and he said to him,

"Arise, carl MacCeochd, thou art whole of sores, I have laid a wager on thee."

The carl got up whole and healthy, and he went out, and he was at three springs at the cap of gold, and he left the leeches far behind.

Then the leeches only asked that they might get their lives. Promise of that they got not (but) the leech's lad got in order.

He snatched his holly in his fist, and he seized the grey hand plane that was on the after side of his haunch, and he took under them, over them, through and amongst them; and left no man to tell a tale, or earn bad tidings, that he did not kill.*

When the carl was healed he sent word for the nobles and for the great gentles of Eirinn to the wedding of his daughter and the Champion, and they were gathering out of each quarter.

"What company is there?" said the leeches' lad.

"There is the company of thine own wedding, and they are gathering from each half and each side," said the carl MacCeochd.

"Be this from me!" said he; "O'Conachar the Shelly (or of Sligo) has a year's service against me," and he put a year's delay on the wedding.

> "Out he went as Voorveel o Voorveel
> And as Veerevuil o Veerevuill,
> As a furious winter wind,
> So swiftly, sprucely, cheerily,
> Right proudly,
> Through glens and high tops.
> And no stop did he make
> Till he struck in the door
> Of Conachar of Sligo."

"Who's that?" said O'Conachar of Sligo.

"I," said he, "Goodherd."

"Let in Goodherd," said O'Conachar of Sligo, for great is my need of him here."

They let him in.

"What couldst thou do here?" said O'Conachar.

"I am hearing," said he, to O'Conachar of Sligo, "that the chase is upon thee. If thou wilt keep out the chase, I will keep in the spoil," said Goodherd.

"What wages wilt thou take?" said O'Conachar of Sligo.

"The wages I will take is that thou shouldst not make half cups with me till the end of a day and year," said Goodherd.

* This seems like mock heroics, an imitation of such tales as the Knight of the Red Shield and Murachadh MacBrian.

O'Conachar made this covenant with him, and the herdsman went to herd.

The chase broke in on O'Conachar of Sligo, and they betook themselves to where the herdsman was, to lift the spoil. When the herdsman saw that they had broken in, he took the holly in his fist, and seized the grey hand-plane that was on the after side of his haunch, and left no man to tell a tale, or earn bad tidings, that he did not kill. He went into a herd's bothy, and he (was) hot, and he saw O'Conachar Sligheach just done drinking a boyne of milk and water.

"Witness, gods and men, that thou hast broken thy promise," said Goodherd.

"That fill is no better than another fill," said O'Conachar Sligheach.

"That selfsame fill thou didst promise to me," said Goodherd.

He took anger at O'Conachar Sligheach, and he went away, and he reached the house of the carl MacCeochd. The daughter of the carl made him a drink of green apples and warm milk, and he was choked.

And I left them, and they gave me butter on a cinder, porridge kail in a creel, and paper shoes; and they sent me away with a big gun bullet, on a road of glass, till they left me sitting here within.

AN CEATHAIRNEACH CAOL, RIABHACH.

Bha duine bochd a bha ann an Aird na h-Uamha a chòmhnuidh, agus rugadh mac dha, 's thug e sgoil a's ionnsachadh dha gus an robh e ceithir bliadhna deug a dh' aois thuirt e r'a athair, "Athair, 's mithidh domhsa 'bhith deànadh air mo shon fhèin; na'n d' thugadh thu domh slat-iasgaidh as basgaid," Fhuair an duine bochd a' h-uile cothrom gus an d' fhuair e slat-iasgaidh as basgaid da.

Nur a fhuair e'n t slat-iasgaidh 's bhasgaid chaidh e ma'n cuairt Loch Aird na h-Uamha, 's ghabh e 'nuas Loch Thòrabais, 's an deigh dha Loch Thòrabais a chliabairt thàinig e gu Loch Phort an Eilean, 's an deigh dha Loch Phort an Eilean iasgach roimhe ghabh e 'mach Loch Allalaidh. Dh' fhan e 'san oidhche 'n Aird Eileastraidh, 's a' h-uile breac a bh' aige dh' fhàg e aig boireannach bochd a bha 'n sin eud.

An la'r na mhàireach smaointich e gu'n togadh e 'mach agus gun d' thugadh e Eirinn air. Thàinig e gu gàradh Aird Inneasdail agus spìon e leis sè ubhla deug, 's thàinig e'n sin gu Maol na h-Otha.

Thilg e ubhal a mach 's an fhairge 's thug e ceum urra. Thilg e 'n ath tè agus thug e ceum eil' urra. Thilg e, mur seo, té an deigh té, gus an d' thàinig e gus an t-sèathamh té deug, 's thug an t-seatho té deug air tir an Eirinn e.

Nur a bha e air tir chrath e chluasan, a's smaointich e nach b' ann an àite suarrach a dh' fhanadh e.

> Ghluais e mar mhuir-mhill o mhuir-mhill,
> 'S mar mhire-bhuill o mhire-bhuill;
> Mar ghaoith ghailbheach gheamhraidh,
> Gu sitheach, sothach, sanntach,
> Sàr-mheamnach,
> Trìd ghleanntann as ard-mhullach;
> 'S cha d' rinneadh stad leis
> Gus an d' thàinig e
> Gu cuirt agus cathair O Domhnuill.
> Thug e leum sunndach, soilleir
> Thar bàrr agus baideil
> Cùirt agus cathair
> O Domhnuill.

Ghabh O Dòmhnuill mòran feirg agus corruich a leithid de shrutha dhona, ao-dhealbhach a tighinn a stigh d' a chùirt, agus dorsair a bhith aige fèin r'a bhaile.

"Cha chreid mi féin," ars' an ceathairneach, "Nach 'eil thu 'gabhail feirg agus corruich O Domhnuill?"

"Mata tha," ors' O Domhnuill, "Na'm biodh fios agam co ris a liginn a mach e?"

"A dhuine mhath," ors' an Ceathairneach, "cha b' fhasa dhomhsa tighinn a stigh na dol e mach a rìs."

"Cha d' theid thu 'mach," ors' O Domhnuill, "gus an innis thu dhomhsa co as a thàinig thu."

> Thàinig mi o ghriobhaill o ghrabhaill,
> O bhun an tobair dhìlinn,
> O ghleann àluinn ealaich;
> Oidhch' an Ile 's oidhch' am Manainn;
> Oidhch' air charna fuara faire;
> An aodann monaidh
> Am baile righ Alba
> Rugadh mi;
> Ceàrnach suarrach, salach mi,
> Gad thàrladh air a' bhaile seo mi.

"Dé," urs' O Domhnuill, "a cheathairnich a dhèanadh thusa? 's cinnteach, 's na 'shiubhail thu 'dh' astar gu'n deanadh thu rudeigin."

"Bha mi uair," urs' esan, "agus sheinninn cruit."

"Mata," urs' O Domhnuill, " 's ann agam féin a tha na cruitearan a's fheàrr ann an còig chòigeamh na h-Eireann, na'n Drochaid-cheudan na Mìth; mar a tha Ruairidh O Cridheagan, Tormaid O Giollagan, agus Taog O Chuthag."

"Cluinneam a' seinn eud," urs' an Ceathairneach. Thòisich na clàrsairean.

> Sheinneadh eud puirt, agus uirt, agus orgain,
> Nitheanna tearmad, teudan tairteil;
> Curaidhean, laoich, as aoig air an casan;
> Aoig, as àinn, as galair, as fiabhrais;
> Chuireadh eud 'nan sìon sioram suain
> An saoghal mòr gu léir,
> Le binnead nam port shìogaidh
> A sheinneadh na clàrsairean.

Cha do chòrd an ceòl ris a' Cheathairneach. Rug e air na clàrsaichean, 's phronn e fo a chasan eud, 's chuir e air teinidh eud, 's rinn e gharadh, 's a chruaidh-gharadh riu.

Ghabh O Domhnuill mòran àrdain gun d' thànaig duine 'stigh do 'n chuirt aige 'dhèanadh a leithid seo air na clàrsaichean.

"Cha chreid mi fhéin a dhuine mhath nach 'eil thu' gabhail corruich," ars' an Ceathairneach.

"Mata tha, nam biodh fhios'am co ris a liginn a mach e."

"Air 'ur n-ais a dhuine mhath! Cha b' fhasa dhomhsa do chlàrsaichean a brisdeadh na'n slànachadh a rìs!" ars' an Ceathairneach.

"Bheir mi ni sam bith seachad airson an slànachadh a rìs," ars' O Domhnuill.

"Air chòig mhairg da uair, ni mise do chlàrsaichean cho math sa bha eud roimhid," urs' an Ceathairneach.

"Gheibh thu sin," ars' O Domhnuill.

Thug O Domhnuill na mairg da agus rug e air làn a dha bhoise do 'n luaith, 's rinn e clàrsach do Ruairidh O Cridheagan, 's té do Thormaid O Giollagan, 's té do Thaog O Chuthag agus clàrsach mhòr, choirealach da fhé.

"Cluinneam do cheòl," ars' O Domhnuill.

"Cluinnidh tu sin a dhuine mhath," urs' an Ceathairneach.

Thòisich an Ceathairneach air seinn, as, och! b' e 'm balach air chùl na clàrsaich e!

Sheinneadh e puirt, agus uirt, agus orgain,
Nitheanna tearmad; teudan tairteil;
Curaidhean, laoich, as aoig air an casan;
Aoig, as àinn, as galair, as fiabhrais.
'S gun cuirte 'nan sìon sioram suain,
An saoghal mòr gu léir,
Le binnead a' phuirt shìogaidh,
A sheinneadh an Ceathairneach.

" 'S binn thus' a Cheathairnich," ars' O Domhnuill.

Nur a chuala na clàrsairean an Ceathairneach a' seinn thùg eud seombar 'eil' orra, 's gad a leanadh e fhathasd cha d' thigeadh eud an làthair.

Dh' fhalbh O Domhnuill 's chuir e còmhnainn bhìdh thun a Ceathairnich.

"Abraibh ris an duine mhath nach bi 'n uibhir sin aige r'a mhùigheadh ormsa nur a dh' fholbhas mi air a' mheadhon lath' am màireach," urs' an Ceathairneach.

Ghabh O Domhnuill moran àrdain a leithid de dhuine 'tighinn a staigh d'a chùirt, 's nach gabhadh e biadh uaidh. Chuir e nìos léin air ialtan 's madal donnain. "Cà' 'bheil seo a' dol?" urs' an Ceathairneach. "A t' ionnsuidh-sa, 'Cheathairneach," urs' eudsan. "Abraibh-se ris an duine mhath nach bi 'n uibhir sin aige r'a mhùigheadh ormsa nur a dh' fholbhas mi air a' meadhan lath' an la'r na màireach," urs' an Ceathairheach. Ghabh O Domhnuill mòran feirg agus corruich, a leithid de duine 'thighinn a staigh d'a chùirt, 's nach ghabhadh e aona-chuid, biadh na aodach uaidh. Chuir e 'nìos còig ciad galloglach a dh' fhaire 'Cheathairnich, air alt 's nach biodh masladh air a thoirt do dh' O Domhnuill le e 'dhol a mach, rathad sam bith ach air an dorus."

"Cà' 'bheil sibhse 'dol?" ars' an Ceathairneach.

"A t' fhaire-sa 'Cheathairnich, air alt 's nach fhalbh thu, 'thoirt masladh do dh' O Domhnuill, gun do ligeil a mach ach mar is còir duit," urs' eudsan.

"Laidhibh sios ann an sin," ars' an Ceathairneach, " 's nur a bhios mise 'g imeachd bheir mi fios duibh."

Ghabh eud a chomhairle, 's laidh eud sìos làmh ris, 's nur a bhrisd am fàire chaidh an Ceathairnich 'na éideadh.

"Càite 'bheil mo luchd faire-sa, tha mi 'g imeachd," ars' na Ceathairneach.

"Na 'n carachadh thu," urs' an gall-oglach mòr, "dhèanainn crupan geur, goirt dhiot leis a' bhòrd-urchair so a'm làimh."

Leum an Ceathairneach air barraibh a phuthag's chaidh e thar barr agus baideil cùirt agus cathair O Domhnuill. Thilg an galloglach am bòrd-urchair a bha 'na laimh, 's mharbh e ceithir pearsanna fichead de dh' fhìor-mhuinntir O Domhnuill.

Co 'choinnich an Ceathairneach ach gille-leantainn O Domhnuill, 's thuirt e ris, "Seo dhuit luigh bheag, bhiorach, ghlas, 's theirig a staigh, 's rub ri bilean na fheadhnach a mharbhadh i, 's thoir beò eud, 's coisinn duit fhéin fichead mart laoigh, 's amhairc as do dhèigh, nur a dhealachas tu riumsa, co 'chi thu teachd."

Nur a rinn an gille-leantainn seo cha 'n fhac e neach a' teachd; ach chunnaic e 'n Ceathairneach tri mìle deug an taobh thall de Luimineach.

> Ghluais e mar mhuir-mhill o mhuir-mhill,
> 'S mar mhire-bhuill o mhire-bhuill;
> Mar ghaoith ghailbheach gheamhraidh,
> Gu sitheach, sothach, sanntach,
> Sàr-mheamnach,
> Trìd ghleanntan as ard-mhullach;
> 'S cha d' rinneadh stad leis,
> Gus an d' ràinig e
> Mac Seathain, an t-Iarl deas.

Bhuail e anns an dorusd. Thuirt MacSeathain an t-Iarl Deas ris, "Co siod 'san dorusd?"

"Tha mise, Dùradan O Dùradan," urs' an Ceathairneach.

Thuirt MacSeathan, an t-Iarl Deas, "Ligibh a staigh Dùradan O Dùradan; cha 'n fhaod neach a bhith a'm' dhorusd-sa 'bualadh gun faotainn a staigh."

Lig eud a staigh e. "Dé 'dhèanadh thusa' Dhuradain O Dùradan?" ars' an t-Iarl Deas.

"Bha mi uair 's dhèanainn cleas," ars esan.

"Mata 's ann agam fhéin a tha 'n aona chleasaiche 's fheàrr ann an còig chòigeamh na h-Eireann, na 'n Drochaid cheudan nam Mith, mar a tha Taog pratach Mac a Cheallaich."

Fhuair eud a nìos an cleasaiche. "Dé," ursa 'n t-Iarl Deas, "an cleas a dhèanadh thusa, Dhuradain O Dùradan.

Mata bha mi uair 's bhogainn a' chluas bhàr mo leithcheinn," ars' esan.

Dh' fholbh an Ceathaireach 's thugar a' chluas bhàr a leithcheinn.

Orsa Taog pratach a' Cheallaich, "Dhèanainn fhéin sin."

Dh' fholbh e 's thug e 'nuas a chluas, 's a suas cha d' thugadh e i! ach chuir an Ceathairneach a suas a chluas fhéin mar a bha i roimhid!

Ghabh an t-Iarla mòran feirg agus corruich a' chluas a bhith d'a chleasaiche.

"Air chòig mhairg da uair," ars' an Ceathairneach, "chuirinnsa 'chluas mar a bha i roimhid."

Fhuair e na còig mhairg da uair, 's chuir e 'chluas air' a chleasaiche mar a bha i roimhid.

"Tha mi 'faicinn," ars' an t-Iarla, "gur leat fhéin cleasachd na h-oidhche nochd."

Dh' fholbh Taog pratach, 's gad a dh' fhanadh eud an sin fad na h-oidhche, cha d' thigeadh e a 'n còir.

Dh' fholbh an Ceathairneach an sin, 's chuir e dreumaire mòr suas ris a' ghealaich; 's chuir e ann an aon àite dheth cù agus gearraidh; 's chuir e ann an àite eile dheth bodach agus caile. Treis as a dhéigh seo dh' fhosgail e 'n toiseach far an do chuir e 'n cù agus an gearradh; 's bha 'n cù 'g itheadh a' ghearraidh. Bhuail e buille de dh' oir a bhois' air a' chù, 's thilg e 'n ceann deth. Dh' fhosgail e' rithisd far an robh am bodach 's a' chaile; 's bha 'm bodach a' pògadh na caile. Bhuail e buille de dh' oir a bhois' air 's thilg e 'n ceann deth.

"Cha bu gheamha leam," ars' an t-Iarl, "air mòran, cù agus bodach a bhith air am marbhadh ann a' m' chùirt."

"Thoir còig mhairg da nair airson gach aon diu 's cuiridh mise na cinn orra 'rìs," urs' Ceathairneach.

"Gheibh thu sin," ars' an t-Iarl Deas.

Fhuair e na còig mhairg da uair, 's chuir e 'n ceann air a' chù 's air a' bhodach mar a bha eud roimhid; 's gad a bhiodh eud beò gus an seo, cha d' thugadh a cù làmh air gearraidh, na 'm bodach air caile, air eagal gun tug-te na cinn diu.

An la 'r na mhàireach, an déigh am bidh, anns a'mhaidinn, chaidh e 'shealgaireachd leis an Iarla. Nur a bha eud feadh na coille chual eud coireal ann an tom.

"Bhuam seo," ursa Dùradan O Dùradan! feumaidh mi dol a dh' amharc cas a' Bhodaich 'Ic Ceochd.

> Ghabh e 'mach,
> 'S ghluais e mar mhuir-mhill o mhur-mhill,
> 'S mar mhire-bhuill o mhire-bhuill;
> Mar ghaoith ghailbheach gheamhraidh,
> Gu sitheach, sothach, sanntach,
> Sàr-mheamnach,

Trìd ghleanntan as ard-mhullach;
Agus stad cha d' rinneadh leis,
Gus an d'ràinig e,
Taigh a' Bhodaich 'Ic Ceochd.

Bhuail e anns an dorusd. "Co siod?" urs' am Bodach Mac Ceochd.

"Mis?" urs' esan, "Gill' an Léigh."

"Mata," urs' am bodach, " 's iomadh léigh dugh, dona 'tighinn, 's cha 'n 'eil eud a' dèanadh mir feum domhsa."

"Thugaibh fios do 'n bhodach, mar an lig e 'staigh mi, gu'm bi mi 'g imeachd," ars' an Ceathairneach.

"Ligibh a staigh Gill' an Léigh, cha lughaide gur h-ann ann a tha mo chobhair," ars' am Bodach Mac Ceochd.

Lig eud a staigh e.

"Eirich suas a Bhodaich 'Ic Ceochd, tha thu saor o chreuchdan," urs' an Ceathairneach.

Dh' éiridh am Bodach Mac Ceochd suas, 's cha robh duin' an Eirinn a bu luaithe 's a bu làidireacha na e!

"Laidh sìos a Bhodaich 'Ic Ceochd tha thu làn chreuchdan," ars' an Ceathairneach. Laidh am Bodach Mac Ceochd sìos 's bha e na bu mhiosa na bha e riabh!

" 'S olc a rinn thu," urs' am Bodach Mac Ceochd, "mo leigheas agus mo mhilleadh a rìs."

"A dhuine seo," ursa Gill' an Léigh; "cha robh mi ach a' ligeil fhaicinn duit gum b'urrainn mi do leigheas!"

"Cha 'n 'eil agam," urs' am Bodach Mac Ceochd, "ach an aon nighean rìs an t-saoghal, 's geobh thu i, 's leith 's na th'agam, 's mo chuid air fad nur a shiubhlas mi, agus leighis mo chas."

"Cha'n e sin mar a bhitheas, ach cùir fios air a' h-uile léigh a bh'agad, 's gum faighinn-sa 'bhith bruidhinn riutha," arsa Gill' an Léigh!

Chuir eud fios le gillean-ruith, feadh chòig chóigeamh na h-Eireann, airson nan lighichean a bha 'feitheamh air a' bhodach; 's thàinig eud air fad, a saoilsinn gu'faigheadh eud pàigheadh. Agus nur a thàinig eud, a'marcachd gu taigh a' Bhodaich, chaidh an Ceathairneach a mach 's thuirt e riu.

"Dé 'thug dhuibhse cas a' Bhodaich 'Ic Ceochd a mhilleadh, 's e fhéin a chur fo ainbheach mur seo?"

"Mata," urs' eudsan, "Na'n togamaide luach ar cungan, gun tighinn air luach ar saoithreach, cha 'n fhàgamaid luach a bhròg aige ris an t-saoghal."

Ursa Gill' an Leigh! "Cuiridh mi geall ruibh; agus 's e sin làn mo churraichd do dh' òr a chur aig ceann na dalach ud shuas, 's nach 'eil gin an Eirinn a bhios aige na 's luaithe na'm Bodach Mac Ceochd!"

Chuir e'n currachd làn òir aig ceann na dalach; 's chuir na leighean geall ris nach b'urrainn siod a bhith.

Chaidh e 'staigh far an robh 'm Bodach Mac Ceochd, 's thuirt e ris.

"Eirich a Bhodaich 'Ic Ceochd, tha thu slàn 'o chreuchdan! Chuir mi geall as do leith." Dh'eiridh am Bodach Mac Ceochd gu slàn, fallan, s' chaidh e mach, 's bha e thri ceumannan aig a' churrachd òir, 's dh fhàg e fad' air deireadh na leighean.

Cha d' iarr na leighean an seo ach na 'm faigheadh eud am beatha leo! Gealladh air a' siod cha d'fhuair eud! Chaidh gill' an leigh air dòigh!

Sparr e 'chuilionn 'na dhorn, as ghlac e'n làmh-lochdair liath a bh'air taobh piar a thòine, 's thug e fòcha 's tharta, 's frìd as rompa; 's cha d' fhàg e fear innseadh sgeoil na chosnadh tuarasdail nach do mharbh e!

Nur a bha 'm bodach leighiste chuir e fios air maithibh 's air mòr-uaislean na h-Eireann thun banais a nighinn 's a' Cheathairnich, 's bha eud a' cruinneachadh as gach ceàrn.

"De 'chuideachd a tha 'n siod?" arsa Gill' an Leigh! "Tha 'n siod cuideachd na bàinns' agad fhein, 's eud a cruinneachadh as gach leith agus as gach taobh," urs' am Bodach Mac Ceochd. "Bhuam seo," ars' esan, "tha fasdadh bliadhn' aig O Conachar an Sligeach orm;" 's chuir e dàil bliadhna 's a' phòsadh.

> Ghabh e 'mach mar mhuir-mhill o mhuir-mhill,
> 'S mar mhire-bhuill o mhire-bhuill;
> Mar ghaoith ghailbheach gheamhraidh;
> Gu sitheach, sothach, sanntach,
> Sàr-mheamnach,
> Trìd ghleanntan as ard-mhullach;
> 'S cha d' rinneadh stad leis,
> Gus an do bhuail e ann an dorusd
> O Conachar Sligeach.

"Co siod?" urs' O Conachar Sligeach.

"Mis'," urs' esan, "Buachaille Math." "Ligibh a staigh Buachaille Math," ars' O Conachar Sligeach;" chionn tha feum mòr agams' air anns an am seo."

Lig eud a staigh e.

"Dé 'dheanadh thusa 'Bhuachaill?" ors' O Conachar Sligeach.

"Tha mi 'cluinntinn," ors' e ri O Conachar Sligeach, "gu 'bheil an toir ort." "Tha," urs' O Conachar Sligeach. "Ma chumas tusa mach an tòir; cumaidh mise staigh a' chreach?" arsa Buachaille Math! "Dé 'n tuarasdal a ghabhas tu?" ars' O Conachar Sligeach.

"Se 'n tuarasdal a ghabhas mi, nach dèan thu leath-chomaith orm gu ceann lath' as bliadhna," arsa Buachaille Math!

Rinn O Conachar Sligeach an cùmhnanta seo ris. Chaidh am buachaille 'bhuachailleachd.

Bhrisd an tòir a staigh air O Conachar Sligeach, 's thug eud orra far an robh 'm buachaill' a thogail na creiche. Nur a chunnaic am buachaille gun do bhrisd eud a staigh, ghabh e 'chuilionn 'na dhorn, as ghlac e 'n lamh-lochdair liath a bh' air taobh piar a thòine; 's cha d'fhag e fear innseadh sgeoil na 'chosnadh tuarasdail an sin nach do mharbh e! Chaidh e staigh do bhothag àirich, agus e teith, 's chunnaic e O Conachar Sligeach an déigh miodar buirn agus bainne 'chriochanachadh d'a òl.

"Fhiannis air Dia 's air daoine gu 'n do bhrisd thu do ghealladh!" arsa Buachaille Math!

"Cha 'n fheàrr an làn 'ud na làn eile," ars' O Conachar Sligeach.

"An làn ud fhéin gheall thu dhomhsa," arsa Buachaille Math!

Ghabh e corruich ri O Conachar Sligeach, 's dh' fholbh e 's ràinig e taigh a' Bhodaich 'Ic Ceochd. Rinn nighean a' bhodaich deoch dha de dh' ubhlan rèim 's de bhainne blàth, 's thachdadh e.

'S dhealaich mise riu; 's thug eud dhomh im air eibhleig, 's brochan-càil an créileig, 's bròga pàipeir, 's chuir eud air folbh mi le peileir gunna-mhòir 'air rathad-mòr gloine gus an d' fhàg eud a'm' shuidhe 'staigh an seo mi.

SECOND VERSION

THE HISTORY OF THE CEABHARNACH

From John Campbell, Strath Gearloch, Ross-shire.

On the day when O'DONULL came out to hold right and justice, he saw a young chap coming. His two shoulders were through his old SUAINAICHE (sleeping coat?) his two ears through his old AIDE, hat, his two squat kick-er-ing tatter-y shoes full of cold roadway-ish water, three feet of his sword sideways on the side of his haunch, after the scabbard had ended.

He blest with easy true-wise maiden's words.

O'Donull blest him in the like of his own words.

O'Donull asked him what was his art?

"I could do harping," said the Ceabharnach.

"There are twelve men with me," said O'Donull, "and we will go to look on them."

"I am willing to do that," said the Ceabharnach.

When they went in O'Donull asked them to begin. "Hast thou ever heard music, oh Ceabharnach, finer than that?"

"I came past by the Isle of Cold, and I did not hear a screech in it that was more hideous than that."

"Wouldst thou play a harp thyself, Ceabharnach?" said O'Donull.

"Here is her player, and who should not play!"

"Give him a harp," said O'Donull.

"Well canst thou play a harp," said O'Donull.

"It is not as thou pleasest but as I please myself, since I am at work."

The music of the Ceabharnach put every harper O'Donull had asleep.

"I will be taking fare thee well," said the Ceabharnach to O'Donull.

"Thou wilt not do that to me," said O'Donull, "thou must awaken my men."

"I am going to take a turn through Eirinn," said the Ceabharnach; "if I come the way they will see, and if I come not they will be thus with thee."

He left him, and he met with one herding. "Thy master's harpers are asleep, and they will not wake till they are awakened. Go thou and awaken them, and thou wilt get what will make a rich man of thee!"

"How shall I do that?" asked the herd.

"Take a tuft of that grass and dip it in water, and shake it on them, and thou wilt awaken them."

He left the man, and he reached SEATHAN MOR MAC AN IARLE, great Seathan the son of the Earl, thirteen miles on the western side of Lumraig.

He saw a young chap coming; his two shoulders were through his old coat, his two ears through his old hat, his shoes full of cold roadway-ish water, three feet of his sword sideways on the side of his haunch after the scabbard was ended.

He asked him what was his trade? He said that he could do juggling.

"I have jugglers myself; we will go to look on them."

"I am willing enough," said the Ceabharnach.

"Shew thy juggling," said the great Seathan, "till we see it."

He put three straws on the back of his fist and he blew them off it.

"If I should get half five marks," said one of the king's lads, "I would make better juggling than that."

"I will give thee that," said the Ceabharnach.

He put three straws on the back of his fist and the fist went along with the straws.

"Thou art sore, and thou wilt be sore," said his master; "my blessing on the hand that gave it to thee."

"I will do other juggles for thee," said the Ceabharnach.

He caught a hold of his own ear, and he gave a pull at it.

"If I could get half five marks," said another of the king's lads, "I would make a better juggle than that."

"I will give thee that," said the Ceabharnach.

He gave a pull at the ear and the head came away with the ear.

"I am going away," said the Ceabharnach.

"Thou wilt not leave my set of men so."

"I am for taking a turn through Eirinn. If I come the way I will see them, and if I come not they will be so along with thee."

He went away, and he met with a man threshing in a barn. He asked him if his work could keep him up.

"It was no more than it could do."

"I," said the Ceabharnach, "will make thee a free man for thy life. There are two of thy master's lads, one with his fist off, and one with his head off. Go there and put them on again, and thy master will make thee a free man for life."

"With what shall I bring them alive?"

"Take a tuft of grass, hold it in water, shake it on them, and thou wilt heal them."

He went away and he came to FEAR CHUIGEAMH MUGHA,* a nasty man that could not bear a man to go the way of his house, to look at him when he was taking his food. There were twelve men with axes at the outer gate, and twelve men of swords on the inner gate; a porter at the great door.

They saw a young chap coming, his two shoulders through his old coat, his two ears through his old hat, his two squat kick-ering tatter-y shoes full of cold roadway-ish water.

He asked their license in to see Fear Chuigeamh Mugha.

One of them raised his axe to drive his head off, but so it was that he struck it on his own comrade.

They arose on each other till they killed each other; and he came to the men of the sword, one raised his sword to strike off his head, but he cut the head off his comrade with it, and they all fell to slaying each other. He reached the porter; he caught him by the small of the legs, and he struck his head on the door.

He reached the great man as he sat at his dinner; he stood at the end of the board.

"Oh evil man," said the king, "great was thy loss before thou camest here," as he rose to catch hold of his sword to strike his head off. His hand stuck to the sword, and his seat stuck to the chair, and he could not rise; no more could his wife leave her own place. When he had done all he wished he went away, and he met a poor man that was travelling the world.

"If thou wilt take my advice," said the Ceabharnach, "I will make a lucky man of thee as long as thou art alive."

"How wilt thou do that?" said the man.

"The king and the queen are fast in their chairs; go thou and loose them, and the king will make a great man of thee."

"How shall I loose them?"

* The man of Munster, Cuige mumhe.

"Shake water on them and they will arise."

He went out of that, and he reached ROB MAC SHEOIC MHIC LAGAIN with a pain in his foot for seven years.

He struck palm to bar. The porter asked "Who was there?"

He said there was a leech.

"Many a leech has come," said the porter. "There is not a spike on the town without a leech's head but one, and may be it is for thy head that one is."

"It might not be," said the Ceabharnach. "Let me in."

"What is putting upon thee, Rob?" said the Ceabharnach.

"My foot is taking to me these seven years. She has beat the leech and leeches."

"Arise and stretch out thy foot with the stitch," said the Ceabharnach; "and let's try if thou canst catch the twelve leeches, or if the twelve leeches will catch thee."

He arose, no man could catch him; and he himself could catch every other one.

"I have but one begotten, a champion of a girl, and I will give her to thee and half my realm."

"Be she good or bad," said the Ceabharnach, "let her be mine or thine."

An order was made for a wedding for the Ceabharnach; but when they had got the wedding in order, he was swifter out of the town than a year-old hare. He came to TAOG O-CEALLAIDH, who was going to raise the spoil of CAILLICHE BUIDHNICHE.

A young chap was seen coming, his two shoulders through his old coat, his two ears through his old hat, his two squat kick-ering tatter-y shoes full of cold roadway-ish water, three feet of his sword sideways on the side of his haunch after the scabbard was ended.

"What's this that puts on thee?" said the Ceabharnach. "Hast thou need of men?"

"Thou wilt not make a man for me," said O-Ceallaidh.

"Shall I not get a man's share if I do a man's share?"

"What's thy name?" said Taog.

"There is on me (the name of) Ceabharanach Saothrach Suarach Siubhail—the servile, sorry, strolling kern."

"What art thou seeking for thy service?"

"I am but asking that thou shouldst not forget my drink."

"Whence camest thou?"

"From many a place; but I am an Albanach."

They went to raise the raid of the carlin. They raised the spoil, but they saw the following coming.

"Be stretching out," said great Taog to the Ceabharnach. "Thou wilt not make thy legs at least. Whether wouldst thou rather turn the chase or drive the spoil with thy set of men?"

"I would not turn the chase, but if the chase would turn, we would drive the spoil at least."

The Ceabharnach cut a sharp, hard whistle, and the drove lay down on the road.

He turned to meet them. He caught each one of the slenderest legs, and the biggest head, and he left them stretched legs on head. He returned after the spoil.

"Thyself and thy lot of men can hardly drive the spoil."

"The spoil will never get up," said Taog.

He cut a whistle: the drove got up, and he drove it home.

It happened that the great man forgot to give the first drink to the Ceabharnach.

"Mine is the half of the spoil," said the Ceabharnach.

"That is more than much for thee," said the king.

"Many a time was I," said the Ceabharnach, "and Murcha MacBrian hewing shields and splitting blades; his was the half of the spoil, and mine was the other half."

"If thou art a comrade of that man, thou shalt have half the spoil," said Taog.

But he went away, and he left themselves and the spoil.

"Health be with thee, oh Ceabharnach. Arise not for ever."

EACHDRAIDH A' CHEABHARNAICH

An latha 'n d' thàinig O Domhnuill a mach a chumail còir agus ceartais, chunnaic e òglach a' tighinn. Bha 'dha ghuallainn trid a sheann suanaiche; a dha chluais trìd a sheann aide; a dha bhròig cheigeanach, bhreabanach, riobanach, làn a dh' uisge fuar ròdanach; tri triodhean dhe'n chlaidheamh air an taobh siar dhe 'thoin, an deigh dh'an scabard teireachduinn. Bheannaich e le briathraibh farasda, fior-ghlic, mìne, maighdeana. Bheannaich O Domhnuill, dha air chomain a bhriathraibh féin. Dh'fheòràich O Domhnuill deth ciod bu nòs da. "Dhèanainn clàrsaireachd,' ars' an Ceabharnach. "Tha da fhear dheug agam fhéin," ars' O Domhnuill, " 's theid sinn a shealtainn orra." "Tha mi toileach sin a dheanamh," ars' an Ceabharnach.

An uair a chaidh iad a steach dh' iarr O Domhnuill orra tòiseachadh, 's thoisich iad. "An cual thu ceòl riamh, a Ceabharnaich a 's brèagha

na sin?" ars' O Domhnuill. "Thàinig mi seachad air Ifrinn; 's cha
chuala mi sgread innte 's gràinnde na sin!" ars' an Ceabharnach.

"An seinneadh tu féin cruit, a Cheabharnaich," ars' O Domhnuill.

"So a sheinneadair!—agus cò nach seinneadair!! ars' an
Ceabharnach!

"Thugaibh cruit dha," ars' O Domhnuill.

"Is math a sheinneas tusa cruit!" ars' O Domhnuill.

"Cha'n ann mar thogras tusa, ach mar a thogras mi féin; oir is
mi 'tha 'g obair," ars' esan.

Chuir ceòl a Cheabharnaich na-h-uile clàrsair a bh' aig O
Domhnuill 'na chadal.

"Bithidh mis' a gabhail slàn leat," ars an Ceabharnach ri O
Domhnuill.

"Cha dèan thu sin ormsa," ars' O Domhnuill; "feumaidh tu mo
dhaoine 'dhùsgadh."

"Tha mi 'dol a thoirt sgrìob feadh Eirinn," ars' an Ceabharnach;
"ma thig mi'n rathad chi iad, agus mur d' thig biodh iad mar sin
agad féin."

Dh' fhàg se e agus thachair e air fear a buachailleachd.

"Tha clàrsairean do mhaighstir 'nan cadal," ars' an Ceabharnach
ris a' bhuachaille, "agus cha dùisg iad gus an dùisgear iad. Falbh
thus' agus dùisg iad, 's gheibh thu na ni duine beartach dhìot."

"Cionnus a ni mi sin?" thuirt am buachaille.

"Gabh bad de'n fheur sin, agus tum ann an uisg'e, agus crath
orr' e, 's dùisgidh tu iad," ars' an Ceabharnach. Dh' fhàg e'n duine,
's ràinig e Seathan mòr Mac an Iarla, tri mìle deug an taobh siar de
Lumraig.

Chunnaic e òglach a' tighinn. Bha 'dha ghualainn trìd a sheann
suanaiche, a dha chluais trìd a sheann aide, a dha bhròig làn a dh'
uisge fuar, ròdanach, tri troidhean dhe 'n chlaidheamh air an taobh
siar dhe thòin, an déigh dh'an scabard teireachdainn.

Dh' fheoraich e dheth ciod bu nòs dha. Thuirt e gu'n dèanadh e
cleasachd.

"Tha cleasaichean agam fein; theid sinn a dh' amharc orra."

"Tha mi glé dheònach," ars' an Ceabharnach.

"Nochd do chleasachd," ars' an Seathan mòr," ach am faic sinn
e. Chuir e tri stràbhan air cùl a dhuirn agus shéid e dheth iad.

"Na 'm faighinn-sa," orsa fear de ghillean an rìgh," leith chùig
mhairg, dhèanainn cleasachd b' fhearr na sin.

"Bheir mise sin duit," ars' an Ceabharnach.

Chuir e tri stràibhean air cùl a dhùrin, agus dh' fhalbh an dorn
maille ris na stràibhean.

"Tha thu goirt, agus bidh tu goirt," ars' a mhaighstir. "Mo bheannachd air an làimh a thug dhuit e."

"Ni mi cleasachd eile dhuit," ars' an Ceabharnach.

Rug e air a' chluais aige féin, agus thug e tarruinn oirre.

"Na 'm faighinn-sa leith chùig mheirg," arsa fear eil' de ghillean' an rìgh, "dhèannain cleasachd a b' fheàrr na sin."

"Bheir mise sin duit," ars' an Ceabharnach.

Thug e tarruinn air a chluais, 's thàinig an ceann leis a chluais.

"Tha mi 'falbh," ars' an Ceabharnach.

"Cha 'n fhàg thu mo chuid daoine-sa agam mar sin."

"Tha mi 'dol a thoirt sgrìob feadh Eirinn; ma thig mi 'n rathad chi mi iad, agus mar d' thig biodh iad mar sin agad féin," ars' an Ceabharnach.

Dh' fhalbh e agus thachair e air duine 'bualadh ann an sabhal, agus dh' fheòraich e dheth am b' urrainn 'obair a chumail suas.

"Cha mhòr nach b' uilear dhomh e," ars' am fear bualaidh.

"Ni mis'," ars an Ceabharnach, "duine saor dhìot ri d' bheò. Tha dithis de ghillean do mhaigstir, 's fear 's an dorn dheth, agus fear eile 's an ceann deth; falbh thus' agus cuir orr' iad, 's ni do mhaighstir duine saoibhir dhìot ri d' bheò."

"Co leis a bheir mi beò iad?" ars' am fear a bha 'bualadh.

"Gabh bad fodair; tum ann an uisg 'e, crath orr' e, agus ni thu 'n leigheas," ars' an Ceabharnach.

Dh' fhalbh e, agus thainig e gu fear chùigeamh Mhumha, duine mosach nach fuilingeadh do dhuine 'dhol rathad a thaighe; gu h-àraid an uair a bhiodh e 'gabhail a bhìdhe. Bha dha dheug a luchd-thuadhan air a' gheata 'muigh; a dha dheug a luchd-chlàidhean air a' gheata 'staigh; dorsair air an dorus mhòr.

Chunnaic iad òglach a' tighinn; a dha ghualainn trìd a sheann suanaiche; a dha chluais trid a sheann aide; a dha bhròig cheigeanach, bhreabanach, riobanach, làn a dh' uisge fuar, rodanach.

Dh' iarr e 'chead orra 'staigh a dh' fhaicinn Fear Chuigeamh Mhumha. Thog fear dhiu a thuadh gus an ceann a chur dheth, ach 's ann a bhuail e air a chompanach i. Dh' éirich iad air a chéile, gus an do mharbh iad a chéile. Thàinig e gu luchd nan clàidhean. Thog fear a chlaidhe gus an ceann a chur dheth, ach ghearr e 'n ceann d'a chompanach, agus dh' eirich iad uile 'mharbhadh a chéile. Ràinig e 'n dorsair. Rug e air chaol chasan air agus bhuail e cheann ris an dorus. Ràinig e 'n duine mòr, agus e 'na shuidhe aig a dhithit. Sheas e aig ceann a' bhùird.

"O'Dhroch Dhuine!" ars' an rìgh, "bu mhòr do chall mu 'n d'

thàinig thu 'n so!" agus e 'g éiridh 's a' breith air a' chlaidhe, gus a'
cheann a thoirt deth. Lean a làmh ris a chlaidhe, agus lean a mhàs
ris a' chaithir, agus cha b' urrainn a bhean a h-àite féin fhàgail.

An uair a rinn e na h-uile ni 'bu mhiann leis dh' fhalbh e, agus
thachair e air duine bochd a bha 'falbh an t-saoghail. "Ma ghabhas
tu mo chomhairle-sa," ars' an Ceabharnach ris an duine bhochd,
"Ni mi duine sona dhìot fhad 's is beò thu."

"Cionnus a ni thu sin?" ars' an duine bochd.

"Tha 'n rìgh agus a' bhan-rìgh le 'm màsan ceangailte ri 'n
caithrichean; falbh thus' agus fuasgail iad, agus ni 'n rìgh duine mòr
dhìot," ars' an Ceabharnach.

"Cionnus a dh' fhuasglas mis' iad?" ars' an duine bochd.

"Crath uisg' orra agus eiridh iad," ars' an Ceabharnach.

"Dh' fhalbh e as a' sin, agus ràinig e Rob Mac Sheoic Mhic a'
Lagain, agus e fuidh eucail 'na chois fad sheachd bliadhna. Bhuail'
e bas ri crann. Dh' fheòraich an dorsair co 'bh' ann. Thuirt esan gu
'robh leighiche.

" 'S iomadh leighiche 'thàinig," ars' an dorsair; "cha 'n 'eil ceann
stop 's a' bhaile gun cheann leighich' ach an t-aon; agus, dh'
fhaododh e 'bhith gur h-ann airson do chinn-sa 'tha 'm fear sinn."

"Cha 'n fhaodadh," ars' an Ceabharnach; "leig a stigh mi."

"Ciod a tha 'cur ort a Rob?" ars' an Ceabharnach.

"Tha, mo chas a' gabhail rium o cheann sheachd bliadhna. Dh'
fhairtlich i air leigh agus leighichean," arsa Rob Mac Sheoic 'Ic a'
Lagain.

"Sìn do chas uait," ars' an Ceabharnach, "dh' fheuchainn am
beir thu air an da leigh dheug, no 'm beir an da leigh dheug ort."

Dh' eirich e. Cha bheireadh duine sam bith airsan, agus
bheireadh e fein air nan h-uile fear eile!

"Cha 'n eil agam ach aon-ghin buadhach nighinn," orsa Rob,
"agus bheir mi dhuit i, agus leith mo rioghachd."

"Math no olc," i, ars' an Ceabharnach, "bidh agamsa no agad
fein."

Chaidh àrd a chur air banais do 'n Cheabharnach; ach 'nuair a
bha iad an deigh a' bhanais ullachadh, bu luaith' e as a' bhaile na
geàrr-bhliadhnach. Thàinig e gu Taog mòr O Ceallaidh, agus e 'dol
a thogail creach na cailliche Buidhniche.

> Chuncas òglach a' tighinn,
> A dha ghualainn trìd a sheann suanaiche;
> A dha chluais trìd a sheann aide;
> A dha bhròig cheigeanach, bhreabanach, riobanach,

Làn a dh' uisge fuar, rodanach;
Tri troidhean dhe 'n chlaidheamh
Air an taobh siar d'a dheireadh.
An déigh do 'n truaill teireachdainn.

"Ciod so 'tha 'cur ort?" ars' an Ceabharnach ri Taog mor O
Ceallaidh, "Am bheil feum dhaoin' ort?"

"Cha dèan thusa duine dhomh," ars' O Ceallaidh.

"Nach faigh mi cuid fir ma ni mi cuid fir?" ars' an Ceabharnach.

"C' ainm a th' ort?" arsa Taog.

"Tha Ceabharnach saothrach, suarach siubhail orm," ars' esan.

"Ciod a tha thu 'g iarraidh airson do sheirbhis?" arsa Taog. "Cha
'n 'eil ach gun thu dhèanamh dearmad dibh' orm," ars' an
Ceabharnach.

"Co as a thàinig thu?" arsa Taog.

"A iomadh àit", ach is Albannach mi," ars' esan.

Dh' fholbh iad a thogail creach na cailliche. Thog iad a' chreach,
ach chunnaic iad an tòir a' tighinn.

"Bi 'sìneadh as," arsa Taog mòr ris a' Cheabharnach. "Cha dean
thusa do chasan co-dhiu. Co 'is fèarr leat an tòir a philleadh na
'chreach iomain le d' chuid daoine."

"Cha phillear an toir ach na 'm pilleadh an toir dh' iomaineamaid
a' chreach co-dhiu."

Gheàrr an Ceabharnach fead chaol, chruaidh, 's luidh a chreach
air an rathad-mhor. Phill e 'n coineamh na toir.

Rug e air na h-uile fear a bu chaoile cas agus a bu mho ceann, 's
dh' fhàg e iad 'nan sìneadh cas air cheann. Phill e 'n déidh na
creiche.

"Is dona 'dh' iomaineas tu féin agus do chuid daoine chreach,"
ars' an Ceabharnach.

"Cha 'n éirich a' chreach gu bràth," arsa Taog.

Ghearr e fead, 's dh' èirich a' chreach, 's dh' iomain e dhachaidh
iad.

Thachair gu 'n do dhearmaid an duine mor an dibh a thoirt air
tus do Cheabharnach.

"Is leamsa leith na creiche," ars' an Ceabharnach.

"Tha 'n sin tuilleadh a's cus duit," ars' an rìgh.

"Is minig a bha mis'," ars' an Ceabharnach, "agus Murchadh
MacBrian a gearradh sgiath 's a' sgoltadh lann; bu leis-san leith na
creiche, agus bu leam-sa an leith eile," ars' an Ceabharnach.

"Ma 's companach thu do 'n duine sin gheibh thu leith na
creiche," arsa Taog.

Ach dh' fhalbh e, 's dh' fhàg e iad fèin agus a chreach.
Slàn leat a' Cheabharnaich; na eirich gu bràth.

3.   A third version of this curious tale was told to me in South
Uist, by MacPhie. It was very like the version told by James Wilson,
blind fiddler in Islay.

It is evidently a composition fallen to bits, and mended with prose,
and it is equally clear that it points to Ireland, though the hero was
made a Scotchman by the three old men.

As a picture of bygone manners, this is curious, and I know nothing
at all like it in any collection of popular tales.

I believe it to be some bardic recitation half-forgotten. It is said
that in the mouth of one reciter in Islay, the story used to last for four
hours.

I lately (September 1860) heard MacPhie repeat his version in
part. It was a mixture of the two versions here given, and a fifth, Irish
grandee, was added.

17d.

THE TALE OF THE SHIFTY LAD, THE WIDOW'S SON.
From John Dewar, Arrochar, June, 1860.

There was at some time or other before now a widow, and she had one son. She gave him good schooling, and she was wishful that he should choose a trade for himself; but he said he would not go to learn any art, but that he would be a thief.

His mother said to him: "If that is the art that thou art going to choose for thine ownself, thine end is to be hanged at the bridge of Baile Cliath,* in Eirinn."

But it was no matter, he would not go to any art, but to be a thief; and his mother was always making a prophecy to him that the end of him would be, hanging at the Bridge of Baile Cliath, in Eirinn.

On a day of the days, the widow was going to the church to hear the sermon, and was asking the Shifty Lad, her son, to go with her, and that he should give over his bad courses; but he would not go with her; but he said to her: "The first art of which thou hearest mention, after thou hast come out of the sermon, is the art to which I will go afterwards."

She went to the church full of good courage, hoping that she would hear some good thing.

He went away, and he went to a tuft of wood that was near to the church; and he went in hiding in a place where he could see his mother when she should come out of the church; and as soon as she came out he shouted, "Thievery! thievery! thievery!" She looked about, but she could not make out whence the voice was coming, and she went home. He ran by the way of the short cut, and he was at the house before her, and he was seated within beside the fire when she came home. He asked her what tale she had got;

* Dublin.

and she said that she had not got any tale at all, but that "thievery, thievery, thievery, was the first speech she heard when she came out of the church."

He said "That was the art that he would have."

And she said, as she was accustomed to say: "Thine ending is to be hanged at the bridge of Baile Cliath, in Eirinn."

On the next day, his mother herself thought, that as nothing at all would do for her son but that he should be a thief, that she would try to find him a good aid-to-learning; and she went to the gadaiche dubh of Aachaloinne, the black gallows bird of Aachaloinne, a very cunning thief who was in that place; and though they had knowledge that he was given to stealing, they were not finding any way for catching him. The widow asked the Black Rogue if he would take her son to teach him roguery. The Black Rogue said, "If he were a clever lad that he would take him, and if there were a way of making a thief of him that he could do it;" and a covenant was made between the Black Rogue and the Shifty Lad.

When the Shifty Lad, the widow's son, was making ready for going to the Black Rogue, his mother was giving him counsel, and she said to him: "It is against my will that thou art going to thievery; and I was telling thee, that the end of thee is to be hanged at the bridge of Baile Cliath, Eirinn;" but the Shifty Lad went home to the Black Rogue.

The Black Rogue was giving the Shifty Lad every knowledge he might for doing thievery; he used to tell him about the cunning things that he must do, to get a chance to steal a thing; and when the Black Rogue thought that the Shifty Lad was good enough at learning to be taken out with him, he used to take him out with him to do stealing; and on a day of these days the Black Rogue said to his lad—

"We are long enough thus, we must go and do something. There is a rich tenant near to us, and he has much money in his chest. It was he who bought all that there was of cattle to be sold in the country, and he took them to the fair, and he sold them; he has got the money in his chest, and this is the time to be at him, before the people are paid for their lot of cattle; and unless we go to seek the money at this very hour, when it is gathered together,* we shall not get the same chance again."

The Shifty Lad was as willing as himself; they went away to the house, they got in at the coming on of the night, and they went up

* Round to each other.

upon the loft,* and they went in hiding up there; and it was the night
of SAMHAIN, Halloween; and there assembled many people within
to keep the Savain hearty as they used to do. They sat together, and
they were singing songs, and at fun burning the nuts† and at
merry-making.

The Shifty Lad was wearying that the company was not scatter-
ing; he got up and he went down to the byre, and he loosed the
bands off the necks of the cattle, and he returned and he went up
upon the loft again. The cattle began goring each other in the byre,
and roaring. All that were in the room ran to keep the cattle from
each other till they could be tied again; and in the time while they
were doing this, the Shifty Lad went down to the room and he stole
the nuts with him, and he went up upon the loft again, and he lay
down at the back of the Black Rogue.

There was a great leathern hide at the back of the Black Rogue,
and the Shifty Lad had a needle and thread, and he sewed the skirt
of the Black Rogue's coat to the leathern hide that was at his back;
and when the people of the house came back to the dwelling room
again, their nuts were away; and they were seeking their nuts; and
they thought that it was some one who had come in to play them a
trick that had taken away their nuts, and they sat down at the side
of the fire quietly and silently.

Said the Shifty Lad to the Black Rogue, "I will crack a nut."

"Thou shalt not crack (one)," said the Black Rogue; "they will
hear thee, and we shall be caught."

Said the Shifty Lad, "I never yet was a Savain night without
cracking a nut," and he cracked one.

Those who were seated in the dwelling-room heard him, and they
said,

"There is some one up on the loft cracking our nuts, we will go
and catch them."

When the Black Rogue heard that, he sprang off the loft and he
ran out, and the hide dragging at the tail of his coat. Every one of
them shouted that there was the Black Rogue stealing the hide with
him. The Black Rogue fled, and the people of the house after him;
and he was a great distance from the house before he got the hide
torn from him, and (was able) to leave them. But in the time that
the people of the house were running after the Black Rogue, the
Shifty Lad came down off the loft; he went up about the house, he

* The loft meant, is the space in the roof of a cottage which is above the rafters, and
is used as a kind of store.
† See Dewar's note at the Gaelic for his account of this.

hit upon the chest where the gold and the silver was; he opened the chest, and he took out of it the bags in which the gold and silver was, that was in the chest; and he took with him a load of the bread and of the butter, and of the cheese, and of everything that was better than another which he found within; and he was gone before the people of the house came back from chasing the Black Rogue.

When the Black Rogue reached his home, and he had nothing, his wife said to him, "How hast thou failed this journey?"

Then the Black Rogue told his own tale; and he was in great fury at the Shifty Lad, and swearing that he would serve him out when he got a chance at him.

At the end of a little while after that, the Shifty Lad came in with a load upon him.

Said the wife of the Black Rogue, "But, I fancy that thou art the better thief!"

The Black Rogue said not a word till the Shifty Lad shewed the bags that he had full of gold and silver; then, said the Black Rogue, "But it is thou that wert the smart lad!"

They made two halves of the gold and silver, and the Black Rogue got the one half, and the Shifty Lad the other half. When the Black Rogue's wife saw the share that came to them, she said, "Thou thyself art the worthy thief!" and she had more respect for him after that, than she had for the Black Rogue himself.

At the end of a few weeks after that, a wedding was to be in the neighbourhood; and it was the custom of the country, when any who were well off were asked, that they should send some gift or other to the people of the wedding. There was a rich tenant, and he was asked; and he desired his herd to go to the mountain moor and bring home a wether for the people of the wedding. The herd went up the mountain and he got the wether, and he was going home with it; and he had it on his back when he was going past the house of the Black Rogue.

Said the Shifty Lad to his master, "What wager wilt thou lay that I do not steal the wether from the back of that man yet, before he reaches the house."

Said the Black Rogue, "I will lay thee a wager of a hundred marks that thou canst not; how shouldst thou steal the thing that is on his back!"

"Howsoever I do it, I will try it," said the Shifty Lad. "Well, then, if thou dost it," said the Black Rogue, "I will give thee a hundred marks."

"It is a bargain," said the Shifty Lad; and with that he went away after the herd.

The herd had to go through a wood, and the Shifty Lad took the ground that was hidden from him until he got before him; and he put some dirt in his shoe, and he set his shoe on the road before the herd, and he himself went in hiding; and when the herd came forward, and he saw the shoe, he said, "But thou art dirty, and though thou art, if thy fellow were there I would clean thee;" and he went past.

The Shifty Lad lifted the shoe, and he ran round about and he was before the herd, and he put his other shoe on the road before him. When the herd came forward and saw the other shoe on the road before him, he said to himself, "But there is the fellow of the dirty shoe."

He set the wether on the ground, and he said to himself, "I will return back now, and I will get the dirty shoe, and I shall clean it, and I shall have two good shoes for my trouble;" and he ran swiftly back again.

The Shifty Lad ran swiftly, and he stole with him the wether, and he took with him the two shoes; and he went home to his master, and he got a hundred marks from his master.

The herd went home and he told his own master himself how it had befallen him. His master scolded the herd; and the next day he sent him again up the mountain to seek a kid, instead of the wether he had lost.

The herd went away to the hill and he got hold of a kid, and he tied it; he put it on his back, and he went away to go home with it. The Shifty Lad saw him, and he went to the wood, and he was there before the herd; and he went in hiding, and he began at bleating like the wether. The herd thought that it was the wether that was in it; and he put the kid off him, and he left it at the side of the road, and he went to seek the wether. At the time when the herd was seeking the wether, the Shifty Lad went and he stole the kid with him, and he went home with it to the Black Rogue.

When the herd went back to where he had left the kid, the kid was gone, the kid was not in it; he sought the kid, and when he could not find the kid, he went home and he told his master how it had befallen him; and his master scolded him, but there was no help for it.

On the next day the tenant asked his herd to go up the mountain and bring home a stot; to be sure that he did not lose it. The herd went up the mountain, and he got a good fat stot, and he was driving it home. The Shifty Lad saw him, and he said to the Black Rogue, "Tiugain, come along, and we will go and try to steal the stot from the herd when he is going through the wood with it."

The Black Rogue and the Shifty Lad went away to the wood before the herd; and when the herd was going through the wood with the stot, the Black Rogue was in one place baa-ing, and the Shifty Lad in another bleating like a goat. The herd heard them, and he thought that he would get the wether and the kid again. He tied the stot to a tree, and went all about the wood seeking the wether and the kid, and he sought them till he was tired. While he was seeking the wether and the kid, the Shifty Lad went, and he stole with him the stot, and he took it home with him to the house of the Black Rogue. The Black Rogue went home after him, and they killed the stot, and they put it in hiding, and the Black Rogue's wife had good puddings for them that night. When the herd came back to the tree where he had left the stot tied, the stot was not there. He knew that the stot had been stolen. He went home and he told his master how it had happened, and his master scolded him, but there was no help for it.

On the next day his master asked the herd to go up the mountain and to bring home a wether, and not let it come off his back at all till he should come home, whatever he might see or hear. The herd went away, and he went up the mountain and he got the wether, and he succeeded in taking that wether home.

The Black Rogue and the Shifty Lad went on stealing till they had got much money, and they thought that they had better buy a drove (of cattle) and go to the fair with it to sell, and that people would think that it was at drovering they had made the money that they had got. The two went, and they bought a great drove of cattle, and they went to a fair that was far on the way from them. They sold the drove, and they got the money for them, and they went away to go home. When they were on the way, they saw a gallows on the top of a hill, and the Shifty Lad said to the Black Rogue, "Come up till we see the gallows; some say that the gallows is the end for the thieves at all events."

They went up where the gallows was, and they were looking all about it. Said the Shifty Lad, "Might we not try what kind of death is in the gallows, that we may know what is before us, if we should be caught at roguery. I will try it myself first."

The Shifty Lad put the cord about his own neck, and he said to the Black Rogue, "Here, draw me up, and when I am tired above I will shake my legs, and then do thou let me down."

The Black Rogue drew the cord, and he raised the Shifty Lad aloft off the earth, and at the end of a little blink the Shifty Lad shook his legs, and the Black Rogue let him down."

The Shifty Lad took the cord off his neck, and he said to the Black Rogue, "Thou thyself hast not ever tried anything that is so funny as hanging. If thou wouldst try once, thou wouldst have no more fear for hanging. I was shaking my legs for delight, and thou wouldst shake thy legs for delight too if thou wert aloft."

Said the Black Rogue, "I will try it too, so that I may know what it is like."

"Do," said the Shifty Lad; "and when thou art tired above, whistle and I will let thee down."

The Black Rogue put the cord about his neck, and the Shifty Lad drew him up aloft; and when the Shifty Lad found that the Black Rogue was aloft against the gallows, he said to him, "Now, when thou wantest to come down, whistle, and if thou art well pleased where thou art, shake thy legs."

When the Black Rogue was a little blink above, he began to shake his legs and to kick; and the Shifty Lad would say, "Oh! art thou not funny! art thou not funny! art thou not funny! When it seems to thee that thou art long enough above whistle."

But the Black Rogue has not whistled yet. The Shifty Lad tied the cord to the lower end of the tree of the gallows till the Black Rogue was dead; then he went where he was, and he took the money out of his pouch, and he said to him, "Now, since thou hast no longer any use for this money, I will take care of it for thee." And he went away, and he left the Black Rogue hanging there. Then he went home where was the house of the Black Rogue, and his wife asked where was his master?

The Shifty Lad said, "I left him where he was, upraised above the earth."

The wife of the Black Rogue asked and asked him about her man, till at last he told her, but he said to her, that he would marry her himself. When she heard that, she cried that the Shifty Lad had killed his master, and he was nothing but a thief. When the Shifty Lad heard that he fled. The chase was set after him; but he found means to go in hiding in a cave, and the chase went past him. He was in the cave all night, and the next day he went another way, and he found means to fly to Eirinn.

He reached the house of a wright, and he cried at the door, "Let me in."

"Who art thou?" said the wright.

"I am a good wright, if thou hast need of such," said the Shifty Lad.

The wright opened the door, and he let in the Shifty Lad, and the Shifty Lad began to work at carpentering along with the wright.

When the Shifty Lad was a day or two in their house, he gave a glance thither and a glance hither about the house, and he said, "O choin! what a poor house you have, and the king's store-house so near you."

"What of that," said the wright.

"It is," said the Shifty Lad, "that you might get plenty from the king's store-house if you yourselves were smart enough."

The wright and his wife would say, "They would put us in prison if we should begin at the like of that."

The Shifty Lad was always saying that they ought to break into the king's store-house, and they would find plenty in it; but the wright would not go with him; but the Shifty Lad took with him some of the tools of the wright, and he went himself and he broke into the king's store-house, and he took with him a load of the butter and of the cheese of the king, and he took it to the house of the wright. The things pleased the wife of the wright well, and she was willing that her own husband should go there the next night. The wright himself went with his lad the next night, and they got into the store-house of the king, and they took with them great loads of each thing that pleased them best of all that was within in the king's store-house.

But the king's people missed the butter and the cheese and the other things that had been taken out of the store-house, and they told the king how it had happened.

The king took the counsel of the Seanagal about the best way of catching the thieves and the counsel that the Seanagal gave them was that they should set a hogshead of soft pitch under the hole where they were coming in. That was done, and the next night the Shifty Lad and his master went to break into the king's storehouse.

The Shifty Lad put his master in before him, and the master went down into the soft pitch to his very middle, and he could not get out again. The Shifty Lad went down, and he put a foot on each of his master's shoulders, and he put out two loads of the king's butter and of the cheese at the hole; and at the last time when he was coming out, he swept the head off his master, and he took the head with him, and he left the trunk in the hogshead of pitch, and he went home with the butter and with the cheese, and he took home the head, and he buried it in the garden.

When the king's people went into the storehouse, they found a body without a head into the hogshead of pitch; but they could not make out who it was. They tried if they could find any one at all that could know him by the clothes, but his clothes were covered with pitch so that they could not make him out. The king asked the counsel of the Seanagal about it; and the counsel that the Seanagal gave was, that they should set the trunk aloft on the points of the spears of the soldiers, to be carried from town to town, to see if they could find any one at all that would take sorrow for it; or to try if they could hear any one that would make a painful cry when they should see it; or if they should not see (one crying) one that should seem about to make a painful cry when the soldiers should be going past with it. The body was taken out of the hogshead of pitch, and set on the points of the spears; and the soldiers were bearing it aloft on the points of their long wooden spears, and they were going from town to town with it; and when they were going past the house of the wright, the wright's wife made a tortured scream, and swift the Shifty Lad cut himself with the adze; and he kept saying to the wright's wife, "The cut is not so bad as thou thinkest."

The commander-in-chief, and his lot of soldiers, came in and they asked,

"What ailed the housewife?"

Said the Shifty Lad, "It is that I have just cut my foot with the adze, and she is afraid of blood;" and he would say to the wife of the wright, "Do not be so much afraid; it will heal sooner than thou thinkest."

The soldiers thought that the Shifty Lad was the wright, and that the wife whom they had was the wife of the Shifty Lad; and they went out, and they went from town to town; but they found no one besides, but the wife of the wright herself that made cry or scream when they were coming past her.

They took the body home to the king's house; and the king took another counsel from his Seanagal, and that was to hang the body to a tree in an open place, and soldiers to watch it that none should take it away, and the soldiers to be looking if any should come the way that should take pity or grief for it.

The Shifty Lad came past them, and he saw them; he went and he got a horse, and he put a keg of whisky on each side of the horse in a sack, and he went past the soldiers with it, as though he were hiding from them. The soldiers thought that it was so, that he had taken something away from them, or that he had something which he ought not to have; and some of them ran after him and they caught the old horse and the whisky; but the Shifty Lad fled, and he left the horse and the whisky with them. The soldiers took the horse and the kegs of whisky back to where the body was hanging against the mast. They looked what was in the kegs; and when they understood that it was whisky that was in them, they got a drinking cup, and they began drinking until at last every one of them was drunk, and they lay and they slept. When the Shifty Lad saw that, that the soldiers were laid down and asleep and drunk, he returned and he took the body off the mast. He set it crosswise on the horse's back, and he took it home; then he went and he buried the body in the garden where the head was.

When the soldiers awoke out of their sleep, the body was stolen away; they had for it but to go and tell it to the king. Then the king took the counsel of the Seanagal; and the Seanagal said to them, all that were in his presence, that his counsel to them was, to take out a great black pig that was there, and that they should go with her from town to town; and when they should come to any place where the body was buried, that she would root it up. They went and they got the black pig, and they were going from farm to farm with her, trying if they could find out where the body was buried. They went from house to house with her till at last they came to the house where the Shifty Lad and the wright's widow were dwelling. When they arrived they let the pig loose about the grounds. The Shifty Lad said that he himself was sure that thirst and hunger was on them; that they had better go into the house and that they would get meat and drink; and that they should let their weariness from off them, in the time when the pig should be seeking about his place.

They went in, and the Shifty Lad asked the wright's widow that she should set meat and drink before the men. The widow of the wright set meat and drink on the board, and she set it before them; and in the time while they were eating their meat, the Shifty Lad went out to see after the pig; and the pig had just hit upon the body in the garden; and the Shifty Lad went and he got a great knife and he cut the head off her, and he buried herself and her head beside the body of the wright in the garden.

When those who had the care of the pig came out, the pig was not to be seen. They asked the Shifty Lad if he had seen her; he said that he had seen (her), that her head was up and she was looking upwards, and going two or three steps now and again; and they went with great haste to the side where the Shifty Lad said that the pig had gone.

When the Shifty Lad found that they had gone out of sight, he set everything in such a way that they should not hit upon the pig. They on whom the care of the pig was laid went and they sought her every way that it was likely she might be. Then when they could not find her, they had nothing for it but to go to the king's house and tell how it had happened.

Then the counsel of the Seanagal was taken again; and the counsel that the Seanagal gave them was, that they should set their soldiers out about the country at free quarters; and at whatsoever place they should get pig's flesh, or in whatsoever place they should see pig's flesh, unless those people could show how they had got the pig's flesh that they might have, that those were the people who killed the pig, and that had done every evil that had been done.

The counsel of the Seanagal was taken, and the soldiers sent out to free quarters about the country; and there was a band of them in the house of the wright's widow where the Shifty Lad was. The wright's widow gave their supper to the soldiers, and some of the pig's flesh was made ready for them; and the soldiers were eating the pig's flesh, and praising it exceedingly. The Shifty Lad understood what was the matter, but he did not let on. The soldiers were set to lie out in the barn; and when they were asleep the Shifty Lad went out and he killed them. Then he went as fast as he could from house to house, where the soldiers were at free quarters, and he set the rumour afloat* amongst the people of the houses, that the soldiers had been sent out about the country to rise in the night and kill the people in their beds; and he found (means) to make the people of the country believe him, so that the people of each house killed all the soldiers that were asleep in their barns; and when the soldiers did not come home at the time they should, some went to see what had happened to them; and when they arrived, it was so that they found the soldiers dead in the barns where they had been asleep; and the people of each house denied that they knew how the soldiers had been put to death, or who had done it.

The people who were at the ransacking for the soldiers, went to the king's house, and they told how it had happened; then the king sent word for the Seanagal to get counsel from him; the Seanagal came, and the king told how it had happened, and the king asked counsel from him. This is the counsel that the Seanagal gave the king, that he should make a feast and a ball, and invite the people of the country; and if the man who did the evil should be there, that

* Cuir e an ceil.

he was the man who would be the boldest who would be there, and that he would ask the king's daughter herself to dance with him. The people were asked to the feast and the dance; and amongst the rest the Shifty Lad was asked. The people came to the feast, and amongst the rest came the Shifty Lad. When the feast was past, the dance began; and the Shifty Lad went and he asked the king's daughter to dance with him; and the Seanagal had a vial full of black stuff, and the Seanagal put a black dot of the stuff that was in the vial on the Shifty Lad. But it seemed to the king's daughter that her hair was not well enough in order, and she went to a side chamber to put it right; and the Shifty Lad went in with her; and when she looked in the glass, he also looked in it, and he saw the black dot that the Seanagal had put upon him. When they had danced till the tune of music was finished, the Shifty Lad went and he got a chance to steal the vial of the Seanagal from him unknown to him, and he put two black dots on the Seanagal, and one black dot on twenty other men besides, and he put the vial back again where he found it.

Between that and the end of another while, the Shifty Lad came again and he asked the king's daughter to dance. The king's daughter had a vial also, and she put a black dot on the face of the Shifty Lad; but the Shifty Lad got the vial whipped out of her pocket, unknown to her; and since there were two black dots on him, he put two dots on twenty other men in the company, and four black dots on the Seanagal. Then when the dancing was over, some were sent to see who was the man on whom were the two black dots, When they looked amongst the people, they found twenty men on whom there were two black dots, and there were four black dots on the Seanagal; and the Shifty Lad found (means) to go swiftly where the king's daughter was, and to slip the vial back again into her pocket. The Seanagal looked and he had his black vial; the king's daughter looked and she had her own vial; then the Seanagal and the king took counsel; and the last counsel that they made was that the king should come to the company, and say, that the man who had done every trick that had been done, must be exceedingly clever; if he would come forward and give himself up, that he should get the king's daughter to marry, and the one half of the kingdom while the king was alive, and the whole of the kingdom after the king's death. And every one of those who had the two black dots on their faces came and they said that it was they who had done every cleverness that had been done. Then the king and his high council went to try how the matter should be settled; and the matter which they settled was, that all the men who had the two black dots on their faces should be put together in a chamber, and they were to get a child, and the king's daughter was to give an apple to the child, and the child was to be put in where the men with the two black dots on their faces were seated and to whatsoever one the child should give the apple, that was the one who was to get the king's daughter.

That was done, and when the child went into the chamber in which the men were, the Shifty Lad had a shaving and a drone (sliseag us dranndan), and the child went and gave him the apple. Then the shaving and the drone were taken from the Shifty Lad, and he was seated in another place, and the apple was given to the child again; and he was taken out of the chamber, and sent in again to see to whom he would give the apple; and since the Shifty Lad had the shaving and the drone before, the child went where he was again, and he gave him the apple. Then the Shifty Lad got the king's daughter to marry.

And shortly after that the king's daughter and the Shifty Lad were taking a walk to Baile Cliabh; and when they were going over the bridge of Baile Cliabh, the Shifty Lad asked the king's daughter what was the name of that place; and the king's daughter told him that it was the bridge of Baile Cliabh, in Eirinn; and the Shifty Lad said—

"Well, then, many is the time that my mother said to me, that my end would be to be hanged at the bridge of Baile Cliabh, in Eirinn; and she made me that prophecy many a time when I might play her a trick."

And the king's daughter said, "Well then, if thou thyself shouldst choose to hang over the little side (wall) of the bridge, I will hold thee aloft a little space with my pocket napkin."

And they were at talk and fun about it; but at last it seemed to the Shifty Lad that he would do it for sport, and the king's daughter took out her pocket napkin, and the Shifty Lad went over the bridge, and he hung by the pocket napkin of the king's daughter as she let it over the little side (wall) of the bridge, and they were laughing to each other.

But the king's daughter heard a cry, "The king's castle is going on fire!" and she started, and she lost her hold of the napkin; and the Shifty Lad fell down, and his head struck against a stone, and the brain went out of him; and there was in the cry but the sport of children; and the king's daughter was obliged to go home a widow.

SGEULACHD A GHILLE CHARAICH MAC NA BANTRACH.

Bha uair eigeinn ann roimh so Bantrach, agus bha aona mhac aic. Thug i d à sgoil mhath, agùs bha i los gu 'n taghadh e ceaird air a shon fein, ach thubhairt esan, nach rachadh e a dh' ionnsaidh ealdhain air bith, ach gu 'm bitheadh e na mhearlach.

Thubhairt a mhathair ris, "Ma is è sin an ealdhain a tha thu a dol a thaghadh dhuit fein, is e is deireadh dhuit, a bhi air do chrochadh aig drochaid Bhaile-cliabh an Eirinn." Ach bu choma cò dhuibh, cha rachadh esan gu ealdhain air bith, ach gu a bhith ann na mhearlach. Agus bhitheadh a mhathair daonnan a deanamh fàisinneachd dà, gu 'm e bu deireadh dhàsan a bhith air a chrochadh aig drochaid Bhaile-cliabh an Eirinn. Latha do na laitheanan bha a Bhantrach a dol do 'n eaglais, a dh' eisdeachd searmoin, agus bha i ag iarraidh air a' ghille-charrach a mac e a dhol leatha, 's e a thoirt thairis do a dhroch stiùireanan, ach cha rachadh e leatha, ach thuirt e rithe, "Is e a chiad ealdhain air an cluimn thusa iomradh, an deigh dhuit tighinn a mach o 'n t-searmoin, an ealdhain gu 's an teid mise a rithis."

Dh fhalbh ise do 'n eaglais, 's i làn misnich an dùil gù 'n cluinneadh i rud-eiginn math. Dh' fhalbh esan 's chaidh e do bhad coille a bha dlùth do 'n eaglais, 's chaidh e 'm fallach ann an àite far am faiceadh e a mhathair, a nuair a thigeadh i a mach as an eaglais. Agus cho luath is a thainig i a mach, ghlaodh esan; "Mèirle, mèirle, mèirle." Sheall ise ma'n cuairt, ach cha b' urrainn di aithneachadh cia as a bha 'n guth a tighinn, 's dh' fhalbh i dachaidh. Ruith esan rathad ath-ghiorra, 's bha e aig an tigh air thoiseach oirre 's bha e na shuidhe a stigh taobh an teine tra a thainig i dachaidh. Dh' fharraid e di, cia-dé an sgeul a fhúair i? Thubhairt ise, nach d-fhuair i sgeul air bith, ach gu 'm b'e méirle, méirle, méirle, a' chiad chainnt a chual' i tra thainig i a mach as an eaglais. Thubhairt esan, gu 'm b'e sin an ealdhain a bhitheadh aigesan, s thubhairt ise mar a b' àbhaist di a ghradh, "Is e is deireadh dhuit a bhith air do chrochadh aig drochaid Bhaile-cliabh an Eirinn." An ath latha smuaintich a mhathair, bho nach deanadh nì air bith tuille gnothach le a mac, ach e a bhith ann na mhèirlach, gu 'm feuchadh i ri oide-ionnsaich math fhaotuinn dà. Agus chaidh i a dh' ionnsaidh gadaiche dubh Achalòine, meirleach anbharra seolta, a bha ann 'san àite sin. Agus ged a bha fios aca gu 'n robh e ri goid, cha robh iad a faotuinn doigh air bith air beireachd air. Dh' fharraid a' bhantrach do 'n ghadaiche dhubh an gabhadh e an gille-carrach a mac gus a ghadachd ionnsachadh dha. Thubhairt an gadaiche dubh, ma bha e 'na ghille tapaidh gu 'n gabhadh, agus ma bha doigh air mèirleach a dheanamh dheth, gu 'n deanadh esan e, agus chaidh cumhnant a dheanamh eadar an gadaiche dubh, a's an gille-carrach. Tra bha an gille-carrach mac na bantraich a deanamh deis gu dol chun a' ghaduiche dhuibh, bha a mhathair a toirt chomhairlean air, agus thuirt i ris. "Is ann an aghaidh mo thoil-sa a tha thu a' dol thun na mèirle, agus tha mi ag innse dhuit, gur è is deireadh dhuit a bhith air do chrochadh aig drochaid Bhaile-cliabh an Eirinn." Ach chaidh an gille carrach dachaidh thun a' ghadaiche dhuibh.

Bha an gadaiche dubh a tabhairt na h-uile foghlum a dh' fhaodadh e do 'n ghille-charrach air mèirle a dheanamh. Bhitheadh e ag innse dhà ma 'n t-seoltachd a dh' fheumadh e a dheanamh, gus an coram fhaotuinn air rud a ghoid. Agus tra bha leis a' ghadaiche dhubh, gu 'n robh an gille-carrach glé mhath air fhoghlum, gu e a bhith air a thoirt a mach leis, bhitheadh e ga thoirt a mach leis gu goid a dheanamh. Agus latha do na laithean sin thubhairt an gaduiche dubh, ri a ghille—

"Tha sinn gle fhada mar so, is fheudar duinn dol a dheanamh rudaiginn; tha tuathanach beartach dlùth dhuinn, agus tha mòran airgid aige 'na chiste, is e a cheannaich na bha do chrodh ri reic ann 'san duthaich, agus thug e chum na faidhir iad, 's chreic e iad, tha an t-airgoid aige 'na chiste, agus 'se so an t-am gu bhith aige, ma'n teid na daoine a phaidh air son an cuid cruidh, 's mur teid sinn a dh iarraidh an airgiod an ceart uair, tra a tha e cruinn ri cheile, cha'n fhaigh sinn an coram ciadna a rithis."

Bha an gille-carrach cho toileach ris fein. Dh' fhalbh iad chum an taigh 'us fhuair iad a stigh aig tighinn na h-oidhche, agus chaidh iad an aird air an fharadh, 's chaidh iad am fallach gu h-àrd ann an sin. Agus is è oidhche Shamhnadh a bha 'nn, agus chruinnich mòran do fheadhainn a stigh a ghleidheadh na Samhuinn gu cridheil mar a b' abhaist doibh. Shuidh iad comhla, agus bha iad a seinn oran, a 's ri aighear, agus a' losgadh nan cnò,* agus ri abhachd.

* One of the amusements which Highland people used to entertain themselves with, is what they call burning nuts on Hallow-eve, the last night of October. A party of young people would collect together in one house for to make merry; one of their amusements was, they would propose a marriage between some lad and lass, and they would name a nut for each of them. The two nuts would be placed beside each other in the fire. If the two nuts burned together, and blazed over each other, that was called a good omen; it was a sign that the party for whom the nuts was named were to be married yet, and live happy together; but if either of the nuts puffed, or flew away, that was a sign that the person for whom that nut was named was proud, and would not accept of the other party.

Bha an gille-carrach a gabhail fadail nach robh a chuideachd a sgaoileadh; dh' eirich e 's chaidh e sios do'n bhàthaich, 's dh fhuasgail e na naisg far amhaichean a chruidh, 's thill e 's chaidh e air an fharadh a rithis. Thòisich an crodh air purradh a cheile ann 'sa bhàthaich, 's air raoiceadh, ruidh na bha anns a chearnadh, a chumail a' chruidh o 'cheile gus an rachadh an ceangal a rithis. An tiom a bha iadsan a deanamh sin, chaidh an gille-carrach sios do 'n chearnadh, 's ghoid e leis na cno'n, 's chaidh e an àird air an fharadh a rithisd, agus luidh e air cùlamh a ghadaiche dhuibh.

Bha seiche mhòr leathraich aig cùlamh a ghadaiche dhuibh, 's bha snathad agus snathainn aig a ghille-charrach agus dh' fhuaigh e iomall còta a ghadaiche dhuibh, ris an t-seiche leathraich a bha aig a cùlamh, agus tra thainig muinntir an taighe air an ais do 'n chearnadh a rithisd, bha na cno'n aca air falbh, agus bha iad ag iarraidh nan cno'n, agus shaoil iad gu 'm b'e cuid-eiginn a thainig a stigh a dheanamh chleas orra, a thug air falbh na cno'n, agus shuidh iad aig taobh an teine gu sàmhach tosdach.

Thubhairt an gille-carrach ris a ghadaiche dhubh, "Cnacaidh mi cno."

"Cha chnac," thuirt an gadaiche-dubh, "cluinnidh iad thu 's theid beireachd oirnn."

Thubhairt an gille-carrach, "cha robh mi-fein riamh roimh oidhche Shamhnadh gu 'n chnò a chnacadh." Agus chnachd e te.

Chuala an fheadhainn a bha 'nan suidhe 's a chearnadh e, 's thubhairt iad, "Tha cuid-eiginn gu h-ard air an fharadh, a cnacadh nan cnò'n again, theid sinn agus beiridh sìnn orra."

Tra chuala an gadaiche—dubh sin, leum e far an fharaidh, 's ruith e a mach, 's an t-seiche an slaodadh ris. Theich an gadaiche-dubh 's muinntir an taighe as a dheigh, 's bha e astar mor o'n tigh ma'n d' fhuair e an t-seiche a reubadh deth agus a fàgail. Ach an tiom a bha muinntir an taighe a ruith a ghadaiche-dhuibh, thainig an gille-carrach a nuas fàr an fharaidh, chaidh e air feadh an taighe, dh' amais e air a chiste far an robh an t-òr 's an t-airgiod aig an tuathanach ga ghleidheadh dh' fhosgail e a chiste, 's thug e a mach aiste na builg ann 'san robh an t-airgiod a bha innte, agus thug e innte, agus thug e leis eallach do 'n aran 's do'n chàise, a's do na h-uile nì a b' fhearr na cheile a fhuair e a stigh. Agus bha esan air falbh, ma 'n d' thainig muinntir an taighe air an ais o bhith a ruith a ghadaiche-dhuibh.

Nuair a rainig an gadaiche-dubh dachaidh, 's nach robh nì air bith aige, thubhairt a bhean ris:—"Cia-mar a chaidh fairsleachadh ort air an turus so?"

An sin dh' innis an gadaiche-dubh a sgeul fein, agus bha fearg
mor air ris a ghille-charrach, 's e a boideachadh, gu 'n deanadh e
dioltas tra gheibheadh e coram air. Aig ceann uine ghoirid na
dheigh sin thainig an gille-carrach a stigh, agus eallach air.
Thubhairt bean a ghadaiche dhuibh, "Ach tha duil agam gur tusa
meirleach is fheàrr."

Cha dubhairt an gadaiche-dubh diog, gus gu'n do leig an gille-
carach fhaicinn na builg a bha aige lan do òr s do airgiod, an sin
thubhairt an gadaiche-dubh "Ach bu tù an gille tapaidh!"

Rinn iad dà leth air an òr, 's air an airgiod, 's fhuair an gadaiche
dubh an darna leth, agus an gille carrach an leth eile. Tra a chunnaic
bean a ghadaiche dhuibh an roinn a thainig oirre thubhairt i, "Is tu
fein am meirleach fiachail," s bha tuille meas aic air na dheigh sin
na bha aic air a ghadaiche-dhubh e fein."

Aig ceann beagan sheachdainnean na dheigh sin, bha banais gu
bhith ann sa coimhearsnachd agus b' è fasan na duthcha, tra
rachadh feadhainn a bhitheadh saoibhir a chuireadh, gu 'n cuireadh
iad tabhartas a thaobhaiginn a dh ionnsaidh muinntir na bainse.
Bha tuathanach beartach ann a chaidh a chuireadh, agus dh' iarr e
air a bhuachaille aige e a dhol ris a mhonadh, 's e a thoirt dachaidh
molt air son muinntir na bainse. Chaidh am buachaille ris a
mhonadh, 's fhuair e am molt 's bha e a dol dachaidh leis, 's e aige
air a dhruim, a nuair a bha e a dol seachad air tigh a ghadaiche
dhuibh. Thubhairt an gille carrach ri mhaighstir "Cia-dè an geall
a chuireas tu nach goid mì am molt far druim an fhir sin, ma 'n ruig
e an tigh fhathasd?" Thubhairt an gadaiche dubh, "Cuiridh mi geall
ciad marg nach urrainn duit, ciamar a ghoideadh tu an rud a tha
air a dhruim?"

"Cia air bhith mar a nì mi e feuchaidh mi ris," orsa an gille-carrach.

"Ma ta ma nì thu a, thuirt an gadaiche dubh, bheir mise dhuit
ciad marg." "Is bargain e," orsa an gille carrach, a's le sin dh' fhalbh
e an deigh a bhuachaille. Bha aig a bhuachaille ri dol troimh choille,
agus ghabh an gille carrach falacha-talmhainte air, gus gu'n d'
fhuair e air thoiseach air, agus shalaich e 'na bhròig, 's chuir e a
bhròg air an rathad air thoiseach air a buachaille, 's chaidh e fein
am fallach. An uair a thainig am buachaille air aghaidh, a's a
chunnaic e a bhròg thubhairt e, "Ach tha thu salach 's ged do thà,
na 'm bitheadh do leth-bhreac ann, ghlanainn thu," 's chaidh e
seachad.

Thog an gille carrach a' bhròg, 's ruidh e ma 'n cuairt, 's bha e
air thoiseach air a' bhuachaille, 's chuir e bhròg eile air an rathad

air thoiseach air. Thubhairt e ris fhein, "ach tha ann an sin leth-bhreac na bròige salaiche."

Chuir e am molt air làr, agus thubhairt e ris-fein, "Tillidh mi an nis 's ghoibh mi a bhrog shalach, 's glanaidh mi i, 's bithidh dà bhroig mhath agam air son mo shaoireach," 's ruith e gu luath air ais. Ruith an gille-carrach gu luath 's ghoid e leis am molt, 's thug e leis an da bhroig, 's chaidh e dachaidh chum a mhaighistir, 's fhuair e a chiad marg o a mhaighistir.

Chaidh am buachaille dachaidh, 's dh' innis e do a mhaighistir fein mar a thachair dà. Throid a mhaighistir ris a bhuachaille. An ath latha chuir an tuathanach a rithis ris a mhonadh e a dhiarraidh eirionnach an àite a mhuilt a chaill e. Dh' fhalbh am buachaille ris a mhonadh, 's fhuair e greim air eirionnach, cheangail se e, chuir e air a dhruim e, 's dh-fhalbh e gu dol dachaidh leis. Chunnaic an gille carrach e, 's chaidh e do'n choille, 's bha e an sin air thoiseach air a bhuachaille, 's chaidh e am falach, 's thòisich e air mèilich coltach ris a' mholt. Shaoil am buachaille gu 'm b'e am molt a bha ann, 's chuir e deth an t-eirionnach, 's dh' fhàg se aig taobh an rathaid e, 's chaidh e a dh iarraidh a mhuilt. An tiom a bha am buachaille ag iarraidh a' mhoilt' chaidh an gille carrach 's ghoid e leis an t-eirionnach, 's dh' fhàg se aig taobh an rathaid e, 's chaidh e dachaidh leis chum a ghadaiche-dhuibh. Tra chaidh am buachaille air ais far an d' fhàg e an t-eirionnach, bha an t-eirionnach air falbh, cha robh an t-eirionnach ann, dh' iarr e air son an eirionnach ann. Dh' iarr e air son an eirionnach, 's a nuair nach b'urrainn d'a an t-eirionnach fhaotuinn, chaidh e dachaidh 's dh' innis e do a mhaighistir mar a dh' eirich da, agus throid a mhaighistir ris, ach cha robh comas air. An ath latha dh' iarr an tuathanach air a bhuachaille aige, e a dhol ris a mhonadh, agus e a thoirt dachaidh damh, e a bhith cinnteach nach cailleadh se e. Chaidh am buachaille ris a mhonadh, 's fhuair e damh math reamhar, 's bha e ga iomain dachaidh. Chunnaic an gille carrach e, s' thubhairt e ris a' ghadaiche-dhubh, "Tiugainn, 's theid sinn a dh fheuchainn ris an damh a ghoid o'n bhuachaille, tra a bhitheas e a dol troimh an choille leis."

Dh' fhalbh an gadaiche-dubh as an gille-carrach do 'n choille air thoiseach air a bhuachaille. Agus tra bha am buachaille a dol troimh an choille leis an damh, bha an gadaiche dubh an aon àite, s è a mèailich, 's an gille-carrach an àite è eile, s è a migeartaich coltach ri gabhar. Chula am buachaille iad, 's shaoil e gu 'm faigheadh e am molt, agus an t-eirionnach a rithisd. Cheangail e an damh ri craoibh, 's chaidh e air feadh na coille, ag iarraidh a' mhuilt agus

an eirionnaich. 'S dh' iarr e iad gus gus 'n robh e sgìth. An tiomsa
bha esan ag iarraidh a mhuilt 's an eirionnaich, chaidh an gille-carach 's ghiod e leis an damh 's thug e leis dachaidh e chum tigh a
ghadaiche dhuibh. Chaidh an gadaiche dubh dachaidh as a dheigh,
's mharbh iad an damh, 's chuir iad am fallach e, 's bha maragan
math aig bean a ghadaiche dhuibh an oidhche sin. Tra thainig am
buachaille air ais thun na craoibh, far an d' fhàg e an damh
ceangailte, cha robh an damh ann. Dh' aithnich e gu 'n deach an
damh a ghoid, chaidh e dachaidh 's dh' innis e do a mhaighistir mar
a thachair, agus throid a mhaighistir ris, ach cha robh comas air.

An ath latha dh' iarr a mhaighistir air a bhuachaille aige e a dhol
ris a mhonadh, 's e a thoirt dachaidh molt, 's gu 'n e ga leigidh far
a dhruim idir, gus gu 'n tigeadh e dachaidh, cia air bith a chiteadh
na a chluinneadh e. Dh' fhalbh am buachaille, 's chaidh e ris a
mhonadh, 's fhuair e am molt, 's chaidh aige air a mholt sin a thoirt
dachaidh.

Ghabh an gadaiche-dubh 's an gille-carrach air an aghaidh ri goid
gus gu 'n robh moran airgid aca, agus smuaintich iad gu 'm b' fhearr
doibh dròbh a cheannach, 's dol chum faidhir leo gu'n creic, agus
gu 'n saoileadh feadhainn gu'm b'ann air an dròbhaireachd a rinn
iad an t-airgiod. Chaidh an dithis agus cheannaich iad drobh mor
cruidh. Agus chaidh iad a dh' ionnsaidh faidhir a bha fad air astar
leo. Chreic iad an dròbh, 's fhuair iad an t-airgiod air an son, 's dh'
fhalbh iad gu dol dachaidh. Tra a bha iad air an rathad, chunnaic
iad croich air mullach cnoic agus thubhairt an gille-carach ris a'
ghadaiche dhubh, "Tiugainn an àird is gu 'm faic sin a' chroich,
tha feadhainn ag ràdh, gur h-i a' chroich is deireadh do na mèirlich
co-dhiubh."

Chaidh iad an àird far an robh a' chroich, 's bha iad a' sealtuinn
ma 'n-cuairt oirre. Thubhairt an gille-carach, "Nach fhaodamaid
fheuchainn cia-dé an seòrsa bàis a tha ann sa' chròchadh, gu 'm bi
fios againn cia-dé a a tha romhainn ma bheirear oirnn ri gadachd;
feuchaidh mi-fein an toiseach e."

Chuir an gille-carach an còrd ma amhaich fein, 's thubhairt e ris
a' ghadaiche-dhubh, "So tarruing an àird mi, 's tra bhitheas mi sgìth
gu h-àrd crathaidh mi mo chas'n, 's an sin leig thusa a nuas mi."

Tharruing an gadaiche-dubh an còrd, 's thog e an gille-carach an
àird far an talmhainte, agus aig ceann seal beag chrath an gille
carach a chas'n, leig an gadaiche-dubh a nuas e.

Chuir an gille carach an còrd far amhaich, 's thubhairt e ris a'
ghadaiche-dhubh, "Cha d' fheuch thu-fhein nì riamh, a tha cho
eibhinn ris a' chrochadh, na 'm feuchadh tu aon uair e cha

bhitheadh eagal ort romh 'n chrochadh tuille, bha mise a crathaidh mo chasan leis an a' oibhinneas 's chrathadh tusa do chasan leis an aoibhneas cuideachd na 'm bitheadh tu gu h-ard."

Thuirt an gadaiche dubh, "Feuchaidh mise e cuideachd, 's gu 'm bith fios agam co ris a's coltach e."

"Dean," orsa gille-carach, " 's tra a bhitheas tu sgìth gu h-ard, dean fead 's leigidh mise an nuas thu."

Chuir an gadaiche-dubh an còrd ma amhaich, 's tharruing an gille-carach an àird e, 's tra fhuair an gille-carach gu 'n robh an gadaiche-dubh gu h-ard ris a' chroich, thuirt e ris, "An nis tra bhitheas tu ag iarraidh a nuas dean fead, 's, ma tha thu toilichte far am bheil thu, crath do chas'n."

Tra a bha an gadaiche dubh seal beag gu h-àrd, thòisich e air crathadh a chasan, 's air breabadh, 's theireadh an gille-carach, "O! nach aighearach thu, nach aighearach thu. O, nach aighearach thu, tra bhithis leat gu 'm bheil thu glé fhada gu h-àrd dean fead."

Ach cha do rinn an gadaiche-dubh fead fhathast; cheangail an gille-carach an còrd ri iochdar crann na croiche, gus gu 'n robh an gadaiche-dubh marbh. An sin, chaidh an gille-carach far an robh e, 's thug e as a phòc an t-airgiod, 's thubhairt se ris, "An nis bho nach eil feum agadsa air an airgiod so na is faide, gabhaidh mise cùram deth air do shon." 'S dh' fhalbh e 's dh fhag e an gadaiche-dubh, a crochadh ann an sin. An sin chaidh e dachaidh far an robh tigh a ghadaiche dhuibh, 's dh' fharraid bean a ghadaiche-duibh deth, c'aite an robh a mhaighistir? Thuirt an gille-carach, "Dh' fhàg mise e far an robh e air ardachadh os-ceann an talaimh." Dh' fharraid, agus dh' fharraid bean a' ghadaiche deth ma dèidhinn a fir, gus ma dheireadh gu 'n d' innis e d' i, ach thuirt e rithe gu 'm pòsadh e-fhein i. Tra chuala ise sin ghlaodh i gu 'n do mharbh an gille-carach a mhaighistir is nach robh ann ach meàrlach. Tra chuala an gille-carach sin theich e. Chaidh an toir a chuir air a dheigh, ach fhuair esan dol am falach ann an uaimh, 's chaidh an tòir seachad air. Bha e 'san uaimh fad na h-oidhche, agus an ath latha chaidh se rathad eile, 's fhuair e teicheadh do dh' Eirinn.

Rainig e tigh saoir, 's ghlaodh se aig an dorus, "Leigibh a stigh mi."

"Co thusa?" orsa an saor.

"Thà saor math, ma tha a leithid a dhìth ort," orsa an gille carach.

Dh' fhosgail an saor an dorus 's leig e a stigh an gille-carach, 's thòisich an gille-carach air obair air an t-saorsaineachd comhla ris an t-saor.

Tra a bha an gille-carach latha na dhà anns an tigh aca, thug e sealladh a null, 's sealladh an nall air feadh an taighe 's thubhairt e, "O chòin is bochd an tigh agaibh a's tigh-taisg an righ cho dluth oirbh."

"Cia-dé dheth sin?" orsa an saor.

"Thà," arsa an gille carach, "gu 'm faodadh sibh am pailteas fhaotuinn as tigh stòir an righ na 'm bitheadh sibh fein glé thapaidh."

Theireadh an saor 's a bhean, "Chuireadh iad ann priosan sinn na 'n tòisicheadh sinn air a leithid sin."

Bha an gille-carach daonnan ag radh gu 'm bu chòirr dòibh dol a bhristeadh a stigh do thigh-taisg an righ, 's gu 'm faigheadh iad am pailteas ann, ach cha rachadh an saor leis. Ach thug an gille-carach leis pairt do dh' acfhuinn an t-saoir, a's chaidh e fhein is bhrisd e a stigh do thigh-taisg an righ, 's thug e leis ealach do 'n im 's do 'n chàise aig an righ, 's thug e do thigh an t-saoir e. Thaitinn na gnothaichen gu math ri bean an t-saoir, 's bha i toileach gu 'n rachadh am fear aic' e fhein ann an ath oidhche. Chaidh an saor e-fhein le a ghille an ath oidhche, 's fhuair iad a stigh do thigh-taisg an righ, 's thug iad leo eallachan mòra dò gach nì a b'fhearr a thaitinn riu do na bha stigh ann an tigh taisg an righ. Ach dh' ionndrainn muinntir an righ an t-im 's an càise, 's na rudan eile a chaidh a thoirt as an tigh-thaisg, 's dh' innis iad do 'n righ mar a thachair.

Ghabh an righ comhairle an t-seanaghail ma 'n doigh a b' fhearr gu beireachd air na mèirleich. Agus is è a chomhairle a thug an seanghall orra, iad a chuir togsaid làn do phic bhog fo'n toll far an robh iad a' tighinn a stigh. Chaidh sin a dheanamh. Agus an ath oidhche chaidh an gille-carach 's a mhaighistir a bhrisdeadh a stigh do thigh-taisg an righ. Chuir an gille-carrach a mhaighistir a stigh air thoiseach air, agus chaidh am maighistir sios anns a' phic bhog gu a theis-meadhion, 's cha n fhaigheadh e as a righisd. Chaidh an gille carach sios, 's chuir e cas air gach gualann aig a mhaighistir, 's chuir e a mach dà eallach do 'n chàise aig an righ air an toll, 's an uair ma dheireadh tra a bha e a tighinn a mach sgiud e an ceann far a mhaighistir, 's thug e leis an ceann, 's dh fhàg e a cholunn anns an togsaid phic, a's chaidh e dachaich leis an im 's leis a' chàise, agus thug e dachaidh an ceann, agus dh' adhlaic e anns a ghàrradh e.

Tra a chaidh muinntir an righ a stigh do 'n tigh-thaisg fhuair iad colunn gu 'n cheann anns an togsaid phic. Ach cha b' urrainn doibh aithneachadh cò é. Dh' fheuch iad am faigheadh iad h-aon air bith a dh' aithneachadh air aodach e, ach bha aodach comhdaichte le pic, air doigh is nach b' urrainn doibh aithneachadh. Dh fharraid an righ comhairle an t-sheanghal ma dheidhinn. Agus is e a chomhairle a thug an seanaghall orra iad a chuir na coluinn an aird air bharr shleaghan, 's na saighdearan gu a giullan o bhaile gu baile, a sheall am faiceadh iad h-aon air bith a ghabhadh truadhas deth, na a dh' fheuchainn an cluinneadh iad a h-aon air bith a dheanamh glaodh gointe tra chithcadh iad é, na ged nach faiceadh, gu m bitheadh iad ealamh gu glaodh gointe a dheanamh, tra bhitheadh na saighdearan a dol seachad leis. Chaidh a choluinn a thoirt as an togsaid phic, 's a cuir air bharr nan sleaghan, 's bha na saighdearan g'a ghiùlan an aird air bharr nan sleaghan fada crannach aca, 's iad a dol o bhaile gu baile leis. Agus tra bha iad a dol seach tigh an t-saoir, rinn bean an t-saoir sgreuch ghointe, agus ghrad ghearr an gille-carach e-fein leis an tàl, 's theireadh e ri bean an t-saoir, "Cha 'n 'eil an gearradh cho dona is a tha thu a smuainteachadh."

Thainig an ceannard 's cuid do na saighdearan a stigh agus dh' fharraid iad, "Cia dé a dh' aithrich bean an taighe." Thubhairt an gille-carach, "Thà gu 'm bheil mise air gearradh mo choise leis an tàl, agus tha eagal aice romh fhuil." Agus theiridh e ri bean an t-saoir, "Na bitheadh na h-uibhir eagail ort, leigheisidh e na is luaith na tha thu a smaointeachadh."

Shaoil na saighdearan gu 'm b'e an gille-carach an saor, agus gu 'm e a bhean a bha aig an t-saor bean a ghille-charaich, agus dh' fhabh iad a mach, 's chaidh iad o bhaile gu baile, ach cha d' fhuair iad a h-aon tuille, ach banntrach an t-saoir i fhein a rinn glaodh na sgreuch tra a bha iad a tighinn seachad orra.

Thug iad a cholunn dachaidh chum tigh an righ. Agus ghabh an righ comhairle eile on t-seanaghail aige, 's b'e in a cholunn a chrochadh ri crann ann an àite follaiseach, agus saighdearan a chuir a thabhairt aire air nach tugadh gin air falbh e, as na saighdearean gu a bhith a shealltinn an tigeadh feadhainn air bith an rathad a ghabhadh truaigheas na doilghios deth.

Thainig an gille-carach seachad orra, agus chunnaic se iad, chaidh e agus fhuair e each, agus chuir e buideal uisge-bheatha air gach taobh do 'n each, ann an sachd, 's chaidh e seach na saighdearan leis, 's e mar gu 'm bitheadh e a' fuireachd am falach orra. Shaoil na saighdearan gu 'm b' ann a thug se rudaiginn air falbh orra, na gu 'n robh rudaiginn aige nach bu chòir d'a a bhith aige, agus ruith cuid diubh air a dheigh, 's bheir iad air an t-seann each s air an uisge-bheatha, ach theich an gille-carach, 's dh' fhàg e an seann each 's an t uisge-beatha aca.

Thug na saighdearan an t each 's na buideil uisge-bheath' air ais far an robh a' cholunn an crochadh ris a' chrann. Sheall iad cia-dé a bha anns na buideil, 's tra thuig iad gur e uisge-beatha a bha ann fhuair iad còrn, 's thòisich iad air òl, gus ma dheireadh, gu 'n robh na h-uile h-aon diubh air mhisg, 's luidh 's chaidil iad. Tra chunnaic an gille-carach gu 'n robh na saighdearean, 'nan luidh 's nan cadal air a mhisg, thill e 's thug e a nuas a' cholunn fàr a' chroinn, chuir e crosgach air druim an eich e 's thug e dachaidh e, chaidh e an sin agus dh' adhlaic e a' cholunn anns a ghàradh far an robh an ceann.

Tra a dhùisg na saighdearan as an cadal, bha a cholunn air a goid air falbh. Cha robh aca air ach dol 's innse do 'n righ. An sin ghabh an righ comhairle an t-seanaghal. Agus thubhairt an seanaghal riutha, na bha anns an lathair, gu 'm b'-e a chomhairle doibh, iad a thoirt a mach muc mhòr dhubh a bha an siod, a iad a dh' fhalbh leatha o bhaile gu baile, agus tra thigeadh iad thun an àite far am bitheadh a' cholunn adhlaicte, gu 'm buraicheadh i an àird é. Chaidh iad 's fhuair iad a mhuc dhubh, 's bha iad a dol o bhaile gu baile leatha, a dh' feuchainn am faigheadh i am mach caite an robh a' cholunn air a h-adhlac. Chaidh iad o' thigh gu tigh leatha, gus ma dheìreadh gu'n d' thainig iad gus an tigh far an robh an gille-carach agus banntrach an t-saoir a chomhnuich. A nuair a rainig iad, leig iad a mhuc mar sgaoil air feadh an talmhuinn. Thubhairt an gille-carach riutha, gu 'n robh e-fein cinnteach gu 'm bitheadh paghadh 's acras orra, gu 'm b' fhearr doibh dol a stigh do 'n tigh, 's gu 'm faigheadh iad biadh 's deoch, 's iad a leigeil an sgìtheas dhiubh, an tiom a bhitheadh a mhuc ag iarraidh ma thimchioll an àite aige-san. Chaidh iadsan a stigh, 's dh' iarr an gille-carach air bantrach an t-saoir i a chur biadh 's deoch air beulamh nan daoine. Chuir bantrach an t-saoir biadh 's deoch air bòrd, 's chuir i air am beulamh e, 's an tiom a bha iadsan ag itheadh am biadh, chaidh an gille-carach a mach a shealltuinn an deigh na muice, 's bha a mhuc air amas air a choluinn anns a ghàradh, 's chaidh an gille-carach agus fhuair e sgian mhòr, agus ghearr e an ceann di, agus dh' adhlaic e i-fein a 's a ceann, lamh-ris a choluinn aig an t-saor anns a ghàrradh. Tra a thainig an fheadhainn air an robh cùram na muic' a mach, cha robh a mhuc ri fhaicinn. Dh' fharraid iad do 'n ghille-charach am faca e i. Thubhairt esan gu 'm faca, gu 'n robh a ceann an àird agus i ag amharc suas, agus a dol da na tri a cheumannan an dràsda is a rithisd. Agus dh' fhalbh iadsan le cabhaig mhòir, an taobh a thubhairt an gille-carach a chaidh a' mhuc. Tra fhuair an gille-carach gu 'n deach iadsan as an t-sealladh, chuir e gach nì air doigh nach amaiseadh iadsan air a mhuic. Chaidh an fheadhainn air an robh curam na muic e agus dh

iarr iad i na h-uile rathad anns am bu coltach i a bhith. An sin tra
nach b' urrainn doibh a faotuinn, cha robh aca air ach dol gu tigh
an righ, agus innse mar a thachair.

An sin chaidh comhairle an t-seanaghail a ghabhail a rithisd.
Agus is e a' chomhairle a thug an seanaghal orra, iad a chuir nan
saighdeirean a mach air feadh na duthcha air cheithearnan, agus
cia aite air bith am faigheadh iad muic-fheoil, na cia aite air bith
am faiceadh iad muic-fheoil; mar b'-urrainn da n fheadhainn sin, a
leigeadh fhaicinn cia mar a fhuair iad a mhuic-fheoil a bhitheadh
aca, gu 'm b' iad sin an fheadhainn a mharbh a mhuc 's a rinn na
h-uile cron a chaidh a dheanamh. Chaidh comhairle an t-seanaghail
a ghabhail 's na saighdearan a chur a mach air cheithearnan air
feadh na duthcha, 's bha bhuidheann diubh ann an tigh banntrach
an t-saoir far an robh an gille-carach. Thug banntrach an t-saoir an
t-suipeair do na saighdearan, 's bha cuid do 'n mhuic-fheoil air a
deanamh deas doibh, agus bha na saighdearan ag itheadh na
mhuic-fheoil, agus ga sàr mholadh. Thuig an gille-carach cia-dé a
bha air an aire, ach cha do leig e air. Chaidh na saighdearan a chuir
a luidh a mach anns an t-sabhal, agus tra bha iad 'nan cadal, chaidh
an gille-carach a mach agus mharbh se iad. An sin chaidh e cho
luath as a b' urrainn da o thigh gu tigh far an robh na saighdeirean
air cheithearnan, agus chuir e an céill do mhuinntir nan taighean,
gu 'm b' ann a chaidh na saighdearan a chuir a mach air feagh na
duthcha, gu iad a dh'eiridh air feadh na h-oidhche, agus an sluagh
a mharbhadh anns na leapaichean aca, agus fhuair e a thoirt air
muinntir na duthcha chreidsinn gun do mharbh muinntir gach
tighe na bha do shaighdeirean 'nan cadal anns na sabhailean aca.
Agus an uair nach d' thainig na saighdeirean dachaidh aig an tiom
bu chòir doibh, chaidh feadhainn a shealltuinn cia-dé a thainig
riutha. Agus tra rainig iadsan is ann a fhuair iad na saighdeirean
marbh anns na saibhlean, far an robh iad 'nan cadal. Agus dh
aicheidh muinntir gach tighe gu 'n robh fios aca cia mar a chaidh
na saighdeirean a chur gu bàs, na cò a rinn e.

Chaidh na daoine a bha ris an rannsachadh air son nan
saighdeirean gu tigh an righ, agus dh' innis iad mar a thachair. An
sin chuir an righ fios air an t-seanaghal, a dh' fhaotuinn comhairle
uaidh. Thainig an seanaghal, agus dhinnis an righ dhà mar a
thachair, agus dh' iarr an righ comhairle air. Agus is e a chomhairle
a thug an seanaghal air an righ, e a dheanamh cuirm agus iob-dan-
nsa (a ball) 's e chuireadh sluagh na duthcha, agus nam bitheadh
am fear a rinn an cron an sin, gu 'm b'e am e fear bu dana a bithidh
an sin, agus gun iarradh e nighean an righ fein a dhannsa leis.

Chaidh an sluagh iarraidh a chum na cuirm, 's an dannsaidh. Agus
a measg chaich chaidh an gille carach iarraidh. Thainig an sluagh
a chum na cuirm, agus a measg chaich thainig an gille-carach. Tra
a bha a' chuirm seachad thòisich an dannsa, agus chaidh an
ghille-carach is dh' iarr e nighean an righ gu dannsa leis, agus bha
searrag làn do rudh dubh aig an t-seanaghal, agus chuir an
seanaghal ball dubh de'n rud a bha anns an t-searrag air a ghille-
charach, ach bha le nighean an righ nach robh a flat glé mhath ann
an òrdugh, 's chaidh i do sheòmar taobhaidh gus a chuir ceart, agus
chaidh an gille-carach a stigh leatha, 's tra sheall ise anns a ghloine
sheall easan cuideachd ann, 's chunnaic e am ball dubh a chuir an
seanaghal air. Tra dhannsiad gus an robh am port ciuil seachad
chaidh an gille carach agus fhuair e cothrom air an t-searag aig an
t-seanaghall a ghoid uaidh gun fhios d'a, agus chuìr esan da bhall
dubh air an t sheanaghal, agus aon a bhall dubh air fichead fear eile
g'a thuile, 's chuir e an t-shearag air ais a rithis far an d' fhuair se i.
Eadar sin 's ceann a ghreis, thainig an gille-carach a rithis 's dh' iarr
e nighean an righ gu dannsa. Bha searag aig nighean an righ
cuideachd, 's chuir i ball dubh air aodann a ghille-charaich ach
fhuair an gille-carach an t-searag a thiulpa as a poca gu 'n fhios di,
agus bho 'n a bha dà bhall aire-san, chuir e da bhall air fichead fear
eile anns a chuideachd, agus ceithir buill dhubh air an t-seanaghal.
An sin tra a bha an dannsa seachad, chaidh feadhainn a chuir a dh'
fhaicin cò e am fear air an robh an dà bhall dhubh. Tra sheall iadsan
air feadh an t-sluaigh fhuair iad fichead fear, air an robh da bhall
dhubh, agus bha ceithir buill dhubh, air an t-seanaghal, 's fhuair an
gille-carach ealadh far an robh nighean an righ, agus an t-searag a
thiulpa na poca a rithis. Sheall an seanaghal agus bha searagan
diubh aige, sheall nighean an righ 's bha a searaig fein aicse, an sin
ghabh an seanaghal a's an righ comhairle, agus is e a chomhairle
sinn a rinn iad, an righ a thighinn do 'n chuideachd, agus e a ghradh
gu 'm b' anabharra tapaidh a dh fheumadh am fear a rinn na h-uile
cleas a chaidh a dheanamh a bhith, na n tigeadh e air aghaidh s e
fein a thoirt suas, gu 'm faighidh e nighean an righ ri phòsadh agus
dàrna leth na rioghachd an fheadh is a bhithidh an an righ beò, agus
an t iomalain do n rioghachd an deigh bàs an righ. Agus thainig na
h-uile gin do n fheadhainn aig an robh an da bhall dhubh air an
aodann, agus thubhairt iad gu'm b' iadsan a rinn na h-uile tapadh
a chaidh a dheanamh. An sin chaidh an righ 's an àrd chomhairle,
a dh' fheuchainn cia-mar a ghabhadh a chuis socrachadh, agus is è
a chuis a shocruich iad, na h-uile fear aig an robh an da bhall dubh
air an aodann a chuir comhla ann an seomar, agus bha iad gu pàisde

fhaotuinn, agus bha nighean an righ gus ubhall a thoirt do 'n phàisde agus bha am pàisde gus a chuir a stigh far an robh na fir aig an robh na buill dhubh air an aodann, nan suidh, agus ge b'è h-aon air bith do 'n tugadh am pàisde an t-ubhall, b'e sin an t-aon a bha gus nighean an righ fhaotuinn.

Chaidh sin a dheanamh, agus tra chaidh am pàisde a chuir a stigh do 'n t seomar anns an robh na fir, bha sliseag 's dranndan aig a ghille-charrach 's chaidh am paisde 's thug se an t-ubhall d'a. Chaidh an sin an t-sliseag 's an dranndan, a thoirt o 'n gille-charach agus a chuir na shuidh ann an àite eile, agus chaidh an t-ubhall a thoirt do 'n phàisde a rithis, agus a thoirt a mach as am t-seomar, 's a chuir a stigh a rithis a sheall cò dh'à a bheiridh e an t-ubhall, agus fun a bha an t sliseag 's an dranndan aig a ghille-charach roimh, chaidh am pàisde far an robh e a rithis, s thug se dh à an t-ubhall. An sin fhuair an gille-carach nighean an righ ri phòsadh.

Agus goirid na dheigh sin bha nighean an righ 's an gille-carach a ghabhail sràide do Bhaile-cliabh, agus a nuair a bha iad a dol thairis air drochaid Bhaile-chiabh, dh' fharraid an gille carach de nighean an righ, cia ainm a bha air an aite sin, agus dh innis, nighean an righ gun robh drochaidh Baile-claibh ann an Eirinn, agus thubhairt an gille-carach—

"Ma ta is tric a thubhairt mo mhathair riumsa gu am bu e bu deireadh dhomh a bhith rir mo chrochadh aig drochaid Bhaile-cliabh an Eirinn, 's rinn i an fhàisineachd sin domh iomadh uair, tra bhithinn a deanamh phrat oirre."

Agus thubhairt nighean an righ, "Mata mo shanntaich thu fein crochadh thairis air taobhann an drochaid, cumaidh mise an àird thu tacan beag le mo napaigean poca."

Agus bha iad ri cainnt 's ri aighear ma deidhinn, ach ma-dheireadh bha leis a ghille-charach gu 'n deanadh se e, air son abhachd, agus thug nighean an righ a mach a neapaigean poca, agus chaidh an gille-carach thair an drochaid, agus chroch e ri neapaignean poca nighean an righ, 's i ga leigeadh fhein thairis air taobhan na drochaid, 's iad a gairichdeich ri cheile.

Ach chuala nighean an righ eubh, "Tha caisteal an righ a dol ri-theine," agus chlisg i, agus chaill i a greim air an neapaigean agus thuit an gille-carach sios, agus bhuail a cheann ri cloich, 's chaidh an eanchainn as, 's cha robh anns an eubh ach fàlrasg claoine 's b' eiginn do nighean an righ dol dachaidh na banntraich.

From Kate Macfarlane, in or near the year 1810; A. Campbell, Roseneath, 1860; and J. M'Nair, Clachaig, 1860.

Some incidents in this story I have known as long as I can remember. They used to be told me as a child by John Campbell, piper. Some of them were told me in 1859 by John Mackenzie at Inverary, who said they were part of a long story of which he could not repeat the rest. Others are alluded to in the Sutherland collection as known in that county. The version given came to me with the pedigree given above, and is unaltered, except in orthography and punctuation here and there.

It may be compared with a very great many stories in many languages, but I know none exactly like it. (See note on No. 40, vol. ii.)

Some of the incidents are very like part of the story of Rampsintus (Rawlinson's Herodotus, vol. ii. p. 191), which were told to Herodotus more than two thousand years ago by priests in Egypt, and the most natural conclusion to arrive at is, that these incidents have been spread amongst the people by those members of their families who study the classics at the Scotch universities, and who might well repeat what they had learned over a winter fire in their father's cottages, as their share of a night's entertainment.

But the incidents of this story, which resemble the classical tale, are associated with a great many other incidents which are *not* in Herodotus. Some of these have a resemblance to incidents in the Norse story of "The Master Thief;" and, according to Mr. Dasent's introduction, these have a resemblance to Sanscrit stories, which are not within my reading. They have a relation to Italian stories in Straparola, and, according to a note in Rawlinson's Herodotus, the story of Rampsintus "has been repeated in the Pecorone of Ser Giovanni, a Florentine of the fourteenth century, who substitutes a Doge of Venice for the king."

I am told that the barrel of pitch and the marks on the men are introduced into an old German story; but there are several incidents such as that of the pig which was to discover the dead body, as pigs now do truffles, and the apple which as usual is mystical, which so far as I know are in Gaelic only.

On the whole, then, there seems to me nothing for it but to admit this to be the Gaelic version of a popular tale, traditionally preserved for ages, altering as times roll on, and suiting itself to the manners of the narrators of the time.

To suppose it to be derived from books is to suppose that these books have all been read at some time so widely in Scotland as to have become known to the labouring population who speak Gaelic, and so long ago as to have been forgotten by the instructed, who speak English and study foreign languages.

Either this is a traditional popular tale, or learning must have been much more widely spread in the west at some former period than it is at present.

 My own opinion is that the tale is traditional, but there is room enough for speculation. On the 25th and 27th of August, I heard parts of the story told by Dewar, and MacNair, and John Mackenzie. Hector Urquhart told me that his father used to tell it in Ross-shire when he was a child. In his version, the storehouse was a treasury full of gold and silver, and the entrance a loose stone in the wall; the man was caught in "CEP," a gin for catching foxes. The pig was a hungry boar, and the lad killed him with an arrow. Even John the tinker, who was present, knew the story, though not well enough to repeat it. It is manifestly widely spread in the Highlands.

 The Gaelic is somewhat peculiar, and there are some errors in it which have not been corrected.

18

THE CHEST.

From Mrs MacGeachy, Islay.

Before this there was a king, and he wished to see his son with a wife before he should depart. His son said he had better go for a wife; and he gave him half a hundred pounds to get her. He went forward in to a hostelry to stay in it. He went down to a chamber with a good fire in front of him; and when he had gotten meat, the man of the house went down to talk to him. He told the man of the house the journey on which he was. The man of the house told him he need not go further; that there was a little house opposite to his sleeping chamber; that the man of the house had three fine daughters; and if he would stand in the window of his chamber in the morning, that he would see one after another coming to dress herself. That they were all like each other, and that he could not distinguish one from the other, but that the eldest had a mole. That many were going to ask for them, but that none got them, because whoever wished for one, must tell whether the one he liked best was younger or older; and if he made her out, that she would cost him a hundred pounds. "I have but half a hundred," said the king's son. "I will give thee another half hundred," said the man of the house, "if thou wilt pay me at the end of a day and a year; and if thou dost not pay me, a strip of skin shall come from the top of thy head to the sole of thy foot."

On the morrow when he rose he went to the window; he saw the girls coming to dress themselves; and after meat in the morning, he went over to the house of their father. When he went in he was taken down to a chamber, and the man of the house went down to talk to him. He told the journey on which he was, and he said to him, "They tell me that thou hast three fine daughters." "I have that same, but I am afraid that it is not thou who wilt buy them."

"I will give them a trial, at all events," said he. The three were sent down before him, and it was said to him "Whether she, the one he liked best, was the elder or younger." He thought he would take the one with the mole, because he knew she was the eldest. She then was much pleased that it was she herself he was for. He asked her father how much she would be, and her father said she would be a hundred pounds. He bought her, and he took her to the house of his father, and they married. Shortly after they married his father departed.

A day or two after the death of the old king, the young king was out hunting; he saw a great ship coming in to the strand; he went down to ask the captain what he had on board. The captain said, "That he had a cargo of silk." "Thou must," said he, "give me a gown of the best silk thou hast for my wife." "Indeed!" said the captain, "thou must have an exceedingly good wife when thou must have a gown of the best silk I have on board." "I have that," said the king, "a wife many of whose equals are not to be got." "Wilt thou lay a wager," said the captain, "that with all her goodness I will not get leave to enter thy chamber?" "I will lay a wager, anything thou desiredst, that thou wilt not." "What wager wilt thou lay?" said the captain. "I will put the heirship in pledge," said the king. Said the captain: "I will put all the silk in ship in pledge to thee that I will." The captain came on shore and the king went on board.

The captain went where the hen-wife was, to try if she could make any way to get in with to king's chamber that night. The hen-wife thought a while, and she said "That she did not think that there was any way that would succeed." The captain rose here, and he was going. "Stop thou!" said she, "I have thought on a way: her maid servant and I are well with each other; I will say to her that I have got word from a sister of mine that I will scarce find her alive; I will say to the king's wife that I must go to see my sister; that I have a big kist, of good worth, and I should like if she would oblige me and let it into her own sleeping chamber till I come back." She went where the queen was, she asked her this, and she got leave. Here the captain was put into the kist, and the king's gillies were gathered, and the kist put in the chamber. The king's wife was within by herself wearying, for the king was not coming home. At last she went to bed; when she was going to bed she put a gold ring that was on her finger, and a gold chain that was about her neck, on a board that was opposite to the bed. When the man who was in the kist thought that she had time to be asleep, he rose and he took with him the chain and the ring, and he went into the kist again. At the mouth of day came the hen-wife to ask for the kist; the gillies were gathered, and the kist was taken down. When every one went from the house, as soon as he could, the captain rose and he went down to the ship; he shook the chain and the ring at the king. Then the king thought that the captain had been with his wife, or that he could not have the chain and ring. He said to the captain, "Would he put him over to the other side of the loch?" The captain said, "That he would." When the captain got him over he returned himself, and he went to dwell in the king's house. Then the king's wife did not know what to do with herself, for that the king had not come home. She went that day and she dressed herself in man's clothes, and she went down to the strand; she met with a boat, and she said to them, "Would they put her over on the other side?" They put her over, and she went on forward till she reached the house of a gentleman; she struck in the door, and the maid servant came down. She said to her, "Did she know if her master wanted a stable gillie?" The maid servant said, "That she did not know, but that she would ask." The maid servant went and she asked her master if he wanted a stable gillie. He said, "He did;" and he asked that he should come in; he engaged her, and she stayed working about the stable. There was a herd of wild beasts coming every night, and going into an empty barn that the gentleman had; a wild man after them, and his face covered with beard. She kept asking her master to send a man with her, and that they would catch him. Her master said, "That he would not; that they had no business with them; and that he had not done any harm to them." She went out one night by herself, and she stole with her the key of the barn door; she lay hid in a hole till the wild man and the beasts went in; she took with her the gillies, and they caught the wild man. They brought him in and they took off his beard; when the beard came off him she knew him, but she took no notice; and he did not know her. On the morrow he was about to go, but she spoke to her master to keep him; that the work was too heavy on her, and that she needed help. Her master ordered her to keep him. She kept him with her, and he himself and she were cleaning the stable.

A short time after this she spoke to her master for leave to go home on a trip to see her friends. Her master gave her leave. She said she would like well to have her gillie with her, and the two best horses that were in the stable.

When they went, she was questioning him by the way what had made him go with these wild beasts; or what he was at before the

day. He would not tell her anything. They went on forward till they
came to the hostelry where he had got the half hundred pounds.
When she set her face down to the house, he refused to go into it.
She said to him, "Did he do anything wrong, as he was refusing to
go into it." He said, "That he had got half a hundred pounds from
the man of the house." She said to him, "Had he paid them;" and
he said, "That he had not paid, and that a strip of skin was to come
from the top of his head to the sole of his foot, if it was not paid at
the end of a day and a year." She said, "It would be well deserved;
but that she was going to stay the night in the hostelry, and that she
must go down." She asked him to put the horses into the stable,
and they went in to the hostelry. He was standing in the door of the
stable, and his head was bent. The man of the house came out, and
he saw him. "My big gillie, I have thee here," said the man of the
house; "art thou going to pay me to-day?" "I am not," said he. Then
he went in, and they were going to begin to cut the strip of skin.
She heard the noise, and she asked what they were going to do to
her gillie. They said, "They were going to cut a strip of skin off him
from his crown to his sole." "If that was to be done," said she, "he
was not to lose a drop of blood; send up here a web of linen, let
him stand on it, and if a drop of blood comes out of him, another
strip of skin shall come off thee." Here there was nothing for it but
to let him go; they could not make anything of it. Early on the
morrow she took him over with her to the house of her father. If he
was against going to the hostelry the night before, he was seven
times as much when going to her father's house. "Didst thou do
harm here too, as thou art against going in?" "I got a wife here such
a time since." "What came of her?" "I don't know." "No wonder
whatever happens to thee, thou hast only to put up with all that
comes thy way." When her father saw him, he said: "I have thee
here! Where is thy wife?" "I don't know where she is." "What didst
thou to her?" said her father. He could not tell what he had done
to her. Now there was nothing to be done but to hang him to a tree.
There was to be a great day about the hanging, and a great many
gentlemen were to come to see it. She asked her father what they
were going to do to her gillie. Her father said, "That they were going
to hang him; he bought a wife from me, and he does not know what
has happened to her." She went out to see the gentles coming in to
the town; she asked of the one of the finest horse, what was his
worth. "Five score," said he. "Though he were five hundreds, he's
mine," said she. She told her servant to put a shot in the horse. She
asked her father if he had paid for his wife. He said he had paid. "If

he paid," said she, "thou hast no business with him, he might do what he liked with her; I bought the finest horse that came into the town to-day; I made my gillie put a shot in him, and who dares to say that it is ill." Here there was nothing to be done but to let him loose. They could do nothing to him because he had bought her.

Here she went in to her father's house, and she told one of her sisters to give her a gown. "What art thou going to do with a gown?" said she. "Never mind, if I spoil it I'll pay for it." When she put on the gown her father and sisters knew her. Her father and sisters told him that it was she was with him, and he did not believe them. She put off the woman's clothes and put on the man's clothes again. They went, herself and he; they went on forward till they were near his own old house. "Now," said she, "we will stay here to-night; do thou sit at the top of the stair, and thou shalt set down all the talk that I and the man of the house will have." When they went in and sat, she and the man of the house began to talk together. "I thought," said she to the captain, "that a king was dwelling here; how didst thou get it?" "He was that who was here before; but I am thinking, as thou art a stranger, that I may tell thee how I got it." "Thou mayest," said she, "I will not make a tale of thee, the matter does not touch me." He told her every turn, how the hen wife had put him in the kist, and the rest of the matter, to the going of the king on the morrow.

Very early on the morrow the man of the house was going to court: he said to her "That if she was not in a hurry to go away, that she might go with him to listen to the court." She said "she would be willing, and she would like well that her gillie should be with her." She went in the coach with the captain, and her gillie rode after her. When the court was over she said, "That she had got a word or two to say, if it were their pleasure to let her speak." They said to her, "To let them hear what she had to say." She said to her gillie, "Rise up and give them the paper thou wrotest last night." When they read the paper, she said, "What should be done to that man?" "Hang him, if he were here," said they.

"There you have him," said she, "do with him what you will." Herself and the king got back to their own house, and they were as they were before.

URSGEUL.

Bha righ ann roimhe so, 's bha toil aige bean fhaicinn aig a mhac ma'n siùbhladh e. Thuirt e r'a mhac gum b'fheàrra dha folbh airson mnatha, 's thug e dha leith chiad punnd airson a faotainn. Choisich e air aghaidh fad latha; 's nur a thàinig an oidhche chaidh e stigh do thigh òsd' airson fantainn ann. Chaidh e sios do sheombar, 's gealbhan math air a bheulthaobh; 's nur a fhuair e 'bhiadh chaidh fear an tighe sios a chomhnadal ris. Dh' innis e do' dh' fhear an tighe an turas air an robh e. Thuirt fear an tighe ris nach ruigeadh e leas dol na b' fhaide; gu' robh tigh beag ma choinneamh an t-seombair chadail aige; gu robh tri nigheanan gasd' aig fear an tighe; agus na 'n seasadh e 'n uinneag a sheombair anns a' mhadainn, gu' faiceadh e te an déigh te 'tighinn a 'h-éideadh féin. Gu' robh iad air fad cosmhuil r'a' chéile, 's nach aithneachadh e eadar te seach te; ach an te 'bu shine, gu' robh ball dòrain urra. Gu robh móran a' dol g'an iarraidh, ach nach robh gin 'gam faotainn; a thaobh gu' feumadh neach a bhiodh air son h-aon diu innseadh co dhiu a b'i an te d'an robh taitneachd aige b' òige na' bu shine; 's na'n déanadh e mach i gun cosdadh i dha ciad punnd. "Cha 'n 'eil agams' ach leith chiad," ursa mac an rìgh. "Bheir mise dhuit leith chiad eile," ursa fear an tighe, "ma phàigheas thu mi 'n ceann la is bliadhna; 's mar am pàigh thig iall o mhullach do chinn gu bonn do choise." Nur a dh' éiridh e 'n la 'r na mhàireach chaidh e gus an uinneig. Chunnaic e na nigheanan a' tighinn a'n éideadh fein, 's an déigh a bhidh 'sa mhadainn chaidh e nunn gu tigh an athar. Nur a chaidh e stigh chaidh a thoirt sios do sheombar, 's chaidh fear an tighe sìos a chomhnadal ris. Dh' innis e 'n turus air an robh e, 's thuirt e ris, "Tha iad ag ràdh rium gu' bheil tri nigheanan bréagh agad." "Tha sin féin agam; ach tha eagal orm nach tusa 'cheannaicheas iad." "Bheir mi feuchainn dhaibh," urs' esan. Chaidh an tri chuir sìos ma 'choinneamh, 's a ràdh ris, cò'ca a b'i 'n te d'an gabhadh e taitneachd an te bu shine na 'n te b' òige. Smaoinich e gu'n gabhadh e té a' bhall dòrain; o'n a bha fhios aige gur h-i 'bu shine. Ghabh ise an sin toil-inntinn mhòr gur h-i féin a bha e air a shon. Dh' fheòraich e d'a h-athair co mhìod a bhitheadh i, 's thuirt a h athair gum biodh i ciad punnd. Cheannaich e i, 's thug e leis i gu tigh athar, 's phòs iad. Goirid an déigh dhaibh pòsadh shiubhail athair.

Latha na dha an déigh bàs àn t-sean rìgh, bha 'n rìgh òg a mach a' sealgaireachd. Chunnaic e long mhòr a' tighinn a stigh thun a' chladaich. Chaidh e sìos a dh' fheòraich de 'n chaibhtinn de 'bha aige air bòrd. Thuirt an caibhtinn gu' robh luchd sìoda. "Feumaidh tu," urs' esan, "guthann de 'n t-sìoda 's fheàrr a th' agad a thoirt dhòmhsa airson mo mhnatha." "Seadh," urs' an caibhtinn, "feumaidh gu' bheil bean fhuathasach mhath agadsa, nur a dh' fheumas i guthann de'n t-sìoda is fheàrr a th' agamsa air bòrd." "Tha sin agam," urs' an rìgh, "bean nach 'eil mòran d'a leithidean r'a fhaotainn." "An cuir thu geall," urs' an caibhtinn, "a' h-uile mathas a th' urra, nach fhaigh mise dol a laidhe leatha nochd?" "Cuiridh mi geall, ni 'sam bith a shanntaicheas thu, nach fhaigh." "Dé 'n geall a chuireas tu?" urs' au caibhtinn. "Cuiridh mi 'n oighreachd an geall," urs' an righ. Urs' an caibhtinn, "Cuiridh mise na bheil de shioda 'san long an geall riutsa gu'm faigh." Thàinig an caibhtinn air tír, 's chaidh an righ air bòrd. Chaidh an caibhtinn far an robh cailleach nan cearc feuch an dèanadh i dòigh 'sam bith air 'fhaotainn a stigh le bean an righ an oidhche sin. Smaointich cailleach nan cearc tacan, 's thuirt i nach robh dùil aice gu' robh dòigh 'sam bith a dhéanadh feum. Dh' éirich an caibhtinn an sin, 's bha e 'falbh. "Stad ort," urs' ise, "smaointich mi air dòigh. Tha 'n searbhannt aice 's mi féin gu math mòr. Their mi rithe gu'n d' fhuair mi fios o phiuthar dhomh nach beirinn beò urra. Their mi ri bean an rìgh gu' feum mi folbh a dh' fhaicinn mo pheathar; gu 'bheil cisde mhòr agam gu math luachar, a bu mhath leam, na'n lughasachadh i dhomh, a leigeil d'a seombar-cadail féin gus an till mi." Chaidh i far an robh 'bhanrighinn; dh' fheòraich i so dhi, 's fhuair i cead. Chaidh an so an caibhtinn a chur a stigh do'n chisde, 's gillean an righ a chruinneachadh, 's a' chisde' chur do 'n t-seombar. Bha bean an righ a stigh leatha féin, 's fadal urra nach robh an rìgh a' tighinn dachaidh. Ma dheireadh chaidh i 'laidhe. Nur a bha i 'dol a laidhe chuir i fainne òir a bha air a meur, agus slabhraidh òir a bha ma 'muineal, air bòrd a bha ma choinneamh na leapa. Nur a smaointich am fear a bha 's a' chisde gu' robh ùine aice 'bhi 'na cadal, dh' éirich e, s thug e leis an t-slabhraidh 's am fainne, 's chaidh e stigh do'n chisde a rithisd. Am beul an latha thàinig cailleach nan cearc a dh' iarraidh a cisde. Chaidh na gillean a chruinneachadh 's a' chisde 'thoirt a nuas. Nur dh' fholbh a' h-uile duine o'n tigh, cho luath sa' bu leur dha, dh' éirich an caibhtinn, 's dh' fholbh e sìos thun na luinge. Chrath e'n t-slabhraidh 's am fainne ris an rìgh. Smaointich an rìgh an sin gun d'fhuair an caibhtinn a stigh le a bhean, no nach biodh an t-slabhraidh 's am fainne aige. Thuirt e ris a' chaibhtinn an cuireadh e nunn e gus an taobh eile de'n loch. Thuirt an caibhtinn gun cuireadh. Nur a fhuair an caibhtinn thairis e, thill e féin 's chaidh e 'chòmhnuidh do thigh an rìgh.

Bha bean an rìgh an sin 's gun fhios aice dé a dhèanadh i rithe féin, o'n nach d'thàinig an rìgh dhachaidh. Dh'fholbh i 'n latha sin, 's dh' éid i i féin ann an aodach fir, 's chaidh i sìos thun a' chladaich. Thachair bàta urra, 's thuirt i riu an cuireadh iad ise a nunn air an taobh eile. Chuir iad a nunn i, 's ghabh i air a h-aghaidh gus an d' ràinig i tigh duine uasail. Bhuail i 'san dorus, 's thàinig an searbhannt' a nuas. Thuirt i rithe an robh fhios aice an robh gille stàbuill a dhìth air a maighstir. Thuirt an searbhannta nach robh fhios aice, ach gu 'foighneachdadh i. Chaidh an searbhanta 's dh' fheòraich i d'a maighstir, an robh gille stàbuill a dhìth air. Thuirt e gun robh, agus dh' iarr e e 'thighinn a stigh. Dh' fhasdaidh e i, 's dh' fhan i 'g obair ma'n stàbull. Bha 'n sin treud de bheathaichean fiadhaich a' tighinn a' h-uile h-oidhche, 's a' dol a stigh do shabhal fàs a bha aig an duine uasal, 's duine fiadhaich as an déigh, 's aod-ann còmhdaichte le feusaig. Bha ise ag iarraidh air a maighstir na'n cuireadh iad duine leatha, gum beireadh iad air. Thuirt a maighstir nach cuireadh, nach robh gnothach aca ris, 's nach d' rinn e coire 'sam bith orra. Dh' fholbh ise mach oidhche leatha féin, 's ghoid i leatha iuchair doruis an t-sabhail. Laidh i 'm falach ann an toll gus an deachaidh an duine fiadhaich agus na beathaichean a stigh. Thug i leatha na gillean, 's rug iad air an duine fhiadhaich. Thug iad a stigh e, 's thug iad dheth an fheusag. Nur a thàinig an fheusag dheth dh' aithnich ise e, ach cha do leig i rud sam bith urra, 's cha d' aithnich esan ise. An la 'r na mhàireach bha e' dol a dh' fholbh, ach bhruidhinn ise r'a maighstir airson a ghleidheadh, gu'n robh an obair tuillidh is trom urra, 's gu 'feumadh i cuideachadh. Dh' òrduich a maighstir dhi 'ghleidheadh. Ghléidh i leath' e, 's bha e fein agus ise a' glanadh an stàbuill.

Beagan ùine 'na dhéigh so bhruidhinn i r'a maighstir, airson cead a dhol dhachaidh air sgrìob a dh' fhaicinn a càirdean. Thug a maighstir cead dhi. Thuirt i gu'm bu mhath leatha a gille, 's an da each a b' fheàrr a bh' ann 's an stàbull a bhi leatha. Nur a dh' fholbh iad bha i 'ga cheasnachadh air an rathad; dé thug dha bhi folbh leis na beathaichean ud, na de bha e ris an toiseach a latha. Cha 'n innseadh e ni sam bith dhi. Ghabh iad air an aghaidh gus an d' thàinig iad gus an tigh òsda far an d' fhuair esan an leith chiad punnd. Nur a thug ise a h-aghaidh sìos gus an tigh, dhiult esan a dhol ann. Thuirt i ris an d' rinn e ni sam bith ceàrr, nur a bha e diùltainn dol ann. Thuirt e gun d' fhuair e leith chiad punnd o fhear an tighe. Thuirt i ris an do phaigh e iad, 's thuirt e nach do phàigh, 's gu'n robh iall ri tighinn o mhullach a chinn gu bonn a choise, mar am biodh e pàighte an ceann la is bliadhna. Thuirt i gum bu mhath an airidh' ach gu' robh ise a' dol a dh' fhantainn 's an tigh òsda 'san oidhche, 's gu' feumadh e dol sìos. Dh' iarr i air na h-eich a chur a stigh 'san stàbull, 's chaidh eud a stigh do 'n tigh òsda. Bha esan na sheasamh ann an dorus an stàbuill, 's a cheann crom. Thàinig fear an tighe mach 's chunnaic e e. "Mo ghille mòr tha thu an so agam," ursa fear an tighe. "Am bheil thu' dol am' phàigheadh an diugh?" "Cha 'n 'eil," urs' esan. Chaidh e 'sin a stigh, 's bha iad a' dol a thòiseachd air an iall a ghearradh. Chual ise an fhuaim, 's dh' fheòraich i gu dé 'bha iad a' dol a dhèanadh air a gille. Thuirt iad gun robh iad a' dol a ghearradh iall deth o mhullach gu bonn. "Ma bha sin r'a dhèanadh," urs' ise, "cha robh e ri deur fola a chall." "Cuir an nuas an so lìon aodach, a's seasadh e air, 's ma thig deur fola as thig iall eile dhìotsa." Cha robh an so ach a leigeil ma sgaoil. Cha b' urrainn iad stugh a dhèanadh dheth. Mochthradh an la'r na mhàireach thug i leatha nunn e gu tigh a h-athar. Ma bha e 'n aghaidh dol a'n tigh òsda an oidhche roimhid, bha e seachd uairean na bu mhotha 'n aghaidh dol do thigh a h-athar. "An do rinn thu cron an so cuideachd nur a tha thu 'n aghaidh dol ann?" "Fhuair mi bean an so o cheann a leithid do dh' ùine." "De 'thàinig urra?" "Cha 'n 'eil fhios'am." "Cha 'n iongantach dé dh' éireas duit! cha 'n 'eil agad ach gabhail ris na thig a'd' rathad!" Nur a chunnaic a h-athair e thuirt e, "Tha thu 'so agam; càit a' bheil do bhean?" "Cha 'n 'eil fhìosam càit' a' bheil i." "Dé a rinn thu rithe?" urs' a h-athair. Cha b'urrainn e innseadh dé a rinn a rithe. Cha robh 'nis ach a chrochadh ri craoibh. Bha latha mòr ri 'bhi timchioll a chrochaidh, 's bha mòran de dhaoine uaisle ri tighinn a 'fhaicinn. Dh' fheòraich ise d'a h-athair dé 'bha iad a dol a dhèanadh r'a gille. Thuirt a h-athair gu'n robh iad a' dol da chrochadh. "Carson," urs' ise, "a tha e r'a chrochadh." "Cheannaich 'e bean uamsa, 's cha 'n 'eil fhios aige dé 'thàinig rithe. Dh' fholbh i 'mach a dh' fhaicinn nan uaislean a' tighinn a stigh do'n bhaile. Dh' fheòraich i de 'n fhear a bu chiataich' each de 'b' fhiach dha." "Coig fichead," urs' esan. "Ged a bhiodh e coig ciad 's leamsa e," urs' ise. Thuirt i r'a gille urchair a chur 'san each. Dh' fheòraich i d'a h-athair an do phàigh e 'bhean. Thuirt e gun do phàigh. "Ma phàigh," urs' ise, "cha 'n 'eil gnothach agadsa ris; dh' fhaodadh e 'roighinn a dhèanadh rithe. Cheannaich mise an t-each a bu chiataiche a thàinig a stigh do 'n bhaile an diugh. Thug mì air mo ghille urchair a chur ann, 's co aig a' bheil a chridhe a ràdh gur olc." Cha u robh 'so ach a leigeil ma sgaoil. Cha b' urrainn iad stugh a dhèanadh air o'n a cheannaich e i.

Chaidh i an sin a stigh do thigh a h-athar, 's thuirt i ri h-aon d'a peathraichean guthann a thoirt dhi. "De 'tha thusa 'dol a dhèanadh do ghuthann?" urs' ise. "Nach coma leatsa. Ma ni mi milleadh air pàighidh mi e." Nur a chuir i urra an guthann dh' aithnich a h-athair's a peathraichean i. Dh' innis a h-athair 's a peathraichean dha gur h-i 'bha leis, 's cha robh e gan creidsinn. Chuir i dhi an t-aodach mnatha, 's chuir i urra an t-aodach fir a rithisd. Dh' fholbh i féin is esan, 's ghabh iad air an aghaidh gus an robh iad dlùth air a shean tigh féin. "Nis," urs' ise, "feumaidh sin fuireachd an so an nochd. Suidhidh tusa air bràigh na staighreach, agus cuirridh tu sìos gach comhnadal a bhios agams' agus aig fear an tighe. Nur a chaidh iad a stigh 's a shuidh iad, thòisich i fein agus fear an tighe air comhradh. "Shaoil mi," urs' i ris a' chaibhtinn, "gum b' e rìgh a bha 'chòmhnuidh an so. Démur 'fhuair thusa e?" " 'Se sin a bha roimhid an so; ach tha mi smaointeachadh, o'n a tha thusa a'd' choigreach, gum faod mi innseadh dhuit démur a fhuair mi e." "Faodaidh," urs' ise, "cha dèan mise sgeul ort; cha bhoin an gnothach dhomh." Dh' innis e dhi 'h-uile car mar a chuir cailleach nan cearc a stigh 'sa chisd' e, 's a' chuid eile de'n chùis; 's gun d' fholbh an rìgh an la 'r na mhàireach.

Mochthrath an la 'r na mhàireach bha fear an tighe 'dol gu cùirt. Thuirt e rithese, mar an robh deifir urra a dh' fholbh, gum faodadh i dol leisean a dh' éisdeachd na cùirt. Thuirt i gum biodh i toileach, 's gum bu mhath leatha a gille 'bhi leatha. Chaidh ise anns a' charbad leis a chaibhtinn, 's mharcaich a gille 'na déigh. Nur a bha 'chùirt seachad, thuirt i gun robh facal na dha aicese r'a ràdh, n'am b' e'n toil leigeil leatha bruidhinn. Thuirt iad rithe leigeil a chluinntinn daibh gu dé 'bha aice r'a ràdh. Thuirt i r'a gille. "Eiridh suas 's thoir dhaibh am paipeir sin a sgriobh thu 'rair." Nur a leubh iad am paipeir, thuirt i dé 'bu chòir a dhèanadh air an fhear sin. "A chrochadh na'm biodh e 'n so," urs' iadsan. "Sin agaibh e," urs' ise, 's deanaibh bhur roighinn ris." Fhuair i féin 'san rìgh tilleadh air an ais d'an tigh féin, 's bha iad mar a bha iad roimhid.

This was written, April 1859, by Hector MacLean, "from the dictation of Catherine Milloy, a Cowal woman, married to a farmer at Kilmeny, Islay—one Angus MacGeachy. Mrs. MacGeachy learned the story from a young man who resides in Cowal, Robert MacColl."

May 1860.—No other version of this story has come to me as yet. It resembles Cymbeline in some of the incidents; and one incident, that of the blood, is like Portia's defence in the Jew of Venice. It is worth remark that the scene of Cymbeline is partly laid in Britain, partly in Italy.

In the Decameron, 2nd day, novel 9, is the Italian story from which Cymbeline is supposed to have originated. "Bernard of Genoa is imposed upon by one Ambrose, loses his money, and orders his wife, who is quite innocent, to be put to death. She makes her escape, and goes in man's dress into the service of the Sultan; there she meets with the deceiver, and, sending for her husband to Alexandria, has him punished; she then resumes her former habit, and returns with her husband rich to Genoa."

In the Decameron, the Italian merchants dispute at Paris, and lay a bet. "A poor woman who frequented the house," replaces the Gaelic "Hen wife." The man who was hid in the chest took a ring, a girdle, a purse, and a gown, and in the Gaelic he takes a ring and a chain. The wife disguises herself as a man in both, but the service which she undertakes is different; and "the Sultan" is replaced by "a gentleman." In both stories she discloses the cheat in open Court,— in the one, before "the Sultan's court;" in the other, "in a court"— "to them." But though there are such resemblances, the two stories differ widely in spirit, in incident, in scene, and in detail. Those who hold that old stories are handed down traditionally, will probably consider this to be one of the kind; and if so, Shakspeare *may* have gathered his incidents at home. On the other hand, so well known a book as the Decameron, translated into English, 1566, might well account for part of the story.

In either case it is curious to trace the resemblance and the difference in these three versions of what appears to be the same popular tale; told by Boccaccio, Shakspeare, and a farmer's wife in the Highlands. If traditional, the story would seem to belong to a forgotten state of society. It is not *now* the custom to buy a wife, and thereby acquire the right to shoot her; and yet this right is insisted on, and acknowledged, and the story hinges on it. It seems that the Gauls had the power of life and death over their families, and that there was a custom very like the purchase of a wife among the old Icelanders.

There used to be, and probably there still are, certain ceremonies about betrothals, both in Norway and in the Highlands, which look like the remains of some such forgotten practice.

In the Highlands, a man used to go on the part of the bridegroom to settle the dower with the bride's father, or some one who acted for him. They argued the point, and the argument gave rise to much fun and rough wit. For example, here is one bit of such a discussion, of which I remember to have heard long ago.

"This is the youngest and the last, she must be the worst; you must give me a large dower, or I will not take her."

"Men always sell the shots first when they can; this is the best—I should give no dower at all."

The first knotty point settled, and the wedding day fixed, the bridegroom, before the wedding day, sent a best man and maid to look after the bride, and gathered all his friends at home. The bride also gathered her friends, and her party led the way to church, the bride was supported by the best-man and best-maid, and a piper played before them. The bridegroom's party marched first on the way home; and then there was a jollification, and a ball, and some curious ceremonies with a stocking.

The strip of skin to be cut from the debtor is mentioned in other stories; and I believe such a mode of torture can be traced amongst the Scandinavians who once owned the Western Islands.

In another story which I have heard, a man was to be punished by cutting IALL, a thong, from his head to his heels, another from his forehead to his feet, a thong to tie them, and a thong to make all fast.

TIGH-OSDA is the word commonly used for an inn. It is probably derived from the same root as Hostelry; Spanish, Osdal; French, Hôtel.

SEOMBAR is pronounced almost exactly like the French chambre—the only difference being that between the French *a* and the Gaelic *o*.

SEARBHANNT is very near the French servante.

19

THE INHERITANCE.

From Donald Macintyre, Benbecula.

There was once a farmer, and he was well off. He had three sons. When he was on the bed of death he called them to him, and he said, "My sons, I am going to leave you: let there be no disputing when I am gone. In a certain drawer, in a dresser in the inner chamber, you will find a sum of gold; divide it fairly and honestly amongst you, work the farm, and live together as you have done with me;" and shortly after the old man went away. The sons buried him; and when all was over, they went to the drawer, and when they drew it out there was nothing in it.

They stood for a while without speaking a word. Then the youngest spoke, and he said—"There is no knowing if there ever was any money at all;" the second said—"There was money surely, wherever it is now;" and the eldest said—"Our father never told a lie. There was money certainly, though I cannot understand the matter." "Come," said the eldest, "let us go to such an old man; he was our father's friend; he knew him well; he was at school with him; and no man knew so much of his affairs. Let us go to consult him."

So the brothers went to the house of the old man, and they told him all that had happened. "Stay with me," said the old man, "and I will think over this matter. I cannot understand it; but, as you know, your father and I were very great with each other. When he had children I had sponsorship, and when I had children he had gostji. I know that your father never told a lie." And he kept them there, and he gave them meat and drink for ten days.

Then he sent for the three young lads, and he made them sit down beside him, and he said—

"There was once a young lad, and he was poor; and he took love for the daughter of a rich neighbour, and she took love for him; but because he was so poor there could be no wedding. So at last they pledged themselves to each other, and the young man went away, and stayed in his own house. After a time there came another suitor, and because he was well off, the girl's father made her promise to marry him, and after a time they were married. But when the bridegroom came to her, he found her weeping and bewailing; and he said, 'What ails thee?' The bride would say nothing for a long time; but at last she told him all about it, and how she was pledged to another man. 'Dress thyself,' said the man, 'and follow me.' So she dressed herself in the wedding clothes, and he took the horse, and put her behind him, and rode to the house of the other man, and when he got there, he struck in the door, and he called out, 'Is there man within?' and when the other answered, he left the bride there within the door, and he said nothing, but he returned home. Then the man got up, and got a light, and who was there but the bride in her wedding dress.

" 'What brought thee here?' said he. 'Such a man,' said the bride. 'I was married to him to-day, and when I told him of the promise we had made, he brought me here himself and left me.'

" 'Sit thou there,' said the man; 'art thou not married?' So he took the horse, and he rode to the priest, and he brought him to the house, and before the priest he loosed the woman from the pledge she had given, and he gave her a line of writing that she was free, and he set her on the horse, and said, 'Now return to thy husband.'

"So the bride rode away in the darkness in her wedding dress. She had not gone far when she came to a thick wood where three robbers stopped and seized her. 'Aha!' said one, 'we have waited long, and we have got nothing, but now we have got the bride herself.' 'Oh,' said she, 'let me go: let me go to my husband; the man that I was pledged to has let me go. Here are ten pounds in gold—take them, and let me go on my journey.' And so she begged and prayed for a long time, and told what had happened to her. At last one of the robbers, who was of a better nature than the rest, said, 'Come, as the others have done this, I will take you home myself.' 'Take thou the money,' said she. 'I will not take a penny,' said the robber; but the other two said, 'Give us the money,' and they took the ten pounds. The woman rode home, and the robber left her at her husband's door, and she went in, and showed him the line—the writing that the other had given her before the priest, and they were well pleased."

"Now," said the old man, "which of all these do you think did best?" So the eldest son said, "I think the man that sent the woman to him to whom she was pledged, was the honest, generous man: he did well." The second said, "Yes, but the man to whom she was pledged did still better, when he sent her to her husband." "Then," said the youngest, "I don't know myself; but perhaps the wisest of all were the robbers who got the money." Then the old man rose up, and he said, "Thou hast thy father's gold and silver. I have kept you here for ten days; I have watched you well. I know your father never told a lie, and thou hast stolen the money." And so the youngest son had to confess the fact, and the money was got and divided.

I know nothing like No. 19. No. 20 begins like a German story in Grimm; but the rest is unlike anything I have read or heard. The first part has come to me in another shape, from Ross-shire; and some men whom I met in South Uist seemed to know these incidents.

The two belong to the class referred to in the Introduction, page xxxv. as fourth. Many of the novels in Boccaccio might be ranked with the same class; they are embryo three-volume novels, which only require nursing by a good writer to become full-grown books. There are plenty of the kind throughout the Highlands, and, as it seems to me, they are genuine popular traditions, *human* stories, whose incidents would suit a king or a peasant equally well. Without a wide knowledge of books, it is impossible to say whence these stories came; or whether they are invented by the people. MacIntyre said he had learned those which he told me from old men like himself, in his native island; and all others whom I have questioned say the same of their stories.

20

THE THREE WISE MEN.

From Donald MacIntyre, Benbecula.

There was once a farmer, and he was very well off, but he had never cast an eye on the women, though he was old enough to be married. So one day he took the horse and saddle, and rode to the house of another farmer, who had a daughter, to see if she would suit him for a wife, and when he got there the farmer asked him to come in, and gave him food and drink, and he saw the daughter, and he thought she would suit him well. So he said to the father, "I am thinking it is time for me to be married, I am going to look for a wife"—(here there was a long conversation, which I forget). So the man told his wife what the other had said, and she told her daughter to make haste and set the house in order, for that such a man was come and he was looking for a wife, and she had better show how handy she was. Well never mind, the daughter was willing enough, so she began to set the house in order, and the first thing she thought of was to make up the fire, so she ran out of the house to the peat-stack. Well, while she was bent down filling her apron with peats, what should fall but a great heap from the top of the stack on her head and shoulders. So she thought to herself, "Oh, now, if I were married to that man, and about to be a mother, and all these peats fallen on my head, I should now be finished and all my posterity;" and she gave a great burst of weeping, and sat down lamenting and bewailing. The mother was longing for her daughter to come back, so she went out and found her sitting crying in the end of the peat-stack, and she said, "What is on thee?" and the daughter said, "Oh, mother, the peat-stack fell on my head, and I thought if I were now married to that man, and about to be a mother, I was done, and all my posterity;" and the mother said, "That is true for thee, my daughter; that is true, indeed," and she sat down and cried too. Then the father was getting cold, so he too went out, wondering what kept the women, and when he found them, they told him what happened, and he said, "That would have been unfortunate indeed," and he began to roar and cry too. The wooer at last came out himself, and found them all crying in the end of the peat-stack, and when they had told him why they were lamenting, he said, "Never you mind. It may be that this may never happen at all. Go you in-doors, and cry no more." Then he took his horse and saddle, and rode home; and as he went, he thought, "What a fool I am to be stopping here all my life. Here I sit, and know no more of the world than a stock. I know how to grow corn, and that is all I know. I will go and see the world, and I will never come home till I find thee as wise as those were foolish whom I left crying in the peat-stack." And so when he got home, he set everything in order, and took the horse and went away. And he travelled the Gældom and the Galldom Highlands and strange lands for many a day, and got much knowledge. At last, one fine evening he came to a pretty plot of green ground in a glen, by a river; and on it there were three men standing. They were like each other, and dressed alike. Their dress was a long coat with short brigis, and a broad belt about the middle, and caps on their heads. (What dress is that? That is the dress they used to wear here. I remember my father well; he always wore it.) So he put Failte on them (saluted them). The three men never answered a word. They looked at him, and then they bent their heads slowly towards each other—(here the narrator bent his own head, and spoke solemnly)—and there they staid with their heads bowed for ten minutes. Then they raised their heads, and one said, "If I had without what I have within, I would give thee a night's share;" the second said, "If I had done what is undone, I would give thee a night's share;" and the third said, "I have nothing more than usual, come with me." So the farmer followed the old man to his house, wondering what all this should mean. When they had gone in and sat down, he wondered still more, for his host never offered him a drink till he had told him all about his journey. Then he said, "Quicker is a drink than a tale;" and the old man gave a laugh, and struck the board, and a fine woman came and gave him a great cup of ale, and that was good. And he drank it, and thought to himself, "If I had that woman for my wife, she would be better than the one I left weeping in the peat-stack." The old man laughed again, and he said, "If two were willing that might be." The farmer wondered that this old man should know his thoughts, and answer them, but he held his tongue. Then the old man struck the board, and a girl came in, and he thought, "If I had that one for my wife, she would be better than the girl I left howling in the peat-stack." The old man gave another little laugh, and he said, "If three were willing that might be too," and the girl set a small pot on the fire. The farmer looked at it, and thought, "This man must have a small company." "Ah," said the man, "it will go about."

"Now," said the farmer, "I *must* know what all this means. I will neither eat nor drink in this house unless you tell me. I saluted you, and you bent your heads, and never answered for ten minutes. When you did speak, I could not understand you, and now you seem to understand my thoughts." Then the old man said, "Sit down, and I will explain it all. Our father was a very wise man. We never knew how wise he was till long after he went away. We are three brothers, and on the bed of death our father left us this pretty place, and we have it amongst us, and plenty besides. Our father made us swear that we would never talk on important matters but in whispers. When thou camest, we bent our heads and whispered, as we always do, for men cannot dispute in a whisper, and we never quarrel. My first brother had the corpse of his mother-in-law within; he was unwilling to ask a stranger to a house of sorrow. She is to be buried to-morrow—If that were out which he had within, he had given thee a night's share. My second brother has a wife who will do nothing till she gets three blows of a stick. Then she is like other women, and a good wife; he did not like a stranger to see the blows given, and he knew she would do nothing without them—If he had done what was undone, he had given thee a night's share. I had nothing to do more than usual. Thou didst tell thy news, and when my wife came in, I knew thy thought. If I were dead, and thou and she were willing, you might be married. So if I, and thou, and my daughter were willing, you might be married too. Now, then, said the old man, sit and eat. The little pot will go about; it will serve for us. My company eat without." On the morrow, the old man said, "I must go to the funeral to my brother's house, do thou stay here." But he said, "I will not stay in any man's house when he is away. I will go with you to the funeral." When they came back he staid some time in the old man's house. He married the daughter, and got a good share of the property. And, now, was not that a lucky peat-stack for the farmer.

This story and No. 19 were told to me on the 6th of September 1859, in the inn at the Sound of Benbecula, by a man whose name would sound to Saxon ears like Dolicolichyarlich; a Celt would know it for Donald MacDonald MacCharles, and his surname is MacIntyre; he is a cotter, and lives in Benbecula.

Donald is known as a good teller of tales, so I walked six miles to his house and heard him tell a long version of the tale of Conal Gulbanach.

It lasted an hour, and I hope to get it written some day; I have other versions of the same incidents. There was an audience of all the people of the village who were within reach, including Mr. Torrie, who lives there near Baile nan Cailleach, which is probably so called from an old nunnery. After the story, the same man recited a fragment of a poem about Fionn and his companions. A man returning from battle with a vast number of heads on a withy, meets a lady who questions him, he recites the history of the heads, and how their owners died. The poem was given rapidly and fluently. The story was partly told in measured prose; but it was very much spun out, and would have gained by condensation.

I told the old man that he had too many leaves on his tree, which he acknowledged to be a fair criticism. He followed me to the inn afterwards, and told me other stories; the household being assembled about the door, and in the room, and taking a warm interest in the proceedings. After a couple of glasses of hot whisky and water, my friend, who was well up in years, walked off home in the dark; and I noted down the heads of his stories in English, because my education, as respects Gaelic writing, was never completed. They are given as I got them, condensed, but unaltered. Donald says he has many more of the same kind.

21

A PUZZLE.

From Kenneth M'Lennan, Turnaid, Ross-shire.

There was a custom once through the Gældom, when a man would
die, that the whole people of the place would gather together to the
house in which the dead man was—Tigh aire faire (the shealing of
watching), and they would be at drinking, and singing, and telling
tales, till the white day should come. At this time they were gathered
together in the house of watching, and there was a man in this
house, and when the tale went about, he had neither tale nor song,
and as he had not, he was put out at the door. When he was put
out he stood at the end of the barn; he was afraid to go farther. He
was but a short time standing when he saw nine, dressed in red
garments, going past, and shortly after that he saw other nine going
past in green dresses; shortly after this he saw other nine going past
in blue dresses. A while after that came a horse, and a woman and
a man on him. Said the woman to the man, "I will go to speak to
that man who is there at the end of the barn." She asked him what
he was doing standing there? He told her? "Sawest thou any man
going past since the night fell?" said she. He said that he had; he
told her all he had seen. "Thou sawest all that went past since the
night fell," said she. "Well then," said she, "the first nine thou
sawest, these were brothers of my father, and the second nine
brothers of my mother, and the third nine, these were my own sons,
and they are altogether sons to that man who is on the horse. That
is my husband; and there is no law in Eirinn, nor in Alaba, nor in
Sasunn that can find fault with us. Go thou in, and I myself will
not believe but that a puzzle is on them till day;" and she went and
she left him.

TOIMHSEACHAN.

Bha cleachdadh aon uair air feadh na Gaeltachd, dar a Bhasaich-
eadh duine, gu tionaladh sluagh a' bhaile uile gu leir, dho'n tigh
sam bitheag an duine marbh, tigh *aire faire*, agus bhithag iad ag' òl
's ag òran 's aginnse sgeulachdan, gus an digadh, an latha geal. Air
an am so bha iad cruinn 'san tigh fhaire, agus bha duine anns an
tigh so, agus dar a chaidh an sgeulachd mu 'n cuairt cha robh aon
chuid aige, sgeulachd, na òran, agus bho'n nach robh chaidh a chur
a mach air an dorus. Dar a chaidh, sheas e aig ceann an t-sabhail,
bha eagal air dol ni b' fhaide. Cha robh e ach goirid na sheasaidh
dar a chunnaic e naodhnar air an sgeadachadh ann an trusgain
dhearga a' dol seachad, agus goirid na dheighe sin chunnaic e
naodhnar eile a' dol seachad ann an deiseachan uaine; began an
deighe so chunnaic e naodhnar eile a' dol seachad ann an
deiseachan gorma; tacan an déigh so thàinig each, 's bean 's duine
air a mhuin. Thuirt a' bhean ris an duine, "Théid mi 'bhruidhinn
ris an fhear a tha 'siud, aig ceann an t-sabhail." Dh' fhoighnichd i
ris dé bha e dianamh an siud 'na sheasamh. Dh' innis e dhi. "Am
faca tu duine air bhith a' dol seachad bho thuit an oidhche?" os ise.
Thuirt gu 'fac. Dh' innis e dhi na chunnaic e. "Chunna tu na chaidh
seachad bho thuit an oidhche," os ise. "Mata," os ise, "Na ceud
naodhnar a chunna tu 'se sin bràithrean m' athar, agus an darna
naodhnar bràithrean mo mhàthair, agus an treas naodhnar 'se sin
mo mhic fhéin; agus 's mic dha n' duine ud a tha air muin an eich
iad uile gu léir. 'Se sin an duine agamsa; agus cha 'n 'eil lagh ann
an Eirinn, na 'n Allaba, na 'n Sasunn a's urrainn coir' fhaotainn
dhuinn.

"Folbh thusa a nis a steach; 's cha chreid mise nach 'eil toimhseachan orra gu latha." 'S dh' fholbh i 's dh' fhàg i e.

Written by Hector Urquhart. The answer is founded on a mistaken
belief that it is lawful for a woman to marry her grandmother's
husband. I am told that there are numerous puzzles of the same kind
now current in India.

22

THE RIDERE (KNIGHT) OF RIDDLES.

From John Mackenzie, fisherman, near Inverary.

There was a king once, and he married a great lady, and she departed on the birth of her first son. And a little after this the king married another one, and he had a son by this one too. The two lads were growing up. Then it struck in the queen's head that it was not her son who would come into the kingdom; and she set it before her that she would poison the eldest son. And so she sent advice to the cook that they would put poison in the drink of the heir; but as luck was in it, so it was that the youngest brother heard them, and he said to his brother not to take the draught, nor to drink it at all; and so he did. But the queen wondered that the lad was not dead; and she thought that there was not enough of poison in the drink, and she asked the cook to put more in the drink on this night. It was thus they did: and when the cook made up the drink, she said that he would not be long alive after this draught. But his brother heard this also, and he told this likewise. The eldest thought he would put the draught into a little bottle, and he said to his brother—"If I stay in this house I have no doubt she will do for me some way or other, and the quicker I leave the house the better. I will take the world for my pillow, and there is no knowing what fortune will be on me." His brother said that he would go with him, and they took themselves off to the stable, and they put saddles on two horses and they took their soles out of that.

They had not gone very far from the house when the eldest one said—"There is no knowing if poison was in the drink at all, though we went away. Try it in the horse's ear and we shall see." The horse went not far when he fell. "That was only a rattle-bones of a horse at all events," said the eldest one, and together they got up on the one horse, and so they went forwards. "But," said he, "I can scarce believe that there is any poison in the drink, let's try it on this horse." That he did, and they went not far when the horse fell cold dead. They thought to take the hide off him, and that it would keep them warm on this night for it was close at hand. In the morning when they woke they saw twelve ravens coming and lighting on the carcase of the horse, and they were not long there when they fell over dead.

They went and lifted the ravens, and they took them with them, and the first town they reached they gave the ravens to a baker, and they asked him to make a dozen pies of the ravens. They took the pies with them, and they went on their journey. About the mouth of night, and when they were in a great thick wood that was there, there came four and twenty robbers out of the wood, and they said to them to deliver their purses; but they said that they had no purse, but that they had a little food which they were carrying with them. "Good is even meat!" and the robbers began to eat it, but they had not eaten too boldly when they fell hither and thither. When they saw that the robbers were dead, they ransacked their pockets, and they got much gold and silver on the robbers. They went forward till they reached the Knight of Riddles.

The house of the Knight of Riddles was in the finest place in that country, and if his house was pretty, it was his daughter was pretty (indeed). Her like was not on the surface of the world altogether; so handsome was she, and no one would get her to marry but the man who would put a question to this knight that he could not solve. The chaps thought that they would go and they would try to put a question to him; and the youngest one was to stand in place of gillie to his eldest brother. They reached the house of the Knight of Riddles with this question—"One killed two, and two killed twelve, and twelve killed four and twenty, and two got out of it;" and they were to be in great majesty and high honour till he should solve the riddle.

They were thus a while with the Ridere, but on a day of days came one of the knight's daughter's maidens of company to the gillie, and asked him to tell her the question. He took her plaid from her and let her go, but he did not tell her, and so did the twelve maidens, day after day, and he said to the last one that no creature had the answer to the riddle but his master down below. No matter! The gillie told his master each thing as it happened. But one day after this came the knight's daughter to the eldest brother, and she was so fine, and she asked him to tell her the question. And now there was no refusing her, and so it was that he told her, but he kept her plaid. And the Knight of Riddles sent for him, and he solved the riddle. And he said that he had two choices: to lose his head, or to be let go in a crazy boat without food or drink, without oar or scoop. The chap spoke and he said—"I have another question to put to thee before all these things happen." "Say on," said the knight. "Myself and my gillie were on a day in the forest shooting. My gillie fired at a hare, and she fell, and he took her skin off, and let her go; and so he did to twelve, he took their skins off and let them go. And at last came a great fine hare, and I myself fired at her, and I took her skin off, and I let her go." "Indeed thy riddle is not hard to solve, my lad," said the knight. And so the lad got the knight's daughter to wife, and they made a great hearty wedding that lasted a day and a year. The youngest one went home now that his brother had got so well on his way, and the eldest brother gave him every right over the kingdom that was at home.

There were near the march of the kingdom of the Knight of Riddles three giants, and they were always murdering and slaying some of the knight's people, and taking the spoil from them. On a day of days the Knight of Riddles said to his son-in-law, that if the spirit of a man were in him, he would go to kill the giants, as they were always bringing such losses on the country. And thus it was, he went and he met the giants, and he came home with the three giants' heads, and he threw them at the knight's feet. "Thou art an able lad doubtless, and thy name hereafter is the Hero of the White Shield." The name of the Hero of the White Shield went far and near.

The brother of the Hero of the White Shield was exceedingly strong and clever, and without knowing what the Hero of the White Shield was, he thought he would try a trick with him. The Hero of the White Shield was now dwelling on the lands of the giants, and the knight's daughter with him. His brother came and he asked to make a comhrag (fight as a bull) with him. The men began at each other, and they took to wrestling from morning till evening. At last and at length, when they were tired, weak, and given up, the Hero of the White Shield jumped over a great rampart, and he asked him to meet him in the morning. This leap put the other to shame, and he said to him "Well may it be that thou wilt not be so supple about this time to-morrow." The young brother now went to a poor little bothy that was near to the house of the Hero of the White Shield tired and drowsy, and in the morning they dared the fight again. And the Hero of the White Shield began to go back, till he went backwards into a river. "There must be some of my blood in thee before that was done to me." "Of what blood art thou?" said the

youngest. " 'Tis I am son of Ardan, great King of the Albann."
" 'Tis I am thy brother." It was now they knew each other. They
gave luck and welcome to each other, and the Hero of the White
Shield now took him into the palace, and she it was that was pleased
to see him—the knight's daughter. He stayed a while with them,
and after that he thought that he would go home to his own
kingdom; and when he was going past a great palace that was there
he saw twelve men playing at shinny over against the palace. He
thought he would go for a while and play shinny with them; but
they were not long playing shinny when they fell out, and the
weakest of them caught him and he shook him as he would a child.
He thought it was no use for him to lift a hand amongst these twelve
worthies, and he asked them to whom they were sons. They said
they were children of the one father, the brother of the Hero of the
White Shield, but that no one of them had the same mother. "I am
your father," said he; and he asked them if their mothers were all
alive. They said that they were. He went with them till he found
the mothers, and when they were all for going, he took home with
him the twelve wives and the twelve sons; and I don't know but that
his seed are kings on Alba till this very day.

RIDERE NAN CEIST.

Bha righ ann uair, 's phòs e ban-tighearna mhòr, agus shiubhail i
air a cheud mhac, ach bha am mac bèo; agus beagan na dhéigh so,
phòs an rìgh tè eile, 's bha mac aige rithe so cuideachd. Bha 'n dà
ghille cinntinn suas. An sin bhuail an ceann na banrigh, nach b'è
macse a thigeadh a stigh air an rìoghachd, agus chuir i roimpe gu
'm puinseanaicheadh i 'm mac bu shine, agus mar so chuir i
comhairle ris a chòcaire, gu 'n cuireadh iad pùinsean ann an deoch
an oighre; ach mar bha sonas an dàn, chual' am bràthair a b' òige
iad, agus thubhairt e ri 'bhràthair, gun an deoch a ghabhail na idir
a h-òl; agus mar so rinn e. Ach bha iongontas air a bhan-righ nach
robh an gille marbh, agus smaoinich i nach robh na leòir a
phùinsean anns an deoch, 's dh' iarr i air a chòcaire tuillidh a chuir
'san deoch air an oidhche so. Is ann mar so a rinn iad, agus a nuair
a rinn an còcaire suas an deoch, thubhairt i nach bitheadh e fada
beo an déigh na dibhe so; ach chual' bhràthair so cuideachd 's dh'
innis e so mar an ceudna. Smaoinich e gu' cuireadh e 'n deoch ann
am botul beag, agus thubhairt e ri' bhrathair, "Ma dh' fhanas mi
'san tigh cha 'n 'eil teagamh agam nach cuir i as domh dòigh a

thaobhaigin, 's mar is luaithe dh' fhàgas mi 'n tigh, 'se is feàrr. Bheir mi an saoghal fo' m' cheann, 's cha 'n 'eil fios de 'm fortan a bhitheas orm." Thubhairt a bhràthair gu' falbhadh e leis, 's thug iad orra do 'n stàbull, 's chuir iad diollaid air dà each, 's thug iad na buinn asda. Cha deach iad glé fhad' o'n tigh, dur a thubhairt am fear bu shine, "Cha 'n 'eil fios an robh puinsean idir san deoch ged a dh' fhalbh sinn; feuch ann an cluais an eich e, 's chì sinn." Cha b' fhada chaidh an t-each dur a thuit e. "Cha robh an sud, ach gliogaire do dh' each co dhiu," thubhairt am fear bu sine, agus le' chéile ghabh iad air muin an aoin eich 's mar so chaidh iad air an aghaidh. "Ach," ars' esan, " 's gann orm a chreidsinn, gu' bheil pùinsean sam bith 'san deoch; feucham i air an each so." Sinn a rinn e, agus cha deach iad fada nuair a thuit an t-each fuar, marbh. Smaonich iad an t-seiche 'thabhairt dheth 's gu cumadh i blàth iad air an oidhche oir bha i dlùth làimh. 'Sa' mhaduinn, 'n uair a dhùisg iad, chunnaic iad dà fhitheach dheug a tighinn, 's laidh iad air closaich an eich. Cha b' fhada' bha iad an sin, 'n uair a thuit iad thairis marbh. Dh' fhalbh iad 's thog iad na fithich, 's thugar leo iad, agus a cheud bhaile a ràinig iad, thug iad na fithich do dh' fhuineadair 's dh' iarr iad air dusan pìth a dheanamh do na fithich. Thug iad leo na pithean, 's dh' fhalbh iad air an turus. Mu bheul na h-oidhche, 's iad ann an coille mhòr dhùmhail a bha sin thàinig ceithir thar fhichead do robairean a mach as a choille, 's thubhairt iad riu, "Iad a liobhairt an sporain;" ach thubhairt iadsan, "Nach robh sporan aca, ach gu 'n robh beagan bìdh a bha iad a giulan leo." " 'S maith biadh fhéin," agus thoisich na robairean air itheadh. Ach cha deach iad ro dhàna 'n uair a thuit fear thall sa bhos dhiubh. A nuair a chunnaic iad gu'n robh na robairean marbh, rannsaich iad na pocaichean aca, 's fhuair iad mòran òr 's airgiod air na robairean. Dh' fhalbh iad air an aghaidh gus an dràinig iad Ridire nan Ceist. Bha tigh Ridire nan Ceist anns an àite bu bhrèagha san dùthaich sin, agus ma bha 'n tigh bòidheach, 'se bha bòidheach a nighean. Cha robh a leithid air uachdar an t-saoghail gu léir, co maiseach rithe. 'S cha 'n fhaigheadh a h-aon ri phòsadh i, ach fear a chuireadh ceist air an ridire so nach b'urrainn da fhuasgladh. Smaonich na fleasgaich gu 'n rachadh iad 's gu feuchadh iad ceist a chuir air; agus bha 'm fear a b' òige gu seasadh an àite gille d'a bhràthair bu sine. Ràinig iad tigh Ridire nan Ceist, leis a cheist so, "Mharbh a h-aon, dithis, 's mharbh dithis a dha-dheug 's marbh dha-dheug, ceithir thar-fhichead, 's thàinig dithis as; 's bha iad gu bhi air bhòrt mòr 's àirde onair gus am fuasgladh e a cheist. Bha iad greis mar so leis an ridire; ach oidhche do na h-oidhchean, thàinig te do na maighdeannan

coimhideachd aig nighean an ridire, gu leaba 'ghille, 's thubhairt i
ris, "N' an innseadh e à cheist dhith gu' rachadh i luidhe leis, agus
mar sin fhéin rinn i; ach mu 'n do leig e air falbh i, thug e a léine
dhi, ach cha do dh' innis e dhi a cheist; agus mar sin rinn an da
mhaighdean dhèug, oidhch' an déigh oidhche agus thubhairt e ris
an te mu dheireadh, "Nach robh fios an toimhseachan aig neach
air bith ach aig a mhaighstir san a mhàin." Coma co-dhiù dh' innis
an gille gach ni mar a bha' tachairt da mhaighstir; ach aon oidhch'
an déigh so, thàinig nighean an ridire do sheòmar a bhrathair bu
sine, 's thubhairt i gu'n rachadh i luidhe leis na 'n innseadh e a'
cheist dhi. Nise cha robh na chomas a diùltadh, agus 's ann mar so
a bha, chaidh i luidhe leis, ach anns a mhaduinn, thug e a léine dhi,
's leig e air falbh i, 's co luath 'sa dh'éirich Ridire nan Ceist, chuir
e fios air, 's dh' fhuasgail e a' cheist, 's thubhairt e ris, "Gun robh
a dha roghainn aige, an ceann a chall, na' leigeil air falbh ann an
eithear, gun bhiadh gun deoch, 's gun ràmh na taoman." Labhair
am fleasgach, 's thubhairt e, "Tha ceist eil agam ri chuir ort mu 'n
tachair na h-uile nithibh so." "Abair romhad," thuirt an ridire.
"Bha mi fein 's mo ghille, latha ann am frìdh a' sealg; loisg mo ghille
air maigheach 's thuit i; thug e 'n craiceann dhi, 's leig e air falbh i.
Rinn e mar sin air a dha-dheug; thug e 'n craiceann diubh 's leig e
air falbh iad, agus mu dheireadh, thainig maigheach mhòr
bhrèagha, 's loisg mi féin oirre, 's thug mi 'n craiceann dhi, 's leig
mi air falbh i." "Moire, cha 'n 'eil do cheist duillich fhuasgladh
òganaich," thirt an ridire, "tha sin ag innseadh gu'n do luidh do
ghille le dà mhaighdean dheug mo nighinn-sa, agus thu fein le mo
nighean 's gu'n d' thug sibh na léintean dhiubh. Sin agad do
thoimhseachain mo ghille maith, agus feuma tu 'pòsadh." Agus se
sin a rinn iad 's banais mhòr, ghreadhnach a mhair latha 's bliadhna.
Dh' fhalbh am fear a b-òige dhachaidh an so, 'n uair a fhuair e a
bhràthair co maith air a dhòigh, 's thug am bràthair bu sine dha na
h-uile còir air an rioghachd a bha aig an tigh. Bha dlùth do dh'
fhearann Ridire nan Ceist triùir fhamhairean, agus iad daonnan a'
mort 'sa' marbhadh cuid do dhaoine an Ridire, 'sa tabhairt uapa
spùill. Latha do na laithean, thuirt Ridire nan Ceist ri chliamhuinn,
na 'm biodh spiorad duin' ann, gu'n rachadh e a mharbhadh nam
famhairean. Agus 's ann mar so a bha, dh' fhalbh e, 's choinnich e
na famhairean agus thainig e dhachaidh le ceann nan tri
famhairean, 's thilg e iad aig casan an ridire. " 'S òlach tapaidh thu
gun teagamh, agus 'se is ainm dhuit na dheigh so, Gaisgeach na
sgiath bàine." Chaidh ainm Gaisgeach na sgiath bàine am fad 's an
goirid. Bha bràthair Gaisgeach na sgiath bàine anabarrach laidir,

tapaidh, agus gun fhios aige co e Gaisgeach na sgiath bàine, smaoinich e gun rachadh e dh' fheuchainn cleas ris. Bha Gaisgeach na sgiath-bàine a' gabhail còmhnuidh air fearann an fhamhair a nis, 's nighean an ridire leis. Thàinig a bhràthair 's dh' iarr e còmhrag a dhèanamh ris. Thòisich na fir air a' chéile, agus thug iad air gleachd bho mhaduinn gu feasgar. Mu dheireadh thall 'n uair a bha iad sgìth, fann, 's air toirt thairis, leum Gaisgeach na sgiath bàine am Baideal mòr, 's dh' iarr e air coinneachainn ris sa mhaduinn. Chuir an leum so am fear eile fuidh sprochd, 's thubhairt e, "Math dh' fhaoidte nach bi thu co subailte mu 'n am so am màireuch." Chaidh am bràthair òg a nise do bhothan beag, bochd a bha dlùth do thigh Gaisgeach na sgiath-bàine, gu sgith, airsnealach; agus anns a mhaduinn, dh' ùraich iad an tuasid agus thòisich Gaisgeach na sgiath-bàine air dol air ais, gus an deach e 'n coimhir a chùil ann an abhuinn. "Feumaidh e gu' bheil cuid do m' fhuil annad mu 'n deanadh tu so ormsa." "Co 'n fhuil da 'm bheil thu?" thuirt am fear a b' òige. " 'S mise mac [?] Ardan rìgh mòr na h-Albann." " 'S mise do bhràthair." 'S ann an so a dh' aithnich iad a' chéile. Chuir iad fàilte 's furan air a chéile, 's thug Gaisgeach na sgiathe-bàine an so a stigh e do 'n lùchairt, agus 's e 'bha toileach fhaicinn nighean an ridire. Dh' fhan e car tamull maille riu, agus 'na dheigh sin, smaoinich e gun rachadh e dhachaidh d'a rìoghachd féin, agus a nuair a bha e gabhail seachad air pàileas mòr a bha' sin, chunnaic e dà fhear dheug a' camanachd fa chomhair a phàileis. Smaoinich e gun rachadh e greis a chamanachd leo, ach cha b' fhad' a bha iad a' camanachd 'n uair a chaidh iad a mach air a' chéile, agus rug am fear bu suarraiche dhiubh air, agus chrath 'se e mar gu'n deanadh e air pàisde. Smaoinich e nach robh math dha' làmh a thogail, am measg an dà cheathairneach dheug so, agus dh' fheoraich e dhiubh, co dha bu mhic iad? Thubhairt iad, "Gu 'm b'e clann aon athar iad, bràthair do Ghaisgeach na sgiath-bàine, agus nach b'e an aon mhàthair a bh' aig a h-aon dhiubh." " 'S mise bhur n-athair," thubhairt esan; is dh' fharraid e dhiubh, "An robh am màthraichean, uile beo?" Thuirt iad gu 'n robh. Chaidh e leo gus an d'fhuair e na màthraichean, agus a nuair a bha iad uile gu falbh thug e leis dhachaidh an dà bhean dèug 's a' dhà mhac dhèug, agus cha 'n 'eil fios agamsa nach e 'n sliochd a tha 'nan righrean air Alba gus a' latha 'n diugh.

Written down from the recitation of John Mackenzie, fisherman at Inverary, who says that he learned the tale from an old man in Lorn many years ago. He has been thirty-six years at Inverary. He first told me the tale fluently, and afterwards dictated it to me; and the words written are, as nearly as possible, those used by Mackenzie on the first occasion.

April, 1859.

HECTOR URQUHART.

The word pronounced Rēet-djĕ-rĕ--, and variously spelt Ridir, Righdir, and Righdeire, is explained in a manuscript history of the Campbells, written about 1827, as Righ, king—dei, after—Ri, king. If this be correct, the word would mean a following or minor king. It may equally be a corruption of Ritter, or Reiter; and I have translated it by *knight*, because it is now applied to all knights.

The author of the manuscript says:—The term is handed down even in Gaelic tales, and mentions several which were then current, Righdiere nan Spleugh, and an Righdeiri Ruadh; he adds, that Righdeirin dubh Loch Oigh (the Black Knights of Loch Awe) was the name then used by old Highlanders in mentioning the chiefs of the Duin (Campbells), and that the ruins of Eredin Castle were then known by no other name than Larach tai nan Righdeirin—the ruins of the house of the knights.

The writer argues from old manuscript histories, charters, etc., that the term was brought from Ireland by the colony who settled in Cantire at a very early period, and who spread thence over Argyllshire, and founded a kingdom, of which frequent mention is made in Irish annals as the Dalreudinan, or Scoto-Irish colonization of Argyll, Cantire, Lorn, and Islay. It is supposed to have taken place about A.D. 503, under Laorn, Fergus, and Angus, three sons of Eric, the descendant of Cairbre Ruadh, a son of Conary II., who ruled as chief king of Ireland A.D. 212. Be that as it may, all the Gaelic traditions now current in the Isles point at an Irish migration which took place in the year of grace *once upon a time*, and the word Righdeire occurs continually, where it seems to mean a small king, and a king of Erin; for example, "there was a king (Ree) and a Reet-djer—as there was and will be and, as grows the fir-tree, some of them crooked and some of them straight—and he was a king of Erin." Even the word Albanach, now used for Scotchman, means Wanderer. When the king's son changes his name, after killing the giants, it seems as if he were made a knight.

This tale, then, would seem to be some mythological account of events which may be traced in Grimm's stories, in the Classics, and elsewhere, mixed up with names and titles belonging to the colonization of Argyllshire by Irish tribes, and all applied to the kings of Scotland in the last sentence. It is a fair representation of the strange confusion of reality and fancy, history and mythology, of which I believe these stories to be composed.

The nearest story to it which I know is Das Räthsel, in Grimm, No. 22. Several versions are given in the third volume, which seem to vary from each other, about as much as this Gaelic version varies from them all.

There is something like the fight between Romulus and his brother. Alba means Scotland.

23

THE BURGH.

From Alexander M'Donald, tenant, and others, Barra,
July 1859.

Four were watching cattle in Baileburgh (Burgh Farm). They were
in a fold. The four were Domhnull MacGhilleathain, Domhnull
Mac-an-t-Saoir, Calum MacNill, and Domhnull Domhnullach.
They saw a dog. Calum MacNill said that they should strike the
dog. Said Domhnull MacGhilleathain, "We will not strike. If thou
strikest him thou wilt repent it." Calum MacNill struck the dog,
and his hand and his arm lost their power. He felt a great pain in
his hand and his arm, and one of the other lads carried his stick
home; he could not carry it himself. He was lamenting his hand,
and he went where there was an old woman, Nic a Phi, to get
knowledge about his hand. She said to him that he would be so till
the end of a day and a year; and at the end of a day and year, to go
to the knoll and say to it, "If thou dost not let with me the strength
of my hand, I or my race will leave neither stick nor stone of thee
that we will not drive to pieces."

At the end of a day and year his comrades said, "There is now a
day and year since thou hast lost the power of thy hand, come to
the knoll till thy hand get its power, as the woman said." He went
himself and his comrades. They reached the hill. He drew his stick,
and he said to the knoll, "If thou dost not let with me the strength
of my hand, I myself or my race will leave neither stick nor stone
of thee that we will not drive to pieces." And he got the power of
his hand.

———

BAILE BHUIRGH.

Bha ceathrar a' faire cruidh ann am Baile bhuirgh. Bha iad ann an

cuidh. B'e 'cheathrar Domhnull MacGhilleathain, Domhnull
Man-an-t-Saoir, Calum MacNill, agus Domhnull Domhnullach.
Chunnaic iad cù. Thuirt Calum MacNill gum buaileadh eud an cù.
Thuirt Domhnull MacGhilleathain. "Cha bhuail, ma bhuaileas tu
e bidh aithreachas ort." Bhuail Calum MacNill an cù agus chaill a
làmh agus a ghàirdean an lùgh. Bha e mothachainn cràdh mòr 'na
làimh agus 'na ghàirdean, agus ghiùlain h-aon de na gillean eile
dachaidh am bata, cha b' urrainn e fhìu a ghiùlan. Bha e 'gearan a
làimhe, 's chaidh e far an robh seana bhean, Nic a Phì, airson eolas
fhaotainn ma làimh. Thuirt i ris gum biodh e mur sin gu ceann la
as bliadhna, 's an ceann la a's bliadhna e dhol gos a' chnoc, 's a
radh ris "Mar an lig thu leamsa lùgh mo làimhe cha n fhag mise,
na mo shliochd, clach na crann diot nach cuir sin as a chéile." An
ceann la a's bliadhna thuirt a chompanaich ris, "Tha nis la a's
bliadhna o'n a chaill thu lùgh na làimhe, thalla gos a' chnoc, 's go'm
faigheadh do làmh a lùgh mar a thuirt a' bhean." Dh' fholbh e fhin
's a chompanaich, 's ràinig eud an cnoc. Tharruinn e'm bata 's
thuirt e ris a' chnoc, "Mar an lig thu leamsa lùgh mo làimhe cha 'n
fhàg mi fhìn, na mo shliochd, clach na crann diot nach d' thoir sin
as a cheile." Fhuair e lùgh na làimhe.

Written by Hector MacLean, from the telling of a man in Barra.
This may be compared with the Manks tradition about the Black
Dog, at Peel Castle.

24

THE TULMAN.

From Alexander M'Donald, tenant, and others, Barra.
July 1859.

There was a woman in Baile Thangusdail, and she was out seeking a couple of calves; and the night and lateness caught her, and there came rain and tempest, and she was seeking shelter. She went to a knoll with the couple of calves, and she was striking a tether-peg into it. The knoll opened. She heard a gleegashing as if a pot-hook were clashing beside a pot. She took wonder, and she stopped striking the tether-peg. A woman put out her head and all above her middle, and she said, "What business hast thou to be troubling this tulman in which I make my dwelling?" "I am taking care of this couple of calves, and I am but weak. Where shall I go with them?" "Thou shalt go with them to that breast down yonder. Thou wilt see a tuft of grass. If thy couple of calves eat that tuft of grass, thou wilt not be a day without a milk cow as long as thou art alive, because thou hast taken my counsel."

As she said, she never was without a milk cow after that, and she was alive fourscore and fifteen years after the night that was there.

AN TULMAN.

Bha boireannach ann am Baile Thangasdail, 's bha i mach aig iarraidh caigionn laogh, agus rug an oidhche 'san t-anmoch urra, agus thàinig sileadh agus sìon, 's bha i 'g iarraidh fasgaidh. Chaidh i go cnoc leis a' chaigionn laogh 's bha i 'bualadh a' chipein ann. Dh' fhosgail an cnoc. Chual i gliogadaich, mar go'm biodh buthal a' gleadhraich taobh poite. Ghabh i ionghantas. Stad i 'bhualadh a' chipein. Chuir boireannach a mach a ceann, 's na robh as cionn a miadhoin, 's thuirt i rithe. "Dé 'n gnothach a th' agad a bhi 'cur dragh air an tulman so 's a' bheil mise 'gabhail comhnuidh?" "Tha mi 'toirt an air' air a' chaigionn laogh so, 's cha 'n 'eil mi ach lag, ca' n d' théid mi leo?" "Théid thu leo 'ionnsuidh an uchd 'ud shias, chi thu bad feoir an sin. Ma dh' itheas do chaigionn laogh am bad feoir sin cha bhi thu latha gun mhart bainne fhad 's is beo thu, o'n a ghabh thu mo chomhairle." Mar a thubhairt i, cha robh i riabh gun mhart bainn' as a dhéigh so, 's bha i beò còig deug agus ceithir fichead bliadhna 'n déigh na h' oidhche 'bha 'n siod.

Written by Hector MacLean, from the dictation of a man in Barra.

25

THE ISLE OF PABAIDH.

From Alexander M'Donald, tenant, and others, Barra.
July 1859.

There came a woman of peace (a fairy) the way of the house of a man in the island of Pabaidh, and she had the hunger of mother-hood on her. He gave her food, and that went well with her. She staid that night. When she went away, she said to him, "I am making a desire that none of the people of this island may go in childbed after this." None of these people, and none others that would make their dwelling in the island ever departed in childbed from that time.

EILEAN PHABAIDH.

Thainig boireannach sìth rathad tigh duin' ann an eilean Phabaidh, agus acras na laidhe shiùbhl' urra. Thug e biadh dhi, 's ghabh sin go math aice. Dh' fhan i 'n oidhche sin. Nur a dh' fhalbh i thuirt i ris, "Tha mise deanadh iarrtas nach fhalbh gin de dhaoin' an eilean so ann an leaba na siùbhla as a dhéigh so." Cha d' fhalbh gin riabh de na daoine sin, 'na gin eile bhiodh a' gabhail comhnuidh 'san eilean uaidhe sin, ann an leaba na siùbla.

Written by Hector MacLean, from the telling of a man in Barra.

26

SANNTRAIGH.

From Alexander M'Donald, tenant, and others, Barra.
July 1859.

There was a herd's wife in the island of Sanntraigh, and she had a kettle. A woman of peace (fairy) would come every day to seek the kettle. She would not say a word when she came, but she would catch hold of the kettle. When she would catch the kettle, the woman of the house would say—

> A smith is able to make
> Cold iron hot with coal.
> The due of a kettle is bones,
> And to bring it back again whole.

The woman of peace would come back every day with the kettle and flesh and bones in it. On a day that was there, the housewife was for going over the ferry to Baile a Chaisteil, and she said to her man, "If thou wilt say to the woman of peace as I say, I will go to Baile Castle." "Oo! I will say it. Surely it's I that will say it." He was spinning a heather rope to be set on the house. He saw a woman coming and a shadow from her feet, and he took fear of her. He shut the door. He stopped his work. When she came to the door she did not find the door open, and he did not open it for her. She went above a hole that was in the house. The kettle gave two jumps, and at the third leap it went out at the ridge of the house. The night came, and the kettle came not. The wife came back over the ferry, and she did not see a bit of the kettle within, and she asked, "Where was the kettle?" "Well then I don't care where it is," said the man; "I never took such a fright as I took at it. I shut the door, and she did not come any more with it." "Good-for-nothing wretch, what didst thou do? There are two that will be ill off—thyself and I." "She will come to-morrow with it." "She will not come."

She hasted herself and she went away. She reached the knoll, and
there was no man within. It was after dinner, and they were out in
the mouth of the night. She went in. She saw the kettle, and she
lifted it with her. It was heavy for her with the remnants that they
left in it. When the old carle that was within saw her going out, he
said,

> Silent wife, silent wife,
> That came on us from the land of chase,
> Thou man on the surface of the "Bruth,"
> Loose the black, and slip the Fierce.

The two dogs were let loose; and she was not long away when she
heard the clatter of the dogs coming. She kept the remnant that was
in the kettle, so that if she could get it with her, well, and if the dogs
should come that she might throw it at them. She perceived the
dogs coming. She put her hand in the kettle. She took the board
out of it, and she threw at them a quarter of what was in it. They
noticed it there for a while. She perceived them again, and she threw
another piece at them when they closed upon her. She went away
walking as well as she might; when she came near the farm, she
threw the mouth of the pot downwards, and there she left them all
that was in it. The dogs of the town struck (up) a barking when they
saw the dogs of peace stopping. The woman of peace never came
more to seek the kettle.

SEANNTRAIGH.

Bha bean fir coimhead ann an eilean Shanntraigh agus bha coir'
aice. Thigeadh bean shìth h-uile latha dh' iarraidh a' choire. Cha
chanadh i smid nur a thigeadh, i ach bheireadh i air a' choire. Nur
a bheireadh i air a' choire theireadh bean an tighe.

> 'S treasaiche gobha gual
> Go iarrunn fuar a bhruich;
> Dleasnas coire cnàimh
> 'Sa thoirt slàn go tigh.

Thigeadh a' bhean shìth air a h-ais 'h-uile latha leis a' choire, agus
feoil as cnàmhan ann. Latha bha 'n sin bha bean an tighe airson dol
thar an aiseig do Bhail' a Chaisteil, agus thuirt i r'a fear, "Ma their
thusa ris a' bhean shìth mar a their mise, falbhaidh mi 'Bhaile
Chaisteil." "U! their," urs' esan, " 's cinnteach gur mi 'their." Bha

e sniamh siamain fraoich gos a chur air an tigh. Chunnaic e bean a' tighinn 's faileas as a casan, 's ghabh e eagal roimhpe. Dhruid e 'n dorusd as stad e d'a obair. Nur a thàinig ise do 'n dorusd cha d' fhuair i 'n dorusd fosgailte, 's cha d' fhosgail esan di e. Chaidh i as cionn toll a bha 's an tigh. Thug an coire da leum as, agus air an treas leum dh' fhalbh e mach air drìom an tighe. Thàinig an oidhche, 's cha d' thàinig an coire. Thill a' bhean thar an aiseig, 's cha 'n fhac i dad de 'n choire stigh, agus dh' fhoighnichd i ca 'n robh 'n coire. "Mata 's coma leam ca' bheil e," urs' a fear, "cha do ghabh mi riabh a leithid de dh' eagal 's a ghabh mi roimhe. Ghabh mi eagal, 's dhùin mi 'n dorusd, 's cha d' thàinig i tuillidh leis." "A dhonain dhona, dè rinn thu? 's dithisd a bhios gu don' thu fhìn agus mise." "Thig i 'm màireach leis." "Cha d' thig."

Sgioblaich i i fhìn, 's dh' fhalbh i 's ràinig i 'n cnoc, 's cha robh duine stigh. Bha e 'n déigh na dinnearach, 's bha eud a mach am bial na h-oidhche. Ghabh i stigh. Chunnaic i 'n coire 's thog i leath' e. Bha e trom aice, 'san còrr a dh' fhag eud ann. Nur a chunnaic am bodach a bha stigh i dol amach, thuirt e,

A bhean bhalbh, a bhean bhalbh,
A thàinig oirnn a tir nan sealg;
Fhir a tha 'n uachdar a' bhruth,
Fuasgail an Dugh 's lig an Garg.

Ligeadh an da chù ma sgaoil, 's cha b' fhada bha is' air falbh nur a chual i strathail nan con a' tighinn. Ghléidh i 'n còrr a bha 's a' choire air alt 's na 'm faigheadh i leath' e gum bu mhath, 's na 'n d' thigeadh na coin gun tilgeadh i orr' e. Dh' fhairich i na coin a' tighinn, 's chuir i làmh sa' choire, 's thug i 'm bòrd as, 's thilg i orra ceathra de na bh' ann. Thug eud an aire treis air an siud. Dh' fhairich i rìs eud, 's thilg i pìos' eil' orra nur a chas eud urra. Dh' fhalbh i coiseachd cho math 's a dh' fhaodadh i. Nur thàinig i dlùth air a' bhaile thilg i 'bhial fodha, 's dh' fhàg i 'n siud aca na bh' ann. Bhuail coin a' bhail' air comhartaich nur a chunnaic eud na coin shith 'stad. Cha d' thàinig a' bhean shìth riabh tuillidh a dh' iarraidh a' choire.

Written by Hector MacLean, from the telling of a man in Barra.

27

CAILLIACH MHOR CHLIBHRICH.

From W. Ross, stalker.

This celebrated witch was accused of having enchanted the deer of the Reay forest, so that they avoided pursuit. Lord Reay was exceedingly angry, but at a loss how to remedy the evil. His man, William (the same who braved the witch and sat down in her hut) promised to find out if this was the case. He watched her for a whole night, and by some counter enchantments managed to be present when in the early morning she was busy milking the hinds. They were standing all about the door of the hut till one of them ate a hank of blue worsted hanging from a nail in it. The witch struck the animal, and said, "The spell is off you; and Lord Reay's bullet will be your death to-day." William repeated this to his master to confirm the tale of his having passed the night in the hut of the great hag, which no one would believe. And the event justified it, for a fine yellow hind was killed that day, and the hank of blue yarn was found in its stomach.

This is one of nearly a hundred stories, gathered amongst the people of Sutherland by a very talented collector, whose numerous accomplishments unfortunately do not include Gaelic. This resembles an account of a Lapp camp (see Introduction). It also bears some affinity to a story published by Grant Stewart, in which a ghost uses a herd of deer to carry her furniture.

28

THE SMITH AND THE FAIRIES.

From the Rev. Thomas Pattieson, Islay.

Years ago there lived in Crossbrig a smith of the name of
MacEachern. This man had an only child, a boy of about thirteen
or fourteen years of age, cheerful, strong, and healthy. All of a
sudden he fell ill; took to his bed and moped whole days away. No
one could tell what was the matter with him, and the boy himself
could not, or would not, tell how he felt. He was wasting away fast;
getting thin, old, and yellow; and his father and all his friends were
afraid that he would die.

At last one day, after the boy had been lying in this condition for
a long time, getting neither better nor worse, always confined to
bed, but with an extraordinary appetite,—one day, while sadly
revolving these things, and standing idly at his forge. with no heart
to work, the smith was agreeably surprised to see an old man, well
known to him for his sagacity and knowledge of out-of-the-way
things, walk into his workshop. Forthwith he told him the occur-
rence which had clouded his life.

The old man looked grave as he listened; and after sitting a long
time pondering over all he had heard, gave his opinion thus—"It is
not your son you have got. The boy has been carried away by the
'Daoine Sith,' and they have left a *Sibhreach* in his place." "Alas!
and what then am I to do?" said the smith. "How am I ever to see
my own son again?" "I will tell you how," answered the old man.
"But, first, to make sure that it is not your own son you have got,
take as many empty egg shells as you can get, go with them into the
room, spread them out carefully before his sight, then proceed to
draw water with them, carrying them two and two in your hands as
if they were a great weight, and arrange when full, with every sort
of earnestness round the fire." The smith accordingly gathered as

many broken egg-shells as he could get, went into the room, and proceeded to carry out all his instructions.

He had not been long at work before there arose from the bed a shout of laughter, and the voice of the seeming sick boy exclaimed, "I am now 800 years of age, and I have never seen the like of that before."

The smith returned and told the old man. "Well, now," said the sage to him, "did I not tell you that it was not your son you had: your son is in Brorra-cheill in a digh there (that is, a round green hill frequented by fairies). Get rid as soon as possible of this intruder, and I think I may promise you your son."

"You must light a very large and bright fire before the bed on which this stranger is lying. He will ask you 'What is the use of such a fire as that?' Answer him at once, 'You will see that presently!' and then seize him, and throw him into the middle of it. If it is your own son you have got, he will call out to save him; but if not, this thing will fly through the roof."

The smith again followed the old man's advice; kindled a large fire, answered the question put to him as he had been directed to do, and seizing the child flung him in without hesitation. The "Sibhreach" gave an awful yell, and sprung through the roof, where a hole was left to let the smoke out.

On a certain night the old man told him the green round hill, where the fairies kept the boy, would be open. And on that night the smith, having provided himself with a bible, a dirk, and a crowing cock, was to proceed to the hill. He would hear singing and dancing and much merriment going on, but he was to advance boldly; the bible he carried would be a certain safeguard to him against any danger from the fairies. On entering the hill he was to stick the dirk in the threshold, to prevent the hill from closing upon him; "and then," continued the old man, "on entering you will see a spacious apartment before you, beautifully clean, and there, standing far within, working at a forge, you will also see your own son. When you are questioned, say you come to seek him, and will not go without him."

Not long after this, the time came round, and the smith sallied forth, prepared as instructed. Sure enough as he approached the hill, there was a light where light was seldom seen before. Soon after a sound of piping, dancing, and joyous merriment reached the anxious father on the night wind.

Overcoming every impulse to fear, the smith approached the threshold steadily, stuck the dirk into it as directed, and entered.

Protected by the bible he carried on his breast, the fairies could not touch him; but they asked him, with a good deal of displeasure, what he wanted there. He answered, "I want my son, whom I see down there, and I will not go without him."

Upon hearing this, the whole company before him gave a loud laugh, which wakened up the cock he carried dozing in his arms, who at once leaped up on his shoulders, clapped his wings lustily, and crowed loud and long.

The fairies, incensed, seized the smith and his son, and throwing them out of the hill, flung the dirk after them, "and in an instant a' was dark."

For a year and a day the boy never did a turn of work, and hardly ever spoke a word; but at last one day, sitting by his father and watching him finishing a sword he was making for some chief, and which he was very particular about, he suddenly exclaimed, "That is not the way to do it;" and taking the tools from his father's hands he set to work himself in his place, and soon fashioned a sword, the like of which was never seen in the country before.

From that day the young man wrought constantly with his father, and became the inventor of a peculiarly fine and well-tempered weapon, the making of which kept the two smiths, father and son, in constant employment, spread their fame far and wide, and gave them the means in abundance, as they before had the disposition to live content with all the world and very happily with one another.

The walls of the house where this celebrated smith, the artificer of the "Claidheamh Ceann-Ileach," lived and wrought, are standing to this day, not far from the parish church of Kilchoman, Islay, in a place called Caonis gall.

Many of the incidents in this story are common in other collections; but I do not know any published story of the kind in which the hero is a smith. This smith was a famous character, and probably a real personage, to whom the story has attached itself.

The gentleman who has been kind enough to send me this tale, does not say from whom he got it, but I have heard of the Islay smith, who could make wonderful swords, all my life, and of the "Swords of the Head of Islay." The Brewery of Egg-shells, and the Throwing of the Fairy Changeling into the Fire, are well-known popular tales in collections from Ireland, Scotland, Wales, and, I think, Brittany. The man carried into the hill and there remaining for a long time, is also an incident common to many races, including the Jews, and one which I have heard in the Highlands ever since I can remember, though I do not remember to have heard any of the peasantry tell it as a story.

The belief that "the hill" opened on a certain night, and that a light shone from the inside, where little people might be seen dancing, was too deeply grounded some years ago to be lightly spoken of; even now, on this subject, my kind friend Mrs. MacTavish writes—"You may perhaps remember an old servant we had at the manse who was much offended if any one doubted these stories—(*I remember her perfectly*). I used to ask her the reason why such wonders do not occur in our day, to which she replied, that religious knowledge having increased, people's faith was stronger than it was in the olden time. In the glebe of Kilbrandon in Lorn is a hill called Crocan Corr—the good or beautiful hill where the fairies even in my young days were often seen dancing around their fire. I sometimes went out with others to look, but never succeeded in seeing them at their gambols.

"Are you aware that——'s mother was carried away by the fairies—(*I know—— well*). So convinced were many of this absurdity, which I remember perfectly well, that it was with difficulty they got a nurse for his brother——, who being a delicate child, was believed to have been conveyed away along with his mother, and a fairy left instead of him during his father's absence * * * The child however throve when he got a good nurse, and grew up to be a man, which, I suppose, convinced them of their folly. Mr.——minister of——had some difficulty in convincing a man whose wife was removed in a similar manner (*she died in childbed*), that his son, a boy twelve years of age, must have been under some hallucination when he maintained that his mother had come to him, saying she was taken by fairies to a certain hill in Muckairn, known to be the residence of the fairies.

"If any one is so unfortunate as to go into one of these hills, which are open at night, they never get out unless some one goes in quest of them, who uses the precaution of leaving a GUN or SWORD across the opening, which the fairies cannot remove. A certain young woman was decoyed into one of these openings, who was seen by an acquaintance dancing with the merry race. He resolved on trying to rescue her, and leaving his gun at the entrance, went forward, and seizing the young woman by the hand, dragged her out before they could prevent him. They pursued them, but having got her beyond the gun, they had no longer power to keep her. She told him she had nearly dropped down with fatigue, but she could not cease dancing, though she felt it would soon kill her. The young man restored her to her friends, to their great joy."

(*I remember exactly the same incident told of a hill called Bencnock in Islay, and one similar of another hill called Cnock-down.*) "When poor women are confined, it is unsafe to leave them alone till their children are baptised. If through any necessity they must be left alone, the Bible left beside them is sufficient protection.

"Many were the freaks fairies were guilty of. A family who lived in Gaolin Castle, Kerrera, near Oban, had, as they supposed, a delicate child; it was advancing in years but not growing a bit; at length a visitor from Ireland came to the castle, and recognized her as the fairy sweetheart of an Irish gentleman of his acquaintance. He addressed her in Gaelic or Irish, saying—'THA THUSA SIN A SHIRACH BHEAG LEANNAN BRIAN MACBRAODH.'—There thou art, little fairy sweetheart of Brian MacBroadh. So offended was the elf at being exposed, that she ran out of the castle and leaped into the sea from the point called RUTHADH NA SIRACH, the fairies' point, to this day.

"Fairies were very friendly to some people whom they favoured, but equally mischievous where they took a dislike. A hill in the farm of Dunvuilg in Craignish was one of their favourite haunts, and on a certain occasion they offered to assist an honest tenant's wife in the neighbourhood, for whom they had a kindness, to manufacture a quantity of wool she had for clothing for her family. She was very glad to have their services, and being always an active race, they set to work directly, repeating 'CIRADH, CARDADH, TLAMADH, CUIGEAL, BEARTIGUE GU LUATH BURN LUAIDH AIR TEINE CORR IONNDRAIDH MHOR MHAITH BEAN AN TIGHE FHIN.' Teazing, carding, mixing, distaff, weaving loom, water for waulking on the fire, the thrifty housewife herself is the best at sitting up late.

"In the heat of their operations an envious neighbour came to the door crying—'DUNBHUILG RA THEINE,' Dunvuilg on fire! Dunvuilg is on fire! Dunvuilg is on fire! was re-echoed by all the little company. 'M' UIRD IS M' INNEAN! M' UIRD IS' M' INEANN! MO CHLANN BHEAG S' MO DHAOINE MORA! MO CHLANN BHEAG S' MO DHAOINE MORA!'— 'Dunvuilg on fire; my hammers and my anvil—my hammers and my anvil; my little children and my grown men—my little children and my grown men!' and they all scampered off, but not till they had nearly finished the housewife's web.

"There is a field in the farm in which I was born, said to have been the scene of fairy operations. They were seen at work, and heard encouraging each other with 'CAOL ACHADH MHAIDH BUANADH GU TETH.' The corn in the field was found in stooks in the morning.

"It is quite common to remark, that the fairies are at some meal as the time of day may indicate when there is rain with sunshine, but I never heard the reason why.—(*In England it is the d——l beating his wife.*)

"The night following the 13th of May, or May-day, old style, is a particularly busy season with both fairies and witches. Then every herd and dairy-maid and cannie housewife uses various arts to ward off the many evils the enemy has the power of inflicting. One device

which I have seen used was putting a little tar in the right ear of each
cow beast in the byre; but all these charms or giosragan, as they are
called, had always some reason. Tar has a disinfecting quality, as is
well known, and used to be put on clothing under the arms when a
person had to go into a house where there was any infectious
disease."

The Dunbhulaig story is all over the Highlands, and there seem
to be many places so called. Mr. John MacLean, Kilchamaig, Tarbert, Argyle, has sent me a version which varies but little from that
told by Mrs. MacTavish. The scene is laid on the Largie side of
Kintyre. The farmer's wife was idle, and called for the fairies, who
wove a web for her and shouted for more work. She first set them to
put each other out, and at last got rid of them by shouting
"Dunbhulaig on fire!" The fairies' rhyme when working was—

> "Is fad abhras 'n aon laimh air dheradh,
> Ciradh cardadh tlamadh cuigel,
> Feath a bhearst fithidh gu luath,
> 'S uisge luaidh air teine
> Obair, obair, obair, obair,
> Is fad abhras 'n aon laimh air dheradh."

Which Mr. MacLean translates freely—

> "Work, work, for a single hand
> Can but little work command,
> Some to tease, and card, and spin;
> Some to oil and weave begin;
> Some the water for waulking heat,
> That we may her web complete.
> Work, work, for a single hand
> Can but little work command."

The rhyme, when they depart in hot haste, is—

> "Mo mhullachan caise m'ord a's m innean,
> Mo bhean's mo phaisde s' mo gogan ima,
> Mo bho s' mo gobhair s' mo chiste beag mine,
> Och, och, ochone gur truagh tha mise!"

Freely translated thus by Mr. MacLean—

> "My wife, my child, alas, with these,
> My butter pail and little cheese,
> My cow, my goat, my meal-chest gone,
> My hammers too, och, och, ochone!"

Or more closely thus—

> "My mould of cheese, my hammer, and anvil,
> My wife and my child, and my butter crock;
> My cow and my goat, and my little meal kist;
> Och, och, ochone, how wretched am I!"

I heard another version of the same story in Lewis from a medical gentleman, who got it from an old woman, who told it as a fact, with some curious variations unfit for printing. And my landlady in Benbecula knew the story, and talked it over with me in September this year. The versions which I have of this story vary in the telling as much as is possible, and each is evidently the production of a different mind, but the incidents are nearly the same in all, and the rhyme varies only in a few points. Dunbhulaig is the same in Kintyre, Lorn, Lewis, and Benbecula. I am not aware that the story has ever before been reduced to writing.

The Man in the Hill is equally well known in Kirkcudbright, but the *hill*, has become a *mill*, and the fairies Brownies. The fairies of Kirkcudbright seem to have carried off children, like the Island Elves; to have borrowed meal, like those of Sutherland, and to have behaved like their brethren elsewhere. The following four stories were got for me by the sisters of Miss Mary Lindsay, who has lived so long with us as to have become one of the family.

KIRKCUDBRIGHT.

Kirkcudbright, Tuesday, Feb. 1859.

My Dear Mary,—I went to Johnny Nicholson last night, and he told me the following fairy story. I must give it in his own words:—

1. "You have been often at the Gatehouse," said he, "well, you'll mind a flat piece of land near Enrick farm; well, that was once a large loch; a long way down from there is still the ruin of a mill, which at that time was fed from this loch. Well, one night about the Hallowe'en times, two young ploughmen went to a smiddy to get their socks (of their ploughs) and colters repaired, and in passing the said mill on their way home again they heard music and dancing, and fiddling, and singing, and laughing, and talking; so one of the lads would be in to see what was going on; the other waited outside for hours, but his companion never came out again, so he went home assured that the brownies had got hold of him. About the same time the following year, the same lad went again to the smiddy on the same errand, and this time he took another lad with him, but had the precaution to put the Bible in his pocket.

Well, in passing the mill the second time, he heard the same sounds of music and dancing. This time, having the Bible in his hand, he ventured to look in, when who should he see but his companion whom he had left standing there that day twelvemonths. He handed him the Bible, and the moment he did so, the music and dancing ceased, the lights went out, and all was darkness; but it is not said what his companion had seen, or had been doing all that time."

2. Another story he told me was about a boy of the name of Williamson, whose father, an Irish linen packman, was drowned on his way from Ireland, where he had gone to purchase linen; so the boy was brought up by his mother and grandfather, an old man of the name of Sproat, who lived in Borgue. The boy disappeared often for two and three, and often ten days at a time, and no one knew where he went, as he never told when he returned, though it was understood the fairies took him away. Upon one occasion the Laird of Barmagachan, was getting his peats cast, and all the neighbours round were assisting. At this time the boy had been away for ten days, and they were all wondering where he could be, when lo and behold, the boy is sitting in the midst of them. "Johnny," said one of the company, who were all seated in a ring, eating their dinner, "where did ye come from?" "I came with our folks," said the boy (meaning the fairies). "Your folks; who are they?" "Do you see yon barrow of peats a couping into yon hole? there's where I came from." An old man of the name of Brown, ancestor of the Browns of Langlands, who are still living in Borgue, advised the grandfather to send the boy to the Papist priest, and he would give him something that would frighten away the fairies; so they accordingly sent the boy, and when he returned home he wore a cross hung round his neck by a bit of black ribbon. When the minister and kirk-session heard of it they excommunicated the old grandfather and old Brown for advising such a thing. They believed in fairies, but not in anything a Papist priest could do. However, the boy was never after taken away; and some of the oldest men now alive remember that boy as an old man. The whole affair is recorded in the books of the kirk-session of Borgue, and can be seen any day.

3. One day as a mother was sitting rocking her baby to sleep, she was surprised, on looking up, to see a lady of elegant and courtly demeanour, so unlike any one she had ever seen in that part of the country, standing in the middle of the room. She had not heard any one enter, therefore you may judge it was with no little surprise, not unmingled with curiosity, that she rose to welcome her strange

visitor. She handed her a chair, but she very politely declined to be seated. She was very magnificently attired; her dress was of the richest green, embroidered round with spangles of gold, and on her head was a small coronet of pearls. The woman was still more surprised at her strange request. She asked, in a rich musical voice, if she would oblige her with a basin of oatmeal. A basinful to overflowing was immediately handed to her, for the woman's husband being both a farmer and miller, had plenty of meal at command. The lady promised to return it, and named the day she would do so. One of the children put out her hand to get hold of the grand lady's spangles, but told her mother afterwards that she felt nothing. The mother was afraid the child would lose the use of her hands, but no such calamity ensued. It would have been very ungrateful in her fairy majesty if she had struck the child powerless for touching her dress, if indeed such power were hers. But to return to our story, the very day mentioned, the oatmeal was returned, not by the same lady, but by a curious little figure with a yelping voice; she was likewise dressed in green. After handing the meal she yelped out, "Braw meal, it's the top pickle of the sin corn." It was excellent; and what was very strange, all the family were advised to partake of it but one servant lad, who spurned the fairy's meal; and he dying shortly after, the miller and his wife firmly believed it was because he refused to eat of the meal. They also firmly believed their first visitor was no less a personage than the Queen of the Fairies, who having dismissed her court, had not one maid of honour in waiting to obey her commands. A few nights after this strange visit, as the miller was going to bed, a gentle tap was heard at the door, and on its being opened by him, with a light in his hand, there stood a little figure dressed in green, who, in a shrill voice, but very polite manner, requested him to let on the water and set the mill in order, for she was going to grind some corn. The miller did not dare to refuse, so did as she desired him. She told him to go to bed again, and he would find all as he had left it. He found everything in the morning as she said he would. So much for the honesty of fairies.

4. A tailor was going to work at a farm-house early one morning. He had just reached it, and was going to enter, when he heard a shrill voice call out, "Kep fast, will ye?" and on looking quickly round, he was just in time to receive in his arms a sweet, little, smiling baby of a month old, instead of a little lady in green, who was standing to receive the child. The tailor turned and ran home as fast as he could, for tailors are generally nimble kind of folks, and giving the baby to his wife, ran off again to his work, leaving his

better half in no pleasant mood with the little intruder, as she very politely termed the little innocent. Having reached the farm-house, the tailor found the inhabitants all thrown into confusion by the screaming, yelping, little pest, as they called their little nurseling, for the little woman in green had given in exchange this little hopeful for their own sweet little one, which was safe with the tailor's wife. They found out afterwards it was the nurse who had done it. The doctor was sent for, but all was in vain; day nor night rest they got none. At last one day, all being absent but the tailor, who was there following his trade, he commenced a discourse with the child in the cradle. "Will hae ye your pipes?" says the tailor. "They're below my head," says the tenant of the cradle. "Play me a spring," says the tailor. Like thought, the little man, jumping from the cradle, played round the room with great glee. A curious noise was heard meantime outside; and the tailor asked what it meant. The little elf called out, "It's my folk wanting me," and away he fled up the chimney, leaving the tailor more dead than alive. Their own child was brought home, and the guilty nurse dismissed, and the tailor's wife amply rewarded for the care of the child. She was heard to say, "It was a glad sight the wee bit bairn."

5. The Macgowans of Grayscroft in Tongland, and latterly of Bogra, had the power of witchcraft to a considerable extent, and it descended from one generation to another. At the time we refer to, Abraham Macgowan and his daughter Jenny resided at Grayscroft. Jenny had an unlimited power from Old Nick to act as she pleased. The ploughmen at that time in their employ were Harry Dew and Davie Gordon, young men about twenty-two years of age; they had been there for the last twelve months; and conversing one day together, the following took place:—

Harry—"Losh man, Davie, what makes ye sae drowsy, lazy, and sleepy-like the day, for I am verra sure ye work nae mair than I do; ye eat the same and sleep the same as I do, and yet ye are so thin and wearied and hungry-like, I dinna ken ava what ails ye; are ye weel eneugh, Davie?" "I'm weel eneugh, Harry, but it's a' ye ken about it; sleep a night or twa at the bedside, and maybe you'll no be sae apt to ask me sic questions again. Harry—"The bedside, Davie! what differ will that make? I hae nae mair objections to sleep there than at the wa'." This being agreed to, they exchanged places. Nothing occurred to disturb either of them till the third night, although Harry kept watch: their bed was on the stable loft, when, about midnight, the stable door was opened cautiously, and some one was heard (by Harry only) coming up the ladder and to the

Popular Tales of the West Highlands

bedside, with a quiet step. A bridle was held above the one next the bedside, and the words, "Up horsey," whispered in his ear; in one moment Harry was transformed into a horse at the stable door. The saddle was got on with some kicking and plunging, but Jenny gets mounted, and off they set by the Elfcraigs, Auld Brig o' Tongland, the March Cleughs, and on till they reach the Auld Kirk of Buittle. Harry was tied to the gate along with others. Meg o' Glengap was there on her dairymaid, now a bonny mare, neat in all her proportions. "Tib" o' Criffle came on her auld ploughman, rather windbroken. "Lizzy," frae the Bennan, came on her cot wife, limping with a swelled knee. "Moll o' the Wood" came on a herd callant frae the "How o' Siddick." When all the horses were mustered, there was some snorting and kicking and neighing amongst them. Fairies, witches, brownies, and all met in the kirk and had a blithe holiday, under the patronage of his Satanic majesty, which continued till the crowing of the cock. Wearied with his gallop, Harry, when the charmed bridle was taken off, found himself in his own bed and in his own shape. Harry is determined to be revenged; he finds the charmed bridle in a hole in the kitchen in a week after; he tries it on Jenny, using the same words, when Jenny is transformed into the auld brown mare of the farm; he takes her to the neighbouring smithy, and gets her, after much ado, shod all round, when he returns and leaves her, after securing the wonderful bridle.

Next morning Harry is ordered to go for a doctor, as his mistress is taken ill. He goes into the house to ask for her; pulls the bed clothes off her, and discovers there was a horse shoe on each hand and foot, when Harry says, "Jenny, my lass, that did ye." Jenny played many more similar tricks on her neighbour lads and lasses.

SUTHERLAND.

In Sutherland the fairy creed is much the same as elsewhere in Scotland, but there is a generic term for supernatural beings, which is rarely used in West Country Gaelic. Here are a few of a large and very good collection of Sutherland stories.

1. Duncan, surnamed More, a respectable farmer in Badenoch, states as follows:—"A matter of thirty summers ago, when I was cutting peats on the hill, my old mother that was, was keeping the house. It was sowens she had in her hand for our supper, when a little woman walked in and begged a lippie of meal of her. My mother, not knowing her face, said, 'And where do you come from?'

'I come from my own place and am short of meal.' My mother, who had plenty by her in the house, spoke her civil, and bound her meal on her back, following her a few steps from the door. She noticed that a little kiln in the hill side was smoking. The wife saw this too, and said, 'Take back your meal, we shall soon have meal of our own.' My mother pressed ours on her; but she left the pock lying; and when she came to the running burn went out of sight; and my mother just judged it was a fairy."

2. Once upon a time there was a tailor and his wife, who owned a small croft or farm, and were well to do in the world; but had only one son, a child, that was more pain than pleasure to them, for it cried incessantly and was so cross that nothing could be done with it. One day the tailor and his helpmeet meant to go to a place some miles distant, and after giving the child its breakfast, they put it to bed in the kitchen, and bid their farm servant look to it from time to time; desiring him also to thrash out a small quantity of straw in the barn before their return. The lad was late of setting to work, but recollected before going off to the barn, that he must see if the child wanted for anything. "What are you going to do now?" said the bairn sharply to Donald, as he opened the kitchen door. "Thrash out a pickle of straw for your father; lie still and do not *girr*, like a good bairn." But the bairn got out of bed, and insisted then and there in being allowed to accompany the servant. "Go east, Donald," said the little master, authoritatively, "Go east, and when ye come to the big brae, chap ye (anglicè *rap*) three times; and when *they* come, say ye are seeking Johnnie's flail." The astonished Donald did as he was bid, and by rapping three times, called up a fairy ("little man") who, giving him the flail, sent him off with it in an unenviable state of terror.

Johnny set to with a will, and in an hour's time, he and Donald had thrashed the whole of the straw in the barn; he then sent Donald back to the brae, where the flail was restored with the same ceremony, and went quietly back to bed. At dusk the parents returned; and the admiration of the tailor at the quantity and quality of the work done, was so great, that he questioned Donald as to which of the neighbours had helped him to thrash out so much straw. Donald, trembling, confessed the truth; and it became painfully evident to the tailor and his wife that the child was none of theirs. They agreed to dislodge it as soon as possible, and chose as the best and quickest way of doing so, to put it into a creel (open basket), and set it on the fire. No sooner said than done; but no sooner had the child felt the fire, than starting from the creel, it vanished up the chimney. A low crying noise at the door attracted their attention; they opened, and a bonny little bairn (which the mother recognised by its frock to be her own), stood shivering outside. It was welcomed with rapture from its sojourn among "the little people," and grew up to be a douse and wise-like *lad*, says my informant.

3. The burn of Invernauld, and the hill of Durchâ, on the estate of Rosehall, are still believed to be haunted by the fairies, who once chased a man into the sea, and destroyed a new mill, because the earth for the embankment of the mill-dam had been dug from the side of their hill. The hill of Durchâ is also the locality assigned for the following tale:—

4. A man, whose wife had just been delivered of her first-born, set off with a friend to the town of Lairg, to have the child's birth entered in the session-books, and to buy a cask of whisky for the christening fête. As they returned, weary with a day's walk, or as it is called in the Highlands "*travelling*," they sat down to rest at the foot of this hill, near a large hole, from which they were, ere long, astonished to hear a sound of piping and dancing. The father feeling very curious, entered the cavern, went a few steps in, and disappeared. The story of his fate sounded less improbable *then* than it would now; but his companion was severely animadverted on; and when a week elapsed, and the baptism was over, and still no signs of the lost one's return, he was accused of having murdered his friend. He denied it, and again and again repeated the tale of his friend's disappearance down the cavern's mouth. He begged a year and a day's law to vindicate himself, if possible; and used to repair at dusk to the fatal spot, and call and pray. The term allowed him had but one more day to run, and as usual, he sat in the gloaming by the cavern, when, what seemed his friend's *shadow*, passed within it. He went down, heard reel tunes and pipes, and suddenly descried the missing man tripping merrily with the fairies. He caught him by the sleeve, stopped him, and pulled him out. "Bless me! why could you not let me finish my reel, Sandy?" "Bless me!" rejoined Sandy, "have you not had enough of reeling this last twelvemonth?" "Last twelvemonth!" cried the other, in amazement; nor would he believe the truth concerning himself till he found his wife sitting by the door with a yearling child in her arms, so quickly does time pass in the company of THE "*good people*."

5. Of the Drocht na Vougha or Fuoah—the bridge of the fairies or kelpies, now called the Gissen Briggs, a bar across the mouth of the Dornoch Firth—it is said that the Voughas being tired of

crossing the estuary in cockle shells, resolved to build a bridge across its mouth. It was a work of great magnificence, the piers and posts, and all the piles being headed and mounted with pure gold. Unfortunately, a passer by lifted up his hands and blessed the workmen and the work; the former vanished; the latter sank beneath the green waves, where the sand accumulating, formed the dangerous quicksands which are there to this day.

6. The Highlanders distinguish between the water and land or *dressed* fairies. I have given one story which shows that they are supposed to be "spirits in prison;" it is not the only legend of the kind. In a Ross-shire narrative, a beautiful green lady is represented as appearing to an old man reading the Bible, and seeking to know, if for such as her, Holy Scripture held out any hope of salvation. The old man spoke kindly to her; but said, that in these pages there was no mention of salvation for any but the sinful sons of Adam. She flung her arms over her head, screamed, and plunged into the sea. They will not steal a baptized child; and "Bless you!" said to an unbaptized one, is a charm against them. A woman out shearing had laid her baby down under a hedge, and went back from time to time to look at it. She was going once to give it suck, when it began to yell and cry in such a frightful way that she was quite alarmed. "Lay it down and leave it, as you value your child," said a man reaping near her; half an hour later she came back, and finding the child apparently in its right mind again, she gave it the breast. The man smiled, told her that he had seen her own infant carried off by the "good people," and a fairy changeling left in its place. When the "folk" saw that their screaming little imp was not noticed, and got nothing, they thought it best to take it back and replace the little boy.

As fairies are represented as having always food, and riches, and power, and merriment at command, it cannot be *temporal* advantages that they seek for their children, probably some spiritual ones are hoped for by adoption or marriage with human beings, as in the romantic legend of Undine; and that this tempts them to foist their evil disposed little ones on us. They never maltreat those whom they carry away.

BADENOCH.

The Badenoch account of the fairies is much the same. I have received eight stories from a Highland minister, who has been kind enough to interest himself in the matter, at the request of the Countess of Seafield. These show, that according to popular belief, fairies commonly carried off men, women, and children, who seemed to die, but really lived underground. In short, that mortals were separated from fairies by a very narrow line.

1. A man sees fairies carding and spinning in a shealing where he is living at the time. Amongst them is Miss Emma MacPherson of Cluny, who had been dead about one hundred years.

2. A woman, benighted, gets into a fairy hill, where she promises to give her child, on condition that she is let out. She gives her child when it is born, and is allowed to visit it "till such time as the child, upon one occasion, looked at her sternly in the face, and in a very displeased mood and tone upbraided her for the manner in which she had acted in giving her child over unto those amongst whom it was now doomed to dwell." The mother scolded, found herself standing on the hillock outside, and never got in again.

3. A lad recognizes his mother, who had been carried off by fairies, but who was believed to be dead. She was recovered from the fairies by a man who threw his bonnet to a passing party, and demanded an exchange. The rescuer gave up the wife, and she returned home. Of this story I have several versions in Gaelic and in English, and I believe it is in print somewhere.

4. An old woman meets her deceased landlord and landlady, who tell her that the fairies have just carried off a young man, who is supposed to be dead. They advise her not to be out so late.

5. The young Baron of Kincardine is entertained by fairies, who steal his father's snuff for him when he asks for a pinch.

6. The young baron meets a bogle with a red hand, tells, and is punished.

7. The baron's dairymaid, when at a shealing, has a visit from a company of fairies, who dance and steal milk.

8. "A man, once upon a time, coming up from Inverness late at night, coming through a solitary part called Slockmuic, was met by crowds of people, none of whom he could recognize, nor did they seem to take any notice of him. They engaged in close conversation, talked on subjects not a word of which he could pick up. At length accosting one individual of them, he asked who they were? 'None of the seed of Abram nor of Adam's race; but men of that party who lost favour at the Court of Grace.' " He was advised not to practise late at night travelling in future.

Thomas MacDonald, gamekeeper at Dunrobin, also gives me a fairy tale, which is "*now commonly believed in Badenoch.*"

9. A man went from home, leaving his wife in child-bed. Her temper had never been ruffled. He found her a wicked scold. Thinking all was not right, he piled up a great fire, and threatened to throw in the occupant of the bed, unless she told him "where his own wife had been brought." She told him that his wife had been carried to Cnoc Fraing, a mountain on the borders of Badenoch and Strathdearn, and that she was appointed successor.

The man went to Cnoc Fraing. He was suspected before of having something supernatural about him; and he soon found the fairies, who told him his wife had been taken to Shiathan Mor, a neighbouring mountain. He went there and was sent to Tom na Shirich, near Inverness. There he went, and at the "Fairy Knoll" found his wife and brought her back. *The person who related this story pretended to have seen people who knew distant descendants of the woman.*"

ROSS.

The Ross-shire account of fairies is again much the same. The people say very little about them, and those who have been kind enough to note stories picked up amongst their less instructed neighbours, have only sent fresh evidence to prove that the fairy creed is the same there as everywhere, and that it is not quite extinct.

1. I have a story, got through the kindness of Mr. Osgood Mackenzie, in which a Lowland minister speaks slightingly of the fairies. "He was riding home through a dark glen, and through an oak wood, where there was many a green tolman (mound). He was surrounded by a squad of little men, leaping before him and dancing behind him. They took him off the horse and carried him up through the skies, his head under him now, and his feet under again, the world running round; and at last they dropped him near his own house."

2. In another story, a lot of fairies borrow a weaver's loom at night, without his leave, and make a web of green cloth from stolen wool.

BEARNAIRIDH.

There was in Beàrnairidh in the Harris, a man coming past a knoll, and taking the road, and he heard churning in the hill. Thirst struck him. "I had rather," said he, "that my thirst was on the herdswoman." He had not gone but about twenty rods away when a woman met him, and she had a fine green petticoat on tied about her waist, and she had a vessel of warm milk between her two hands. She offered him a draught, and he would not take it.

"Thou one that sought my draught, and took not my draught, mayest thou not be long alive."

He went to the narrows, and he took a boat there over; and coming over the narrows he was drowned.

Bha aunn am Beàrnairidh aunns na h-Earadh, fear a' tighinn seachad air cnoc a' gabhail an rathaid agus chual e aunns a' chnoc maistreadh. Bhuail am pathadh e. "B' fheàrr leom," ars' esan, "gon robh mo phathadh air a' bhanachaig." Cha deach e ach mu thuaiream fichead slat air falbh, an uair a choinnich boireannach e, agus còta briagh, uain' urr' air a cheanghal mu 'miadhon, agus cuman blàthaich aic' eadar a da làimh. Thairg i da deoch, 's cha ghabhadh e i. "Fhir a dh' iarr mo dheoch, 's nach do ghabh mo dheoch, na mu fada 'bhios thu beò." Ghabh e 'ionnsuidh a chaolais, agus ghabh e bàt' a sin thairis, 's a' tighinn thairis air a' chaolas chaidh a bhàthadh.

From Malcolm MacLean, who learnt it from his grandfather, Hugh MacLean.

North Uist, August 11, 1859.

The Argyllshire stories, which I can well remember as a child, are of the same stamp. The fairies lived in hills, they came out now and then and carried people away; and they spent their time inside their dwellings in dancing to the pipes. They stole milk, and they were overcome by charms, which men sold to those who believed in them. They could not withstand a rowan-tree cross; nor could they follow over a running stream.

There is a small waterfall in a wood which I know, where it used to be said that the fairies might be seen on moonlight nights, fishing for a magic chain from boats of sedge leaves. They used to drag this chain through the meadows where the cattle fed, and the milk came all to them, till a lad, by the advice of a seer, seized one end of the chain and ran for his life, with the fairy troop in pursuit; he leaped the lin and dropped the chain; and the lin is called the chain lin still.

MAN.

The Manks fairy creed is again the same. Similar beings are supposed to exist, and are known by the name of FERISH, which a Manksman assured me was a genuine Manks word. If so, fairy may be old Celtic, and derived from the same root as Peri, instead of being derived from it.

The fairies in the Isle of Man are believed to be spirits. They are not supposed to throw arrows as they are said still to do in the Highlands. None of the old peasants seemed to take the least interest in "elf shots," the flint arrows, which generally lead to a story when shown elsewhere. One old man said, "The ferish have no body, no bones;" and scorned the arrow heads. It is stated in Train's history, that no flint-arrow heads have ever been found in the Isle of Man; but as there are numerous barrows, flint weapons may yet be discovered when some one looks for them.

Still these Manks fairies are much the same as their neighbours on the main land. They go into mills at night and grind stolen corn; they steal milk from the cattle; they live in green mounds; in short, they are like little mortals invested with supernatural power, thus: There was a man who lived not long ago near Port Erin, who had a LHIANNAN SHEE. "He was like other people, but he had a fairy sweetheart; but he noticed her, and they do not like being noticed, the fairies, and so he lost his mind. Well, he was quite quiet like other people, but at night he slept in the barn; and they used to hear him talking to his sweetheart, and scolding her sometimes; but if any one made a noise he would be quiet at once."

Now, the truth of this story is clear enough; the man went mad; but this madness took the form of the popular belief, and that again attributed his madness to the fairy mistress. I am convinced that this was believed to be a case of genuine fairy intercourse; and it shows that the fairy creed still survives in the Isle of Man.

DEVONSHIRE.

The same is true of Devonshire. In May 1860 I was told that many of the farmers "are so superstitious as to believe in PISKIES" they are "Never seen, but they are often heard laughing at people in the dark, and they lead them away." My informant said that when he was young he used to hear so many stories about piskies from

the old women about the fireside, that he used to be frightened to
go out at night.

"When the young colts are out running wild, their manes get
rough and hang down on both sides, and get tangled with the wind
like; not like manes of horses that are well kept (here the speaker
pointed with his whip at the sleek pair which he was driving); and
when the farmers find stirrups like in the hair of the mane, they say
the piskies has been a ridin' of them."

In short, this notice of fairy belief might be extended to fill
volumes; every green knoll, every well, every hill in the Highlands,
has some fairy legend attached to it. In the west, amongst the
unlearned, the legends are firmly believed. Peasants never talk about
fairies, for they live amongst them and about them. In the east the
belief is less strong, or the believers are more ashamed of their creed.
In the Lowlands, and even in England, the stories survive, and the
belief exists, though men have less time to think about it. In the south
the fairy creed of the peasants has been altered, but it still exists, as
is proved occasionally in courts of law. There is a ghost which walks
under the North Bridge in Edinburgh; and even in the cultivated
upper strata of society in this our country, in France, and elsewhere,
fairy superstition has only gone down before other stronger beliefs,
in which a table is made the sole partition between this world and
the next. Whether we are separated from the other world by a deal
board or a green mound, does not seem to make much difference;
and yet that is the chief difference between the vagrant beliefs of the
learned and unlearned.

An old highlander declared to me that he was once in a boat with
a man who was struck by a fairy arrow. He had the arrow for a long
time; it was slender like a straw for thickness. He himself drew it out
of the temple of the other man, where it was stuck in the skin through
the bonnet. They were then miles from the shore, fishing. A man,
whom the fairies were in the habit of carrying about from island to
island, told him that he had himself thrown the dart at the man in
the boat by desire of *them*; "*they* made him do it."

My informant evidently believed he was speaking truth, as my
more educated friends do when they tell me sgeulachd about Mr.
Hume.

For my own part, I believe *all* my friends; but I cannot believe in
fairies, or that my forbears have become slaves of a table to be
summoned at the will of a quack. I believe that there is a stock of old
credulity smouldering near a store of old legends, in some corner of
every mind, and that the one acts on the other, and produces a fresh
legend and a new belief whenever circumstances are favourable to
the growth of such weeds. At all events, I am quite sure that the fairy

creed of the peasantry, as I have learned it from them, is not a whit more unreasonable than the bodily appearance of the hand of Napoleon the First to Napoleon the Third in 1860, as it is described in print; and the grave books which are written on "Spiritual Manifestations" at home and abroad. What is to be said of the table which became so familiar with a young lady, that it followed her upstairs and jumped on to the sofa!

29

THE FINE.

The Feen were once, and their hunting failed, and they did not know what they should do. They were going about strands and shores gathering limpets, and to try if they should fall in with a pigeon or a plover. They were holding counsel together how they should go to get game. They reached a hill, and sleep came on them. What should Fionn see but a dream. That it was at yon crag of rock that he would be, the longest night that came or will come; that he would be driven backwards till he should set his back to the crag of rock. He gave a spring out of his sleep. He struck his foot on Diarmid's mouth, and he drove out three of his teeth. Diarmid caught hold of the foot of Fionn, and he drove an ounce of blood from every nail he had. "Ud! what didst thou to me?"—"What didst thou thyself to me?"—"Be not angry, thou son of my sister. When I tell thee the reason, thou wilt not take it ill."—"What reason?"—"I saw a dream that at yonder crag I would pass the hardest night I ever passed; that I should be driven backwards till I should set my back to the crag, and there was no getting off from there." "What's our fear! Who should frighten us! Who will come!" "I fear, as we are in straits just now, that if this lasts we may become useless." They went and they cast lots who should go and who should stay. The Feinn altogether wished to go. Fionn was not willing to go, for fear the place should be taken out before they should come (back). "I will not go," said Fionn. "Whether thou goest or stayest, we will go," said they.

The rest went, but Fionn did not go. They stopped, on the night when they went, at the root of a tree; they made a booth, and they began to play at cards. Said Fionn, when the rest were gone, "I put him from amongst heroes and warriors any man that will follow me out." They followed after Fionn. They saw a light before them, and they went forward where the light was. Who were here but the others playing at cards, and some asleep; and it was a fine frosty night. Fionn hailed them so stately and bravely. When they heard the speaking of Fionn, those who were laid down tried to rise, and the hair was stuck to the ground. They were pleased to see their master. Pleasant to have a stray hunting night. They went home. Going past a place where they used to house, they saw a house. They asked what house was that. They told them there was the house of a hunter. They reached the house, and there was but a woman within, the wife of the fine green kirtle. She said to them, "Fionn, son of Cumal, thou art welcome here." They went in. There were seven doors to the house. Fionn asked his gillies to sit in the seven doors. They did that. Fionn and his company sat on the one side of the house to breathe. The woman went out. When she came in, she said, "Fionn, son of Cumal, it is long since I was wishing thy welfare, but its little I can do for thee to-night. The son of the king of the people of Danan is coming here, with his eight hundred full heroes, this night." "Yonder side of the house be theirs, and this side ours, unless there come men of Eirinn." Then they came, and they sat within. "You will not let a man on our side," said Fionn, "Unless there comes one that belongs to our own company." The woman came in again, saying, "The middle son of the king of the people of Danan is coming, and his five hundred brave heroes with him." They came, and more of them staid without on a knoll. She came in again, saying, "The youngest son of the king of the people of Danan is coming, and his five hundred swift heroes with him." She came in again, saying, "That Gallaidh was coming, and five hundred full heroes."— "This side of the house be ours, and that be theirs, unless there come of the men of Eirinn." The people of Danan made seven ranks of themselves, and the fourth part of them could not cram in. They were still without a word. There came a gillie home with a boar that had found death from leanness and without a good seeming, and he throws that in front of Fionn with an insult. One of Fionn's gillies caught hold of him, and he tied his four smalls, and threw him below the board, and they spat on him. "Loose me, and let me stand up; I was not in fault, though it was I that did it, and I will bring thee to a boar as good as thou ever ate."—"I will do that," said Fionn; "but though thou shouldst travel the five-fifths of Eirinn, unless thou comest before the day comes, I will catch thee." They loosed him; he went away, and gillies with him.

They were not long when they got a good boar. They came with
it, and they cooked it, and they were eating it. "A bad provider of
flesh art thou," said Gallaidh to Fionn. "Thou shalt not have that
any longer to say;" and the jawbone was in his hand. He raised the
bone, and he killed seven men from every row of the people of
Danan, and this made them stop. Then a gillie came home, and
the black dog of the people of Danan with him, seeking a battle of
dogs. Every one of them had a pack of dogs, and a dozen in every
pack. The first one of them went and slipped the first dozen. The
black dog killed the dozen; he killed them by the way of dozen and
dozen, till there was left but Bran in loneliness. Said Fionn to
Conan, "Let slip Bran, and, unless Bran makes it out, we are
done." He loosed him. The two dogs began at each other. It was
not long till Bran began to take driving; they took fear when they
saw that; but what was on Bran but a venomous claw. There was
a golden shoe on the claw of Venom, and they had not taken off
the shoe. Bran was looking at Conan, and now Conan took off the
shoe; and now he went to meet the black dog again; and at the
third "spoch" he struck on him; he took his throat out. Then he
took the heart and the liver out of his chest. The dog took out to
the knoll; he knew that foes were there. He began at them. A
message came in to Fionn that the dog was doing much harm to
the people without. "Come," said Fionn to one of the gillies, "and
check the dog." The gillie went out, and (was) together with the
dog; a message came in that the gillie was working worse than the
dog. From man to man they went out till Fionn was left within
alone. The Feen killed the people of Danan altogether. The lads
of the Feen went out altogether, and they did not remember that
they had left Fionn within. When the children of the king saw that
the rest were gone, they said that they would get the head of Fionn
and his heart. They began at him, and they drove him backwards
till he reached a crag of rock. At the end of the house he set his
back to it, and he was keeping them off. Now he remembered the
dream. He was tightly tried. Fionn had the "Ord Fianna," and
when he was in extremity it would sound of itself, and it would be
heard in the five-fifths of Eirinn. The gillies heard it; they gathered
and returned. He was alive, and he was no more. They raised him
on the point of their spears: he got better. They killed the sons of
the king, and all that were alive of the people, and they got the
chase as it ever was.

NA FEINNE.

Bha 'n Fhìnn uair agus cheileadh an t-seilg orra, 's cha robh fios aca dé dhianadh eud. Bha eud a' falbh feadh tragha as cladach a' cruinneachadh bhàirneach, 's feuch an aimscadh calman na feadag orra. Bha eud a' gabhail comhairle comhla airson gum falbhadh eud airson seilg fhaotainn. Ràinig eud cnoc 's thàinig cadal orra. Dé chunnaic Fionn ach bruadar, gur h' ann aig a' charragh chreig' ud shìos a bhiodh e 'n oidhche a b' fhaide leis a thig na 'thàinig. Gum biodh e 'ga iomain air ais gus an cuireadh e 'dhriom ris a' charragh chreige. Thug e leum as a chadal, 's bhuail e chas air bial Dhiarmaid, 's chuir e tri fiaclan as. Rug Diarmaid air cas Fhinn 's chuir e unnsa fala bhàr h' uile fin' a bh' aige. "Ud dé rinn thu orm?" "De rinn thu fhin ormsa?" "Na gabh thusa mìothlachd a mhic mo pheathar; nur a dh' innseas mi duit an reusan cha gabh thu gu don' e." "De 'n reusan?" "Chunna mi bruadar gur h-ann aig a' charragh sin shìos a chuirinn seachad an oidhche bu doirbhe chuir mi riabh; gum bithinn air m' iomain air m' ais gus an cuirinn mo dhriom ris a' charragh, 's cha robh dol as an sin." "De 's eagal duinn? Co chuireadh eagal oirnn? Co thig?" arsa Diarmaid. "Tha eagal orm, a's sinn air anacothrom an drasd, ma leanas so gum fagar gun fheum sinn," arsa Fionn. Dh' fhalbh eud 's thilg eud croinn co dh' fhalbhadh 's co dh' fhanadh 's co dh' fhanadh. Bha 'n Fhéinn uil' airson folbh. Cha robh Fionn deònach folbh, eagal gun d' thugt' amach an t-àite ma 'n d' thigeadh eud. "Cha n fholbh mi," ursa Fionn. "Còca dh' fholbhas na dh' fhanas thu falbhaidh sinne," ursa iadsan. Dh' fholbh càch, ach cha d' fholbh Fionn. Stad eud, an oidhche sin a dh' fholbh eud, aig bonn craoibhe. Rinn eud bùth agus thòisich eud air iomairt chairtean. Ursa Fionn nur dh' fholbh càch, "Tha mi 'ga chur a cuid laoich na gaisgich duine sam bith a leanas a mach mi." Dh' fholbh eud as déigh Fhinn. Chunnaic eud solusd rompa. Ghabh eud air an aghaidh far an robh 'n solusd. Co bha 'n so ach cách a' cluichd air chairtean, 's oidhche bhriagh reothaidh ann. Chuir Fionn fàilt orra go flathail, fialaidh. Nur a chual eud bruidhinn Fhinn thug an fheadhain a bha na'n laidhe làmh air éiridh, 's bha 'n gruag air leantail ris a' ghrannd. Bha eud toilicht' am maighstir fhaicinn. Taitneach còrr oidhche seilg fhaotainn, chaidh eud thun a' bhaile. 'Dol seachad air àite 'b' àbhaist daibh a bhi tighich chunnaic eud tigh, dh' fheoraich eud dé 'n tigh a bha 'n siud. Thuirt eud riu gun robh tigh sealgair. Ràinig eud an tigh, 's cha robh stigh ach boireannach. Bean a chòta chaoil

uaine. Urs' i riu, "Fhinn Mhic Cumhail 'se do bheatha an so."
Chaidh eud a stigh. Bha seachd dorsan air an tigh. Dh' iarr Fionn
air a ghillean suidhe ann an seachd dorsan an tighe. Rinn eud sin.
Shuidh Fionn 'sa chuideachd san darna taobh de n tigh a ligeil an
analach. Chaidh a' bhean a mach. Nur a thàinig i stigh thuirt i,
"Fhinn Mhic Cumhail's fhad' o'n a bha mi 'g altachadh le slàinte
dhuit, ach 's beag is urra mi dheanadh riut a nochd; tha mac righ
sluagh de Danainn a' tighinn an so a nochd agus ochd ciad làn
ghaisgeach aige." "An taobh ud de 'n tigh acasan, 'san taobh so
againne, mar an d' thig e dh' fhearaibh Eirinn." Thàinig eud an sin
's shuidh eud a stigh. "Cha lig sibh duin' air ar taobhne," ursa
Fionn, "mar an d' thig duine 'bhoineas d'ar cuideachd fhìn."
Thàinig a' bhean a stigh a rithisd ag ràdh. "Tha mac miadhonach
righ Sluagh de Dana 'tighinn agus còig ciad treun ghaisgeach aige."
Thàinig eud 's dh' fhan còrr dhiu mach air cnoc. Thàinig i stigh a
rithisd ag ràdh, "Tha mac is òige righ Sluagh de Dana tighinn agus
còig ciad lùgh-ghaisgeach leis." Thàinig i stigh a ris ag ràdh gun
robh Gallaidh a' tighinn agus còig ciad làn ghaisgeach leis. "An
taobh so' n tigh againne, 's an taobh sin acasan, mar an d' thig e
dh' fhearaibh Eirinn," arsa Fionn. Rinn an Sluagh de Dana seachd
streathan dhiu fhìn, 's cha do theachd an ceathramh cuid a stigh
dhiu. Bha eud na 'n tàmh gun smid. Thàinig gille dachaidh le torc
a fhuair bàs leis a' chaoile, gun sgath math, 's tilgear siud air
bialthaobh Fhinn le tàmailt. Rug h-aon de ghillean Fhinn air agus
cheanghail e cheithir chaoil; thilg e fo 'n bhòrd e 's bha eud a
caitheadh smugaidean air. "Fuasgail mis' agus lig 'nam sheasamh
mi, cha mhi bu choireach gad is mi rinn e, agus bheir mi go torc
thu cho math 's a dh' ith thu riabh." "Ni mise sin," arsa Fionn,
"ach gad a shiùbhla tu còig chòigeabh na h-Eireann, mar an d' thig
thu man d' thig an latha, beiridh mis' ort." Dh' fhuasgail eud e.
Dh' fhalbh e 's gillean leis. Cha b' fhada bha eud nur a fhuair eud
deagh thorc. Thàinig eud leis, 's bhruich eud e, 's bha eud 'ga
itheadh. "S dona 'm biataiche feòl' thu," ursa Gallaidh ri Fionn.
"Cha bhi sin agadsa na 's fhaide r'a ràdh," arsa Fionn agus cnàimh
a' chiobhuill aige 'na laimb. Chaith e 'n cnàimh, agus mharbh e
seachd daoin' as gach streath de n t-Sluagh de Dana, agus chuir so
eud 'nan stad. Thàinig gille an sin dachaidh, 's cù dugh Sluagh de
Dana leis' aig iarraidh còmhrag chon. Bha lodhainn chon aig a'
h-uile fear diusan, as dusan anns a' h-uile lodhainn, agus dh' fhalbh
a' chiad fhear diu agus dh' fhuasgail e chiad dusan. Mharbh an cù
dugh an dusan. Mharbh e eud a lìon dusan a's dusan, gus nach d'
fhàgadh ach Bran 'na ònrachd. Ursa Fionn ri Conan, "Lig

fuasgladh do Bhran, agus mar dian Bran deth e tha sin deth." Dh' fhuaisgail e e. Thòisich an da chù air a chéile. Cha b' fhada gos an do thòisich Bran air gabhail iomanach. Ghabh eud eagal nur a chunnaic eud sin; ach dé bha air Bran ach crudha nimhe. Bha bròg òir air a' crudha nimhe, 's cha d' thug eud deth a' bhròg. Bha Bran ag amharc air Conan; 's thug Conan deth a' nis a' bhròg. Chaidh e nis an dàil a' choin duigh a rìs, 's air an treas spoch a bhuail e air, thug e 'n sgòrnan as. Thug e 'n sin an cridhe 's an gruan a mach as an uchd aige. Ghabh an cù mach thun a' chnoic; dh' aithnich gur h-e naimhdean a bh' aun; thòisich e orra. Thàinig brath a stigh go Fionn, gon robh 'n cù dianadh mòran cron air an t-sluagh a muigh. "Thalla," ursa Fionn, ri fear de na gillean, "agus caisg an cù." Chaidh an gille mach comhla ris a' chù. Thàinig brath a stigh gon robh an gille 'g obair na bu mhiosa na 'n cù. O fhear go fear chaidh eud a mach gos an d' fhàgadh Fionn a stigh 'na ònrachd. Mharbh an Fhìnn an Sluagh de Danainn uile. Dh' fhalbh gillean na Fìnne mach uile, 's cha do chuimhnich eud gun d' fhàg eud Fionn a stigh. Nur a chunnaic clann an righ gon d' fhalbh càch air fad 'thuirt eud gom faigheadh eud ceann Fhìnn 'sa chridhe. Thòisich eud air, agus dh' iomain eud air ais e 'gos an d' ràinig e carragh creige aig ceaunn an tighe. Chuir e dhriom ris, 's bha e 'gan cumail deth. Chuimhnich e 'n so air a' bhruadar. Bha e air fheuchainn go teaunn. Bha aig Fionn an t-òrd Fianna, 's nur a bhiodh e 'na éigin sheinneadh e leis fhìn, agus chluint' aunn an còig chòigeabh na h-Eireann e. Chual na gillean e; chruinnich eud 's thill eud. Bha e beò, 's cha robh tuillidh air. Thog eud e air bharraibh nan sleagh. Chaidh e 'na b' fheàrr. Mharbh eud mic an righ 's na bha beò d' an sluagh. Fhuair eud an t-seilg mur a bha i riabh.

This story is one of the kind usually called SEANACHAS NA FEINE,—that is, the tradition, conversation, or tale or old stories, or ancient history, history or biography (Macalpine) of the people, best known to English readers as the Fingalians. These are called by a collective name, and are spoken of as *the* Feen or Fain. They are generally represented as hunters and warriors in Eirinn, but their country is the Feen. Bran's battle and his venomous claw in a golden shoe, is more like the fight of a tiger or cheetah than an Irish deer-hound.

The people of Danan are called Tuatha de danan, in manuscripts and books, and are supposed to be Scandinavians. The name, by a slight change in pronunciation, might mean the daring Northerns, the tenants of Danan, or the people of Danan, as here. Fionn, in various inflections, is pronounced Feeun, Een, Eeun. ORD FIANNA would seem to mean hammer of the Feean; if so, Fin may have acquired some of his gear of Thor, or he may be the same personage. The "ord Fiannar" is generally supposed to be a whistle, which sounded of itself, and was heard over the five-fifths of Erin.

This tale, and No. 24, 25, 26, 27, and the two which follow, were told to Hector MacLean "by four individuals, ALEXANDER MAC-DONALD, tenant, Barra, BAILEBHUIRGH, who heard them from his grandmother, Mary Gillies, about forty years ago, when she was more than eighty; NEILL MACLEAN, tenant, ditto, who learnt them from Donald MacNeill, who died about five years ago, about eighty years of age; JOHN CAMERON, ditto, who heard them from many, but cannot name any in particular. They state that these tales were very common in their younger days. They are pretty common still. They can tell nothing respecting the tales beyond the persons from whom they learnt them; of those from whom they learnt them they know nothing."

There are numerous prose tales of the Fingalians in Gaelic manuscripts, now in the Advocates' Library in Edinburgh (according to an abstract lent by W. F. Skene, Esq.) One is probably the same as this tale; it is No. 4 of the manuscript numbered 4, called THE BOOTH OF EOCHAIDH DEARG—a tale of Fingal decoyed into a tent, and his combats with monsters, giants, armies, etc.

Of this manuscript the author of the abstract, Ewen MacLachlan, says (1812):—"This volume is evidently a transcript, perhaps not older than half a century. The language bespeaks high antiquity."

With the exception of a few words, the language in this Barra tale is the ordinary language of the people of the island. It seems then, that this is a remnant of an old tale, rapidly fading from memory and mixing with the manners of the day, but similar to tales in manuscripts about one hundred years old, and to tales now told in Ireland. See Poems of Ossin, Bard of Erin, 1857.

30

THE TWO SHEPHERDS.

There were out between Lochaber and Baideanach two shepherds who were neighbours to each other, and the one would often be going to see the other. One was on the east side of a river, and another on the west. The one who was on the west side of the river came to the house of the one who was on the east of it on an evening visit. He staid till it was pretty late, and then he wished to go home. "It is time to go home," said he. "It is not that which thou shalt do, but thou shalt stay to-night," said the other, "since it is so long in the night." "I will not stay at all events; if I were over the river I don't care more." The houseman had a pretty strong son, and he said, "I will go with thee, and I will set thee over the river, but thou hadst better stay."—"I will not stay at all events."—"If thou wilt not stay I will go with thee." The son of the houseman called a dog which he had herding. The dog went with him. When he set the man on the other side of the river, the man said to him, "Be returning now, I am far in thy debt." The strong lad returned, and the dog with him. When he reached the river as he was returning back home, he was thinking whether he should take the stepping-stones, or put off his foot-clothes and take below. He put off his foot-clothes for fear of taking the stepping-stones, and when he was over there in the river, the dog that was with him leaped at the back of his head. He threw her off him; she leaped again; he did the same thing. When he was on the other side of the river, he put his hand on his head, and there was not a bit of a bonnet on it. He was saying whether should he return to seek the bonnet, or should he go home without it. "It's disgusting for me to return home without my bonnet; I will return over yet to the place where I put my foot-clothes off me; I doubt it is there that I left it." So he returned to the other side of the river. He saw a right big man seated where he had been, and his own bonnet in his hand. He caught hold of the bonnet, and he took it from him. "What business hast thou there with that?—It is mine, and thou hadst no business to take it from me, though thou hast got it." Over the river then they went, without a word for each other, fiercely, hatingly. When they went over, then, on the river, the big man put his hand under the arm of the shepherd, and he began to drag the lad down to a loch that was there, against his will and against his strength. They stood front to front, bravely, firmly on either side. In spite of the strength of the shepherd's son, the big man was about to conquer. It was so that the shepherd's son thought of putting his hand about an oak tree that was in the place. The big man was striving to take him with him, and the tree was bending and twisting. At last the tree was loosening in the earth. She loosened all but one of her roots. At the time when the last root of the tree slipped, the cocks that were about the wood crowed. The shepherd's son understood that when he heard the cocks crowing that it was on the short side of day. When they heard between them the cocks crowing, the big man said, "Thou has stood well, and thou hadst need, or thy bonnet had been dear for thee." The big man left him, and they never more noticed a thing near the river.

AN DA CHIOBAIR.

Bha, mach eadar Lochabar agus Bàideanach, da chìobair a bha 'nan nàbaidhean aig a chéile, 's bhiodh an darna fear, gu bicheanta, dol a dh' amharc an fhir eile. Bha fear air taobh na h-aird an iar de 'n abhainn, 's fear eile air taobh na h-aird an ear. Thàinig am fear a bh' air taobh na h-aird an iar de 'n abhainn 'ionnsuidh tigh an fhir a bh' air taobh na h-aird an ear di, air cheilidh. "Dh' fhan e gos an robh e go math anmoch, 's bha e 'n sin deònach air dol dachaidh. "Tha 'n t-am dol dachaidh," urs' esan. "Cha 'ne sin a ni thu ach fanaidh tu noch," urs' am fear eile, "on a tha e cho fada 's an oidhche." "Cha 'n fhan mi codhiu; na 'm bithinn thar na h-abhne thu; ach 's fheàrra duit fantail." "Cha 'n fhan mi codhiu." "Mar am fan falbhaidh mise leat." Dh' eubh mac fir an tighe air galla 'bh' aig' a' cìobaireachd. Dh' fhalbh a' ghalla leis. Nur a chuir e null an duin' air an taobh eile de 'n abhainn thuirt an duine ris. "Bi tilleadh a nis tha mi fad ann a'd' chomain." Thill an gille làidir agus a' ghalla comhla ris. Nur a rìnig e 'n abhainn, agus e tilleadh air ais dachaidh, bha e smaointeachadh còca a ghabhadh e na sìnteagan, na chuireadh e dheth a chaisbheart agus a ghabhadh e go h-ìseal. Chur e dheth a chaisbheart eagal na sìnteagan a ghabhail, 's nur a bha e null anns an abhainn, leum a' ghalla bha leis ann an cùl a chinn. Thilg e deth i. Leum i rithisd. Rinn e 'n ni cianda. Nur bha e 'n taobh thall de 'n abhainn, chuir e làmh air a cheann, 's cha robh spìdeag de 'n bhoinneid air. Bha e 's an ag a gradh còca thilleadh e dh' iarraidh no boinneid, na rachadh e dhachaidh as a h' ioghnais. " 'S ceacharra domh fhìn gun till mi dachaidh gun mo bhoinneid; tillidh mi null fhathasd gos an àite an do chuir mi dhiom mo chaisbheart; 's ann ann a tha amharus agam a dh' fhàg mi i." Thill e 'n so go taobh thaull na h-aibhne. Chunnaic e fear ro mhòr 'na shuidhe far an robh e, 'sa bhoinneid fhìn 'na làimh. Rug e air a' bhoinneid 's thug e uaidh' i. "Dé do ghnothach sa ris a sin?" "Mo chuid fhìn a th' ann, 's nach robh gnothach agadsa toirt uam, gad a tha i agad." Null, an sin, thar an abhainn dh' fhalbh eud, 's gun facal aca r'a chéile, go fiachach fuachach. Nur a chaidh eud a null, an sin, air an abhainn chuir am fear mòr a làmh fo achlais a' chìobair, 's thòisich e air a' ghille a tharuinn a sìos gu loch a bha 'n sin, an aghaidh a thoil 's an aghaidn a neart. Sheas eud aghaidh ri aghaidh, go treun calm' air gach taobh. A dh' aindeoin cho làidir 's a bha mac a' chìobair bha 'm fear mòr a' brath buadhachadh. 'Se smaointich mac a' chìobair a nis a làmh a chur timchioll air craobh dharaich a bha 'san àite. Bha 'm fear mòr a' strìth ra thoirt leis, 's bha chraobh a' lùbadh 's a' fàsgadh. Fo dheireadh bha chraobh a' fuasgladh as an talamh. Dh' fhuasgail i ach aon fhreumhach di. 'San am an d' fhuasgail an fhreumhach ma dheireadh de 'n chraoibh, ghairm na coilich a bha feadh na coille. Thuig mac a' chìobair, nur a chual e na coilich a' gairm, gon robh e air an taobh ghoirid de 'n latha. Nur a chual eud eatorra na coilich a' gairm thuirt am fear mòr, " 'S math a sheas thu, 's bha feum agad air, airneo, bhiodh do bhoinneid daor duit." Dhealaich am fear mòr ris, 's cha d' fhairich eud sgath riabh tuillidh a chòir na n-aibbne.

There is a bogle story in W. Grant Stewart's "Highland Superstitions" (published 1823 and 1851), in which a man is dragged towards a river by a supernatural being, whom he kills with his dirk.

2. I have another story like this, which was sent to me by a young gentleman, a member of the Ossianic Society of Glasgow. It has some likeness to No. 28, The Smith, and is a good illustration of this part of popular mythology. When the people of Kintyre, MUINTIR CHEAN TIREADH were coming home from the northern airt from

fighting against Prince Charles, under their chieftain, the man of Skipnish, they were going together, each band that was nearest as neighbours. So one little company staid behind the great band, in CEAN LOCH GILP, Lochgilphead. The one who was hindmost of this company, who was called by the nickname of IAN DUBH MOR, Big Black John, heard an unearthly noise, when he was come in front of a fall that was at A MHAOIL DUBH, on the northern side of TAIRBAIRT CHEANTIREADH, Tarbert (which may be rendered Land's-end draw-boat.)

He went on, and in a burn below the fall, a terrible being met him; he drew his blade. Said the being to him, "Strike me." "I will not strike, thou monster," said John; but BRODAIDH MI THU, "I will prod thee."

"Prod me," the being would say. "I will not prod thee, monster, but I will strike thee," John would say.

They fought thus for a great time till the cock crew; and the being said to Ian, "Thou wilt now be going, but before thou goest, take thy choice of the two following things—EALAN GUN RATH NO, RATH GUN EALAIN, speechless art, or artless speech."

John chose speechless art, and so it happened. He was a black-smith, as skilful as ever drew hammer on anvil; but he was not much better for that; there was no penny he earned that he would not spoil, and that would not go in some way that was not easily explained. As an instance of art, he could mend a saw, though thou hadst a bit in either hand, in such a way that it could not be seen where it was broken; and a gun in the same way. There would be a covering on the smithy windows when he would be mending such things.

Big Black John got great power over witchcraft, BUITSEACHAS, and evil eye.

There was a man in Skipnish who had made money by smuggling, but he began to lose his money, for his malt refused to yield its product, till at last he lost the whole of what he had made; and he was a poor man. He went at last to IONARAIR, Ayr, where John was dwelling at that time. John told him that it was enmity that was doing the ill. He did not learn who was spoiling him. He said to him, "Go home and thou wilt get back the produce of the malt;" and so he did. Each TOGAIL (mashing) he made began to give more than the other, till the produce he got frightened him. He followed on thus till the loss was made up, and after that he got but the usual product.

The following are stories of the same kind. The prevailing notions are, that supernatural beings exist which cannot withstand the power of iron, and that there are men and women who deal with them. These are from Mr. Hector Urquhart, written in English, and given in his own words.

3. One day last week, as I was walking up Glenfyne, I overtook an

old man who was carting coals up to the Lodge. "Good day to you, John." "Good day to yourself," says John. From good days to showery days, I asked John if there was any virtue in iron against witchcraft or fairy spells. "Indeed, and that's what there is," says John. So, when we came to the Lodge, I wrote the following story from his telling:—"On a certain year and me a young lad, all our cows lost the milk, one after one; we guessed what was wrong with them, and my big brother lost no time in going to Appin, to consult the man of the RED BOOK. He no sooner entered his house than the man told him what moved him from home. 'It's your own neighbour's wife,' says he, 'that spoilt your cows; she is this moment in your house, inquiring whether you went from home to-day, and where did you go to; and to make it double sure to you, that it's her who spoilt your cows, she will meet you under the lintel of your door coming out as you are going in. Go you now home, and take a shoe of an entire horse, and nail it to your byre-door; but let no living person know of it.'

"My brother came home, and as the man of the red book told him, this identical woman met him on the threshold as he was going in to the house. I do not know how he managed to get hold of the laird's stallion, but the shoe was nailed on our byre door before sunrise next morning, so our cows had plenty milk from that day forth."

4. "This must be a wonderful book, John," says I; "do you know how this man came to have it?" "Well," says John, "I'll tell you that."

"Once upon a time, there lived a man at Appin, Argyllshire, and he took to his house an orphan boy. When the boy was grown up, he was sent to herd; and upon a day of days, and him herding, there came a fine gentleman where he was, who asked him to become his servant, and that he would give him plenty to eat and drink, clothes, and great wages. The boy told him that he would like very much to get a good suit of clothes, but that he would not engage till he would see his master; but the fine gentleman would have him engaged without any delay; this the boy would not do upon any terms till he would see his master. 'Well,' says the gentleman, 'in the meantime write your name in this book.' Saying this, he put his hand into his oxter pocket, and pulling out a large red book, he told the boy to write his name in the book. This the boy would not do; neither would he tell his name, till he would acquaint his master first. 'Now,' says the gentleman, 'since you will neither engage, or tell your name, till you see your present master, be sure to meet me about sunset to-morrow, at a certain place.' The boy promised that he would be sure to meet him at the place about sun-setting. When the boy came home he told his master what the gentleman said to him. 'Poor boy,' says he, 'a fine master he would make; lucky for you that you neither engaged nor wrote your name in his book; but since you promised to meet him, you must go; but as you value your life, do as I tell you.' His master gave him a sword, and at the same time he told him to be sure and be at the place mentioned a while before sunset, and to draw a circle round himself with the point of the sword in the name of the Trinity. 'When you do this, draw a cross in the centre of the circle, upon which you will stand yourself; and do not move out of that position till the rising of the sun next morning.' He also told him that he would wish him to come out of the circle to put his name in the book; but that upon no account he was to leave the circle; 'but ask the book till you would write your name yourself, and when once you get hold of the book keep it, he cannot touch a hair of you head, if you keep inside the circle.'

"So the boy was at the place long before the gentleman made his appearance; but sure enough he came after sunset; he tried all his arts to get the boy outside the circle, to sign his name in the red book, but the boy would not move one foot out of where he stood; but, at the long last, he handed the book to the boy, so as to write his name therein. The book was no sooner inside the circle than it fell out of the gentleman's hand inside the circle; the boy cautiously stretches out his hand for the book, and as soon as he got hold of it, he put it in his oxter. When the fine gentleman saw that he did not mean to give him back the book, he got furious; and at last he transformed himself into a great many likenesses, blowing fire and brimstone out of his mouth and nostrils; at times he would appear as a horse, other times a huge cat, and a fearful beast (uille bheast); he was going round the circle the length of the night; when day was beginning to break he let out one fearful screech; he put himself in the likeness of a large raven, and he was soon out of the boy's sight. The boy still remained where he was till he saw the sun in the morning, which no sooner he observed, than he took to his soles home as fast as he could. He gave the book to his master; and this is how the far-famed red book of Appin was got."

I have heard many old people say that they went from all parts to consult the red book of Appin, though this is the best story I heard about it. You ask if there were virtue in iron; you must know that iron was the principal safeguard against evil spirits, etc., etc.; which I shall show in my next letter on the fairies.

5. The next is from thé telling of a dancing master, a north country Highlander, and written by my friend Mr. John Campbell of Kilberry, in Argyllshire. The supernatural being described as Bauchan, is probably BOCAN, a little buck, a hobgoblin, a ghost, a sprite, spectre (Armstrong and other Dic.); and he seems but a half-tamed specimen of the same genus as the terrible being before described.

COLUINN GUN CHEANN, The Headless Trunk. Coluinn gun

Cheann was a very celebrated Bauchkan, who favoured the family of the Macdonals of Morar, for ages immemorial, and was frequently seen about their residence, Morar House; which is situated on the main land, opposite the point of Slaate, in the Island of Skye. Though a protector of the family, he was particularly hostile to the neighbourhood, and waged war, especially with all the strong men he could meet with; for this purpose he particularly haunted the "Mile Reith," or "Smooth Mile," one end of which was not above 200 yards from the Mansion (I know the place well); the other end of the Mile terminated at a large stream, called the River Morar, famed in history for salmon fishing; after sunset, people did wisely to avoid that part, for then the "COLUINN GUN CHEANN" was sure to keep his vigils; and any stray man who passed was sure to become a victim, the bodies being always found dead, and in the majority of instances mutilated also. As he took care never to appear, except to a solitary passenger, it was in vain to send a party against him. He was seldom, if ever, seen by women, and did no harm either to them or to children. Once it happened that a distant relative, but intimate friend *of Raasay's*, dared his fate, and remained a victim on the ground. This came to the ears of "IAN GARBH, MACGILLIE CHALLUM, RAASAY," "Big John, the son of M'Leod of Raasay;" he was celebrated for his prowess and strength, and never had been vanquished in any fight, though he had tried with the strongest. He told his step-mother of the news he had heard from the Mainland, and asked her advice, as he usually did, before he undertook any exploit of the kind. She advised him to go, and avenge the blood of his friend. After his preparations were made, and not without a blessing from the Oracle, he set out on his circuitous journey, and met the "COLUINN" after sunset, on the Mile Reith, and a battle did ensue, and I daresay it was a very stiff one. Before sunrise it was necessary for the Coluinn to be off, as he never could be seen in daylight. Whether finding he made no progress discouraged him or not, we can't say, but Ian got the victory. Being determined to get a sight of the Coluinn, and also to prove his victory to others, Ian tucked him under his arm, to carry him to the nearest light. The Coluinn had never been heard to speak; but being in this predicament, called out, "LEIG AS MI," "Let me go." "CHA LEIG MI AS THU," "I will not let thee go." Leig as mi, he repeated; but still the answer was Cha leig mi as thu. "Leig as mi, agus chan fheachear an so mi gu brath tuileadh." "Let me go, and I shall never be seen here any more." "Ma bhoidachais thu air a leobhar, air a chonail, agus air a stocaidh dhubh, bi falbh." "If thou swear that on the book, on the candle, and on the black stocking, begone!" After making the Coluinn promise this on his knees, Ian liberated him. The Coluinn flew off, singing the following doleful words—"S fada uam fein bonn

beinn Hederin, s fada uam fein bealach a bhorbhan," which we can
only translate by—

> "Far from me is the hill of Ben Hederin,
> Far from me is the pass of murmuring."

This lament was repeated as long as Ian could hear, and these words
are still sung by women in that country to their children, to the
following notes, which tradition says was the very air:—

In the next, from the same source, the same being appears fully
tamed; still supernatural, still possessed of extraordinary strength,
but attached to a family, and a regular brownie.

6. In the neighbourhood of Loch Traig, in Lochaber, Callum Mor
MacIntosh held a little farm. There were rumours of his having
intercourse with a mysterious personage called a bauchan, but of his
first acquaintance with him there are no authentic accounts. One
thing, however, is certain, that on some occasions he was supernat-
urally aided by this bauchan, while at others, having in some way
excited his displeasure, Callum was opposed in all his schemes, and
on several occasions they came the length of fighting hand to hand,
Callum never suffering much injury. On one occasion, as Callum
was returning from Fort-William market, he met his friend the
bauchan within a short distance of his own house, and one of these
contests took place, during which Callum lost his pocket-handker-
chief, which, having been blessed and presented to him by the priest,
was possessed of a peculiar charm. The fight being ended, Callum
hurried home; but, to his dismay, found that he had lost his charmed
handkerchief, for which he and his wife in vain sought. Callum felt
certain he had to thank the bauchan for this mishap, and hurried
back to the scene of action. The first object that met his view was
the bauchan, busily engaged in rubbing a flat stone with the identical

handkerchief. On seeing Callum, he called out, "Ah! you are back; it is well for you, for if I had rubbed a hole into this before your return you were a dead man. No doctor on earth or power could save you; but you shall never have this handkerchief till you have won it in a fair fight." "*Done*," said Callum, and at it they went again, and Callum recovered his handkerchief. Peats were almost unknown at that time, and Callum, when the weather grew cold, took his axe, and felled a large birch tree in the neighbouring forest, the branches supplied wood for the fire for several days, and Callum did not trouble himself to lay in a store nearer hand—when, lo! a snow storm came on, and blocked up the country, so that he was cut off from his supply. There was no means of access to the tree; and careful as Callum's wife was, the last branch was almost consumed, and the fire burnt low. Up started Callum with an exclamation, "Oh! wife, would that we had the tree I felled in the forest! it would keep us warm this night." Hardly had he spoken when the house was shaken and the door rattled; a heavy weight had fallen near the door. Callum rushed to see what the cause was, and there was the wished-for tree, with the Bauchan grinning at him—"S ma am Bauchan fathast, ged a sgain an Sagart"—(the Bauchan is still kind, though the Priest should burst)—said the wife. On another occasion it happened that Callum left the farm he was in and went to one adjoining which he had taken carrying with him his wife and all his furniture. In the night-time Callum turned to his wife and said, "Well, it is well we have all with us; only one thing have we forgotten, the hogshead in which the hides are being barked; *that* we have forgotten." "No matter for that," said the wife; "there is no one to occupy the place yet a while, and we have time to get it home safe enough;" and so the matter rested; but on going round the end of the house next morning, what did Callum see but his own identical hogshead, hides and all. It had been transported the distance of five miles of most rugged, rocky district. None but a goat could have crossed the place, and in the time it would have bothered one to do it, but the Bauchan managed it, and saved Callum a most troublesome journey. If you will go and take a look at it—the spot is there yet—and I would like to see how soon you would manage it, let alone the hogshead.

Poor Callum, however, was obliged, with many of his neighbours, to leave Lochaber; indeed, he was amongst the first embarking at Arisaig for New York. The passage was a tedious one, but it ended at last, and without any particular adventures; but on arriving they had to perform a quarantine of many days. On getting pratique, Callum was in the first boat which landed, and happened to have stowed himself in the bows of the boat, and when she grounded, was the first man to jump on shore. Directly his feet touched the ground, who should meet him in the shape of a goat but the Bauchan, "Ha,

ha Callum, ha mi sho air thoseach orst." Ha, Malcolm, I am here
before thee. Here ends our story; but rumour says that Callum was
the better of the Bauchan's help in clearing the lands of his new
settlement, and that, till he was fairly in the way of prosperity, the
Bauchan abstained from teasing and provoking poor Callum.

The next makes the supernatural beings robbers, and is a further
argument in favour of the theory that all these traditions are fictions
founded on fact; recollections of wild savages living in mountain
fastnesses, whose power, and strength, and cavern dwellings were
enlarged and distorted into magic arts, gigantic stature, and the
under-ground world. I translate the story from Gaelic, written by
Hector MacLean from the telling of JOHANNA MACCRIMMON in
Berneray, August 1859. This woman is a native of Skye, and descended from the celebrated pipers. Her father, grandfather, and
uncles were pipers. She learned the story from her grand-uncle
Angus MacCrimmon.

7. A gentleman had AIREACH, a herd's dwelling, and he was out in
a far-off glen long in the year with his herd women and his calf herd.
They had every man they needed, and they were there till the middle
of summer was. Then the herd woman said that she must go to seek
things that she wanted.

The herd woman went away, and she had a great distance to go
before she should reach the farm.

She said to the herd, in spite of the length of the path, that she
would try to be back that night. When the evening was coming, the
herd was wearying that the herd woman was not coming. Then he
put the cattle to rights AGUS BHLIGH E EUD, and he milked them, and
there were wild showers of snow in the beginning of the night. He
went home when the beginning of night was, and he set in order his
own food, after he had taken a thought—DUIL A THOIRT DETH—that
the herd woman would not come. He took his foods and he shut the
door as well as he could, thinking that no man would come near him
that night. He put NA BEAIRTEAN FRAOICHE (the bundles of heather)
behind the CÒMHLA (door),* and then he sat to toast himself at the
fire because the SIDE (weather) was so cold. He was taking his dinner
there, when he heard a great TARTAR (noise) coming towards the
door. Then he got up from the door with great fear, and he noticed
a being striking the door again. He was thinking, and he did not know
what to do, that if the door were struck a third time it would be in.

He got up, and the door was struck a third time. Then he crouched
in a corner at the lower end of the shealing when he saw the door
being driven in.

* It is quite common in Highland cottages to keep a large bundle of heather or
brushwood to stuff into the doorway on the windward side; sometimes it is the sole
door.

He did not know now whether he should stay as he was or hide himself. When he noticed the door being pushed in, there came in a beast, and she went up to the fire.

The heather took fire and he saw this nasty beast standing at the fire. And she had a great long hair, and that creature was—A CNAMH A CIR—chewing the cud, as though there were a sheep or a cow. The horns that were on her were up to the top of the shealing. The poor man that was within thought that it was time for him to take his legs along with him, and he went out through the night and the winnowing and snow in it.

He found one of the horses, and he reached his master's house before the day came. Here there he struck in the door of his master furiously, and his master awoke and he went where he was, and he told his master the UAMHAS—terrible wonder that had come upon him since the herd woman left him.

The master went, and the eldest son he had and himself, and they took a gun with them. They went as fast as they could to try to catch the beast to kill her. There was the worth of much money in the shealing, and they thought it a loss that they should want it. Then when they were coming near the shealing the gentleman put a charge in the gun, to be all ready—DEISEAL.—(This word is said to be derived from South—about the old practice being to make a turn sun-wise before doing anything of importance).

They reached the shealing, and they let off a shot in. Though he let off the shot he did not notice a thing, and fear would not let one of them search within. They were thus at the door and they perceived the beast showing herself out. It was hardly that she dragged herself out of the door of the shealing.

There out went they—the gentleman and his son! They went in such a great perturbation, that they did not remember the horses; but they stretched out on foot, fleeing before the beast that was there. What but that the beast followed after them till they reached the house, and they thought she would have finished them before they should arrive. When they reached the farm, one of the gentlemen's men met him, and the gentleman told him that he was almost dead at all events, that he had hopes of reaching the house, and that he should go to try to meet the beast, and keep her back a space.

The man went to meet the beast that was here, and she full of the snow; and he looked keenly at her. He returned to his master to tell him what sort of beast it was, and he said, "Come out here that you may come and see the beast."

When they went out to see the beast, what was here but the buck goat, full of the snow, and the master was shamed that he should have fled from the like of that beast.

The herd fled by the way of the banks of the shore; when he saw

his master running away, and they had no tale of him. Three of the
servants were sent about the glen to try if they could find him; and
they were not finding him at all.

He was lost thus for three days and three nights, and they had no
hope that they would find him for ever. On the third day he was going
at the side of the shore, and water-horses and wild beasts coming on
land on the shores. What should he fall in with but a dwelling-place
there. He went in. There was no man there but a little russet man.
The little russet man put welcome on him, and he asked him to come
forward—that he was welcome. He asked of the little russet man
what was the meaning of his staying in such a place, that there was
no man with him.

"Oh," said the little russet man, "it is not allowed me to tell
anything."

"I will tell thee," said the herd, "what sent me in here. It is that I
fled from UAMHAS—a terrible wonder."

"This is the thing thou shalt do," said the little russet man. "Thou
shalt stretch thyself on this bed up here, and thing or thing that thou
seest in thy sleep, remember on thy death that thou dost not tell it."

Then when he went to stretch himself in the bed, what should
meet him in the bed but the body of a man; and he took to trembling
with fear, but he did not move. He thought he would stay as he was;
that the dead man was not to touch him at all events. Then he heard
great speaking coming towards the house; he was not long so till he
noticed a great clatter coming, and what was this but—SEISEAR FEAR
(collective singular noun of number, six man)—six men coming in
and a cow with them. The master that was over the six, said to the
little russet man, "Didst thou see or perceive a man coming this way
since early earliness."

"I did not see," said he, "he might come the way unknown to me."

"Shut the door," said the big man, "and all without be they
without, and all within within."

Then they put the cow on the fire in a great caldron after they had
torn it asunder in quarters. When they had put this on the fire it was
not long till they noticed the next clatter, and what was here but
another band coming.

What should this band have but another cow flayed, and they had
a pit within, and there they salted her. When the flesh that was in the
kettle was cooked, they took their supper all together.

The poor man that was here in the bed did not know on earth what
he should do for fear. Here when it was coming near on the mouth
of the day, the little russet man went out to look what likeness was
on the night.

When he came in, said they to him, "What seeming is on the
night?" "There is a middling seeming," said he; but it is I who saw

the terrible man DUINE FUATHASACH since I went out, as though he were listening to you. I think that it is FHUAMHAIR CHREIG DALLAIG the giant of crag dallag, who is there.

There out went every man of them, and the one that would not wait on his bow he would seize on his sword to kill him.

When the little russet man, who was within, thought that they had hurried well from the house, he said to the one who was in the bed, "Thou one that art up come down as fast as thou didst ever." Then he stretched to the poor man who was in the bed, as fast as ever he did, a stocking full of dollars, and he gave him bread and cheese. "If thou ever didst it, do it now," said the little russet man to the herdsman. The herdsman went, and he reached the house of his master whole and healthy.

The moral of this tale seems to be, that he who runs away from fancied danger may fall into real peril; but what bears upon the theory of the origin of such stories is, that the *real* peril is from "water-horses" and "robbers," who have a little red (RUAGH) man who plays the part of the enchanted princess, and the friendly cat, and the woman who is the slave of the giants, and the robbers; the character which appears in all collections of popular tales to befriend the benighted stranger, or the wandering prince. And what is more, the *fancied* danger was from a creature under the form of a goat. Why a man should be frightened by a goat, appears from the last of following two stories, translated from the Gaelic of Hector Urquhart, and written from the telling of John Campbell in Strath-Gairloch, Ross-shire. He is now (1859) sixty-three.

8. At some time of the world the lord of Gearloch TIGHEARNA GHEARLOCH had a CEATHEARNACH, who used to be slaying FUATHAN, bogles, and routing out the spoilers. The name of this stalwart man was UISTEAN MOR MAC GHILLE PHADRIG. Uistean was on a day hunting, and he saw a great wreath of mist above him, and heard the sweetest music he ever heard, but he was not seeing a thing but the mist itself. He cast a shot that was in his gun at the wreath of mist, and the very finest woman he ever saw fell down at his side. He took her with him to his own house, but there was not a word of speech in her; and she was thus for a year with him, and she never saw a thing that she could not do. And Uistean was thus in the mountain as usual slaying the bogles, FUATHAN, and on a day at the end of a year, and he in the mountain, the night come on him as he was coming home. There he saw a light in a hill; he reached where the light was, and he stood in the door, and NA SITHICHEAN, the fairies, were within making music and dancing, and the butler that they had going round about amongst them and giving them the drink. Uistean was looking at this: and the butler said, "It is a year from this night's night that we lost the daughter of Iarla Anndrum,

the Earl of Antrim. She has the power of the draught on her that she does not speak a word, till she gets a drink from the cup that is in my hand." And the butler was going round about till he reached where Uistean was, and he gave the CORN (cup) to Uistean. No sooner got Uistean a hold of the cup in his hand than he took his soles out (of that), and they after him. They were here coming close to (shearing on) Uistean, and when they were come within sight of the town the cock crowed. One said, "It is as well for us to return;" but another said, "It is but BOGAG FOGHAIR, a Spring soft one." At the end of a while another cock crowed. "But it is time to return now; this is the black cock of March"—and they returned; but Uistean did not let go the cup till they reached his own house, and till he had given a draught to her from the cup, and as soon as she had drunk a draught from the cup, she had speech as well as another. And Uistean went on the spot, back with the cup, and he left it on the hill; and when Uistean came back to his own house she told him that she was the daughter of the Earl of Antrim, and that the fairies had taken her from childbed. Uistean gave her two choices, whether would she rather stay by him, or be sent back to Eirinn; and she had rather go home. They went, and when they reached the house of the Earl of Antrim, she stayed in a little house that was near upon the castle for that night, and when they began to give them news, the housewife told them that the daughter of the Earl of Antrim was exceedingly ill, and that there was no leech in Eirinn that could do her good. Uistean said that he was the great doctor of the King of the Gaeldom, and that he would heal her, and that he would not ask payment till she should be healed.

The Earl was right well pleased his like to be come about, and it was told to the one who was on the bed, that a great Scottish doctor was come to her town that could cure her. But this did not please her at all, and she would not let him come near her. But Uistean said that he would go there though it was ill with her; and he went where she was, with his naked sword in his hand. She who was in the bed cast an eye on him, and she said, "If I had been to put my thumb on the apple of thy throat on the night that thou wert born, thou couldest not do this to me this day."

And when Uistean went to the bed, she went as a flame of fire out at the end of the house.

Then Uistean gave his own daughter by the hand to the Earl of Antrim, whole and healthy. The Earl of Antrim gave Uistean his two choices, that he should stay with him, or a bag of gold and go home. Uistean took the bag of gold, and he came home; and he began at killing Fuathan, as he was before.

This story joins Fairies and Fuathan, and has many relations in other languages, and the next joins the whole to the French Loup

Garou, of which I heard from a peasant in France in November 1859, but the wolf is a goat in the Highlands.

9. Some time after this, word went to Uistean that there was a Fuath on TOMBUIDHE GHEARRLOCH on the yellow knoll of Gairloch, and this Fuath was killing much people, and sending others out of the husk (or the gates) of their hearts, A COCHAIL AN CRIDHE, because no man could take the path after the night or darkness should come.

Uistean came, and on the way at the foot of the knoll Uistean went into the house of a yellow-footed weaver that was living there. Said the weaver to Uistean, "Thou hadst best stop the night."

"Well, I will do that," said Uistean; "I am going to kill the Fuath of Tombuidh to-night."

"Perhaps that is not so easy," said the weaver; "with what wilt thou kill Gabhair Mhoil-Bhui, the goat of Maol-buidh?"

"With the gun," said Uistean.

"What," said the weaver, "if the gun will not suit?"

"If it will not suit," said he, "I will try the sword on her."

"What," said the weaver, "if the sword will not come out of the sheath?"

"Well," said Uistean, "I will try my mother's sister on her."

And on every arm that Uistean named, the weaver laid ROSAD, a spell, but on the dirk which he called his mother's sister the weaver could not lay a spell. Then Uistean went up to the top of the knoll, and on the top of the knoll was a pit in which the goat used to dwell.

She let out a MEIGAID bleat, and Uistean said, "Dost thou want thy kid thou skulker?"

"If I do, I have got it now," said she. Then Uistean laid hands on his gun, but she would not give a spark. Then he laid hands on his sword, but it would not come out of the sheath.

"Where now is thy mother's sister?" said the goat.

When Uistean heard this he sprang on the goat, and the first thrust he gave her with the BIODAG dirk, she let out a roar.

"It seems odd to me, poor beast, if I do not give thy kid milk now."

And he did not see the goat any more. Uistean turned back to the weaver's house, and when he kindled a light, he found the weaver under the loom pouring blood.

"If it was thou who madest so much loss on the yellow knoll, thou shalt not get off any farther," said Uistean.

Then he killed the weaver under the loom, and no man was slain on the yellow knoll since then, by the goat or bogle.

These two stories are certain enough. It was by my mother I heard them, and many a tale there is of Uistean, if I had mind of them.

JOHN CAMPBELL, Strath Gairloch, Ross-shire.

10. I have another version of this same tale written by a school-master, at the request of Mr. Osgood Mackenzie. It is in very good Gaelic, but to translate it would be repetition, for it is almost the identical. I do not mention the name of the writer, for it might be displeasing to him. The narrator is Alexander Macdonald, In-verasdale. The goat is called GABHAR MHOR RHIBEAGACH FHEUSAGACH, a great hairy-bearded goat; and the dirk is called CATRIONA PUITHAR MO SHEANA MHATHAIR, Catherine, my grandmother's sister. He finds the BREABADAIR weaver in bed, with a wound in his thigh, and gives him his death thrust there.

I have given these specimens of a particular class of tales which are common enough, as they came to me, because they seem to be fair illustrations of the popular creed as to spirits; and to show that the so-called spirits are generally very near mortal men. My belief is, that bocan, bodach, fuath, and all their tribe, were once savages, dressed in skins, and that gruagach was a half-tamed savage hanging about the houses, with his long hair and skin clothing; that these have gradually acquired the attributes of divinities, river gods, or forest nymphs, or that they have been condemned as pagan superstitions, and degraded into demons; and I know that they are now remem-bered, and still somewhat dreaded, in their last character. The tales told of them partake of the natural and supernatural, and bring fiction nearer to fact than any class of tales current in the Highlands, unless it be the fairy stories of which a few are given under number 28, etc.

31

OSEAN AFTER THE FEEN.

From Barra.

Oisean was an old man after the (time of the) Feen, and he (was) dwelling in the house of his daughter. He was blind, deaf, and limping, and there were nine oaken skewers in his belly, and he ate the tribute that Padraig had over Eirinn. They were then writing the old histories that he was telling them.

They killed a right big stag; they stripped the shank, and brought him the bone. "Didst thou ever see a shank that was thicker than that in the Feen?" "I saw a bone of the black bird's chick in which it would go round about."—"In that there are but lies." When he heard this, he caught hold of the books with rage, and he set them in the fire. His daughter took them out and quenched them, and she kept them. Ossian asked, with wailing, that the worst lad and dog in the Feen should lay weight on his chest. He felt a weight on his chest. "What's this?"—"I MacRuaghadh" (son of the red, or auburn one). "What is that weight which I feel at my feet?"— "There is MacBuidheig" (the son of the little yellow). They stayed as they were till the day came. They arose. He asked the lad to take him to such a glen. The lad reached the glen with him. He took out a whistle from his pocket, and he played it. "Seest thou anything going past on yonder mountain?"—"I see deer on it."—"What sort dost thou see on it?"—"I see some slender and grey on it."—"Those are the seed of the Lon Luath, swift elk; let them pass."—"What kind seest thou now?"—"I see some gaunt and grizzled."—"Those are the seed of Dearg dasdanach, the red Fierce: let them pass."— "What kind seest thou now?"—"I see some heavy and sleek."— "Let the dog at them Vic Vuiaig!" MacBhuieig went. "Is he dragging down plenty?"—"He is."—"Now, when thou seest that he has a dozen thou shalt check him." When he thought he had them, he played the whistle, and he checked the dog. "Now if the pup is sated with chase, he will come quietly, gently; if not, he will come with his gape open." He was coming with his gape open, and his tongue out of his mouth. "Bad is the thing which thou hast done to check the pup unsated with chase."—"When he comes, catch my hand, and try to put it in his gape, or he will have us." He put the hand of Oisean in his gape, and he shook his throat out. "Come, gather the stags to that knoll of rushes." He went, and that is done; and it was nine stags that were there, and that was but enough for Oisean alone; the lad's share was lost. "Put my two hands about the rushy knoll that is here;" he did that, and the great caldron that the Feen used to have was in it. "Now, make ready, and put the stags in the caldron, and set fire under it." The lad did that. When they were here ready to take it, Oisean said to him, "Touch thou them not till I take my fill first." Oisean began upon them, and as he ate each one, he took one of the skewers out of his belly. When Oisean had six eaten, the lad had three taken from him. "Hast thou done this to me?" said Oisean. "I did it," said he; "I would need a few when thou thyself hadst so many of them."—"Try if thou wilt take me to such a rock." He went down there, and he brought out the chick of a blackbird out of the rock. "Let us come to be going home." The lad caught him under the arm, and they went away. When he thought that they were nearing the house, he said, "Are we very near the house?" "We are," said the lad. "Would the shout of a man reach the house where we are just now?"*—"It would reach it."—"Set my front straight on the house." The lad did thus. When he was coming on the house, he caught the lad, and he put his hand in his throat, and he killed him. "Now," said he, "Neither thou nor another will tell tales of me." He went home with his hands on the wall, and he left the blackbird's chick within. They were asking him where he had been since the day came; he said he had been where he had often passed pleasant happy days. "How didst thou go there when thou art blind?"—"I got a chance to go there this day at all events. There is a little pet yonder that I brought home, and bring it in." They went out to look, and if they went, there did not go out so many as could bring it home. He himself arose, and he brought it in. He asked for a knife. He caught the shank, he stripped it, and then took the flesh off it. He broke the two ends of the bone. "Get now the shank of the dun deer that you said I never saw the like of in the Feen." They got this for him, and

* A Lapp measure of distance is "a dog's bark."

he threw it out through the marrow hole. Now he was made
truthful. They began to ask more tales from him, but it beat them
ever to make him begin at them any more.

OISEAN AN DEIGH NA FEINNE.

Bha Oisean 'na shean duin' an déigh na Finne 's e fuireachd an tigh
a nighinne. Bha e daull, bodhar, bacach, 's bha naoidh deilg daraich
'na bhroinn, 's e 'g itheadh na càin a bh' aig Pàdraig air Eirinn. Bha
eud an sin a' sgrìobhadh na seann eachdraidh a bha e 'g innseadh
dhaibh. Mharbh eud damh ro mhòr; rùisg eud an calpa, 's thug eud
a 'ionnsuidh an cnàimh. "A nis am faca tu calpa riabh a bu ghairbhe
na sin 'san Fhìnn." "Chunna mi cnàimh isein an lòn duigh, 's
rachadh e ma 'n cuairt an taobh a stigh dheth." "Cha n 'eil an sin
ach na briagan." Nur a chual e so rug e air na leabhraichean le
corraich, agus chuir e 'san tein' eud. Thug a nighean as an tein'
eud, 's chuir i as eud, 's ghléidh i eud.

Dh' iarr Oisean de dh' achanaich an gill' agus an cù bu mhiosa
bha 'san Fhìnn a chur cudthrom air uchd. Dh' fhairich e cudthrom
air uchd. "Dé so?" "Mise Mac na Ruaghadh." "De 'n cudthrom
ud a tha mi faotainn aig mo chasan?" "Tha MacBuidheig." Dh'
fhan eud mur a bha eud gos an d' thàinig a latha. Nur a thàinig an
latha dh' éiridh eud. Dh' iarr e air a ghille 'thoirt go leithid so de
ghleann. Ràinig an gille an gleann leis. Thug e mach fideag a a
phòca 's sheinn e i. "Am faic thu dad sam bith a dol seachad air an
aonadh ud shuas?" "Chi mi feidh ann." Dé 'n seòrsa a chi thu ann?"
"Chi mi feadhain chaola ghlas ann." "Sin agad sìol na Luine
luaithe; lig seachad eud." "Dé 'n seòrsa chi thu 'n dràsd?" "Ch mi
feadhain sheanga riabhach." "Sinn agad sìol na Deirge dàsanaich;
lig seachad eud." "Dé 'n fheadhain a chi thu 'n dràsd?" "Chi mi
feadhain throma loma." "Lig an cù thuca Mhic Bhuidheig!" Dh'
fhalbh Mac Bhuidheig. "A bheil e leagail na leoir?" "Tha." "Nur a
chi thu nis aon dusan aige caisgidh thu e." Nur a shaoil e gun robh
eud aige sheinn e 'n fhìdeag 's chaisg e 'n cù. "Nis ma tha 'n cuillean
buidheach seilge thig e gu modhail, socair; mur 'eil thig e 's a chraos
fosgailt." Bha e tighinn 'sa chraos fosgailte 'sa theanga mach air a
bhial. " 'S dona 'n rud a rinn thu an cuilean a chasg 's gun e
buidheach seilg. Nur a thig e beir air mo làimhsa 's fiach an cuir
thu stigh na chraos i, no bidh sinn aige." Chuir e stigh làmh Oisein
'na chraos 's chrath e 'n sgòrnan as. "Thalla, cruinnich na daimh
'ionnsuidh an tom luachrach." Dh' fhalbh e 's dianar siud, agus 'se

naoidh daimh a bh' ann, agus cha b' uilear do dh' Oisean siud 'na
onrachd, 's bha cuid a' ghill air chaull. "Cuir mo dha laimhsa ma
'n tom luachrach a tha 'n so." Rinn e siud 's bha 'n coire mòr a
b'àbhaist a bhi aig an Fhìnn ann, "Dian anis deas 's cuir na daimh
anns a' choire 's cuir gealbhan foidhe." Rinn an gille siud. Nur a
bha eud an so deas airson an gabhail, urs' Oisean ris. "Na bean
thusa dhaibh gos an gabh mise mo dhial an toiseach." Thòisich
Oisean orra, 'sa h-uile fear a dh' itheadh e bheireadh e fear de na
deilg as a bhroinn. Nur a bha sia aig Oisean air an itheadh bha tri
aig a ghill' air an toirt uaidhe. "An d' rinn thu so orm?" urs' Oisean.
"Rinn," urs' esan, "dh' fheumainnsa beagan, nur a bha mòran agad
fhìn diu." "Fiach an d' thoir thu mis' ionnsuidh a leithid so do
chreag." Rinn e siud. Chaidh e sios an sin 's thug e mach isean lòn
duigh as a' chreig. "Thugainn a bhi falbh dachaidh." Rug an gill'
air achlais air 's dh' fhalbh eud. Nur a bha e smaointeachadh gon
robh eud a' teannadh air an tigh thuirt e. "A bheil sinn a' teannadh
goirid o'n tigh." "Tha," urs' an gille, "An ruigeadh- eubh duin' air
an tigh far a bheil sin an dràsd." "Ruigeadh." "Cuir m' aghaidhsa
dìreach air an tigh." Rinn an gille siud. Nur a bha e tigh'n air an
tigh rug e air a' ghille 's chuir e làmh 'na sgòrnan 's mharbh e e.
"So," urs' esan, "cha bhi thusa na fear eile 'g innseadh eachdraidh
a'm' dhéigh-sa." Chaidh e dachaidh 's a làmhan 's a' bhalla 's dh'
fhàg e isean an lòn duigh a stigh. Bha eud a' feòraidh deth càit' an
robh e o thàinig an latha. Thuirt e gon robh e far am minig an do
chuir e làithean sòlasach, toilichte seachad. "Demur a chaidh thus'
an sin 's thu daull?" "Fhuair mi cothrom air a dhol ann an diugh
co dhiu. Tha PEATA beag an siud a thug mi dachaidh 's thugaibh a
steach e." Dh' fhalbh eud a mach a choimhead, 's ma dh' fhalbh,
cha deach a mach na bheireadh dachaidh e. Dh' eiridh e fhìn a mach
's thug e steach e. Dh' iarr e corc. Rug e air a chalpa, 's rùisg e e,
's thug e 'n fheòil deth. Bhris e da cheann a' chnàimh. "Faighibh a
nis calp' an daimh odhair a bha sibh ag radh nach fhaca mise riabh
a leithid 's an Fhinn." Fhuair eud so dha 's thilg e mach romh tholl
an smior aig e. Bha e 'n so air a dhianadh firinneach. Thòisich eud
air iarraidh tuillidh eachdraidh air, ach dh' fhairtlich orra riabh toirt
air tòiseachadh orra tuillidh.

2. A version of this was told to me by an old tinker at Inverary,
but, according to him, the books were destroyed. I took it to be the
popular account of the Ossian controversy. Ossian, MacPherson,
Dr. Smith, and their party, fused into "Ossian," Dr. Johnson, and
his followers, condensed into "Padraig." The famous Red Book of

Clanrannald has also become mythical. Its true history will be found in the book by the Highland Society. I was told in Benbecula how a man had found a book, containing the history of the Feen, in a moss; and how he had parted with it to a blind beggar, who had sold part to a clergyman, the rest was in America. "The book was not dug up; it was *on* the moss. It seemed as if the ancestors had sent it."

3. This story of the Blackbird's bone is common. I heard it myself from several men in South Uist, with variations. According to one, the deer's bone was to turn round on end in the blackbird's shank. Another version has been sent to me from Sutherland. According to J. H. Simpson, a similar tale is now told by the peasantry of Mayo. (Poems of Ossin, Bard of Erin, from the Irish, 1857, page 191.) Mr. MACLEAN very ingeniously suggests that the word which now means Blackbird (Londubh) may originally have meant Black-ELK. Armstrong's Dictionary gives LÒN, a meadow; LÒN, a diet, a dinner, a store, provision, food; LON, an ousel, a blackbird, an *Elk;* LON, greed, prattle, hunger; also, a rope of raw hides used by the people of St. Kilda. The word, then, may mean almost anything that can be eaten by man or beast in general; and an elk in particular.

There are plenty of elks still living in Scandinavia. Their gigantic fossil bones are found in Irish bogs, and in the Isle of Man; a whole skeleton is to be seen in the British Museum; and it is supposed that men and elks existed together in Ireland. (See Wilson's Pre-historic Annals of Scotland, page 22: 1851.) The story probably rests on a foundation of fact—namely, the discovery of fossil bones—mixed up with the floating traditions about the Feen which pervade both Ireland and Scotland, and which have been woven into poems for centuries in both countries. These *may* date from the days when men hunted elks in Erin, as they now do in Scandinavia. "Padraig" probably slipped in when that curious dialogue was composed, of which several versions are still extant in old manuscripts.

4. The Sutherland version is as follows:—

The last of the giants lived among the Fearn Hills (Ross-shire, and within sight of the windows of Skibo); he had an only daughter, married not to a giant, but to a common man.

His son-in-law did not always treat him well, for he was sometimes very hungry, and had to wear a hunger-belt.

One day at dinner his son-in-law said to him, "Did you ever, amongst the giants, eat such good beef, or from so large an ox?"

"Amongst us," said the last of the giants, "the legs of the birds were heavier than the hind quarters of your ox."

They laughed him to scorn, and said, that it was because he was blind that he made such mistakes; so he called to a servant and bid him bring his bow and three arrows, and lead him by the hand to a corrie which he named in the Balnagowan forest.

"Now," said he, "do you see such and such a rock?"

"Yes," said the servant.

"And is there a step in the face of it?"

"Yes," said the servant.

"Are there rushes at the foot of it?"

"Yes," said the servant.

"Then, take me to the steps, and put me on the first of them."

The servant did so.

"Look now, and tell me what comes."

"I see birds," said the fellow.

"Are they bigger than common?"

"No bigger than in Fearn," said the servant.

A little after, "What do you see?"

"Birds still," said the servant.

"And are they no bigger than usual?"

"They are three times bigger than eagles."

A little later, "Do you see any more birds?" said the giant.

"Yes, birds that the air is black with them, and the biggest is three times as big as an ox."

"Then guide my hand to the bow," said the blind giant; and the boy guided him so well that the biggest bird fell at the foot of the rock amongst the rushes.

"Take home a hind quarter," said the giant, and they carried it home between them.

When they came to the house of his son-in-law, he walked in with it, and aimed a tremendous blow at the place where his son-in-law usually sat. Being blind he did not see that the chair was empty; it was broken to pieces; but the son-in-law lived to repent, and treat the blind giant better.

I have another version written in English by Mr. Hugh MacColl, gardener at Ardkinglass, from which it appears that the blind old giant was Ossian, and that his father-in-law was Paul na nooi clerach, Paul of the nine clerks (whom I strongly suspect to be St. Patrick). They questioned him about deer; and this shows how stories alter, for DAMH means *ox* and *stag*, and in Sutherland it has become ox.

5. They would not believe that Ossian's black birds were so large. He got a boy and went to a hill, and pulled a tuft of rushes; and here again is another change in the translation from Gaelic to English; for TOM means a *knoll* and a *bush*. Under the tuft they find a yellow dog, and under another, firelocks and spades; which is another curious change from the bow and arrows. Then they go to a *hill* covered with wood, which suits the country about Stirling; and the lad is made to dig a hole with the spade, and put his head into it. The old giant whistles, and nearly splits the boy's head; and he does this thrice. The first time the boy sees deer as big as peat-stacks; the second, as

large as house; the third, as large as hills; and they slip "cue baie mac kill e buiach," the yellow dog after them.

Then they kindle a fire and roast the deer. Here the bettle has dropped out, and the boy eats some, and old giant is furious; for if he had eaten all he could have recovered his sight. Then he took the boy to a wood, and made him shoot a blackbird on its nest, and he took home a leg, which was so heavy that it broke the table.

Then they tried to get the old man to tell them more about the Faen, but he would not, because they would not believe him; and the next day they went with the boy to a well, and wrung his neck, to keep him silent also.

Here, as in all the versions which I have got, the black *bird* seems to be hauled in to account for the Gaelic word, which is but rarely used, and whose meaning is forgotten. LON DUBH means black *bird* or black *Elk*; and surely deer as big as hills might have done to prove the wonders of the olden time. These three versions of the same story show, as well as any which I have, how the same tale changes in various localities, and why.

In Stirling and in Sutherland Gaelic is fading rapidly. Elks have ceased to exist in Scotland; and the tradition has changed with the times, and shapes itself to suit the ideas of the narrators, and the country about them.

32

THE BARRA WIDOW'S SON.

From Alexander MacNeill, tenant and fisherman, then at Tangual, Barra.

There was a poor widow in Barra, and she had a babe of a son, and Iain was his name. She would be going to the strand to gather shell-fish to feed herself and her babe. When she was on the strand on a day, what did she see but a vessel on the west of Barra. Three of those who were on board put out a boat, and they were not long coming on shore.

She went to the shore and she emptied out the shell-fish beside her. The master of the vessel put a question to her, "What thing was that?" She said that it was strand shell-fish the food that she had. "What little fair lad is this?"—"A son of mine."—"Give him to me and I will give thee gold and silver, and he will get schooling and teaching, and he will be better off than to be here with thee."—"I had rather suffer death than give the child away."—"Thou art silly. The child and thyself will be well off if thou lettest him (go) with me." With the love of the money she said that she would give him the child. "Come hither, lads, go on board; here's for you the key. Open a press in the cabin, and you will bring me hither a box that you will find in it." They went away, they did that, and they came. He caught the box, he opened it, he emptied it with a gush (or into her skirt), and he did not count it all, and he took the child with him.

She staid as she was, and when she saw the child going on board she would have given all she ever saw that she had him. He sailed away, and he went to England. He gave schooling and teaching to the boy till he was eighteen years on the vessel. It was Iain Albanach the boy was called at first, he gave him the name of Iain Mac a Maighstir (John, master's son), because he himself was master of the vessel. The "*owner*" of the vessel had seven ships on sea, and

seven shops* on shore—each one going to her own shop with her
cargo. It happened to the seven ships to be at home together. The
owner took with him the seven skippers to the house, "I am growing
heavy and aged," said he; "you are there seven masters; I had none
altogether that I would rather than thou. I am without a man of
clan though I am married; I know not with whom I will leave my
goods, and I have a great share; there was none I would rather give
it to than thee, but that thou art without clan as I am myself." "I,"
said the skipper, "have a son eighteen years of age in the ship, who
has never been let out of her at all."—"Is not that wonderful for
me, and that I did not hear of it!"—"Many a thing might the like
of me have, and not tell it to you."—"Go and bring him down hither
to me that I may see him." He went and he brought him down, and
he set him in order. "Is this thy son?"—"It is," said the skipper.
"Whether wouldst thou rather stay with me, or go with thy father
on the sea as thou wert before, and that I should make thee an heir
for ever?"—"Well then, it was ever at sea that I was raised, and I
never got much on shore from my youth; so at sea I would rather
be; but as you are determined to keep me, let me stay with yourself."

"I have seven shops on shore, and thou must take thy hand in
the seven shops. There are clerks at every one of the shops," said
he. "No one of them will hold bad opinion of himself that he is not
as good as I. If you insist that I take them, I will take the seventh
one of them."

He took the seventh one of the shops, and the first day of his
going in he sent word through the town, the thing that was before
a pound would be at fifteen shillings; so that everything in the shop
was down, and the shop was empty before the ships came. He (the
owner) went in, he counted his money, and he said that the shop
was empty. "It is not wonderful though it were, when the thing that
was before a pound is let down to fifteen shillings."—"And, my
OIDE, are you taking that ill? Do you not see that I would put out
all in the shop seven times before they could put it out once."—
"With that thou must take the rest in hand, and let them out so."
Then he took the rest in hand, and he was a master above the other
clerks. When the ships came the shops altogether were empty. Then
his master said, "Whether wouldst thou rather be master over the
shops or go with one of the seven ships? Thou wilt get thy choice
of the seven ships."—"It is at sea I was ever raised and I will take
a ship." He got a ship. "Come, send hither here to me the seven

* Buthanan, Booths.

skippers." The seven skippers came. "Now," said he to the six skippers that were going with Iain, "Iain is going with you, you will set three ships before and three behind, and he will be in the middle, and unless you bring him whole hither to me, there is but to seize you and hang you."—"Well, then, my adopted father," said Iain, "that is not right. The ships are going together, a storm may come and drive us from each other; let each do as best he may." The ships went, they sailed, and it was a cargo of coal that Iain put in his own. There came on them a great day of storm. They were driven from each other. Where did Iain sail but to Turkey. He took anchorage in Turkey at early day, and he thought to go on shore to take a walk. He was going before him walking; he saw two out of their shirts working, and as though they had two iron flails. What had they but a man's corpse! "What are you doing to the corpse?"—"It was a Christian; we had eight marks against him, and since he did not pay us while he was alive, we will take it out of his corpse with the flails."—"Well then, leave him with me and I will pay you the eight marks." He seized him, he took him from them, he paid them, and he put mould and earth on him. It was soon for him to return till he should see more of the land of the Turk. He went on a bit and what should he see there but a great crowd of men together. He took over where they were. What did he see but a gaping red fire of a great hot fire, and a woman stripped between the fire and them. "What," said he, "are you doing here?" "There are," said they, "two Christian women that the great Turk got; they were caught on the ocean; he has had them from the end of eight years. This one was promising him that she would marry him every year: when the time came to marry him she would not marry him a bit. He ordered herself and the woman that was with her to be burnt. One of them was burnt, and this one is as yet unburnt."

"I will give you a good lot of silver and gold if you will leave her with me, and you may say to him that you burnt her." They looked at each other. They said that he would get that. He went and he took her with him on board, and he clothed her in cloth and linen.

"Now," said she, "thou hast saved my life for me; thou must take care of thyself in this place. Thou shalt go up now to yonder change-house. The man of the inn will put a question to thee what cargo thou hast. Say thou a cargo of coal. He will say that would be well worth selling in the place where thou art. Say thou it is for selling it that thou art come; what offer will he make for it. He will say, to-morrow at six o'clock there would be a *waggon* of gold going down, and a waggon of coal coming up, so that the ship might be kept in the same *trim*,* till six o'clock on the next night. Say thou that thou wilt take that; but unless thou art watchful they will come in the night when every man is asleep, with muskets and pistols; they will set the ship on the ground; they will kill every man, and they will take the gold with them."

He went to the man of the inn, and agreed with him as she had taught him. They began on the morrow, in the morning, to put down the gold, and take up the coal. The skipper had a man standing looking out that the vessel should be in trim. When the coal was out, and the ship was as heavy with the gold as she was with the coal; and when he was on shore, she got an order for the sailors to take her advice till he should come. "Put up," said she, "the sails, and draw the anchors. Put a rope on shore." They did that. He came on board; the ship sailed away through the night; they heard a shot, but they were out, and they never caught them more.

They sailed till they reached England. Three ships had returned, and the three skippers were in prison till Iain should come back. Iain went up and he reached his adopted father. The gold was taken on shore, and the old man had two thirds and Iain a third. He got chambers for the woman, where she should not be troubled.

"Art thou thinking that thou wilt go yet?" said the woman to him. "I am thinking that I have enough of the world with that same."— "Thou wentest before for thine own will, if thou wouldst be so good as to go now with my will."—"I will do that."—"Come to that shop without; take from it a coat, and a brigis, and a waistcoat; try if thou canst get a cargo of herring and thou shalt go with it to Spain. When the cargo is in, come where I am before thou goest."

When he got the cargo on board he went where she was. "Hast thou got the cargo on board?"—"I have got it."

"There is a dress here, and the first Sunday after thou hast reached the Spain thou wilt put it on, and thou wilt go to the church with it. Here is a whistle, and a ring, and a book. Let there be a horse and a servant with thee. Thou shalt put the ring on thy finger; let the book be in thine hand; thou wilt see in the church three seats, two twisted chairs of gold, and a chair of silver. Thou shalt take hold of the book and be reading it, and the first man that goes out of the church be thou out. Wait not for man alive, unless the King or the Queen meet thee."

He sailed till he reached the Spain; he took anchorage, and he

* Trump.

went up to the change-house. He asked for a dinner to be set in order. The dinner was set on the board. They went about to seek him. A trencher was set on the board, and a cover on it, and the housewife said to him—"There is meat and drink enough on the board before you, take enough, but do not lift the cover that is on the top of the trencher." She drew the door with her. He began at his dinner. He thought to himself, though it were its fill of gold that were in the trencher, or a fill of "daoimean,"* nothing ever went on board that he might not pay. He lifted the cover of the trencher, and what was on the trencher but a couple of herring. "If this be the thing she was hiding from me she need not," and he ate one herring and the one side of the other. When the housewife saw that the herring was eaten,—"Mo chreach mhor! my great ruin" said she; "how it has fallen out! Was I never a day that I could not keep the people of the realm till to-day?"—"What has befallen thee?"— "It is, that I never was a day that I might not put a herring before them till to-day."—"What wouldst thou give for a barrel of herrings?"—"Twenty Saxon pounds."—"What wouldst thou give for a ship load?"—"That is a thing that I could not buy."—"Well, then, I will give thee two hundred herring for the two herring, and I wish the ship were away and the herrings sold."

On the first Sunday he got a horse with a bridle and saddle,† and a gillie. He went to the church; he saw the three chairs. The queen sat on the right hand of the king, and he himself sat on the left; he took the book out of his pocket, and he began reading. It was not on the sermon that the king's looks were, nor the queen's, but raining tears. When the sermon skailed he went out. There were three nobles after him, shouting that the king had a matter for him. He would not return. He betook himself to the change-house that night. He staid as he was till the next Sunday, and he went to sermon; he would not stay for any one, and he returned to the change-house. The third Sunday he went to the church. In the middle of the sermon the king and queen came out; they stood at each side of the (bridle) rein. When the king saw him coming out he let go the rein; he took his hat off to the ground, and he made manners at him. "By your leave; you needn't make such manners at me. It is I that should make them to yourself."—"If it were your will that you should go with me to the palace to take dinner."—"Ud! Ud! it is a man below you with whom I would go to dinner." They reached the palace. Food was set in the place of eating, drink in the

---

* Diamonds.
† All riders have not these luxuries.

place of drinking, music in the place of hearing. They were plying
the feast and the company with joy and gladness,* because they had
hopes that they would get news of their daughter. "Oh, skipper of
the ship," said the queen, "hide not from me a thing that I am going
to ask thee. Any thing that I have that I can tell I will not hide it
from you." "And hide not from me that a woman's hand set that
dress about your back, your coat, your brigis, and your waistcoat,
and gave you the ring about your finger, and the book that was in
your hand, and the whistle that you were playing." "I will not hide
it. With a woman's right hand every whit of them was reached to
me." "And where didst thou find her? 'Tis a daughter of mine that
is there." "I know not to whom she is daughter. I found her in
Turkey about to be burned in a great gaping fire." "Sawest thou a
woman along with her?" "I did not see her; she was burned before
I arrived. I bought her with gold and silver. I took her with me, and
I have got her in a chamber in England." "The king had a great
general," said the queen, "and what should he do but fall in love
with her. Her father was asking her to marry him, and she would
not marry him. She went away herself and the daughter of her
father's brother with a vessel, to try if he would forget her. They
went over to Turkey; the Turk caught them, and we had not hope
to see her alive for ever."

"If it be your pleasure, and that you yourself are willing, I will set
a ship with you to seek her; you will get herself to marry, half the
realm so long as the king lives, and the whole realm when he is
dead." "I scorn to do that; but send a ship and a skipper away, and
I will take her home; and if that be her own will, perhaps I will not
be against it."

A ship was made ready; what should the general do but pay a lad
to have him taken on board unknown to the skipper; he got himself
hidden in a barrel. They sailed far; short time they were in reaching
England. They took her on board, and they sailed back for Spain.
In the midst of the sea, on a fine day, he and she came up on deck,
and what should he see but an island beyond him; it was pretty calm
at the time. "Lads, take me to the island for a while to hunt, till
there comes on us the likeness of a breeze." "We will." They set
him on shore on the island; when they left him on the island the
boat returned. When the general saw that he was on the island, he
promised more wages to the skipper and to the crew, for that they
should leave him there; and they left Iain on the island.

* This passage is one common to many reciters, and spoiled by translation.

When she perceived that they had left Iain on the island, she went mad, and they were forced to bind her. They sailed to Spain. They sent word to the king that his daughter had grown silly, as it seemed, for the loss of the form of her husband and lover. The king betook himself to sorrow, to black melancholy, and to woe, and to heart-breaking, because of what had arisen; and (because) he had but her of son or daughter.

Iain was in the island, hair and beard grown over him; the hair of his head down between his two shoulders, his shoes worn to pulp, without a thread of clothes on that was not gone to rags; without a bite of flesh on him, his bones but sticking together.

On a night of nights, what should he hear but the rowing of a boat coming to the island. "Art thou there, Iain Albanich?" said the one in the boat. Though he was, he answered not. He would rather find death at the side of a hill than be killed.

"I know that thou hearest me, and answer; it is just as well for thee to answer me, as that I should go up and take thee down by force." He went, and he took himself down. "Art thou willing to go out of the island?" "Well, then, I am; it is I that am that, if I could get myself taken out of it." "What wouldst thou give to a man that would take thee out of this?" "There was a time when I might give something to a man that would take me out of this; but to day I have not a thing." "Wouldst thou give one half of thy wife to a man that would take thee out of this?" "I have not that." "I do not say if thou hadst, that thou wouldst give her away." "I would give her." "Wouldst thou give half thy children to a man that would take thee out of this." "I would give them." "Down hither; sit in the stern of the boat." He sat in the stern of the boat. "Whether wouldst thou rather go to England or Spain?" "To Spain." He went with him, and before the day came he was in Spain.

He went up to the change-house; the housewife knew him in a moment. "Is this Iain!" said she. "It is the sheath of all that there was of him that is here."

"Poorly has it befallen thee!" said she. She went and she sent a message to a barber's booth, and he was cleansed; and word to a tailor's booth, and clothes were got for him; she sent word to a shoemaker's booth, and shoes were got for him. On the morrow when he was properly cleansed and arrayed, he went to the palace of the king, and he played the whistle. When the king's daughter heard the whistle she gave a spring, and she broke the third part of the cord that bound her. They asked her to keep still, and they tied more cords on her. On the morrow he gave a blast on the whistle, and she broke two parts of all that were on her. On the third day when she heard his whistle, she broke three quarters; on the fourth day she broke what was on her altogether. She rose and she went out to meet him, and there never was a woman more sane than she. Word was sent up to the king of Spain, that there never was a girl more sane than she; and that the bodily presence of her husband and lover had come to her.

A "coach" was sent to fetch Iain; the king and his great gentles were with him; he was taken up on the deadly points.* Music was raised, and lament laid down; meat was set in the place of eating, drink in the place of drinking, music in the place for hearing; a cheery, hearty, jolly wedding was made. Iain got one half of the realm; after the king's death he got it altogether. The general was seized; he was torn amongst horses; he was burned amongst fires; and the ashes were let (fly) with the wind.

After the death of the king and queen, Iain was king over Spain. Three sons were born to him. On a night he heard a knocking in the door. "The asker is come," said he. Who was there but the very man that took him out of the island. "Art thou for keeping thy promise?" said the one who came, "I am," said Iain. "Thine own be thy realm, and thy children and my blessing! Dost thou remember when thou didst pay eight merks for the corpse of a man in Turkey; that was my body; health be thine; thou wilt see me no more."

MAC NA BANTRAICH BHARRACH.

Bha bantrach bhochd ann am Barra, agus bha leanabh mic aice, agus 's e Iain a b' ainm dha. Bhiodh i dol do 'n tràigh a chruinneachadh maoraich airson i fhìn 's an leanabh a bheathachadh. Nur a bha i 'san tràigh latha bha 'n sin dé chunnaic i ach soitheach air an aird an Iar de Bharra. Chuir triuir de na bha air bòrd a mach bàta 's cha b' fhada bha eud a' tigh'n air tir. Chaidh ise gos a' chladach 's dhòirt i 'm maorach làmh riutha. Chuir Maighstir an t-soithich ceisd urra de 'n rud a bha 'n siud. Thuirt i go 'n robh maorach cladaich, am biadh a bh' aice. "Dè 'n gille beag, bàn a tha 'n so?" "Mac domh." "Thoir dhomhs' e, agus bheir mi dhuit òr agus airgiod, agus gheibh e sgoil as ionnsachadh, 's bidh e na 's fheàrr 'na bhi agads' an so." " 'S fheàrr leam bàs fhuileann na

* This I take to be a phrase wrongly used; an old phrase, meaning that the personage was raised on spears. The passage is common.

'm pàisd' a thoirt seachad." "Tha thu gòrrach, bidh thu fhìn 's an leanabh go math ma ligeas tu leam e." Le gaol an airgid thuirt i gon d' thugadh i 'n leanabh da. "Thallaibh an so ghillean. Theirigibh air bòrd; so duibh iuchair; fosglaibh *press* anns a *chabin*, 's bheir sibh thugamsa bòsdan a gheibh sibh ann." Dh'fhalbh eud; rinn eud siud's thàinig eud. Rug e air bosca' dh' fhosgail e e—dhoirt e 'na sguirt e 's cha do chunnd e idir e, 's thug e leis an leanabh. Dh' fhan ise mur a bha i, 's nur chunnaic i 'n leanabh a dol air bòrd, bheireadh i na chunnaic i riabh go 'n robh e aice. Sheòl esan air falbh agus ghabh e go ruige Sasunn. Thug e sgoil a's ionnsachadh do 'n bhalach gos an robh e ochd bliadhna diag, air an t-soitheach. 'Se Iain Albannach a bh' air a' bhalach an toiseach. Thug esan Iain Mac a Mhaighstir air, a thaobh gom be fhìn maighstir au t-soithich. Bha aig *owner* an t-soithich seachd soithichean air muir, agus seachd bùthannan air tir—a' h-uile té gabhail thun a bùth fhìn le a luchd. Thachair do na seachd loingeas a bhi aig an tigh comhla. Thug an sealbhadair suas leis na seachd sgiobairean thun an tighe. "Tha mi 'fas trom aosd'," urs' esan. "Tha sibh an sin seachd maighstirean—cha robh gin agam gu léir a bu docha leam na thusa—tha mi gon duine cloinne gad a tha mi pòsda. Cha 'n 'eil fhios'am co aig a dh' fhàgas mi mo chuid, agus cuid mhòr agam. Cha robh gin a bu docha leam a thoirt da na thusa, ach go 'bheil thu gon chlann mar mi fhín." "Tha agams'," urs' an sgiobair, "mac ochd bliadhna diag a dh' aois anns an t-soitheach gon a liginn aisd' idir." "Nach neònach leamsa sin agad 's gon mise g'a chluintinn riabh." " 'S iomadh rud a dh' fhaodadh a bhi aig mo leithidsa nach bithinn aig innseadh dhuibhse." "Falbh 's thoir thugams' a nuas e 's gom faicinn e." Dh' fhalbh e 's thug e nuas e, 's chuir e 'n òrdugh e. "An e so do mhacsa?" " 'S e," urs' an sgiobair. "Còca 's fheàrr leat fuireachd agamsa, na falbh le t' athair air a' mhuir mur a bha thu roimhid, 's gun dian mise dìleabach dìot go bràthach." "Mata's ann air muir a fhuair mi mo thogail riabh, 's cha d' fhuair mi dad o m' òig air tìr; le sin 's ann air muir a b' fheàrr leam a bhi; ach o 'n tha sibhs' a' cur roimhibh go 'n cum sibh mi 'gom fan mi agaibh fhìn." "Tha seachd bùthannan agam air tìr, agus feumaidh tu làmh a ghabhail anns na seachd bùthannan." "Tha cléireach aig a h-uile fear riabh de na bùthannan," urs' esan; "cha gabh h-aon aca droch bharail orra fhìn, nach 'eil eud cho math riumsa; ma tha sibh a cur mar fhiachaibh ormsa go 'n gàbh mi eud, gabhaidh mi 'n seachdamh fear diu.

Ghabh e 'n seachdamh fear de na bùthannan, 'sa chiad latha da dol ann 'chuir e fios feadh a' bhaile, an rud a bha roimhid punnd gom biodh e air còig tasdain diag, air alt 's gon d' thàinig 'h-uile rud a bhà a' bhùth nuas 's gon robh 'm bùth falamh ma'n d' thàinig na soithichean. Chaidh e stigh, chunndais e chuid airgid, 's thuirt e go 'n robh 'm bùth falamh. "Cha n' ioghnadh gad a bhitheadh, san rud a bha roimhid air punnd thu g'a ligeil sòis go còig tasdain diag." "Agus, oide, 'bheil sibhse 'ga ghabhail sin go h-olc; nach 'eil sibh a' faicinn gon cuirinnsa mach na bh' anns a bhùth seachd uairean ma 'n cuireadh eudsan a mach aon uair e." "Leis an sin feumaidh tu làmh a ghabhail ri càch agus an ligeil a mach mur sin." Ghabh e n sin làmh ri càch, agus bha e 'na mhaighstir as cionn nan cléireach eile. Nur a thàinig na soithichean bha na bùthannan go léir falamh.

Thuirt a mhaighstir ris a nis, "Còca 's fheàrr leat a bhi 'd' mhaighstir thar nam bùthannan, na falbh le h-aon de na seachd soithichean; gheibh thu do roighinn de na seachd soithichean." " 'S ann air muir a thogadh riabh mi 's gabhaidh mi soitheach." Fhuair e soitheach. "Thallaibh, cuiribh thugamsa na seachd sgiobairean." Thàinig na seachd sgiobairean a 'ionnsuidh. "Nis," urs' esan, ris na sia sgiobairean a bha dol le Iain. "Tha Iain a' dol leibh—cuiridh sibh tri soithichean air thoiseach, 's tri air deireadh, 's bidh esan 'sa mhiadhon; 's mur an d' thoir sibh thugamsa slàn e cha 'n 'eil ach breith oirbh 's 'ur crochadh." "Mata m' oide," urs' Iain, "cha 'n 'eil sin freagarrach. Tha na soithichean a' falbh comhla; faodaibh stoirm tighinn agus ar fuadach o chéile. Dianadh h-uile h-aon mar is fheàrr a dh' fhao-das e."

Dh' fhalbh na soithichean—sheòl eud—agus 'se luchd guail a chuir Iain a stigh na thé fhin. Thàinig latha mòr stoirm orra. Dh' fhuadaicheadh o chéil' eud. C' a 'n do sheòl Iain ach do 'n Tuirc. Ghabh e acair 's an Tuirc trath latha. Smaoinich e dol air tìr a ghabhail sràid. Bha e gabhail roimhe 'coiseachd. Chunnaic e dithisd as an léintean ag obair, 's mar gom biodh da shùisid iaruinn aca. Dé bh' ac' ach corp duine. "Dé tha sibh a dianadh ris a' chorp." " 'Se Crìosdaidh a bh' ann. Bha ochd mairg againn air, 's o'n nach do phàigh e sinn nur a bha e beo bheir sinn a a chorp leis na sùisdean e." "Mata ligibh leams' e agus pàighidh mi dhuibh na h-ochd mairg." Rug e air—thug e uath'e—phaigh a eud agus chuir e ùir as talamh air.

Bha e luath leis tilleadh air ais gos am faiceadh e tuillidh de dh' fhearann na Tuirc. Ghabh e air aghaidh treis, agus dé chunnaic e 'n sin ach grunnan mòr dhaoine cruinn. Ghabh e null far an robh eud. Dé chunnaic e ach craoslach mòr teine, de theine mhor leathann, agus boireannach rùisgt' eadar an teine 's eud fhìn. "De," urs' esan "a tha sibh a dianadh an so." "Tha," urs' eudsan, "da bhana Chriosdaidh a fhuair an Turcach mòr. Rugadh orra air a' chuan. Tha eud o cheann ochd bliadhna aige. Bha 'n te so 'gealltainn da gom pòsadh i e h-uile bliadhna. Nur thàinig an t-am cha phòsadh i bad doth. Dh' òrdaich e i fhìn 's am boireannach a bha comhla rithe 'losgadh. Loisgeadh an darna té dhiu 's tha i so gon losgadh fhathasd." "Bheir mi fhìn duibh tiodhlac math airgid agus òir ma ligeas sibh leam i, agus faodaidh sibh a ràdh ris gon do loisg sibh i." Sheall eud air a chéile. Thuirt eud gom faigheadh e siud. Dh' fhalbh e 's thug e leis air bord i, agus sgeadaich e i 'n aodach 's an anart.

"Nis," urs' ise, "shabhail thu mo bheatha dhomh. Feumaidh tu 'n aire thoirt ort fhìn 's an àite so. Théid thu suas a nis do 'n tigh sheins' ud shuas. Cuiridh fear an tigh sheinse ceisd ort dé 'n luchd a th' agad. Abraidh tusa luchd guail. Abraidh esan gor math a mhiadh siud 'san àite a bheil thu airson a reic. Abraidh tusa gor ann airson a reic a thàinig thu; dé 'n tairgse bheir e air. Their esan, "A màireach air sia uairean bidh *waggon* òir a' dol a sios 's *waggon* guail a' dol a suas, air alt 's gon cumar an soitheach anns an aon *trump* go sia uairean an ath oìdch.' " Abair thusa gon gabh thu siud; ach anns an oidhche' mur am bi thusa a'd-earalas thig eud 's an oidhche, nur a tha h-uile duine na 'n cadal, le musgannan 's le dagannan; cuiridh eud an soitheach air a ghrund; marbhaidh eud a h-uile duine, 's 'bheir eud leo an t-òr." Chaidh e far an robh fear an tigh sheise agus chòrd e ris mar a sheòl is' e. Thòisich eud an la'r na mhàireach 'sa mhadainn air cur sìos an òir 's air toirt suas a' ghuail. Bha fear aig an sgiobair 'na sheasamh ag amharc gom biodh an soitheach ann an trump. Nur a bha 'n gual a mach, 'sa bha 'n soitheach cho trom leis an òr 's a bha i leis a ghual, 's nur a bha esan air tìr, fhuair is' òrdan na seòladairean a ghabhail a comhairle gos an d' thigeadh esan. "Cuiribh suas," urs' ise, "Na siuil, 's tàirnibh na h' acraichean. Cuiribh ròp' air tir." Rinn eud siud. Thàinig esan air bòrd. Sheòl an soitheach air falbh feadh na h-oidhche. Chual eud urchair; ach bha eudsan a mach 's cha d' rug eud orra tuillidh. Sheòl eud go ruige Sasunn. Bha tri soithichean àir tilleadh, 's bha na tri sgiobairean am prìosan gos an tilleadh Iain. Ghabh Iain suas 's ràinig e oide. Chaidh an t-òr a thoirt air tìr, 's bha da dhrian aig a bhodach, 's drian aig Iain. Fhuair e seombraichean do 'n bhoireannach far nach cuirte dragh urra.

"A bheil thu smaointeachadh go falbh thu fhathasd," urs' am boireannach ris. "Tha mi smaointeachadh go bheil na leoir dhe 'n t-saoghal agam siud fhìn." "Dh' fhalbh thu roimhid le t' thoil fhìn;

na 'm biodh tu cho math 's gom falbhadh thu nis le 'm thoilsa."
"Ni mi sin." "Thalla do 'n bhuth ud a muigh, thoir as còt, agus
brigis, agus peitean. Feuch am faigh thu luchd sgadain, agus théid
thu do 'n Spàin leis. Nur a bhios an luchd a stigh thig far a bheil
mise ma 'm falbh thu."

Nur a fhuair e 'n luchd air bòrd chaidh e far an robh i. "An d'
fhuair thu 'n luchd air bord?" "Fhuair." "Tha deise 'n so, 's a chiad
Domhnach an déigh dhuit an Spàin a ruigheachd, cuiridh tu umad
i, agus theid thu do 'n eaglais leatha. So fideag, agus fàinne, agus
leobhar. Bidh each agus gille leat. Cuiridh tu 'm fàinne air do mhiar,
bidh an leobhar a' d' làimh. Chi thu anns an eaglais tri cathraichean,
da chathair amluidh òir, agus cathair airgid. Beiridh tu air an
leabhar 's bidh thu 'ga leubhadh; 's a' chiad duin' a théid a mach as
an eaglais bi thus' amach; na fan ri duine beo mur an coinnich an
righ sa bhan-righ thu."

Sheòl e go ruig an Spàin, ghabh e acarsaid, 's ghabh e suas do 'n
tigh sheinse. Dh'iarr e dinneir a chur air dòigh. Chuireadh an
dinnear air a bhòrd. Dh' iadhaicheadh sìos 'ga iarraidh. Chuireadh
a sìos *trinsear* air a' bhòrd, agus mias air a mhuinn, agus thuirt bean
an tigh sheinse ris, "Tha biadh a's deoch na leoir air a bhòrd ma 'r
coinneamh; gabhaibh 'ur leoir, ach na togaibh a mhias a th' air
muinn an *trinseir*." Tharruinn i 'n doras leatha. Thòisich e air a
dhinneir. Smaoinich e aige fhìn gad a b' e 'làn òir a bhiodh anns an
trinseir, na 'làn daoimean, nach deachaidh sgath riabh air a' bhòrd
nach fhaodadh e phàigheadh. Thog e mhias bhàr an trinseir, 's dé
bh' air an trinsear ach da sgadan. "Ma 's e so rud a bha i falach orm
cha ruigeadh i leas e." Dh' ith e aon sgadan 's na darna taobh do
'n fhear eile. Nur chunnaic bean an tighe gan robh 'n sgadan ithte,
"Mo chreach mhòr," urs' ise, "mar a dh' éiridh domh; nach robh
mi latha riabh nach fhaodainn muinntir na rioghachd a ghleidheadh
gos an diugh. De dh' éiridh dhuit?" "Tha nach robh mi latha riabh
nach faodainn sgadan a chur air am bial-thaobh gos an diugh." "Dé
bheireadh thu air baraille sgadan?" "Fichead punnd Sasnach." "Dé
bheireadh thu air luchd soithich?" "Sin rud nach b' urra mi
'cheannach." "Mata bheir mise duit da chiad sgadan airson an da
sgadain. B' fhearr leam gon robh 'n soitheach air falbh 's na sgadain
creicte."

A chiad Di Domhnaich fhuair e each le strian as dìollaid, agus
gille. Dh' fhalbh e do 'n eaglais. Chunnaic e na tri cathraichean.
Shuidh a bhanrigh air an làimh dheas de 'n righ 's shuidh e fhìn air
an làimh thosgail. Thug e mach an leobhar a a phòca 's thòisich e
air leubhadh. Cha b' ann air searmoin a bha àir' aig an rìgh na aig

a bhanrigh, ach a' sileadh nan diar. Nur a sgaoil an t-searmoin
ghabh e mach. Bha triuir stàtan as a dhéigh, aig eubhach ris gon
robh gnothach aig an righ ris. Cha tilleadh e. Thug e 'n tigh seins'
an oidhche sin air. Dh' fhan e mar a bha e gos an ath Dhomhnach.
Chaidh e 'n t-searmoin, cha 'n fhanadh e ri duine, 's thill e do 'n
thigh sheinse. An treas Domhnach chaidh e do 'n eaglais. Am
miadhan na searmoin thàinig an righ 's a' bhanrigh a mach. Sheas
eud aig gach taobh do 'n t-sréin. Nur chunnaic an righ esan a tigh
'n a mach, lig e as an t-srian, thug e ada dheth do làr, 's rinn e modh
dha. "Le 'r cead cha ruig sibh a leas a leithid sin de mhodh a
dhianadh dhomhsa, 's ann a bu chòir dhomhsa dhianadh dhuibh
fhin." "Na 'm b' e 'ur toil gon rachadh sibh leinn a ghabhail dinnear
do 'n *phaileas.*" "Ud ud 's e duine sòis uaibhse rachainns 'ghabhail
dinnearach leis!"

Ràinig eud am paileas. Chuireadh biadh an àite 'chaitheadh
dhaibh, agus deoch an àite 'h-òl, 's ceòl an àit' éisdeachd. Bha eud
a' caitheadh na cuirme 's na cuideachd le solas 's le toil-inntinn, ri
linn dùil a bhi aca gom faigheadh eud naigheachd air an nighinn.
"A sgiobair na luinge," urs' a bhanrigh, "Na ceil orm dad a tha mi
dol a dh' fhoighneachd dìot." "Dad sam bith a th' agams' is urrainn
mi innseadh dhuibh cha cheil mi oirbh." "Na ceilibh orm nach làmh
boireannaich a chuir a' chulaidh sin ma'r driom, bhur cota, bhur
brigis, 's 'ur peitean; 's a thug dhuibh am fàinne bha mu'r miar, 's
an leobhar a bha 'nur làimh, 's an fhideag a bha sibh a' seinn." "Cha
cheil mi. Le làimh dheas boireannaich a shineadh a h-uile sgath
dhiu sin domhsa." " 'S c'àit' an d' fhuair thu i? 's nighean leams' a
tha 'n sin." "Cha 'n 'eil fios agamsa co da 'n nighean i. Fhuair mis'
i anns an Tuirc a' dol g'a losgadh ann an craoslach mòr teine." "Am
fac thu boireannach comhla rithe?" "Cha 'n fhac. Bha i'n deigh a
losgadh ma 'n d' ràinig mi. Cheannaich mi ise le h-òr 's le airgiod,
thug mi leam i, 's tha i ann an seombar an Sasunn." "Bha Seanailear
mòr aig an righ," ars' a' bhanrigh, " 's dé rinn e ach gaol a ghabhail
urra. Bha h-athair aig iarraidh urra phòsadh 's cha phòsadh i e. Dh'
fhalbh i fhìn 's nighean bhràthar a h-athar le soitheach, fiach an
ligeadh e air diochuimhn' i. Chaidh eud thairis do 'n Tuirc. Ghlac
an Turcach eud, 's cha robh dùil againn a faicinn beò go
bràthach.

Ma 'se 'ur toils' e, 's go bheil sibh fhìn deònach, cuiridh mise
long leibh a 'h iarraidh; gheibh sibh i fhìn a' pòsadh, leith na
rioghachd fad 's is beò an righ, 's an rioghachd uile nur a bhios e
marbh." "Cha 'n fhiach leam sin a dhianadh, ach cuiridh sibhse
soitheach agus sgiobair air falbh, 's bheir mise dachaidh i, 's ma 's

e sin a toil fhìn dh' fhaoidte nach bi mise 'na aghaidh." Chaidh soitheach a dhianadh deas. Dé rinn an Seanailear ach gille phàigheadh' airson a thoirt air bòrd gon fhios do 'n sgiobair. Fhuair e 'san am, e fhìn fhalach ann am baraille. Sheòl eud, fada goirid gon robh eud, go ruige Sasunn. Thug eud is' air bòrd 's shèol eud air an ais airson na Spàin. Am miadhon a' chuain, latha briagh, thàinig esan agus ise nìos air an *deck*. Dè chunnaic e ach eilean an taobh thall deth. Bha e go math fèitheil 'san am. "Ghillean," ars' esan, "thugaibh mis' air an eilean treis a shealg, gos an d' thig coslas soirbheis oirnn." "Bheir," ars' àdsan. Chuir eud air tir air an eilean e. Nur a dh' fhàg eud air an eilean e thill am bàta. Nur chunnaic an Seanailear gon robh e air an eilean, gheall e tuillidh tuarasdail do 'n sgiobair agus don sgiobadh, 's eud a 'fhàgail an siud agus dh'fhàg eud Iain air an eilean. Nur a mhothaich ise gon d' fhàg eud air an eilean e, chaidh i air a choitheach, s b' eigin a ceangal. Sheòl eud do 'n Spàin.

Chuir eud fios 'ionnsuidh an rìgh gon robh a nighean an déigh fas gòrach, a réir coslais, airson call aobhar a fir's a leannain. Chaidh an rìgh go mulad, 's go leann-dugh, 's go bròn, 's go bristeadh cridhe; chionn mur a dh' éiridh dha, 's gon a bhi aig' ach i do mhac na 'nighean.

Bha Iain 'san eilean, fhionna 's fhiasag air dol thairis air, a ghruag sios eadar a dha shlinnean, na brògan air an cnàmh, 's gun snàthainn aodaich air nach robh air falbh na bhìdeagan, gon ghreim feòl air, ach na cnàmhan a' leantail ra cheile. Oidhche de na h-oidhchean dé chual e ach iomram bàta tigh 'n thun an eilean. "A bheil thu 'n sin Iain Albannaich?" ars' am fear a bha 's a bhàta. Gad a bha cha do fhreagair. B' fheàrr leis bàs fhaotainn taobh cnoic na gom biodh e air a mharbhadh. "Tha fhios' am go bheil thu 'gam chluinntinn agus freagair, 's cearta cho math dhuit mise fhreagairt, 's mi dhol suas, 's gon d' thoir mi nuas gon taing thu." Dh' fhalbh e 's ghabh e sìos. "A bheil thu deònach falbh as an eilean?" "Mata tha, 's mi tha 'sin, na 'm faighinn mo thoirt as." "Dé bheireadh thu do dhuine bheireidh as an so thu?" "Bha uair 's dh' fhaodoinn rud a thoirt do dhuine bheireadh as an so mi; ach an diugh cha 'n 'eil sgath agam." "An d'thoireadh thu dha leith do rioghachd?" "Cha bhi rioghachd am feasd agam, na 'm bitheadh bheireadh." "An d' thugadh thu 'n darna leith de d' mhnaoi do dhuine bheireadh as an so thu?" "Cha 'n 'eil sin agam." "Cha 'n 'eil mise 'g radh gad a bhitheadh gon d' thugadh thu seachad i." "Bheireadh." "An d' thugadh thu leith do chloinne do dhuine bheireadh as an so thu?" "Bheireadh." "Nuas, suidh an deireadh a' bhàta." Shuidh e 'n

deireadh a bhàta. "Co dhiu 's fheàrr leat dol do Shasunn na do 'n
Spàin?" "Do 'n Spàin." Dh' fhalbh e leis, 's ma 'n d'thàinig an latha
bha e 'san Spàin.

Ghabh e suas do 'n tigh sheinse. Dh' aithnich bean an tigh
sheinse 'sa mhionaid e. "An e so Iain?" ars' ise. " 'Se 'n truaill de
na bh' ann deth a th' ann," ars' esan. " 'S bochd mur a dh' éiridh
dhuit," ars' ise. Dh' fhalbh i 's chuir i fios go buth bearradair s
ghlanadh e, chuir i fios go bùth tàilleir 's fhuàradh aodach da, chuir
i fios go bùth griasaich 's fhuaradh brògan da.

An la 'r na mhàireach, nur a bha e air a ghlanadh, 's air a
sgeadachadh go dòigheil, chaidh e thun pàileas an righ, 's sheinn e
'n fhìdeag. Nur chual nighean an righ an fhìdeag thug i leum aisde,
's bhris i 'n treas earrann de 'n t sreang a bha 'ga ceangal. Dh' iarr
eud urra fuireachd socair 's cheangail eud tuillidh sreang urra. An
la 'r na mhàireach thug esan sgàl air an fhideig 's bhris i da earrann
de na bh' urra. An treas latha, nur a chual i 'n fhìdeag, bhris i tri
earrannan. Air a' cheathramh latha bhris i na bh' urra go léir. Dh'
éiridh i 's chaidh i mach 'na chomhdhail, 's cha robh boireannach
riabh a bu stòldacha na i. Chuireadh brath suas thun rìgh na Spàin
nach robh nighean riabh na bu stòldacha na bha i, 's gon d' thàinig
aobhar a fir 'sa leannain a 'h ionnsuidh.

Chuireadh *coach* a dh' iarraidh Iain. Bha 'n rìgh 's a mhòr uaislean
comhla ris. Thugadh suas air bhàrr bas e. Thogadh ceòl 's leagadh
bròn. Chuireadh biadh an àit' a chaithidh, deoch an àit' a h-òl, 's
ceòl an àit' éisdeachd. Rinneadh banais, shunndach, eibhinn,
aighearach. Fhuair Iain an darna leith de 'n rioghachd. An déigh
bàis an righ bha 'n rioghachd uile go léir aige. Rugadh air an
t-Seanailear, riasladh eadar eachaibh e, loisgeadh eadar thinean e,
's ligeadh an luath leis a' ghaoith.

An déigh bàis an righ 's na banrigh bha Iain 'na rìgh air an Spàin.
Rugadh triuir mac da. Oidhche bha 'n sin chual e bualadh 'san
dorus. "Tha 'n t-iarrtaich air tighinn," urs' esan. Dé bh' ann ach a
cheart duin' a thug as an eilean e. "A bheil thu airson do ghealladh
a chumail?" ars' am fear a thàinig. "Tha," ars' Iain. "Biodh do
rioghachd 's do chlann agad fhìn 's mo bheannachdsa. A bheil
cuimhn' agad nur a phàigh thu na h-ochd mairg airson cuirp an
duin' anns an Tuirc? B'e sin mo chorp-sa. Slàn leat' cha 'n fhaic
thu mise tuillidh."

Got this tale from Alexander MacNeill, tenant and fisherman, then
at Tangval, Barra. Heard his father, Roderick MacNeill, often recite
it. Roderick MacNeill died about twenty years ago, about the age of

eighty years. Heard it from many other old men in youth, and says
it was pretty common then.

July, 1859.

H. MacLean.

The landscape, and the ways of the poor of Barra, are painted from
nature: the flat strand, the shell-fish, the ship in the offing, the boat
at the edge of the sea. Then comes the popular romance, in which
the poor man is to become a prince. The life of shops and ships,
dimly seen, but evident enough. Turkey and Spain fairly lost in a
distant haze. The commercial principle laid down, that small profits
make quick returns; and that men should buy in the cheapest, and
sell in the dearest market; and all this woven with a love story, and
mixed up with an old tale which Grimm found in Germany, and
which Hans Andersen has made the foundation of one of his best
tales. Alas! Why did not the King of Spain send for the Barra widow
to make it complete.

33

THE TALE OF THE QUEEN WHO SOUGHT A DRINK FROM A CERTAIN WELL.

From Mrs. MacTavish, Port Ellen, Islay.

There was before now, a queen who was sick, and she had three daughters. Said she to the one who was eldest, "Go to the well of true water, and bring to me a drink to heal me."

The daughter went, and she reached the well. A LOSGANN (frog or toad) came up to ask her if she would wed him, if she should get a drink for her mother. "I will not wed thee, hideous creature! on any account," said she. "Well then," said he, "thou shalt not get the water."

She went away home, and her mother sent away her sister that was nearest to her, to seek a drink of the water. She reached the well; and the toad came up and asked her "if she would marry him if she should get the water." "I wont marry thee, hideous creature!" said she. "Thou shalt not get the water, then," said he.

She went home, and her sister that was youngest went to seek the water. When she reached the well the toad came up as he used, and asked her "if she would marry him if she should get the water." "If I have no other way to get healing for my mother, I will marry thee," said she; and she got the water, and she healed her mother.

They had betaken themselves to rest in the night when the toad came to the door saying:—

"A CHAOMHAG, A CHAOMHAG,	"Gentle one, gentle one,
AN CUIMHNEACH LEAT	Rememberest thou
AN GEALLADH BEAG	The little pledge
A THUG THU AIG	Thou gavest me
AN TOBAR DHOMH,	Beside the well,
A GHAOIL, A GHAOIL."	My love, my love."

When he was ceaselessly saying this, the girl rose and took him in, and put him behind the door, and she went to bed; but she was not long laid down, when he began again saying, everlastingly:—

> "A hàovaig, a hàovaig,
> An cuineach leat
> An geallug beag
> A hoog oo aig
> An tobar gaw,
> A géule, a géule."

Then she got up and she put him under a noggin; that kept him quiet a while; but she was not long laid down when he began again, saying:—

> "A hàovaig, a hàovaig,
> Au cuineach leat
> An geallug beag
> A hoog oo aig
> An tobar gaw,
> A géule, a géule."

She rose again, and she made him a little bed at the fireside; but he was not pleased, and he began again saying, "A chaoimheag, a chaoimheag, an cuimhneach leat an gealladh beag a thug thu aig an tobar dhomh, a ghaoil, a ghaoil." Then she got up and made him a bed beside her own bed; but he was without ceasing, saying, "A chaoimheag, a chaoimheag, an cuimhneach leat an gealladh beag a thug a thug thu aig an tobar dhomh, a ghaoil, a ghaoil." But she took no notice of his complaining, till he said to her, "There is an old rusted glave behind thy bed, with which thou hadst better take off my head, than be holding me longer in torture."

She took the glave and cut the head off him. When the steel touched him, he grew a handsome youth; and he gave many thanks to the young wife, who had been the means of putting off him the spells, under which he had endured for a long time. Then he got his kingdom, for he was a king; and he married the princess, and they were long alive and merry together.

SGEULACHD BAN-RIGH A DH' IARR DEOCH A TOBAR ARAID.

Bha banrigh ann roimhe so a bha tinn, agus bha triùir nighean aice. Thubhairt i ris an té 'bu shine, "Falbh do 'n tobar fhìor-uisg', agus

thabhair do m' ionnsuidh deoch gu m' leigheas." Dh' fhalbh an
nighean agus ràinig i 'n tobar. Thàinig losgann a nìos a dh' fharraid
di am pòsadh i e na 'm faighheadh i deoch d'a màthair. "Cha phòs
mis' thu 'chreutair ghrànnda! air aon chor." "Mata," ars' esan, "cha
'n fhaigh thu 'n t-uisge." Dh' fhalbh i dhachaidh, agus chuir a
màthair air falbh a piuthar a b' fhaisge dhi a dh' iarraidh deoch do
'n uisge. Ràinig i 'n tobar, agus thàinig an losgann a nìos, agus dh'
fharraid e dhi am pòsadh i e, na 'm faigheadh i 'n t-uisge. "Cha
phòs mis' thu 'chreutair ghrànnd," ars' ise. "Cha 'n fhaigh thu 'n
t-uisge mata," urs' esan. Thill i dhachaidh, agus chaidh a piuthar
a b' òige 'dh' iarraidh an uisge. An uair a ràinig i 'n tobar thàinig
an losgann à nìos mar a b' àbhaist, agus dh' fharraid e dhi am
pòsadh i e na 'm faigheadh i 'n t-uisge. "Mar am bheil sèol eil' agam
air leigheas fhaotainn do 'm mhàthair pòsaidh mi thu," ars' ise, agus
fhuair i 'n t-uisge, agus shlànaicheadh a màthair.

Bha iad an déigh gabhail mu thàmh 'san oidhche an uair a thàinig
an losgann do 'n dorus aig ràdh, "A chaomhag, a chaomhag an
cuimhneach leat an gealladh beag a thug thu aig an tobar dhomh?
A ghaoil! a ghaoil!" An uair a bha e gun tàmh aig ràdh mar so, dh'
éiridh an nighean agus thug i stigh e, agus chuir i cùl an doruis e,
agus chaidh i 'laidhe; ach cha robh i fada 'na luidhe an uair a
thòisich e rithis air a ràdh, a choidh, "A chaomhag, a chaomhag an
cuimhneach leat an gealladh beag a thug thu aig an tobar dhomh?
A ghaoil! a ghaoil!" Dh' éirich i 'n sin agus chuir i fo noigean e.
Chum sin sàmhach e tacan; ach cha robh i fada 'na luidhe an uair
a thòisich e rithis air a ràdh, "A chaomhag, a chaomhag an
cuimhneach leat an gealladh beag a thug thu aig an tobar dhomh?
A ghaoil! a ghaoil!" Dh' éirich i rithis agus rinn i leaba bheag dha
taobh an teine; ach cha robh e toilichte. Co luath agus a bha i 'na
leaba thòisich e rithis air a ràdh, "A chaoimheag, a chaoimheag
nach cuimhneach leat an gealladh beag a thug thu aig an tobar
dhomh? A ghaoil! a ghaoil!" Dh' éirich i 'n sin agus rinn i leaba dha
làmh ri 'leaba féin; ach bha e gun tàmh aig ràdh, "A chaoimheag,
a chaoimheag an cuimhneach leat an gealladh beag a thug thu aig
an tobar dhomh? A ghaoil! a ghaoil!" Ach cha robh i' tabhairt feairt
air a ghearan gus an dubhairt e rithe, "Tha seana chlaidheamh
meirgeach cùl do leapa leis an fheàrra dhuit an ceann a thabhairt
dhìom, na 'bhith 'gam' chumail am péin ni 's faide." Ghabh i 'n
claidheamh agus gheàrr i 'n ceann deth. An uair a bhoin an stàilinn
da dh' fhàs e 'na òganach dreachmhor, agus thug e iomadh
buidheachas do 'n ògbhean a bha 'na meadhon an druidheachd,
foidh an robh e ré uin' fhad' a' fulann, a chur dheth. Fhuair e 'n sin

a rìoghachd, oir bu rìgh righ e, agus phòs e 'bhana phrionnsa, agus bha iad fada beò gu subhach còmhla.

The lady who has been so kind as to write down this, and other stories, is one of my oldest friends. She has brought up a large family, and her excellent memory now enables her to remember tales, which she had gathered during a long life passed in the West Highlands, where her husband was a respected minister. The story is evidently a Celtic version of the Wearie Well at the Warldis End, of which Chambers has published one Scotch version, to which Grimm refers in notes "Der Froschkônig," in his third volume. There are many versions still current in Scotland, told in broad Scots; and it can be traced back to 1548. According to Grimm, it belongs to the oldest in Germany. This version clearly belongs to the Gaelic language, for the speech of the frog is an imitation of the gurgling and quarking of spring frogs in a pond, which I have vainly endeavoured to convey to an English reader by English letters; but which is absurdly like, when repeated in Gaelic with this intention. The persevering, obstinate repetition of the same sounds is also exceedingly like the habit of frogs, when disturbed, but not much frightened. Let any one try the experiment of throwing a stone into the midst of a frog concert, and he will hear the songsters, after a moment of stillness, begin again. First a half-smothered GUARK GUARK; then another begins, half under water, with a gurgle, and then more and more join in till the pond is in full chorus once again. GUARK, GUARK, GOOILL GOOARK GOOILL

Holy healing wells are common all over the Highlands; and people still leave offerings of pins and nails, and bits of rag, though few would confess it. There is a well in Islay where I myself have, after drinking, deposited copper caps amongst a hoard of pins and buttons, and similar gear, placed in chinks in the rocks and trees at the edge of the "Witches' Well." There is another well with similar offerings, freshly placed beside it in an island in Loch Maree, in Ross-shire; and similar wells are to be found in many other places in Scotland. For example, I learn from Sutherland, that "a well in the black Isle of Cromarty, near Rosehaugh, has miraculous healing powers. A country woman tells me, that about forty years ago, she remembers it being surrounded by a crowd of people every first Tuesday in June, who bathed or drank of it *before* sunrise. Each patient tied a string or rag to one of the trees that overhung it before leaving. It was sovereign for headaches. Mr.——remembers to have seen a well here called Mary's Well, hung round with votive rags."

Well worship is mentioned by Martin. The custom in his day, in the Hebrides, was to walk south about round the well.

Sir William Betham in his Gael and Cymbiri (Dublin: W. Curry, jun., & Co., 1834), says at page 235, "The Celtæ were much addicted to the worship of fountains and rivers as divinities. They had a deity called Divona, or the river god."

Divona Celtarum lingua fons addite Divii (*Ausonius*).

He quotes from "The Book of Armagh, a MS. of the seventh century,"—"And he (St. Patrick) came to *Fina Malge*, which is called *Slane*, because it was intimated to him that the *Magi honoured this fountain*, and made donations to it as gifts to a god." *For they sacrificed gifts to the fountain, and worshipped it like a god.*

The learned author explains how wells are now venerated in Ireland, and traces their worship back to remote ages; and to the East, by way of Spain, Carthage, and Egypt, Tyre and Sidon, Arabia, Chaldea, and Persia, where men still hang bits of rag on trees near wells. Baal, according to some of the authorities quoted, is mixed up with the well worship of the Irish Segli Divona the river god or Baal may therefore have degenerated into a toad; and the princess who married him may once have been a Celtic divinity, whose story survives as a popular tale in Germany and in Scotland.

The following story bears on the same subject, and may explain why gifts were left when a drink was taken from a well. The story was told to me long ago, while seated under shelter of a big stone waiting for ducks on the shore. It was told in Gaelic, and the pun upon the name of the lake is lost in any other language. The meaning of the name might be the weasel lake, or the lake of the falls; or perhaps the lake of the island; but the legend gives a meaning, which the sound of the name will bear, and it ought to be right if it is not.

34

THE ORIGIN OF LOCH NESS.

From Mr. Thomas MacDonald, now gamekeeper at Dunmbin.

Where Loch Ness now is, there was long ago a fine glen. A woman went one day to the well to fetch water, and she found the spring flowing so fast that she got frightened, and left her pitcher and ran for her life; she never stopped till she got to the top of a high hill; and when there, she turned about and saw the glen filled with water. Not a house or a field was to be seen! "Aha!" said she, "Tha Loch ann a nis." (Ha Loch an a neesh). There is a lake in it now; and so the lake was called Loch Ness (neesh).

35

CONALL.

From Alexander MacNeill, tenant and fisherman, Barra.

There was an old king before now in Erin,* and a sister of his, whose name was MAOBH, had three sons. The eldest of them was Ferghus, the middlemost Lagh an Laidh, and the youngest one Conall.

He thought he would make an heir of the eldest one, Ferghus. He gave him the schooling of the son of a king and a "ridere," and when he was satisfied with school and learning he brought him home to the palace. Now they were in the palace.

Said the king, "I have passed this year well; the end of the year is coming now, and trouble and care are coming on with it."

"What trouble or care is coming on thee?" said the young man. "The vassals of the country are coming to reckon with me to-day." "Thou hast no need to be in trouble. It is proclaimed that I am the young heir, and it is set down in papers and in letters in each end of the realm. I will build a fine castle in front of the palace for thee. I will get carpenters, and stonemasons, and smiths to build that castle."

"Is that thy thought, son of my sister?" said the king. "Thou hadst neither claim nor right to the realm unless I myself had chosen to give it to thee with my own free will. Thou wilt not see thyself handling Erin till I go first under the mould."

"There will be a day of battle and combat before I let this go on," said the young man.

He went away, and he sailed to Alba. A message was sent up to the king of Alba that the young king of Erin was come to Alba to see him. He was taken up on the deadly points.† Meat was set in the

---

* In this tale Erin is spelt instead of Eirinn and Eireann; Alba and Sassun, *Scotland* and *England*, express the sound of the Gaelic words.
† Probably lifted on spears.

place for eating; drink in the place for drinking; and music in the place for hearing; and they were plying the feast and the company.

"Oh! young king of Erin," said the king of Alba, "it was not without the beginning of some matter that thou art come to Alba."

"I should not wish to let out the knowledge of my matter till I should first know whether I may get it."

"Anything I have thou gettest it, for if I were seeking help, perhaps I would go to thee to get it."

"There came a word with trouble between me and my mother's brother. It was proclaimed out that I was king of Erin; and he said to me that I should have nothing to do with anything till a clod should first go on him. I wish to stand my right, and to get help from thee."

"I will give thee that," said the king; "three hundred swift heroes, three hundred brave heroes, three hundred full heroes; and that is not bad helping."

"I am without a chief over them, and I am as ill off as I was before; but I have another small request, and if I might get it, I would wish to let it out."

"Anything I have that I can part from, thou shalt get it," said the king; "but the thing I have not, I cannot give it to thee. Let out thy speech, and thou shalt have it."

"It is Boinne Breat, thy son, at their head."

"My torture to thee! had I not promised him to thee, thou hadst not got him. But there were not born in Alba, nor in Erin, nor in Sassun, nor in any one place (those) who would gain victory over my son if they keep to fair play. If my son does not come back as he went, the word of an Eriannach is never again to be taken, for it is by treachery he will be overcome."

They went away on the morrow, and they sailed to the king of Sassun. A message went up to the king of Sassun that the young king of Erin had come to the place. The king of Sassun took out to meet him. He was taken up on the deadly points; music was raised, and lament laid down in the palace of the king of Sassun; meat was set in the place for eating; drink in the place for drinking; music in the place of hearing; and they were plying the feast and the company with joy and pleasure of mind.

"Oh! young king of Erin," said the king of Sassun, "it is not without the end of a matter that thou art come here."

"I got the schooling of the son of a king and a ridere. My mother's brother took me home. He began to speak about the vassals of the country and the people of the realm; that care and trouble were on him; and that he had rather the end of the year had not come at all. Said I to him, 'I will build thee a palace, so that thou shalt have but to wash thy face, and stretch thy feet in thy shoes.' Said he, 'My sister's son, thou hadst no right to the realm, and thou gettest it not till a clod goes on me, in spite of everything.' Said I, 'There will be a day of battle and combat between thee and me, before the matter is so.' I went away; I took my ship; I took a skipper with me; and I sailed to Alba. I reached Alba, and I got three hundred swift heroes, three hundred brave heroes, and three hundred full heroes; now I am come to thee to see what help thou wilt give me."

"I will give thee as many more, and a hero at their head," said the king of Sassun.

They went away, and they sailed to Erin. They went on shore on a crag in Erin, and the name of Carrig Fhearghuis is on that rock still. He reached the king. "Brother of my mother, art thou now ready?"—"Well, then, Fhearghuis, though I said that, I thought thou wouldst not take anger; but I have not gathered my lot of people yet."—"That is no answer for me. Thou hast Erin under thy rule. I am here with my men, and I have neither place, nor meat, nor drink for them."

"Oo!" said the king, "the storehouses of Erin are open beneath thee, and I will go away and gather my people."

He went away. He went all round Erin. He came to a place which they called "An t' Iubhar" (Newry). There was but one man in Iubhar, who was called Goibhlean Gobha (Goivlan Smith). He thought to go in, for thirst was on him; and that he would quench his thirst, and breathe a while. He went in. There was within but the smith's daughter. She brought him a chair in which he might sit. He asked for a drink. The smith's daughter did not know what she should do, for the smith had but one cow, which was called the Glas Ghoibhlean (Grey Goivlan), with the vessel he had for the milk of the cow; three times in the day it would go beneath the cow; three times in the day thirst would be on him; and he would drink the vessel each time, and unless the daughter had the vessel full she was not to get off. She was afraid, when the king asked for a drink, that unless she had the vessel full her head would be taken off. It was so that she thought the vessel should be set before the king at all hazards. She brought down the vessel, and she set it before him. He drank a draught; he took out the fourth part, and he left three quarters in it. "I would rather you should take it out altogether than leave it. My father has made an oath that unless I have the vessel full, I have but to die."

"Well, then," said the king, "it is a spell of my spells to leave the vessel as full as it was before."

He set the vessel on the board, he struck his palm on it, and he struck off as much as was above the milk, and the vessel was full; and before he went away, the girl was his own.

"Now, thou art going, oh king of Erin, and I am shamed; what wilt thou leave with me?"

"I would give thee a thousand of each hue, a thousand of each kind, a thousand of each creature."

"What should I do with that, for I wilt not find salt in Erin to salt them?"

"I would give thee glens and high moors to feed them from year to year."

"What should I do with that? for if Fearghus should kill you, he will take it form me, unless I have it with writing, and a drop of blood to bind it."

"I am in haste this night, but go to-morrow to the camp to Croc Maol Nam Muc," said the king; and he left his blessing with her.

Her father came.

"Far from thee—far from thee be it, my daughter! I think that a stranger has been to see thee here this day."

"How dost thou know that?"

"Thou hadst a maiden's slow eyelash when I went out; thou hast the brisk eyelash of a wife now."

"Whom wouldst thou rather had been here?"

"I never saw the man I would rather be here than the king of Erin."

"Well, it was he; he left me a thousand of each hue, a thousand of each kind, a thousand of each creature.

" 'What,' said I, 'shall I do with them, as I cannot get in Erin as much salt as will salt them?'

"Said he, 'I would give thee glens and high moors to feed them from year to year.'

" 'What shall I do if Fearghus should kill you? I will not get them.'

"He said, 'I should have writing and a drop of his own blood to bind it.' "

They slept that night as they were. If it was early that the day came, it was earlier that the smith arose. "Come, daughter, and let us be going." She went, herself and the smith, and they reached the king in his camp.

"Wert thou not in the Iubhar yesterday?" said the smith to the king, "I was; and hast thou mind of thy words to the girl?"

"I have; but the battle will not be till to-morrow. I will give thee, as I said, to the girl; but leave her."

The smith got that, and he went away.

That night, when she had slept a while, she awoke, for she had seen a dream. "Art thou waking?"

"I am; what wilt thou with me? I saw a dream there: a shoot of fir growing from the heart of the king, one from my own heart, and they were twining about each other." "That is our babe son." They slept, and it was not long till she saw the next dream.

"Art thou waking, king of Erin?" "I am; what wilt thou with me?" "I saw another dream. Fearghus coming down, and taking the head and the neck out of me."

"That is, Fearghus killing me, and taking out my head and neck." She slept again, and she saw another dream.

"Art thou sleeping, king of Erin?"

"I am not; what wilt thou with me now?"

"I saw Erin, from side to side, and from end to end, covered with sheaves of barley and oats. There came a blast of wind from the east, from the west, from the north; every tree was swept away, and no more of them were seen."

"Fearghus will kill me, and he will take the head and neck out of me. As quickly as ever thou didst (anything), seize my set of arms, and keep them. A baby boy is begotten between thee and me. Thou shalt suckle and nurse him, and thou shalt set him in order. Keep the arms. When thou seest that he has speech, and can help himself, thou shalt send him away through the world a wandering, till he find out who he is. He will get to be king over Erin; his son will be king over Erin; his grandson will be king over Erin. His race will be kings over Erin till it reaches the ninth knee. A child will be born from that one. A farmer will come in with a fish; he will cook the fish; a bone will stick in his throat, and he will be choked."

Maobh, the king's sister, the mother of Fearghus, had two other sons, and the battle was to be on the morrow. Lagh and Laidh and Connal; and Lagh an Laidh was the eldest.

"Whether," said Lagh an Laidh, "shall we be with our mother's brother or with Fearghus?"

"I know not. If our mother's brother wins, and we are with Fearghus, it is a stone in our shoe for ever; but if Fearghus wins, he will turn his back to us, because we were on the other side."

"Well, then, it is not thus it shall be; but be thou with Fearghus, and I will be with our mother's brother."

"It shall not be so; we will leave it to our mother."

"Were I a man," said Maobh, "I would set the field with my own brother."

"Well, then, I will be with Fearghus," said Lagh an Laidh, "and be thou with Fearghus, oh Connal!"

Fearghus went to Fionn; he blessed him in calm, soft words. Fionn blessed him in better words; and if no better, they were no worse.

"I heard that there was a day of battle and combat between thyself and thy mother's brother," said he.

"That is to be, and I came to you for help."

"It is but bold for me to go against thy mother's brother, since it was on his land that I got my keep. If thy mother's brother should win, we shall get neither furrow nor clod of the land of Erin as long as we live. I will do thus. I will not strike a blow with thee, and I will not strike a blow against thee."

Fearghus went home on the morrow, and they set in order for the battle. The king's company was on one side, and the company of Fearghus on the other. Fearghus had no GAISGICH heroes but Boinne Breat and his company. The great Saxon hero and his company, and Lagh an Laidh. Boinne Breat drew out to the skirt of the company; he put on his harness of battle and hard combat. He set his silken netted coat above his surety* shirt; a booming shield on his left side; how many deaths were in his tanned sheath!

He strode out on the stern steps like a sudden blaze; each pace he put from him was less than a hill, and greater than a knoll on the mountain side. He turned on them, cloven and cringing. Three ranks would he drive of them, dashing them from their shields, to their blood and their flesh in the skies.† Would he not leave one to tell the tale, or report bad news; to put in a land of holes or a shelf of rock. There was one little one-eyed russet man, one-eyed, and on one knee and one handed. "Thou shalt not be to tell a tale of me;" he went and he took his head off. Then Boinne Breat shunned the fight, and he took his armour off.

"Go down, Fearghus, and take off the head of thy mother's brother, or I will take it off."

Fearghus went down, he caught hold of his mother's brother, and he took his head off. The smith's daughter went to the arms, and she took them with her.

Lagh an Laidh kept on his armour. When he saw Fearghus going

* CORR, the epithet applied to a shirt, is a word which gives the meaning of greatness or excess; and in *corran*, means an iron weapon, or a sickle. "A shirt of armour."
† This passage is common; I am not certain that it is correctly rendered.

to take off the head of his mother's brother, he took a frenzy. Lagh an Laidh went about the hill to try if he could see Boinne Breat, who was unarmed. Boinne Breat thought that man was drunk with battle. He thought that he would turn on the other side of the hill to try if he could come to his own place. Lagh an Laidh turned on the other side against him. He thought to turn again to try if the battle frenzy would abate. The third time he said he would not turn for all who were in Albuin, or Eirinn, or Sassun. "It is strange thou, man, that wert with me throughout the battle, to be against me? I will not believe but that thou hast taken the drunkenness of battle," said Boinne Breat.

"I am quite beside myself."

"Well, then," said he, "though I am unarmed, and thou under arms, remember that thou art no more to me than what I can hold between these two fingers."

"I will not be a traiter to thee, there behind thee are three of the best heroes in Albuin, or Eirinn, or Sassun."

He gave a turn to see the three heroes, and when he turned Lagh an Laigh struck off his head.

"My torture," said Fearghus, "I had rather my own head were there. An Eireannach is not to be taken at his word as long as a man shall live. It is a stone in thy shoe every day for ever, and a pinch of the land of Eirinn thou shalt not have."

Lagh an Laidh went away and he went to the mountain. He made a castle for himself there, and he stayed in it.

The smith's daughter came on well till she bore a babe-son. She gave him the name of Conal Mac Righ Eirinn. She nourished him well, and right well. When speech came and he could walk well, she took him with her on a wet misty day to the mountain amongst high moors and forests. She left him there astray to make out a way for himself, and she went home.

He did not know in the world what he should do, as he did not know where to go, but he found a finger of a road. He followed the road. What should he see but a little hut at the evening of the day at the wayside. He went into the hut: there was no man within: he let himself down at the fire-side. There he was till a woman came at the end of the night, and she had six sheep. She saw a great slip of a man beside the fire, who seemed to be a fool. She took great wonder when she saw him, and she said that he had better go out of that, and go down to the king's house, and that he would get something amongst the servants in the kitchen. He said he would not go, but if she would give him something that he might eat, that he would go to herd the sheep for herself. What should be the name of the woman but CAOMHAG Gentle. "If I thought that, I would give thee meat and drink," said she. On the morrow he went away with the sheep. "I have not a bite of grass for them," said she, "but a road; and thou shalt keep them at the edge of the road, and thou shalt not let them off it."

At the time of night he came home with them; on the morrow he went away with the sheep. There were near to the place where he was with them three fields of wheat that belonged to three gentlemen. The sheep were wearing him out. He went and he levelled the dyke, and he let them in from one to the other till they had eaten the three fields. On a day of days, the three gentlemen gathered. When they came, he had let the fields be eaten by the sheep.

"Who art thou? Thou hast eaten the fields?"

"It was not I that ate them at all; it was the sheep that ate them."

"We will not be talking to him at all; he is but a fool. We will reach Caomhag to see if the sheep are hers."

They reached Caomhag. They took her with them to the court. This was the first court that Fearghus had made after he got the crown.

The kings had a heritage at that time. When they did not know how to split justice properly, the judgment-seat would begin to kick, and the king's neck would take a twist when he did not do justice as he ought.

"I can make nothing of it," said the king, "but that they should have the tooth that did the damage.

"The judgment-seat would begin to kick, and the king's neck took a turn. Come here one of you and loose me; try if you can do justice better than that." Though there were thousands within, none would go in the king's place. They would not give the king such bad respect, as that any one of them would go before him.

"Is there a man that will loose me?"

"There is not, unless the herd of Caomhag himself will loose thee."

Caomhag's herd was set down.

"Loose for me, my little hero, and do justice as it should (be done), and let me out of this."

"(Nor) right nor justice will I do before I get something that I may eat."

Then he got something which he ate.

"What justice didst thou do thyself?" said he.

"I did but (doom) the tooth that did the damage to be theirs."

"What was in the way that thou didst not give death to Caomhag? This is what I would do:—Caomhag has six sheep, and though the six sheep were taken from her, they would not pay the gentlemen. Caomhag will have six lambs, the gentlemen shall have the six lambs, and she herself shall have the sheep to keep."

The turn went out of the king's neck. He went away, and they did not ask who he was, and he got no skaith.

There was another gentleman, and he had a horse, and he sent him to a smithy to be shod. The smith had a young son and a nurse under the child. What should it be but a fine day, and it was without that the horse was being shod, and she never saw a horse shod before; and she went out to see the shoeing of the horse. She sat opposite to the horse, and he took the nail and the shoe, and he did not hit the hoof with the nail but he put it in the flesh, and the horse struck the child, and drove the cup of his head off. They had but to go to justice again to the king, and the justice the king made for them was, that the leg should be taken off the horse. The judgment-seat began to kick again, and the king's neck took a twist. The herd of Caomhag was there, and they asked him to loose the king. He said that he would not do a thing till he should first get something to eat.

He got that. He went where the king was.

"What law didst thou make?"

"The leg to be taken off the horse?"

"That will not pay the smith. Send hither to me the *groom* that broke the horse, and the gentleman to whom he belongs. Send over here the smith and the nurse."

The gentleman and the groom came.

"Well then, my gentleman, didst thou make this groom break this horse as he should?"

The groom said that he had done that as well as he knew (how to do it).

"No more could be asked of thee. Well, smith, didst thou give an order to the nurse to stay within without coming out of her chamber?"

"I did not give it," said the smith, "but (she might do) as she chose herself."

"My gentleman," said he, "since thou art best kept, I will put a third of the EIRIC of the smith's son on thee, and another third on the smith himself, because he did not measure the nail before he put it to use, and another third on the nurse and the groom because she did not stay within her chamber, and in case he left some word or other untaught to the horse."

The gentleman went away and the smith; the judgment-seat stopped, and she hadn't a kick; the turn came out of the king's neck, and they let him go as usual.

Said the king—"If he has travelled over the universe and the world, there is a drop of king's blood in that lad; he could not split the law so well as that if it were not in him. Let the three best heroes I have go, and let them bring me his head."

They went after him. He gave a glance from him and what should he see coming but they. They came where he was. "Where are you going?"—"We are going to kill thyself. The king sent us to thee."

"Well, then, that was but a word that came into his mouth, and it is not worth your while to kill me."

"He is but a fool," said they.

"Since he sent you to kill me, why don't you kill me?"

"Wilt thou thyself kill thyself, my little hero?" said they.

"How shall I kill myself?"

"Here's for thee a sword and strike it on thee about the neck, and cast the head off thyself," said they.

He seized on the sword, and gave it a twirl in his fist. "Fall to killing thyself, my little hero."

"Begone," said he, "and return home, and do not hide from the king that you did not kill me."

"Well, then, give me the sword," said one of them.

"I will not give it; there are not in Erin as many as will take it from my fist," said he.

They went and they returned home. As he was going by himself, he said, "I was not born without a mother, and I was not begotten without a father. I have no mind (of) ever coming to Erin, and I know that it was in Erin I was born. I will not leave a house in which there is smoke or fire in Erin till I know who I (am)."

He went to the Iubhar. What was it but a fine warm day. Whom did he see but his mother washing. He was coming to a sort of understanding, so that he was thinking that it was his mother who was there. He went and he went behind her, and he put his hand on her breast. "Indeed," said he, "a foster son of thy right breast am I." She gave her head a toss. "Thy like of a *tarlaid* drudge, I never had as a son or a foster son."—"My left hand is behind thy head, and a sword in my right hand, and I will strike off thy head unless thou tell me who I am."—"Still be thy hand, Conall, son of the king of Erin."

"I knew myself I was that, and that there was a drop of the blood of a king's son in me; but who killed my father?"

"Fearghus killed him; and a loss as great as thy father was slain on the same day—that was Boinne Breat, son of the king of Alba."

"Who slew Boinne Breat?"—"It is a brother of Fearghus, whom they call Lagh an Laidh."

"And where is that man dwelling?"

"He could not get a bit on the land of Erin when once he had slain Boinne Breat; he went to the hills, and he made him a 'còs'* in the forest, amongst '*uille biaste*,' monsters, and untamed creatures."

"Who kept my father's arms?"—"It is I."

"Go fetch them, and bring them hither to me." She brought them.

He went and put the arms on him, and they became him as well as though they had been made for himself.

"I eat not a bit, and I drink not a draught, and I make no stop but this night, until I reach where that man is, wheresoever he may be."

He passed that night where he was. In the morning, on the morrow he went away; he went on till there was black upon his soles and holes in his shoes. The white clouds of day were going, and the black clouds of night coming, and without his finding a place of staying or rest for him. There he saw a great wood. He made a "còs," in one of the trees above in which he might stay that night. In the morning, on the morrow he cast a glance from him. What should he see but the very *uile bheist*, whose like was never seen under the sun, stretched without clothing, without foot coverings, or head covering, hair and beard gone over him. He thought, though he should go down, that he could not do for him. He put an arrow in a "*crois*," and he "fired" at him. He struck him with it on the right fore-arm, and the one who was below gave a start. "Move not a sinew of thy sinews, nor a vein of thy veins, nor a bit of thy flesh, nor a hair of thy locks, till thou promise to see me a king over Erin, or I will send down of slender oaken darts enough to sew thee to the earth." The uile bheist did not give him yielding for that. He went and he fired again, and he struck him in the left fore-arm. "Did I not tell thee before, not to stir a vein of thy veins nor a bit of thy flesh, nor a hair of thy locks till thou shouldst promise to see me king over Erin."—"Come down then, and I will

* Còs, a hollow or cave; here a kind of dwelling scooped out in the side of a hill.

see thyself or myself that before this time to morrow night." He came down.

"If I had known that it was thy like of a drudge that should dictate thus to me, I would not do it for thee for anything; but since I promised thee I will do it, and we will be going."

They went to the palace of the king. They shouted Battle or Combat to be sent out, or else the head of Fearghus, or himself a captive.

Battle and combat they should get, and not his head at all, and they could not get himself a captive.

There were sent out four hundred swift heroes, four hundred full heroes, and four hundred strong heroes.

They began at them. The one could not put from the other's hand as they were killed.

They shouted battle or combat again, or else the head of Fearghus to be sent out, or himself a captive.

"It is battle and combat thou shalt have, and not at all my head, and no more shalt thou get myself a captive."

There were sent out twelve hundred swift heroes, twelve hundred full heroes, and twelve hundred stout heroes.

The one could not put from the other's hand as they killed of them.

They shouted battle and combat, or else the head of Fearghus, or himself a captive.

Battle and combat they should have, and not the head of Fearghus at all, nor himself a captive.

There were sent out four hundred score to them. The one could not put from the other as they killed.

They shouted battle and combat.

"Those who are without," said Fearghus, "are so hard (to please) that they will take but my head, and unless they get (it) they will kill all there are in Erin and myself after them. Take one of you a head from one of those who were slain, and when Lagh an Laidh comes and asks my head, or myself a captive, give it to him, and he will think it is my head."

The head was given to Lagh an Laidh. He went where Conall was with it.

"What hast thou there?" said Conall.

"The head of Fearghus."

"That is not the head of Fearghus yet. I saw him a shorter (time) than thyself, but turn and bring hither to me the head of Fearghus."

Lagh an Laidh returned.

"Let another go to meet him in the king's stead, and say that it is his head he shall get, not himself a captive."

This one went to meet Lagh an Laidh. He seized him and took the head out of his neck.

He reached Conall. "What hast thou there?"—"The head of Fearghus."

"That is not the head of Fearghus yet; turn and bring to me the head of Fearghus."

Lagh an Laidh returned.

"The one who is without is so watchful, and the other is so blind, that there is no man in Erin but they will kill unless they get myself."

"Where art thou going, Lagh an Laidh?" said Fearghus.

"I am going to seek thy head, or thyself as a captive."

"It's my head thou shalt get, and not myself as a captive; but what kindness art thou giving thy brother?

"The kindness that thou gavest thyself to me, I will give it to thee."

He took the head out of his neck, and he took it with him. He came where Conall was.

"What hast thou there?"—"The head of Fearghus."—"It is not."—"Truly it is."—"Let me see it."

He gave it to him. He drew it, and he struck him with it, and he made two heads of the one. Then they began at each other.

They would make a bog on the rock, and a rock on the bog. In the place where the least they would sink, they would sink to the knees, in the place where the most they would sink, they would sink to the eyes.

Conall thought it would be ill for him to fall after he had got so near the matter.

He drew his sword, and he threw the head off Lagh an Laidh.

"Now I am king over Erin, as I myself had a right to be."

He took his mother and her father from the Iubhar, and took them to the palace; and his race were in it till the ninth knee. The last one was choked, as a babe, with a splinter of bone that went crosswise into his throat, and another tribe came in on EIRINN.

———

CONALL.

Bha sean righ roimhe so ann an Eirinn agus bha triùir mac aig piuthar dha. Be 'm fear a bu shine dhiu Fearghus, am fear a bu mhiadhonaiche Lagh an Làigh, 's am fear a b' òige Conall.

Smaointich e gon dianadh e oighre do 'n fhear a bu shine Fearghus.
Thug e sgoil mhic righ agus ridire dha, agus nur a bha e buidheach
sgoil agus ionnsachaidh thug e dhachaidh e do 'n phàileas. Bha eud
an so anns a' phaileas. Urs' an righ, "Chuir mi seachad a' bhliadhna
so go math. Tha ceann na bliadhna nis a' tighinn 's tha trioblaid
agus cùram a' tigh 'n orm leatha." "Dé 'n trioblaid na 'n cùram a
tha tigh 'n ort?" urs' am fear òg. "Tha tuath na duthcha tigh 'n a
chunndas rium an diugh." "Cha ruig thu leas cùram a bhi ort 'tha
e air eubhach a mach gor mis' an t-oighr' òg 's air a chur sìos ann
am paipeirean 's an litrichean anns gach ceàrn de 'n rioghachd.
Togaidh mise caisteal bòidheach air bialthaobh a' phàileas duit.
Gheibh mi saoir agus clachairean agus goibhnean gos a' chaisteal
sin a thogail." "An e sin smaointinn a th' agad a mhic mo pheathar,"
ars' an Righ, "cha robh ceart na còir agad air an rioghachd fhaotainn
mar an tograinn fhìn a toirt duit le m' thoil fhìn. Cha 'n fhaic thusa
laimhseachadh Eirinn agad gos an d' théid mise an toiseach fo 'n
ùir." "Bidh latha blàir agus batailt ann ma 'n lig mise sin air
aghaidh," urs' am fear òg.

Dh' fhalbh e agus sheòl e go ruig Alba. Chuireadh brath a suas
thun righ Alba gon robh rìgh òg Eirinn air tigh 'n go ruig Alba g'a
choimhead. Thugadh suas air bharraibh bas e. Chuireadh biadh an
àit' a chaithidh, deoch an ait a h-òl, agus ceòl an àit' éisdeachd. Bha
eud a' caitheadh na cuirm agus na cuideachd.

"A rìgh òg Eirinn," ursa righ Alba, "cha n' ann gon cheann
gnothaich a thàinig thusa go ruig Alba." "Cha bu mhath leam fios
mo gnothaich a ligeil a mach gos am biodh fhios'am am faighinn
an toiseach e." "Dad 's am bith a th' agamsa gheibh thus' e, chionn
na'm bithinn aig iarraidh cuideachaidh cha lughaide gon rachainn
a t' ionnsuidh-s' airson fhaotainn." "Facal a thàinig ann an
doilgheas eadar mis' agus brath 'r mo mhàthar." "Bha e air eubhach
a mach go 'm bu mhi righ Eirinn; 's thuirt e rium nach biodh
gnothach agam ri ni gos an rachadh plochd airsan an toiseach. Tha
toil agam mo chòir a sheasamh agus cuideachadh fhaotainn uaitse."
"Bheir mise sin duit," ars' an Righ, "tri chiad lùgh ghaisgeach, tri
chiad treun-ghaisgeach, agus tri chaid làn-ghaisgeach, 's cha don'
an cuideachadh sin." "Tha mise gon cheannard as an cionn, 's tha
mi cho dona 's a bha mi roimhid; ach tha iarrtas beag eil' agam,
agus na 'm faighinn e bhithinn deònach air a ligeil a mach." "Rud
sam bith a th' agamsa," ars' an Righ, " 's is urra mi dealachadh ris
gheibh thu e, ach rud nach 'eil agam cha n' urra mi 'thoirt duit; ach
lig amach do chainnt 's gheibh thu e." " 'Se sin Boinne Breat do
mhac air an ceann." "Mo ghonadh dhuit, na 'm bithinn gon a

ghealltainn duit cha n' fhaigheadh thu e; ach cha do rugadh an Albainn, na 'n Eirinn, na 'n Sasunn, na 'n aon àite na gheibheadh buaidh air mo mhacsa, ach fantainn aig ceartas; mar an d' thig mo mhacs' air ais mar a dh' fhalbh e cha 'n 'eil facal Eireannaich ri ghabhail tuillidh, chionn 's ann am foill a thight' air."

Dh' fhalbh eud an la 'r na mhàireach 's sheòl eud 'ionnsuidh righ Shasuinn. Chaidh brath suas go righ Shasuinn gon robh righ òg Eirinn an déigh tigh 'n do 'n àite. Ghabh righ Shasuinn 'na chomhdhail's thugadh suas air bharraibh bas e. Thogadh ceòl 's leagadh bron ann am pàileas righ Shasuinn. Chuireadh biadh an àit' a chaitheadh, deoch an àit' a h-òl, agus ceòl an àit' éisdeachd. Bha eud a' caitheadh na cuirm 's na cuideachd le aighear 's le toilinntinn.

"A righ òg Eirinn," ursa righ Shasuinn, "cha n' ann gon cheann gnothaich a thàinig thu 'n so." "Fhuair mise sgoil mhic righ agus ridire. Thug brath 'r mo mhàthar dachaidh mi. Thòisich e air bruidhinn mo thuath na duthcha 's mo mhuinntir na rioghachd, gon robh curam agus trioblaid air, 's gom b'fhearr leis nach d' thàinig ceann na bliadhn' idir. Ursa mise ris togaidh mise paileas duit, air alt 's nach bi agad ach t' aodann a nigheadh 's do chasan a shineadh ann a'd' bhrògan. Urs' esan, "A mhic mo pheathar cha robh còir agad air an rioghachd, 's cha 'n fhaigh thu i, gos an d' theid plochd ormsa, aona chuid a dheoin na dh' aindeoin." Ursa mi ris, "Bidh latha blàir agus batailt eadar mis' agus thusa ma 'm bi chùis mur sin." Dh' fhalbh mi, ghabh mi go long, thug mi leam sgioba, agus sheòl mi go ruig Alba. Ràinig mi Alba, 's fhuair mi tri chiad lùgh-ghaisgeach, tri chiad treun-ghaisgeach, agus tri chiad làn-ghaisgeach. Nis thàinig mi 't' ionnsuidhsa fiach de 'n cuideachadh a bheir thu dhomh." "Bheir mise dhuit urad eile agus gaisgeach air an ceann," ursa Righ Shassuinn.

Dh' fhalbh eud agus sheòl eud go Eirinn. Chaidh eud air tir aig Carraig an Eirinn 's tha Carraig Fhearghuis mar ainm air a' charraig sin fhathasd. Ràinig e 'n righ. "A bhrath'r mo mhàthar, a' bheil thu nis deas." "Mata Fhearghuis gad a thuirt mise siud shaoil mi nach gabhadh thu corruich; ach tha mise gon mo chuid sluaigh a chruinneachadh fhathasd." "Cha fhreagair sin domhsa, the Eirinn agadsa fo d' smachd, tha mise 'n so le m' dhaoine 's cha 'n eil àite, na biadh, na deoch agam dhaibh." "U!" urs' an righ, "Fhearghuis tha taighean taisg Eirinn fosgailte fodhad, agus falbhaidh mise's cruinnichidh mi mo chuid sluaigh.

Dh'fhalbh an righ, chaidh e ma 'n cuairt Eirinn. Thàinig e go àite ris an canadh eud an t-Iubhar. Cha robh ach aon duine 'san Iubhar

ris an canadh eud Goibhlean Gobha. Smaointich e gabhail a stigh
's am pathadh air, 's gon caisgeadh e phathadh 's gon ligeadh e treis
analach. Ghabh e stigh. Cha robh stigh ach nighean a' ghobha.
Thug i a 'ionnsuidh cathair air an suidheadh e. Dh'iarr e deoch.
Cha robh fios aig nighean a' ghobha dé dhianadh i. Cha robh aig
a' ghobh ach an aon mhart ris an abradh eud a' Ghlas Ghoibhlean.
Leis a' chòrn a bh' aige ri bainne na bà, 's tri uairean 's an latha a
rachte fo 'n mhart. Tri uairean 'san latha bhiodh pathadh airsan, 's
dh' òladh e 'n còrn air a h-uile siubhal. Mar am biodh an còrn Iàn
aig a nighinn cha robh ri dol as a chionn aice. Bha eagal urra, nur
a dh' iarr an righ deoch, mur am biodh an còrn Iàn aice gom biodh
an ceann air a thoirt dith. 'Se smaointich i gom bu chòir an còrn a
chur air bialthaobh an righ codhiu. Thug i nuas an corn 's chuir i
air a bhialthaobh e. Dh'òl e deoch, 's thug e 'n ceathramh cuid as,
's dh' fhàg e tri earrannan ann. "B' fhearr leam sibh a 'thoirt as go
léir na fhàgail. Thug m' athair mionnan mar am bi 'n corn Iàn nach
eil agam ri dol go chionn." "Mata," ars' an righ, " 's geas de m'
gheasans' an còrn fhàgail cho Iàn 'sa bha e roimhid." Chuir e 'n
corn air a' bhord, bhuail e bhas air, 's chuir e dheth na bha as cionn
a' bhainne, 's bha 'n corn Iàn. Man d'fhalbh an righ fhuair e 'n
nighean da fhìn. "Tha thu falbh a righ Eirinn 's mise an deigh mo
mhaslachaidh; dè tha thu fàgail agam?" "Bheireamsa sin duit mil'
as gach dath, mil' as gach seòrsa, mil' as gach creutair." "Dé ni mise
deth sin, 's nach fhaigh mi 'shalann an Eirinn na shailleas sin?"
"Bheiream dhuit glinn a's monaidh a bheothaicheas eud o
bhliadhna go bliadhna." "Dé ni mise dheth sin? ma mharbhas
Fearghus sibhse 'màireach bheir e uam e, o 'n nach robh e agam le
sgriobhadh agus boinne fala 'ga cheanghal." "Tha orms' a nochd
cabhag, ach theirig am màireach do 'n champ go Cnoc maol nam
Muc," ars' an righ, agus dh' fhàg e beannachd aice. Thàinig a
h-athair. "Bhuais e, bhuais e nighean, cha 'n eil dùil' am fhìn nach
robh arbhalach ga d' choimhead an so an diugh." "Cémur a tha thu
'g aithneachadh sin?" "Bha rasg maull maighdinn agad nur a chaidh
mi mach; tha rasg brisg mnà agad an dràsd." "Co b' fhearr leat a
bhi ann?" "Cha 'n fhaca mi duine riabh a b'fhearr leam a bhi ann
na righ Eirinn." "Mata 's e bh' ann. Dh' fhàg e agam mìl as gach
dath, mil' as gach seòrsa, mìl' as gach creutair. De, ursa mise, ni
mise dhiu, 's nach fhaigh mi de shalann an Eirinn na shailleas eud?
Urs' esan, "Bheiream duit glinn agus monaidhean a bheathaicheas
eud o bhliadhna go bliadhna." Dé ni mi ma mharbhas Fearghus
sibhse, cha 'n fhaigh mi sin? Thuirt e rium gom faighinn sgriobhadh
's boinne da fhuil fhìn 'ga cheanghal."

Chaidil eud an oidhche sin mar a bha eud. Ma bu mhoch a thainig an latha bu mhoiche na sìn a dh' éiridh an gobha. "Thalla'nighean, bitheamaid a' falbh." Dh' fhalbh i fhìn 's an gobha 's ràinig eud an righ anns a' champ. "Nach robh thu anns an Iubhar an dé?" urs' an gobha ris an righ. "Bha." "Bheil cuimhn' agad air do bhriathran ris an nighinn so. "Tha, ach cha bhi 'm blar ann gos am màireach, bheir mi dhuit mar a thuirt mi ris an nighinn ach go fag thu ise," Fhuair an gobha siud agus dh' fhalbh e.

An oidhche sin, nur a bha ise treis na cadal, dhùisg i, 's i 'n déigh aislig fhaicinn. "A' bheil thu 'd' dhùsgadh?" "Tha, dé do ghnothach domh?" "Chunnaic mi aislig an siud, gathar giubhais a' fàs a cridh' an righ, fear a m' chridhe fhìn, 's eud a' snaomadh 'na chéile. "Sin leanabh mic an déigh a ghineach eadar thus' a's mis' a nochd." Chaidil eud an uair sin, 's cha b' fhada chaidil eud gos am fac i 'n ath aislig. "A bheil thu 'd' dhùsgadh a righ Eirinn?" "Tha, dé do ghnothach domh?" "Chunnaic mi aislig eile, Fearghus a' tigh 'n a nuas 'sa toirt a' chinn 's an amhuich agam fhìn asam." "Sin Fearghus gam mharbhadhsa 'sa toirt a' chinn 's an amhùich asam." Chaidil i rìs agus chunnaic i aislig eile. "A bheil thu 'd' chadal a righ Eirinn?" "Cha 'n 'eil, dé do ghnothach domh an drasd?" "Chunnaic mi Eirinn, o thaobh go taobh agus o cheann go ceann, air a chomhdach le sguaban eòrn' agus coirce; thàinig oiteag shoirbheis o 'n ear, o 'n iar, a 'n tuath; sguabadh air falbh a h-uile craobh, 's cha 'n fhacas gin riabh tuillidh dhiu." "Marbhaidh Fearghus mise 's bheir e 'n ceann 's an amhach asam; co luath 's a rinn thusa riabh beir air mo chuid arm, agus gléidh eud. Tha leanabh mic air a ghineach eadar mis' a's thusa. Bheir thu cìoch a's altram da, 's cuiridh thu 'n òrdugh e. Gléidh na h-airm. Nur a chi thu gom bi cainnt as comhnadal aige cuiridh tu air falbh e, feadh an t-saoghail, air seachran, gos am faigh e mach co e fhìn. Gheibh esan 'na righ air Eirinn, bidh a mhac 'na righ air Eirinn, bidh otha 'na righ air Eirinn, bidh a shliochd na 'n righrean air Eirinn, gos an ruig an naoidheamh glùn. Bidh leanabh air a bhreith do 'n fhear sin, thig tuathanach a stigh le iasg, bruichidh e 'n t-iasg, 's théid cnàimh 'na amhuich, 's tachdar e."

Bha dithisd mac eil' aig Maobh (Piuthar an righ, màthair Fhearghuis) 's bha 'm blàr ri bhi ann a màireach, Lagh an làidh agus Conall, agus 'se Lagh an làidh a bu shine. "Co dhiu," ursa Lagh an làidh, "a bhios sinn le brath'r ar màthar na le Fearghus?" "Cha 'n 'eil fhios 'am; ma bhuidhneas Bràthair ar màthar agus gom bi sinn le Fearghus, 's clach 'nar bròig go bràth'ch e; ach ma bhuidhneas Fearghus cuiridh e cùl ruinn, o 'n a bha sinn air ann taobh eile." "Mata cha 'n ann mar sin a bhitheas, ach bi thusa le Fearghus, 's bidh mise le bràthair ar màthar." "Cha 'n ann mur sin a bhitheas, ligidh sinn g' ar màthair e." "Na 'm bithinnsa 'm fhirionnach," ursa Maobh, "bhithinn a' cur a bhlàir le m bhràthair fhin." "Mata bidh mis' aig Fearghus," ursa Lagh an làidh, " 's bi thus' aig Fearghus a Chonaill."

Dh' fhalbh Fearghus 'ionnsuidh Fhinn, 's bheannaich e dha ann am briathran ciuine, mìne. Bheannaich Fionn da ann am briathran a b'fheàrr; mur am b' eud a b' fheàrr cha b' eud a bu mhiosa. "Chuala mi gon robh latha blàir agus batailt eadar thu fhìn agus bràthair do mhàthar," ars' esan. "Tha sinn ri bhi ann 's thainig mi 'ur ionnsuidhsa airson cuideachaidh." "Cha 'n 'eil e ach dàna domhsa dol an aghaidh bhràthair do mhàthar, 's gur ann air fhearann a fhuair mi mo chumail; ma bhuidhneas bràthair do mhàthar cha 'n fhaigh sinn sgrìob na plochd de dh' fhearann Eirinn a neas 's is beò sinn. 'S e so a ni mi, cha bhuail mi buille leat, 's cha bhuail mi buille 't' aghaidh."

Chaidh Fearghus dachaidh an la 'r na mhàireach. Chuir eud an òrdugh airson a' bhlàir. Bha cuideachd an righ air an darna taobh 's cuideachd Fhearghuis air an taobh eile. Cha robh 'ghaisgich aig Fearghus ach Boinne Breat 'sa chuideachd, an gàisgeach mòr Sasunnach 's a chuideachd, agus Lagh an làidh.

Tharruinn Boinne Breat a mach an iomall na cuideachd. Chaidh e na chulaidh chath agus chruaidh-chomhrag. Chuir e 'chòtan sròl sìoda air uachdar a chòrr-léine, sgiath bhucaideach air a thaobh clì gom bu lianar oideadhar 's an truaill chairtidh. Theann e mach air na ceumannan moiteil mur bhoillsgeadh. Gach ceum a chuireadh e uaidhe, bu lugh' e na beinn, 's bu mhoth' e na meall-chnoc sléibhe. Thionndàidh e riutha go gìogach, gagach; tri dithean gon cuireadh e dhiu; gan cailceadh o 'n sgiathan g'am fuil agus g'am feoil, anns ann iarmailt; nach fhàgadh e fear innsidh sgeoil na chaitheadh tuairisgeil, a chur an talamh toll, na 'n sgeilpidh chreag. Bha aon fhear beag, càm, ruadh ann, air leith shùil 's air leith ghlùn 's air leith làimh. "Cha bhi thus' ann a dh' innseadh sgeoil ormsa." Dh' fhalbh e 's thug e 'n ceann deth. Dh' òb Boinne Breat 's chuir e dheth airm. "Falbh sios Fhearghuis 's thoir an ceann de bhràthair do mhàthar no bheir mise deth e." Chaidh Fearghus sìos, rug e air bràthair a mhàthar 's thug e 'n ceann deth. Thug nighean a' ghobha thun nan arm 's thug i leath' eud. Chum Lagh an làidh air a chuid armaibh, nur a chunnaic e Fearghus a' dol a thoirt a' chinn de bhràthair a mhàthar. Ghabh e feirg. Chaidh Lagh an làidh ma 'n cuairt a chnuic fiach am faiceadh e Boinne Breat 's e gon armaibh.

Smaointich Boinne Breat gor misg chath a ghabh an duin' ud. Smaointich e gon tilleadh e air an taobh eile de 'n chnoc fiach an d'thigeadh e go àite fhìn. Thiondaidh Lagh an làidh air an taobh eile 'na aghaidh. Smaointich e tilleadh a rìs fiach an traoigheadh e 'mhire-'chatha. An treas uair thuirt e nach tilleadh e airson na bha 'n Albainn, na 'n Eirinn; na 'n Sasunn. " 'S neònach, fhir a bha leam fad an lath', thu bhi 'm' aghaidh." Cha chreid mi nach misg chath a ghabh thu thugad!" "Direach as an aodann a tha mi." "Mata," urs' esan, "gad a tha mise gon armaibh, agus thusa fo armaibh, cuimhnich nach moth' orm thu agus na chumas mi eadar an da mhiar sin." "Cha 'n 'eil mi ri bhi 'm brath foille dhuit; sin air do chùl an triuir ghaisgeach is fhearr an Albainn, na 'n Eirinn, na 'n Sasunn." Thug e tionndadh air a dh' fhaicinn nan triuir ghaisgeach, agus nur a thionndaidh e thug Lagh an làidh an ceann deth. "Mo ghonadh," ursa Fearghus, "b' fhearr leam mo cheann fhìn a bhi ann. Cha 'n 'eil Eireannach ri ghabhail air fhacal a neas is beò duine tuillidh. 'S clach a'd' bhròig e h-uile latha go bràthach, agus greim de dh' fhearann Eirinn cha 'n fhaigh thu."

Dh' fhalbh Lagh an làidh agus chaidh e 'n bheinn. Rinn e caisteal dà fhìn ann agus dh' fhan e ann. Bha nighean a' ghobha tigh'n air a h-aghaidh go math gos an d' rug i leanabh mic. Thug i Conall mac righ Eirinn mar ainm air. Bheathaich i go math 's go ro mhath e. Nur thàinig càinnt a's coiseachd go math dha thug i leath' e, latha bog, ceòthar, do 'n bheinn feadh monaidh agus coille. Dh' fhàg i 'n siud e air seachran, go bhi dianadh an rathaid dha fhìn, agus chaidh ise dachaidh.

Cha robh fios aig air an t-saoghal de dhianadh e, gon fhios aige c'a 'n rachadh e, ach fhuair e miar de rathad mòr, 's lean e 'n rathad. Dé chunnaic e ach bothan beag, feasgar de latha, taobh an rathaid mhòir. Ghabh e stigh do 'n bhothan. Cha robh duine stigh ann. Lig e e fhìn ri taobh an teine, sìos, gon bhiadh gon deoch. Bha e 'n sin gos an d' thàinig boireannach dachaidh an deireadh na h-oidhche agus sia caoraich aice. Chunnaic i stiall mhòr duine taobh an teine cosail ri bhi 'na amadan. Ghabh i iongantas mòr nur a chunnaic i e, 's thuirt i ris, gom b' fhearra dha falbh e siud agus dol sios go tigh an righ, 's gom faigheadh e rud a miosg nan gillean anns a' chidsinn. Thuirt e nach rachadh, ach na 'n tugadh i dha rud a dh' itheadh e, gom biodh e falbh a bhuachailleachd nan caorach air a son fhìn. Dé'n t-ainm a bh' air a bhoireannach ach Caomhag. "N' an saoilinn sin gheibheadh thu biadh a's deoch," ars' ise.

An la 'r na mhaireach dh' fhalbh e leis na caoraich. "Cha 'n 'eil greim feoir agamsa dhaibh," urs' ise, "ach rathad mòr, 's cumaidh

tu eud air iomall an rathaid mhòir, 's cha lig thu dheth eud." An
am na h-oidhche thàinig e dachaidh leo. An la 'r na mhàireach dh'
fhalbh e leis na caoraich. Bha, dlùth air an àite 'n robh e leo, tri
pàircean cruinneachd a bheanadh do thri daoin' uaisle. Bha na
caoraich ga shàrachadh; dh' fhalbh e 's leag e 'n gàrradh, 's lig e
stigh eud o thé go té, gos an d' ith eud na tri pàircean. Latha de na
làithean chruinnich na tri daoin' uaisle. Nur a thàinig eud bha esan
an déigh na pàircean a ligeil itheadh leis na caoraich. "Ciod thuige
dh'ith thu na pàircean." "Cha mhis' a dh' ith eud idir 's ann a dh'
ith na caoraich eud." "Cha bhi sinn a' bruidhinn ris idir, cha 'n 'eil
ann ach amadan, ruige sinn Caomhag fiach an leathaise na
caoraich." Rainig eud Caomhag. Thug eud leo 'ionnsuidh na cùirt
i. B'i so a' chiad chuirt do Fhearghus a dhiànadh an déigh dha 'n
crùn fhaotainn.

Bha fàgail aig na righrean 'san am ud. Nur nach b' aithne dhaibh
an ceartas a sgoltadh dòigheil, thòiseachadh cathair a bhreathanais
air breabadaich, 's rachadh car an amhuich an righ nur nach
dianadh e ceartas mur bu chòir dha.

"Cha 'n urra mise dad a dhianadh," urs' an righ, "ach an fhiacaill
a rinn an sgath i bhi aca." Thoisich cathair a' bhreathanais ri
breabadaich, 's chaidh car an amhuich an righ. "Thigeadh fear
agaibh an so agus fuasglaibh orm, fiach an dian sibh an ceartas na
's fhear na siud." Gad a bhiodh mìltean a stigh cha rachadh gin an
àit' an righ; cha rachadh eud a thoirt do dhroch mhios air an righ
gon rachadh gin diu air a bhialthaobh. "A bheil duin' a dh' fhuasglas
orm?" "Cha n 'eil mar am fusgail buachaille Chaomhaig fhin ort."
Chuireadh sìos buachaille Chaomhaig. "Fuasgail orm a laochain,
's dian an ceartas mur is còir, 's lig a so mi." "Ceartas na còir cha
dian mise gos am faigh mi 'n toiseach rud a dh' itheas mi." Fhuair
e 'n sin rud a dh' ith e. "De 'n ceartas a rinn thu fhìn?" ars' esan.
"Cha d' rinn mis' ach an fhiacaill a rinn an sgath a bhi aca." "Ciod
thuige nach d' thug thu 'm bàs do Chaomhaig? So mur a
dhianainnsa. Tha sia caoraich aig Caomhaig, 's gad a bheirte uaithe
na sia caoraich cha phaigheadh eud na daoin' uaisle. Bidh sia uain
aig Caomhaig, 's gheibh na daoin' uaisle na sia uain' 's bidh na
caoraich aice fhìn a' cumail." Dh' fhalbh an car a amhuich an righ.
Dh' fhalbh esan, 's cha d' fhoighneachd eud co e, 's cha d' fhuair
e sgath.

Bha duin' uasal eil' ann, 's bha each aige, 's chuir e thun ceardach
e gos a bhi air a chrùidheadh. Bha mac òg aig a' ghobha, 's
banaltrum fo 'n leanabh. Dé bh' ann ach latha briagh, 's is ann a
mach a bha 'n t-each 'ga chrùidheadh, 's cha 'n fhac is' each ga

chrùidheadh riabh, 's chaidh i mach a dh' fhaicinn crùidheadh an eich. Shuidh i ma choinnimh an eich, 's thug esan an tairg 'sa chruidh, 's cha d' amais e 'n crodhan leis au tairg ach chuir e 'san fheoil i, agus bhuail an t-each an leanabh, 's chuir e copan a' chinn deth.

Cha robh ac' ach dol go ceartas a rithisd thun an righ. 'Se 'n ceartas a rinn an righ dhaibh a' chas a thoirt bhar an eich. Thòisich cathair a bhreathanais air breabadaich, 's chaidh car an amhuich an righ. Bha buachaille Chaomhaig a làthair. Dh'iarr eud air fuasgladh air an righ. Thuirt e nach dianadh e sgath gos am faigheadh e rud ri itheadh an toiseach. Fhuair e siud. Chaidh e far an robh 'n righ. "Dé 'n lagh a rinn thu?" "A chas a thoirt bhàr an eich." "Cha phàigh sin an gobha." "Cuiribh thugams' an *groom* a dh' ionnsaich an t-each, agus an duin' uasal da 'm bean e." Chuireadh a naull an so an gobha agus a' bhanaltrum. Thàinig an duin' uasal 's an *groom*. "Seadh, a dhuin' uasail, an d' thug thus' air a' *ghroom* an t-each so ionnsachadh mur a bu chòir dha?" Thuirt an groom gon d' rinn e siud cho math 's a b' aithne dha. "Cha b' urrainnear tuillidh iarraidh ort." Seadh a ghobha an d' thug thus' ordugh do d' bhanaltrum fantainn a stigh, gon tigh'n amach as a seombar?" "Cha d' thug," urs' an gobha, "ach mur a thogradh i fhìn." "A dhuin' uasail," ars' esan, "o 'n is tusa 's fhearr cumail, cuiridh mise trian ort de dh' éirig mhic a' ghobha, agus trian eil' air a' ghobha fhìn, o 'n nach do thomhais e 'n tairg ma 'n do chuir e go feum i; agus trian eil' air a bhanaltrum 's air a *ghroom*; o 'n nach d' fhan *is*' a stigh na seombar; 's gon fhios nach d' fhàg *esan* facal air choraigin gon ionnsachadh do 'n each." Dh' fhalbh an duin' uasal agus an gobha; agus stad cathair a' bhreathanais, 's cha robh car aice; thàinig an car e amhuich an righ; 's lig eud esan air falbh mur a b' àbhaist.

Urs' an righ, "ma shiubhail e 'n domhan agus an saoghal tha boinne dh' fhuil mhic righ anns a ghill' ud. Cha b' urrainn e 'n lagh a sgoltadh cho math an siud mar am biodh e ann; falbhadh na tri gaisgich is fhearr á th' agam agus thugadh eud a'm' ionnsuidh a cheann." Dh' fhalbh eud as a dhéigh. Thug e sùil uaidhe, 's dé chunnaic e a' tighinn ach eud. Thàinig eud far an robh e. "C'a' bheil sibh a dol?" "Tha sinn a' dol ad' mharbhadh fhìn; chuir an righ gad' ionnsuidh sinn." "Mata cha 'n 'eil an sin ach rud a thàinig 'na bhial, 's cha ruig sibh a leas mo mharbhadh." "Cha 'n 'eil ann ach amadan," ars' eudsan. "O 'n a chuir esan sibhse gum' mharbhadh, nach marbh sibh mi?" "Am marbh thu fhìn thu fhìn a laochain?" ars' iadsan. "Dé mur a mharbhas mi mi fhìn?" "So dhuit

claidheamh agus buail mu 'n amhuich ort e, 's tilg an ceann dìot
fhìn," ars' iadsan. Rug e air a' chlaidheamh; chuir e car deth 'na
dhorn. "Siud a laochain air thu fhìn a mharbhadh." "Falbhaibh,"
ars' esan, "agus tillibh dachaidh, 's na ceilibh air an righ nach do
mharbh sibh mise." "Mata thoir dhomh an claidheamh," ursa fear
diu. "Cha d' thoir. Cha 'n 'eil an Eirinn na bheir as mo dhorn e,"
ars' esan. Dh'fhalbh eud agus thill eud dachaidh.

Air dha bhi falbh leis fhin thuirt e, "Cha do rugadh mi gon
mhàthair, 's cha do ghineadh mi gon athair. Cha chuimhne leam
tigh'n do dh'Eirinn riabh, agus tha fios agam gur h-ann an Eirinn
a rugadh mi; cha 'n fhàg mi tigh 's a bheil smùid na tein' ann an
Eirinn gos am bi fhios agam co mi."

Chaidh e dha 'n Iubhar. Dé bh' ann ach latha briagh blàth. Co
chunnaic e ach a mhàthair a nigheadaireachd. Bha e tigh'n go seòrs'
aithne, air alt 's gon robh e smaointeachadh gur i mhàthair a bh'
ann. Dh' fhalbh e agus chaidh e air a cùl, 's chuir e 'làmh sìos 'na
broilleach, 's thug e chioch dheas a mach. "Dearbh," urs' esan,
" 's dalta cìche deise dhuit mi." Thug i 'n togail sin air a ceann.
"Do leithid de thàrlaid cha robh agamsa riabh, na mhac, na na
dhalta!" "Tha mo làmh chli ann an cùl do chinn, agus tha
claidheamh ann a'm' laimh dheis, agus cuiridh mi 'n ceann dìot
mar an innis thu domh co mi." "Fois air do laimh a Chonaill mhic
righ Eireann." "Dh' aithnich mi fhìn sin, gom b'e sin mi, 's gon
robh boinne dh' fhuil mhic righ annam; ach co mharbh m' athair?"
"Mharbh Fearghus; agus diùbhail cho mòr ri t' athair mharbhadh
a' cheart latha, b' e sìn Boinne Breat mac righ Alba." "Co mharbh
Boinne Breat?" "Tha bràthair do Fhearghus ris an can eud Lagh
an làidh." " 'S c'àit' a bheil an duine sin a fuireachd?" "Cha 'n
fhaigheadh e sgath air fearann Eirinn aon uair 's gon do mharbh e
Boinne Breat. Chaidh e 'n bheinn, 's rinn e còs 'sa choille miosg
h-uile biast a's creutair mi-ghnàthaichte." "Co ghléidh airm m'
athar?" "Tha mise." "Theirig agus faigh eud 's thoir thugams' eud."
Thug i a 'ionnsuidh eud, dh' fhalbh esan agus chuir e na h-airm
air, agus thigeadh eud dha cho math 's gad a dhèanta dha fhìn eud.
"Cha 'n ith mi greim, 's cha 'n òl mi deoch, 's cha dian mi stad ach
a nochd, gos an ruig mi far a bheil an duine sin, ge b'e àit' a bheil
e." Chuir e 'n oidhche sin seachad far an robh e.

Anns a' mhadainn an la 'r na mhàireach dh' falbh e. Ghabh e air
aghaidh, gos an robh dughadh air a bhonnaibh, agus tolladh air a
bhrògaibh. Bha neoil gheal' an latha 'falbh 's neoil dhugha na
h-oidhche 'tighinn, 's gon e faighinn àite stad na tàmh dha.
Chunnaic e coille mhòr ann an sin. Dhian e còs ann an té de na

craobhan go h-ard anns am fanadh e 'n oidhche sin. Anns a' mhadainn an la 'r na mhàireach thug e sùil uaidhe. Dé chunnaic e ach an aon uilebheist, nach fhacas riabh a leithid fo 'n ghréin, 'na shineadh gon aodach, gon chaisbheart, gon cheann aodach; fhionn' agus fhiasag air dhol thairis air. Smaointich e gad a rachadh e sìos nach dianadh e feum air. Chuir e saighead ann an crois 's loisg e air. Bhuail e anns a ghairdean deas air i, 's thug am fear a bha shìos breab as. "Na gluais féithe de t' fhéithean, na cuisle de t' chuislean, na bìdeag de t' fheoil, na ròinean de d' ghruaig; gos an geall thu gom faic thu mise 'nam righ air Eirinn, no cuiridh mise sìos dheth shleaghan caola, daraich na dh' fhuaigheas ris an talamh thu." Cha d' thug an uilebheist géill dha siud. Dh' fhalbh e agus loisg e rithisd, agus bhuail e anns a ghairdean thoisgeil e. "Nach d' thuirt mi riut roimhid gon cuisle de d' chuislean a ghluasad, na bìdeag de t' fheoil, na ròinean de d' ghruaig, gos an gealladh thu gom faiceadh thu mise nam righ air Eirinn." "Thig a nuas mata, 's chi mi thu fhìn na mi fhìn ann fo 'n am so 'n ath-oidhch." Thàinig e 'nuas. "Nam biodh fhios'am gur e do leithid de thàrlach a chuireadh a leithid mar fhiachaibh orm, cha dianainn duit air chor sam bith e; ach o 'n gheall mi duit e ni mi e, 's bidh sinn a' falbh."

Ghabh eud 'ionnsuidh pàileas an righ. Dh' eubh eud cath na còmhrag a chur amach, air neo ceann Fhearghuis, na e fhìn mar phrìosanach. Cath a's còmhrag a gheibheadh eud, 's cha b'e cheann; 's idir cha 'n fhaigheadh eud e fhìn mar phrìosanach. Chuireadh a mach ceithir chiad lùgh-ghaisgeach, ceithir chiad làn-ghaisgeach, agus ceithir chiad treùn-ghaisgeach. Thòisich eud orra. Cha chuireadh an darna fear o laimh an fhir eile mur a mharbhadh eud. Dh' eubh eud cath as comhrag a ris, air-neo ceann Fhearghuis a chur amach, na e fhìn mar phrìosanach. " 'Se cath as an còmhrag a gheibh thu; 's idir cha 'n fhaigh thu mo cheann, 's cha mhotha 'gheibh thu mi fhìn mar phrìosanach." Chuireadh a mach da chiad diag lùgh-ghaisgeach, da chiad diag làn-ghaisgeach, agus da chiad diag treùn-ghaisgeach. Cha chuireadh an darna fear a laimh an fhir eile mur a mharbhadh eud diu sin. Dh' eubh eud cath as còmhrag, air neo ceann Fhearghuis, na e fhin mar phrìosanach. Cath as comhrag a gheibheadh eud, 's cha b' e ceann Fhearghuis; 's idir cha 'n fhaigheadh eud e fhìn 'na phrìosanach. Chuireadh a mach ceithir chiad fichead a 'n ionnsuidh. Cha chuireadh an darna fear o 'n fhear eile mur a mharbhadh eud. Dh' eubh eud cath na comhrag. "Tha 'n fheadhain a tha mach cho olc," ursa Fearghus, " 's nach gabh eud ach mo cheann, agus mur am faigh eud marbhaidh eud na bheil an Eirinn, 's mi fhìn as an déigh.

Thugadh fear agaibh an ceann bhar aon de na chaidh a mharbhadh, agus nur a thig Lagh an làidh 's a dh' iarras e mo cheann na mi fhìn a'm' phrìosanach, thugaibh dha e, agus saoilidh e g'an e mo cheannsa bhios ann." Thugadh an ceann do Lagh an làidh. Chaidh e far an robh Conall leis. "Dé th' agad an sin?" ursa Conall. "Ceann Fhearghuis." "Cha 'n e sin ceann Fhearghuis fhathasd, 's mise 's giorra chunnaic e na thu fhìn; ach till 's thoir thugamsa ceann Fhearghuis." Thill Lagh an làidh. "Rachadh fear eile 'na choinneamh an àit' an righ, 's abradh e gur e cheann a gheibh e, 's nach e fhìn mar phrìosanach. Chaidh am fear so an coinneamh Lagh an làigh. Rug e air 's thug e 'n ceann as an amhuich aige. Ràinig e Conall. "Dé th' agad an sin?" "Ceann Fhearghuis." "Cha 'n e sin ceann Fhearghuis fhathasd. Till agus thoir am' ionnsuidh ceann Fhearghuis." Thill Lagh an làidh. "Tha 'm fear a tha muigh cho beachdail, 's am fear eile cho daull, 's nach 'eil duin' an Eirinn nach marbh eud mar am faigh eud mi fhìn." "C' a' bheil thu dol a Lagh an làidh?" ursa Fearghus. "Tha mi dol a dh' iarraidh do chinnsa na thu fhìn mar phrìosanach." " 'Se mo cheann a gheibh thu, 's cha mhi fhìn mar phrìosanach; ach dé bhàigh a tha thu toirt do d' bhràthair?" "A bhàigh a thug thu fhin domhsa bheir mise duits' e." Thug e 'n ceann as an amhuich aige 's thug e leis e. Thàinig e far an robh Conall. "Dé th' agad an sin?" "Ceann Fhearghuis." "Cha 'n e." "Go dearbh 's e." "Lig fhaicinn e." Thug e dha e. Tharruinn e e agus bhuail e air, 's rinn e da cheann de 'n aon. Thòisich eud an so air a chéile. Dhianadh eud bogan air a chreagan agus creagan air a bhogan, 's an t-àite bu lugha rachadh eud fodha gan glùinean, 's an t-àite bu mhotha rachadh eud fodha rachadh eud fodha 'gan sùilean. Smaointich Conall go 'm bu dona dha tuiteam 's e 'n déis dol cho goirid do'n ghnothach. Tharruinn e chlaidheamh agus thilg e 'n ceann de Lagh an làidh. Tha mise nis a' m' righ air Eirinn mur bu chòir domh fhìn a bhi.

Thug e mhàthair 's a h' athair as an Iubhar, 's thug e go ruig am pàileas eud. 'S bha shliochd ann gos an naoidheamh glùn. Thacadh an t-aon ma dheireadh, 'na leanabh, le bìdeag de chnaimh a chaidh tarsuinn 'na amhuich, 's thainig treubh eile stigh air Eirinn.

ALEXANDER M'NEILL.

Heard it recited by his father and by several others in his youth.

This story is one of a number, all of which relate to a certain Conall, who was a natural son of a king of Eirinn, and came to be king himself.

There are generally two elder brothers born of the queen (instead

of three uncles), who are less brave than the illegitimate brother. The
mother is generally the daughter of an old man who has magical arts.
The king stays in his house at first for a whole year, and fancies it
one day; all sorts of adventures, and poetical ornaments, and descriptions of dress, and feats of skill are joined to this frame-work, and
the stories are always told with a great deal of the measured prose
which seems to belong to the particular class of which this is a
specimen. They are always long. I think they are the remains of
compositions similar to portions of the manuscripts in the
Advocates' Library and elsewhere—which are a curious jumble of
classical and native allusions woven into a story; which, for want of
a better illustration, may be compared with the old romances of other
tongues.

The story, translated into English, loses part of its merit, which
consists of the rapid utterance of a succession of words which convey,
by their sound and rhythm alone, the idea of the fight which they
describe; the sounds—

> "Dā chĕeăd djĕeăg Lān-gāsh-gāch
> Dā chĕeăd djĕeăg Lōo-gāsh-gāch
> Dā chĕeăd djĕeăg Trāin-gāsh-gāch
>
> Gān cā′lchg-ăg ōn sgēe-ān
> Gām fāil ăgŭs gām feō-īl
> Ans ăn ēeàr-māilt."

By the constant repetition of the sounds *djee*, *gash*, *gach*, suggest the
singing, creaking, clashing, and hacking of blades and armour, and
the rhythm, which varies continually, and must be heard to be
understood, does the same.

The narrator heard it from his father and other old men in his
youth. I have heard similar passages frequently from others, since
the beginning of this year, and I remember to have heard something
of the kind as a child.

One of the names, or one like it, occurs in a MS., said to be of the
twelfth century, in a tale called "The Story of Art MacCuinn, King
of Ireland, and the Battle of Magh Muckruinne," which extends to
forty-three pages. Art MacCon wins a battle and becomes king of
Ireland. All I know of the story is from an abstract; it is said to be
mixed with poetry. The tales about Conall are all over the Highlands,
and those who repeat them are generally old men. I have several
versions written which differ materially from this.

36

MAGHACH COLGAR.

From Alexander MacNeill, Barra.

Fionn, the son of Cumal. FIONN MAC CUMHAIL was in Eirinn, and
the king of Lochlann in Lochlann. The king of Lochlann sent
MAGHACH COLGAR to Fionn to be taught. The king of the SEALG
sent to him his own son, whom they called INNSRIDH MACRIGH
NAN SEALG. They were of age, six years (and) ten. Then they were
in Erin with Fionn, and Fionn taught Maghach, son of the king of
Lochlann, every learning he had.

There came a message from the king of Lochlann, that he was in
the sickness of death for leaving the world; and that the Maghach
must go home to be ready for his crowning. Maghach went away,
and the chase failed with the FEINN, and they did not know what
they should do.

Maghach wrote a letter to Fionn from Lochlann to Eirinn: "I
heard that the chase failed with you in Eirinn. I have burghs on sea,
and I have burghs on shore: I have food for a day and a year in every
burgh of these—the meat thou thinkest not of, and the drink thou
thinkest not of; come thou hither thyself and thy set of
FIANTACHAN. The keep of a day and a year is on thy head."

Fionn got the letter, and he opened it: "He is pitiable who would
not do a good thing in the beginning of youth; he might get a good
share of it again in the beginning of his age. Here is a letter came
from my foster-son from Lochlann that he has burghs on sea and
burghs on shore, food for a day and a year in every one of them—the
drink that we can think of, and the drink that we do not think of;
the meat we can think of; and the meat that we do not think of—and
it is best for us to be going."

"Whom shall we leave," said FIACHERE MACFHINN (the trier

son of Fionn) his son, "to keep the darlings and little sons of Eireann."

"I will stay," said FIACHERE MACFHINN.

"I will stay," said DIARMID O'DUIBHNE, his sister's son.

"I will stay," said INNSRIDH MACRIGH NAN SEALG, his foster-son.

"I will stay," said CATH CONAN MAC MHIC CON.

"We will stay now," said they—the four.

"Thou art going, my father," said Fiachere, "and it is as well for thee to stay; how then shall we get word how it befalls thee in Lochlainn?"

"I will strike the ORD FIANNT (hammer of Fiant) in Lochlainn, and it will be known by the blow I strike in Lochlainn, or in Eirinn, how we shall be."

Fionn and his company went, they reached Lochlainn. Maghach Colgar, son of the king of Lochlainn, went before to meet them.

"Hail to thee, my foster father," said Maghach.

"Hail to thyself, my foster-son," said Fionn.

"There is the business I had with thee; I heard that the chase had failed in Eirinn, and it was not well with me to let you die without meat. I have burghs on sea and burghs on shore, and food for a day and year in every one of them, and which kind wouldst thou rather choose?"

"It is on shore I used to always be, and it is not on sea; and I will take some on shore," said Fionn.

They went into one of them. There was a door opposite to every day in the year on the house; every sort of drink and meat within it. They sat on chairs; they caught every man hold of a fork and of a knife. They gave a glance from them, and what should they see in the "araich" (great half-ruined building), but not a hole open but frozen rime. They gave themselves that lift to rise. The chairs stuck to the earth. They themselves stuck to the chairs. Their hands stuck to the knives, and there was no way of rising out of that.

It was day about that Fiachaire MacFhinn and Innsridh MacRigh nan Sealg were going to keep the chase, and Diarmid O'Duibhne and Conan were going on the other day. On their returning back, what should they hear but a blow of the hammer of Fionn being struck in Lochlainn.

"If he has wandered the universe and the world, my foster-father is in pledge of his body and soul."

Fiachaire MacFhinn and Innsridh MacRigh nan Sealg went from Eirinn, and they reached Lochlainn.

"Who is that without on the burgh?"

"I am," said Fiachaire MacFhinn and Innsridh MacRigh nan Sealg.

"Who is there on the place of combat?"

"There are two hundred score of the GREUGACHAIBH (Greeks) come out and great IALL at their head coming to seek my head to be his at his great meal to morrow."

Fiachaire MacFhinn and Innsridh MacRigh nan Sealg went and they reached the place of combat.

"Where are ye going?" said Fiachaire MacFhinn.

"We are going to seek the head of Mhic Cumhail to be ours at our great meal to-morrow."

"It is often that man's head might be sought and be on my own breast at early morning."

"Close up," said Iall, "and leave way for the people."

"There is a small delay on that," said Fiachaire.

Fiachaire, son of Fhinn, pressed out on the one end of them. Innsridh, son of the king of the Sealg, began in the other end, till the two glaves clashed against each other. They returned, and they reached the burgh.

Co aig a bha 'n càth grannda	"With whom was the hideous fight
A bha air an àth chomhrag	That was on the battle-place
An diugh?	to-day?"

said Fionn.

"With me," said Fiachaire, "and with the son of the king of the Sealg."

"How was my foster-son off there?"

"Man upon man," said Fiachaire. "And if he had not another man, he had lacked none."

"Over the field, to my foster-son," said Fionn; "and his bones but soft yet! but mind the place of combat. Yonder are three hundred score of the Greeks coming out seeking my head to be theirs at their great meal tomorrow."

Fiachaire MacFhinn, and Innsridh MacRigh nan Sealg went, and they reached the place of combat.

"Where are you going?" said Fiachaire MacFhinn.

"Going to seek the head of Mhic Cumhail to be ours at our great meal to-morrow."

"It's often that very man's head might be sought, and be on my own breast at early morning."

"Close up and leave way for the people."

"There is still a small delay on that."

Fiachaire began in the one end of the company, and Innsridh MacRigh nan Sealg in the other, till the two glaves clashed on each other. They returned to the burgh.

"Who is that?" said Fionn.

"I am Fiachaire, thy son, and Innsridh, son of the king of the Sealg, thy foster son,

> With whom was the hideous fight
> That was on the battle place (battle ford)
> To-day.

It was with me and with three hundred score of Greeks."

"Mind the place of battle; there are four hundred score of the Greeks, and a great warrior at their head coming to seek my head to be theirs at their great meal to-morrow."

They went and they reached the place of battle.

"Where are you going?" said Fiachaire MacFhinn to the Greeks.

"Going to seek the head of Mhic Cumhail, to be ours at our great meal to-morrow."

"It's often that man's head might be sought, and be on my own breast at early morning."

"Close up from the way, and leave way for the people."

"There is a small delay on that yet."

He himself and Innsridh MacRigh nan Sealg began at them till they had killed every man of them, and till the two glaves clashed on each other. They returned home, and they reached the burgh.

"Who's that without?" said Fionn.

"I am Fiachaire, thy son, and Innsridh, son of the king of the Sealg, thy foster-son,

> With whom was the hideous fight
> That was at the battle place (ford)
> To-day."

"It was with me and so many of the Greeks."

"How was my foster-son off there?"

"Man upon man, and if there had been no one besides, he had lacked none."

"Mind the place of battle. There are twice as many as came out, a good and heedless warrior at their head, coming to seek my head, to be theirs at their great meal to-morrow."

They reached the place of battle; and when they reached it, there came not a man of the people.

"I won't believe," said Fiachaire MacFhinn, "that there are not remnants of meat in a place whence such bands are coming. Hunger is on myself, and that we ate but a morsel since we ate it in Eirinn. And come thou, Innsridh, and reach the place where they were. They will not know man from another man, and try if thou canst get scraps of bread, and of cheese, and of flesh, that thou wilt bring to us; and I myself will stay to keep the people, in case that they should come unawares."

"Well, then, I know not the place. I know not the way," said Innsridh, son of the king of Sealg, "but go thyself and I will stay."

Fiachaire went, and Innsridh staid, and what should they do but come unawares.

"Where are ye going," said Innsridh?

"Going to seek the head of Mhic Cumhail, to be ours at our great meal to-morrow."

"It is often that man's head might be sought, and be on my own breast at early morning."

"Close up, and leave way for the people."

"There is a small delay on that yet." Innsridh began at them, and he left not one alone.

"What good did it do thee to slay the people, and that I will kill thee," said the great warrior at their head.

"If I had come out, from my meat and from my warmth, from my warmth and from my fire, thou shouldst not kill me." He and the warrior began at each other. They would make a bog of the crag, and a crag of the bog, in the place where the least they would sink they would sink to the knees, in the place that the most they would sink they would sink to the eyes. The great warrior gave a sweep with his glave, and he cut the head off Innsridh MacRigh nan Sealg.

Fiachaire came. The warrior met him, and with him was the head of Innsridh.

Said Fiachaire to the great warrior, "What thing hast thou there?"

"I have here the head of Mhic Cumhail."

"Hand it to me."

He reached him the head. Fiachaire gave a kiss to the mouth, and a kiss to the back of the head.

"Dost thou know to whom thou gavest it?" said Fiachaire to the warrior.

"I do not," said he. "It well became the body on which it was before."

He went and he drew back the head, and strikes it on the warrior's head while he was speaking, and makes one head of the two. He went and he reached (the place) where Fionn was again.

"Who is that without?" said Fionn.

"I am Fiachaire, thy son,

> With whom was the hideous fight
> That was at the battle place
> To-day."

"It was with Innsridh, thy foster-son, and with the Greeks."

"How is my foster-son from that?"

"He is dead without a soul. Thy foster-son killed the Greeks first, and the great Greek killed him afterwards, and then I killed the great Greek."

"Mind the place of combat. There is Maghach, son of the king of Lochlann, and every one that was in the Greek burgh with him."

He went and he reached the place of combat.

"Thou art there, Fiachaire?" said Maghach Colgar.

"I am."

"Let hither thy father's head, and I will give thee a free bridge in Lochlainn."

"My father gave thee school and teaching, and every kind of DRAOCHD (Magic) he had, and though he taught that, thou wouldst take the head off him now, and with that thou shalt not get my father's head, until thou gettest my own head first."

Fiachaire began at the people, and he killed every man of the people.

"Thou has killed the people," said Maghach, "and I will kill thee."

They began at each other.

They would make a bog of the crag, and a crag of the bog, in the place where the least they would sink, they would sink to the knees; in the place where the most they would sink, they would sink to the eyes. On a time of the times the spear of Mhaghach struck Fiachaire, and he gave a roar. What time should he give the roar but when Diarmid was turning step from the chase in Eirinn.

"If he has travelled the universe and the world," said Diarmid, "the spear of the Maghach is endured by Fiachaire."

"Wailing be on thee," said Conan. "Cast thy spear and hit thy foe."

"If I cast my spear, I know not but I may kill my own man."

"If it were a yellow-haired woman, well wouldst thou aim at her."

"Wailing be on thee now; urge me no longer."

He shook the spear, and struck under the shield (chromastaich).

"Who would come on me from behind in the evening, that would not come on me from the front in the morning?" said Maghach.

" 'Tis I would come on thee," said Diarmid, "early and late, and at noon."

"What good is that to thee," said Maghach, "and that I will take the head off Fiachaire before thou comest."

"If thou takest the head off him," said Diarmid, "I will take off thy head when I reach thee."

Diarmid reached Lochlann. Maghach took the head off Fiachaire. Diarmid took the head off the Maghach. Diarmid reached Fionn.

"Who's that without?" said Fionn.

"It is I, Diarmid,

> With whom was the hideous fight
> That was on the battle place
> To-day."

"It was with so many of the Greeks, and with the the Maghach, son of the king of Lochlann, and with Fiachaire, thy son; Fiachaire killed all the Greeks, Maghach killed Fiachaire, and then I killed Maghach."

"Though Maghach killed Fiachaire, why didst thon kill Maghach, and not let him have his life? But mind the place of combat, and all that are in the burghs of the Greeks coming out together."

"Whether wouldst thou rather, Cath Conan, go with me or stay here?"

"I would rather go with thee."

They went, and when they reached the place of combat, no man met them. They reached where they were; they sat there, and what should Cath Conan do but fall asleep, they were so long coming out. It was not long after that till they began to come, and the doors to open. There was a door before every day in the year on every burgh, so that they burst forth all together about the head of Diarmid. Diarmid began at them, and with the sound of the glaves and return of the men, Cath Conan awoke, and he began thrusting his sword in the middle of the leg of Diarmid. Then Diarmid felt a tickling in the middle of his leg. He cast a glance from him, and what should he see but Cath Conan working with his own sword.

"Wailing be on thee, Cath Conan," said Diarmid; "pass by thy own man and hit thy foe, for it is as well for thee to thrust it into yonder bundle* as to be cramming it into my leg. Do not thou plague me now till I hit my foe!"

They killed every man of the people.

They thought of those who were in the burgh, and they without food; each one of them took with him the full of his napkin, and his breast, and his pouches.

"Who's that without?" said Fionn.

"I am Diarmid, thy sister's son."

"How are the Greeks?"

"Every man of them is dead, without a soul."

"Oh, come and bring hither to me a deliverance of food."

"Though I should give thee food, how shouldst thou eat it, and thou there and thee bound?"

He had no way of giving them food, but to make a hole in the burgh above them, and let the food down to them.

"What is there to loose thee from that?" said Diarmid.

"Well, that is hard to get," said Fionn; "and it is not every man that will get it; and it is not to be got at all."

"Tell thou me," said Diarmid, "and I will get it."

"I know that thou wilt subdue the world till thou gettest it; and my healing is not to be got, nor my loosing from this, but with the one thing."

"What thing is it that thou shouldst not tell it to me, and that I might get it?"

"The three daughters of a king, whom they call King Gil; the daughters are in a castle in the midst of an anchorage, without maid, without sgalag (servant), without a living man but themselves. To get them, and to wring every drop of blood that is in them out on plates and in cups; to take every drop of blood out of them, and to leave them as white as linen."

Diarmid went, and he was going till there were holes in his shoes and black on his soles, the white clouds of day going, and the black clouds of night coming, without finding a place to stay or rest in. He reached the anchorage, and he put the small end of his spear under his chest, and he cut a leap, and he was in the castle that night. On the morrow he returned, and he took with him two on the one shoulder and one on the other shoulder; he put the small end of his spear under his chest, and at the first spring he was on shore. He reached Fionn; he took the girls to him; he wrung every

* There is a pun here, which cannot be rendered; a *boot* or a *bundle*, as of hay, or a crowd of men.

drop of blood that was in every one of them out at the finger ends of her feet and hands; he put a black cloth above them, and he began to spill the blood on those who were within, and every one as he spilt the blood on him, he would rise and go. The blood failed, and every one was loosed but one, whom they called Conan.

"Art thou about to leave me here, oh Diarmid."

"Wailing be on thee; the blood has failed."

"If I were a fine yellow-haired woman, its well thou wouldst aim at me?"

"If thy skin stick to thyself, or thy bones to thy flesh, I will take thee out."

He caught him by the hand and he got him loose, but that his skin stuck to the seat, and the skin of his soles to the earth. "It were well now," said they, "if the children of the good king were alive, but they should be buried under the earth." They went where they were, and they found them laughing and fondling each other, and alive. Diarmid went, and took them with him on the shower top of his shoulder, and he left them in the castle as they were before, and they all came home to EIRINN.

MAGHACH COLGAR.

Bha Fionn MacCumhail ann an Eirinn, agus righ Lochlann ann an Lochlann. Chuir righ Lochlann Maghach Colgar thun Fhinn a 'ionnsachadh. Chuir righ nan Sealg a 'ionnsuidh a mhac fhìn ris an canadh eud Innsridh Mac righ nan Sealg. Bha iad aig aois sia bliadhna diag. Bha eud an sin ann an Eirinn aig Fionn. Dh' ionnsuich Fionn do Mhaghach mac righ Lochlann h-uile h-ionnsachadh a bh' aige. Thainig brath o righ Lochlann gon robh e 'n galar a bhàis airson an saoghal fhàgail, 's gom feumadh am Maghach dol dachaidh go bhi 'n làthair airson a chrùnadh. Dh' fhalbh Maghach dachaidh, agus cheileadh an t-seilg air an Fheinn, 's cha robh fios aca dé dhianadh eud.

Sgriobh Maghach litir go Fionn a Lochlainn do dh' Eirinn. "Chuala mi gon do cheileadh an t-seilg oirbh ann an Eirinn. Tha bruighean air muir agam 's tha bruighean air tìr agam, tha lòn la a's bliadhn' agam anns a h-uile brugh dhiu sin, am biadh nach smaointich thu 's an deoch nach smaointich thu. Thig thusa 'n so thu fhìn agus do chuid Fhiantachan. Tha lòn la agus bliadhn' air do chionn."

Fhuair Fionn an litir 's dh' fhosgail e i, " 'S mairg nach dianadh rud math an tùs òige, gheibheadh e rud math an tùs a shine deth rithisd. Tha litir an so air tigh'n o 'm dhalt' a Lochlainn go 'bheil bruighean air muir agus bruighean air tìr aige, lòn la a's bliadhna 's a h-uile té dhiu, an deoch a smaointicheas sinn 's an deoch nach smaointich sinn, am biadh a smaointicheas sinn 's am biadh nach smaointich sinn, agus 's ann is fhearra dhuinn a bhi falbh."

"Co dh' fhàgas sibh," ursa Fiachaire MacFhinn a mhac, "a ghleidheadh mùirn agus màcan na h-Eireann." "Fanaidh mis'," ursa Fiachaire MacFhinn. "Fanaidh mis'," ursa Diarmaid O Duibhne mac a pheathar. "Fanaidh mis'," urs' Innsridh Mac righ nan Sealg a dhalta. "Fanaidh mis'," ursa Cath Conan Mac mhic Con. "Fanaidh sinn a nis," urs' àdsan an ceithrear so.

"Tha thu falbh, m' athair," ursa Fiachaire, "agus tha e cho math dhuit fantail." "Dé nis mur a dh' éireas duit ann an Lochlainn?" "Buailidh mis' an t-ord Fiannt' ann an Lochlainn, 's aithneachar air a bhuill' a bhuaileas mi ann an Lochlainn na 'n Eirinn démur a bhitheas sinn."

Dh' fhalbh Fionn 's a chuideachd. Ràinig eud Lochlainn. Chaidh Maghach Colgar mac righ Lochlainn 'nan coinneamh agus 'nan comhdhail. "Failt' ort m' oide," ursa Maghach. "Failt' ort fhin a dhalta," ursa Fionn. "Siud an gnothach a bh' agam riut, chuala mi gon do cheileadh an t-seilg an Eirinn, 's cha bu mhath leam 'ur ligeadh bàs gon bhiadh. Tha bruighean air muir agam, 's tha bruighean air tìr agam agus lòn la a's bliadhn' anns' a h-uile gin diu; agus co-dhiu feadhain is roighniche leat?" " 'S ann air tìr a chleachd mi bhi riabh, 's cha 'n ann air muir, 's gabhaidh mi feadhain air tìr," ursa Fionn. Ghabh eud a stigh ann a h-aon diu. Bha dorus ma choinneamh h-uile latha sa' bliadhn' air an tigh; h-uile seorsa bìdh a's dibhe stigh ann. Shuidh eud air cathraichean. Rug eud, a h-uile fear, air forc agus air sgithin. Thug eud sùil uatha, 's dé chunnaic eud air an àraich, ach gon toll fosgailte, ach snidhe reòta. Thug eud an togail sinn orra go éiridh. Lean na cathraichean ris an talamh, lean eud fhìn ris na cathraichean, lean na làmhan ris na sgeanan, 's cha robh comas air éiridh as an siud. 'Se latha ma seach a bhiodh Fiachaire MacFhinn agus Innsridh Mac Righ nan Sealg a' falbh a ghleidheadh na seilg, agus bha Diarmaid O Duibhne agus Conan a' falbh an lath eile. Air tilleadh dhaibh air an ais, dé chual eud ach buill' an uird aig Fionn 'ga bhualadh ann an Lochlainn. "Ma shiubhail e 'n domhan agus an saoghal tha m' oid' ann an geall a chuirp agus anama." Dh' fhalbh Fiachaire MacFhinn agus Innsridh Mac Righ nan Sealg a Eirinn agus ràinig eud Lochlainn. "Co siud a mach air a bhruighin?" "Tha mis'," ursa

Fiachaire MacFhinn, "agus Innsridh Mac Righ nan Sealg." "Co tha 'n siud air an àth chomhrag?" "Siud da chiad fhichead de na Greugachaibh air tigh'n a mach, agus Iall mòr air an ceann, a tigh'n a dh' iarraidh mo chinnsa gos a bhi ac' air an diat mhòr a màireach." Dh' fhalbh Fiachaire Mac-Fhinn agus Innsridh Mac Righ nan Sealg agus ràinig eud an t-àth chomhrag. "C' a' bheil sibh a dol?" ursa Fiachaire Mac-Fhinn. "Tha sinn a' dol a dh' iarraidh ceann Mhic Cumhail gos a bhi againn air ar diat mhòr a màireach." " 'S minig a rachadh go 'iarraidh 's gor moch air mhadainn air mo mhinid fhìn e." "Teann," urs' Iall, "agus lig rathad dha 'n t-sluagh." "Tha fuireachd beag air an sin," ursa Fiachaire. Theann Fiachaire Mac-Fhinn a mach anns an darna ceann diu, thòisich Innsridh Mac Righ nan Sealg anns a' cheann eile, gos an do bhuail an da chlaidheamh ri chéile. Thill eud agus ràinig eud am brugh. "Co aig' a bha 'n càth grannd a bh' air au àth chromhrag an diugh?" ursa Fionn. "Agams'," ursa Fiachaire, " 's aig Innsridh Mac Righ nan Sealg."

"Dèmur a bha mo dhalta dheth sinn?" "Fear air an fhear," ursa Fiachaire, " 's mar an robh fear a bharrachd aige, cha robh gin 'na uireasbhuidh." "Thar an àr do 'm dhalt'," ursa Fionn, " 's gon a chnàimh ach maoth fhathasd; ach cuimhnich an t-àth chomhrag. Siud tri chiad fichead de na Greugachaibh a' tigh 'n a mach a dh' iarraidh mo chinnsa go bhi ac' air an diat mhòr a màireach." Dh' fhalbh Fiachaire MacFhinn agus Innsridh Mac Righ nan Sealg agus ràinig eud an t-àth chomhrag. "C' ait' a bheil sibh a dol?" ursa Fiachaire MacFhinn. "Dol a dh' iarraidh ceann Mhic Cumhail gos a bhi againn air ar diat mhòr a màireach." " 'S minig a rachadh a dh' iarraidh ceann an duine sinn fhìn 's gor moch air mhadainn air mo mhinid fhin e." "Teann agus lig rathad do 'n t-sluagh." "Tha fuireachd beag air an sin fhathasd." Thòisich Fiachair' anns an darna ceann de 'n chuideachd, 's Innsridh Mac Righ nan Sealg anns a cheann eile, gos an do bhuail an da chlaidheamh air a cheile.

Thill eud 'ionnsuidh na bruighne a rìs. "Co siud?" ursa Fionn. "Tha mise Fiachaire do mhac, agus Innsridh Mac nan Sealg do dhalta."

"Co aig a bha 'n cath grannd' a bh' air an àth 'n diugh?" "Bha agamsa 's aig tri chiad fichead de na Greugachaibh." "Cuimhnich an t- àth chomhrag; siud ceithir chiad fichead de na Greugachaibh 's gaisgeach mòr air an ceann, a' tigh'n a dh' iarraidh mo chinnsa go bhi ac' air an diat mhòr a màireach." Dh' fhalbh eud 's ràinig eud an t- àth chomhrag. "C' àit' a' bheil sibh a dol?" ursa Fiachaire Mac-Fhinn riś na Greugachaibh. "Dol a dh' iarraidh ceann Mhic Cumhail gos a bhi againn air ar diat mhòr a màireach." " 'S minig a rachadh a dh' iarraidh ceann an duine sin, 's gor moch air madainn air mo mhionaid fhìn e." "Teann as an rathad agus leig rathad dha 'n t-sluagh." "Tha fuireach beag air an sin fhathasd." Thòisich e fhéin agus Innsridh Mac Righ nan Sealg orra, gos an do mharbh eud a h-uile duine dhiùbh, 's an do bhuail an da chlaidheamh air a cheile. Thill eud dachaidh 's ràinig eud am brugh. "Co siud a muigh?" ursa Fionn. "Tha mise, Fiachaire do mhac, agus Innsridh Mac Righ nan Sealg do dhalta." "Co aig a bha 'n cath grannd' a bh' air an àth an diugh?" "Bha agamsa 's aig na h' uiread dheth na Greugachaibh." "Demur a bha mo dhalta dheth an sin?" "Fear air an fhear, 's mur robh fear a bharrachd, cha robh gin 'na uireasbhuidh." "Cuimhnich an t-àth chomhrag. Siud a dha uiread 's a thainig a mach an dé tighinn a mach an diugh, gaisgeach gon chiall air an ceann, a' tighinn a dh' iarraidh mo chinnsa go bhi ac' air dìot mhòr a màireach."

Ràinig eud an t-àth chomhrag, 's nur a ràinig eud cha d' thàinig duine de 'n t-sluagh. "Cha chreid mi," ursa Fiachaire MacFhinn, "a it' as a bheil a leithid siud de bhuidheann a' tighinn, nach bi fuighleach bìdh ann. Tha 'n t-acras orm fhìn, 's nach d' ith sinn mìr o'n a dh'ith sinn ann an Eirinn e, agus thalla thus' Innsridh, 's ruig an t-àit an robh eud, 's cha 'n aithnich eud duine seach duin' eile, agus fiach am faigh thu criomagan de dh' aran, agus de chàis', agus de dh' fheòil a bheir thu g'ar n' ionnsuidh, 's fanaidh mi fhìn a' gleidheadh an t-sluaigh, gon fhios nach d' thigeadh eud gon fhios domh." "Mata cha 'n 'eil mis' eòlach, cha 'n aithne dhomh an rathad," urs' Innsridh Mac Righ nan Sealg, "ach falbh fhéin, agus fanaidh mise."

Dh' fhalbh Fiachaire, agus dh' fhan Innsridh, agus dé rinn àdsan, ach tighinn gon fhios da. "C'a' bheil sibh a dol?" urs' Innsridh. "Dol a dh' iarraidh ceann Mhic Cumhail gos a bhi againn air ar dìot mhòr a màireach." " " 'S minig a dh' iarradh ceann an duine sin, 's gur moch air mhadainn air mo mhionaid fhìn e." "Teann agus lig rathad do 'n t-sluagh." "Tha fuireach beag air an sin fhathasd." Thòisich Innsridh orra 's cha d' fhàg e gin diubh na ònrachd. "Dé 'm maith a rinn e duit an sluagh a mharbhadh 's go marbh mis' thus?" urs' an gaisgeach mòr a bh' air an ceann. "Na 'n d' thiginnsa mach o m' bhiadh, agus o m' bhlàthas, o m' bhlàthas, agus o m' theine, cha mharbhadh thusa mi." Thòisich e fhéin 's an gaisgeach air a chéile. Dhianadh eud bogan de 'n chreagan, agus creagan de 'n bhogan. An t-àite bu lugha 'rachadh eud fodha rachadh eud fodha go 'n glùinean, 's an t-àite bu mho 'rachadh eud fodha, rachadh eud fodha go 'n sùilean. Thug an gaisgeach mór tarruinn

air a' chlaidheamh, 's thilg e 'n ceann bhar Innsridh Mac Righ nan
Sealg.

Thàinig Fiachaire. Choinnich e 'n gaisgeach, 's ceann Innsridh
aige. Ursa Fiachaire ris a' ghaisgeach mhòr, "Dé 'n rud a th' agad
an sin?" "Tha agam an so ceann Mhic Cumhail." "Fiach dhomh
e." Shìn e dha 'n ceann. Thug Fiachaire pòg dà bhial 's pòg do chùl
a chinn. "Am bheil fhios agad co dha thug thu e?" ursa Fiachaire,
ris a' ghaisgeach. "Cha n' eil," urs' esan. "Is maith a thigeadh e air
a cholainn air an robh e roimhe." Dh' fholbh e, agus tharruing e 'n
ceann is buailear air ceann a ghaisgich e, neas a bha e bruidhinn, is
dianar aon cheann de 'n dhà. Dh' fhalbh e, is ràinig e far an robh
Fionn a rìs.

"Co siud a muigh?" ursa Fionn. "Tha mise, Fiachaire do mhac."
"Co aig a bha an cath grannd a bh' air an àth chomhràg an diugh?"
"Bha aig Innsridh do dhalta, is aig na Greugachaibh." "Demur a
tha mo dhalta deth sin?" "Tha e marbh gon anam. Mharbh do
dhalta na Greugaich an toiseach, is mharbh an Greugach mòr esan
a rithisd, is mharbh mis' an sin an Greugach mòr."

"Cuimhnich an t-àth chomhrag. Siud Maghach Mac Righ
Lochlann, is a h-uile gin a bha 's a bhrugh Ghreugach leis." Dh'
fhalbh e is ràinig e 'n t-àth chomhrag. "Tha thu 'an sin Fhiachaire,"
ursa Maghach Colgar. "Tha." "Leig thugam ceann d' athar, is bheir
mi dhuit drochaid shaor ann an Lochlainn." "Thug m' athair duit
sgoil as ionnsachadh, 's a h-uile seorsa draochd a bh' aige, 's gad a
dh ionnsaich e sinn duitse, bheireadh tu an ceann deth rithisd; agus
leis a sin cha 'n fhaigh thusa ceann m' atharsa, gos am faigh thu mo
cheann fhìn an toiseach."

Thòisich Fiachaire air an t-sluagh, is mharbh e h-uile duine de
'n t-sluagh. "Mharbh thus' an sluagh," ursa Maghach, " 's
marbhaidh mis' thusa." Thòisich eud air a cheile. Dhianadh eud
bogan de 'n chreagan agus creagan de 'n bhogan. An t-àite bu lugha
rachadh eud fodha, rachadh eud fodha g'an glùinean, 's an t-àite
bu mho a rachadh eud fodha rachad eud fodha g'an sùilean. Uair
de na h-uairean, bhuail sleagh Mhaghaich Fiachaire is thug e ràn
as. Dé 'n t-am 's an d' thug e ràn as ach mar a bha Diarmaid a
tionndadh ceum o'n t-seilg 'an Eirinn. "Ma shiubhail e 'n domhan
agus an saoghal," ursa Diarmaid, "tha sleagh a Mhaghaich air
giùlan Fhiachaire." "Ambradh ort," ursa Conan, "caith de shleagh,
agus amais do namhaid." "Ma chaitheas mise mo shleagh, cha 'n
'eil fhios' a'm nach ann a mharbhainn mo dhuine fhin." "Nam bu
bhean bhadanach bhuidhe bhiodh ann 's maith a dh' amaiseadh
thu i." "Amhradh ort a nis, na h-athnuadhaich mi na 's fhaide."

Chrath e 'n t-sleagh, 's bhuail e e fo 'n chromastaich. "Co 'thigeadh orm a thaobh mo chùil anns an anmoch, nach d' thigeadh orm a thaobh m' aghaidh anns a' mhadainn?" ursa Maghach. "Mise thigeadh ort," ursa Diarmaid, "moch a's anmoch 's air a mhiadhon latha." "Dé 'm maith a ni sin duitse?" ursa Maghach, " 's gon d' thoir mis' an ceann de dh' Fhiachaire mu 'n d' thig thu." "Ma bheir thus' an ceann deth," ursa Diarmaid, "bheir mise an ceann diotsa nur a ruigeas mi." Ràinig Diarmaid Lochlainn. Thug Maghach an ceann bhàrr Fhiachaire. Thug Diarmaid an ceann bhàrr Mhaghaich. Ràinig Diarmaid Fionn, "Co siud a muigh?" ursa Fionn. "Tha ann mise Diarmaid." "Co aig a bha 'n cath grannd a bh' air an àth chomhrag an diugh?" "Bha e aig no h-uiread de na Greugachaibh, 's aig a Mhaghach Mac Rìgh Lochlann, 's aig Fiachaire do mhac. Mharbh Fiachaire h-uile gin de na Greugachaibh, mharbh Maghach Fiachaire, 's mharbh mis' an sin Maghach." "Gad a mharbh Maghach Fiachaire carson a mharbh thusa Maghach, nach do leig thu leis beo? Ach cuimhnich an t-àth chomhrag, 's a h-uile h-aon am bruighean nan Greugach a tighinn a mach comhla." "Co dhiubh 's fhearr leats', a Chath Conan, falbh leamsa, na fantainn an so?" "Is fhearr leam falbh comhla riutsa." Dh' fhalbh eud, 's 'nur a ràinig eud an t-àth chomhrag cha do choinnich duine eud. Ràinig eud far an robh eud. Shuidh eud an sin is dé rinn Cath Conan ach tuiteam 'na chadal, leis cho fada 's bha eud gon tighinn a mach. Cha b' fhada 'na dheigh sin gos an do thòisich eud ri tighinn, agus na dorsan ri fosgladh. Bha dorus ma choinneamh a h-uile latha 's a bhliadhn' air gach brugh air alt 's gon do mhaom eud a mach uile ma cheann Dhiarmaid. Thòisich Diarmaid orra, agus le fuaim nan claidhean agus le tilleadh nan daoine dhùisg Cath Conan, 's thòisich e air dinneadh a' chlaidheamh ann am miadhon a chalp' aig' Diarmaid. Fhuair Diarmaid an so tachas ann am miadhon a chalp' aige. Thug e sùil uaithe, is dé chunnaic e ach Cath Conan ag obair leis a chlaidheamh aige fhéin? "Amhradh ort, a Chath Conain," ursa Diarmaid, "seachainn do dhuine fhéin, agus amais do namhaid, 's gor co maith dhuit a bhi 'ga dhinneadh anns a bhota ud shuas, 's a bhi 'ga dhinneadh a'm'chalpasa. Na h-athnuadhaich thusa mis' anis, ach an amais mis' air mo namhaid." Mharbh eud a h-uile duine dhe 'n t-sluagh.

Smaointich eud air an fheadhain a bha 's an àraich 's eud gon bhiadh. Thug gach aon diubh leis làn neapaigin, 'sa bhrollaich, 's a phòcaidean. "Co siud a muigh?" ursa Fionn. "Tha mise Diarmaid mac do pheathar." "Démur a tha na Greugaich?" "Tha a h-uile

duine dhiubh marbh gon anam." "O thalla, agus thoir thugam
teanachdas de bhiadh." "Gad a bheirinnsa dhuit biadh demur a
dh'itheadh thu e, 's thu ann an sin, 's thu ceangailte?"

Cha robh saod aig air biadh a thoirt daibh, ach a bhi 'tolladh a'
bhrugh as an cionn, 's a' leigeil a bhìdh sìos a 'n ionnsuidh. "De
tha go d' fhuasgladh as a sin?" ursa Diarmaid. "Mata is deacair sinn
fhaotainn," ursa Fionn, " 's cha 'n e h-uile fear a gheibh e, 's cha
'n 'eil e ri fhaotainn idir." "Innis thusa dhomhs' e," ursa Diarmaid,
"agus gheibh mi e." "Tha fhios' am gon cìosnaich thu 'n saoghal
gos am faigh thu e, agus cha 'n 'eil mo leigheas-sa fhaotainn, na
fuasgladh as an so, ach aon rud." "Dé 'n aon rud a th' ann, nach
innis thu dhomhs' e, 's gom faighinn e?" "Triùir nigheanan righ ris
an can eud Righ Gil." Tha na tri nigheanan ann an caisteal ann am
miadhon acarsaid, gon searbhant, gon sgalag, gon duine beo ach
eud fhìn. Eud sin fhaotainn, 'sa h-uile boinne fala th' annt' fhàsgadh
asda, 's a cuir air trìnsearan, 's ann an copain,—a h-uile diar fal' a
th' annt a thoirt asda, 's am fàgail cho geal ris an anart."

Dh' fhalbh Diarmaid, 's bha e 'falbh gos an robh dubhadh air a
bhonnaibh, agus tolladh air a bhrogan, is neoil gheal an latha 'falbh,
's neoil dhubha na h-oidhche tighinn, is gon e faighinn àite stad na
tàmh dha. Ràinig e 'n acarsaid, 's chuir e ceann caol a shleagh fo
'uchd, 's ghearr e leum, s bha e 'sa chaisteal an oidhche sin. An la
'r na mhàireach thill e. Thug e leis dithisd air an darna guallainn 's
a h-aon air a' ghualainn eile. Chuir e ceann caol a shleagh fo 'uchd,
's air a chiad leum bha e air tìr. Ràinig e Fionn. Thug e d'a
ionnsuidh na nigheanan. Dh' fhàisg e h-uile diar fala bh' anns na
h-uile té riabh a mach air miaraibh a cas agus a làmh. Chuir e brat
dubh air an uachdar. Thòisich e air dortadh na fal' air an fheadhain
a bha stigh, 's a h-uile fear a dhoirteadh e'n fhuil air, dh' eireadh e,
is dh' fhalbhadh e. Theirig an fhuil, is bha h-uile fear air fhuasgladh
ach h-aon ris an canadh eud Conan.

"An ann a brath mis' fhàgail an so a tha thu Dhiarmaid?"
"Amhradh ort, theirig an fhuil." "Nam bu bean bhriagh,
bhadanach, bhuidhe mise, 's maith a dh' amaiseadh tu mi." "Ma
leanas do chraicionn riut fhéin, na do chnamhan ri d' fheoil, bheir
mis' as thu." Dh' fhalbh e, agus rug e air làimh air. Fhuair e ma
sgaoil, ach gon do lean craicionn a mhàis ris an àite shuidhe, agus
craicionn nam bonn ris an talamh. "Bu mhaith a nis," urs' eudsan,
"Na'm biodh clann an righ mhaith beò, ach 's còir an tiodhlacadh
fo 'n talamh." Dh' fhalbh eud far an robh eud, 's fhuair eud eud a
gàireachdaich 's a'beadradh r'a chéile, is eud beo. Dh' fhalbh
Diarmaid, is thug e leis eud air fras mhullach a ghuaillean, 's dh'

fhàg e eud 's a chaisteal mur a bha eud roimhe. Thàinig eud uile
dhachaidh do dh'Eirinn.

Got this tale from Alexander MacNeill, fisherman, then Tangval,
Barra; says he learnt it from his father, and that he heard it recited
by him and others ever since he remembers; says it has been handed
down orally from one person to another from time immemorial.
MacNeill is about sixty years of age, and can neither read, write, nor
speak English. His father died twenty years ago, aged eighty years.

Barra, July 1859.

I know nothing like this anywhere out of the Highlands, but I have
heard similar wild rambling stories there all my life.

The heroes are the heroes of Ossian, with the characters always
assigned to them in Gaelic story. Fionn, the head of the band, but
not the most successful; Diarmaid, the brown-haired admirer of the
fair sex; Conan, the wicked, mischievous character, who would be
the clown in a pantomime, or Loki in Norse mythology. They are
enchanted in a BRUGH, which I have translated burgh, on the
authority of Armstrong; and they fight crowds of Greeks on a place,
if it be A for AITE; or at a ford, if it be ATH, which is pronounced in
the same way. Greeks, GREUGACHIBH, may possibly be GRUAGACH-
ibh, the long-haired people mentioned in the first story, changed into
Greeks in modern times; or "GRUAGACH" may be a corruption from
"Greugach," and this story compounded by some old bard from all
the knowledge he had gathered, including Greeks, just as the fore-
word to the Edda is compounded of Tyrkland, and Troja, and Odin,
and Thor, the Asia men and the Asa, and all that the writer knew.
The story as told is extravagant. Men in Eirinn and in Lochlainn,
Ireland, and Scandinavia, converse and throw spears at each other.
The hammer of Fionn is heard in Ireland when struck in Lochlan.
But one of the manuscripts in the Advocates' Library throws some
light on this part of the tale. If the scene were an island in the
Shannon, men might converse and fight in the ford well enough. The
MS. is a quarto on paper, with no date, containing five tales in prose,
a vocabulary, and poems, and is attributed to the twelfth century.
"Keating considers the subject of Tale 2, which contains forty-two
pages, as authentic history." One of the people mentioned is Aol or
Æul, a son of Donald, king of Scotland, who is probably "Great Iall,"
unless Iall is Iarl, an Earl. Tale 3 sends Cuchullin first to Scotland
to learn feats of agility from Doiream, daughter of King Donald,
thence to Scythia, where a seminary is crowded with pupils from
Asia, Africa, and Europe. He beats them all, goes through wonderful
adventures, goes to Greece, returns with certain Irish chiefs, arrives
in Ireland, and is followed by his son, a half Scythian, whom he kills

at a ford. No. 4, the story of the children of Lir, changed into swans, is very curious.

No. 5 is called the rebellion of MIODACH, son of COLGAR, against Fingal, and seems to resemble Maghach Colgar.

Colgar, king of Lochlin, proposes to assume the title of Sovereign of the Isles, and to subjugate Ireland. He is beaten by Fingal, who gives him a residence *in an island in the Shannon.* After eighteen years he comes to propose riddles to Fingal, and invites him to an entertainment. They, the Fingalians, go, and *are enchanted,* sing their own dirge, are overheard by a friend sent by Ossian. *Some Greek Earls* (Gaelic, Iarla) appear, and there is a great deal of fighting. Ossian dispatches DIARMAD O DUIBHNE and FATHACH CANNACH, who *guard a ford* and perform feats. Oscar, son of Ossian, performs prodigies of valour, and kills Sinnsir.

This abstract of an abstract, lent me by Mr. Skene, is sufficient to shew that this old manuscript tale still exists in fragments, as tradition, amongst the people of the Isles.

The transcriber who copied it into the Roman hand in 1813, considers the MS. to be written in very pure Gaelic. It is referred to the twelfth or thirteenth century, is characterized by exuberant diction, groups of poetical adjectives, each beginning with the same letter as the substantive. In short, Tale 5 seems to be a much longer, better, and older version of the tale of Maghach Colgar. The transcriber makes a kind of apology for the want of truth in these tales at the end of his abstract. He was probably impressed with the idea that Ossian and his heroes sang and fought in Scotland, and that Uirsgeul meant a *new* tale or novel, unworthy of notice. My opinion is that the prose tales and the poems, and this especially, are alike old compositions, founded on old traditions common to all Celts, and perhaps to all Indo-European races, but altered and ornamented, and twisted into compositions by bards and reciters of all ages, and every branch of the race; altered to suit the time and place—adorned with any ornament that the bard or reciter had at his disposal; and now a mere remnant of the past.

It is a great pity that these MSS. in the Advocates' Library are still unpublished. They could not fail to throw light on the period when they were written.

It is remarkable that the so-called Greeks in this story seem to want the head of Fionn for dinner.

37

THE BROLLACHAN.

From Widow M. Calder, a pauper, Sutherland.

In the mill of the Glens, MUILION NA GLEANNAN, lived long ago a cripple of the name of Murray, better known as "Ally" na Muilinn. He was maintained by the charity of the miller and his neighbours, who, when they removed their meal, put each a handful into the lamiter's bag. The lad slept usually at the mill; and it came to pass that one night, who should enter but the BROLLACHAN,* son of the FUATH.

Now the Brollachan had eyes and a mouth, and can say two words only, MI-FHEIN, myself, and THU-FHEIN, thyself; besides that, he has no speech, and alas no shape. He lay all his lubber-length by the dying fire; and Murray threw a fresh peat on the embers, which made them fly about red hot, and Brollachan was severely burnt. So he screamed in an awful way, and soon comes the "Vough," very fierce, crying, "Och, my Brollachan, who then burnt you?" but all he could say was "mee!" and then he said "oo!" (me and thou, mi thu); and she replied, "Were it any other, wouldn't I be revenged."

Murray slipped the peck measure over himself, and hid among the machinery, so as to look as like a sack as possible, ejaculating at times, "May the Lord preserve me," so he escaped unhurt; and the "Vough" and her Brollachan left the mill. That same night a woman going by the place, was chased by the still furious parent, and could have been saved had she not been nimble to reach her own door in time, to leave nothing for the "Vough" to catch but her heel; this heel was torn off, and the woman went lame all the rest of her days.

* Brollachan is a Gaelic expression for any shapeless deformed creature.—COLLEC-TOR. I should translate it breastling, or bantling.—J. F. C.

The word spelt Vough, is probably spelt from ear; but it is the Gaelic word Fuath, which is spelt Fouah in the map of the estate where the mill is. The story was told in Gaelic to D. M., gamekeeper, and written by him in English.

Of the same mill another story was got from the same source, called—

1. MOULION NA FUADH. One of John Bethune's forebears, who lived in Tubernan, laid a bet that he would seize the kelpie of Moulin na Fouah and bring her bound to the inn at Inveran. He procured a brown, right-sided, maned horse, and a brown black-muzzled dog; and, by the help of the latter, having secured the Vough, he tied her on the horse behind him, and galloped away. She was very fierce, but he kept her quiet by pinning her down with an awl and a needle. Crossing the burn at the further side of Loch Midgal, she became so restless that he stuck the shoemaker's and the tailor's weapons into her with great violence. She cried out, "Pierce me with the awl, but keep that slender hair-like slave (the needle) out of me." When he reached the clachan of Inveran, where his companions were anxiously waiting for him, he called to them to come out and see the Vough. Then they came out with lights, but as the light fell upon her she dropt off, and fell to earth like the remains of a fallen star—a small lump of jelly. (These jellies are often seen on the moors; dropt stars resembling the medusie on the shore—COLLECTOR. They are white, do not seem to be attached to the ground, and are always attributed to the stars. They are common on moors, and I do not know what they are.—J. F. C.)

The same creature, or one of her kind.

2. In Beann na Caltuinn, one day called to Donald MacRobb, "Will you eat any charcoal, Donald?" "No," he said; "my wife will give me supper when I go home."

3. And it is said, that a family of Munroes had, many generations ago, married with the Vougha of Beann na Caltuinn. Their descendants had manes and tails till within the last four generations.

4. Four or five miles from Skibo Castle is Loch Nigdal, with a great granite rock of the same name to the north of it; at one end is a burn which passes the mill where the Brollachan entered. It is haunted with a Banshee (that is, female fairy), which the miller's wife saw about three years ago. She was sitting on a stone, quiet, and beautifully dressed in a green silk dress, the sleeves of which were curiously puffed from the wrists to the shoulder. Her long hair was yellow, like ripe corn; but on nearer view she had no nose.

5. A very old, coarse, and dirty Banshee belongs to a small sheep-farm of Mr. Dempster's. A shepherd found her apparently crippled at the edge of the moss, and offered her a lift on his back. In going, he espied her feet, which were dangling down, and seeing

that she was web-footed, he threw her off, flung away the plaid on which she had lain, and ran for his life.

From all these it appears that the Fuath in Sutherland is a water-spirit; that there are males and females; that they have web-feet, yellow hair, green dresses, tails, manes, and no noses; that they marry men, and are killed by light, and hurt with steel weapons; that in crossing a stream they become restless. From the following stories it appears that they are hairy, have bare skin on their faces, and have two large round eyes.

The Rev. Mr. Thomas Pattieson has sent me a story from Islay, which he has written in English, but which he picked up amongst the people. It is as follows; but I have ventured to shorten it a little:—

6. *The Water Horse.*—There is a small island off the Rhinns of Islay, where there is a light-house now, but which was formerly used for grazing cattle only. There is a fearful tide, and it is dangerous to cross the Sound in bad weather. A man and a woman had charge of a large herd of cattle there, and the woman was left alone one night, for the man had to go to the mainland, and a storm coming on, he could not return. She sat at her peat fire in her cabin, when suddenly she heard a sound as of living creatures all about the hut. She knew her fellow-servant could not have returned, and, thinking it might be the cows, she glanced at the window which she had left open. She saw a pair of large round eyes fastened upon her malignantly, and heard a low whining laugh. The door opened, and an unearthly creature walked in. He was very tall and large, rough and hairy, with no skin upon his face but a dark livid covering. He advanced to the fire and asked the girl what her name was. She answered as confidently as she could, "Mise mi Fhin"—me myself. The creature seized the girl, and she threw a large ladle full of boiling water about him, and he, yelling, bounded out. A great noise ensued of wild unearthly tongues, questioning their yelling companion as to what was the matter with him, and who had hurt him. "Mise mi Fhin, Mise mi Fhin—me myself, me myself," shouted the savage; and thereupon arose a great shout of laughter. No sooner did that pass than the girl rushed out in terror, turned one of the cows that was lying outside from its resting-place, and having made a circle about her, lay there herself. The storm raged, and she heard the rushing of many footsteps, loud laughter, and sounds of strife. When morning dawned, she was safe, protected by the consecrated circle, but the cow she had disturbed was dead.

An Islay pilot told me this year that water-horses still haunt a glen near the island. Rattling chains are heard there. An account was published some years ago in newspapers of the appearance of a mermaid near the spot.

7. I myself heard the groundwork of this story long ago from John

Piper; and I heard a similar story this year in Man. (See Introduction.) It is the same as the Brollachan. The creature was scalded by a woman (who had said her name was MI FHIN when he came in), because he wanted to eat her porridge; and when he told his friends Myself had burned him, they said, "Ma 's thu fhin a losg thu fhin bi gad' leigheas fhin thu fhin—If it was thyself burnt thyself, be thyself healing thyself."

8. I again heard a similar story this year from a gentleman whom I met in an inn at Gairloch. He had a large knowledge of Highland tales, and we spent several pleasant evenings together. He has every right to stories, for one of his ancestors was a clever doctor in his day, and is now a magician in legends. Some of his MSS. are in the Advocates' Library.

Mr. Pattieson points out the resemblance which this bear to part of the story of Ulysses, and, for the sake of comparison, here it is from the ninth book of Pope's Odyssey:—

9. Ulysses goes into the cave of the Cyclop with some of his companions. The Cyclop was a one-eyed shepherd, and his cave is described as a dairy; his flocks were goats and sheep, which he milked when he came home:—

"Scarce twenty-four wheeled cars compact and strong.
The massy load could bear or roll along."

He was a giant, therefore, living under ground; and he ate two of the strangers raw. He spoke Greek, but claimed to be of a race superior to the Greek gods. He ate two more Greeks for breakfast, and two for supper. Then got drunk on wine given him by Ulysses, which was better than his own. Ulysses said, "No man is my name;" and the giant promised to eat him last, as a return for his gift of rosy wine, and went to sleep.

Then they heated a stake in the fire, and drilled his eye out. The Cyclops assembled at his "well-known roar," asked what was the matter, and were told—

"Friends, no man kills me, no man in the hour
Of sleep oppresses me with fraudful power.
If no man hurt thee, but the hand divine
Inflicts disease, it fits thee to resign.
To Jove or to thy father Neptune pray,
The brethren cried, and instant strode away."

It seems, then, that the Cyclop was a water-being as well as the Fuath and water-horse of Gaelic story, and the kelpie. There is no word in Gaelic that could be corrupted into Kelpie, but he is the same as Each uisge. The Gaelic tradition may have been taken from

Homer; but if so, the plagiarist must have lived some time ago, for
the story is now widely spread, and his edition must have had some
other reading for ουτιδ, because the Gaelic word is "myself," in all
versions I know.

10. THE CAILLEACH MHORE OF CLIBRICK was a very rich and
wicked old woman (I have already shown that there is some reason
to suppose she was a Lapp; and no Lapp ever offered me anything,
often as I have been amongst them), who, though she had plenty of
the good things of this world, never gave anything away, and never
asked a traveller to sit down in her house. A bold man once laid a
wager that he would circumvent her. He accordingly walked into her
kitchen, when she craved to know whence he came and what was his
destination. "I come from the south and am going north," said he.
"And what is your name?" said the hag of Greyside. "My name is
WILLIAM DEAN SUIDHE." "WILLIAM dean Suidhe!" (sit down) she
repeated; when he flung himself into a chair, and making her a bow,
said, "That will I when the mistress bids me." She was very angry,
and, taking out an enormous bannock as round as the moon, began
to eat without taking any notice of him. "Your piece seems a dry one,
mistress," said William. "The fat side is to me," said the witch. And
indeed she had one side spread with butter about an inch thick. "The
side that is to you shall be to me," he retorted; and caught at the
cake. He called her a satanic old Cailleach, and left the hut carrying
his piece away as a trophy. The old woman was left cursing, and
praying that the cake might kill him; but he had too much sense to
touch it, and his ill-wisher (the hag) foolishly finishing the remainder,
died of its unhallowed effects, to the great relief of her neighbours.

Those who maintain popular stories are as old as the races who
tell them, will probably consider the Brollachan, and the Water-
horse, and the Greek story, as so many versions of an older original.
In this case Homer has a strong claim; but he has an equal claim to
several other stories in this collection, which Grimm and the Arabian
Nights claim as popular lore. Sindbad, and Conal Crobhi, and
Grimms' Robber, if plagiarists, are far more guilty than the
Brollachan; and Murachadh Mac Brian, who follows, is quite as bad.

38

MURACHADH MAC BRIAN.

From Donald Shaw, old soldier, Ballygrant, Islay.

There were three men in the land of Ceann Coire, in Erin—that was Moorchug MacBreean, and Donachug MacBreean, and Breean Borr, their father. They got a call to go to dine in a place which they called MAGH O DORNA. They took with them three-score knives, threescore bridles, and threescore red-eared white horses. They sat at the feast, and no sooner sat they at the feast than they saw the maid of Knock Seanan, in Erin, passing by. Then out would go Moorchug, then out would go Donachug, and then out would go Brian Borr, their father, after them.

They were not long gone when they saw a great lad coming to meet them.

Brian Borr blessed him in the FISNICHE FAISNICHE—soft, flowing, peaceful words of wisdom.

He answered in better words, and if they were no better they were no worse.

"What man art thou?" said Brian Borr. "A good lad am I, seeking a master." "Almighty of the world against thee, beast! Dost thou wish to be hanged with a sea of blood about thine eyes! 'Tis long I would be ere I would hire thee at thy size." "I care not, may be Murachadh would hire me." He reached Murachadh. Murachadh blessed him in the FISNICHE FAISNICHE—soft, flowing, peaceful words of wisdom. The lad answered him in better words, and if no better they were no worse.

"What man art thou?" says Murachadh. "A good lad am I, seeking a master," said he. "What wages will thou be asking?" "Two-thirds of thy counsel to be mine,* and thyself to have but one, till we come from chasing the maiden."

* "Da dhrian de d'comhairle." I am not sure of this translation.

"If thou gett'st that," said Murachadh, "man got it not before, and no man will get it after thee, but sure if thou wouldst not honour it, thou wouldst not ask it."

When they had agreed he took a race after the maiden, and he was not long gone when he came back. "Almighty of the world against thee," said Brian Borr. "Dost thou wish to be hanged with a sea of blood about thine eyes? I knew he was without a gillie in the first of the day the man that hired thee, and had he taken my counsel he had not hired thee."

"I will not do a good turn to-day till the buttons come off my bigcoat." Then they got a tailor, and the tailor had not as much skill as would take the buttons off the greatcoat. Then he took shears out of the rim of his little hat, and he took the buttons off his greatcoat in a trice.

Then he took another race after the maiden, and he was not long away when he came back. "Almighty of the great world against thee," said Brian Borr. "Dost thou wish to be hanged with a sea of blood about thine eyes? I knew that he was without a gillie in the first of the day the man that hired thee, and had he taken my counsel he had not hired thee."

"I wont do a good turn to-day till the buttons go on the bigcoat again, for the women will chase me." They got a tailor, and the shears would not cut a grain, and the needle would not sew a stitch. Then he got shears and a needle himself out of the rim of his little hat, and he sewed the buttons on the bigcoat again. He took another little race after the maiden, and he was not long gone when he came back. "Almighty, &c ... ," said Brian Borr.

"I will not do a good turn to-day till the thorn in my foot comes out." Then they got a leech, but the leech had not skill enough to take the thorn out of the foot. Then he himself took out a little iron that he had in the rim of his little hat, and he took the thorn out of his foot, and the thorn was a foot longer than the shank.

"Oov! oov!" said Brian Borr, "that is a wondrous matter, the thorn to be longer than the shank." "Many a thing," said he, "is more wondrous than that; there is good stretching at the end of the joints and bones." Then he took a little race away, and he was not long gone when he came back, and he had a wild duck roasted on the fire, not a bit burned or raw in her, and she was enough for every one within. "This is the best turn thou hast done yet," said Brian Borr.

"I will not do a good turn to-day till I get a little wink of sleep." They went to the back of Knock Seanan, in Erin, behind the wind and before the sun, where they could see each man, and man could not see them. He slept there; and when he awoke, what but the maid of Knock Seanan was on the top of the hill! He rose, he struck her a low blow of his palm on the ear, and he set her head back foremost. "Almighty, &c... . ," said Brian Borr.

"Set the head right on the maiden."—"If my master asks me that, I will do it, and if he does not ask, I will not do it to-day for thee."

"There she is," said Murachadh, "and do to her as thou wilt." Then struck he a fist on her, and he knocked her brains out. They were not long there when they saw a deer and a dog chasing it. Out after it went they, and the sparks that the hound sent from his toes were hitting Murachadh's gillie right in the face. The sparks that Murachadh's gillie sent from his toes were striking Murachadh right in the face, and the sparks that Murachadh sent from his toes were hitting Donachadh right in the face, and the sparks that Donachadh sent from his toes were hitting Brian Borr right in the face. In the time of lateness Murachadh lost his set of men; nor father, nor brother, nor gillie, nor deer, nor dog, was to be seen, and he did not know to what side he should go to seek them. Mist came on them.

He thought he would go into the wood to gather nuts till the mist should go. He heard the stroke of an axe in the wood, and he thought that it was the man of the little cap and the big bonnet. He went down and it was the man of the little cap who was there. Murachadh blessed him; in the fisniche foisniche, soft flowing peaceful words of wisdom; and the youth blessed him in better words; and if no better they were no worse. "I am thinking, then," said the lad, "that it is of the company of Murachadh Mac Brian thou art." "It is," said he. "Well! I would give thee a night's share for the sake of that man, though there should be a man's head at thy belt." Murachadh feared that he would ask him to put the faggot on his back, and he was right feared that he would ask him to carry the axe home for its size. "Good lad," said he, "I am sure thou art tired enough thyself after thy trouble and wandering. It is much for me to ask thee to lift the faggot on my back; and it is too much to ask thee to take the axe home."

He went and he lifted the faggot of fuel on his own back, he took the axe with him in his hand; they went the two to the house of that man; and that was the grand house! Then the wife of that man brought up a chair of gold, and she gave it to her own man; and she brought up a chair of silver, and she gave it to Murachadh; she brought up a stoup of wine, and she gave it to Murachadh, and he took a drink out of it; he stretched it to the other, and after he had drunk what was in it he broke it against the wall. They were chatting together, and Murachadh was always looking at the housewife. "I am thinking myself," said the man of the house, "that thou art Murachadh Mac Brian's self."—"Well, I am."—"I have done thee two discourtesies since thou camest to the house, and thou hast done one, to me. I sat myself in the chair of gold, and I set thee in the silver chair; I broke the drinking cup; I failed in that I drank a draught from a half-empty vessel. Thou didst me another discourtesy: thou art gazing at my wife there since thou camest into the house, and if thou didst but know the trouble I had about her, thou wouldst not wonder though I should not like another man to be looking at her." "What," said Murachadh, "is the trouble that thou hast had about her that man had not before, and that another man will not have again after thee?"—"Sleep to-night and I will tell thee that to-morrow."—"Not a cloud of sleep shall go on mine eye this night till thou tellest me the trouble that thou hast had."

"I was here seven years with no man with me but myself. The seanagal (soothsayer) came the way one day, and he said to me, if I would go so far as the white Sibearta, that I would get knowledge in it. I went there one fine summer's day, and who was there but the Gruagach of the island and the Gruagach of the dog setting a combat. The Gruagach of the island said to me, if I would go in before her to help her, that she would give me her daughter to marry when we should go home. I went in on her side, I struck a fist on the Gruagach of the dog, and I knocked her brains out. Myself and the Gruagach of the island went home, and a wedding and a marriage was made between myself and her daughter that very night; but, with the hero's fatigue, and the reek of the bowl, I never got to her chamber door. If the day came early on the morrow, 'twas earlier still that my father-in-law arose shouting to me to go to the hunting hill to hunt badgers, and vermin, and foxes. At the time of lifting the game and laying it down, I thought that I had left my own wife without a watch-man to look on her. I went home a hero, stout and seemly, and I found my mother-in-law weeping; and I said to her, 'What ails thee?' 'Much ails me, that three monks have just taken away the woman thou didst marry thyself.'

"Then took I the good and ill of that on myself, and I took the track of the duck on the ninth morn. I fell in with my ship, and she was drawn her own seven lengths on dried dry land, where no wind could stain, or sun could burn, or the scholars of the big town could mock or launch her. I set my back to her, and she was too heavy;

but I thought it was death before or behind me if I did not get my wife, and I set my pith to her, and I put her out. I gave her prow to the sea, and her stern to the land; helm in her stern, sails in her prow, tackle to her ropes, each rope fast and loose, that could make port and anchorage of the sea isle that was there. I anchored my ship, and I went up, and what was there but the three monks casting lots for my wife. I swept their three heads off, I took my wife me and I set her in the stern of the ship; I hoisted the three speckled flapping sails against the tall tough splintery masts. My music was the plunging of eels and the screaming of gulls; the biggest beast eating the beast that was least, and the beast that was least doing as she might. The bent brown buckie that was in the bottom of ocean would play haig on its mouth, while she would cut a slender corn straw before her prow, with the excellence of the steering. There was no stop or rest for me, while I drove her on till I reached the big town of my mother and father-in-law. Music was raised and lament laid down. There were smooth drunken drinks, and coarse drinks drunken. Music in fiddle-strings to the ever-healing of each disease, would set men under evil eye, and women in travail, fast asleep in the great town that night. With the hero's fatigue and the reek of the bowl, I slept far from the wife's chamber.

"If it was early that the day came on the morrow, 'twas still earlier that my father-in-law arose shouting to me to go to the hunting hill to hunt badgers, and vermin, and foxes. At the time of lifting the game and laying it down, I thought that I had left my own wife without a watchman to look on her. I went home a hero, stout and seemly, and I found my mother-in-law weeping. 'What ails thee to-night?' 'Much ails me, that the wet-cloaked warrior has just taken away the bride thou didst marry thyself.'

"Then took I the good and ill of that on myself, and I took the track of the duck on the ninth morn. I fell in with my ship; I set my back to her, and she was too heavy: and I set my pith to her and I put her out. I gave her prow to the sea, and her stern to the land; helm in her stern, sails in her prow, tackle to her ropes, each rope fast and loose, that could make a choice port and anchorage of the big town of the wet-cloaked warrior. I drew my ship her own seven lengths on dry land, where wind could not stain, or sun burn her; and where the scholars of the big town could not play pranks or launch her. I left my harness and my spears under the side of the ship; I went up, and a herd fell in with me. 'What's thy news to-day, herd?' said I to him. 'Almighty, etc.,' said the herd, 'if my news is not good, a wedding and a marriage between the wet-cloaked warrior and the daughter of the Island Gruagach: and that there is neither glad nor sorry in the realm that is not asked to the wedding.' 'If thou wouldst give me the patched cloak on thee, I would give thee this good coat that I have on, and good day besides for that.' 'Almighty, etc... .' 'That is not the joy and wonder that I have to take in it before the sun rises to sky to-morrow.' I struck him a blow of my fist in the midst of his face, and I drove the brains in fiery slivers through the back of his head, I put on the patched cloak, and up I went, and the men had just assembled to the wedding. I thought it was lucky to find them gathered. I went amongst them as falcon through flock, or as goat up rock, or as a great dog on a cold spring day going through a drove of sheep. So I would make little bands of large bands, hardy* castles which might be heard in the four airts of heaven, slashing of blades, shearing heroic shields, till I left not one would tell a tale or withhold bad news; how one would be one-legged, and one one-handed; and though there were ten tongues in their heads, it is telling their own ills and the ills of others that they would be. I took with me my wife, and I set her in the stern of the boat. I gave her prow to sea and her stern to land; I would make sail before, and set helm behind. I hoisted the three speckled flapping sails against the tall tough splintery masts. My music was the plunging of eels and the screaming of gulls; the beast that was biggest eating the beast that was least, and the beast that was least doing as she might; the bent brown buckie that was at the bottom of the sea would play HAIG! on her great mouth, as she would split a slender oat stubble straw with the excellence of the steering.

"We returned to the big town of my father-in-law. Music was raised, and lament laid down. There were smooth drunken drinks and coarse drinks drunken. Music on strings forever healing each kind of ill, would set wounded men and women in travail asleep in the big town that night. With the hero's fatigue and the reek of the bowl, I never got to my bride's chamber that night.

"If it was early that the day came on the morrow, earlier than that my father-in-law arose shouting to me to go to the hunting hill, to go to hunt brocks, and vermin, and foxes. At the time of lifting the game, and of laying it down, I thought that I had left my own bride without a watchman to watch over her. I went home a hero, stout and seemly, and I found my mother-in-law weeping. 'What ails thee?' said I. 'Much ails me,' said she, 'that the great hero, son of

---

* I cannot make sense of this phrase.

the King of SORCHA (light), has just taken the bride that thou didst wed, away; and he was the worst of them all for me.' Let it be taken well and ill, that was for me. I took the track of the duck on the ninth morn. I fell in with my ship; I set my back to her, and she was too heavy for me; I set my back to her again and I set her out. I gave prow to sea, and stern to land; I'd set helm in her stern, and sails in her prow, and tackles in her middle against each rope that was in her loose and fast, to make choice port and anchorage of the big town of the great hero king of Sorcha. I drew my ship her own seven lengths from ebb, on dry land, where wind would not stain, and sun would not burn, the scholars of the big town could make neither plaything or mocking, or launching of her.

"I went up and a begger fell in with me. 'What's thy tale to day, oh begger?' 'Mighty of the world be against thee! dost wish to be hanged with a sea of blood about thine eyes; great and good is my tale; a wedding and a marrying between the great hero, son of the king of Sorcha, and the daughter of the island Gruagach; and that there is neither glad nor sorry in the land that is not called to the wedding.' 'If thou wouldst give me thy cloak, I would give thee good pay and this good coat that I have on for it.' 'Mighty of the world, thou beast, dost wish to be hanged with a sea of blood about thine eyes?' 'That is not the wonder and joy that I am to get from it, before the sun rises in heaven to-morrow,' I struck him a blow of my fist in the midst of his face, and I drove the brain in flinders of flame through the back of his head. The bride knew somehow that I would be there, and she asked that the beggars should first be served. I sat myself amidst the beggars; and each that tried to take bit from me, I gave him a bruise 'twixt my hand and my side; and I'd leave him there, and I'd catch the meat with the one of my hands, and the drink with the other hand. Then some one said that the big beggar was not letting a bit to the heads of the other beggars. The bride said, to be good to the beggars, and they themselves would be finished at last. When all the beggars had enough they went away, but I lay myself where I was. Some one said that the big beggar had laid down drunk. The man of the wedding said, to throw the beast out at the back of a hill, or in the shelter of a dyke, till what was in his maw should ebb. Five men and ten came down, and they set their hand to lifting me. On thy two hands, oh Murachadh; but it was easier for them to set Cairn a Choinnich in Erin from its base, than to raise me from the earth. Then came down one of the men that was wiser than the rest; I had a beauty spot, and there never was man that saw me once but he would know me again. He raised the cap and he knew who it was, That fortune should help you here to-night! 'Here is the upright of Glen feite, the savage* Macallain, pitiless, merciless, fearless of God or man, unless he would fear Murachadh Mac Brian.' When I myself heard that, I rose to put on my tackling for battling and combat; I put on my charmed praying shirt of satin, and smooth yellow silk stretched to my skin, my cloudy coat above the golden shirt, my kindly coat of cotton above the kindly cloak, my boss-covered hindering sharp-pointed shield on my left side, my hero's hard slasher in my right hand, my spawn of narrow knives in my belt, my helm of hardness about my head to cover my comely crown, to go in the front of strife, and the strife to go after it; I put on my hindering, dart-hindering resounding mail, without a flaw, or without outlet, blue-grey, bright blue, "LEUDAR LEOTHAR." Lochliner, the long-light and high-minded; and I left not a man to tell a tale or withhold bad news. If there was not one on one foot, and one one-handed, and though there were ten tongues in their heads, it is telling their own ills, and the ills of the rest that they would be. I took my bride with me, I set her in the ship, I hoisted the three speckled flapping sails against the tall tough splintery trees. My music was the plunging of eels and screaming of gulls; the beast that was biggest eating the beast that was least, and the beast that was least doing as it might; the bent brown buckie that was in the bottom of the sea she would play Haig on her mouth as she would split a slender oat stubble before her prow, with the excellence of the steering. 'Twas no stop or stay for me, as I drove her on till I reached the big town of my father-in-law."

"That was my first rest, Murachadh, and is it wondrous that I dislike any man to be gazing at her?" "Indeed, it is not wonderful," said Murachadh. Murachadh lay down that night, and he found himself on the morrow in the tower of CHINNECOIRE in Erin, where were his father and his grandfather; and the deer and the dog, and his father and his brother, were in before him.

MURACHADH MAC BRIAN.

Bha triùir dhaoine ann an duthaich Chinn a Choire ann an Eirinn; b' e sin Murchadh Mac Brian, agus Donnachadh Mac Brian, agus Brian Bòrr an athair. Fhuair iad cuireadh a dhol gu dinneir gu h-àite ris an abradh iad Magh O Dòrna. Thug iad leotha tri fichead sgian,

---

* FEAMANACH,—Feaman means a tail, but whether this means the man with the tail or not, I do not know.

agus tri fichead srian, agus tri fichead each cluas-dearg, geal. Shuidh iad aig a' chuirm, 's cha luaith shuidh iad aig a' chuirm, na chunnaic iad gruagach Chnoc Seanain an Eirinn a' dol seachad. Siod a mach gabhaidh Murchadh; siod a mach gabhaidh Donnachadh; agus siod a mach gabhaidh Brian Bòrr, an athair 'nan dèigh. Cha b' fhada 'bha iad air folbh nur a chunnaic iad òlach mòr a'tighinn 'nan coinneamh. Bheannaich Brian Bòrr e ann am briathran fisniche, foisniche, file, mile, ciùin an seanachas. Fhreagair esan ann am briathran a b' fheàrr, 's mar am b' iad a b' fheàrr cha b' iad a bu mheasa. "De 'n duine thusa?" ursa Brian Bòrr. "Is gille math mi ag iarraidh maighstir." "Uile chumhachdan an t-saoghail a' t' aghaidh a bhiasd; am math leat do chrochadh is sian fala ma t' shùilean; 's fhada bhithinn fhéin mam fasdainn thu aig do mheud." "Is coma leam cò-aca; dh' fhaoidte gum fasdadh Murchadh mi." Ràinig e Murchadh, 's bheannaich Murchadh e ann am briathran fisniche foisniche, file, mile, ciùin an seanachas. Fhreagair an t-òlach e ann am briathran a b' fheàrr, 's mar am b' iad a b' fhearr cha b' iad a bu mheasa. "De 'n duine thusa?" ursa Murchadh. " 'S gille math mi 'g iarraidh maighstir," urs' esan. "De 'n turasgal a bhios thu 'g iarruidh?" "*Da dhrian de d' chomhairle* gus an d' thig sin o ruith na gruacaich, 's gun a bhi agad féin ach an t-aon." "Ma gheobh thusa sin," ursa Murchadh, "cha d' fhuair fear romhad e, 's cha 'n fhaigh fear a' d' dheigh e; ach 's cinnteach mar am b' airidh thu air nach iarradh thu e."

Nur a chòrd iad thug e roid an dèigh na gruacaich, 's cha b' fhada 'bha e air folbh nur a thill e. "Uile chumhachdan an t-saoghail a' t' aghaidh," ursa Brian Bòrr, "am math leat do chrochadh is sian fala ma t' shùilean? dh' aithnich mi gun robh e gun ghille, toiseach an latha, am fear a dh' fhasdaidh thu, 's nan gabhadh e mo chomhairlesa cha 'n fhasdadh e thu." "Cha dèan mi turn math an diugh gus an d' thig na géineagan bhàr a' chòta mhòir." Fhuair iad an siod tàilleir, 's cha robh de dh' innleachd aig an tàillear na 'bheireadh na géineagan bhàr a' chòta mhòir. Thug e 'n sin siosar a mach a bile na h-ata bige, 's thug e na géineagan bhar a chòta mhòir ann am mionaid. Thug e roid an sin an dèigh na gruacaich a rithisd, 's cha b' fhada bha e air folbh nur a thill e. "Uile chumhachdan an t-saoghail a' t' aghaidh," ursa Brian Bòrr, "am math leat do chrochadh is sian fala ma t' shùilean; dh' aithnich mi gun robh e gun ghille toiseach an latha am fear a dh' fhasdaidh thu, 's na 'n gabhadh e mo chomhairlesa cha d'fhasdaidh e thu." "Cha dèan mi turn math an diugh gus an d' théid na géineagan air a chòta mhòr a rithisd; no ma chi mnathan a' bhaile mi bidh a h-uile te dhiu as mo dhéigh." Fhuair iad tàillear, 's cha ghearradh a shiosar gréim, 's cha 'n fhuaigheadh a shnàthad beum. Thug e fhein an sin siosar is snàthad a bile na h-ata bige, 's chuir e na géineagan air a' chòta mhòr a rithisd. Thug e roid bheag eile an déigh na gruacaich, 's eha b' fhada 'bha e air folbh nur a thill e. "Uile chumhachdan an t-saoghail a' t' aghaidh," ursa Brian Bòrr; "dh' aithnich mi gun robh e gun ghille toiseach an latha am fear a dh' fhasdaidh thu, 's na'n gabhadh e mo chomhairlesa cha d' fhasdaidh e thu." "Cha dèan mi turn math an diugh gus an d' thig am bior a th' ann a'm' chois aisde." Fhuair iad an siod léigh, 's cha robh do dh' innleachd aig an léigh na bheireadh am bior as a chois. Thug e féin iarunn beag a bh' aige am bile na h-ata bige a mach, 's thug e 'm bior as a chios, 's bha 'm bior troigh na b' fhaide na 'n lurga. "Ubh! ubh!" ursa Brian Bòrr, " 's iongantach an gnothach sin, am bior a bhi na b' fhaide na 'n lurga!" " 'S iomadh," urs' esan, "rud is iongantaiche na sin; tha sineadh math an ceann nan alt 's nan cnàmh." Thug e roid bheag air folbh an sin, 's cha b' fhada 'bha e air folbh nur a thill e, 's lach aig air a ròsdadh air an teine, 's gun bhall loisgte na amh innte, 's bha sàith a h-uile duine stigh innte. " 'S e so turn is fhearr a a rinn thu fhathasd," ursa Brian Bòrr.

"Cha dean mi turn math an diugh gus am faigh mi luchdan beag cadail." Dh' fholbh iad air chùl Chnoc Seanain an Eirinn, air chùl gaotha, 's air aghaidh gréine far am faiceadh iad gach duine 's nach faiceadh duine iad. Chaidil e 'n sin, 's nur a dhùisg dé 'bha ach gruagach Chnoc Seanain air mullach a' chnoic. Dh' èiridh e, 's bhuail e buille d'a bhois urra 'sa chluais, 's chuir e 'n ceann cùl air bheul-thaobh. "Uile chumhachdan an t-saoghail a' t' aghaidh," ursa Brian Bòrr, "am math leat do chrochadh is sian fala ma t' shùilean. Cuir an ceann gu ceart air a' ghruagaich." "Ma dh' iarras mo mhaighstir sin orm ni mi e, 's mar an iarr cha dèan mi 'n diugh air do shons' e." "Sin agad i," ursa Murchadh, " 's dean do roghainn rithe." Bhuail e 'n sin a dhòrn urra, 's chuir e 'n t-ionachuinn aisde.

Cha b' fhada 'bha iad an sin nur a chunnaic iad fiadh, agus gadhar 'ga 'ruith. Mach as a dhéigh gabhaidh iad; 's na spreadan a bha 'n gadhar a' cur as a ladharan, bha iad a bualadh gille Mhurchaidh an clàr an aodainn; na spreadan a bha gille Mhurchaidh a' cur as a ladharan, bha iad a' bualadh Mhurchaidh an clàr an aodainn; 's na spreadan a bha Murchadh a' cur as a ladharan, bha iad a bualadh Dhonnachaidh an clàr an aodainn; 's na spreadan a bha Donnachadh a' cur as a ladharan, bha iad a bualadh Bhrian Bòrr an clàr an aodainn. An am an anamoich chaill Murchadh a chuid daoine. Cha robh 'athair, na bhrathair, na 'ghille, na 'm fiadh, na 'n gadhar r'a fhaicinn; 's cha robh fios aige dé 'n taobh a rachadh e a 'n iarraidh. Thàinig ceò orra.

Smaointich e gun rachadh e stigh do 'n choille 'chruinneachadh chnuthan gus am folbhadh an ceò. Chual e buille tuaigh anns a' choille, is smaointich e gum b'e fear na h-ata bige 's na boinneide mòire bh' ann. Ghabh e sios, 's is e fear atan bhig a bh' ann. Bheannaich Murchadh e ann am briathran fisniche, foisniche, file, mile, ciùin an seanachas; 's fhreagair an t-òlach e ann am briathran a b' fheàrr, 's mar am b-iad a b' fheàrr cha b' iad a bu mheasa. "Tha duil am féin," urs' an t-òlach sin, "gur h-ann do chuideachd Mhurchaidh Mhic Brian thu." " 'S ann," urs' esan. "Mata bheirinusa cuid na h-oidhche dhuit airson an duine sin, ged a bhiodh ceann duine air do chrios." Bha eagal air Murchadh gun iarradh e air a' chual a chur air a' mhuinn, 's bha ra eagal air gun iarradh e air an tuagh a ghiùlan dachaidh aig a meud. "Ghille mhath," urs' esan, "tha mi cinnteach gu' bheil thu féin glé sgith an déigh t' allabain is t' ànraidh. Tha e mòr leam iarraidh ort a' chual a thogail air mo mhuinn, 's tha e ra mhòr leam iarruidh ort an tuagh a thoirt dachaidh."

Dh' fholbh e 's thog e chual chonnaidh air a mhuinn fein; thug e leis an tuagh 'na làimh; dh' fholbh iad 'nan dithisd gu tigh an duine sin, 's b' e sin an tigh ciatach. Thug, an sin, bean an duine sin a nios cathair òir, 's thug i d'a fear féin i; 's thug i nios cathair airgid, 's thug i do Mhurchadh i. Thug i nios stòpan fion, 's thug i do Mhurchadh e, 's thug e deoch as. Shin e do 'n fhear eile e, 's an déigh dhàsan na bh' ann òl bhrisd e ris a bhall' e.

Bha iad a' seanachas còmhla, 's bha Murchadh daonnan ag amharc air bean an tighe. "Tha dùil' am féin," ursa fear an tighe, "gur tu Murchadh Mac Brian fein." "Mata 's mi." "Rinn mise da mhiomhodh ortsa o'n a thàinig thu thun an tighe, 's rinn thusa h-aon ormsa. Shuidh mi féin anns a' chathair òir, 's chuir mi thusa anns a chathair airgid. Bhrisd mi 'n còrn dibhe; bha de dh' easbhuidh orm gun deoch òl a soitheach leith fhalamh. Rinn thusa miomhodh eile ormsa; tha thu 'g amharc air a' mhnaoi sin agam, o'n a thainig thu thun an tighe, 's na 'm biodh fhios agad na fhuair mi 'dhragh rithe, cha bhiodh iongantas ort ged nach bu mhath leam duine eile 'bhi 'g amharc urra." "Dé," ursa Murchadh, "an dragh a fhuair thusa rithe, nach d' fhuair fear romhad, 's nach fhaigh fear eile a'd' dheigh?" "Caidil a nochd 's innsidh mi sin duit a màireach." "Cha d' théid neul cadail air mo shuil a nochd, gus an innis thu dhomh dé 'n dragh a fhuair thu rithe."

"Bha mi 'n so seachd bliadhna gun duine leam ach mi fein. Thàinig an seanaghal latha an rathad, 's thuirt e rium na 'n rachainn gus an ruig an sibearta geal gum faighinn fiosrachadh ann. Dh' fholbh mi 'n sin latha bòidheach samhraidh, 's co' bh' ann ach gruagach an eilean, 's gruagach a ghadhair a' cur blàir. Thuirt gruagach an eilean rium na 'n rachainn a stigh air a h-aghaidh a chuideachadh leatha gun d' thugadh i dhomh a nighean r'a pòsadh nur a rachamaid dhachaidh. Chaidh mi stigh air a beulthaobh. Bhuail mi dòrn air gruagach a ghadhair 's chuir mi 'n t-ionachuinn aisde. Chaidh mi féin agus gruagach an eilean dhachaidh, 's rinneadh banais agus pòsadh eadar mi féin agus a nighean an oidhche sin fein; ach le sgios a' ghaisgich, 's athar na pòit, cha d' fhuair mise dol a laidhe leatha an oidhche sin. Ma's moch a thàinig an latha an la 'r na mhàireach, bu mhoiche na sin a dh' éiridh m' athair céile, a ghlaodhach rium, a dhol do 'n bheinn sheilg a dhol a shealg bhrochd, uile, agus shionnach. An am togail na sithinn agus a leagalach smaointich mi gun d' fhàg mi mo bhean féin gun fear faire na coimhid urra. Chaidh mi dhachaidh mar churaidh ro chalma, 's fhuair mi mo mhàthair cheile 'caoineadh, 's thuirt mi rithe, "Dé th' ort?" " 'S mòr a th' orm; an triùir mhanach an déigh a' bhean ud a phòs thu féin a thoirt air folbh."

Ghabh mi olc 's a mhath siod orm féin, 's ghabh mi lorg na lach air an naoidheamr tràth. Thachair mo long orm, 's bha i air a tarruinn a seachd fad féin, air fearann tioram, tràighte, far nach dubhadh gaoith, agus nach loisgeadh grian, 's nach dèanadh agoilearan baile mhoir magadh na fochaid urra. Chuir mi mo dhriom rithe, 's bha i ra throm; ach smaointich mi gum bu bhàs romham agus na 'm dhéighinn e mar am faighinn mo bhean, 's chuir mi mo spionnadh rithe, 's chuir mi mach i. Thug mi 'toiseach do mhuir 's a' deireadh do thir; stiùir 'na deireadh; siuil 'na toiseach; 's beairt na buill; aghaidh gach buill ceangailt, agus fuasgailt'; a' deanadh cala agus acarsaid do dh' eilean mara 'bha sin.

Dh' acraich mi mo long, 's ghabh mi suas; 's dé 'bha 'sin ach an triùir mhanach a' cur crann feuch co leis aca bhiodh i 'san oidhche. Sgrìob mi na tri cinn diu; thug mi leam mo bhean; 's chuir mi ann an deiread na luing i. Thog mi na tri siùil bhreaca, bhaidealach an aodann nan crann fada, fulannach, fiùighidh. 'Se bu cheòl dhomh plubarsaich easgann, 's béiceardaich fhaoileann; a' bhéisd a bu mhotha 'g itheadh na béisd a bu lugha, 's a' bhéisd a bu lugha dèanadh mar a dh' fhaodadh i. An fhaochag chrom, chiar a bha 'n grunnd an aigean, bheireadh i *haig* air a beul mòr. Ghearradh i cuinnlean coirce romh a toiseach le feobhas an stiùraidh. Cha bu stad 's cha b' fhois dhomh, 's mi 'ga 'caitheadh, gus an d' ràinig mi baile-mòr mo mhàthair cheile agus m' athair céile. Thogadh au ceòl, 's leagadh am bròn. Bha deochanna mine, misgeach, 's deochanna garbha 'gan gabhail; ceòl ann an teudan fiodhlach, a' sior leigheas gach galair, a chuireadh fir ghointe agus mnathan siùbhla 'nan cadal air a mhòr-bhaile an oidhche sin. Le athar na pòit, 's le sgios a' ghaisgich, cha do laigh mise leis a' bhean an oidhche sin.

Ma bu mhoch a thàinig an latha an la 'r na mhàireach, bu mhoiche na sin a dh'éiridh m' athair ceile a ghlaodhach rium fein a dhol do 'n bheinn sheilg, a dhol a shealg bhrochd, is uile, is shionnach. An am togail na sithinn is a leagalach, smaointich mi féin gun d' fhàg mi mo bhean gun fear faire na feur choimhead urra. Ghabh mi dhachaidh a'm' churaidh ro chalma, 's fhuair mi mo mhàithair chéile 'caoineadh. "Dé th' ort a nochd?" "Is mòr a th' orm, Macan na Falluinne fluiche an déigh a' bhean ud a phòs thu féin a thoirt air folbh."

Ghabh 'mi a mhath is olc siod orm fein. Ghabh mi lorg an lach air an naoidheamh tràth. Thachair mo long orm. Chuir mi mo dhriom rithe, 's bha i ra throm leam. Chuir mi mo dhriom rithe a rithisd, 's chuir mi mach i. Thug mi 'toiseach do mhuir, 's a deireadh do thir. Dheanainn stiuir 'na deireadh, siuil 'na toiseach; 's beairt 'na buill; aghaidh gach buill a bh' innte ceangailt' agus fuasgailt'; a' deànadh rogha cala agus acarsaid do Bhaile-mòr Macan na Falluinne fliuiche. Tharruinn mi mo long a seachd fad féin air fearann tioram, tràighte, far nach dubhadh gaoith, 's nach loisgeadh grian, 's nach deanadh sgoilearan baile-mhòir culaidh mhagaidh na fhochaid di. Dh' fhàg mi mo luirg 's mo shleaghan fo thaobh na luinge. Chaidh mi suas, 's thachair buachaill' orm. Dé do naigheachd an diugh a bhuachaille? thuirt mi ris. "Uile chumhachdan an t-saoghail a' t' aghaidh a bhiasd, am math leat do chrochadh is sian fala ma t' shùilean; 's mòr 's is math mo naigheachd; banais agus pòsadh eadar Macan na Falluinne fliuiche 's nighean gruagach an eilean, 's nach 'eil mùirne na maird 'san rioghachd nach 'eil cuireadh aca thun na bainnse." "Nan d' thugadh thu domh an lùireach sin ort, bheirinn duit an còta math so 'th' orm féin, 's pàigheadh math a thuillidh air an sin." "Uile chumhachdan an t-saoghail a' t' aghaidh a bhiasd, am math leat do chrochadh is sian fala ma t' shùilean; cha 'n e sin aighear agus *ioghnadh* a th' agam féin r'a ghabhail aisde ma 'n éirich grian air athar am màireach." Bhuail 'mi buill de m' dhorn air an clàr an aodainn 's chuir mi 'n t-ionachainn 'na chùibeanan teine tríd chùl a chinn.

Chuir mi orm an lùireach, 's ghabh mi suas, 's bha na daoine an déigh cruinneachadh thun na bainnse. Smaointich mi gun robh e fortanach dhomh am faotainn cruinn. Ghabh mi na 'm measg mar sheobhaig romh ealt, na mar ghobhair ri creig, na mar chù mòr ann an latha fuar Earraich a' dol romh threud chaorach. Sin mar a dheanainn buidhnichean beaga do bhuidhnichean mòra; caisteil chròdha 'chluinnt 'an ceithir àirdean an athair; slachdarsaich lann a' gearradh nan sgiath sonnalach; gus nàch d' fhàg mi fear innsidh *sgeoil* na chumadh tuairisgeul; mar am biodh fear air leith-chois 's fear air leith-làimh, 's ged a bhiodh deich teangannan 'nan ceann 's ann aig innseadh an uilc féin is uilc chàich a bhitheadh iad. Thug mi leam mo bhean féin, 's chuir mi ann an deireadh na luing i. Thug mi 'toiseach do mhuir 's a deireadh do thir. Dheanainn siùil 'na toiseach, stiuir 'na deireadh. Thog mi na tri siùil bhreaca, bhaidealach an aodann nan crann fada, fulannach, fiughaidh. 'S e bu cheòl dhomh plubarsaich easgann, s béiceardaich fhaoileann; a' bhéisd a bu mhotha 'g itheadh na béisd a bu lugha, 's a' bhéisd a bu lugha 'deanadh mar a dh' fhaodadh i. An fhaochag chrom, chiar a bha 'n grunnd an aigean bheireadh i *haig* air a beul mòr. Ghearradh i cuinnlean caol coirce le feobhas an stiùraidh. Thill sinn gu baile mòr m' athair céile. Thogadh an ceòl 's leagadh am bròn. Bha deochanna mine, misgeach, s deochanna garbha 'gan gabhail; ceòl air teudan, a' sior leigheas gach seorsa galair, a chuireadh fir ghointe agus mnathan siubhla 'nan cadal air a' mhòr-bhaile an oidhche sin. Le sgios a ghaisgich, agus le athar na pòit, cha do laidh mise le m' mhnaoi an oidhche sin.

Ma bu mhoch a thàinig an latha an la 'r na mhàireach, bu mhoiche na sin a dh' éiridh m' athair céile a ghlaodhach rium a dhol do 'n bheinn sheilg, a dhol a shealg bhrochd, is uilc is shionnach. An am togail na sithinn is a leagalach, smaointich mi gun d' fhàg mi mo bhean féin gun fhear faire na fuar choimhead urra. Dh' fholbh mi dhachaidh mar churaidh ro chalma, 's fhuair mi mo mhàthair chéile 'caoineadh. Dé th' ort? " 'S mòr sin, Macan mòr mac righ na Sorcha an déigh a' bhean ud a phòs thu féin a thoirt air folbh." Is e bu mheasa leam aca. Ghabhtar a mhath is olc siod orm fein. Ghabh mi lorg an lach air an naoidheamh tràth. Thachair mo long orm. Chuir mi mo dhriom rithe, 's bha i ra throm leam. Chuir mi mo dhriom rithe a rithisd, 's chuir mi mach i. Thug mi 'toiseach do mhuir 's a deireadh do thir. Dhéanainn stiuir 'na deireadh; siùil 'na toiseach; 's beairt na buillsgean; aghaidh gach buill a bh' innte fuasgailt' agus ceangailte; a' dèanadh rogha cala agus acarsaid do bhaile-mòr Macan mòr righ na Sorcha. Tharruin mi mo long a seachd fad féin o thràigh air fearann tioram, far nach dubhadh gaoith, 's nach loisgeadh grian, 's nach dèanadh sgoilearan baile-mhòir culaidh bhùird, na mhagaidh, na fhochaid di.

Ghabh mi suas 's thachair bleidire orm. "Dé do naigheachd an diugh a bhleidire?" "Cumhachdan an t-saoghail a' t' aghaidh; am math leat do chrochadh is sian fala ma t' shùilean? 's mor agus is math mo naigheachd; banais agus pòsadh eadar Macan mòr righ na Sorcha agus nighean gruagach an eilean; 's nach 'eil mùirne na mairde 'san tir nach 'eil air an cuireadh thun na bainnse." "Na 'n d' thugadh thu féin dhomh do lùireach, bheirinn dhuit paigheadh math, agus an cota math so th' orm air a son?" "Cumhachdan an t-saoghail a' t' aghaidh a bhiasd; am math leat do chrochadh agus sian fala ma t' shùilean; cha 'n e sin aighear agus ioghnadh a th' agam féin r'a ghabhail aisde ma 'n éirich grian air athar am màireach." Bhuail mi buille do m' dhòrn air an clàr an aodainn, 's chuir mi 'n t-ionachainn 'na chùibeanan teine trìd chùl a chinn. Bha fhios aig bean na bainns' air altaigin gum bithinn ann, 's dh' iarr i na bleidirean a riarachadh an toiseach. Shuidh mi féin am meadhon nam bleidirean, 's a h-uile fear a theannadh ri mir a thoirt uam bheirinn bruthadh dha eadar mo làmh 's mo thaobh, 's dh' fhàgainn an siod e, 'scheapainn am biadh leis an darna làmh, 's an deoch leis an làimh eile. Thuirt cuideigin nach robh am bleidire mòr a leigeil mìr an ceann nam bleidirean eile. Thuirt bean na bainnse iadsan a bhi math do na bleidirean, 's gum biodh iad féin réidh air a' cheann ma dheireadh. Nur a fhuair na bleidirean air fad an leòir dh'fholbh iad, ach laidh mi féin far an robh mi. Thuirt cuideigin gun robh am bleidire mòr an déigh laidhe air an daoraich, 's thuirt fear na bainnse a' bhiasd a thilgeil a mach air cùl cnoic na 'n sgàth gàrraidh, gus an traoghadh e na bha 'na bhrainn. Thàinig còig deug de na daoine 'nuas, 's thug iad làmh air mi féin a thogail. Air do dha làimh a Mhurchaidh gum b'fhasa dhaibh Càrn a Choilnnich an Eirinn a chura a bhonn na mise 'thogail o 'n talamh. Thàinig h-aon de na daoine 'bu ghlice na chéile nuas, bha ball seirc orm, 's cha robh duine chunnaic riamh mi nach aithneachadh a rithisd mi, 's thog e 'n currachd, 's dh' aithnich e co 'bh'ann. "Gun cuideachadh am fortan leibh an so a nochd. Tha 'n so Direach Ghleann féite Macallain, am feamanach gun iochd, gun trocair, gun eagal Ni Math, na duine; mar an dèanadh e do Mhurchadh Mac Brian e."

Nur a chuala mi féin siod dh' éiridh mi dhol ann a'm' threallaichean cath agus comhraig. Chuir mi orm mo lèine sheuntaidh, sheumh de 'n t-sròl 's de 'n t-sioda shleamhuinn

bhuidhe, sinte ri m' chraicionn; mo chòta caomh *cotain* air uachdar
a chaomh bhroitinn; mo sgiath bhucaideach, bhacaideach, bharra-
chaol air mo thaobh cli; mo shlachdanta cruaidh curaidh ann a'm'
làimh dheis; m' iuchair sginnichdinn chaol air mo chrios; mo
chlogada cruadhach ma m' cheann a dhìon mo mhaise mhullaich,
a dhol an toiseach na h-iorguill 's an iorghuil a' dol 'na deireadh.
Chuir mi orm mo lùireach thorantach, shith thorantach,
chorraghleusda, gun fhòtas, na gun os, ghormghlas, ghormghlan,
leudar, leòthar, Lochlannach, fhada, aotrom, inntinneach; 's cha d'
fhàg mi fear innsidh sgeoil na chumadh tuairisgeul; mar am biodh
fear air leith-chos ann, 's fear air leith-làimh, 's ged a bhiodh deich
teangannan 'nan ceann, 's ann aig innseadh an uilc fein is uilc
chàich a bhithead iad.

Thug mi leam mo bhean 's chuir mi 'san luing i. Thog mi na tri
siùil bhreaca, bhaidealach an aodann nan cranna fada, fulannach,
fiùghaidh. 'S e bu cheòl dhomh plubarsaich easgann, 's
béiceardaich fhaoileann; a bhéisd a bu mhotha aig itheadh na béisd
a bu lugha, 's a bheisd a bu lugha a' dèanadh mar a dh' fhaodadh
i. An fhaochag chrom, chiar a bha 'n grunnd an aigean bheireadh
i haig air a beul mòr. Ghearradh i cuinlean coirce romh a toiseach
le feobhas an stiùraidh. Cha bu stad 's cha b' fhois dhòmh, 's mi
'ga caitheadh, gus an d' ràinig mi baile-mòr m' athair cèile. Sin agad
a' chiad oidhche a fhuair mise le m' bhean a Mhurchaidh, 's am b'
iongantach ged nach bu mhath leam duine sam bith a bhith 'g
amharc urra. "Gu dearbh cha b'iongantach," ursa Murchadh.
Chaidh Murchadh an oidhche sin a laidhe, 's fhuair e e féin an là'r
na mhàireach ann an tùr Chinn a Choire ann an Eirinn, far an robh
athair agus a sheanair; 's am fiadh, 's an gadhar, is athair, 's a'
bhràthair a stigh air thoiseach tir.

This tale was taken down in May 1859, from the recitation of
Donald Shaw, then aged sixty-eight, a pauper, living at Ballygrant in
Islay, who was in the 42nd Highlanders at Waterloo. He served in
the army about three years. He said that he had learned it from one
Duncan MacMillan, A Colonsay man, well advanced in years, about
fifty years ago. On the 6th of July, Hector MacLean wrote:—"Shaw
died a few days ago, and so far as it can ascertain, there is none in
Islay, Jura, or Colonsay, that can recite the same tale now."

I have only met with one man who knew it by this name; MacPhie,
at the Sound of Benbecula, a very old man, who gave me the outline
of it. Some of the language is exceedingly difficult; some words none
of us can make out; and MacPhie's version, and most of his stories,
were full of such language.

The tale then is found in Islay and South Uist, and traced to Colonsay, and is certainly about fifty years old. I have several other tales which resemble it in some degree.

The little hat with everything in it, and the great coat and buttons, are Irish. There is much communication between Ireland and the Isles at this day. The language spoken on the opposite coasts is all but identical, and this is probably common to Ireland and the Isles.

There is something like it in Mr. Simpson's book; and some of his words resemble words in this story, and seem to have puzzled the Irish translators as much as they have puzzled me. The phrase, "As a falcon through a flock of birds," is in Mr. Simpson's work. The man with the bundle of wood is something like the giant in Grimm's Valiant Tailor. The servant who drew a thorn longer than his leg out of his foot, may be some supernatural personage. The measured prose descriptions of sailing, arming, and fighting, are common all over the West Highlands amongst the eldest and poorest men, and similar passages occur in manuscripts.

For descriptions of costume and for language, the tale is very curious, and worth the labour bestowed on it, which is considerable. I have endeavoured to translate closely, and at the same time to imitate this tale; but it is a very weak attempt, I well know.

The manners described are partly those of the day. The politeness and discourtesy in the house of the man with the little hat, are purely Highland. The breaking of the tumbler is a mark of great respect; no meaner lip should touch the glass drained to an honoured guest; but the glass must be first filled and emptied—no half cups are allowed. The best seat should be the guest's. The telling of the story in the evening is the real amusement of the poorer classes now, and used to be much more common.

The description of the sailing of a boat amongst the fish and birds is true to nature; it is the expression *the track of the duck;* none but a man familiar with the habits of birds on a sea-coast could think of such a phrase. Ducks feed on shore, and return to the sea at daylight.

The experience of the old soldier probably makes the drink wine, not whisky; and *Sibearta* is probably white Siberia, derived from the same source; if not, I can make nothing of it.

The dress described may be the old dress of the Isles, as depicted on tombstones, with a cotton coat slipped in. In an account of the Danes and Norwegians in England and Ireland, by J.J.A. Worsaae, London, 1852, it is stated that Magnus Barfod sat himself at the helm while his ship was drawn over the Peninsula of Tarbet (draw-boat); acquired the sovereignty of the Western Isles; and adopted the dress generally worn there. "They went about the streets (in Norway) with bare legs, and wore short coats and cloaks, whence Magnus was called by his men, Barfod or Barbeen (barefoot or barelegs)," says the Icelandic historian, Snorro Sturleson, who, as well known, lived in the first half of the thirteenth century. It is remarkable enough that this is the oldest account extant of the well-known Scotch Highland dress, whose antiquity is thus proved.

The tale might be taken partly from the Odyssey. The man disguised as a beggar, going to a wedding where his own wife was the bride, and where he knocks out the brains of a beggar with a single blow, and makes a general slaughter afterwards, is very like Ulysses, Penelope, Irus, and the Suitors, but similar incidents are common in popular tales. There is a story in the Decameron which somewhat resembles the incident of the wife carried away. On the whole, I think this story is a remnant of an old bardic composition, of which very little remains.

The word GRUAGACH is here used both for a maiden and for a woman with a daughter; it usually means *a maiden*, rarely a chief; sometimes it seems to mean a conjuror, or philosopher, or instructor; often the being called Brownie. It probably means any one with long hair; from GRUAG, air of the head.

GLOSSARY.

ALLABAN ANRADH, painful, wandering.

ATHAR NA POIT, the evil effect of drinking.

BEART NA BUIL, tackle in the ropes.

BEUCARSAICH, screaming.

BROCHD AGUS OLC, badgers and evil creatures, vermin.

BUCAIDACH, pimply, *boss* covered, or perhaps hollow.

CALA AGUS ACARSAID, port and anchorage.

CNOCK SEANAN, (?) Hill of Jewels, from sean or seun, a jewel.

CRANNA FADA FULANNACH, tress or masts, long-enduring.

FILE, MILE, soft, fluent.

FISNICHE FAISNICHE, words whose meaning is lost in the islands; probably Irish; perhaps knowing, delaying, that is wise, eloquent.

LEUDAR LEOTHAR LOCHLANNACH, (?) perhaps a description of the man; the epithet Lochlannach is the only one of the three which is comprehensible, and this line probably belongs to something else.

LORG NA LACH, the track of the duck; path, towards the sea.

LURACH, a coat of mail, also a patched cloak.

MAGH O DORNA, (?) plain of pebbles, from dornag, a stone, that can be held in dorn, the fist.

NEAM-A-LACH, (?) not to be found in dictionairies.

PLUBARSAICH, an expressive word for plunging about.